English Tourism Council

Official Guide to
Hotels

GW00507903

England

There's something different
around every corner

The English Tourism Council

English Tourism Council is the national body for English Tourism. Its mission is to drive forward the quality, competitiveness and wise growth of England's tourism by providing intelligence, setting standards, creating partnerships and ensuring coherence. ETC sets out: to provide leadership and support for the industry – creating the right framework for tourism to flourish and providing a clear focus for tourism policy and promotion; to raise the quality of English tourism – ensuring consumers expectations are met and that tourism contributes to the quality of life; to improve the competitiveness of the industry; to ensure the wise growth of tourism – helping the tourism industry to take better account of the natural and built environment and the communities within which it operates.

Cover Pictures:
      Front Cover: Wood Norton Hall & Conference Centre, Evesham, Worcestershire
      Front Cover Inset: Mortons House Hotel, Corfe Castle, Dorset
      Back Cover: (from top) Chilston Park Country House Hotel, Lenham, Kent
      Rothay Garth Hotel, Ambleside, Cumbria

Photo Credits:
      Cumbria - Cumbria Tourist Board
      Northumbria - Northumbria Tourist Board, Graeme Peacock, Mike Kipling, Colin Cuthbert and Michael Busselle
      North West - North West Tourist Board, Cheshire County Council, Lancashire County Council, Marketing Manchester
      Yorkshire - Yorkshire Tourist Board
      Heart of England - Heart of England Tourist Board
      East of England - East of England Tourist Board Collection
      South West - South West Tourism
      South of England - Southern Tourist Board,
      Peter Titmuss, Chris Cove-Smith and Iris Buckley
      South East England - South East England Tourist Board, Chris Parker and Iris Buckley

      Published by: The English Tourism Council, Thames Tower, Black's Road, Hammersmith, London W6 9EL.
      ISBN 0 86143 250 9

      Publishing Manager: Michael Dewing
      Production Manager: Iris Buckley
      Technical Manager: Marita Sen
      Compilation, Design & Production: www.jacksonlowe.com
      Typesetting: Tradespools Ltd, Somerset and Jackson Lowe Marketing, Lewes
      Maps: © Maps In Minutes™ (1999)
      Printing and Binding: Mozzon Giutina S.p.A, Florence and Officine Grafiche De Agostini S.p.A, Novara.
      Advertisement Sales: Jackson Lowe Marketing, 173 High Street, Lewes, East Sussex BN7 1EH. (01273) 487487
      © English Tourism Council (except where stated)

Contents

Where to Stay in England 2002

Key to Symbols
A key to symbols can be found on the inside back cover. Keep it open for easy reference.

For short breaks, family holidays, touring holidays or business stop-overs, Where to Stay is all you need. This guide contains details of thousands of places to stay in a wide choice of locations at prices to suit all budgets. Plus places to visit, tourist information centres, maps, events and a whole lot more.

There's no better way to feel refreshed and revitalised than by taking a short break or holiday in England. It offers a rich variety of interest, from dramatic coastal paths, rolling hills and hedgerows to vibrant cities and quality attractions.

Start by looking for a place to stay. The English Tourism Council has assessed all accommodation in this guide for quality, so you can book with confidence that it will meet your expectations.

a warm
welcome

Welcome to our 27th edition -
it's so easy to use, and packed with information.

Get away
and do yourself an English
world of good.

How to use the guide

The guide is divided into the 10 English Regional Tourist Board regions (these are shown on page 14). These regional sections give you all the information you need on the area: accommodation, places to visit, tourist information centres, travel and publications for further information.

Accommodation is listed alphabetically in order of place name. If you would like to know more about the city, town or village in which you wish to stay, you will find brief descriptions at the end of each regional section. Or you can contact the local Tourist Information Centre - the telephone number can be found next to the town name on the accommodation entry pages.

Finding your accommodation

Whether you know exactly where you want to stay or only have an idea of the area you wish to visit, it couldn't be easier to find accommodation:

BY PLACE if you know the town or village look in the index at the back.

BY AREA if you know the area look at the full colour maps starting on page 18. All the places in black offer accommodation featured in this guide.

BY REGION if you know which part of England look in the relevant regional section. These are colour coded at the top of each page. A map showing the regions can be found on page 14.

BY COUNTY if you know which county look at the listing on page 15 to find the region it is in.

Types of accommodation

Hotel accommodation is featured in this guide and each entry includes a description of the property and facilities. There are two special types of hotel accommodation: **Townhouses** are small personally run town centre hotels which concentrate on privacy, luxuriously furnished bedrooms and suites and high quality service. They may not have public rooms or formal dining arrangements but offer additional high quality room service and are usually located in areas well served by restaurants. **Travel Accommodation** includes purpose built bedroom accommodation which you will find along major roads and motorways.

Exclusive hotel listings

Where to Stay is the only guide to contain details of ALL hotels in England which have been quality assessed by the English Tourism Council, giving you the widest choice of accommodation.

Accommodation entries explained

Each accommodation entry contains detailed information to help you decide if it is right for you. This information has been provided by the proprietors themselves, and our aim has been to ensure that it is as objective and factual as possible. To the left of the establishment name you will find the Star rating and quality award, if appropriate.

At-a-glance symbols at the end of each entry give you additional information on services and facilities - a key can be found on the back cover flap. Keep this open to refer to as you read.

1. Listing under town or village with map reference

2. ETC Star rating plus Gold and Silver Awards where applicable

3. Accessible rating where applicable

4. At-a-glance facility symbols

5. Establishment name, address, telephone and fax numbers, e-mail and web site address

6. Prices for bed and breakfast (B&B) and half board (HB) accommodation

7. Months open

8. Hotel group name, if applicable. For a list of central reservation offices see pages 356-357.

9. Accommodation details including credit cards accepted

10. Special Promotions and Themed breaks

Making a Booking

Please remember that changes may occur after the guide is printed. When you have found a suitable place to stay we advise you to contact the establishment to check availability, also to confirm prices and specific facilities which may be important to you. Further advice on how to make a booking can be found at the back of this guide, together with information about deposits and cancellations. It is always advisable to confirm your booking in writing.

Accommodation Ratings & Awards

English Tourism Council

★ ★ ★
HOTEL

Ratings and awards are an indication of quality which will help you find the most suitable accommodation to meet your needs and expectations. You'll find several in this guide:

STAR RATINGS FOR QUALITY

The English Tourism Council's quality assurance standard awards One to Five Stars giving you reliable information about the quality of the accommodation you can expect. (See opposite). You'll find something to suit all budgets and tastes.

SPECIAL AWARDS FOR EXCELLENCE

Gold and Silver Awards - Part of the English Tourism Council standard, Gold and Silver Awards are given to establishments achieving the highest levels of quality within their Star rating. So if you're looking for somewhere special, turn to page 11 for a list of Gold Award holders which have an entry in the regional sections of this guide. Silver award holders are too numerous to list, but they are clearly indicated in the accommodation entries.

The annual Excellence in England awards are the Oscars of the tourism industry. Winners will be announced in Spring 2002, see page 16.

NATIONAL ACCESSIBLE SCHEME FOR SPECIAL NEEDS

Establishments which have a National Accessible rating provide access and facilities for wheelchair users and people who have difficulty walking. Turn to page 12 and 13 for further details.

How do we arrive at a Star rating?

The English Tourism Council has more than 50 trained assessors throughout England who visit properties annually, generally staying overnight as an anonymous guest.

They award ratings based on the overall experience of their stay, and there are strict guidelines to ensure every property is assessed to the same criteria. High standards of housekeeping are a major requirement; heating, lighting, comfort and convenience are also part of the assessment.

THE ASSESSOR'S ROLE - GUEST, ASSESSOR AND ADVISOR

Assessor books their accommodation as a 'normal' guest. They will take into account all aspects of the visiting experience, from how the telephone enquiry is dealt with to the quality of the service and facilities on offer.

During their stay assessors try to experience as many things as possible including the quality of food the knowledge of staff and services, such as room service and dry cleaning if available. They will even check under the bed!

After paying the bill assessors reveals who they are and asks to look round the rest of the establishment. They will then advise the proprietor of the Star rating that has been awarded, discussing the reasons why, as well as suggesting areas for improvement.

So you can see it's a very thorough process to ensure that when you book accommodation with a particular Star rating you can be confident it will meet your expectations. After all, meeting customer expectations is what makes happy guests.

Ratings you can trust

When you're looking for a place to stay, you need a rating system you can trust. The English Tourism Council's ratings give a clear guide to what to expect, in an easy-to-understand form. Properties are visited annually by trained, impartial assessors, so you can have the confidence that your accommodation has been thoroughly checked and rated for quality before you make your booking.

STAR RATING

Ratings are awarded from One to Five Stars. The more Stars, the higher the quality and the greater the range of facilities and level of service provided. The brief explanations of the Star ratings outlined here show what is included at each rating level (note that each rating also includes what is provided at a lower Star rating).

★   Practical accommodation with a limited range of facilities and services, and a high standard of cleanliness throughout (75% of rooms will have en-suite or private facilities). Friendly and courteous staff. A restaurant/eating area offering breakfast and dinner to you and your guests. Alcoholic drinks served in a bar or lounge.

★★   Good accommodation offering a personal style of service with additional facilities. More comfortable bedrooms (all with en-suite or private facilities and colour TV). Food and drink is of a slightly higher standard.

★★★   Very good accommodation with more spacious public areas and bedrooms, all offering a significantly greater quality and higher standard of facilities and services. A more formal style of service with a receptionist. A wide selection of drinks, light lunch and snacks served in a bar or lounge with greater attention to quality. Room service for continental breakfast and laundry service.

★★★★   Accommodation offering excellent comfort and quality. All rooms with en-suite facilities. Strong emphasis on food and drink. Experienced staff responding to your needs and requests. Room service for all meals and 24 hour drinks, refreshments and snacks available.

★★★★★   Spacious and luxurious offering accommodation, extensive facilities, services and cuisine of the highest international quality. Professional, attentive staff, exceptional comfort and a sophisticated ambience.

Gold and Silver Awards

Look out, too, for the English Tourism Council's Gold and Silver Awards, which are awarded to properties achieving the highest levels of quality within their Star rating. While the overall rating is based on a combination of facilities and quality, the Gold and Silver Awards are based solely on quality.

Gold Award

Hotels featured in the regional sections of this Where to Stay guide, which have achieved a Gold Award for an exceptionally high standard of quality, are listed on this page. Please use the Town Index at the back of the guide to find the page numbers for their full entry.

Silver Awards also represent high standards of quality and there are many establishments within this guide which have achieved this. Gold and Silver Awards are clearly indicated in the accommodation entries.

For further information about Gold and Silver Awards, please see page 9.

The Pictures:
1 Lindeth Fell Country House
2 Eastwell Manor
3 Castle House

- **Brockencote Hall,** Chaddesley Corbett, Worcestershire
- **Castle House,** Hereford, Herefordshire
- **Channel House Hotel,** Minehead, Somerset
- **The Chester Grosvenor**, Chester, Cheshire
- **Duxford Lodge Hotel and Le Paradis,** Cambridge, Cambridgeshire
- **Eastwell Manor Hotel,** Ashford, Kent
- **Gilpin Lodge Country House,** Windermere, Cumbria
- **Hotel Riviera,** Sidmouth, Devon
- **Lindeth Fell Country House Hotel,** Windermere, Cumbria
- **Linthwaite House Hotel,** Windermere, Cumbria
- **Little Barwick House,** Barwick, Somerset
- **Lucknam Park,** Bath, Bath and North East Somerset
- **The Milestone Hotel and Apartments,** London, Greater London
- **Millstream Hotel & Restaurant,** Chichester, West Sussex
- **Morston Hall,** Blakeney, Norfolk
- **Northcote Manor Hotel,** Blackburn, Lancashire
- **Nuthurst Grange Country House Hotel,** Hockley Heath, West Midlands
- **Old Bank Hotel,** Oxford, Oxfordshire
- **The Old Vicarage Hotel,** Bridgnorth, Shropshire
- **Rudding Park Hotel & Golf,** Harrogate, North Yorkshire
- **Swinside Lodge Hotel,** Keswick, Cumbria
- **The Vineyard at Stockcross**, Newbury, Berkshire
- **Westover Hall Hotel,** Milford-on-Sea, Hampshire
- **Wood Norton Hall and Conference Centre**, Evesham, Worcestershire

National
Accessible Scheme

The English Tourism Council and National and Regional Tourist Boards throughout Britain assess all types of places to stay, on holiday or business, that provide accessible accommodation for wheelchair users and others who may have difficulty walking.

Accommodation establishments taking part in the National Accessible Scheme, and which appear in the regional sections of this guide are listed opposite. Use the Town Index at the back to find the page numbers for their full entries.

The Tourist Boards recognise three categories of accessibility:

CATEGORY 1   Accessible to all wheelchair users including those travelling independently.

CATEGORY 2   Accessible to a wheelchair user with assistance.

CATEGORY 3   Accessible to a wheelchair user able to walk short distances and up at least three steps.

If you have additional needs or special requirements of any kind, we strongly recommend that you make sure these can be met by your chosen establishment before you confirm your booking.

The criteria the English Tourism Council and National and Regional Tourist Boards have adopted do not necessarily conform to British Standards or to Building Regulations. They reflect what the Boards understand to be acceptable to meet the practical needs of wheelchair users.

The National Accessible Scheme is currently in the process of being updated. Consultation has been conducted throughout 2001 with introduction during 2002.

The National Accessible Scheme forms part of the Tourism for All Campaign that is being promoted by the English Tourism Council and National and Regional Tourist Boards. Additional help and guidance on finding suitable holiday accommodation for those with special needs can be obtained from:

Holiday Care,
2nd Floor, Imperial Buildings,
Victoria Road,
Horley, Surrey RH6 7PZ

Tel: (01293) 774535
Fax: (01293) 784647
Email: holiday.care@virgin.net
Internet: www.holidaycare.org.uk
Minicom: (01293) 776943

CATEGORY 1

- **Bournemouth, Dorset** - Durlston Court Hotel
- **Bracknell, Berkshire** - Coppid Beech Hotel
- **Lowestoft, Suffolk** - Ivy House Farm Hotel
- **Manchester, Greater Manchester**
  - Radisson SAS Hotel Manchester
- **Warkworth, Northumberland**
  - Warkworth House Hotel

CATEGORY 2

- **Ambleside, Cumbria** - Rothay Manor
- **Blakeney, Norfolk** - The Pheasant Hotel
- **Bournemouth, Dorset** - Belvedere Hotel
- **Bridgnorth, Shropshire** - The Old Vicarage Hotel
- **Great Yarmouth, Norfolk** - Horse & Groom Motel
- **Leeds, West Yorkshire**
  - Weetwood Hall Conference Centre & Hotel
- **Greater London** - The Bonnington in Bloomsbury
- **Manchester, Greater Manchester**
  - Novotel Manchester West
- **Norwich, Norfolk** - Beeches Hotel

CATEGORY 3

- **Basildon, Essex** - Campanile Hotel
- **Bath and North East Somerset**
  - Old Malt House Hotel
- **Brockenhurst, Hampshire** - The Watersplash Hotel
- **Cheltenham, Gloucestershire**
  - The Prestbury House Hotel and Restaurant
- **Chester, Cheshire** - Dene Hotel
  - Green Bough Hotel and Restaurant
  - The Chester Grosvenor
- **Chesterfield, Derbyshire** - Abbeydale Hotel
- **Chipping, Lancashire** - Gibbon Bridge Hotel
- **Cirencester, Gloucestershire** - Stratton House Hotel
- **Colchester, Essex** - Rose & Crown
- **Eastbourne, East Sussex** - Congress Hotel
- **Finedon, Northamptonshire** - Tudor Gate Hotel
- **Grange-over-Sands, Cumbria** - Netherwood Hotel
- **Great Yarmouth, Norfolk**
  - Burlington Palm Court Hotel

- **Harrogate, North Yorkshire** - The Boar's Head Hotel
- **Helmsley, North Yorkshire** - Pheasant Hotel
- **Ipswich, Suffolk** - Swallow Belstead Brook Hotel
- **Keswick, Cumbria** - Derwentwater Hotel
- **Kirkby Stephen, Cumbria** - The Black Swan Hotel
- **Langho, Lancashire**
  - Mytton Fold Hotel and Golf Complex
- **Leyburn, North Yorkshire**
  - Golden Lion Hotel & Licensed Restaurant
- **Lytham St Annes, Lancashire** - Chadwick Hotel
- **Margate, Kent** - Lonsdale Court Hotel
- **Newmarket, Suffolk** - Heath Court Hotel
- **Norwich, Norfolk**
  - Marriott Sprowston Manor Hotel & Country Club
  - Old Rectory
- **Nottingham, Nottinghamshire**
  - The Nottingham Gateway Hotel
- **Penzance, Cornwall** - The Queens Hotel
- **Plymouth, Devon** - Novotel Plymouth
- **Preston, Lancashire** - Swallow Hotel
- **Rotherham, South Yorkshire**
  - Best Western Elton Hotel
- **Royal Tunbridge Wells, Kent** - The Spa Hotel
- **Stamford, Lincolnshire** - Garden House Hotel
- **Stonor, Oxfordshire** - The Stonor Arms Hotel
- **Swanage, Dorset** - The Pines Hotel
- **Tenterden, Kent** - Little Silver Country Hotel
- **Torquay, Devon** - Frognel Hall
- **Wareham, Dorset** - Kemps Country House Hotel
- **Warrington, Cheshire**
  - Hanover International Hotel and Club
- **Winchester, Hampshire** - Harestock Lodge Hotel
- **Windermere, Cumbria** - Linthwaite House Hotel
- **Wisbech, Cambridgeshire** - Crown Lodge Hotel
- **Woodhall Spa, Lincolnshire** - Petwood Hotel
- **York, North Yorkshire**
  - Hilton York
  - Savages Hotel
  - The Grange Hotel

(The information contained on these pages
was correct at the time of going to press.)

Regional
Tourist Board
Areas

This Where to Stay guide is divided into 10 regional sections as shown on the map below. To identify each regional section and its page number, please refer to the key below. The county index overleaf indicates in which regional section you will find a particular county.

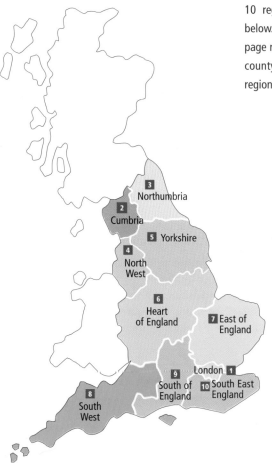

Each of the ten English regions shown here has a Regional Tourist Board which can give you information about things to see or do locally. Contact details are given both at the beginning and end of each regional section.

LOCATION MAPS

Colour location maps showing all the cities, towns and villages with accommodation in the regional sections of this guide can be found on pages 18-30. Turn to the Town Index at the back of this guide for the page number on which you can find the relevant accommodation.

In which region is the county I wish to visit?

COUNTY/UNITARY AUTHORITY	REGION
Bath & North East Somerset	South West
Bedfordshire	East of England
Berkshire	South of England
Bristol	South West
Buckinghamshire	South of England
Cambridgeshire	East of England
Cheshire	North West
Cornwall	South West
Cumbria	Cumbria
Derbyshire	Heart of England
Devon	South West
Dorset (Eastern)	South of England
Dorset (Western)	South West
Durham	Northumbria
East Riding of Yorkshire	Yorkshire
East Sussex	South East England
Essex	East of England
Gloucestershire	Heart of England
Greater London	London
Greater Manchester	North West
Hampshire	South of England
Herefordshire	Heart of England
Hertfordshire	East of England
Isle of Wight	South of England
Isles of Scilly	South West
Kent	South East England
Lancashire	North West
Leicestershire	Heart of England
Lincolnshire	Heart of England
Merseyside	North West
Norfolk	East of England
North East Lincolnshire	Yorkshire
North Lincolnshire	Yorkshire
North Somerset	South West
North Yorkshire	Yorkshire
Northamptonshire	Heart of England
Northumberland	Northumbria
Nottinghamshire	Heart of England
Oxfordshire	South of England
Rutland	Heart of England
Shropshire	Heart of England
Somerset	South West
South Gloucestershire	South West
South Yorkshire	Yorkshire
Staffordshire	Heart of England
Suffolk	East of England
Surrey	South East England
Tees Valley	Northumbria
Tyne & Wear	Northumbria
Warwickshire	Heart of England
West Midlands	Heart of England
West Sussex	South East England
West Yorkshire	Yorkshire
Wiltshire	South West
Worcestershire	Heart of England
York	Yorkshire

UNITARY AUTHORITIES

Please note that many new unitary authorities have been formed - for example Brighton & Hove and Bristol - and are officially separate from the county in which they were previously located. To aid the reader we have only included the major unitary authorities in the list above and on the colour maps.

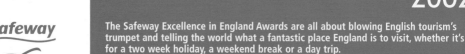

Our Countryside Matters!

Country Code

- Always follow the Country code
- Guard against all risk of fire
- Keep your dogs under close control
- Use gates and stiles to cross fences, hedges and walls
- Take your litter home
- Protect wildlife, plants and trees
- Make no unnecessary noise

- Enjoy the countryside and respect its life and work
- Fasten all gates
- Keep to public paths across farmland
- Leave livestock, crops and machinery alone
- Help to keep all water clean
- Take special care on country roads

We hope the countryside will fully open in 2002. However, given the serious nature of Foot and Mouth Disease please be ready to follow this additional advice and respect any further precautions given in local authority notices:

- Don't go onto farmland if you have handled farm animals in the last 7 days
- Avoid contact with farm animals and keep dogs on a lead where they are present
- If you step in dung, remove it before you leave the field • Don't go on paths with a local authority 'closed' notice.

For more information contact Tourist information Centres or Countryside Agency web site
www.countryside.gov.uk
which links to other local authority web sites providing details about rights
of way and access opportunities across England.

Tourist information
Centres

When it comes to your next England break, the first stage of your journey could be closer than you think. You've probably got a Tourist Information centre nearby which is there to serve the local community – as well as visitors. Knowledgeable staff will be happy to help you, wherever you're heading.

Many Tourist information Centres can provide you with maps and guides, and sometimes it's even possible to book your accommodation, too.

Across the country, there are more than 550 Tourist Information Centres. You'll find the address of your nearest Tourist Information Centre in your local Phone Book.

www.travelengland.org.uk

Log on to travelengland.org.uk and discover something different around every corner. Meander through pages for ideas of places to visit and things to do. Spend time in each region and discover the diversity – from busy vibrant cities to rural village greens; rugged peaks to gentle rolling hills; dramatic coastline to idyllic sandy beaches. England might be a small country but it is brimming with choice and opportunity. Visit www.travelengland.org.uk and see for yourself.

MAP 1

A   B

Location
Maps

Every place name featured in the regional accommodation sections of this Where to Stay guide has a map reference to help you locate it on the maps which follow. For example, to find Colchester, Essex, which has 'Map ref 3B2', turn to Map 3 and refer to grid square B2.

All place names appearing in the regional sections are shown in black type on the maps. This enables you to find other places in your chosen area which may have suitable accommodation - the Town Index (at the back of this guide) gives page numbers.

1

2

3

MAP 5
Newcastle upon Tyne
Carlisle

MAP 4 • York
• Manchester
Lincoln •

Birmingham
Ipswich

MAP 2 Oxford •   MAPS 6&7
MAP 1   • Bristol   • London
Southampton Dover •
Exeter •   MAP 3

Tintagel

A389
Mawgan Porth
Watergate Bay   NEWQUAY
Newquay   A392   Lostwithiel
A30
CORNWALL
St Austell
St Agnes
Truro   Mevagissey
Illogan
Ruan High
Lanes
Penzance
Land's End   Falmouth
A394
Manaccan

ISLES OF SCILLY

Isles of Scilly
(St. Mary's)

MAP 1

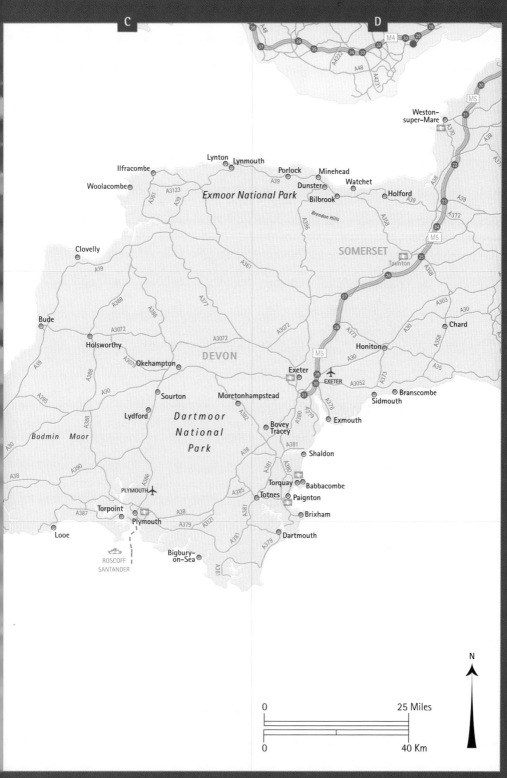

C D

Weston-
super-Mare

Lynton Lynmouth
Ilfracombe Porlock Minehead
Woolacombe Dunster Watchet
Exmoor National Park Bilbrook Holford

Brendon Hills
SOMERSET
Clovelly
Taunton

Bude Chard
Holsworthy Honiton
DEVON
Okehampton EXETER
Exeter Branscombe
Sourton Sidmouth
Lydford Exmouth
Bodmin Moor Dartmoor Bovey
National Tracey
Park Shaldon
PLYMOUTH Torquay Babbacombe
Torpoint Totnes Paignton
Plymouth Brixham
Looe
Dartmouth
ROSCOFF Bigbury-
SANTANDER on-Sea

N

0 25 Miles

0 40 Km

MAP 2

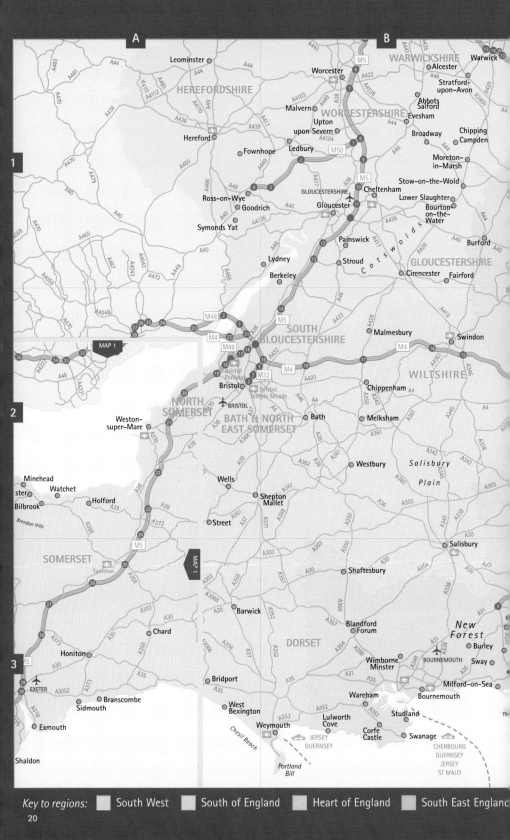

MAP 2

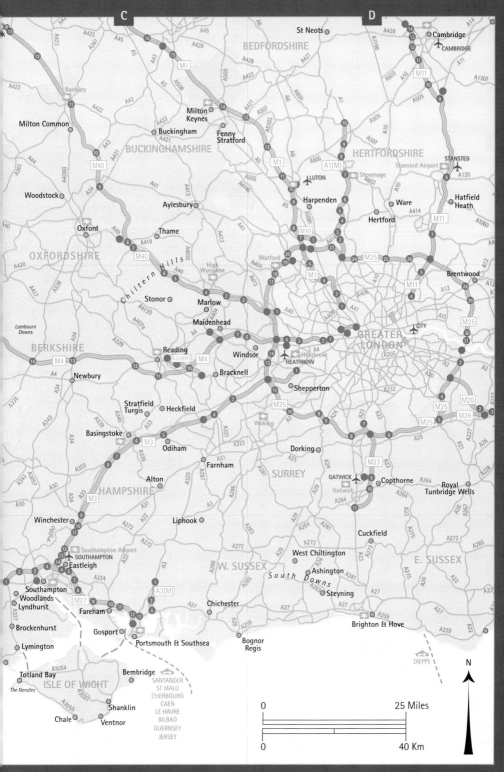

East of England

All place names in black offer accommodation in this guide.

MAP 3

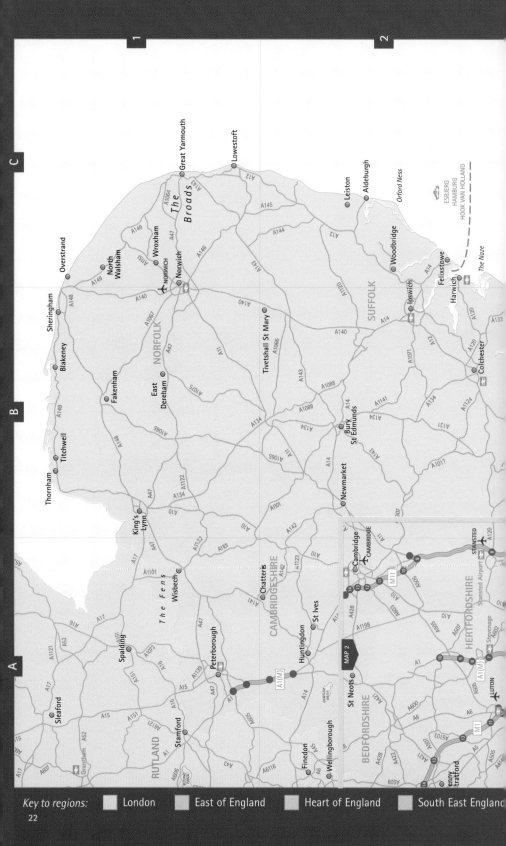

Key to regions: █ London █ East of England █ Heart of England █ South East England

MAP 3

All place names in black offer accommodation in this guide.

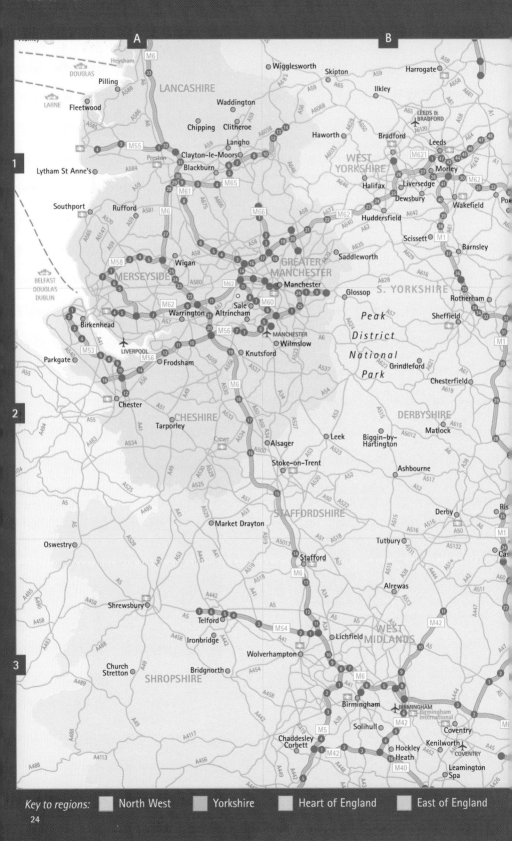

MAP 4

MAP 4

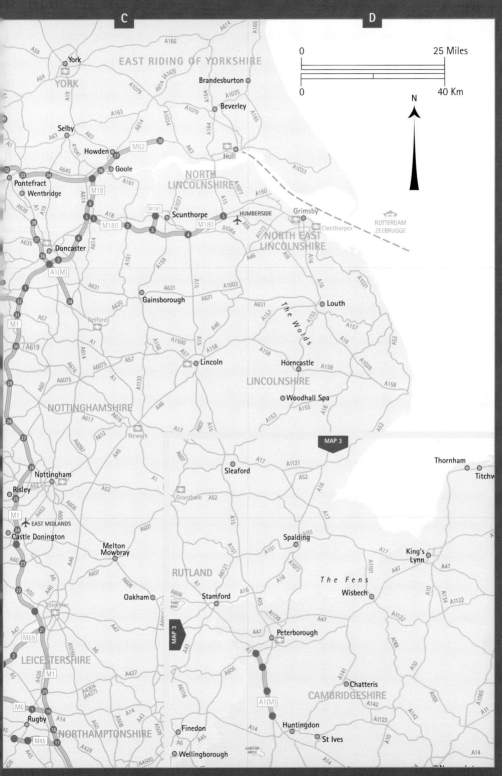

All place names in black offer accommodation in this guide.

MAP 5

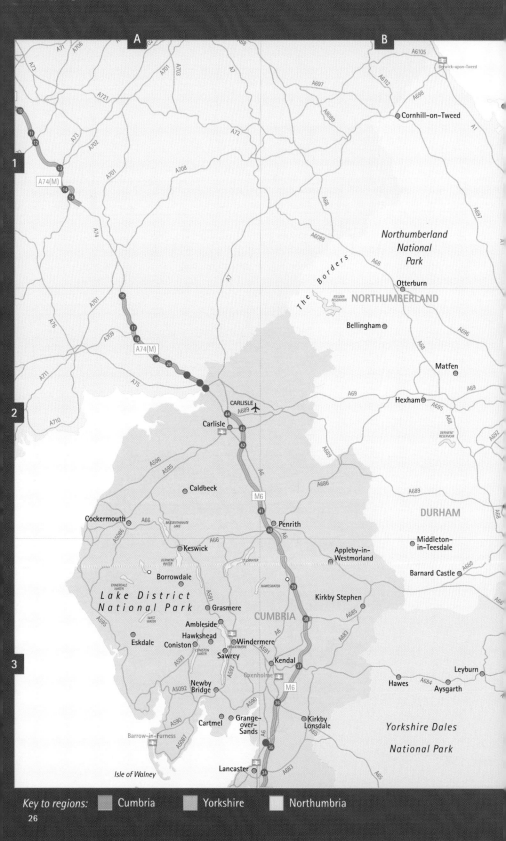

Key to regions: Cumbria   Yorkshire   Northumbria

MAP 5

Holy Island
Farne Islands
Bamburgh

Alnmouth
Warkworth

0   25 Miles
0   40 Km

N

Whitley Bay
NEWCASTLE
Tynemouth
Newcastle upon Tyne

BERGEN
STAVANGER
KIRSTIANSAND
HAUGESUND
AMSTERDAM (Ijmulden)
GOTHENBURG

TYNE & WEAR
Sunderland

Durham
Crook

Sedgefield
Rushyford

TEES VALLEY
Middlesbrough

Darlington
TEESIDE

Whitby

Stokesley

Rosedale Abbey

North York Moors
National Park

Gillamoor
Kirkbymoorside

Scarborough

Bedale
Newby Wiske
Helmsley
Thornton Watlass
Thirsk

Filey

NORTH YORKSHIRE

Markington
Boroughbridge
A1(M)

Bridlington

All place names in black offer accommodation in this guide.

MAP 6

MAP 6

© Arka Cartographics Ltd. 1999

MAP 7

Central London

LONDON

A dynamic mix of history and heritage, cool and contemporary. Great museums, stunning art collections, royal palaces, hip nightlife and stylish shopping, from ritzy Bond Street to cutting-edge Hoxton.

classic sights

St Paul's Cathedral – Wren's famous church
Tower of London – 900 years of British history
London Eye – spectacular views from the world's highest 'big wheel'

arts for all

National Gallery – Botticelli, Rembrandt, Turner and more
Tate Modern – 20th century art in a former power station
Victoria & Albert Museum – decorative arts

city lights

Theatre: musicals – West End; drama – Royal Court and National Theatre;
Music: classical – Wigmore Hall and Royal Festival Hall;
jazz – Ronnie Scott's; ballet & opera – Royal Opera House

insider london

Dennis Severs's House, E1 – candlelit tours of this authentically 18th century house

Greater London, comprising the 32 London Boroughs

FOR MORE INFORMATION CONTACT:
London Tourist Board
6th Floor, Glen House, Stag Place,
London SW1E 5LT
Telephone enquiries - see London Line on page 36
Internet: www.LondonTouristBoard.com

The Pictures:
1 Tower Bridge
2 Hampton Court
3 Piccadilly Circus

Places to Visit - see pages 32-36
Where to Stay - see pages 37-42

31

PLACES to visit

You will find hundreds of interesting places to visit during your stay, just some of which are listed in these pages. Contact any Tourist Information Centre in and around London for more ideas on days out.

Bank of England Museum

Bartholomew Lane, London, EC2R 8AH
Tel: (020) 7601 5545 www.bankofengland.co.uk
The museum is housed within the Bank of England. It traces the history of the Bank from its foundation by Royal Charter in 1694 to its role today as the nation's central bank.

British Airways London Eye

Jubilee Gardens, South Bank, London, SE1
Tel: (0870) 5000 600 www.ba-londoneye.com
At 443 ft (135 m) high, this is the world's highest observation wheel. It provides a 30-minute slow-moving flight over London

British Library

96 Euston Road, London, NW1 2DB
Tel: (020) 7412 7332 www.bl.uk
Exhibition galleries, bookshop, piazza displaying Magna Carta, Gutenberg Bible, Shakespeare's First Folio and illuminated manuscripts, temporary exhibitions.

British Museum

Great Russell Street, London, WC1B 3DG
Tel: (020) 7323 8000 www.thebritishmuseum.ac.uk
One of the great museums of the world, showing the works of man from prehistoric to modern times with collections drawn from the whole world.

Cabinet War Rooms

Clive Steps, King Charles Street, London, SW1A 2AQ
Tel: (020) 7930 6961 www.iwm.org.uk
The underground headquarters used by Winston Churchill and the British Government during World War II. Includes Cabinet Room, Transatlantic Telephone Room and Map Room.

Chessington World of Adventures

Leatherhead Road, Chessington, KT9 2NE
Tel: (01372) 729560 www.chessington.com
Visitors will be in for a big adventure as they explore the theme park's amazing new attractions.

Design Museum

28 Shad Thames, London, SE1 2YD
Tel: (020) 7403 6933 www.designmuseum.org
The Design Museum is one of London's most inspiring attractions, concerned solely with the products, technologies and buildings of the 20thC and 21stC.

Hampton Court Palace

Hampton Court, East Molesey, KT8 9AU
Tel: (020) 8781 9500 www.hrp.org.uk
The oldest Tudor palace in England with many attractions including the Tudor kitchens, tennis courts, maze, State Apartments and King's Apartments.

HMS Belfast

Morgan's Lane, Tooley Street, London, SE1 2JH
Tel: (020) 7940 6300 www.iwm.org.uk
World War II cruiser weighing 11,500 tonnes, now a floating naval museum, with 9 decks to explore.

Imperial War Museum

Lambeth Road, London, SE1 6HZ

Tel: (020) 7416 5320 www.iwm.org.uk

Museum tells the story of 20thC war from Flanders to Bosnia. Special features include the Blitz Experience, the Trench Experience and the World of Espionage.

Kensington Palace State Apartments

Kensington Gardens, London, W8 4PX

Tel: (020) 7937 7079 www.hrp.org.uk

Furniture and ceiling paintings from Stuart-Hanoverian periods, rooms from Victorian era and works of art from the Royal Collection. Also Royal Ceremonial Dress Collection.

Kew Gardens (Royal Botanic Gardens)

Kew Richmond TW9 3AB

Tel: (020) 8940 1171 Rec.

300 acres (121 ha) containing living collections of over 40,000 varieties of plants. Seven spectacular glasshouses, 2 art galleries, Japanese and rock garden.

London Dungeon

28-34 Tooley Street, London, SE1 2SZ

Tel: (020) 7403 7221 www.thedungeons.com

The world's first medieval fully interactive horror attraction. Relive the 'Great Fire of London', unmask 'Jack the Ripper' and take the 'Judgement Day' ride.

London Planetarium

Marylebone Road, London, NW1 5LR

Tel: (0870) 400 3000 www.london-planetarium.com

Visitors can experience a virtual reality trip through space and wander through the interactive Space Zones before the show.

London Transport Museum

Covent Garden Piazza, London, WC2E 7BB

Tel: (020) 7379 6344 www.ltmuseum.co.uk

The history of transport for everyone, from spectacular vehicles, special exhibitions, actors and guided tours to film shows, gallery talks and children's craft workshops.

London Zoo

Regent's Park, London, NW1 4RY

Tel: (020) 7722 3333 www.londonzoo.co.uk

One of the world's most famous zoos and home to over 600 species. Including the new 'Web of Life' exhibition, as well as a full daily events programme.

Madame Tussaud's

Marylebone Road, London, NW1 5LR

Tel: (0870) 400 3000 www.madame-tussauds.com

World-famous collection of wax figures in themed settings which include The Garden Party, 200 Years, Superstars, The Grand Hall, The Chamber of Horrors and The Spirit of London.

National Army Museum

Royal Hospital Road, Chelsea, London, SW3 4HT

Tel: (020) 7730 0717
www.national-armymuseum.ac.uk

The story of the British soldier in peace and war, through five centuries. Exhibits range from paintings to uniforms and from the English Civil War to Kosovo.

National History Museum

Cromwell Road, London, SW7 5BD

Tel: (020) 7942 5000 www.nhm.ac.uk

Home of the wonders of the natural world, one of the most popular museums in the world and one of London's finest landmarks.

The Pictures:
1 London by night, Piccadilly Circus
2 Big Ben
3 Buckingham Palace
4 Albert Hall
5 Harrods
6 Horseguards Parade

National Portrait Gallery

St Martin's Place, London, WC2H 0HE

Tel: (020) 7306 0055 www.npg.org.uk

Permanent collection of portraits of famous men and women from the Middle Ages to the present day. Free, but charge for some exhibitions.

Royal Air Force Museum

Grahame Park Way, Hendon, London, NW9 5LL

Tel: (020) 8205 2266 www.rafmuseum.com

Britain's National Museum of Aviation features over 70 full-sized aircraft, Flight Simulator, 'Touch and Try' Jet Provost Trainer and Eurofighter 2000 Theatre.

Royal Mews

Buckingham Palace, London, SW1A 1AA

Tel: (020) 7839 1377 www.royal.gov.uk

Her Majesty The Queen's carriage horses, carriages and harness used on State occasions (Coronation Coach built 1761).

Royal Observatory Greenwich

Greenwich Park, London, SE10 9NF

Tel: (020) 8858 4422 www.nmm.ac.uk

Museum of time and space and site of the Greenwich Meridian. Working telescopes and planetarium, timeball, Wren's Octagon Room and intricate clocks and computer simulations.

Science Museum

Exhibition Road, London, SW7 2DD

Tel: (0870) 870 4868 www.sciencemuseum.org.uk

See, touch and experience the major scientific advances of the last 300 years. With over 40 galleries, and over 2,000 hands-on exhibits to captivate and inspire all.

Shakespeare's Globe Exhibition and Tour

New Globe Walk, Bankside, London, SE1 9DT

Tel: (020) 7902 1500 www.shakespeares-globe.org

Against the historical background of Elizabethan Bankside, the City of London's playground in Shakespeare's time, the exhibition focuses on actors, architecture and audiences.

St Paul's Cathedral

St Paul's Churchyard, London, EC4M 8AD

Tel: (020) 7236 4128 www.stpauls.co.uk

Wren's famous cathedral church of the diocese of London incorporating the Crypt, Ambulatory and Whispering Gallery.

Tate Britain

Millbank, London, SW1P 4RG

Tel: (020) 7887 8000 www.tate.org.uk

Tate Britain presents the world's greatest collection of British art in a dynamic series of new displays and exhibitions.

Theatre Museum

Russell Street, London, WC2E 7PA

Tel: (020) 7943 4700 www.theatremuseum.org

Five galleries illustrating the history of performance in the United Kingdom. The collection includes displays on theatre, ballet, dance, musical stage, rock and pop music.

Tower of London

Tower Hill, London, EC3N 4AB

Tel: (020) 7709 0765 www.hrp.org.uk

Home of the `Beefeaters' and ravens, the building spans 900 years of British history. On display are the nation's Crown Jewels, regalia and armoury robes.

Victoria and Albert Museum

Cromwell Road, London, SW7 2RL

Tel: (020) 7942 2000 www.vam.ac.uk

The V&A holds one of the world's largest and most diverse collections of the decorative arts, dating from 3000BC to the present day.

Vinopolis, City of Wine

1 Bank End, London, SE1 9BU

Tel: (0870) 241 4040 www.vinopolis.co.uk

Vinopolis offers all the pleasures of wine under one roof. The Wine Odyssey tour includes free tastings from over 200 wines; also 2 restaurants on site.

Westminster Abbey

Parliament Square, London, SW1P 3PA

Tel: (020) 7222 5152 www.westminster-abbey.org

One of Britain's finest Gothic buildings. Scene of the coronation, marriage and burial of British monarchs. Nave and cloisters, Royal Chapels and Undercroft Museum.

Find out more about London

Millennium Wheel

LONDON TOURIST BOARD

London Tourist Board and Convention Bureau
6th Floor, Glen House, Stag Place, London SW1E 5LT
www.LondonTouristBoard.com

TOURIST INFORMATION CENTRES

POINT OF ARRIVAL

- **Heathrow Terminals 1, 2, 3** Underground Station Concourse, Heathrow Airport, TW6 2JA.
  Open: Daily 0800-1800; 1 Jun-30 Sep, Mon-Sat 0800-1900, Sun 0800-1800.

- **Liverpool Street Underground Station,** EC2M 7PN.
  Open: Daily 0800-1800; 1 Jun-30 Sep, Mon-Sat 0800-1900, Sun 0800-1800.

- **Victoria Station Forecourt,** SW1V 1JU.
  Open: 1 Jun-30 Sep, Mon-Sat 0800-2100, Sun 0800-1800; 1 Oct-Easter, daily 0800-1800; Easter-31 May, Mon-Sat 0800-2000, Sun 0800-1800.

- **Waterloo International Terminal**
  Arrivals Hall, London SE1 7LT. Open: Daily 0830-2230.

INNER LONDON

- **Britain Visitor Centre,** 1 Regent Street, Piccadilly Circus, SW1Y 4XT.
  Open: Mon 0930-1830,Tue-Fri 0900-1830, Sat & Sun 1000-1600; Jun-Oct, Sat 0900-1700.

- **Greenwich TIC,** Pepys House, 2 Cutty Sark Gardens, Greenwich SE10 9LW.
  Tel: 0870 608 2000; Fax: 020 8853 4607.
  Open: Daily 1000-1700; 1 Jul-31 Aug, daily 1000-2000.

- **Lewisham TIC,** Lewisham Library, 199-201 Lewisham High Street, SE13 6LG.
  Tel: 020 8297 8317; Fax: 020 8297 9241.
  Open: Mon 1000-1700, Tue-Fri 0900-1700, Sat 1000-1600, Sun closed.

- **Liverpool Street Underground Station,** EC2M 7PN.
  Open: Mon-Fri 0800-1800, Sat 0800-1730, Sun 0900-1730.

- **Southwark Information Centre,**
  London Bridge, 6 Tooley Street, SE1 2SY.
  Tel: 020 7403 8299; Fax: 020 7357 6321.
  Open: Easter-31 Oct, Mon-Sat 1000-1800, Sun 1030-1730; 1 Nov-Easter, Mon-Sat 1000-1600, Sun 1100-1600.

- **Tower Hamlets TIC,** 18 Lamb Street, E1 6EA.
  Fax: 020 7375 2539.
  Open: Mon, Tue, Thu & Fri 0930-1330 & 1430-1630, Wed 0930-1300, Sat closed, Sun 1130-1430.

- **Victoria Station Forecourt,** SW1V 1JU.
  Open: Jan-Feb, Mon-Sat 0800-1900; Mar-May, Mon-Sat 0800-2000; Jun-Sep, Mon-Sat 0800-2100; Oct-Dec, Mon-Sat 0800-2000, Sun 0800-1815.

- **London Visitor Centre, Arrivals Hall,**
  Waterloo International Terminal, London SE1 7LT.
  Open: Daily 0830-2230.

OUTER LONDON

- **Bexley Hall Place TIC,** Bourne Road, Bexley, Kent, DA5 1PQ.
  Tel: 01322 558676; Fax 01322 522921.
  Open: Mon-Sat 1000-1630, Sun 1400-1730.

- **Croydon TIC, Katharine Street,** Croydon, CR9 1ET.
  Tel: 020 8253 1009; Fax: 020 8253 1008.
  Open: Mon, Tues, Wed & Fri 0900-1800, Thu 0930-1800, Sat 0900-1700, Sun 1400-1700.

- **Harrow TIC, Civic Centre,** Station Road, Harrow, HA1 2XF.
  Tel: 020 8424 1103; Fax: 020 8424 1134.
  Open: Mon-Fri 0900-1700, Sat & Sun closed.

- **Heathrow Terminals 1,2,3 Underground Station**
  Concourse, Heathrow Airport, TW6 2JA.
  Open: Daily 0800-1800.

- **Hillingdon TIC,** Central Library, 4-15 High Street, Uxbridge, UB8 1HD.
  Tel: 01895 250706; Fax: 01895 239794.
  Open: Mon, Tue & Thu 0930-2000, Wed 0930-1730, Fri 1000-1730, Sat 0930-1600, Sun closed.

- **Hounslow TIC,** The Treaty Centre, High Street, Hounslow, TW3 1ES.
  Tel: 020 8583 2929; Fax: 020 8583 4714.
  Open: Mon, Wed, Fri & Sat 0930-1730, Tue & Thu 0930-2000, Sun closed.

- **Kingston TIC,** Market House, Market Place, Kingston upon Thames, KT1 1JS.
  Tel: 020 8547 5592; Fax: 020 8547 5594.
  Open: Mon-Fri 1000-1700, Sat 0900-1600, Sun closed.

- **Richmond TIC,** Old Town Hall, Whittaker Avenue; Richmond, TW9 1TP.
  Tel: 020 8940 9125 Fax: 020 8940 6899.
  Open: Mon-Sat 1000-1700; Easter Sunday-end Sep, Sun 1030-1330.

- **Swanley TIC,** London Road, BR8 7AE.
  Tel: 01322 614660; Fax: 01322 666154.
  Open: Mon-Thur 0930-1730, Fri 0930-1800, Sat 0900-1600, Sun closed.

- **Twickenham TIC,** The Atrium, Civic Centre, York Street, Twickenham, Middlesex, TW1 3BZ.
  Tel: 020 8891 7272; Fax: 020 8891 7738.
  Open: Mon-Thu 0900-1715, Fri 0900-1700, Sat & Sun closed.

LONDON LINE

London Tourist Board's recorded telephone information service provides information on museums, galleries, attractions, river trips, sight seeing tours, accommodation, theatre, what's on, changing of the Guard, children's London, shopping, eating out and gay and lesbian London.
Available 24 hours a day. Calls cost 60p per minute as at July 2001. Call 09068 663344.

ARTSLINE

London's information and advice service for disabled people on arts and entertainment. Call (020) 7388 2227.

HOTEL ACCOMMODATION SERVICE

Accommodation reservations can be made throughout London. Call the London Tourist Board's Telephone Accommodation Service on (020) 7932 2020 with your requirements and Mastercard/Visa/Switch details or email your request on book@londontouristboard.co.uk

Reservations on arrival are handled at the Tourist Information Centres at Victoria Station, Heathrow Underground, Liverpool Street Station and Waterloo International. Go to any of them on the day when you need accommodation. A communication charge and a refundable deposit are payable when making a reservation.

WHICH PART OF LONDON?

The majority of tourist accommodation is situated in the central parts of London and is therefore very convenient for most of the city's attractions and night life.

However, there are many hotels in outer London which provide other advantages, such as easier parking. In the 'Where to Stay' pages which follow, you will find accommodation listed under INNER LONDON (covering the E1 to W14 London Postal Area) and OUTER LONDON (covering the remainder of Greater London). Colour maps 6 and 7 at the front of the guide show place names and London Postal Area codes and will help you to locate accommodation in your chosen area of London.

Getting to
London

BY ROAD: Major trunk roads into London include: A1, M1, A5, A10, A11, M11, A13, A2, M2, A23, A3, M3, A4, M4, A40, M40, A41, M25 (London orbital).
London Transport is responsible for running London's bus services and the underground rail network. (020) 7222 1234 (24 hour telephone service; calls answered in rotation).

BY RAIL: Main rail termini:
Victoria/Waterloo/Charing Cross - serving the South/South East;
King's Cross - serving the North East; Euston - serving the North West/Midlands;
Liverpool Street - serving the East; Paddington - serving the Thames Valley/West.

The Pictures:
1 China Town
2 Houses of Parliament

Where to stay in London

Accommodation entries in this region are listed under Inner London (covering the postcode areas E1 to W14) and Outer London (covering the remainder of Greater London) - please refer to the colour location maps 6 and 7 at the front of this guide.

At-a-glance symbols at the end of each accommodation entry give useful information about services and facilities. A key to symbols can be found inside the back cover flap. Keep this open for easy reference.

A complete listing of all the English Tourism Council assessed accommodation covered by this guide appears at the back of the guide.

INNER LONDON
LONDON N1

★★★

JURYS LONDON INN

60 Pentonville Road, Islington, London N1 9LA
T: (020) 7282 5500
F: (020) 7282 5511
E: london_inn@jurysdoyle.com
I: www.jurysdoyle.com

B&B per night:
S Max £102.00
D Max £110.00

OPEN All year round

CR
Utell International

Each of our rooms is equipped to an excellent standard, including air conditioning, direct-dial telephone, tea/coffee facilities, modem points and satellite TV. Situated in Islington, a cultural quarter of London which offers many sights and experiences for the business or leisure traveller.

Bedrooms: 229 double/ twin
Bathrooms: 229 en suite

Lunch available
Evening meal available
CC: Amex, Delta, Diners, Mastercard, Switch, Visa

IMPORTANT NOTE Information on accommodation listed in this guide has been supplied by the proprietors. As changes may occur you are advised to check details at the time of booking.

LONDON N4

★

SPRING PARK HOTEL

400 Seven Sisters Road, London
N4 2LX
T: (020) 8800 6030
F: (020) 8802 5652
E: sphotel400@aol.com
I: www.smoothhound.co.uk/hotels/
springpa.html

Bedrooms: 10 single,
39 double/twin, 1 triple/
multiple
Bathrooms: 36 en suite

Evening meal available
CC: Amex, Delta,
Mastercard, Switch, Visa

B&B per night:
S £40.00–£60.00
D £50.00–£80.00

HB per person:
DY £50.00–£70.00

OPEN All year round

Edwardian villa-style hotel overlooking scenic Finsbury Park. Air conditioned restaurant/ bar. Free car park. Next to Manor House underground station (Piccadilly line).

LONDON SE3

★★

CLARENDON HOTEL

8-16 Montpelier Row, Blackheath, London
SE3 0RW
T: (020) 8318 4321
F: (020) 8318 4378
E: relax@clarendonhotel.com
I: www.clarendonhotel.com

B&B per night:
S £70.00–£85.00
D £80.00–£150.00

HB per person:
DY Min £87.50

OPEN All year round

This Georgian-fronted hotel commands superb views over historic Blackheath and Greenwich. An ideal tourist base for visiting London, Greenwich and the Garden of England, Kent. Make your stay a memorable one: enjoy dinner in the Meridian restaurant, brandy by the log fire or visit our nautical chart bar.

Bedrooms: 36 single,
107 double/twin,
39 triple/multiple; suites
available
Bathrooms: 182 en suite

Lunch available
Evening meal available
CC: Amex, Delta, Diners,
Mastercard, Switch, Visa

Many themed events throughout the year such as Murder Mystery, Buddy Holly Dinner, jazz every Sat. Weekend breaks from £99pp.

LONDON SW1

★★★★
Silver
Award

DOLPHIN SQUARE HOTEL

Dolphin Square, Chichester Street, London
SW1V 3LX
T: (020) 7834 3800 & 0800 616607
F: (020) 7798 8735
E: reservations@dolphinsquarehotel.co.uk
I: www.dolphinsquarehotel.co.uk

B&B per night:
S £155.00–£400.00
D £180.00–£400.00

HB per person:
DY £170.00–£250.00

OPEN All year round

ⓒⓇ
Utell International/
Grand Heritage Hotels

Set in 3.5 acres of private gardens in the heart of London, bordered by Westminster, close to the River Thames. One of the few all-suite hotels in London, each of our 148 suites includes a kitchen or butler's pantry, 1, 2 or 3 bedrooms, and most have a separate lounge.

Bedrooms: 109 double/
twin, 39 triple/multiple,
suites available
Bathrooms: 148 en suite

Lunch available
Evening meal available
CC: Amex, Delta, Diners,
Mastercard, Switch, Visa

Weekend special from £60pp based on 2 sharing, incl breakfast. Minimum 2-night stay, valid Thu-Sun and Bank Hols.

LONDON SW5

★★

BARKSTON GARDENS HOTEL, KENSINGTON

34-44 Barkston Gardens, London
SW5 0EW
T: (020) 7373 7851
F: (020) 7370 6570
E: info@barkstongardens.com
I: www.cairn.hotels.co.uk

Bedrooms: 30 single,
54 double/twin, 9 triple/
multiple
Bathrooms: 93 en suite

Lunch available
Evening meal available
CC: Amex, Delta, Diners,
Mastercard, Switch, Visa

B&B per night:
S £65.00–£95.00
D £75.00–£125.00

OPEN All year round

The Independents

Traditional, friendly hotel situated in garden square. Near Underground and exhibition centre, within easy reach of Hyde Park, Knightsbridge and museums.

LONDON SW5 continued

| ★★★★ Silver Award TOWNHOUSE | THE CRANLEY HOTEL 10-12 Bina Gardens, South Kensington, London SW5 0LA T: (020) 7373 0123 F: (020) 7373 9497 E: karendukes@thecranley.com I: www.thecranley.com | Bedrooms: 4 single, 33 double/twin, 1 triple/ multiple; suites available Bathrooms: 38 en suite | CC: Amex, Delta, Diners, Mastercard, Switch, Visa | B&B per night: S £192.07–£209.70 D £231.40–£313.65 OPEN All year round (CR) Utell International |

Situated in the Royal Borough of Kensington and Chelsea, this delightful townhouse hotel offers complimentary afternoon tea, champagne and canapes.

Ⓜ️🛏️♿️🏨🍴🖥️🖨️📶Ⓢ✂️🅾️⬆️🖥️⊜🔲

| ★★ | ENTERPRISE HOTEL 15-25 Hogarth Road, London SW5 0QJ T: (020) 7373 4502 & 7373 4503 F: (020) 7373 5115 E: ehotel@aol.com I: www.enterprisehotel.com | Bedrooms: 14 single, 61 double/twin, 20 triple/multiple Bathrooms: 95 en suite | Lunch available Evening meal available CC: Amex, Delta, Diners, Mastercard, Switch, Visa | B&B per night: S £50.00–£69.00 D £79.00–£99.00 OPEN All year round (CR) The Independents/ Minotel |

Ideally located with connections by underground to the West End and Knightsbridge. Kensington High Street shops nearby.

Ⓜ️🛏️♿️🖨️Ⓢ🅾️🅾️⬆️🖥️⊜🐴♦

| ★★★ | HOGARTH HOTEL 33 Hogarth Road, Kensington, London SW5 0QQ T: (020) 7370 6831 F: (020) 7373 6179 E: hogarth@marstonhotels.co.uk I: www.marstonhotels.co.uk | Bedrooms: 7 single, 77 double/twin, 1 triple/ multiple Bathrooms: 85 en suite | Lunch available Evening meal available CC: Amex, Delta, Diners, Mastercard, Switch, Visa | B&B per night: S £99.00–£115.00 D £120.00–£145.00 OPEN All year round (CR) Marston Hotels |

Modern hotel near Earl's Court within walking distance of Olympia and Earl's Court Exhibition Centres. Designer bedrooms are well-equipped and have benefited from recent refurbishment.

🛏️♿️🍴🖨️🖥️♦Ⓢ✂️🅾️🅾️⬆️🖥️⊜🍴🐴P

★★★★

SWALLOW INTERNATIONAL HOTEL

Cromwell Road, London SW5 0TH
T: (020) 7973 1000
F: (020) 7244 8194
E: international@swallow-hotels.co.uk
I: www.swallowhotels.com

B&B per night:
S £99.00–£130.00
D £99.00–£130.00

OPEN All year round

Modern hotel centrally located in Kensington. Air-conditioned bedrooms, 2 restaurants and Leisure Club. Car park (chargeable). Rate shown is a breakaway rate, based on a minimum 2 nights' stay and includes £19.95 voucher per couple, subject to availability. Call quoting EN900.

Bedrooms: 28 single, 254 double/twin, 36 triple/multiple; suites available
Bathrooms: 330 en suite

Lunch available
Evening meal available
CC: Amex, Delta, Diners, Mastercard, Switch, Visa

★★★

RAMADA JARVIS KENSINGTON

31-34 Queen's Gate, South Kensington, London SW7 5JA
T: (020) 7584 7222
F: (020) 7589 3910
E: jkensington.rs@jarvis.co.uk
I: www.jarvis.co.uk

B&B per night:
S £80.00–£150.00
D £99.00–£185.00

OPEN All year round

Jarvis Hotels/Utell International

Set in the aristocratic heart of London, the Ramada Jarvis Kensington is ideally situated close to the Royal Albert Hall, the Kensington museums, Harrods, and just a short walk from Hyde Park and Kensington Gardens. The hotel has undergone a complete refurbishment and offers spacious rooms with a contemporary classic feel.

Bedrooms: 7 single, 57 double/twin, 19 triple/multiple; suites available
Bathrooms: 83 en suite

CC: Amex, Delta, Diners, Mastercard, Switch, Visa

Weekend rates from £90pppn (B&B and min 2-nights' stay). Also upgrade packages into townhouse and studio rooms.

★★

ALBRO HOUSE HOTEL
155 Sussex Gardens, London W2 2RY
T: (020) 7724 2931 & 7706 8153
F: (020) 7202 2276
E: joe@albrohotel.co.uk
I: www.albrohotel.co.uk

Bedrooms: 2 single, 12 double/twin, 4 triple/multiple
Bathrooms: 17 en suite

CC: Mastercard, Visa

B&B per night:
S £38.00–£52.00
D £52.00–£72.00

OPEN All year round

Ideally located in pleasant area near public transport. Nice rooms, all en suite. English breakfast. Languages spoken. Friendly and safe. Some parking available.

★★★

CHISWICK HOTEL
73 High Road, London W4 2LS
T: (020) 8994 1712
F: (020) 8742 2585
E: chishot@clara.net
I: www.chiswick-hotel.co.uk

Bedrooms: 28 single, 21 double/twin, 7 triple/multiple; suites available
Bathrooms: 56 en suite

Evening meal available
CC: Amex, Delta, Diners, Mastercard, Switch, Visa

B&B per night:
S £105.00–£115.00
D £138.00–£160.00

OPEN All year round

Large, tastefully converted Victorian hotel. Self-contained apartments available. Relaxed atmosphere. Close to Heathrow Airport and central London.

CONFIRM YOUR BOOKING
You are advised to confirm your booking in writing.

★★★

LONDON LODGE HOTEL
134-136 Lexham Gardens, London W8 6JE
T: (020) 7244 8444
F: (020) 7373 6661
E: info@londonlodgehotel.com
I: www.londonlodgehotel.com

B&B per night:
S £85.00–£128.00
D £98.00–£177.00

HB per person:
DY £68.00–£148.00

OPEN All year round

Newly refurbished townhouse hotel, ideally situated in a quiet residential street in the heart of Kensington. Perfectly placed for business, shopping and seeing London. All rooms individually designed to reflect traditional English elegance. Modern facilities such as satellite television, PC modem lines, mini bar. Executive rooms have whirlpool bath and private safe. Air conditioned rooms available.

Bedrooms: 7 single, 20 double/twin, 1 triple/ multiple
Bathrooms: 28 en suite

Lunch available
Evening meal available
CC: Amex, Delta, Diners, Mastercard, Switch, Visa

Double rooms at £98 per room per night incl breakfast, minimum stay 3 nights. Other offers available-please enquire.

★★★★★
Gold
Award

TOWNHOUSE

THE MILESTONE HOTEL AND APARTMENTS
1 Kensington Court, London W8 5DL
T: (020) 7917 1000
F: (020) 7917 1010
E: guestservices@milestone. redcarnationhotels.com
I: www.themilestone.com

B&B per night:
S £275.00–£430.00
D £305.00–£485.00

OPEN All year round

Unrivalled panoramic views of Kensington Palace. All 57 guest rooms and suites have been designed to the highest standards. Special touches and exceptional attention from all staff contribute to the 'legend'. 'Hideaway' bar, a most elegant restaurant, Chenestons, an al fresco conservatory, modern gym facility, sauna and jacuzzi.

Bedrooms: 57 double/ twin; suites available
Bathrooms: 57 en suite

Lunch available
Evening meal available
CC: Amex, Delta, Diners, Mastercard, Switch, Visa

Weekend breaks and themed packages available throughout the year.

★★★★
Silver
Award

THE KENSINGTON
Richmond Way, London W14 0AX
T: (020) 7674 1000
F: (020) 7674 1050
E: reservations@thekensington.co.uk
I: www.thekensington.co.uk

B&B per night:
S £229.00–£295.00
D £273.00–£311.00

OPEN All year round

Situated in a chic, urban area just across from Holland Park and close to Kensington Palace, the K-WEST hotel offers contemporary, stylised accommodation with all the latest technology, together with our health spa and treatment rooms. Conveniently located for West End shopping and the City and on the doorstep of Olympia and Earls Court exhibition centres.

Bedrooms: 16 single, 210 double/twin; suites available
Bathrooms: 226 en suite

Lunch available
Evening meal available
CC: Amex, Delta, Diners, Mastercard, Switch, Visa

Fri-Sun from £125 plus VAT per room per night. Spa breaks from £111pp incl VAT and 1.5 hours' treatment.

RATING All accommodation in this guide has been rated, or is awaiting a rating, by a trained English Tourism Council assessor.

LONDON WC1

★★★ THE BONNINGTON IN BLOOMSBURY

92 Southampton Row, London WC1B 4BH
T: (020) 7242 2828
F: (020) 7831 9170
E: sales@bonnington.com
I: www.bonnington.com

Bedrooms: 96 single, 101 double/twin, 18 triple/multiple
Bathrooms: 215 en suite

Lunch available
Evening meal available
CC: Amex, Delta, Diners, Mastercard, Switch, Visa

B&B per night:
S £80.00–£117.00
D £120.00–£149.00

OPEN All year round

Between the City and West End. Close to mainline stations and on the underground to Heathrow Airport.

★★★ WAVERLEY HOUSE HOTEL

130-134 Southampton Row, London WC1B 5AF
T: (020) 7833 3691
F: (020) 7837 3485
E: whhres@aquariushotels.co.uk
I: www.aquarius-hotels.com

Bedrooms: 35 single, 69 double/twin, 5 triple/multiple; suites available
Bathrooms: 109 en suite

Lunch available
Evening meal available
CC: Amex, Diners, Mastercard, Switch, Visa

B&B per night:
S £95.00–£120.00
D £120.00–£170.00

OPEN All year round

Elegant, attractive, small hotel in a popular central location, designed to meet the needs of the business and leisure traveller.

OUTER LONDON

CROYDON *Tourist Information Centre Tel: (020) 8253 1009*

★★★★ COULSDON MANOR
Silver Award

Coulsdon Court Road, Coulsdon, Croydon CR5 2LL
T: (020) 8668 0414
F: (020) 8668 3118
E: coulsdonmanor@marstonhotels.co.uk
I: www.marstonhotels.co.uk

Bedrooms: 35 double/twin
Bathrooms: 35 en suite

Lunch available
Evening meal available
CC: Amex, Delta, Diners, Mastercard, Switch, Visa

B&B per night:
S £105.00–£145.00
D £125.00–£185.00

HB per person:
DY £79.50–£95.00

OPEN All year round

Ⓒ Ⓡ
Marston Hotels

Victorian country house hotel in 140 acres of Surrey parkland and golf course. Easy access to Croydon, London and M25/M23. Half-board rate based on minimum 2 nights.

★★★★ SELSDON PARK HOTEL
Silver Award

Addington Road, Sanderstead, South Croydon CR2 8YA
T: (020) 8657 8811
F: (020) 8651 6171
E: caroline.chardon@principalhotels.co.uk
I: www.principalhotels.co.uk

Bedrooms: 58 single, 134 double/twin, 12 triple/multiple; suites available
Bathrooms: 204 en suite

Lunch available
Evening meal available
CC: Amex, Delta, Diners, Mastercard, Switch, Visa

B&B per night:
S £65.00–£105.00
D £118.00–£198.00

HB per person:
DY £75.00–£105.00

OPEN All year round

Ⓒ Ⓡ
Principal Hotels

Neo-Jacobean country house hotel, 10 minutes from the M25, 30 minutes from London and Gatwick, set in 200 acres of parkland. Special weekend rates.

ENFIELD

★★ OAK LODGE HOTEL
Silver Award

80 Village Road, Bush Hill Park, Enfield EN1 2EU
T: (020) 8360 7082 & 83600194
E: oaklodge@FSmail.net
I: www.oaklodgehotel.co.uk

Bedrooms: 6 double/twin, 1 triple/multiple
Bathrooms: 6 en suite, 1 private

Lunch available
Evening meal available
CC: Amex, Delta, Diners, Mastercard, Switch, Visa

B&B per night:
S £70.00–£94.00
D £90.00–£130.00

HB per person:
DY £80.00–£115.00

OPEN All year round

Award-winning country house hotel and candlelit restaurant set in leafy surroundings. Interior furnished with style, elegance and intimacy of an ocean-going yacht.

SUTTON

★★ THATCHED HOUSE HOTEL

135-141 Cheam Road, Sutton SM1 2BN
T: (020) 8642 3131
F: (020) 8770 0684

Bedrooms: 6 single, 26 double/twin
Bathrooms: 28 en suite, 4 private

Lunch available
Evening meal available
CC: Delta, Diners, Mastercard, Switch, Visa

B&B per night:
S £50.00–£80.00
D £65.00–£95.00

HB per person:
DY £60.00–£90.00

OPEN All year round

An old cottage-style thatched hotel, completely modernised. A few minutes from Sutton station and 20 minutes from central London.

CUMBRIA

Cumbria's dramatic and breathtaking landscapes, from the famous Lakes to the rugged mountains and fells, have inspired poets and artists for hundreds of years.

classic sights

Hadrian's Wall – a reminder of Roman occupation
Lake Windermere – largest lake in England

coast & country

Scafell Pike – England's highest mountain
Whitehaven – historic port

literary links

William Wordsworth – The poet's homes: Wordsworth House, Dove Cottage and Rydal Mount
Beatrix Potter – Her home, Hill Top; her watercolours at the Beatrix Potter Gallery and the tales at The World of Beatrix Potter

distinctively different

The Gondola – sail Coniston Water aboard the opulent 1859 steam yacht Gondola
Cars of the Stars Museum – cars from TV and film, including Chitty Chitty Bang Bang and the Batmobile

The county of Cumbria

FOR MORE INFORMATION CONTACT:
Cumbria Tourist Board
Ashleigh, Holly Road, Windermere,
Cumbria LA23 2AQ
Tel: (015394) 44444 Fax: (015394) 44041
Email: mail@cumbria-tourist-board.co.uk
Internet: www.golakes.co.uk

Places to Visit - see pages 44-47
Where to Stay - see pages 48-60

The Pictures:
1 Lake Windermere
2 Muncaster Castle
3 Walking at Wasdale

43

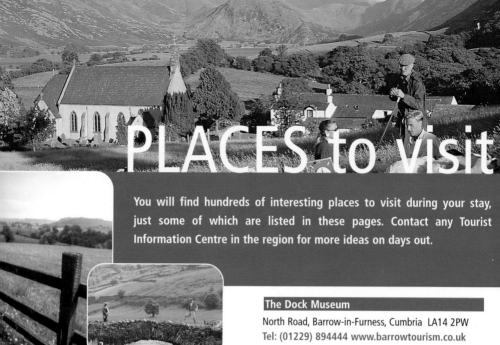

PLACES to visit

You will find hundreds of interesting places to visit during your stay, just some of which are listed in these pages. Contact any Tourist Information Centre in the region for more ideas on days out.

The Beacon
West Strand, Whitehaven, Cumbria CA28 7LY
Tel: (01946) 592302 www.copelandbc.gov.uk
Discover the industrial, maritime and social history of Whitehaven and surrounding area. Includes Meteorology Office weather gallery with satellite-linked equipment.

Birdoswald Roman Fort
Gilsland, Carlisle, Cumbria CA8 7DD
Tel: (016977) 47602
Remains of Roman fort on one of the best parts of Hadrian's Wall with excellent views of the Irthing Gorge. Exhibition, shop, tearooms and excavations.

Brantwood, Home of John Ruskin
Coniston, Cumbria LA21 8AD
Tel: (015394) 41396 www.brantwood.org.uk
Superb lake and mountain views. Works by Ruskin and contemporaries, memorabilia, Ruskin watercolours, craft and picture gallery, gardens.

Cars of the Stars Motor Museum
Standish Street, Keswick, Cumbria CA12 5LS
Tel: (017687) 73757 www.carsofthestars.com
Features TV and film vehicles including the Batmobile, Chitty Chitty Bang Bang, the James Bond collection, Herbie, FAB 1, plus many other famous cars and motorcycles.

The Dock Museum
North Road, Barrow-in-Furness, Cumbria LA14 2PW
Tel: (01229) 894444 www.barrowtourism.co.uk
The museum presents the story of steel shipbuilding, for which Barrow is famous, and straddles a Victorian graving dock. Interactive displays, nautical adventure playground.

Dove Cottage and Wandsworth Museum
Town End, Grasmere, Ambleside, Cumbria LA22 9SH
Tel: (015394) 35544 www.wordsworth.org.uk
Wordsworth's home 1799-1808. Poet's possessions. Museum with manuscripts, farmhouse reconstruction, paintings and drawings. Special events throughout the year.

Eden Ostrich World
Langwathby Hall Farm, Langwathby Hall, Langwathby, Penrith, Cumbria CA10 1LW
Tel: (01768) 881771 www.ostrich-world.com
Working farm with ostriches and other rare breed animals. Play areas, riverside walk, tearooms and gift shop. An enjoyable day out for the whole family.

Furness Abbey
Barrow-in-Furness, Cumbria LA13 0TJ
Tel: (01229) 823420
Ruins of 12thC Cistercian abbey, the 2nd wealthiest in England. Extensive remains include transepts, choir and west tower of church, canopied seats, arches, church.

Gleaston Water Mill

Gleaston, Ulverston, Cumbria LA12 0QH
Tel: (01229) 869244 www.watermill.co.uk
Water-driven corn mill in working order. Impressive wooden machinery and water-wheel. Farm equipment and tools display. Craft workshop, craft videos and rare breeds.

Heron Glass

The Lakes Glass Centre, Oubas Hill, Ulverston, Cumbria LA12 7LY
Tel: (01229) 581121
Heron Glass is a combined visitor centre and workshop where you will find traditional glass-making demonstrations daily with a chance of purchasing glassware at the factory shop.

Hill Top

Near Sawrey, Ambleside, Cumbria LA22 0LF
Tel: (015394) 36269 www.nationaltrust.org.uk
Beatrix Potter wrote many of her popular Peter Rabbit stories and other books in this charming little house which still contains her own china and furniture.

Jennings Brothers, The Castle Brewery

Cockermouth, Cumbria CA13 9NE
Tel: (01900) 821011 www.jenningsbrewery.co.uk
Guided tours of Jennings traditional brewery. The brewery uses the finest well water, malt, hops, sugar and yeast to brew distinctive local beers.

K Village Outlet Centre

Lound Road, Netherfield, Kendal, Cumbria LA9 7DA
Tel: (01539) 732363 www.kvillage.co.uk
Famous named brands such as K-shoes, Van Heusen, Denby, National Trust Shop, Tog24 and Ponden Mill, all at discounts. Open 7 days per week with full disabled access.

The Lake District Coast Aquarium

Maryport South Quay, Maryport, Cumbria CA15 8AB
Tel: (01900) 817760
www.lakedistrict-coastaquarium.co.uk
Purpose-built independent aquarium with over 35 displays. Largest collection of native marine species in Cumbria. Cafe and gift shop.

The Lake District Visitor Centre

Brockhole, Windermere, Cumbria LA23 1LJ
Tel: (015394) 46601 www.lake-district.gov.uk
Interactive exhibitions, audio-visual show, shop, gardens, grounds, adventure playground, dry-stone walling area, trails, events and croquet. Cafe with home-cooked food.

Lakeland Motor Museum

Holker Hall, Cark in Cartmel, Grange-over-Sands, Cumbria LA11 7PL
Tel: (015395) 58509 www.holker-hall.co.uk
Over 10,000 exhibits including rare motoring automobilia. A 1930s garage re-creation and the Campbell Legend Bluebird Exhibition.

Lakeland Sheep and Wool Centre

Egremont Road, Cockermouth, Cumbria CA13 0QX
Tel: (01900) 822673 www.shepherdshotel.co.uk
An all-weather attraction with live sheep shows including working-dog demonstrations. Also large screen and other tourism exhibitions on the area, a gift shop and cafe.

Lakeland Wildlife Oasis

Hale Milnthorpe, Cumbria LA7 7BW
Tel: (015395) 63027 www.wildlifeoasis.co.uk
A wildlife exhibition where both living animals and inanimate hands-on displays are used to illustrate evolution in the animal kingdom. Includes gift shop and cafe.

The Pictures:
1 Kirkstile Inn
2 Watendlath Bridge
3 Loughrigg
4 Shoreline, Derwentwater

Lowther Parklands

Hackthorpe, Penrith, Cumbria CA10 2HG
Tel: (01931) 712523
Attractions include exotic birds and animals, rides, miniature railway, boating lake, play areas, adventure fort, Tarzan trail, international circus and a puppet theatre.

Muncaster Castle, Gardens, Owl Centre and Meadow Vole Maze

Ravenglass, Cumbria CA18 1RQ
Tel: (01229) 717614 www.muncastercastle.co.uk
Muncaster Castle has the most beautifully situated Owl Centre in the world. See the birds fly, picnic in the gardens, and visit the Pennington family home.

Ravenglass and Eskdale Railway

Ravenglass, Cumbria CA18 1SW
Tel: (01229) 717171 www.ravenglass-railway.co.uk
England's oldest narrow-gauge railway runs for 7 miles through glorious scenery to the foot of England's highest hills. Most trains are steam hauled.

Rheged - The Village in the Hill

Redhills, Penrith, Cumbria CA11 0DQ
Tel: (01768) 868000 www.rheged.com
Cumbria's new visitor attraction with Europe's largest grass-covered building. Discover speciality shops, restaurants, artist exhibitions, pottery demonstrations, children's play area and The National Mountaineering Exhibition.

The Rum Story

27 Lowther Street, Whitehaven, Cumbria CA28 7DN
Tel: (01946) 592933 www.rumstory.co.uk
'The Rum Story' - an authentic, heritage-based experience, depicting the unique story of the UK rum trade in the original Jefferson's wine merchant premises

Sizergh Castle

Kendal, Cumbria LA8 8AE
Tel: (015395) 60070 www.nationaltrust.org.uk
Strickland family home for 750 years, now National Trust owned. With 14thC pele tower, 15thC great hall, 16thC wings. Stuart connections. Rock garden, rose garden, daffodils.

South Lakes Wild Animal Park Ltd

Crossgates, Dalton-in-Furness, Cumbria LA15 8JR
Tel: (01229) 466086 www.wildanimalpark.co.uk
Wild zoo park in over 17 acres (7 ha) of grounds. Large waterfowl ponds, cafe, toilets, car/coach park, miniature railway. Over 120 species of animals from all around the world.

South Tynedale Railway

Railway Station, Alston, Cumbria CA9 3JB
Tel: (01434) 381696 www.strps.org.uk
Narrow-gauge railway operating along 2.25 mile line from Alston to Kirkhaugh through the scenic South Tyne Valley. Steam- and diesel-hauled passenger trains.

Steam Yacht Gondola

Pier Cottage, Coniston, Cumbria LA21 8AJ
Tel: (015394) 41962
Victorian steam-powered vessel now National Trust owned and completely renovated with an opulently upholstered saloon. Superb way to appreciate the beauty of Coniston Water.

Theatre by the Lake

Lakeside, Keswick, Cumbria CA12 5DJ
Tel: (017687) 74411 www.theatrebythelake.com
Main auditorium of 400 seats, studio of 80. Exhibitions all year round. Cafe and bar.

Tullie House Museum and Art Gallery

Castle Street, Carlisle, Cumbria CA3 8TP
Tel: (01228) 534781 www.historic-carlisle.org.uk
Major tourist complex housing museum, art gallery, education facility, lecture theatre, shops, herb garden, restaurant and terrace bars.

Windermere Lake Cruises

Lakeside Pier, Newby Bridge, Ulverston, Cumbria LA12 8AS
Tel: (015395) 31188
www.windermere-lakecruises.co.uk
Steamers and launches sail between Ambleside, Bowness and Lakeside with connections for the Steam Railway, Brockhole, Ferry House, Fell Foot and the Aquarium of the Lakes.

Windermere Steamboat Museum

Rayrigg Road, Bowness-on-Windermere, Windermere, Cumbria LA23 1BN
Tel: (015394) 45565 www.steamboat.co.uk
A wealth of interest and information about life on bygone Windermere. Regular steam launch trips, vintage vessels and classic motorboats. Model boat pond, lakeside picnic area.

The World Famous Old Blacksmith's Shop Centre

Gretna Green, Gretna DG16 5EA
Tel: (01461) 338441 www.gretnagreen.com
The original Blacksmith's Shop museum and a shopping centre selling cashmere and woollen knitwear, crystal and china. Taste local produce in the Old Smithy Restaurant.

Find out more about
Cumbria

Further information about holidays and attractions in Cumbria is available from:

CUMBRIA TOURIST BOARD

Ashleigh, Holly Road, Windermere, Cumbria LA23 2AQ.

Tel: (015394) 44444 Fax: (015394) 44041

Email: mail@cumbria-tourist-board.co.uk

Internet: www.golakes.co.uk

The following publications are available from Cumbria Tourist Board:

Cumbria Tourist Board Holiday Guide (free) Tel: 08705 133059

Events Listings (free)

Cumbria The Lake District Touring Map
including tourist information and touring caravan and camping parks - £3.95

Laminated Poster - £4.50

Getting to
Cumbria

BY ROAD: The M1/M6/M25/M40 provide a link with London and the South East and the M5/M6 provide access from the South West. The M62/M6 link Hull and Manchester with the region. Approximate journey time from London is 5 hours, from Manchester 2 hours.

BY RAIL: From London (Euston) to Oxenholme (Kendal) takes approximately 3 hours 30 minutes. From Oxenholme (connecting station for all main line trains) to Windermere takes approximately 20 minutes. From Carlisle to Barrow-in-Furness via the coastal route, with stops at many of the towns in between, takes approximately 2 hours. Trains from Edinburgh to Carlisle take 1 hour 45 minutes. The historic Settle-Carlisle line also runs through the county bringing passengers from Yorkshire via the Eden Valley.

The Pictures:
1 Ullswater
2 Buttermere
3 Lake Windermere

www.travelcumbria.co.uk

Where to stay in Cumbria

Accommodation entries in this region are listed in alphabetical order of place name, and then in alphabetical order of establishment.

Map references refer to the colour location maps at the front of this guide. The first number indicates the map to use; the letter and number which follow refer to the grid reference on the map.

At-a-glance symbols at the end of each accommodation entry give useful information about services and facilities. A key to symbols can be found inside the back cover flap. Keep this open for easy reference.

A brief description of the towns and villages offering accommodation in the entries which follow, can be found at the end of this section.

A complete listing of all the English Tourism Council assessed accommodation covered by this guide appears at the back of the guide.

AMBLESIDE, Cumbria Map ref 5A3 *Tourist Information Centre Tel: (015394) 32582*

★★★

In the heart of the Lake District, a traditional hotel overlooking village centre, beautifully refurbished to provide 42 en suite rooms (9 non-smoking) and many with jacuzzi baths. Comfortable lounge and extended restaurant serving dinners. Excellent bar food lunchtimes and evenings. Free membership of nearby luxury leisure club. A warm welcome assured.

THE AMBLESIDE SALUTATION HOTEL

Lake Road, Ambleside LA22 9BX
T: (01539) 432244
F: (01539) 434157
E: reservations@hotelambleside.uk.com
I: www.hotelambleside.uk.com

Bedrooms: 3 single, 35 double/twin, 4 triple/multiple
Bathrooms: 42 en suite

Lunch available
Evening meal available
CC: Amex, Diners, Mastercard, Switch, Visa

B&B per night:
S £41.00–£54.00
D £82.00–£108.00

HB per person:
DY £55.50–£69.00

OPEN All year round

(CR)
Best Western Hotels

CENTRAL RESERVATIONS OFFICES

The symbol (CR) and a group name in an entry indicate that bookings can be made through a central reservations office. These are listed in a separate section towards the back of this guide.

AMBLESIDE continued

★★★
Silver
Award

LANGDALE HOTEL AND COUNTRY CLUB

Great Langdale, Ambleside	Bedrooms: 46 double/	Lunch available	B&B per night:
LA22 9JD	twin, 19 triple/multiple	Evening meal available	S £70.00–£150.00
T: (01539) 437302	Bathrooms: 65 en suite	CC: Amex, Mastercard,	D £70.00–£210.00
F: (01539) 437130		Switch, Visa	
E: itsgreat@langdale.co.uk			HB per person:
I: www.langdale.co.uk			DY £90.00–£150.00

Winner of 1986 Civic Trust environmental award, in 35 acres of wooded grounds. Indoor country club, large pool, spa-bath, sports facilities, restaurants, bars. Minimum stay 2 nights.

OPEN All year round

★★

QUEENS HOTEL

Market Place, Ambleside LA22 9BU

T: (01539) 432206

F: (01539) 432721

E: queenshotel.ambleside@btinternet.com

I: www.smoothhound.co.uk/hotels/ quecum.html

B&B per night:
S £25.00–£36.00
D £50.00–£72.00

OPEN All year round

Family-owned 18thC hotel in the centre of village, renowned for warm and friendly atmosphere. Log fires, 4-poster and jacuzzi bedrooms. Excellent-value bar meals and a la carte restaurant. Real ales featuring local breweries. Ideally situated, convenient for walking and touring the Lakes.

Bedrooms: 4 single,	Lunch available
17 double/twin, 5 triple/	Evening meal available
multiple	CC: Amex, Delta,
Bathrooms: 26 en suite	Mastercard, Switch, Visa

3-night breaks available Nov-Jun (excl Christmas and New Year).

★★

ROTHAY GARTH HOTEL

Rothay Road, Ambleside LA22 0EE

T: (01539) 432217

F: (01539) 434400

E: enquiries@rothay-garth.co.uk

I: www.rothay-garth.co.uk

B&B per night:
S £34.00–£43.00
D £68.00–£86.00

HB per person:
DY £54.00–£68.00

OPEN All year round

Distinctive Victorian country house with elegant Loughrigg restaurant overlooking lovely gardens. Close to village centre and Lake Windermere; an ideal centre for walking or touring all parts of the Lake District. Resident owners committed to your comfort. Great value all-season breaks.

Bedrooms: 1 single,	Lunch available
11 double/twin, 3 triple/	Evening meal available
multiple; suites available	CC: Delta, Diners,
Bathrooms: 14 en suite,	Mastercard, Switch, Visa
1 private	

Nov-Mar: 3 night candlelit dinner breaks from £116pp. Special Christmas and New Year holidays. Great value all-season breaks.

★★★
Silver
Award

ROTHAY MANOR

Rothay Bridge, Ambleside LA22 0EH

T: (01539) 433605

F: (01539) 433607

E: hotel@rothaymanor.co.uk

I: www.rothaymanor.co.uk

B&B per night:
S Max £80.00
D £115.00–£140.00

HB per person:
DY £78.00–£98.00

OPEN Feb-Dec and New Year

Elegant Regency house standing in its own grounds, quarter mile from the head of Lake Windermere. Personally managed by the Nixon family, it retains the comfortable, relaxed atmosphere of a private house. Internationally renowned for its cuisine, and ideally situated for local attractions and sightseeing. Free use of nearby leisure centre.

Bedrooms: 2 single,	Lunch available
8 double/twin, 8 triple/	Evening meal available
multiple; suites available	CC: Amex, Delta, Diners,
Bathrooms: 18 en suite	Mastercard, Switch, Visa

Special short break rates available. Specialised holidays Nov-May: antiques, music, painting, gardening, walking, photography and bridge.

CUMBRIA

APPLEBY-IN-WESTMORLAND, Cumbria Map ref 5B3 *Tourist Information Centre Tel: (017683) 51177*

★★

ROYAL OAK INN

Bongate, Appleby-in-Westmorland
CA16 6UN
T: (01768) 351463
F: (01768) 352300
E: royaloakinn@mortalmaninns.fsnet.co.uk
I: www.mortal-man-inns.co.uk/royaloak

B&B per night:
S £49.00–£55.00
D £76.00–£90.00

HB per person:
DY £55.00–£65.00

OPEN All year round

The Royal Oak Inn is a beautiful 17thC traditional coaching inn. Well-renowned for its delicious food from the freshest local produce and its beautifully furnished accommodation. Fine wines, real ales and malt whisky on offer. Ideally situated for walking, exploring the Lakes and other activities. A wonderful time guaranteed.

Bedrooms: 2 single, 6 double/twin, 1 triple/multiple
Bathrooms: 7 en suite, 2 private

Lunch available
Evening meal available
CC: Amex, Delta, Mastercard, Switch, Visa

Bargain summer break mid-week 3 nights DB&B £152pp (standard room), £169pp (superior room). Bargain winter break-£149pp (standard room), £163pp (superior room).

BORROWDALE, Cumbria Map ref 5A3

★★

MARY MOUNT HOTEL

Borrowdale, Keswick CA12 5UU
T: (01768) 777223 & 777381
E: marymount@bigfoot.com
I: www.marymount.pcrrn.co.uk

Bedrooms: 1 single, 10 double/twin, 3 triple/multiple
Bathrooms: 14 en suite

Lunch available
Evening meal available
CC: Delta, Mastercard, Switch, Visa

B&B per night:
S £27.00–£33.00
D £54.00–£66.00

OPEN All year round

Set in 4.5 acres of gardens and woodlands on the shores of Derwentwater, 2.5 miles from Keswick. Views across lake to Catbells and Maiden Moor. Families and pets welcome.

CALDBECK, Cumbria Map ref 5A2

★★

PARKEND COUNTRY HOTEL

Parkend, Caldbeck, Wigton
CA7 8HH
T: (01697) 478494 & 07976 741005
F: (01697) 478580
E: carol.parkend@tinyworld.co.uk

Bedrooms: 6 double/twin
Bathrooms: 6 en suite

Lunch available
Evening meal available
CC: Amex, Mastercard, Visa

B&B per night:
S £30.00–£40.00
D £50.00–£60.00

HB per person:
DY £40.00–£55.00

OPEN All year round

17thC farmhouse hotel. Situated in Caldbeck in the wonderful walking country of the northern lakes. Fine food in tranquil surroundings. On the Coast to Coast cycle route.

CARLISLE, Cumbria Map ref 5A2 *Tourist Information Centre Tel: (01228) 625600*

★★★

SWALLOW HILLTOP HOTEL WHITBREAD HOTEL COMPANY

London Road, Carlisle CA1 2PQ
T: (01228) 529255
F: (01228) 525238
E: carlisle@swallow-hotels.co.uk
I: www.swallowhotels.com

Bedrooms: 2 single, 00 double/twin, 2 triple/multiple
Bathrooms: 92 en suite

Lunch available
Evening meal available
CC: Amex, Delta, Diners, Mastercard, Switch, Visa

B&B per night:
S £75.00–£95.00
D £90.00–£105.00

HB per person:
DY Min £52.00

OPEN All year round

Comfortable, modern hotel with excellent leisure facilities. Ideal touring base for Borders, Lakes, Hadrian's Wall, Solway Coast. Half board price based on minimum 2-night stay.

AT-A-GLANCE SYMBOLS

Symbols at the end of each accommodation entry give useful information about services and facilities. A key to symbols can be found inside the back cover flap. Keep this open for easy reference.

CARTMEL, Cumbria Map ref 5A3

★★
Silver
Award

Lovely old manor house, nestling in the historic vale of Cartmel. Personally managed, for 20 years, by the Varley family. An award-winning Georgian dining room, open log fires and elegant lounges create the perfect atmosphere for relaxation. Ideal base for Lakeland and its peninsulas. Recommended in all leading guides.

AYNSOME MANOR HOTEL

Cartmel, Grange-over-Sands LA11 6HH
T: (01539) 536653
F: (01539) 536016
E: info@aynsomemanorhotel.co.uk
I: www.aynsomemanorhotel.co.uk

Bedrooms: 10 double/ twin, 2 triple/multiple
Bathrooms: 12 en suite

Lunch available
Evening meal available
CC: Amex, Delta, Mastercard, Switch, Visa

B&B per night:
S £42.00–£52.00
D £60.00–£85.00

HB per person:
DY £47.00–£65.00

OPEN Feb–Dec

COCKERMOUTH, Cumbria Map ref 5A2 *Tourist Information Centre Tel: (01900) 822634*

★★

ALLERDALE COURT HOTEL
Market Square, Cockermouth
CA13 9NQ
T: (01900) 823654
F: (01900) 823033
E: john-h-carlin@tinyonline.co.uk
I: www.allerdalecourthotel.co.uk

Bedrooms: 10 single,
14 double/twin
Bathrooms: 24 en suite

Evening meal available
CC: Amex, Delta, Diners,
Mastercard, Switch, Visa

B&B per night:
S £45.00–£60.00
D £60.00–£66.00

HB per person:
DY Min £45.00

OPEN All year round

Traditional 17thC building, oak beams. Family-run inn, offering excellent food in 2 renowned restaurants. Refurbished and comfortable en suite bedrooms, well stocked bar.

★★★

TROUT HOTEL
Crown Street, Cockermouth
CA13 0EJ
T: (01900) 823591
F: (01900) 827514
E: enquiries@trouthotel.co.uk
I: www.trouthotel.co.uk

Bedrooms: 1 single,
27 double/twin, 1 triple/
multiple
Bathrooms: 29 en suite

Lunch available
Evening meal available
CC: Amex, Delta,
Mastercard, Switch, Visa

B&B per night:
S £59.95–£130.00
D £89.95–£150.00

HB per person:
DY £60.00–£75.00

OPEN All year round

Attractive black and white listed building, dating from c1670, on banks of River Derwent adjacent to own award-winning gardens. 12 miles west of Keswick off A66.

CONISTON, Cumbria Map ref 5A3

★★

For walkers and talkers, on the hill to Coniston Old Man and beyond, this is a rather good hotel with its very own pub next door. Comfortable and informal. En suite accommodation for 1 to 25. 16thC real ale pub. Conservatory with exceptional views. Large garden and plenty of parking. Call The Sun for availability and brochure.

SUN HOTEL & 16TH CENTURY INN

Coniston LA21 8HQ
T: (01539) 441248
F: (01539) 441219
E: thesun@hotelconiston.com
I: www.smoothhound.co.uk/hotels/sun.html

Bedrooms: 1 single,
6 double/twin, 3 triple/
multiple
Bathrooms: 9 en suite,
1 private

Lunch available
Evening meal available
CC: Amex, Delta,
Mastercard, Switch, Visa

B&B per night:
S £35.00–£50.00
D £70.00–£80.00

OPEN All year round

3 nights for price of 2 Nov-Mar (excl Christmas and New Year). Excellent for receptions, parties and functions. Please call to discuss.

WHERE TO STAY

Please mention this guide when making your booking.

ESKDALE, Cumbria Map ref 5A3

★★

BOWER HOUSE INN

Eskdale, Holmrook CA19 1TD
T: (01946) 723244
F: (01946) 723308
E: info@bowerhouseinn.freeserve.co.uk
I: www.bowerhouseinn.co.uk

B&B per night:
S £40.00–£55.00
D £74.00–£77.00

HB per person:
DY £110.00–£128.00

OPEN All year round

A typical 17thC Lakeland inn set in its own secluded gardens. There is a lovely oak-beamed bar, candlelit restaurant, relaxing lounge and comfortable en suite accommodation. Noted for good food and an ideal centre for walking and touring the area, the inn is popular with locals and visitors.

Bedrooms: 3 single, 18 double/twin, 3 triple/ multiple
Bathrooms: 24 en suite

Lunch available
Evening meal available
CC: Mastercard, Switch, Visa

Christmas breaks, New Year 3 day and 4 day breaks.

GRANGE-OVER-SANDS, Cumbria Map ref 5A3 *Tourist Information Centre Tel: (015395) 34026*

★
Silver
Award

CLARE HOUSE

Park Road, Grange-over-Sands LA11 7HQ
T: (01539) 533026 & 534253

B&B per night:
S £36.00–£38.00
D £72.00–£76.00

HB per person:
DY £51.00–£54.00

Charming hotel in its own grounds, with well appointed bedrooms, pleasant lounges and super bay views, offering peaceful holidays to those who wish to relax and be looked after. Delightful meals, prepared with care and pride from fresh, local produce, will contribute greatly to the enjoyment of your stay.

Bedrooms: 3 single, 13 double/twin, 1 triple/ multiple
Bathrooms: 16 en suite

Lunch available
Evening meal available
CC: Delta, Mastercard, Switch, Visa

★★

HAMPSFELL HOUSE HOTEL

Hampsfell Road, Grange-over-Sands LA11 6BG
T: (01539) 532567
F: (01539) 535995
E: hampsfellhotel@email.msn.com
I: www.hampsfellhotel.com

B&B per night:
S £38.00–£47.00
D £76.00–£120.00

HB per person:
DY £53.00–£60.00

OPEN All year round

Enjoy the pleasant tranquil setting of this Victorian hotel, set in its own private grounds surrounded by woodland away from busy roads. Relax in the comfortable lounges and enjoy the friendly atmosphere. The dining room serves freshly prepared 4-course evening dinner with fine wines. There's ample safe parking.

Bedrooms: 8 double/ twin, 1 triple/multiple
Bathrooms: 9 en suite

Evening meal available
CC: Amex, Delta, Mastercard, Switch, Visa

Special 3-night break with evening meal and glass of wine.

CREDIT CARD BOOKINGS If you book by telephone and are asked for your credit card number it is advisable to check the proprietor's policy should you cancel your reservation.

GRANGE-OVER-SANDS continued

★★★

NETHERWOOD HOTEL
Lindale Road, Grange-over-Sands
LA11 6ET
T: (01539) 532552
F: (01539) 534121
E: blawith@aol.com
I: www.netherwood-hotel.co.uk

Bedrooms: 3 single,
20 double/twin, 5 triple/
multiple
Bathrooms: 28 en suite

Lunch available
Evening meal available
CC: Delta, Mastercard,
Switch, Visa

B&B per night:
S £55.00–£65.00
D £110.00–£130.00

HB per person:
DY £80.00–£90.00

OPEN All year round

Built in 1893 and a building of high architectural and historic interest, with superb oak panelling throughout, set in 14 acres of gardens, overlooking Morecambe Bay.

GRASMERE, Cumbria Map ref 5A3

★★
Silver
Award

THE GRASMERE HOTEL
Broadgate, Grasmere, Ambleside
LA22 9TA
T: (01539) 435277
F: (01539) 435277
E: enquiries@grasmerehotel.co.uk
I: www.grasmerehotel.co.uk

Bedrooms: 1 single,
11 double/twin
Bathrooms: 12 en suite

Evening meal available
CC: Amex, Delta,
Mastercard, Switch, Visa

B&B per night:
S £30.00–£45.00
D £50.00–£60.00

HB per person:
DY £45.00–£65.00

In the midst of beautiful mountain scenery, with award-winning restaurant overlooking secluded garden through which the River Rothay flows.

★★★

GRASMERE RED LION HOTEL
Red Lion Square, Grasmere, Ambleside
LA22 9SS
T: (01539) 435456
F: (01539) 435579
E: enquiries@hotelgrasmere.uk.com
I: www.hotelgrasmere.uk.com

Village centre traditional coaching inn, refurbished to provide 47 delightful en suite rooms – including 12 additional non-smoking rooms built in 1999. Hairdressing salon, fitness centre, mini-gym and free leisure club membership. Enjoy good food served by friendly staff – lunch in the conservatory or dinner in the Courtyard Restaurant.

Bedrooms: 4 single,
39 double/twin, 4 triple/
multiple
Bathrooms: 47 en suite

Lunch available
Evening meal available
CC: Amex, Delta, Diners,
Mastercard, Switch, Visa

B&B per night:
S £42.00–£56.50
D £84.00–£113.00

HB per person:
DY £56.50–£71.50

OPEN All year round

Best Western Hotels

★★★

ROTHAY GARDEN HOTEL
Broadgate, Grasmere, Ambleside LA22 9RJ
T: (01539) 435334
F: (01539) 435723
E: rothay@grasmere.com
I: www.grasmere.com

This 19thC country house is set on the outskirts of picturesque Grasmere village in 2 acres of riverside gardens amidst outstanding scenery and is renowned for very comfortable bedrooms (many with feature beds and whirlpool baths). Superb cuisine, an excellent wine list and friendly, professional service.

Bedrooms: 2 single,
22 double/twin, 1 triple/
multiple
Bathrooms: 25 en suite

Lunch available
Evening meal available
CC: Delta, Mastercard,
Switch, Visa

4-day walking breaks with Blue Badge guide. 4-day food and drink programmes with wine seminars and cooking demonstrations Nov-Mar.

B&B per night:
S £35.00–£67.50
D £70.00–£135.00

HB per person:
DY £60.00–£87.50

OPEN All year round

---

www.travelengland.org.uk
Log on for information and inspiration. The latest information on places to visit, events and quality assessed accommodation.

HAWKSHEAD, Cumbria Map ref 5A3

★★
Silver
Award

QUEENS HEAD HOTEL
Main Street, Hawkshead, Ambleside
LA22 0NS
T: (015394) 36271
F: (015394) 36722
E: enquiries@queensheadhotel.co.uk
I: www.queensheadhotel.co.uk

B&B per night:
S £42.00–£47.00
D £63.00–£84.00

OPEN All year round

Built in the 16thC, low oak-beamed ceilings, panel walls and a log fire. All bedrooms are tastefully decorated, 4-poster beds and family rooms available. Queens Head is best known for the excellent quality of food and extensive menu; our specialities include: Herdwick lamb, fresh fish and vegetarian dishes, all using local produce.

Bedrooms: 11 double/ twin, 2 triple/multiple
Bathrooms: 11 en suite, 2 private

Lunch available
Evening meal available
CC: Delta, Mastercard, Switch, Visa

DB&B breaks available Sun-Thurs, min 3 days stay.

KENDAL, Cumbria Map ref 5B3 *Tourist Information Centre Tel: (01539) 725758*

★★★

MACDONALD RIVERSIDE HOTEL
Stramongate Bridge, Kendal
LA9 4BZ
T: (01539) 734861
F: (01538) 9734863
E: riverside@macdonald-hotels.co.uk
I: www.macdonaldhotels.co.uk

Bedrooms: 36 double/ twin, 11 triple/multiple; suites available
Bathrooms: 47 en suite

Lunch available
Evening meal available
CC: Amex, Delta, Mastercard, Switch, Visa

B&B per night:
S £50.00–£75.00
D £75.00–£95.00

HB per person:
DY £49.50–£52.50

OPEN All year round

A deed dated 3 February 1626 records the sale for £8-4s of a tannery at Stramongate Bridge. This is now the site of our Riverview Restaurant.

KESWICK, Cumbria Map ref 5A3 *Tourist Information Centre Tel: (017687) 72645*

★★★

BORROWDALE HOTEL
Borrowdale, Keswick CA12 5UY
T: (01768) 777224
F: (01768) 777338
E: theborrowdalehotel@yahoo.com
I: www.theborrowdalehotel.co.uk

Bedrooms: 4 single, 26 double/twin, 3 triple/ multiple; suites available
Bathrooms: 33 en suite

Lunch available
Evening meal available
CC: Delta, Mastercard, Switch, Visa

B&B per night:
S £55.00–£60.00
D £90.00–£100.00

HB per person:
DY £62.00–£80.00

OPEN All year round

Traditional, friendly, licensed Lakeland hotel renowned for service and cuisine. All rooms en suite. Family and 4-poster rooms available. Full colour brochure also available.

★★★
Silver
Award

BORROWDALE GATES COUNTRY HOUSE HOTEL AND RESTAURANT
Grange-in-Borrowdale, Keswick CA12 5UQ
T: (01768) 777204
F: (01768) 777254
E: hotel@borrowdale-gates.com
I: www.borrowdale-gates.com

B&B per night:
S £47.50–£69.50
D £85.00–£130.00

HB per person:
DY £60.00–£87.50

Situated in a peaceful setting, amidst the breathtaking scenery of the Borrowdale Valley. This is arguably Lakeland's most beautiful and sought after destination. A charming and unpretentious hotel, which is owner managed. The hotel has gained an enviable reputation for hospitality, service and food in its acclaimed restaurant. Super base for walking and touring.

Bedrooms: 3 single, 26 double/twin
Bathrooms: 29 en suite

Lunch available
Evening meal available
CC: Amex, Delta, Mastercard, Switch, Visa

Winter bargain breaks. Christmas and New Year programmes.

HALF BOARD PRICES Half board prices are given per person, but in some cases these may be based on double/twin occupancy.

KESWICK continued

★★★ Silver Award

DERWENTWATER HOTEL

Portinscale, Keswick CA12 5RE
T: (01768) 772538
F: (01768) 771002
E: reservations@derwentwater-hotel.co.uk
I: www.derwentwater-hotel.co.uk

B&B per night:
S £79.00–£95.00
D £130.00–£190.00

HB per person:
DY £65.00–£95.00

OPEN All year round

The epitome of a Lakeland country house hotel, set in 16 acres of conservation grounds on the shores of Derwent Water. Refurbished to provide high standards of accommodation – sublimely comfortable without being pretentious. Award-winning hospitality, pets welcome, and entry to leisure club, make it the perfect Lakeland retreat.

Bedrooms: 4 single, 41 double/twin, 2 triple/ multiple; suites available
Bathrooms: 47 en suite

Evening meal available
CC: Amex, Delta, Mastercard, Switch, Visa

★★ Silver Award

HIGHFIELD HOTEL

The Heads, Keswick CA12 5ER
T: (01768) 772508
E: highfieldkeswick@talk21.com

B&B per night:
S £30.00–£37.00
D £54.00–£75.00

HB per person:
DY £44.00–£55.00

Quietly situated just a 5-minute walk from the town centre, lake and theatre. Enjoys magnificent lake and mountain views all round. Excellent food, imaginatively prepared and beautifully presented. All bedrooms are tastefully furnished to a high standard, are en suite and non-smoking. Large private car park.

Bedrooms: 2 single, 15 double/twin, 1 triple/ multiple
Bathrooms: 18 en suite

Lunch available
Evening meal available
CC: Amex, Delta, Mastercard, Switch, Visa

3 day breaks DB&B winter £114pp, summer £138pp.

★★ Silver Award

LAIRBECK HOTEL

Vicarage Hill, Keswick CA12 5QB
T: (01768) 773373
F: (01768) 773144
E: WTS@lairbeckhotel-keswick.co.uk
I: www.lairbeckhotel-keswick.co.uk

B&B per night:
S £33.50–£39.50
D £67.00–£79.00

HB per person:
DY £50.00–£56.00

OPEN Mar–Dec

Lairbeck is a traditional country house hotel built of Lakeland stone, in a secluded setting with mountain views, just 10 minutes' walk from Keswick. Friendly, relaxed atmosphere with log fires, full central heating and ample parking. Excellent home cooking. All bedrooms are fully en suite and non-smoking. Special breaks.

Bedrooms: 4 single, 9 double/twin, 1 triple/ multiple
Bathrooms: 14 en suite

Evening meal available
CC: Delta, Mastercard, Switch, Visa

3-day weekend, 4-day mid-week and 7-day HB special breaks available (excl Easter, Bank Hol weekends and Christmas period).

ACCESSIBILITY

Look for the 🦽 ♿ 👨 symbols which indicate accessibility for wheelchair users. A list of establishments is at the front of this guide.

★★★

QUEEN'S HOTEL
Main Street, Keswick CA12 5JF
T: (01768) 773333
F: (01768) 771144
E: book@queenshotel.co.uk
I: www.queenshotel.co.uk

B&B per night:
S £32.00–£39.00
D £60.00–£78.00

OPEN All year round

The Independents

The elegant Queen's Hotel lies at the heart of bustling Keswick. A friendly reception, well appointed rooms and well prepared food will make your stay one to remember. Phone for our brochure now, or look us up on our website. We would be pleased to meet you.

Bedrooms: 5 single, 18 double/twin, 12 triple/multiple
Bathrooms: 35 en suite

Lunch available
Evening meal available
CC: Amex, Delta, Diners, Mastercard, Switch, Visa

★★

SWAN HOTEL AND COUNTRY INN
Thornthwaite, Keswick CA12 5SQ
T: (01768) 778256
F: (01768) 778080
E: bestswan@aol.com
I: www.swan-hotel-keswick.co.uk

B&B per night:
S Min £29.00
D £58.00–£70.00

HB per person:
DY £47.00–£53.00

The Swan Hotel is an attractive 17thC former coaching inn set amidst magnificent Lakeland scenery in a quiet, elevated position overlooking Skiddaw and the Derwent Valley. Rooms available in hotel or converted coach house.

Bedrooms: 18 double/twin, 2 triple/multiple
Bathrooms: 20 en suite

Lunch available
Evening meal available
CC: Mastercard, Visa

Mid-week winter breaks, Nov-Mar: 3 nights £65.
Spring breaks Apr-May 3 nights £75.

★
Gold
Award

SWINSIDE LODGE HOTEL
Grange Road, Newlands, Keswick CA12 5UE
T: (01768) 772948 & 07887 930998
F: (01768) 772948
E: info@swinsidelodge-hotel.co.uk
I: www.swinsidelodge-hotel.co.uk

B&B per night:
S £40.00–£75.00
D £80.00–£127.00

HB per person:
DY £65.00–£95.00

OPEN All year round

Beautifully situated in an idyllic location at the foot of Cat Bells and just 5 minutes' walk from Lake Derwentwater, Swinside Lodge offers peace and tranquillity. This informal, licensed, country house hotel provides the highest standards of comfort, service and hospitality and is renowned, both locally and nationally, for its superb, award-winning cuisine.

Bedrooms: 7 double/twin
Bathrooms: 7 en suite

Evening meal available
CC: Delta, Mastercard, Switch, Visa

Special packages of 2, 3 and 4 days for Christmas and the New Year.

QUALITY ASSURANCE SCHEME
Star ratings and awards were correct at the time of going to press but are subject to change. Please check at the time of booking.

KIRKBY LONSDALE, Cumbria Map ref 5B3 *Tourist Information Centre Tel: (015242) 71437*

★★

PHEASANT INN
Casterton, Kirkby Lonsdale, Carnforth
LA6 2RX
T: (015242) 71230
F: (015242) 71230
E: pheasant.casterton@eggconnect.net
I: www.pheasantinn.co.uk

B&B per night:
S Min £40.00
D Min £76.00

OPEN All year round

Friendly country inn specialising in providing excellent food and en suite accommodation. Situated in the beautiful Lune Valley, 1 mile from Kirkby Lonsdale and ideal for exploring the Lakes, dales and Trough of Bowland.

Bedrooms: 2 single,
9 double/twin
Bathrooms: 11 en suite

Lunch available
Evening meal available
CC: Delta, Diners,
Mastercard, Switch, Visa

★★

WHOOP HALL INN
Burrow with Burrow,
Kirkby Lonsdale, Carnforth LA6 2HP
T: (01524) 271284
F: (01524) 272154
E: info@whoophall.co.uk
I: www.whoophall.co.uk

Bedrooms: 3 single,
14 double/twin, 3 triple/
multiple
Bathrooms: 20 en suite

Lunch available
Evening meal available
CC: Amex, Delta, Diners,
Mastercard, Switch, Visa

B&B per night:
S £45.00–£55.00
D £60.00–£80.00

HB per person:
DY £42.50–£49.50

OPEN All year round

®
Minotel/The
Independents

Renowned 17thC inn with oak beams, log fires and restaurant serving traditional food with local specialities. Ideal base for Lakes and Dales. Only 6 miles from M6 junction 36.

KIRKBY STEPHEN, Cumbria Map ref 5B3 *Tourist Information Centre Tel: (017683) 71199*

★★

THE BLACK SWAN HOTEL
Ravenstonedale, Kirkby Stephen
CA17 4NG
T: (01539) 623204
F: (01539) 623604
E: reservations@blackswanhotel.
com
I: www.blackswanhotel.com

Bedrooms: 1 single,
14 double/twin
Bathrooms: 14 en suite,
1 private

Lunch available
Evening meal available
CC: Amex, Delta, Diners,
Mastercard, Switch, Visa

B&B per night:
S £45.00–£50.00
D £70.00–£85.00

HB per person:
DY £55.00–£65.00

OPEN All year round

®
Minotel

Delightful family-run hotel, set amidst beautiful countryside in a picturesque village. Renowned for food, comfort and hospitality. Private fishing. 5 minutes from M6 junction 38.

NEWBY BRIDGE, Cumbria Map ref 5A3

★★★

WHITEWATER HOTEL
The Lakeland Village, Newby Bridge,
Ulverston LA12 8PX
T: (01539) 531133
F: (01539) 531881
E: enquiries@whitewater-hotel.co.uk
I: www.whitewater-hotel.co.uk

B&B per night:
S £70.00–£87.50
D £100.00–£155.00

HB per person:
DY £60.00–£90.00

OPEN All year round

The Whitewater's fantastic riverside setting, 5 minutes from Lake Windermere, and its superb leisure facilities make it the perfect setting for your relaxing break. On-site health and fitness club offers swimming pool, sauna, steam room, squash, tennis, jacuzzi, solaria, state-of-the-art gym and a full range of beauty treatments in our health spa.

Bedrooms: 2 single,
21 double/twin,
12 triple/multiple
Bathrooms: 35 en suite

Lunch available
Evening meal available
CC: Amex, Delta, Diners,
Mastercard, Switch, Visa

Pamper weekends available. Special mid-week breaks. Family Christmas holiday. Winter jazz festivals. Romantic weekend packages.

IDEAS For ideas on places to visit refer to the introduction at the beginning of this section.

PENRITH, Cumbria Map ref 5B2 *Tourist Information Centre Tel: (01768) 867466*

★★★

WESTMORLAND HOTEL

Westmorland Place, Orton, Penrith
CA10 3SB
T: (01539) 624351
F: (01539) 624354
E: westmorlandhotel@aol.com
I: www.westmorland.com

B&B per night:
S £57.00–£86.00
D £73.00–£100.00

HB per person:
DY £75.00–£102.00

OPEN All year round

At the head of the Lune Gorge lies the hotel – an ideal base to explore the Lakes, the Dales and the high Pennines. Sample our award-winning cuisine in a truly welcoming environment, with breathtaking views over the moors. A place to rest and recharge the batteries.

Bedrooms: 44 double/ twin, 9 triple/multiple
Bathrooms: 53 en suite

Lunch available
Evening meal available
CC: Amex, Delta, Diners, Mastercard, Switch, Visa

Ⓜ🐎♿☎🖥📞♨Ⓢ✂🅿Ⓞ⊞🏨🛆🍴♻☀🐾🐕🐾P

SAWREY, Cumbria Map ref 5A3

★★

SAWREY HOTEL

Far Sawrey, Ambleside LA22 0LQ
T: (01539) 443425
F: (01539) 443425

B&B per night:
S Min £29.50
D Min £59.00

HB per person:
DY Min £39.50

OPEN All year round

Country inn on the quieter side of Lake Windermere. One mile from the car ferry on the Hawkshead road B5285. It has been run by the Brayshaw family for over 30 years and a warm welcome awaits guests all year with special rates between November and March.

Bedrooms: 2 single, 13 double/twin, 3 triple/ multiple
Bathrooms: 18 en suite

Lunch available
Evening meal available
CC: Delta, Mastercard, Switch, Visa

Any 3 nights DB&B Apr-Oct £114pp. Any 4 nights DB&B Oct-Mar (Sun-Fri) £110pp. Any 2 nights £78pp.

Ⓜ🐎♿☎Ⓓ♨Ⓢ✂🅸🏨🛆🍴♻🐾🐾🚗🏨P

WINDERMERE, Cumbria Map ref 5A3 *Tourist Information Centre Tel: (015394) 46499*

★★
Silver
Award

CEDAR MANOR HOTEL

Ambleside Road, Windermere LA23 1AX
T: (01539) 443192
F: (01539) 445970
E: cedarmanor@fsbdial.co.uk
I: www.cedarmanor.co.uk

B&B per night:
S £42.00–£55.00
D £64.00–£90.00

HB per person:
DY £34.00–£62.00

OPEN All year round

Situated close to Windermere village and Lake, Cedar Manor is a haven for food lovers and those who enjoy the good things in life. The hotel has won many awards for food and service. For those who like to work off the calories we have leisure facilities nearby.

Bedrooms: 10 double/ twin, 2 triple/multiple
Bathrooms: 10 en suite

Lunch available
Evening meal available
CC: Mastercard, Visa

Ⓜ🐎♿🏨☎🖥♨Ⓢ✂🅸Ⓞ🏨🛆U🍴♻☀🐾🚗♻🏨P

SPECIAL BREAKS

Many establishments offer special promotions and themed breaks. These are highlighted in red. (All such offers are subject to availability.)

WINDERMERE continued

★★

CRANLEIGH HOTEL

Kendal Road, Bowness-on-Windermere,
Windermere LA23 3EW
T: (01539) 443293
F: (01539) 447283
E: mike@thecranleigh.com
I: www.thecranleigh.com

B&B per night:
S £35.00–£72.00
D £52.00–£120.00

HB per person:
DY £39.00–£90.00

OPEN All year round

Our hotel is friendly and comfortable, 2 minutes' walk lake and village centre. Ample breakfasts, good value dinners, bar, garden. Free leisure facilities for that rainy day! Four-poster beds available and mountain bike hire for the energetic. Ideal base for exploring. For full details ring for our colour brochure.

Bedrooms: 11 double/ twin, 4 triple/multiple
Bathrooms: 14 en suite, 1 private

Lunch available
Evening meal available
CC: Delta, Mastercard, Switch, Visa

Golfers' (2 for 1) discount green fee vouchers available when booking 2 nights or more, based on double room occupancy.

★★★
Gold
Award

GILPIN LODGE COUNTRY HOUSE HOTEL AND RESTAURANT

Crook Road, Windermere LA23 3NE
T: (015394) 88818
F: (015394) 88058
E: hotel@gilpin-lodge.co.uk
I: www.gilpin-lodge.co.uk

B&B per night:
S £80.00–£105.00
D £90.00–£210.00

HB per person:
DY £65.00–£125.00

OPEN All year round

Pride of Britain

Elegant, friendly, relaxing, country house hotel and restaurant in 20 tranquil acres of woodland, moors and gardens 2 miles from Lake Windermere and 12 miles from M6. Sumptuous bedrooms, 4-posters, jacuzzi baths, etc. Award-winning food. See our comprehensive website or phone for brochure.

Bedrooms: 14 double/ twin
Bathrooms: 14 en suite

Lunch available
Evening meal available
CC: Amex, Delta, Diners, Mastercard, Switch, Visa

Year-round breaks from £175pp for 3 nights DB&B; 3 nights plus 2 games of golf (Windermere) from £260.

★★

HIDEAWAY HOTEL
Phoenix Way, Windermere
LA23 1DB
T: (01539) 443070
F: (01539) 448664
E: enquiries@hideaway-hotel.co.uk
I: www.hideaway-hotel.co.uk

Bedrooms: 3 single, 9 double/twin, 3 triple/ multiple
Bathrooms: 15 en suite

Evening meal available
CC: Amex, Delta, Mastercard, Switch, Visa

B&B per night:
S £35.00–£60.00
D £60.00–£130.00

HB per person:
DY £48.00–£78.00

Friendly, small hotel away from the main road, with a pleasant garden, well-trained chefs, open fires and well-equipped, comfortable en suite bedrooms.

★★★
Silver
Award

HILLTHWAITE HOUSE

Thornbarrow Road, Windermere LA23 2DF
T: (01539) 443636 & 446691
F: (01539) 488660
E: reception@hillthwaite.com
I: www.hillthwaite.com

B&B per night:
S £35.00–£69.50
D £70.00–£119.00

HB per person:
DY £43.00–£85.00

OPEN All year round

Extended country house overlooking lake and fells, nestling in 3 acres of gardens. Fine cuisine. Some 4-poster rooms with jacuzzi baths. Swimming pool, sauna, steam room. A warm welcome awaits you.

Bedrooms: 3 single, 33 double/twin, 1 triple/ multiple
Bathrooms: 37 en suite

Lunch available
Evening meal available
CC: Delta, Mastercard, Switch, Visa

★★
Gold
Award

At the top of a tree-lined drive, Lindeth Fell stands in magnificent gardens on the hills above Lake Windermere. One of the most beautifully situated hotels in Lakeland, Lindeth Fell offers brilliant views, stylish surroundings and superb English cooking.

LINDETH FELL COUNTRY HOUSE HOTEL

Lyth Valley Road, Bowness-on-Windermere, Windermere LA23 3JP
T: (015394) 43286 & 44287
F: (015394) 47455
E: kennedy@lindethfell.co.uk
I: www.lindethfell.co.uk

Bedrooms: 2 single, 10 double/twin, 2 triple/ multiple; suites available
Bathrooms: 14 en suite

Lunch available
Evening meal available
CC: Delta, Mastercard, Switch, Visa

Special breaks available early Nov–Mar (excl weekends and hols). Free fishing on local waters, golf nearby.

B&B per night:
S £52.00–£67.00

HB per person:
DY £72.50–£89.00

OPEN Feb–Dec

★★★
Gold
Award

Spectacular views over Lake Windermere, friendly unstuffy staff, unwind and exercise your eyes. Attractions: wonderful hiking, golf, boating. Homes, houses and gardens: Beatrix Potter, Wordsworth, John Ruskin, Muncaster and Sizergh Castles, Levens and Holker Halls. Antiques, galleries, quality shopping widely available. Yorkshire Dales, Hadrian's Wall 1 hour.

LINTHWAITE HOUSE HOTEL

Crook Road, Windermere LA23 3JA
T: (01539) 488600
F: (01539) 488601
E: admin@linthwaite.com
I: www.linthwaite.com

Bedrooms: 1 single, 25 double/twin; suites available
Bathrooms: 26 en suite

Lunch available
Evening meal available
CC: Amex, Delta, Mastercard, Switch, Visa

Romantic breaks: chilled champagne, handmade chocolates and a bunch of red roses in your room ready for your arrival. Just add £60.

B&B per night:
S £85.00–£115.00
D £90.00–£210.00

HB per person:
DY £59.00–£130.00

OPEN All year round

Grand Heritage Hotels

★★

Traditional Lakeland-stone built home from the late 19thC. Family-owned and run hotel offering a warm welcome, relaxed surroundings and excellent home-cooked food. Ideally situated with easy access to all parts of the National Park and the many attractions on offer for all ages.

RAVENSWORTH HOTEL

Ambleside Road, Windermere LA23 1BA
T: (01539) 443747
F: (01539) 443070
E: ravenswth@aol.com
I: www.ravensworthhotel.co.uk

Bedrooms: 2 single, 11 double/twin, 1 triple/ multiple
Bathrooms: 14 en suite

Evening meal available
CC: Amex, Delta, Mastercard, Switch, Visa

Reductions of up to 25% on multiple-night stays.

B&B per night:
S £22.00–£30.00
D £44.00–£80.00

HB per person:
DY £50.00–£72.00

OPEN Feb–Dec

CHECK THE MAPS

The colour maps at the front of this guide show all the cities, towns and villages for which you will find accommodation entries. Refer to the town index to find the page on which they are listed.

A brief guide to the main Towns and Villages offering accommodation in Cumbria

A AMBLESIDE, CUMBRIA - Market town situated at the head of Lake Windermere and surrounded by fells. The historic town centre is now a conservation area and the country around Ambleside is rich in historic and literary associations. Good centre for touring, walking and climbing.

- **APPLEBY-IN-WESTMORLAND, CUMBRIA** - Former county town of Westmorland, at the foot of the Pennines in the Eden Valley. The castle was rebuilt in the 17th C, except for its Norman keep, ditches and ramparts. It now houses a Rare Breeds Survival Trust Centre. Good centre for exploring the Eden Valley.

B BORROWDALE, CUMBRIA - Stretching south of Derwentwater to Seathwaite in the heart of the Lake District, the valley is walled by high fellsides. It can justly claim to be the most scenically impressive valley in the Lake District. Excellent centre for walking and climbing.

C CALDBECK, CUMBRIA - Quaint limestone village lying on the northern fringe of the Lake District National Park. John Peel, the famous huntsman who is immortalised in song, is buried in the churchyard. The fells surrounding Caldbeck were once heavily mined, being rich in lead, copper and barytes.

- **CARLISLE, CUMBRIA** - Cumbria's only city is rich in history. Attractions include the small red sandstone cathedral and 900-year-old castle with a magnificent view from the keep. Award-winning Tullie House Museum and Art Gallery brings 2,000 years of Border history dramatically to life. Excellent centre for shopping.

- **CARTMEL, CUMBRIA** - Picturesque conserved village based on a 12th C priory with a well-preserved church and gatehouse. Just half a mile outside the Lake District National Park, this is a peaceful base for walking and touring, with historic houses and beautiful scenery.

- **COCKERMOUTH, CUMBRIA** - Ancient market town at confluence of Rivers Cocker and Derwent. Birthplace of William Wordsworth in 1770. The house where he was born is at the end of the town's broad, tree-lined main street and is now owned by the National Trust. Good touring base for the Lakes.

- **CONISTON, CUMBRIA** - The 803m fell Coniston Old Man dominates the skyline to the east of this village at the northern end of Coniston Water. Arthur Ransome set his 'Swallows and Amazons' stories here. Coniston's most famous resident was John Ruskin, whose home, Brantwood, is open to the public. Good centre for walking.

E ESKDALE, CUMBRIA - Several minor roads lead to the west end of this beautiful valley, or it can be approached via the east over the Hardknott Pass, the Lake District's steepest pass. Scafell Pike and Bow Fell lie to the north and a miniature railway links the Eskdale Valley with Ravenglass on the coast.

G GRANGE-OVER-SANDS, CUMBRIA - Set on the beautiful Cartmel Peninsula, this tranquil resort, known as Lakeland's Riviera, overlooks Morecambe Bay. Pleasant seafront walks and beautiful gardens. The bay attracts many species of wading birds.

- **GRASMERE, CUMBRIA** - Described by William Wordsworth as 'the loveliest spot that man hath ever found', this village, famous for its gingerbread, is in a beautiful setting overlooked by Helm Grag. Wordsworth lived at Dove Cottage. The cottage and museum are open to the public.

H HAWKSHEAD, CUMBRIA - Lying near Esthwaite Water, this village has great charm and character. Its small squares are linked by flagged or cobbled alleys and the main square is dominated by the market house, or Shambles, where the butchers had their stalls in days gone by.

K KENDAL, CUMBRIA - The 'Auld Grey Town' lies in the valley of the River Kent with a backcloth of limestone fells. Situated just outside the Lake District National Park, it is a good centre for touring the Lakes and surrounding country. Ruined castle, reputed birthplace of Catherine Parr.

- **KESWICK, CUMBRIA** - Beautifully positioned town beside Derwentwater and below the mountains of Skiddaw and Blencathra. Excellent base for walking, climbing, watersports and touring. Motor-launches operate on Derwentwater and motor boats, rowing boats and canoes can be hired.

- **KIRKBY LONSDALE, CUMBRIA** - Charming old town of narrow streets and Georgian buildings, set in the superb scenery of the Lune Valley. The Devil's Bridge over the River Lune is probably 13th C.

- **KIRKBY STEPHEN, CUMBRIA** - Old market town close to the River Eden, with many fine Georgian buildings and an attractive market square. St Stephen's Church is known as the 'Cathedral of the Dales'. Good base for exploring the Eden Valley and the Dales.

N NEWBY BRIDGE, CUMBRIA - At the southern end of Windermere on the River Leven, this village has an unusual stone bridge with arches of unequal size. The Lakeside and Haverthwaite Railway has a stop here, and steamer cruises on Lake Windermere leave from nearby Lakeside.

P PENRITH, CUMBRIA - Ancient and historic market town, the northern gateway to the Lake District. Penrith Castle was built as a defence against the Scots. Its ruins, open to the public, stand in the public park. High above the town is the Penrith Beacon, made famous by William Wordsworth.

S SAWREY, CUMBRIA - Far Sawrey and Near Sawrey lie near Esthwaite Water. Both villages are small but Near Sawrey is famous for Hill Top Farm, home of Beatrix Potter, now owned by the National Trust and open to the public.

W WINDERMERE, CUMBRIA - Once a tiny hamlet before the introduction of the railway in 1847, now adjoins Bowness which is on the lakeside. Centre for sailing and boating. A good way to see the lake is a trip on a passenger steamer. Steamboat Museum has a fine collection of old boats.

Finding
accommodation
is as easy as 1 2 3

Where to Stay makes it quick and easy to find a place to stay. There are several ways to use this guide.

1

Town Index
The town index, starting on page 366, lists all the places with accommodation featured in the regional sections. The index gives a page number where you can find full accommodation and contact details.

2

Colour Maps
All the place names in black on the colour maps at the front have an entry in the regional sections. Refer to the town index for the page number where you will find one or more establishments offering accommodation in your chosen town or village.

3

Accommodation listing
Contact details for **all** English Tourism Council assessed accommodation throughout England, together with their national Star rating are given in the listing section of this guide. Establishments with a full entry in the regional sections are shown in blue. Look in the town index for the page number on which their full entry appears.

NORTHUMBRIA

Romans, sailors and industrial pioneers have all left their mark here. Northumbria's exciting cities, castle – studded countryside and white-sanded coastline make it an undiscovered gem.

classic sights

Lindisfarne Castle – on Holy Island
Housesteads Roman Fort – the most impressive Roman fort on Hadrian's Wall

coast & country

Kielder Water and Forest Park – perfect for walking, cycling and watersports
Saltburn – beach of broad sands
Seahouses – picturesque fishing village

maritime history

HMS Trincomalee – magnificent 1817 British warship
Captain Cook – birthplace museum and replica of his ship, *Endeavour*
Grace Darling – museum commemorating her rescue of shipwreck survivors in 1838

arts for all

Angel of the North – awe-inspiring sculpture by Antony Gormley

distinctively different

St Mary's lighthouse – great views from the top

The counties of County Durham, Northumberland,
Tees Valley and Tyne & Wear

FOR MORE INFORMATION CONTACT:
Northumbria Tourist Board
Aykley Heads, Durham DH1 5UX
Tel: (0191) 375 3009 Fax: (0191) 386 0899
Internet: www.visitnorthumbria.com

The Pictures:
1 Lindisfarne Castle, Holy Island
2 Bamburgh, Northumberland
3 Washington Old Hall,
    Tyne & Wear

Places to Visit - see pages 64-67
Where to Stay - see pages 68-75

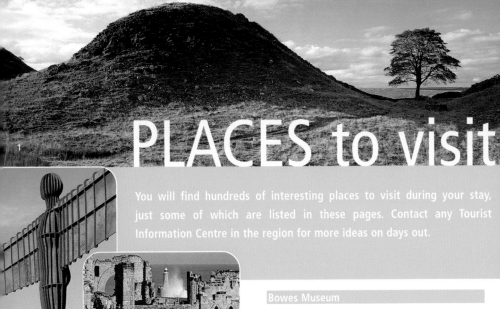

PLACES to visit

You will find hundreds of interesting places to visit during your stay, just some of which are listed in these pages. Contact any Tourist Information Centre in the region for more ideas on days out.

Bowes Museum

Barnard Castle, Durham DL12 8NP
Tel: (01833) 690606 www.bowesmuseum.org.uk
French-style chateau housing art collections of national importance and archaeology of south west Durham.

Captain Cook Birthplace Museum

Stewart Park, Marton, Middlesbrough, Cleveland TS7 6AS
Tel: (01642) 311211
Early life and voyages of Captain Cook and the countries he visited. Temporary exhibitions. One person free with every group of 10 visiting.

Alnwick Castle

The Estate Office, Alnwick, Northumberland NE66 1NQ
Tel: (01665) 510777 www.alnwickcastle.com
Largest inhabited castle in England, after Windsor Castle, and home of the Percys, Dukes of Northumberland since 1309.

Chesters Roman Fort (Cilurnum)

Chollerford, Hadrian's Wall, Humshaugh, Hexham, Northumberland NE46 4EP
Tel: (01434) 681379
Fort built for 500 cavalrymen. Remains include 5 gateways, barrack blocks, commandant's house and headquarters. Finest military bath house in Britain.

ARC

Dovecot Street, Stockton-on-Tees, Stockton TS18 1LL
Tel: (01642) 666600 www.arconline.co.uk
Arts venue which aims to provide the region with an extensive and innovative programme. Two theatres, a dance studio, recording studio and rehearsal rooms.

Bamburgh Castle

Bamburgh, Northumberland NE69 7DF
Tel: (01668) 214515 www.bamburghcastle.com
Magnificent coastal castle completely restored in 1900. Collections of china, porcelain, furniture, paintings, arms and armour.

Cragside House, Gardens and Estate

Cragside, Rothbury, Morpeth, Northumberland NE65 7PX
Tel: (01669) 620333 www.nationaltrust.org.uk
House built 1864-84 for the first Lord Armstrong, a Tyneside industrialist. Cragside was the first house to be lit by electricity generated by water power.

Bede's World

Church Bank, Jarrow, Tyne & Wear NE32 3DY
Tel: (0191) 489 2106 www.bedesworld.co.uk
Discover the exciting world of the Venerable Bede, early medieval Europe's greatest scholar. Church, monastic site, museum with exhibitions and recreated Anglo-Saxon farm.

Discovery Museum

Blandford House, Blandford Square, Newcastle upon Tyne, Tyne & Wear NE1 4JA
Tel: (0191) 232 6789
The Museum is currently undergoing a £10.7 million redevelopment. Visit the Science Maze, Fashion Works, Live Wires, Maritime Gallery, A Soldier's Life Gallery and The Newcastle Story (the new John George Jolcey Museum).

Durham Castle

Palace Green, Durham DH1 3RW
Tel: (0191) 374 3863 www.durhamcastle.com
Castle founded in 1072, Norman chapel dating from 1080, kitchens and great hall dated 1499 and 1284 respectively. Fine example of motte-and-bailey castle.

Durham Cathedral

The Chapter Office, The College, Durham DH1 3EH
Tel: (0191) 386 4266 www.durhamcathedral.co.uk
Durham Cathedral is thought by many to be the finest example of Norman church architecture in England. Visit the tombs of St Cuthbert and The Venerable Bede.

Gisborough Priory

Church Street, Guisborough, Redcar & Cleveland TS14 6HG
Tel: (01287) 633801
Remains of a priory founded by Robert de Brus in AD1119. A priory for Augustinian canons in the grounds of Guisborough Hall. Main arch and window of east wall virtually intact.

Hall Hill Farm

Lanchester, Durham DH7 0TA
Tel: (01388) 730300 www.hallhillfarm.co.uk
Family fun set in attractive countryside with an opportunity to see and touch the animals at close quarters. Farm trailer ride, riverside walk, teashop and play area.

Hartlepool Historic Quay

Maritime Avenue, Hartlepool, Cleveland TS24 0XZ
Tel: (01429) 860006 www.thisishartlepool.com
Hartlepool Historic Quay is an exciting reconstruction of a seaport of the 1800s with buildings and lively quayside, authentically reconstructed.

Housesteads Roman Fort (Vercovicum)

Hadrian's Wall, Haydon Bridge, Hexham, Northumberland NE47 6NN
Tel: (01434) 344363
Best preserved and most impressive of the Roman forts. Vercovicium was a 5-acre fort for an extensive 800 civil settlement. Only example of a Roman hospital.

Killhope, The North of England Lead Mining Museum

Cowshill, Weardale, St John's Chapel, Bishop Auckland, County Durham DL13 1AR
Tel: (01388) 537505 www.durham.gov.uk/killhope
Most complete lead mining site in Great Britain. Mine tours available, 10m (34ft) diameter water-wheel, reconstruction of Victorian machinery, miners lodging and woodland walks.

Kirkleatham Old Hall Museum

Kirkleatham, Redcar, Redcar & Cleveland TS10 5NW
Tel: (01642) 479500
Displays depicting local life, industry, commerce, local history, sea rescue, artists, social and natural history and the story of Kirkleatham.

Laing Art Gallery

New Bridge Street, Newcastle upon Tyne, Tyne & Wear NE1 8AJ
Tel: (0191) 232 7734
Paintings, including watercolours by Northumbrian-born artist John Martin. Award-winning interactive displays 'Art on Tyneside' and 'Children's Gallery'. Cafe and shop.

Life Interactive World

Times Square, Scotswood Road, Newcastle upon Tyne, Tyne & Wear NE1 4EP
Tel: (0191) 243 8210 www.lifeinteractiveworld.co.uk
Life Interactive World is an amazing action-packed journey. Experience the longest motion ride in the world, magical 3D, theatre shows, virtual games and interactives.

The Pictures:
1 Hadrian's Wall
2 The Angel of the North, Gateshead
3 Tynemouth Priory and Castle, Tyne & Wear
4 Dunstanburgh, Northumberland
5 Boulby Cliff, Cleveland
6 Kielder Water, Northumberland

National Glass Centre

Liberty Way, Sunderland, Tyne & Wear SR6 0GL

Tel: (0191) 515 5555 www.nationalglasscentre.com

A large gallery presenting the best in contemporary and historical glass. Master craftspeople will demonstrate glass-making techniques. Classes and workshops available.

Nature's World at the Botanic Centre

Nature's World at the Botanic Centre
Ladgate Lane, Acklam, Middlesbrough,
Tees Valley TS5 7YN

Tel: (01642) 594895 www.naturesworld.org.uk

Demonstration gardens, wildlife pond, white garden, environmental exhibition hall, shop, tearooms and River Tees model now open. Hydroponicum and visitor exhibition centre.

Newcastle Cathedral Church of St Nicholas

St Nicholas Street, Newcastle upon Tyne,
Tyne & Wear NE1 1PF

Tel: (0191) 232 1939

www.newcastle-ang-cathedral-stnicholas.org.uk

13thC and 14thC church, added to in 18thC-20thC. Famous lantern tower, pre-reformation font and font cover, 15thC stained glass roundel in the side chapel.

The North of England Open Air Museum

Beamish, County Durham DH9 0RG

Tel: (0191) 370 4000 www.beamish.org.uk

Visit the town, colliery village, working farm, Pockerley Manor and 1825 railway, recreating life in the North East in the early 1800s and 1900s.

Ormesby Hall

Church Lane, Ormesby, Middlesbrough TS7 9AS

Tel: (01642) 324188 www.nationaltrust.org.uk

Georgian, 18thC mansion. Impressive contemporary plasterwork. Magnificent stable block attributed to Carr of York. Model railway exhibition and layout.

Raby Castle

PO Box 50, Staindrop, Darlington, County Durham DL2 3AH

Tel: (01833) 660202 www.rabycastle.com

The medieval castle, home of Lord Barnard's family since 1626, includes a 200-acre deer park, walled gardens, carriage collection, adventure playground, shop and tearooms.

Sea Life Aquarium

Grand Parade, Tynemouth, Tyne & Wear NE30 4JF

Tel: (0191) 257 6100

More than 30 hi-tech displays provide encounters with dozens of sea creatures. Journey beneath the North Sea and discover thousands of amazing creatures.

South Shields Museum and Art Gallery

Ocean Road, South Shields, Tyne & Wear NE33 2JA

Tel: (0191) 456 8740

Discover how the area's development has been influenced by its natural and industrial past through lively hands-on displays. Exciting programme of temporary exhibitions.

Thomas Bewick Birthplace Museum

Cherryburn, Station Bank, Mickley, Stocksfield, Northumberland NE43 7DB

Tel: (01661) 843276

Birthplace cottage (1700) and farmyard. Printing house using original printing blocks. Introductory exhibition of the life, work and countryside.

Vindolanda (Chesterholm)

Chesterholm Museum, Hadrian's Wall, Bardon Mill, Hexham, Northumberland NE47 7JN

Tel: (01434) 344277 www.vindolanda.com

Visitors may inspect the remains of the Roman fort and settlement, and see its extraordinary finds in the superb museum. Full-scale replicas of Roman buildings.

Washington Old Hall

The Avenue, District 4, Washington, Tyne & Wear NE38 7LE

Tel: (0191) 416 6879

From 1183 to 1399 the home of George Washington's direct ancestors, remaining in the family until 1613. The manor, from which the family took its name, was restored in 1936.

Wet 'N Wild

Rotary Way, Royal Quays, North Shields,
Tyne & Wear NE29 6DA

Tel: (0191) 296 1333 www.wetnwild.co.uk

Tropical indoor water park. A fun water playground providing the wildest and wettest indoor rapid experience. Whirlpools, slides and meandering lazy river.

Wildfowl and Wetlands Trust

Washington, District 15, Washington, Tyne & Wear NE38 8LE

Tel: (0191) 416 5454 www.wwt.org.uk

Collection of 1,000 wildfowl of 85 varieties. Viewing gallery, picnic areas, hides and winter wild bird-feeding station, flamingos and wild grey heron. Food available.

Find out more about Northumbria

Dunstanburgh Castle

Further information about holidays and attractions in Northumbria is available from:

NORTHUMBRIA TOURIST BOARD
Aykley Heads, Durham DH1 5UX.
Tel: (0191) 375 3009 Fax: (0191) 386 0899
Internet: www.visitnorthumbria.com

The following publications are available from Northumbria Tourist Board unless otherwise stated:

Northumbria 2002
information on the region, including hotels, bed and breakfast and self-catering accommodation, caravan and camping parks, attractions, shopping, eating and drinking

Going Places
information on where to go, what to see and what to do. Combined with the award-winning Powerpass promotion which offers 2-for-1 entry into many of the region's top attractions

Group Travel Directory
guide designed specifically for group organisers, detailing group accommodation providers, places to visit, suggested itineraries, coaching information and events

Educational Visits
information to help plan educational visits within the region. Uncover a wide variety of places to visit with unique learning opportunities

Discover Northumbria on two wheels
information on cycling in the region including an order form allowing the reader to order maps/leaflets from a central ordering point

Freedom
caravan and camping guide to the North of England. Available from Freedom Holidays, tel: 01202 252179

Getting to Northumbria

BY ROAD: The north/south routes on the A1 and A19 thread the region as does the A68. East/west routes like the A66 and A69 easily link with the western side of the country. Within Northumbria you will find fast, modern interconnecting roads between all the main centres, a vast network of scenic, traffic-free country roads to make motoring a pleasure and frequent local bus services operating to all towns and villages.

BY RAIL: London to Edinburgh InterCity service stops at Darlington, Durham, Newcastle and Berwick upon Tweed. 26 trains daily make the journey between London and Newcastle in just under 3 hours. The London to Middlesbrough journey takes 3 hours. Birmingham to Darlington 3 hours 15 minutes. Bristol to Durham 5 hours and Sheffield to Newcastle just over 2 hours. Direct services operate to Newcastle from Liverpool, Manchester, Glasgow, Stranraer and Carlisle. Regional services to areas of scenic beauty operate frequently, allowing the traveller easy access. The Tyne & Wear Metro makes it possible to travel to many destinations within the Tyneside area, such as Gateshead, South Shields, Whitley Bay and Newcastle International Airport, in minutes.

Where to stay in Northumbria

Accommodation entries in this region are listed in alphabetical order of place name, and then in alphabetical order of establishment.

Map references refer to the colour location maps at front of this guide. The first number indicates the map to use; the letter and number which follow refer to the grid reference on the map.

At-a-glance symbols at the end of each accommodation entry give useful information about services and facilities. A key to symbols can be found inside the back cover flap. Keep this open for easy reference.

A brief description of the towns and villages offering accommodation in the entries which follow, can be found at the end of this section.

A complete listing of all the English Tourism Council assessed accommodation covered by this guide appears at the back of the guide.

ALNMOUTH, Northumberland Map ref 5C1

★★

SADDLE HOTEL
24-25 Northumberland Street,
Alnmouth, Alnwick NE66 2RA
T: (01665) 830476

Bedrooms: 7 double/
twin, 1 triple/multiple
Bathrooms: 8 en suite

Lunch available
Evening meal available
CC: Delta, Mastercard,
Switch, Visa

B&B per night:
S £31.00–£36.00
D £52.00–£58.00

HB per person:
DY £38.00–£45.00

OPEN All year round

Personally supervised by owners and offering a high standard of accommodation. One of Alnmouth's premier eating houses, with many good food awards.

♪⅏✆🖳▱💧🖬☒⌷▦◨☕♨↻🐎

BAMBURGH, Northumberland Map ref 5C1

★★★

WAREN HOUSE HOTEL
Waren Mill, Belford NE70 7EE
T: (01668) 214581
F: (01668) 214484
E: enquiries@warenhousehotel.co.uk
I: www.warenhousehotel.co.uk

B&B per night:
S £40.50–£105.00
D £80.50–£135.00

HB per person:
DY £65.50–£130.00

OPEN All year round

Traditional, beautifully restored and renovated, award-winning country house hotel in 6 acres of wooded grounds and walled garden on edge of Budle Bay overlooking Holy Island. Superb accommodation, excellent food, choice of over 250 reasonably priced wines. Two miles Bamburgh Castle, 5 miles Farne Islands. Children over 14 welcome.

Bedrooms: 10 double/
twin; suites available
Bathrooms: 10 en suite

Evening meal available
CC: Amex, Delta, Diners,
Mastercard, Switch, Visa

Short breaks-dinner, room and breakfast from £62pppn.

♪⅏14🏠✆🖳▱💧🖬☒🏡▦◨☕↻⌷❄🐎🚲🐾⌂P

BARNARD CASTLE, Durham Map ref 5B3 *Tourist Information Centre Tel: (01833) 690909*

★★★

JERSEY FARM HOTEL
Darlington Road, Barnard Castle DL12 8TA
T: (01833) 638223
F: (01833) 631988
E: enquiries@jerseyfarm.co.uk
I: www.jerseyfarm.co.uk

B&B per night:
S £55.00–£68.00
D £70.00–£90.00

OPEN All year round

One mile east of Barnard Castle in an Area of Outstanding Natural Beauty. The Watsons created the hotel in 1978 after previously farming the land. Comfortable rooms with panoramic views. The Meadow Restaurant is famous for a la carte and carvery meals with plenty of it! Residents' lounge, bar and conservatory, all tastefully decorated.

Bedrooms: 1 single, 15 double/twin, 4 triple/ multiple; suites available
Bathrooms: 20 en suite

Lunch available
Evening meal available
CC: Delta, Mastercard, Switch, Visa

Mini-breaks available all year, Murder Mysteries, various theme nights-special brochure available on forthcoming events.

BELLINGHAM, Northumberland Map ref 5B2 *Tourist Information Centre Tel: (01434) 220616*

★★

RIVERDALE HALL HOTEL
Bellingham, Hexham NE48 2JT
T: (01434) 220254
F: (01434) 220457
E: iben@riverdalehall.demon.co.uk

B&B per night:
S £46.00–£48.00
D £69.00–£84.00

HB per person:
DY £54.00–£67.00

OPEN All year round

CR
The Independents

Spacious Victorian country hall in large grounds. All bedrooms en suite with TV, telephone and hospitality trays. Indoor swimming pool, sauna, fishing, cricket field and golf nearby. Award-winning restaurant. Kielder Water, Pennine Way and Hadrian's Wall nearby. The Cocker family's 23rd year.

Bedrooms: 3 single, 13 double/twin, 4 triple/ multiple
Bathrooms: 20 en suite

Lunch available
Evening meal available
CC: Delta, Diners, Mastercard, Switch, Visa

Golfing, fishing and cricketing breaks arranged. Free place for organiser for parties of 15 or more.

BERWICK-UPON-TWEED, Northumberland Map ref 5B1 *Tourist Information Centre Tel: (01289) 330733*

Rating
Applied For

MARSHALL MEADOWS COUNTRY HOUSE HOTEL
Berwick-upon-Tweed TD15 1UT
T: (01289) 331133
F: (01289) 331438
E: stay@marshallmeadows.co.uk
I: www.marshallmeadows.co.uk

B&B per night:
S Min £75.00
D £85.00–£100.00

OPEN All year round

This stylish Georgian mansion set in attractive woodland gardens is located off the A1 just a few minutes' drive north of Berwick. Magnificent public rooms and comfortable, well-equipped bedrooms are offered, together with excellent service and tempting menus drawing on local produce, in a relaxing country house atmosphere.

Bedrooms: 3 single, 16 double/twin; suites available
Bathrooms: 19 en suite

Lunch available
Evening meal available
CC: Delta, Mastercard, Switch, Visa

Weekend breaks available throughout the year.

PRICES
Please check prices and other details at the time of booking.

CORNHILL-ON-TWEED, Northumberland Map ref 5B1

★★★
Silver
Award

TILLMOUTH PARK COUNTRY HOUSE HOTEL

Cornhill-on-Tweed TD12 4UU
T: (01890) 882255
F: (01890) 882540
E: reception@tillmouthpark.f9.co.uk
I: www.tillmouthpark.co.uk

B&B per night:
D £130.00–£170.00

HB per person:
DY £90.00–£120.00

OPEN All year round

Grand Heritage Hotels

A magnificent mansion house set in 15 acres of secluded parkland gardens above the River Till. Fourteen fully appointed en suite bedrooms, spacious and individually styled. Award-winning restaurant and informal bistro with a well-stocked bar. Exceptional hospitality, comfort and service. A perfect venue for country pursuits or peace and tranquility.

Bedrooms: 1 single,
13 double/twin, 1 triple/
multiple
Bathrooms: 15 en suite

Lunch available
Evening meal available
CC: Amex, Delta, Diners,
Mastercard, Switch, Visa

Border break: 3 nights' DB&B from £192pp.
Telephone hotel for fishing & golfing packages.

CROOK, Durham Map ref 5C2

★★★

HELME PARK HALL COUNTRY HOUSE AND RESTAURANT HOTEL

Fir Tree, Crook DL13 4NW
T: (01388) 730970
F: (01388) 730970

B&B per night:
S £40.00–£46.00
D £70.00–£75.00

HB per person:
DY £43.50–£69.00

OPEN All year round

Comfortable, privately owned, recently refurbished hotel offering a welcoming atmosphere with spectacular views over the dales. Food is of the highest quality with plentiful bar meals, table d'hote or a la carte meals. Easily accessible with good parking. With its 2 acres of grounds it offers a haven of peace and tranquillity.

Bedrooms: 2 single,
11 double/twin
Bathrooms: 13 en suite

Lunch available
Evening meal available
CC: Amex, Delta,
Mastercard, Switch, Visa

Weekend special break offers and evening
entertainment on selected weekends. Christmas and
New Year breaks.

DARLINGTON, Durham Map ref 5C3 *Tourist Information Centre Tel: (01325) 388666*

★★★

HEADLAM HALL HOTEL AND RESTAURANT

Headlam, Gainford, Darlington DL2 3HA
T: (01325) 730238
F: (01325) 730790
E: admin@headlamhall.co.uk
I: www.headlamhall.co.uk

B&B per night:
S £69.00–£99.00
D £84.00–£114.00

HB per person:
DY £57.00–£62.00

OPEN All year round

Charming Jacobean mansion located in a picturesque hamlet in rural lower Teesdale. Set in 4 acres of formal gardens, the hotel offers high quality accommodation, a superb restaurant and leisure facilities including pool, sauna, tennis court, gym and fishing. Conveniently located for the region's main towns and attractions.

Bedrooms: 32 double/
twin, 4 triple/multiple;
suites available
Bathrooms: 36 en suite

Lunch available
Evening meal available
CC: Amex, Delta, Diners,
Mastercard, Switch, Visa

Winter, easter and summer breaks.

SYMBOLS The symbols in each entry give information about services and facilities. A key to these symbols appears at the back of this guide.

DURHAM, Durham Map ref 5C2 *Tourist Information Centre Tel: (0191) 384 3720*

★★
KENSINGTON HALL HOTEL
Kensington Terrace, Willington,
Crook DL15 0PJ
T: (01388) 745071
F: (01388) 745800
E: kensingtonhall@cs.com
I: ourworld.cs.com/kensingtonhall

Bedrooms: 7 double/
twin, 3 triple/multiple
Bathrooms: 10 en suite

Lunch available
Evening meal available
CC: Amex, Delta, Diners,
Mastercard, Switch, Visa

B&B per night:
S £40.00–£42.00
D £50.00–£52.00

HB per person:
DY £52.00

Comfortable family-run hotel, lounge bar, restaurant and function suite. Excellent meals. South-west of Durham on A690 to Crook. Easy access to Durham Cathedral, Beamish Museum and Weardale.

OPEN All year round

★★★
Silver
Award
LUMLEY CASTLE HOTEL
Chester-le-Street DH3 4NX
T: (0191) 389 1111
F: (0191) 389 1881
E: lumcastle@netcomuk.co.uk
I: www.lumleycastle.com

Bedrooms: 14 single,
42 double/twin, 2 triple/
multiple; suites available
Bathrooms: 58 en suite

Lunch available
Evening meal available
CC: Amex, Delta, Diners,
Mastercard, Switch, Visa

B&B per night:
S £105.00–£147.00
D £155.00–£210.00

HB per person:
DY £89.50–£99.50

14thC castle on the River Wear, in 9 acres of parkland. Five miles from Durham and 13 miles from Newcastle, easily accessible from the A1(M).

OPEN All year round

HAMSTERLEY FOREST

See under Barnard Castle, Crook

HEXHAM, Northumberland Map ref 5B2

★★★

BEAUMONT HOTEL
Beaumont Street, Hexham NE46 3LT
T: (01434) 602331
F: (01434) 606184
E: beaumont.hotel@btinternet.com
I: www.beaumont-hotel.co.uk

B&B per night:
S £75.00–£85.00
D £100.00–£110.00

HB per person:
DY £60.00–£75.00

OPEN All year round

Attractive refurbished hotel overlooking the delightful park and abbey. Two comfortable bars and an a la carte restaurant. Lunch/dinner, morning coffee and afternoon teas served daily. Lift to all floors. In the heart of Hadrian's Wall country. Superb golf with 3 of the North's finest courses close-by.

Bedrooms: 6 single,
18 double/twin, 1 triple/
multiple
Bathrooms: 25 en suite

Lunch available
Evening meal available
CC: Amex, Delta, Diners,
Mastercard, Switch, Visa

Best Western Hotels

★★★

LANGLEY CASTLE
Langley-on-Tyne, Hexham NE47 5LU
T: (01434) 688888
F: (01434) 684019
E: manager@langleycastle.com
I: www.langleycastle.com

B&B per night:
S £99.50–£139.50
D £125.00–£195.00

HB per person:
DY £67.50–£97.50

OPEN All year round

A genuine 14thC castle, set in own woodland estate. All rooms with private facilities, some with window seats set into 7ft thick walls, sauna and 4-poster beds. The magnificent drawing room, with blazing log fire, complements the intimate Josephine Restaurant. Perfect to explore Northumberland, Bamburgh Castle, Holy Island, the Borders.

Bedrooms: 18 double/
twin; suites available
Bathrooms: 18 en suite

Lunch available
Evening meal available
CC: Amex, Delta, Diners,
Mastercard, Switch, Visa

REGIONAL TOURIST BOARD The ♠ symbol in an
establishment entry indicates that it is a Regional Tourist Board member.

HOLY ISLAND, Northumberland Map ref 5C1

★

LINDISFARNE HOTEL
Holy Island, Berwick-upon-Tweed
TD15 2SQ
T: (01289) 389273
F: (01289) 389284

Bedrooms: 2 single,
4 double/twin, 2 triple/
multiple
Bathrooms: 6 en suite

Evening meal available
CC: Amex, Delta, Diners,
Mastercard, Switch, Visa

B&B per night:
S £22.00–£30.00
D £52.00–£65.00

HB per person:
DY £39.00–£45.50

OPEN All year round

Small, comfortable, family-run hotel providing dinner, bed and breakfast. An ideal place for ornithologists and within walking distance of Lindisfarne Castle and Priory.

⋔☎⚐☎✆◻♨♦⑂Ⓢ↙⛱▥◲◳🔍✽⬡P

KIELDER FOREST

See under Bellingham

MATFEN, Northumberland Map ref 5B2

★★★
Silver
Award

MATFEN HALL
Matfen, Newcastle upon Tyne NE20 0RH
T: (01661) 886500
F: (01661) 886055
E: info@matfenhall.com
I: www.matfenhall.com

B&B per night:
S £95.00–£135.00
D £120.00–£205.00

HB per person:
DY £75.00–£117.50

OPEN All year round

Built in the 1830s Matfen Hall has been lovingly restored into a luxurious hotel, which lies in the heart of Northumberland's most beautiful countryside. With panoramic views over its 18-hole golf course, the hotel offers splendid facilities, combining modern features with traditional opulence whilst retaining all its original character.

Bedrooms: 31 double/
twin; suites available
Bathrooms: 31 en suite

Lunch available
Evening meal available
CC: Amex, Delta,
Mastercard, Switch, Visa

⋔☎⚐☎✆◻♨♦⑂Ⓢ↙▣◐▥◲◳🍴🝆✽🐎⛳⬡P

MIDDLESBROUGH, Tees Valley Map ref 5C3

★★★

BALTIMORE HOTEL
250 Marton Road, Middlesbrough
TS4 2EZ
T: (01642) 224111
F: (01642) 226156
E: info@lincoln-group.co.uk

Bedrooms: 18 single,
12 double/twin, 1 triple/
multiple; suites available
Bathrooms: 31 en suite

Lunch available
Evening meal available
CC: Amex, Delta, Diners,
Mastercard, Switch, Visa

B&B per night:
S £38.00–£71.00
D £51.00–£84.00

HB per person:
DY £50.00–£83.00

OPEN All year round

ⓒⓡ
Utell International

Close to the heart of both commercial and residential Middlesbrough and 1 mile from the central station. Teesside Airport 18 miles.

⋔☎⚐✆◼◻♨♦⑂Ⓢ◐▥◲◳🍴⚅★✽⬡P

MIDDLETON-IN-TEESDALE, Durham Map ref 5B3

★★

THE TEESDALE HOTEL
Market Place, Middleton-in-Teesdale,
Barnard Castle DL12 0QG
T: (01833) 640264 & 640537
F: (01833) 640651
I: www.teesdalehotels.com

B&B per night:
S Max £42.50
D Max £65.00

HB per person:
DY £48.25–£62.50

OPEN All year round

Tastefully modernised, family-run 18thC coaching inn serving home cooking and fine wines. All rooms with telephone, radio and TV. Dogs welcome free of charge.

Bedrooms: 2 single,
8 double/twin
Bathrooms: 10 en suite

Lunch available
Evening meal available
CC: Amex, Delta,
Mastercard, Switch, Visa

Buy 2 nights' DB&B £96.50pp (excl Christmas and New Year).

⋔☎⚐✆◻♨♦⑂Ⓢ◲▥◲◳🍴♿✽🐎🐕⬡⬡P

MAP REFERENCES
Map references apply to the colour maps at the front of this guide.

NEWCASTLE UPON TYNE, Tyne and Wear Map ref 5C2 *Tourist Information Centre Tel: (0191) 277 8000*

★★ **GROSVENOR HOTEL**

Grosvenor Road, Jesmond,
Newcastle upon Tyne NE2 2RR
T: (0191) 281 0543
F: (0191) 281 9217
E: info@grosvenor-hotel.com
I: www.grosvenor-hotel.com

Bedrooms: 14 single,
36 double/twin, 3 triple/
multiple
Bathrooms: 51 en suite,
2 private

Lunch available
Evening meal available
CC: Amex, Delta, Diners,
Mastercard, Switch, Visa

B&B per night:
S £25.00–£35.00
D £50.00–£65.00

HB per person:
DY £35.00–£45.00

Friendly hotel in quiet residential suburb, offering a wide range of facilities. Close to city centre. Bar restaurant, 24-hour service. Easy parking.

OPEN All year round

⚞🎠♿🍴🛏🖥💧🕄⑤🔀🔌①🛏🖨🍽🐾🅿

★★★
Silver
Award

SURTEES HOTEL LTD

12-18 Dean Street,
Newcastle upon Tyne NE1 1PG
T: (0191) 261 7771
F: (0191) 230 1322
E: surtees@milburn.net
I: www.surteeshotel.co.uk

Bedrooms: 12 single,
15 double/twin
Bathrooms: 27 en suite

Lunch available
Evening meal available
CC: Amex, Delta, Diners,
Mastercard, Switch, Visa

B&B per night:
S £59.50–£79.50
D £79.50–£89.50

OPEN All year round

City-centre hotel within walking distance of Eldon Square, the Quayside and station, with a 24-hour multi-storey car park adjacent. Cocktail and public bar, restaurant and nightclub.

⚞🎠🍴🖥💧🕄⑤🔌①🛏🖨🍽🚐🐾🏛

TOWN INDEX

This can be found at the back of this guide. If you know where you want to stay, the index will give you the page number listing accommodation in your chosen town, city or village.

MIDDLESBROUGH

Quality Hotel and Conference Centre Middlesbrough
Paul Morrison
Ormesby Road, Middlesbrough TS3 7SF
Tel: 01642 203 000 Fax: 01642 232 003
Email: info@tad-centre.co.uk Internet: www.tad-centre.co.uk

40 spacious en-suite rooms with tea and coffee making facilities, direct-dial telephone, hairdryer, cable/satellite T.V. 14 meeting rooms and computer resource room, conference theatre with state-of-the-art facilities seating up to 170 delegates. Video conferencing. Nursery attached to conference centre. Banqueting facilities for up to 200 guests. Licensed to hold civil wedding ceremonies. 155-seater restaurant serves superb quality food. Bar. 24-hour secure car parking for 150 cars.
From A19, take A66E to Middlesbrough, 2M take A172 and turn left at roundabout. Take next right, over roundabout, hotel on the right. Teeside Airport: 7M, Train: 2M, leisure and fitness facilities; ¹/₂M, Whitby: 20M, North Yorkshire Moors: 5M, Middlesbrough F.C, Cellnet Riverside Stadium a short car ride away. Metrocentre (shopping): 40M

Quality

English Tourism Council
★★★
HOTEL

40 Rooms
Rates from
£45.00 to £65.00

★★★

Elegantly furnished hotel, with traditionally styled bedrooms, cocktail bar, lounge and leisure club with pool. Free car park. One mile from Newcastle centre. Rates shown are Breakaway rates, based on a minimum 2-night stay and subject to availability. Call, quoting EN900, to request a breakaway brochure full of great deals.

SWALLOW IMPERIAL HOTEL

Jesmond Road, Newcastle upon Tyne
NE2 1PR
T: (0191) 281 5511
F: (0191) 281 8472
E: jesmond@swallow-hotels.co.uk

Bedrooms: 49 single, 67 double/twin, 6 triple/ multiple
Bathrooms: 122 en suite

Lunch available
Evening meal available
CC: Amex, Delta, Diners, Mastercard, Switch, Visa

HB per person:
DY Min £54.00

OPEN All year round

OTTERBURN, Northumberland Map ref 5B1 *Tourist Information Centre Tel: (01830) 520093*

★★★
Silver
Award

OTTERBURN TOWER HOTEL
Otterburn, Newcastle upon Tyne
NE19 1NS
T: (01830) 520620 &
(01670) 772287
F: (01830) 521504
E: reservations@otterburntower.co.
uk
I: www.otterburntower.co.uk

Bedrooms: 16 double/ twin, 1 triple/multiple; suites available
Bathrooms: 17 en suite

Lunch available
Evening meal available
CC: Delta, Mastercard, Switch, Visa

B&B per night:
S Min £60.00
D £90.00–£160.00

HB per person:
DY £60.00–£95.00

OPEN All year round

Grade II Listed 13thC country house fronted by formal gardens and surrounded by pastures, rivers and woodland. Award-winning restaurant. Fishing and rural sports available.

RUSHYFORD, Durham Map ref 5C2

★★★

17thC former coaching inn, 8 miles south of Durham. Facilities include leisure club with pool, Lord Eldon restaurant renowned for fine food, and recently refurbished bedrooms. Rates shown are Breakaway rates, based on a minimum 2-night stay and subject to availability. Call, quoting EN900, to request a Breakaway brochure full of great deals.

SWALLOW EDEN ARMS HOTEL

Rushyford, Ferryhill DL17 0LL
T: (01388) 720541
F: (01388) 721871
E: edenarmsswallow@whitbread.com
I: www.swallowhotels.co.uk

Bedrooms: 13 single, 27 double/twin, 5 triple/ multiple; suites available
Bathrooms: 45 en suite

Lunch available
Evening meal available
CC: Amex, Delta, Diners, Mastercard, Switch, Visa

3 for 2 offer-stay Fri/Sat DB&B receive Sun B&B free. Spoil yourselves with upgrade packages from £10pppn.

B&B per night:
S £38.00–£85.00
D £76.00–£115.00

HB per person:
DY £53.00–£105.00

OPEN All year round

SEDGEFIELD, Durham Map ref 5C2

★★★

HARDWICK HALL HOTEL
Sedgefield, Stockton-on-Tees
TS21 2EH
T: (01740) 620253
F: (01740) 622771

Bedrooms: 17 double/ twin
Bathrooms: 17 en suite

Lunch available
Evening meal available
CC: Amex, Delta, Diners, Mastercard, Switch, Visa

B&B per night:
S £56.00–£110.00
D £65.00–£120.00

OPEN All year round

The former home of Lord Boyne standing in 22 acres of lovely parkland. 52 luxury bedrooms plus a superb conference and banqueting centre. Outstanding location.

TYNEMOUTH, Tyne and Wear Map ref 5C2

★★★
GRAND HOTEL
Grand Parade, Tynemouth,
North Shields NE30 4ER
T: (0191) 293 6666
F: (0191) 293 6665
E: info@grandhotel-uk.com
I: www.grandhotel-uk.com

Bedrooms: 34 double/
twin, 11 triple/multiple
Bathrooms: 45 en suite

Lunch available
Evening meal available
CC: Amex, Delta, Diners,
Mastercard, Switch, Visa

B&B per night:
S £70.00–£95.00
D £75.00–£100.00

OPEN All year round

Built in 1872 as a summer residence for the Duchess of Northumberland, this Victorian hotel is located on a cliff top overlooking Tynemouth Longsands beach.

WARKWORTH, Northumberland Map ref 5C1

★★

WARKWORTH HOUSE HOTEL
16 Bridge Street, Warkworth, Morpeth
NE65 0XB
T: (01665) 711276
F: (01665) 713323
E: welcome@warkworthhousehotel.co.uk
I: www.warkworthhousehotel.co.uk

B&B per night:
S £53.00–£55.00
D £90.00–£95.00

HB per person:
DY £55.00–£65.00

OPEN All year round

Minotel

Delightful country house set in the heart of a small picturesque village. The house, like the village has a wealth of history, with many stories to tell. Ideal for those seeking old world charm, comfort, alongside our established reputation for service and cuisine. We look forward to welcoming you.

Bedrooms: 1 single,
13 double/twin
Bathrooms: 14 en suite

Lunch available
Evening meal available
CC: Amex, Delta, Diners,
Mastercard, Switch, Visa

3 nights for the price of 2, Oct-Apr (excl bank hols). Wine weekends. Pudding weekends. Celebration weekends.

WHITLEY BAY, Tyne and Wear Map ref 5C2 *Tourist Information Centre Tel: (0191) 200 8535*

★★★

THE ESPLANADE HOTEL
The Esplanade, Whitley Bay NE26 2AW
T: (0191) 252 1111
F: (0191) 252 0101

B&B per night:
S £50.00–£55.00
D £60.00–£65.00

OPEN All year round

Seafront hotel originally built in 1908 in Edwardian splendour. Interior recently completely refurbished to ultra-modern standards, with a Scandinavian blonde ash accent throughout. First floor seaview restaurant offering good food at reasonable prices. Excellent base for exploring Northumbria, whether for business or pleasure.

Bedrooms: 1 single,
44 double/twin, 5 triple/
multiple
Bathrooms: 50 en suite

Lunch available
Evening meal available
CC: Amex, Delta, Diners,
Mastercard, Switch, Visa

★★★
WINDSOR HOTEL
South Parade, Whitley Bay
NE26 2RF
T: (0191) 2518888
F: (0191) 2970272
E: info@windsorhotel-uk.com
I: www.windsorhotel-uk.com

Bedrooms: 2 single,
67 double/twin
Bathrooms: 69 en suite

Lunch available
Evening meal available
CC: Amex, Delta, Diners,
Mastercard, Switch, Visa

B&B per night:
S £45.00–£65.00
D £55.00–£75.00

OPEN All year round

Privately owned and newly-refurbished hotel with beautifully appointed bedrooms, situated between the seafront and town centre. First choice for business or pleasure.

QUALITY ASSURANCE SCHEME
Star ratings and awards are explained at the back of this guide.

A brief guide to the main Towns and Villages offering accommodation in Northumbria

A ALNMOUTH, NORTHUMBERLAND - Quiet village with pleasant old buildings, at the mouth of the River Aln where extensive dunes and sands stretch along Alnmouth Bay. 18th C granaries, some converted to dwellings, still stand.

B BAMBURGH, NORTHUMBERLAND - Village with a spectacular red sandstone castle standing 150ft above the sea. On the village green the magnificent Norman church stands opposite a museum containing mementoes of the heroine Grace Darling.

BARNARD CASTLE, DURHAM - High over the Tees, a thriving market town with a busy market square. Bernard Baliol's 12th C castle (now ruins) stands nearby. The Bowes Museum, housed in a grand 19th C French chateau, holds fine paintings and furniture. Nearby are some magnificent buildings.

BELLINGHAM, NORTHUMBERLAND - Set in the beautiful valley of the North Tyne close to Kielder Forest, Kielder Water and lonely moorland below the Cheviots. The church has an ancient stone wagon roof fortified in the 18th C with buttresses.

BERWICK-UPON-TWEED, NORTHUMBERLAND - Guarding the mouth of the Tweed, England's northernmost town with the best 16th C city walls in Europe. The handsome Guildhall and barracks date from the 18th C. Three bridges cross to Tweedmouth, the oldest built in 1634.

C CORNHILL-ON-TWEED, NORTHUMBERLAND - Pretty border village on the River Tweed which divides it from Coldstream, of Regimental Guards fame. This area is notable for its connections with the Battle of Flodden Field, the last battle to be fought between England and Scotland in 1513.

CROOK, DURHAM - Pleasant market town sometimes referred to as 'the gateway to Weardale'. The town's shopping centre surrounds a large, open green, attractively laid out with lawns and flowerbeds around the Devil's Stone, a relic from the Ice Age.

D DARLINGTON, DURHAM - Largest town in County Durham, standing on the River Skerne and home of the earliest passenger railway which first ran to Stockton in 1825. Now the home of a railway museum. Originally a prosperous market town occupying the site of an Anglo-Saxon settlement, it still holds an open market.

DURHAM, DURHAM - Ancient city with its Norman castle and cathedral, now a World Heritage site, set on a bluff high over the Wear. A market and university town and regional centre, spreading beyond the market-place on both banks of the river.

H HEXHAM, NORTHUMBERLAND - Old coaching and market town near Hadrian's Wall. Since pre-Norman times a weekly market has been held in the centre with its market-place and abbey park, and the richly-furnished 12th C abbey church has a superb Anglo-Saxon crypt.

HOLY ISLAND, NORTHUMBERLAND - Still an idyllic retreat, tiny island and fishing village and cradle of northern Christianity. It is approached from the mainland at low water by a causeway. The clifftop castle (National Trust) was restored by Sir Edwin Lutyens.

M MIDDLESBROUGH, TEES VALLEY - Boom-town of the mid 19th C, today's Teesside industrial and conference town has a modern shopping complex and predominantly modern buildings. An engineering miracle of the early 20th C is the Transporter Bridge which replaced an old ferry.

MIDDLETON-IN-TEESDALE, DURHAM - Small stone town of hillside terraces overlooking the river, developed by the London Lead Company in the 18th C. Five miles up-river is the spectacular 70-ft waterfall, High Force.

N NEWCASTLE UPON TYNE, TYNE AND WEAR - Commercial and cultural centre of the North East, with a large indoor shopping centre, Quayside market, museums and theatres which offer an annual 6 week season by the Royal Shakespeare Company. Norman castle keep, medieval alleys, old Guildhall.

O OTTERBURN, NORTHUMBERLAND - Small village set at the meeting of the River Rede with Otter Burn, the site of the Battle of Otterburn in 1388. A peaceful tradition continues in the sale of Otterburn tweeds in this beautiful region, which is ideal for exploring the Border country and the Cheviots.

R RUSHYFORD, DURHAM - Small village on the old Great North Road.

S SEDGEFIELD, DURHAM - Ancient market town, a centre for hunting and steeplechasing, with a racecourse nearby. Handsome 18th C buildings include the town council's former Georgian mansion and the rectory. The church with its magnificent spire has 17th C wood-carvings by a local craftsman.

T TYNEMOUTH, TYNE AND WEAR - At the mouth of the Tyne, old Tyneside resort adjoining North Shields with its fish quay and market. The pier is overlooked by the gaunt ruins of a Benedictine priory and a castle. Splendid sands, amusement centre and park.

W WARKWORTH, NORTHUMBERLAND - A pretty village overlooked by its medieval castle. A 14th C fortified bridge across the wooded Coquet gives a superb view of 18th C terraces climbing to the castle. Upstream is a curious 14th C Hermitage and in the market square is the Norman church of St Lawrence.

WHITLEY BAY, TYNE AND WEAR - Traditional seaside resort with long beaches of sand and rock and many pools to explore. St Mary's lighthouse is open to the public.

NORTH WEST

Home of pop stars, world famous football teams, Blackpool Tower and Coronation Street, the great North West has vibrant cities, idyllic countryside and world class art collections too.

classic sights

Blackpool Tower & Pleasure Beach – unashamed razzamatazz
Football – museums and tours at Manchester United and Liverpool football clubs
The Beatles – The Beatles Story, Magical Mystery Tour Bus and Macca's former home

coast & country

The Ribble Valley – unchanged rolling landscapes
Formby – a glorious beach of sand dunes and pine woods
Wildfowl & Wetlands Trust, near Ormskirk – 120 types of birds including flamingoes

arts for all

The Tate Liverpool – modern art
The Lowry – the world's largest collection of LS Lowry paintings

distinctively different

Granada Studios – tour the home of many TV classics

The counties of Cheshire, Greater Manchester, Lancashire, Merseyside and the High Peak District of Derbyshire

FOR MORE INFORMATION CONTACT:

**North West Tourist Board
Swan House, Swan Meadow Road,
Wigan Pier, Wigan WN3 5BB
Tel: (01942) 821222 Fax: (01942) 820002
Internet: www.visitnorthwest.com**

The Pictures:
1 Manchester United
   Football Club
2 Healey Dell, Rochdale
3 Blackpool Beach

Places to Visit - see pages 78-81
Where to Stay - see pages 82-93

77

PLACES to visit

You will find hundreds of interesting places to visit during your stay, just some of which are listed in these pages. Contact any Tourist Information Centre in the region for more ideas on days out.

The Albert Dock Company Limited

Suite 22, Edward Pavilion, Albert Dock, Liverpool, Merseyside L3 4AF
Tel: (0151) 708 7334 www.albertdock.com
Britain's largest Grade I Listed historic building. Restored four-sided dock including shops, bars, restaurants, entertainment, marina and the Maritime Museum.

The Beatles Story

Britannia Vaults, Albert Dock, Liverpool, Merseyside L3 4AA
Tel: (0151) 709 1963
Liverpool's award-winning visitor attraction with a replica of the original Cavern Club. Available for private parties.

Beeston Castle

Beeston, Tarporley, Cheshire CW6 9TX
Tel: (01829) 260464
A ruined 13thC castle situated on top of the Peckforton Hills, with views of the surrounding countryside. Exhibitions are also held featuring the castle's history.

Blackpool Pleasure Beach

525 Ocean Boulevard, South Shore, Blackpool, Lancashire FY4 1EZ
(0870) 444 5577
www.blackpoolpleasurebeach.co.uk
Europe's greatest show and amusement park. Blackpool Pleasure Beach offers over 145 rides and attractions, plus spectacular shows.

Blackpool Sea Life Centre

The Promenade, Blackpool, Lancashire FY1 5AA
Tel: (01253) 622445
Tropical sharks up to 8 ft (2.5 m) housed in a 100,000-gallon (454,609-litre) water display with an underwater walkway. The new 'Lost City of Atlantis' is back with the feature exhibition.

Blackpool Tower

The Promenade, Blackpool, Lancashire FY1 4BJ
Tel: (01253) 622242 www.blackpoollive.com
Inside Blackpool Tower you will find the Tower Ballroom, a circus, entertainment for the children, the Tower Top Ride and Undersea World.

Boat Museum

South Pier Road, Ellesmere Port, Cheshire CH5 4FW
Tel: (0151) 355 5017
Over 50 historic crafts, largest floating collection in the world with restored buildings, traditional cottages, workshops, steam engines, boat trips, shop and cafe.

Bridgemere Garden World

Bridgemere, Nantwich, Cheshire CW5 7QB
Tel: (01270) 520381
Bridgemere Garden World, 25 fascinating acres (10 ha) of plants, gardens, greenhouses and shop. Coffee shop, restaurant and over 20 different display gardens in the Garden Kingdom.

Camelot Theme Park

Park Hall Road, Charnock Richard, Chorley, Lancashire PR7 5LP
Tel: (01257) 453044 www.camelotthemepark.co.uk
The magical kingdom of Camelot is a world of thrilling rides, fantastic entertainment and family fun, with over 100 rides and attractions to enjoy.

CATALYST: The Museum of Chemical Industry

Gossage Building, Mersey Road, Widnes, Cheshire WA8 0DF
Tel: (0151) 420 1121
Catalyst is the award-winning family day out where science and technology come alive.

Chester Zoo

Upton-by-Chester, Chester, Cheshire CH2 1LH
Tel: (01244) 380280 www.demon.co.uk/chesterzoo
Chester Zoo is one of Europe's leading conservation zoos, with over 5,000 animals in spacious and natural enclosures. Now featuring the new 'Twilight Zone'.

Dunham Massey Hall Park and Garden

Altrincham, Cheshire WA14 4SJ
Tel: (0161) 941 1025 www.thenationaltrust.org.uk
An 18thC mansion in a 250-acre (100ha) wooded deer park with furniture, paintings and silver. A 25-acre (10ha) informal garden with mature trees and waterside plantings.

East Lancashire Railway

Bolton Street Station, Bury, Greater Manchester BL9 0EY
Tel: (0161) 764 7790 www.east-lancs-rly.co.uk
Eight miles of preserved railway, operated principally by steam. Traction Transport Museum close by.

Gawsworth Hall

Gawsworth, Macclesfield, Cheshire SK11 9RN
Tel: (01260) 223456 www.gawsworthhall.com
Gawsworth Hall is a Tudor half-timbered manor-house with tilting ground. Featuring pictures, sculpture and furniture and an open-air theatre.

Jodrell Bank Science Centre, Planetarium and Arboretum

Lower Withington, Macclesfield, Cheshire SK11 9DL
Tel: (01477) 571339 www.jb.man.ac.uk/scicen
Exhibition and interactive exhibits on astronomy, space, energy and the environment. Planetarium and the world-famous Lovell telescope, plus a 35-acre (14-ha) arboretum.

Knowsley Safari Park

Prescot, Merseyside L34 4AN
Tel: (0151) 430 9009 www.knowsley.com
A 5-mile safari through 500 acres (202 ha) of rolling countryside, and the world's wildest animals roaming free – that's the wonderful world of freedom you'll find at the park.

Lady Lever Art Gallery

Port Sunlight Village, Higher Bebington, Wirral, Merseyside CH62 5EQ
Tel: (0151) 478 4136 www.nmgm.org.uk
The 1st Lord Leverhulme's magnificent collection of British paintings dated 1750-1900, British furniture, Wedgwood pottery and oriental porcelain.

The Pictures:
1 The River Ribble and Pendle Hill, Lancashire
2 Japanese Garden, Tatton Park
3 Lytham, Lancashire
4 Pavilion Gardens, Buxton
5 Blackpool Pleasure Beach

Lancaster Castle

Shire Hall, Castle Parade, Lancaster, Lancashire LA1 1YJ
Tel: (01524) 64998
www.lancashire.gov.uk/resources/ps/castle/index.htm
Shire Hall has a collection of coats of arms, a crown
court, a grand jury room, a 'drop room' and dungeons.
Also external tour of castle.

Lyme Park

Disley, Stockport, Greater Manchester SK12 2NX
Tel: (01663) 762023 www.nationaltrust.org.uk
Lyme Park is a National Trust country estate set in 1,377
acres (541 ha) of moorland, woodland and park. This
magnificent house has 17 acres (7 ha) of historic gardens.

The Museum of Science & Industry, in Manchester

Liverpool Road, Castlefield, Manchester M3 4FP
Tel: (0161) 832 1830 www.msim.org.uk
The Museum of Science and Industry in Manchester is
based in the world's oldest passenger railway station
with galleries that amaze, amuse and entertain.

National Football Museum

Deepdale Stadium, Preston, Lancashire PR1 6RU
Tel: (01772) 908442
www.nationalfootballmuseum.com
The Football Museum exists to explain how and why
football has become the people's game.

Norton Priory Museum and Gardens

Tudor Road, Runcorn, Cheshire WA7 1SX
Tel: (01928) 569895 www.nortonpriory.org
Medieval priory remains, purpose-built museum,
St Christopher's statue, sculpture trail and award-winning
walled garden, all set in 39 acres (16 ha) of beautiful
gardens.

Quarry Bank Mill

Styal, Wilmslow, Cheshire SK9 4LA
Tel: (01625) 527468
www.rmplc.co.uk/orgs/quarrybankmill
A Georgian water-powered cotton-spinning mill, with
four floors of displays and demonstrations and 300 acres
(121 ha) of parkland surroundings.

Rufford Old Hall

Rufford, Ormskirk, Lancashire L40 1SG
Tel: (01704) 821254 www.nationaltrust.org.uk
One of the finest 16thC buildings in Lancashire with a
magnificent hall, particularly noted for its immense
moveable screen.

Sandcastle

South Promenade, Blackpool, Merseyside FY4 1BB
Tel: (01253) 343602
Wave pool, leisure pools, giant water flumes, white-
knuckle water slides, kiddies' safe harbour, play area,
catering, bar, shops and amusements.

Smithills Hall & Park Trust

Smithills Hall, Smithills Dean Road, Bolton,
Greater Manchester BL1 7NP
Tel: (01204) 332377
Smithills Hall is a fascinating example of the growth of a
great house which mirrors the changes in fashion and
living conditions from the late 14thC.

Southport Zoo and Conservation Trust

Princes Park, Southport, Merseyside PR8 1RX
Tel: (01704) 538102
Zoological gardens and conservation trust. Southport Zoo
has been run by the Petrie family since 1964. Talks on
natural history are held in the schoolroom.

Stapley Water Gardens & Palms Tropical Oasis

London Road, Stapeley, Nantwich, Cheshire CW5 7LH
Tel: (01270) 623868
www.stapeleywatergardens.com
Large water garden centre filled with display lakes, pools
and fountains. Trees and shrubs, pot plants, gifts, garden
sundries and pets. Thousand of items on display.

Tate Liverpool

Albert Dock, Liverpool, Merseyside L3 4BB
Tel: (0151) 702 7445 www.tate.org.uk
The Tate at Liverpool exhibits the National Collection of
Modern Art.

Tatton Park

Knutsford, Cheshire WA16 6QN
Tel: (01625) 534400 www.tattonpark.org.uk
Historic mansion with a 50-acre (20-ha) garden,
traditional working farm, Tudor manor-house, 2,000-acre
(809-ha) deer park and children's adventure playground.

Wigan Pier

Trencherfield Mill, Wigan, Lancashire WN3 4EF
Tel: (01942) 323666 www.wiganmbc.gov.uk
Wigan Pier combines interaction with displays and
reconstructions and the Wigan Pier Theatre Company.
Facilities include shops and a cafe.

Find out more about the
North West

Further information about holidays and attractions in the North West is available from:

NORTH WEST TOURIST BOARD
Swan House, Swan Meadow Road, Wigan Pier, Wigan WN3 5BB.
Tel: (01942) 821222 Fax: (01942) 820002
Internet: www.visitnorthwest.com

The following publications are available from North West Tourist Board:

Best of the North West
a guide to information on the region including hotels, self-catering establishments, caravan and camping parks. Also includes attractions, major events, shops and restaurants

Discovery Map
a non-accommodation guide, A1 folded to A4 map including list of visitor attractions, what to see and where to go

Bed and Breakfast Map
forming part of a family of maps for England, this guide provides information on bed and breakfast establishments in the North West region

Freedom
forming part of a family of publications about caravan and camping parks in the north of England

Stay on a Farm
a guide to farm accommodation in the north of England

Group Travel Planner
a guide to choosing the right accommodation, attraction or venue for group organisers

Venues
a 6-monthly newsletter about conference venues in the North West region

Schools Out
a 6-monthly newsletter aimed at schools providing information about where to go and what to see

Getting to the
North West

BY ROAD:
Motorways intersect within the region which has the best road network in the country. Travelling north or south use the M6 and east or west the M62.

BY RAIL:
Most North West coastal resorts are connected to InterCity routes with trains from many parts of the country and there are through trains to major cities and towns.

he Pictures:
Derbyshire
Barca Cafe Bar, Manchester

Where to stay in the North West

Accommodation entries in this region are listed in alphabetical order of place name, and then in alphabetical order of establishment.

Map references refer to the colour location maps at front of this guide. The first number indicates the map to use; the letter and number which follow refer to the grid reference on the map.

At-a-glance symbols at the end of each accommodation entry give useful information about services and facilities. A key to symbols can be found inside the back cover flap. Keep this open for easy reference.

A brief description of the towns and villages offering accommodation in the entries which follow, can be found at the end of this section.

A complete listing of all the English Tourism Council assessed accommodation covered by this guide appears at the back of the guide.

ALSAGER, Cheshire Map ref 4B2

★★★ **THE MANOR HOUSE HOTEL**

Audley Road, Alsager, Stoke-on-Trent ST7 2QQ
T: (01270) 884000
F: (01270) 882483
E: mhres@compassmotels.co.uk
I: www.compasshotels.co.uk

Bedrooms: 9 single, 44 double/twin, 4 triple/ multiple
Bathrooms: 57 en suite

Lunch available
Evening meal available
CC: Amex, Delta, Diners, Mastercard, Switch, Visa

B&B per night:
S £68.00–£99.00
D £68.00–£109.00

HB per person:
DY £64.00–£120.00

OPEN All year round

Beautifully converted 300-year-old farmhouse and outbuildings. Located minutes from exit 16 of the M6. Swimming pool and games room.

Best Western Hotels

ALTRINCHAM, Greater Manchester Map ref 4A2 *Tourist Information Centre Tel: (0161) 912 5931*

★★ **OASIS HOTEL**

46-48 Barrington Road, Altrincham WA14 1HN
T: (0161) 928 4523
F: (0161) 928 1055
E: enquiries@oasishotel.co.uk
I: www.oasishotel.co.uk

Bedrooms: 14 single, 16 double/twin, 3 triple/ multiple
Bathrooms: 32 en suite, 1 private

Evening meal available
CC: Amex, Delta, Diners, Mastercard, Switch, Visa

B&B per night:
S £30.00–£37.00
D £40.00–£48.00

HB per person:
DY £28.00–£46.00

OPEN All year round

Independent hotel within easy reach of Manchester Airport and city centre. Chinese restaurant providing high quality meals. Lounge bar with Sky TV. Full English breakfast.

MAP REFERENCES The map references refer to the colour maps at the front of this guide. The first figure is the map number; the letter and figure which follow indicate the grid reference on the map.

BIRKENHEAD, Merseyside Map ref 4A2 *Tourist Information Centre Tel: (0151) 647 6780*

★

CENTRAL HOTEL
Clifton Crescent, Birkenhead
CH41 2QH
T: (0151) 647 6347 &
07812 378565
F: (0151) 647 5476

Bedrooms: 15 single,
19 double/twin, 2 triple/
multiple
Bathrooms: 29 en suite

Lunch available
Evening meal available
CC: Amex, Delta,
Mastercard, Switch, Visa

B&B per night:
S £39.90–£42.50
D £49.90–£54.90

HB per person:
DY Min £49.90

Town centre hotel opposite railway station with direct service to Liverpool and Chester. Near Liverpool tunnel entrance. Three bars, restaurant, regular entertainment.

OPEN All year round

℗
The Independents

BLACKBURN, Lancashire Map ref 4A1 *Tourist Information Centre Tel: (01254) 53277*

★★★
Gold
Award

NORTHCOTE MANOR HOTEL
Northcote Road, Old Langho,
Blackburn BB6 8BE
T: (01254) 240555
F: (01254) 246568
E: admin@northcotemanor.com
I: www.northcotemanor.com

Bedrooms: 14 double/
twin
Bathrooms: 14 en suite

Lunch available
Evening meal available
CC: Amex, Delta,
Mastercard, Switch, Visa

B&B per night:
S £100.00–£120.00
D £130.00–£150.00

HB per person:
DY £160.00–£190.00

Privately-owned refurbished manor house with outstanding restaurant, offering the best in hospitality. 9 miles from M6 junction 31, off A59. Special gourmet breaks.

OPEN All year round

CHESTER, Cheshire Map ref 4A2 *Tourist Information Centre Tel: (01244) 402111*

Rating
Applied For

THE CHESTER CRABWALL MANOR
Parkgate Road, Mollington, Chester
CH1 6NE
T: (01244) 851666
F: (01244) 851400
E: crabwallmanor@marstonhotels.
com
I: www.marstonhotels.com

Bedrooms: 47 double/
twin, 1 triple/multiple;
suites available
Bathrooms: 48 en suite

Lunch available
Evening meal available
CC: Amex, Delta, Diners,
Mastercard, Switch, Visa

B&B per night:
S £120.00–£135.00
D £135.00–£165.00

HB per person:
DY £89.50–£95.00

Country-house hotel with individually designed bedrooms, award-winning restaurant. Leisure spa and beauty retreat. Golf club, only 100 yards from the hotel. Half-board rate based on minimum 2 nights.

OPEN All year round

℗
Marston Hotels

★★★★★
Gold
Award

THE CHESTER GROSVENOR
Eastgate, Chester CH1 1LT
T: (01244) 324024 & 895614
F: (01244) 313246
E: chesgrov@chestergrosvenor.co.
uk
I: www.chestergrosvenor.co.uk

Bedrooms: 85 double/
twin; suites available
Bathrooms: 85 en suite

Lunch available
Evening meal available
CC: Amex, Delta, Diners,
Mastercard, Switch, Visa

B&B per night:
S £185.00–£205.00
D £265.00–£320.00

OPEN All year round

℗
Small Luxury Hotels/
Pride of Britain

De luxe city-centre hotel, owned by the Duke of Westminster. Two highly-acclaimed restaurants, leisure facilities and outstanding service. Ideal for touring North Wales.

★★

CURZON HOTEL
52-54 Hough Green, Chester CH4 8JQ
T: (01244) 678581
F: (01244) 680866
E: curzon.chester@virgin.net
I: www.chestercurzonhotel.co.uk

B&B per night:
S £45.00–£50.00
D £65.00–£75.00

HB per person:
DY £47.50–£52.50

OPEN All year round

The Curzon is a family-run Victorian townhouse hotel. Unwind in the lounge bar and sample our excellent cuisine in the splendid restaurant. Sleep peacefully in one of the 16 individually designed guest rooms. There is ample private parking and we are within easy reach of the city centre.

Bedrooms: 9 double/
twin, 7 triple/multiple
Bathrooms: 16 en suite

Evening meal available
CC: Amex, Delta,
Mastercard, Switch, Visa

'Deva Break'-any 2 nights DB&B £45pppn; 3 nights or more £42.50pppn. 'Winter Warmers' from Oct.

CHESTER continued

DENE HOTEL
★★

Hoole Road, Chester CH2 3ND
T: (01244) 321165
F: (01244) 350277
E: denehotel@btconnect.com
I: www.denehotel.com

Bedrooms: 7 single,
37 double/twin, 5 triple/
multiple
Bathrooms: 49 en suite

Lunch available
Evening meal available
CC: Amex, Delta,
Mastercard, Switch, Visa

B&B per night:
S £40.00–£46.00
D £50.00–£59.00

HB per person:
DY £36.50–£53.00

OPEN All year round

Ideally located to explore Chester and the picturesque Welsh countryside. Recently refurbished rooms with welcome tray and Sky TV. Francs brasserie recommended by 'Les Routier' – fresh food at affordable prices. Ample parking.

★★★
Silver
Award

GREEN BOUGH HOTEL AND RESTAURANT

60 Hoole Road, Chester CH2 3NL
T: (01244) 326241
F: (01244) 326265
E: greenboughhotel@cwcom.net
I: www.smoothhound.co.uk/hotels/greenbo.html

B&B per night:
S £64.50–£94.50
D £85.00–£135.00

HB per person:
DY £62.50–£87.50

OPEN All year round

A de luxe, family-run, fully refurbished Victorian hotel with friendly, relaxed atmosphere. The owners and their staff are dedicated to giving quality service to guests. The hotel and lodge are tastefully decorated with many antique furnishings. The award-winning Olive Tree Restaurant is a must. No smoking venue.

Bedrooms: 16 double/
twin; suites available
Bathrooms: 16 en suite

Lunch available
Evening meal available
CC: Amex, Delta, Diners,
Mastercard, Switch, Visa

2 nights with 3-course dinner free of charge at various times of year.

★★★

GROSVENOR–PULFORD HOTEL

Wrexham Road, Pulford, Chester CH4 9DG
T: (01244) 570560
F: (01244) 570809
E: enquiries@grosvenorpulfordhotel.co.uk
I: www.grosvenorpulfordhotel.co.uk

B&B per night:
S £70.00–£90.00
D £95.00–£120.00

HB per person:
DY £60.00–£80.00

OPEN All year round

Ideally located only minutes from Chester but within easy access to Wales and Snowdonia. Magnificent leisure club includes 18m pool, whirlpool, steam and sauna rooms, gymnasium, solarium and snooker room. First-class function suite. Bar and restaurant serving a wide range of food from bar snacks to a la carte.

Bedrooms: 4 single,
61 double/twin, 7 triple/
multiple; suites available
Bathrooms: 72 en suite

Lunch available
Evening meal available
CC: Amex, Delta, Diners,
Mastercard, Switch, Visa

★★★★

MOLLINGTON BANASTRE HOTEL

Parkgate Road, Mollington, Chester
CH1 6NN
T: (01244) 851471
F: (01244) 851165
E: mollington@arcadianhotels.co.uk
I: www.mollingtonbanastre.co.uk

Bedrooms: 3 single,
54 double/twin, 6 triple/
multiple
Bathrooms: 63 en suite

Lunch available
Evening meal available
CC: Amex, Delta, Diners,
Mastercard, Switch, Visa

B&B per night:
S £65.00–£85.00
D £90.00–£120.00

HB per person:
DY £90.00–£111.00

OPEN All year round

Best Western Hotels

Country house hotel in its own grounds, only 1.5 miles from historic Chester. Leisure complex.

IMPORTANT NOTE Information on accommodation listed in this guide has been supplied by the proprietors. As changes may occur you are advised to check details at the time of booking.

CHESTER continued

★★★ **HOTEL ROMANO**

51 Lower Bridge Street, Chester
CH1 1RS
T: (01244) 325091 & 320841
F: (01244) 315628
E: hotelromano@aol.com
I: www.hotel-romano.co.uk

Bedrooms: 22 double/
twin, 6 triple/multiple
Bathrooms: 28 en suite

Lunch available
Evening meal available
CC: Amex, Delta, Diners,
Mastercard, Switch, Visa

B&B per night:
S £45.00–£55.00
D £65.00–£75.00

HB per person:
DY £52.00–£65.00

OPEN All year round

17thC listed building decorated in Romano/Italian style. Languages spoken: English, Italian, Spanish and French. Children and group bookings welcome.

CHIPPING, Lancashire Map ref 4A1

★★★★
Silver
Award

GIBBON BRIDGE HOTEL

Chipping, Preston PR3 2TQ
T: (01995) 61456
F: (01995) 61277
E: reception@gibbon-bridge.co.uk
I: www.gibbon-bridge.co.uk

B&B per night:
S £70.00–£100.00
D £100.00–£230.00

HB per person:
DY £60.00–£90.00

OPEN All year round

This award-winning privately owned hotel and restaurant is in the heart of some of Lancashire's finest countryside – The Forest of Bowland, AONB. Elegant restaurant, private dining, stylish meeting rooms, magnificent gardens. Leisure facilities, beauty salon. A genuine warm welcome, personal service, and value for money. Perfect for a tranquil break.

Bedrooms: 2 single,
23 double/twin, 4 triple/
multiple; suites available
Bathrooms: 29 en suite

Lunch available
Evening meal available
CC: Amex, Delta, Diners,
Mastercard, Switch, Visa

CLAYTON-LE-MOORS, Lancashire Map ref 4A1

★★★ **SPARTH HOUSE HOTEL**

Whalley Road, Clayton-le-Moors,
Accrington BB5 5RP
T: (01254) 872263
F: (01254) 872263

Bedrooms: 15 double/
twin, 1 triple/multiple;
suites available
Bathrooms: 16 en suite

Lunch available
Evening meal available
CC: Amex, Delta, Diners,
Mastercard, Switch, Visa

B&B per night:
S £55.00–£85.00
D £65.00–£99.00

HB per person:
DY £69.00–£115.00

OPEN All year round

Built in 1740 and set in its own peaceful grounds, the hotel offers the perfect location for short stays, conferences and functions alike.

CLITHEROE, Lancashire Map ref 4A1 *Tourist Information Centre Tel: (01200) 425566*

★★ **SHIREBURN ARMS HOTEL**

Whalley Road, Hurst Green,
Clitheroe BB7 9QJ
T: (01254) 826518
F: (01254) 826208
E: sales@shireburn-hotel.co.uk
I: www.shireburn-hotel.co.uk

Bedrooms: 1 single,
14 double/twin, 3 triple/
multiple
Bathrooms: 18 en suite

Lunch available
Evening meal available
CC: Amex, Delta,
Mastercard, Switch, Visa

B&B per night:
S £45.00–£65.00
D £65.00–£85.00

HB per person:
DY £58.95–£78.95

OPEN All year round

Ⓒ
Minotel

16thC family-run hotel, with unrivalled views, renowned for food and comfort, log fires, real ale, bar food. Within easy reach of the motorway network.

FLEETWOOD, Lancashire Map ref 4A1 *Tourist Information Centre Tel: (01253) 773953*

★★★
Silver
Award

NORTH EUSTON HOTEL

Esplanade, Fleetwood FY7 6BN
T: (01253) 876525
F: (01253) 777842
E: admin@northeustonhotel.co.uk
I: www.northeustonhotel.co.uk

Bedrooms: 6 single,
44 double/twin, 3 triple/
multiple
Bathrooms: 53 en suite

Lunch available
Evening meal available
CC: Amex, Delta, Diners,
Mastercard, Switch, Visa

B&B per night:
S £57.50–£67.50
D £87.00–£107.00

HB per person:
DY £71.00–£81.00

OPEN All year round

Elegant Victorian hotel with panoramic views of Morecambe Bay and the Lakeland hills. Family owned for 21 years.

FRODSHAM, Cheshire Map ref 4A2

★★★

FOREST HILLS HOTEL

Overton Hill, Frodsham WA6 6HH
T: (01928) 735255
F: (01928) 735517
E: info@foresthillshotel.com
I: www.foresthillshotel.com

B&B per night:
S Min £55.00
D Min £45.00

HB per person:
DY Min £55.00

OPEN All year round

Situated just off the M56 amidst beautiful Cheshire countryside, superb leisure facilities include a luxurious pool and spa, sauna, steam room, solarium, gymasium and snooker room. The perfect location for conferences, civil weddings and leisure breaks.

Bedrooms: 50 double/
twin, 8 triple/multiple
Bathrooms: 58 en suite

The hotel has an ongoing programme of events incl live entertainment, Murder Mystery Dinners, gourmet evenings and quiz nights.

Lunch available
Evening meal available
CC: Amex, Delta, Diners,
Mastercard, Switch, Visa

KNUTSFORD, Cheshire Map ref 4A2 *Tourist Information Centre Tel: (01565) 632611*

★★

LONGVIEW HOTEL AND RESTAURANT

Manchester Road, Knutsford WA16 0LX
T: (01565) 632119
F: (01565) 652402
E: enquiries@longviewhotel.com
I: www.longviewhotel.com

B&B per night:
S £50.00–£82.00
D £69.50–£135.00

OPEN All year round

Friendly hotel of character, with cosy cellar bar, open log fires and high quality en suite bedrooms. Comfortable, relaxed dining room offers a value for money menu. Ideally situated overlooking heath, only a short stroll from Knutsford's many good restaurants and pubs. Close to Manchester, its airport and M6 motorway.

Bedrooms: 5 single,
21 double/twin; suites
available
Bathrooms: 26 en suite

Evening meal available
CC: Amex, Diners,
Mastercard, Visa

★★★★

MERE COURT HOTEL

Mere, Knutsford WA16 0RW
T: (01565) 831000
F: (01565) 831001
E: sales@merecourt.co.uk
I: www.merecourt.co.uk

B&B per night:
S £75.00–£135.00
D £85.00–£155.00

OPEN All year round

Built as a private residence in 1903 but now lovingly and skilfully restored to a fine country house hotel standing in 7 acres with a private lake. The main house offers 4-poster room and suites, some with double jacuzzi spa baths and Victorian claw baths. Rooms all individually designed and furnished.

Bedrooms: 34 double/
twin; suites available
Bathrooms: 34 en suite

Weekend breaks available Fri/Sat/Sun.

Lunch available
Evening meal available
CC: Amex, Delta, Diners,
Mastercard, Switch, Visa

LANCASTER, Lancashire Map ref 5A3 *Tourist Information Centre Tel: (01524) 32878*

★

SCARTHWAITE COUNTRY HOUSE HOTEL

Crook O'Lune, Caton, Lancaster
LA2 9HR
T: (01524) 770267
F: (01524) 770711

Bedrooms: 6 double/
twin, 1 triple/multiple
Bathrooms: 7 en suite

Lunch available
Evening meal available
CC: Delta, Mastercard,
Switch, Visa

B&B per night:
S Max £39.50
D Max £58.00

OPEN All year round

Large Victorian house on an extensive wooded estate facing the River Lune. All bedrooms en suite. Fully licensed. New conservatory restaurant open to non residents.

LANGHO, Lancashire Map ref 4A1

★★★

MYTTON FOLD HOTEL AND GOLF COMPLEX

Whalley Road, Langho, Blackburn
BB6 8AB
T: (01254) 240662
F: (01254) 248119
E: enquiries@myttonfold.co.uk
I: www.myttonfold.co.uk

Bedrooms: 27 double/
twin, 1 triple/multiple
Bathrooms: 28 en suite

Lunch available
Evening meal available
CC: Amex, Delta,
Mastercard, Switch, Visa

B&B per night:
S £45.00–£52.00
D £74.00–£82.00

OPEN All year round

Mytton Fold, a tranquil, friendly oasis. Lovingly created colourful gardens. Private 18-hole golf course. 15 minutes M6, M65. 28 en suite rooms. Free golf for residents after 4.00pm.

LYTHAM ST ANNES, Lancashire Map ref 4A1 *Tourist Information Centre Tel: (01253) 725610*

★★★

CHADWICK HOTEL

South Promenade, Lytham St Annes
FY8 1NP

T: (01253) 720061
F: (01253) 714455
E: sales@thechadwickhotel.com
I: www.thechadwickhotel.com

B&B per night:
S £40.00–£47.00
D £60.00–£68.00

HB per person:
DY £39.50–£46.50

OPEN All year round

Panoramic views across the Ribble estuary and Irish Sea. Award-winning family hotel provides excellent cuisine, comforts and facilities unsurpassed for value. Exclusive health and leisure suite. Children's soft play amenities. Great for relaxing short breaks or longer. Dinner dances and theme weekend parties. Truly a hotel for all seasons.

Bedrooms: 10 single,
40 double/twin,
25 triple/multiple
Bathrooms: 75 en suite

Lunch available
Evening meal available
CC: Amex, Delta, Diners,
Mastercard, Switch, Visa

★★★

DALMENY HOTEL

19-33 South Promenade,
Lytham St Annes FY8 1LX
T: (01253) 712236
F: (01253) 724447
E: info@dalmenyhotel.com
I: www.dalmenyhotel.com

Bedrooms: 1 single,
50 double/twin,
79 triple/multiple
Bathrooms: 120 en suite

Lunch available
Evening meal available
CC: Amex, Delta, Diners,
Mastercard, Switch, Visa

B&B per night:
S £80.00–£95.00
D £96.00–£136.00

HB per person:
DY £61.00–£81.00

OPEN All year round

The Dalmeny is ideally situated on the seafront in St Annes, overlooking the promenade and gardens and within walking distance of the town centre.

★★

LINDUM HOTEL

63-67 South Promenade, Lytham St Annes
FY8 1LZ

T: (01253) 721534 & 722516
F: (01253) 721364
E: info@lindumhotel.co.uk
I: www.lindumhotel.co.uk

B&B per night:
S £30.00–£55.00
D £50.00–£75.00

HB per person:
DY £40.00–£55.00

OPEN All year round

A warm welcome awaits at this family-run seafront hotel, opposite all promenade amenities including cinemas, casino, swimming pools and mini golf. The hotel is renowned for its excellent food and comfortable accommodation. Close to fine shops and championship golf courses. Five miles from Blackpool centre.

Bedrooms: 10 single,
46 double/twin,
22 triple/multiple
Bathrooms: 78 en suite

Lunch available
Evening meal available
CC: Amex, Delta,
Mastercard, Switch, Visa

Theatre trips, racing weekends, bridge holidays,
Christmas/New Year breaks, weekend and mid-week
offers throughout the year.

COLOUR MAPS Colour maps at the front of this guide pinpoint all places under which you will find accommodation listed.

LYTHAM ST ANNES continued

★★ **ST IVES HOTEL**
7 South Promenade,
Lytham St Annes FY8 1LS
T: (01253) 720011
F: (01253) 722873
E: book@st-ives-hotel.co.uk
I: www.st-ives-hotel.co.uk

Bedrooms: 1 single,
21 double/twin,
43 triple/multiple; suites
available
Bathrooms: 65 en suite

Lunch available
Evening meal available
CC: Amex, Delta, Diners,
Mastercard, Switch, Visa

B&B per night:
S £30.00–£40.00
D £60.00–£80.00

HB per person:
DY £40.00–£50.00

OPEN All year round

Clean and child-friendly seafront hotel with a reputation for excellent food and entertainment facilities. Open all year and offering many special break packages for families and group bookings.

MANCHESTER, Greater Manchester Map ref 4B1 *Tourist Information Centre Tel: (0161) 234 3157*

★★★ **CASTLEFIELD HOTEL**
Liverpool Road, Castlefield,
Manchester M3 4JR
T: (0161) 832 7073
F: (0161) 837 3534
E: info@castlefield-hotel.co.uk
I: www.castlefield-hotel.co.uk

Bedrooms: 3 single,
45 double/twin
Bathrooms: 48 en suite

Lunch available
Evening meal available
CC: Amex, Delta, Diners,
Mastercard, Switch, Visa

B&B per night:
S £49.00–£78.00
D £59.00–£84.00

HB per person:
DY £59.00–£88.00

OPEN All year round

City-centre hotel situated by the water's edge in the Castlefield basin. Offers excellent restaurant, bar, conference and leisure facilities.

★★★

GARDENS HOTEL
55 Piccadilly, Manchester M1 2AP
T: (0161) 236 5155
F: (0161) 228 7287
E: gardensman@hotmail.com
I: www.cairn-hotels.co.uk

B&B per night:
S £60.00–£89.00
D £70.00–£100.00

OPEN All year round

This modern hotel, only 9 years old, is situated in the heart of the city, overlooking Piccadilly Gardens and a few minutes from Piccadilly railway station which has direct trains to the airport. All parts of the country can be easily accessed.

Bedrooms: 12 single,
87 double/twin
Bathrooms: 99 en suite

Lunch available
Evening meal available
CC: Amex, Delta, Diners,
Mastercard, Switch, Visa

★★★

JURYS INN MANCHESTER
56 Great Bridgewater Street, Manchester
M1 5LE
T: (0161) 953 8888
F: (0161) 953 9090
I: www.jurysdoyle.com

B&B per night:
S £73.00–£75.00
D £81.00–£83.00

HB per person:
DY £89.25–£91.25

OPEN All year round

Utell International

A modern hotel located in the city centre, beside the Bridgewater Hall, the G-Mex and Manchester International Convention Centre. Each room can accommodate up to 3 adults or 2 adults and 2 children. All rooms have air conditioning, modem points, en suite bathrooms, satellite TV and tea/coffee-making facilities.

Bedrooms: 97 single,
101 double/twin,
167 triple/multiple
Bathrooms: 365 en suite

Lunch available
Evening meal available
CC: Amex, Delta, Diners,
Mastercard, Switch, Visa

Special weekend rates (Fri/Sat/Sun) £39 room only, strictly subject to availability.

CENTRAL RESERVATIONS OFFICES
The symbol ⓒⓡ and a group name in an entry indicate that bookings can be made through a central reservations office. These are listed in a separate section towards the back of this guide.

MANCHESTER continued

★★★ **NOVOTEL MANCHESTER WEST**

Worsley Brow, Worsley, Manchester
M28 2YA
T: (0161) 799 3535
F: (0161) 703 8207
E: h0907@accor-hotels.com
I: www.novotel.com

Bedrooms: 38 single,
76 double/twin, 5 triple/
multiple
Bathrooms: 119 en suite

Lunch available
Evening meal available
CC: Amex, Diners,
Mastercard, Switch, Visa

B&B per night:
S £65.00–£85.00

OPEN All year round

Modern hotel, restaurant, banqueting and conference centre. Ideal for business or pleasure. Junction 13 on M60. Restaurant open 0600-midnight. For early risers, breakfast available from 0430.

★★★ **PRINCESS HOTEL**

101 Portland Street, Manchester
M1 6DF
T: (0161) 236 5122
F: (0161) 236 4468
E: admin@princesshotels.co.uk
I: www.princesshotels.co.uk

Bedrooms: 5 single,
80 double/twin
Bathrooms: 85 en suite

Lunch available
Evening meal available
CC: Amex, Delta, Diners,
Mastercard, Switch, Visa

B&B per night:
S £69.50–£96.50
D £81.50–£133.00

OPEN All year round

City centre hotel catering for business and holiday clients. Professional service, personal approach. Easily accessed by major motorway, road and rail networks, Manchester Airport and metro link.

★★★★ **RADISSON SAS HOTEL MANCHESTER AIRPORT**

Chicago Avenue,
Manchester Airport, Manchester
M90 3RA
T: (0161) 490 5000
F: (0161) 490 5100
E: sales@manzq.rdsas.com
I: www.radissonsas.com

Bedrooms: 360 double/
twin; suites available
Bathrooms: 360 en suite

Lunch available
Evening meal available
CC: Amex, Delta, Diners,
Mastercard, Switch, Visa

B&B per night:
S £79.00–£165.00
D £89.00–£180.00

OPEN All year round

Located between terminals 1 and 2 and the railway station. 360 air-conditioned bedrooms in 4 different themes. Health club with gym and swimming pool. Limited parking.

MANCHESTER AIRPORT

See under Altrincham, Knutsford, Manchester, Sale, Wilmslow

PARKGATE, Cheshire Map ref 4A2

★★ **SHIP HOTEL**

The Parade, Parkgate, South Wirral
CH64 6SA
T: (0151) 336 3931
F: (0151) 336 3931
I: www.the-shiphotel.co.uk

Bedrooms: 9 single,
13 double/twin, 2 triple/
multiple
Bathrooms: 24 en suite

Lunch available
Evening meal available
CC: Amex, Delta,
Mastercard, Switch, Visa

B&B per night:
S £35.00–£55.00
D £60.00–£70.00

OPEN All year round

A comfortable inn with beautiful views across the marshes of the Dee Estuary and local attractions.

QUALITY ASSURANCE SCHEME

For an explanation of the quality and facilities represented by the Stars please refer to the front of this guide. A more detailed explanation can be found in the information pages at the back.

★★★

SPRINGFIELD HOUSE HOTEL AND RESTAURANT

Wheel Lane, Pilling, Preston PR3 6HL
T: (01253) 790301
F: (01253) 790907

Manor house built in 1840, in its own grounds. Award-winning gardens, full facilities in all rooms. Enjoy the tranquility of surrounding countryside. Well renowned for superb food and value for money. All the food is prepared from local fresh produce grown in the Fylde area.

E: recep@springfieldhouse.uk.com
I: www.springfieldhouse.uk.com

Bedrooms: 4 double/twin, 4 triple/multiple
Bathrooms: 8 en suite

Lunch available
Evening meal available
CC: Amex, Delta, Mastercard, Switch, Visa

2-night break incl DB&B with traditional afternoon tea on arrival.

B&B per night:
S £35.00–£40.00
D £59.50–£65.00

OPEN All year round

★★★

SWALLOW HOTEL

Preston New Road, Samlesbury, Preston PR5 0UL
T: (01772) 877351 & 872703
F: (01772) 877424
E: swallow.preston@whitbread.com
I: www.swallowhotels.com

Modern, comfortable hotel set in countryside, ideal base for North West attractions. Relax in leisure club before enjoying fine cuisine and wines in the restaurant. Rates shown are Breakaway rates, based on a minimum 2-night stay and subject to availability. Call to request a Breakaway brochure full of great deals.

Bedrooms: 6 single, 72 double/twin
Bathrooms: 78 en suite

Lunch available
Evening meal available
CC: Amex, Delta, Diners, Mastercard, Switch, Visa

B&B per night:
S £60.00–£82.00
D £62.00–£105.00

HB per person:
DY £46.00–£68.00

OPEN All year round

See under Chipping, Clitheroe, Langho

★★

RUFFORD ARMS HOTEL

380 Liverpool Road, Rufford L40 1SQ
T: (01704) 822040
F: (01704) 821910
E: ruffordarmshotel@hotmail.com

Family-run hotel offering comfortable value for money accommodation. Restaurant and bar offer a large selection of dishes to meet both taste and budget. Set in the rural background of Rufford but only 10 minutes' from major road network of M6, M61. Close to Southport, Liverpool and Preston.

Bedrooms: 12 double/twin, 2 triple/multiple
Bathrooms: 14 en suite

Lunch available
Evening meal available
CC: Delta, Mastercard, Switch, Visa

Breakaway deals-2 nights DB&B for only £129.95 per couple, Fri-Sat or Sat-Sun (based on 2 people sharing).

B&B per night:
S £34.95–£37.95
D £44.95–£54.95

OPEN All year round

CONFIRM YOUR BOOKING
You are advised to confirm your booking in writing.

SADDLEWORTH, Greater Manchester Map ref 4B1 *Tourist Information Centre Tel: (01457) 870336*

★★★

A family-owned hotel set in one of Saddleworth's villages with picturesque surroundings of the Pennine Hills, yet only 5 minutes from M62 motorway. This ideal location, together with our log fires and friendly atmosphere, is perfect for your stay. Our restaurant offers a la carte, home-made pizzas and bar snacks.

LA PERGOLA HOTEL AND RESTAURANT
Rochdale Road, Denshaw, Oldham OL3 5UE
T: (01457) 871040
F: (01457) 873804
E: reception@lapergola.freeserve.co.uk
I: www.hotel-restaurant.uk.com

B&B per night:
S £38.50–£54.00
D £56.00–£67.00

OPEN All year round

The Independents

Bedrooms: 2 single, 21 double/twin, 4 triple/ multiple; suites available
Bathrooms: 27 en suite

Lunch available
Evening meal available
CC: Amex, Delta, Diners, Mastercard, Switch, Visa

SALE, Greater Manchester Map ref 4A2

★★

LENNOX LEA HOTEL
Irlam Road, Sale M33 2BH
T: (0161) 973 1764
F: (0161) 969 6059
E: info@lennoxlea.co.uk
I: www.lennoxlea.co.uk

Bedrooms: 19 single, 10 double/twin, 2 triple/ multiple
Bathrooms: 31 en suite

Evening meal available
CC: Amex, Diners, Mastercard, Switch, Visa

B&B per night:
S £35.00–£52.95
D £40.00–£72.95

OPEN All year round

A small and friendly family-run hotel featuring the acclaimed Alexander's bistro. Close to M60, Manchester city centre/sports arenas/exhibition centres and Metrolink.

SOUTHPORT, Merseyside Map ref 4A1 *Tourist Information Centre Tel: (01704) 533333*

★★

DUKES FOLLY HOTEL
11 Duke Street, Southport PR8 1LS
T: (01704) 533355
F: (01704) 530065
E: mjatdukesfoll@bluecarrots.co.uk
I: www.dukesfolly.co.uk

Bedrooms: 4 single, 14 double/twin
Bathrooms: 18 en suite

Lunch available
Evening meal available
CC: Amex, Mastercard, Visa

B&B per night:
D £68.00–£78.00

HB per person:
DY £48.50–£65.00

OPEN All year round

Licensed family-run hotel noted for its high standards and friendly atmosphere. On the corner of Duke Street and Lord Street and within easy reach of all local amenities.

★★

METROPOLE HOTEL
3 Portland Street, Southport PR8 1LL
T: (01704) 536836
F: (01704) 549041
E: metropole.southport@ btinternet.com
I: www.btinternet.com/~metropole. southport

Bedrooms: 11 single, 8 double/twin, 4 triple/ multiple
Bathrooms: 23 en suite

Lunch available
Evening meal available
CC: Amex, Delta, Mastercard, Switch, Visa

B&B per night:
D £44.00–£66.00

OPEN All year round

Fully licensed, centrally located, family-owned hotel offering traditional standards of comfort and courtesy. Fifty yards Lord Street shopping boulevard. Golf breaks a speciality.

USE YOUR *i*s

There are more than 550 Tourist Information Centres throughout England offering friendly help with accommodation and holiday ideas as well as suggestions of places to visit and things to do. You'll find TIC addresses in the local Phone Book.

TARPORLEY, Cheshire Map ref 4A2

★★★

WILLINGTON HALL HOTEL

Willington, Tarporley CW6 0NB
T: (01829) 752321
F: (01829) 752596
E: enquiries@willingtonhall.co.uk
I: www.willingtonhall.co.uk

B&B per night:
S £67.50–£70.00
D £100.00–£120.00

HB per person:
DY £80.00–£87.50

OPEN All year round

Country house hotel built in 1829. Set in 17 acres of formal gardens and parkland with good views over surrounding countryside. Renowned for good food in restaurant and bar and warm informal hospitality. An ideal touring base for Chester and North Wales.

Bedrooms: 1 single, 9 double/twin
Bathrooms: 10 en suite

Lunch available
Evening meal available
CC: Amex, Delta, Mastercard, Switch, Visa

2 night breaks for 2 people DB&B £215.

WADDINGTON, Lancashire Map ref 4A1

★★

THE MOORCOCK INN
Slaidburn Road, Waddington, Clitheroe BB7 3AA
T: (01200) 422333
F: (01200) 429184

Bedrooms: 11 double/twin
Bathrooms: 10 en suite, 1 private

Lunch available
Evening meal available
CC: Amex, Delta, Diners, Mastercard, Switch, Visa

B&B per night:
S £38.00–£40.00
D £60.00–£62.00

OPEN All year round

Friendly, family-run inn with panoramic views of Ribble Valley. En suite rooms. Fresh home-cooked food available in bar and restaurant. Banqueting facilities.

WARRINGTON, Cheshire Map ref 4A2

★★★★

HANOVER INTERNATIONAL HOTEL AND CLUB
Stretton Road, Stretton, Warrington WA4 4NS
T: (01925) 730706
F: (01925) 730740
E: hotel@park-royal-int.co.uk
I: www.hanover-international.com

Bedrooms: 2 single, 125 double/twin, 15 triple/multiple; suites available
Bathrooms: 142 en suite

Lunch available
Evening meal available
CC: Amex, Delta, Diners, Mastercard, Switch, Visa

B&B per night:
S £62.50–£111.75
D £72.50–£132.00

HB per person:
DY £59.00–£131.70

OPEN All year round

Best Western Hotels

Set in the heart of Cheshire, minutes from junction 10 M56. Exclusive health and leisure spa. Deluxe bedrooms. Award-winning restaurant. Weekend rates available.

WIGAN, Greater Manchester Map ref 4A1 *Tourist Information Centre Tel: (01942) 825677*

★★★

BURRIDGES HOTEL AND RESTAURANT

Standishgate, Wigan WN1 1XA
T: (01942) 741674
F: (01942) 741683
E: reception@burridges.co.uk
I: www.burridges.co.uk

B&B per night:
D £60.00–£70.00

OPEN All year round

This family-run hotel is located in a beautifully refurbished former church building. 10 luxury en suite bedrooms, together with an award-winning a la carte restaurant and friendly and efficient staff all help towards making your stay with us as pleasurable as possible whilst visiting the many local attractions.

Bedrooms: 9 double/twin, 1 triple/multiple; suites available
Bathrooms: 10 en suite

Lunch available
Evening meal available
CC: Amex, Delta, Diners, Mastercard, Switch, Visa

Special weekend rates and packages available. Please contact us for details.

CREDIT CARD BOOKINGS If you book by telephone and are asked for your credit card number it is advisable to check the proprietor's policy should you cancel your reservation.

★★★
Silver
Award

STANNEYLANDS HOTEL

Stanneylands Road, Wilmslow SK9 4EY
T: (01625) 525225
F: (01625) 537282
E: email@stanneylands.co.uk
I: www.stanneylandshotel.co.uk

B&B per night:
S £69.00–£99.00
D £99.00–£120.00

HB per person:
DY £65.00–£80.00

OPEN All year round

Exclusive country house hotel set in several acres of beautiful gardens. All rooms en suite with satellite TV, radio, trouser press and telephone. Rosettes for fine cuisine, in addition to many awards for excellence. Ideal base for exploring Cheshire and the Peak District. Twenty minutes from Manchester City Centre and 3 miles from airport.

Bedrooms: 1 single, 28 double/twin, 3 triple/ multiple; suites available
Bathrooms: 32 en suite

Lunch available
Evening meal available
CC: Amex, Delta, Diners, Mastercard, Switch, Visa

Park and fly–£53pp sharing (room only). Incl 15 days free car parking, plus courtesy coach to airport between 0800 and 2300.

CR
Utell International

WIRRAL

See under Birkenhead, Parkgate

COUNTRY CODE

Always follow the Country Code ⍟
Enjoy the countryside and respect
its life and work ⍟ Guard against
all risk of fire ⍟ Fasten all gates
⍟ Keep your dogs under close control
⍟ Keep to public paths across
farmland ⍟ Use gates and stiles to
cross fences, hedges and walls ⍟
Leave livestock, crops and machinery
alone ⍟ Take your litter home ⍟
Help to keep all water clean ⍟
Protect wildlife, plants and trees ⍟
Take special care on country roads ⍟
Make no unnecessary noise ⍟

A brief guide to the main Towns and Villages offering accommodation in the North West

A ALSAGER, CHESHIRE - Small suburban town, mostly late Victorian and Edwardian, with pleasant parkland adjoining.

• **ALTRINCHAM, GREATER MANCHESTER** - Historic market town developed as a residential area in the 19th C. Preserves the best of the old at its fascinating Old Market Place, with the best of the new on pedestrianised George Street. International fashion and high style interior design rub shoulders with boutiques and speciality shops.

B BIRKENHEAD, MERSEYSIDE - Founded in the 12th C by monks who operated the first Mersey ferry service, Birkenhead has some fine Victorian architecture and one of the best markets in the north west. Attractions include the famous Mersey Ferry and Birkenhead Park, opened in 1847, the first public park in the country.

• **BLACKBURN, LANCASHIRE** - North East Lancashire town. Architecture reflects Victorian prosperity from the cotton industry. Daniel Thwaites, founder of Thwaites Brewery, is buried in St John's churchyard. Lewis Textile Museum is dedicated to the history of the textile industry.

C CHESTER, CHESHIRE - Roman and medieval walled city rich in treasures. Black and white buildings are a hallmark, including 'The Rows' - two-tier shopping galleries. 900-year-old cathedral and the famous Chester Zoo.

• **CHIPPING, LANCASHIRE** - Charming, well-preserved 17th C village, on the edge of the Forest of Bowland on the Pendle Witches' Trail. Ancient church, pub, craft shops, superb base for walking and touring the area. Best Kept Village award.

• **CLAYTON-LE-MOORS, LANCASHIRE** - Small industrial town, 5 miles north-east of Blackburn.

• **CLITHEROE, LANCASHIRE** - Ancient market town with an 800-year-old castle keep and a wide range of award-winning shops. Good base for touring Ribble Valley, Trough of Bowland and Pennine moorland. Country market on Tuesdays and Saturdays.

F FLEETWOOD, LANCASHIRE - Major fishing port and resort bounded by the sea on 3 sides. Fine sands, bathing and large model-yacht pond. Good views across Morecambe Bay and peaks of Lake District.

• **FRODSHAM, CHESHIRE** - Spacious, tree-lined main street flanked by 17th, 18th and 19th C buildings. Near Delamere Forest and Sandstone Trail, close to Mersey estuary and overlooked by Overton Hill.

K KNUTSFORD, CHESHIRE - Delightful town with many buildings of architectural and historic interest. The setting of Elizabeth Gaskell's 'Cranford'. Annual May Day celebration and decorative 'sanding' of the pavements are unique to the town. Popular Heritage Centre.

L LANCASTER, LANCASHIRE - Interesting old county town on the River Lune with history dating back to Roman times. Norman castle, St Mary's Church, Customs House, City and Maritime Museums, Ashton Memorial and Butterfly House are among places of note. Good centre for touring the Lake District.

• **LANGHO, LANCASHIRE** - This parish can trace its history back to Saxon times when in 798 AD a battle was fought at Billangohoh from which the names of Billington and Langho were derived. A flourishing community of mainly cattle farms, near both the River Ribble and the River Calder.

• **LYTHAM ST ANNES, LANCASHIRE** - Pleasant resort famous for its championship golf-courses, notably the Royal Lytham and St Annes. Fine sands and attractive gardens. Some half-timbered buildings and an old restored windmill.

M MANCHESTER, GREATER MANCHESTER - The Gateway to the North, offering one of Britain's largest selections of arts venues and theatre productions, a wide range of chain stores and specialist shops, a legendary, lively nightlife, spectacular architecture and a plethora of eating and drinking places.

P PARKGATE, CHESHIRE - Once a busy port on the Dee Estuary, Parkgate was the scene of Handel's departure for the great performance of 'Messiah' in Dublin in 1741. The George Inn where he stayed is now Mostyn House School.

• **PRESTON, LANCASHIRE** - Scene of decisive Royalist defeat by Cromwell in the Civil War and later of riots in the Industrial Revolution. Local history exhibited in Harris Museum. Famous for its Guild and the celebration that takes place every 20 years.

S SADDLEWORTH, GREATER MANCHESTER - The stone-built villages of Saddleworth are peppered with old mill buildings and possess a unique Pennine character. The superb scenery of Saddleworth Moor provides an ideal backdrop for canal trips, walking and outdoor pursuits.

• **SALE, GREATER MANCHESTER** - Located between Manchester and Altrincham, Sale owes its name to the 12th C landowner Thomas de Sale. It is now home to Trafford Water Sports Centre and Park which offers the best in aquatic leisure and countryside activities.

• **SOUTHPORT, MERSEYSIDE** - Delightful Victorian resort noted for gardens, sandy beaches and 6 golf-courses, particularly Royal Birkdale. Attractions include the Atkinson Art Gallery, Southport Railway Centre, Pleasureland and the annual Southport Flower Show. Excellent shopping, particularly in Lord Street's elegant boulevard.

T TARPORLEY, CHESHIRE - Old town with gabled houses and medieval church of St Helen containing monuments to the Done family, a historic name in this area. Spectacular ruins of 13th C Beeston Castle nearby.

W WADDINGTON, LANCASHIRE - One of the area's best-known villages, with a stream and public gardens gracing the main street.

• **WARRINGTON, CHESHIRE** - Has prehistoric and Roman origins. Once the 'beer capital of Britain' because so much beer was brewed here. Developed in the 18th and 19th C as a commercial and industrial town. The cast-iron gates in front of the town hall were originally destined for Sandringham.

• **WIGAN, GREATER MANCHESTER** - Although a major industrial town, Wigan is an ancient settlement which received a royal charter in 1246. Famous for its pier distinguished in Orwell's 'Road to Wigan Pier'. The pier has now been developed as a major tourist attraction.

• **WILMSLOW, CHESHIRE** - Nestling in the valleys of the Rivers Bollin and Dane, Wilmslow retains an intimate village atmosphere. Easy to reach attractions include Quarry Bank Mill at Style. Lindow Man was discovered on a nearby common. Romany's caravan sits in a memorial garden.

YORKSHIRE

Yorkshire combines wild and brooding moors with historic cities, elegant spa towns and a varied coastline of traditional resorts and working fishing ports.

classic sights

Fountains Abbey & Studley Royal – 12th century Cistercian abbey and Georgian water garden
Nostell Prior – 18th century house with outstanding art collection
York Minster – largest medieval Gothic cathedral north of the Alps

coast & country

The Pennines – dramatic moors and rocks
Whitby – unspoilt fishing port, famous for jet (black stone)

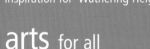

literary links

Brontë parsonage, Haworth – home of the Brontë sisters; inspiration for 'Wuthering Heights' and 'Jane Eyre'

arts for all

National Museum of Photography, Film and Television – hi-tech and hands-on

distinctively different

The Original Ghost Walk of York – spooky tours every night

The counties of North, South, East and West Yorkshire, and Northern Lincolnshire

FOR MORE INFORMATION CONTACT:
Yorkshire Tourist Board
312 Tadcaster Road, York YO24 1GS
Tel: (01904) 707070 (24-hr brochure line) Fax: (01904) 701414
Email: info@ytb.org.uk Internet: www.yorkshirevisitor.com

The Pictures:
1 Roseberry Topping
2 Skidby Windmill
3 The Beach at Bridlington

Places to Visit - see pages 96-99
Where to Stay - see pages 100-122

PLACES to visit

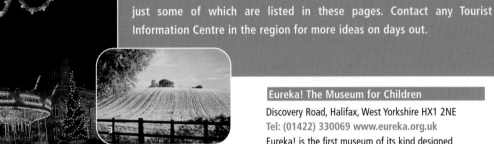

You will find hundreds of interesting places to visit during your stay, just some of which are listed in these pages. Contact any Tourist Information Centre in the region for more ideas on days out.

Eureka! The Museum for Children

Discovery Road, Halifax, West Yorkshire HX1 2NE
Tel: (01422) 330069 www.eureka.org.uk
Eureka! is the first museum of its kind designed especially for children up to the age of 12 with over 400 hands-on exhibits.

Beningbrough Hall & Gardens

Beningbrough, York, North Yorkshire YO30 1DD
Tel: (01904) 470666
Handsome Baroque house, built in 1716, with 100 pictures from the National Portrait Gallery, Victorian laundry, potting shed and restored walled garden.

Flamingo Land Theme Park, Zoo and Holiday Village

Kirby Misperton, Malton, North Yorkshire YO17 6UX
Tel: (01653) 668287 www.flamingoland.co.uk
One-price family funpark with over 100 attractions, 7 shows and Europe's largest privately owned zoo. Europe's only triple-looping coaster, Magnum Force.

Camp Modern History Theme Museum

Malton, North Yorkshire YO17 6RT
Tel: (01653) 697777 www.edencamp.co.uk
Modern history theme museum depicting civilian way of life during World War II. Millennium features.

Fountains Abbey and Studley Royal

Studley Park, Ripon, North Yorkshire HG4 3DY
Tel: (01765) 608888 www.fountainsabbey.org.uk
Largest monastic ruin in Britain, founded by Cistercian monks in 1132. Landscaped garden laid between 1720-40 with lake, formal water garden, temples and deer park.

Cusworth Hall Museum of South Yorkshire Life

Cusworth Hall, Cusworth Lane, Doncaster,
South Yorkshire DN5 7TU
Tel: (01302) 782342
www.museum@doncaster.gov.uk
Georgian mansion in landscaped park containing Museum of South Yorkshire Life. Special educational facilities.

Hornsea Freeport

Rolston Road, Hornsea,
East Riding of Yorkshire HU18 1UT
Tel: (01964) 534211
Set in 25 acres (10 ha) of landscaped gardens with over 40 quality high-street names all selling stock with discounts of up to 50%, licensed restaurant. Leisure attractions.

The Deep

79 Ferensway, Hull, Kingston upon Hull HU2 8LE
Tel: (01482) 615789 www.hull.ac.uk
The Deep consists of 4 elements: a visitor attraction, learning centre, research facility and a business centre.

Last of the Summer Wine Exhibition (Compo's House)

30 Huddersfield Road, Holmfirth, Huddersfield,
West Yorkshire HD6 1JS
Tel: (01484) 681408
Collection of photographs and memorabilia connected with the television series 'Last of the Summer Wine'.

Leeds City Art Gallery

The Headrow, Leeds, West Yorkshire LS1 3AA
Tel: (0113) 247 8248
www.leeds.gov.uk/tourinfo/attract/museums/artgall.html
Art gallery containing British paintings, sculptures, prints and drawings of the 19thC and 20thC. Henry Moore gallery with permanent collection of 20thC sculpture.

Lightwater Valley Theme Park

North Stainley, Ripon, North Yorkshire HG4 3HT
Tel: (01765) 635321 www.lightwatervalley.net
Set in 175 acres (71 ha) of parkland, Lightwater Valley features a number of white-knuckle rides and children's rides along with shopping malls, a restaurant and picnic areas.

Magna

Sheffield Road, Templeborough, Rotherham,
South Yorkshire S60 1DX
Tel: (01709) 720002 www.magnatrust.org.uk
Magna is the UK's first science adventure centre set in the vast Templeborough steelworks in Rotherham. Fun is unavoidable here with giant interactives.

Midland Railway Centre

Butterley Station, Ripley, North Yorkshire DE5 3QZ
Tel: (01773) 747674
Over 50 locomotives and over 100 items of historic rolling stock of Midland and LMS origin with a steam-hauled passenger service, a museum site, country and farm park.

Mother Shipton's Cave & the Petrifying Well

Prophesy House, High Bridge, Knaresborough,
North Yorkshire HG5 8DD
Tel: (01423) 864600 www.mothershipton.co.uk
Mother Shipton's Cave and Petrifying Well are the oldest tourist attractions in Britain, opened in 1630. Cave, well, museum, playground and 12 acres (5 ha) of riverside grounds.

National Museum of Photography, Film & Television

Bradford, West Yorkshire BD1 1NQ
Tel: (01274) 202030 www.nmpft.org.uk
This fascinating and innovative museum houses the three types of media that have transformed the 20thC. Millennium grant awarded.

National Railway Museum

Leeman Road, York, North Yorkshire YO26 4XJ
Tel: (01904) 621261 www.nrm.org.uk
For a fun-packed family day out come along to the National Railway Museum and experience the incredible story of the train.

North Yorkshire Moors Railway

Pickering Station, Park Street, Pickering,
North Yorkshire YO18 7AJ
Tel: (01751) 472508 www.nymr.demon.co.uk
Evening and Sunday lunchtime dining service trains offer a unique and nostalgic experience with a wonderful selection of menus to suit all tastes.

The Pictures:
1 Boats in harbour, Whitby, North Yorkshire
2 Hull Fair
3 Countryside near Grimsby
4 The Humber Bridge
5 Flamborough Head
6 Felixkirk, North York Moors

Piece Hall

Halifax, West Yorkshire HX1 1RE
Tel: (01422) 358087 www.calderdale.gov.uk
Built in 1779 and restored in 1976, this Grade I Listed building forms a unique and striking monument to the wealth and importance of the wool trade.

Pleasure Island Family Theme Park

Kings Road, Cleethorpes, North East Lincolnshire DN35 0PL
Tel: (01472) 211511 www.pleasure-island.co.uk
The East Coast's biggest fun day out, with over 50 rides and attractions. Whatever the weather, fun is guaranteed with lots of undercover attractions. Shows from around the world.

Ripley Castle

Ripley, Harrogate, North Yorkshire HG3 3AY
Tel: (01423) 770152 www.ripleycastle.co.uk
Ripley Castle, home to the Ingilby family for over 26 generations, is set in the heart of a delightful estate with Victorian walled gardens, deer park and pleasure grounds.

Royal Armouries Museum

Armouries Drive, Leeds, West Yorkshire LS10 1LT
Tel: (0870) 510 6666 www.armouries.org.uk
Experience more than 3,000 years of history covered by over 8,000 spectacular exhibits and stunning surroundings. Arms and armour.

Sheffield Botanical Gardens

Clarkehouse Road, Sheffield, South Yorkshire S10 2LN
Tel: (0114) 250 0500 www.sbg.org.uk
Extensive gardens with over 5,500 species of plants, Grade II Listed garden pavilion (now closed).

Skipton Castle

Skipton, North Yorkshire BD23 1AQ
Tel: (01756) 792442 www.skiptoncastle.co.uk
Fully-roofed Skipton Castle is in excellent condition. One of the most complete and well-preserved medieval castles in England.

Temple Newsam House

Leeds, West Yorkshire LS15 0AE
Tel: (0113) 264 7321 www.leeds.gov.uk
Tudor/Jacobean house, birthplace of Lord Darnley. Paintings, furniture by Chippendale and others. Gold and silver c1600 onwards. Ceramics, especially Leeds pottery.

Thirsk Museum

14-16 Kirkgate, Thirsk, North Yorkshire YO7 1PQ
Tel: (01845) 527707
Exhibits of local life and industry and cricket memorabilia. The building was the home of Thomas Lord, founder of Lords cricket ground in London.

The Viking City of Jorvick

Coppergate, York, North Yorkshire YO1 9WT
Tel: (01904) 643211 www.jorvik-viking-centre.co.uk
Technology of the 21stC transforms real archaeological evidence into a dynamic vision of the City of York in the10thC.

Wensleydale Cheese Visitor Centre

Wensleydale Creamery, Gayle Lane, Hawes, North Yorkshire DL8 3RN
Tel: (01969) 667664
Museum, video and interpretation area, viewing gallery. Handmade Wensleydale cheese, licensed restaurant, specialist cheese shop, farm animals in natural environment.

Wigfield Farm

Haverlands Lane, Worsbrough Bridge, Barnsley, South Yorkshire S70 5NQ
Tel: (01226) 733702
Open working farm with rare and commercial breeds of farm animals including pigs, cattle, sheep, goats, donkeys, ponies, small animals, snakes and other reptiles.

York Castle Museum

The Eye of York, York, North Yorkshire YO1 9RY
Tel: (01904) 653611 www.york.gov.uk
England's most popular museum of everyday life including reconstructed streets and period rooms.

York Dungeon

12 Clifford Street, York, North Yorkshire YO1 9RD
Tel: (01904) 632599 www.thedungeons.com
Set in dark, musty, atmospheric cellars and featuring life-size tableaux of Dark Age deaths, medieval punishments and persecution/torture of heretics.

York Minster

Deangate, York, North Yorkshire YO1 7HH
Tel: (01904) 557200 www.yorkminster.org
York Minster is the largest medieval Gothic cathedral north of the Alps. Museum of Roman/Norman remains. Chapter house.

Find out more about Yorkshire

Further information about holidays and attractions in Yorkshire is available from:

YORKSHIRE TOURIST BOARD
312 Tadcaster Road, York YO24 1GS.
Tel: (01904) 707070 (24-hour brochure line)
Fax: (01904) 701414
Email: info@ytb.org.uk
Internet: www.yorkshirevisitor.com

The following publications are available from Yorkshire Tourist Board:

Yorkshire Visitor Guide 2002
information on the region, including hotels, self-catering, caravan and camping parks.
Also attractions, shops, restaurants and major events

Yorkshire - A Great Day Out
non-accommodation A5 guide listing where to go, what to see and where to eat,
the list goes on! Including map

Bed & Breakfast Touring Map
forming part of a 'family' of maps covering England, this guide provides information on
bed and breakfast establishments in Yorkshire

Group Operators' Guide 2002
a guide to choosing the right venue for travel trade and group organisers including hotels,
attractions and unusual venues

Conference and Venue Guide 2002
a full-colour, comprehensive guide to conference facilities in the region

The Pictures:
1 Walker in the Yorkshire Dales
2 York Minster

Getting to Yorkshire

BY ROAD: Motorways: M1, M62, M606, M621, M18, M180, M181, A1(M). Trunk roads: A1, A19, A57, A58, A59, A61, A62, A63, A64, A65, A66.

BY RAIL: InterCity services to Bradford, Doncaster, Harrogate, Kingston upon Hull, Leeds, Sheffield, Wakefield and York. Frequent regional railway services city centre to city centre including Manchester Airport service to Scarborough, York and Leeds.

Where to stay in Yorkshire

Accommodation entries in this region are listed in alphabetical order of place name, and then in alphabetical order of establishment.

Map references refer to the colour location maps at front of this guide. The first number indicates the map to use; the letter and number which follow refer to the grid reference on the map.

At-a-glance symbols at the end of each accommodation entry give useful information about services and facilities. A key to symbols can be found inside the back cover flap. Keep this open for easy reference.

A brief description of the towns and villages offering accommodation in the entries which follow, can be found at the end of this section.

A complete listing of all the English Tourism Council assessed accommodation covered by this guide appears at the back of the guide.

AYSGARTH, North Yorkshire Map ref 5B3

★★

THE GEORGE & DRAGON INN
Aysgarth, Leyburn DL8 3AD
T: (01969) 663358
F: (01969) 663773

B&B per night:
S £34.50
D £59.00

HB per person:
DY £46.50

OPEN All year round

Delightful 17thC inn, with old beams and antiques, in a pretty village amongst glorious scenery, perfectly situated for exploring the magnificent dales. Indulge in superb food, freshly prepared from local ingredients whenever possible, locally brewed ales, charming hospitality and beautiful, well-appointed bedrooms – all in a welcoming, congenial atmosphere.

Bedrooms: 6 double/
twin, 1 triple/multiple
Bathrooms: 7 en suite

Lunch available
Evening meal available
CC: Delta, Mastercard,
Switch, Visa

3 nights for price of 2 during winter months
provided dinner purchased each evening.

---

www.travelengland.org.uk
Log on for information and inspiration. The latest information on places to visit, events and quality assessed accommodation.

BARNSLEY, South Yorkshire Map ref 4B1 *Tourist Information Centre Tel: (01226) 206757*

★★★
Silver
Award

TANKERSLEY MANOR HOTEL
Church Lane, Upper Tankersley,
Tankersley, Barnsley S75 3DQ
T: (01226) 744700
F: (01226) 745405
E: tankersley@marstonhotels.com
I: www.marstonhotels.com

Bedrooms: 69 double/
twin
Bathrooms: 69 en suite

Lunch available
Evening meal available
CC: Amex, Delta, Diners,
Mastercard, Switch, Visa

B&B per night:
S £85.00–£105.00
D £110.00–£135.00

HB per person:
DY £69.50–£79.50

OPEN All year round

17thC manor set in its own grounds with excellent motorway access. Ten meeting rooms for small meetings, exhibitions and conferences. Half-board rate based on minimum 2 nights.

BEDALE, North Yorkshire Map ref 5C3

★★

WHITE ROSE HOTEL
Bedale Road, Leeming Bar,
Northallerton DL7 9AY
T: (01677) 422707 & 424941
F: (01677) 425123
E: royston@whiterosehotel.co.uk
I: www.whiterosehotel.co.uk

Bedrooms: 9 single,
7 double/twin, 2 triple/
multiple
Bathrooms: 18 en suite

Lunch available
Evening meal available
CC: Amex, Delta, Diners,
Mastercard, Switch, Visa

B&B per night:
S Min £39.50
D Min £52.00

OPEN All year round

Family-run private hotel centrally situated half a mile from A1 in village on A684 – the road to the Dales. 'Heartbeat' Country, historic city of York, coastal resorts within easy reach.

BEVERLEY, East Riding of Yorkshire Map ref 4C1 *Tourist Information Centre Tel: (01482) 867430*

★★★

TICKTON GRANGE HOTEL & RESTAURANT
Tickton Grange, Tickton, Beverley
HU17 9SH
T: (01964) 543666
F: (01964) 542556
E: maggy@tickton-grange.demon.
co.uk
I: www.ticktongrange.co.uk

Bedrooms: 14 double/
twin, 3 triple/multiple
Bathrooms: 17 en suite

Lunch available
Evening meal available
CC: Amex, Delta, Diners,
Mastercard, Switch, Visa

B&B per night:
S £65.00–£75.00
D £75.00–£95.00

OPEN All year round

A beautiful Georgian country house hotel set in 3 acres of rose gardens, 3 miles from historic Beverley. Award-winning modern British cuisine.

BOROUGHBRIDGE, North Yorkshire Map ref 5C3

★★★

CROWN HOTEL
Horsefair, Boroughbridge, York YO51 9LB
T: (01423) 322328
F: (01423) 324512
E: sales@crownboroughbridge.co.uk
I: www.crownboroughbridge.co.uk

B&B per night:
S £68.50–£76.00
D £84.00–£99.50

HB per person:
DY £60.25–£70.75

OPEN All year round

The Independents/Best
Western Hotels

Based in the heart of North Yorkshire, the Crown really offers its guests something a little bit special. We have a fine a la carte restaurant, bars with real ales and fires and newly refurbished bedrooms. New leisure centre, pool, sauna, steam and jacuzzi, fitness suites. Make the Crown Hotel your first choice.

Bedrooms: 2 single,
32 double/twin, 3 triple/
multiple
Bathrooms: 37 en suite

Lunch available
Evening meal available
CC: Amex, Delta, Diners,
Mastercard, Switch, Visa

ACCESSIBILITY
Look for the 🔲🔲🔲 symbols which indicate accessibility for wheelchair users. A list of establishments is at the front of this guide.

★★★★
Silver
Award

The Hanover International Hotel offers a unique mixture of modern design and friendly, quality service. Close to the dales and the many delights of Yorkshire, its location is ideal. Extensive leisure facilities, international restaurant and beautifully appointed bedrooms make the Cedar Court an excellent choice for your weekend break.

HANOVER INTERNATIONAL HOTEL & CLUB

Mayo Avenue (top of the M606), Off Rooley Lane, Bradford BD5 8HZ
T: (01274) 406606
F: (01274) 406600
E: sales.bradford@hanover-international.com
I: www.hanover-international.com

Bedrooms: 124 double/ twin, 7 triple/multiple; suites available
Bathrooms: 131 en suite

Lunch available
Evening meal available
CC: Amex, Diners, Mastercard, Switch, Visa

Weekend breaks from only £49pppn DB&B, available Fri, Sat & Sun, minimum 2 nights.

B&B per night:
S £74.75–£114.75
D £84.50–£124.50

HB per person:
DY £61.75–£134.25

OPEN All year round

★★

'It's like staying in the country!' This elegant Victorian residence in its delightful woodland setting is just 1.5 miles from the city centre. Enjoy delicious home cooking, friendly personal service and a peaceful night's sleep. Visit Bronte Parsonage, National Museum of Photography, Yorkshire Dales, 'Emmerdale', Salts Mill or Royal Armouries.

PARK DRIVE HOTEL

12 Park Drive, Heaton, Bradford BD9 4DR
T: (01274) 480194
F: (01274) 484869
E: info@parkdrivehotel.co.uk
I: www.parkdrivehotel.co.uk

Bedrooms: 5 single, 5 double/twin, 1 triple/ multiple
Bathrooms: 11 en suite

Evening meal available
CC: Amex, Delta, Diners, Mastercard, Switch, Visa

B&B per night:
S £35.00–£52.00
D £49.00–£62.00

HB per person:
DY £38.00–£65.00

OPEN All year round

Ⓒ
The Independents

★★

PARK GROVE HOTEL AND RESTAURANT

Park Grove, Frizinghall, Bradford BD9 4JY
T: (01274) 543444
F: (01274) 495619
E: enquiries@parkgrovehotel.co.uk
I: www.parkgrovehotel.co.uk

Bedrooms: 5 single, 9 double/twin, 1 triple/ multiple
Bathrooms: 15 en suite

Evening meal available
CC: Amex, Delta, Mastercard, Switch, Visa

B&B per night:
S £25.00–£40.00
D £35.00–£50.00

HB per person:
DY £35.00–£50.00

OPEN All year round

Ⓒ
Minotel

Victorian establishment in a secluded preserved area of Bradford, 1.5 miles from the city centre. Gateway to the dales.

CHECK THE MAPS

The colour maps at the front of this guide show all the cities, towns and villages for which you will find accommodation entries. Refer to the town index to find the page on which they are listed.

BRANDESBURTON, East Riding of Yorkshire Map ref 4D1

★★

BURTON LODGE HOTEL
Brandesburton, Driffield YO25 8RU
T: (01964) 542847
F: (01964) 544771
E: email@burtonlodgefsnet.co.uk

B&B per night:
S £34.00–£37.00
D £49.00–£53.00

HB per person:
DY £48.00–£52.00

OPEN All year round

Charming country hotel set in 2 acres of grounds adjoining Hainsworth Park Golf Course (18 holes and 1st tee from the hotel grounds). Nine en suite bedrooms including 2 family, and 2 ground floor bedrooms. Fine English cooking and carefully chosen wine list. Comfortable lounge/bar with open fire. Situated on the A165, 8 miles from Beverley.

Bedrooms: 1 single, 6 double/twin, 2 triple/ multiple
Bathrooms: 9 en suite

Evening meal available
CC: Amex, Delta, Mastercard, Switch, Visa

BRIDLINGTON, East Riding of Yorkshire Map ref 5D3 *Tourist Information Centre Tel: (01262) 673474*

★★★

EXPANSE HOTEL
North Marine Drive, Bridlington YO15 2LS
T: (01262) 675347
F: (01262) 604928
E: expanse@brid.demon.co.uk
I: www.expanse.co.uk

B&B per night:
S £33.00–£58.00
D £62.00–£84.00

HB per person:
DY £40.00–£110.00

OPEN All year round

Superbly positioned, overlooking the beach and sea, with panoramic views of the bay and Heritage Coast, together with easy access to coastal walks, the Expanse is an ideal hotel in which to relax or to use as a touring base. Every room is as individual as you.

Bedrooms: 13 single, 31 double/twin, 4 triple/ multiple
Bathrooms: 48 en suite

Lunch available
Evening meal available
CC: Amex, Delta, Mastercard, Switch, Visa

★★★

THE FERNS HOTEL
Main Street, Carnaby, Bridlington YO16 4UJ
T: (01262) 678961
F: (01262) 400712
E: the.ferns_hotel@virgin.net
I: www.fernshotel.co.uk

B&B per night:
S £39.25–£44.25
D £59.75–£65.75

OPEN All year round

Family-run hotel with a bias towards health and fitness. Gym, indoor pool, sauna, solarium, steam room and spa bath are all included with your stay. Large public bar and restaurant serving a superb selection of hot and cold meals. All rooms en suite with several satellite channels.

Bedrooms: 3 single, 9 double/twin
Bathrooms: 11 en suite, 1 private

Lunch available
Evening meal available
CC: Delta, Mastercard, Switch, Visa

Weekend specials from £23.95 pppn, based on 2 sharing a double room for a minimum of two nights (Fri, Sat or Sun).

QUALITY ASSURANCE SCHEME
Star ratings and awards were correct at the time of going to press but are subject to change. Please check at the time of booking.

DEWSBURY, West Yorkshire Map ref 4B1

★★★ **HEATH COTTAGE HOTEL & RESTAURANT**

Wakefield Road, Dewsbury	Bedrooms: 9 single,	Lunch available	B&B per night:
WF12 8ET	17 double/twin, 3 triple/	Evening meal available	S £38.00–£54.00
T: (01924) 465399	multiple	CC: Delta, Mastercard,	D £63.00–£75.00
F: (01924) 459405	Bathrooms: 29 en suite	Switch, Visa	
E: Bookings@heathcottage.co.uk			HB per person:
I: www.heathcottage.co.uk			DY £46.45–£52.45

Impressive Victorian house in well-kept gardens. On the A638, 2.5 miles from M1 junction 40. Conference/banquet facilities. Large car park. Civil weddings.

OPEN All year round

DONCASTER, South Yorkshire Map ref 4C1 *Tourist Information Centre Tel: (01302) 734309*

★★★

REGENT HOTEL
Regent Square, Doncaster DN1 2DS
T: (01302) 364180 & 364336
F: (01302) 322331
E: admin@theregenthotel.co.uk
I: www.theregenthotel.co.uk

B&B per night:
S £50.00–£80.00
D £75.00–£85.00

HB per person:
DY £65.00–£100.00

OPEN All year round

A charming Victorian building overlooking a secluded Regency park. Ideally situated within easy reach of Doncaster's vibrant town centre, business centres, market, historic racecourse and exhibition centre. Founded in 1935 and family-run since, the hotel has the distinctive air of 'home from home', with a choice of public areas to suit.

Bedrooms: 21 single,
24 double/twin, 5 triple/
multiple
Bathrooms: 50 en suite

Lunch available
Evening meal available
CC: Amex, Delta, Diners,
Mastercard, Switch, Visa

Jun and Jul 'summer special' rates. B&B from £27.50pp in our budget and economy rooms.

FILEY, North Yorkshire Map ref 5D3

★★
Silver
Award
THE DOWNCLIFFE HOUSE HOTEL

The Beach, Filey YO14 9LA	Bedrooms: 1 single,	Lunch available	B&B per night:
T: (01723) 513310	7 double/twin, 2 triple/	Evening meal available	S £40.00–£50.00
F: (01723) 513773	multiple	CC: Delta, Mastercard,	D £80.00–£100.00
E: downcliffe@2filey.co.uk	Bathrooms: 10 en suite	Switch, Visa	

Recently refurbished seafront hotel with magnificent views over Filey Bay. All rooms en suite with telephone, satellite TV and tea-making facilities.

HB per person:
DY £60.00–£80.00

★★ **SEA BRINK HOTEL**

3 The Beach, Filey YO14 9LA	Bedrooms: 1 single,	Lunch available	B&B per night:
T: (01723) 513257	5 double/twin, 3 triple/	Evening meal available	S £31.00–£45.00
F: (01723) 514139	multiple	CC: Delta, Mastercard,	D £61.00–£66.00
E: seabrink@supanet.com	Bathrooms: 9 en suite	Switch, Visa	
I: www.seabrink.co.uk			HB per person:
			DY £40.00–£46.00

Licensed seafront hotel with nine delightful, full facility, en suite rooms, many overlooking panoramic Filey Bay. Children and pets welcome. German spoken. Dinner available. Closed January.

OPEN Feb–Dec

GILLAMOOR, North Yorkshire Map ref 5C3

Rating
Applied For
ROYAL OAK INN

Gillamoor, York YO62 7HX	Bedrooms: 6 double/	Lunch available	B&B per night:
T: (01751) 431414	twin	Evening meal available	S £32.00–£36.00
F: (01751) 431414	Bathrooms: 6 en suite	CC: Delta, Mastercard,	D £44.00–£56.00
		Switch, Visa	

Old country inn on the edge of the North York Moors. Tastefully renovated, with plenty of character and charm. Open log fires. Excellent a la carte menu.

OPEN All year round

RATING All accommodation in this guide has been rated, or is awaiting a rating, by a trained English Tourism Council assessor.

GOOLE, East Riding of Yorkshire Map ref 4C1

★★
Silver
Award

CLIFTON HOTEL
Boothferry Road, Goole DN14 6AL
T: (01405) 761336
F: (01405) 762350
E: cliftonhotel@telinco.co.uk
I: www.cliftonhotel.cwc.net

Bedrooms: 4 single,
4 double/twin, 1 triple/
multiple
Bathrooms: 8 en suite,
1 private

Evening meal available
CC: Amex, Delta, Diners,
Mastercard, Switch, Visa

B&B per night:
S £32.00–£42.00
D £44.00–£52.00

OPEN All year round

Friendly and attentive service provided at this well-furnished and comfortable hotel. Restaurant menu includes healthy options.

🐎 📞 📺 ▢ 👜 ⚑ Ⓢ ⌘ ⌥ 🖥 ⚓ ⏺ 🐕 🚗 P

Ⓒ
The Independents

HALIFAX, West Yorkshire Map ref 4B1 *Tourist Information Centre Tel: (01422) 368725*

★★

THE HOBBIT HOTEL
Hob Lane, Norland, Halifax HX6 3QL
T: (01422) 832202
F: (01422) 835381
E: info@hobbit-hotel.co.uk
I: www.hobbit-hotel.co.uk

Bedrooms: 2 single,
13 double/twin, 5 triple/
multiple
Bathrooms: 20 en suite

Lunch available
Evening meal available
CC: Amex, Delta, Diners,
Mastercard, Switch, Visa

B&B per night:
S £38.00–£63.00
D £50.00–£68.00

OPEN All year round

Country hotel with panoramic views. Restaurant and bistro have reputation for good food at affordable prices. Friendly inn-type atmosphere. 'Murder Mysteries' featured regularly.

♨ 🐎 🛏 📞 📺 ▢ 👜 ⚑ Ⓢ ⌥ 🖥 ⚓ ⏺ ∪ ▶ ✷ 🐕 🚗 P

★★★

THE ROCK INN HOTEL & PALMER'S RESTAURANT
Holywell Green, Halifax HX4 9BS
T: (01422) 379721
F: (01422) 379110
E: the.rock@dial.pipex.com
I: www.rockinnhotel.com

Bedrooms: 28 double/
twin, 2 triple/multiple;
suites available
Bathrooms: 30 en suite

Lunch available
Evening meal available
CC: Amex, Delta, Diners,
Mastercard, Switch, Visa

B&B per night:
S £50.00–£140.00
D £65.00–£140.00

OPEN All year round

Privately-owned hostelry offering attractions of a wayside inn plus sophistication of a first class hotel and conference centre. Rural setting 1.5 miles junction 24 of M62.

♨ 🐎 🛏 📞 📺 ▢ 👜 ⚑ Ⓢ ⌥ Ⓞ 🖥 ⚓ ⏺ ∪ ▶ ✷ 🐕 🚗 P

HARROGATE, North Yorkshire Map ref 4B1 *Tourist Information Centre Tel: (01423) 537300*

★★
Silver
Award

ASCOT HOUSE HOTEL
53 Kings Road, Harrogate HG1 5HJ
T: (01423) 531005
F: (01423) 503523
E: admin@ascothouse.com
I: www.ascothouse.com

B&B per night:
S £53.00–£63.00
D £78.00–£88.00

HB per person:
DY £49.00–£56.00

OPEN All year round

Ⓒ
Minotel

Delightful, refurbished hotel with lovely Victorian decorative features, within easy walking distance of Harrogate's renowned shops and gardens. Relax in our comfortable lounge bar. Enjoy quality cuisine and great value wines. All bedrooms en suite with telephone, TV, radio/alarm, hairdryer and tea/coffee facilities. Great selection of local attraction brochures. Car park.

Bedrooms: 4 single,
14 double/twin, 1 triple/
multiple
Bathrooms: 19 en suite

Evening meal available
CC: Amex, Delta, Diners,
Mastercard, Switch, Visa

Fawlty Towers comedy nights with professional actors. Please ring for dates and information.

♨ 🐎 🛏 📞 📺 ▢ 👜 ⚑ Ⓢ 🖥 ⚓ ⏺ ✷ 🐕 🏛 P

★★★

BALMORAL HOTEL
Franklin Mount, Harrogate HG1 5EJ
T: (01423) 508208
F: (01423) 530652
E: info@balmoralhotel.co.uk
I: www.balmoralhotel.co.uk

Bedrooms: 3 single,
17 double/twin; suites
available
Bathrooms: 20 en suite

Lunch available
Evening meal available
CC: Amex, Delta,
Mastercard, Switch, Visa

B&B per night:
S Min £69.00
D Min £95.00

HB per person:
DY Min £61.50

OPEN All year round

Exclusive townhouse with beautifully furnished rooms and a relaxed, tranquil ambience. Nine 4-poster rooms. Award-winning restaurant with modern English menu. Special weekend rates.

♨ 🐎 🛏 📞 📺 ▢ 👜 ⚑ Ⓢ ⌥ Ⓞ 🖥 ⚓ ▶ ✷ 🐕 P

WHERE TO STAY
Please mention this guide when making your booking.

HARROGATE continued

★★★ Silver Award

THE BOAR'S HEAD HOTEL
Ripley Castle Estate, Ripley,
Harrogate HG3 3AY
T: (01423) 771888
F: (01423) 771509
E: reservations@boarsheadripley.
co.uk
I: www.ripleycastle.co.uk

Bedrooms: 25 double/
twin
Bathrooms: 25 en suite

Lunch available
Evening meal available
CC: Amex, Delta, Diners,
Mastercard, Switch, Visa

B&B per night:
S £99.00–£120.00
D £120.00–£140.00

OPEN All year round

ⓒⓡ
Grand Heritage Hotels

At the heart of the historic Ripley Castle estate, overlooking the cobbled market square. Renowned restaurant and fine village pub. One of the great inns of Britain.

★★★★ Gold Award

RUDDING PARK HOTEL & GOLF
Rudding Park, Follifoot, Harrogate
HG3 1JH
T: (01423) 871350
F: (01423) 872286
E: sales@ruddingpark.com
I: www.ruddingpark.com

Bedrooms: 48 double/
twin, 2 triple/multiple;
suites available
Bathrooms: 50 en suite

Lunch available
Evening meal available
CC: Amex, Delta, Diners,
Mastercard, Switch, Visa

B&B per night:
S £120.00–£280.00
D £150.00–£280.00

HB per person:
DY £125.00–£310.00

OPEN All year round

ⓒⓡ
Grand Heritage Hotels

In its own 2000-acre estate, just 2 miles south of Harrogate, this contemporary hotel boasts the award-winning Clocktower restaurant and 18-hole parkland golf course.

★★★

WHITE HART HOTEL
Cold Bath Road, Harrogate HG2 0NF
T: (01423) 505681
F: (01423) 568354
E: pwalker@whitehart.net
I: www.whitehart.net

B&B per night:
S £60.00–£65.00
D £80.00–£85.00

OPEN All year round

The White Hart is beautifully situated overlooking The Stray. Around the corner are the Valley Gardens, shops and Betty's. Situated in the centre of Harrogate, the hotel, an historic building tastefully upgraded, is an ideal base for touring the dales.

Bedrooms: 27 single,
26 double/twin
Bathrooms: 53 en suite

Lunch available
Evening meal available
CC: Delta, Mastercard,
Switch, Visa

Weekend breaks £50 single B&B, £75 twin/double B&B.

HAWES, North Yorkshire Map ref 5B3 *Tourist Information Centre Tel: (01969) 667450*

★★

STONE HOUSE HOTEL
Sedbusk, Hawes DL8 3PT
T: (01969) 667571
F: (01969) 667720
E: daleshotel@aol.com
I: www.stonehousehotel.com

B&B per night:
S £40.00–£93.00
D £70.00–£93.00

HB per person:
DY £56.50–£68.00

Fine Edwardian country house hotel set amidst beautiful gardens with panoramic views of upper Wensleydale. Well-appointed en suite bedrooms (5 with private conservatories on the ground floor). Delicious food, fine wines, log fires. Dogs welcome. Superb walking. This really is the perfect venue from which to explore the Dales!

Bedrooms: 1 single,
20 double/twin, 1 triple/
multiple; suites available
Bathrooms: 21 en suite,
1 private

Evening meal available
CC: Delta, Mastercard,
Switch, Visa

Bargain breaks Oct-Apr. Special interest courses-wine tasting, embroidery, painting, malt whisky tasting. Murder mystery weekdends-Jan.

SPECIAL BREAKS
Many establishments offer special promotions and themed breaks. These are highlighted in red. (All such offers are subject to availability.)

YORKSHIRE

HAWORTH, West Yorkshire Map ref 4B1 *Tourist Information Centre Tel: (01535) 642329*

★★

OLD WHITE LION HOTEL
Main Street, Haworth, Keighley BD22 8DU
T: (01535) 642313
F: (01535) 646222
E: enquiries@oldwhitelionhotel.com
I: www.oldwhitelionhotel.com

B&B per night:
S £48.00–£58.00
D £65.00–£75.00

HB per person:
DY £60.00–£70.00

OPEN All year round

Family-run centuries old coaching inn situated at the top of the charming cobbled Main Street. Fourteen en suite rooms most commanding spectacular views of surrounding countryside. Candlelit a la carte restaurant, oak beamed bars serving traditional ales and home cooked food. As featured on BBC Holiday programme 2001.

Bedrooms: 3 single,
9 double/twin, 2 triple/
multiple
Bathrooms: 14 en suite

Lunch available
Evening meal available
CC: Amex, Delta, Diners,
Mastercard, Switch, Visa

Special bargain breaks available. Great value and good food in old world surroundings.

ⁿ P

HELMSLEY, North Yorkshire Map ref 5C3

★★

THE CROWN HOTEL
Market Place, Helmsley, York
YO62 5BJ
T: (01439) 770297
F: (01439) 771595

Bedrooms: 2 single,
9 double/twin, 1 triple/
multiple
Bathrooms: 12 en suite

Lunch available
Evening meal available
CC: Delta, Mastercard,
Switch, Visa

B&B per night:
S £28.00–£35.00
D £56.00–£70.00

HB per person:
DY £40.00–£49.00

OPEN All year round

16thC inn with a Jacobean dining room offering traditional country cooking. Special breaks available. Dogs welcome. Run by the same family for 41 years.

★★

FEATHERS HOTEL
Market Place, Helmsley, York YO62 5BH
T: (01439) 770275
F: (01439) 771101
E: feathers@zen.co.uk
I: www.feathershotel.co.uk

B&B per night:
S Max £45.00
D Max £60.00

OPEN All year round

An old world country inn offering a delightful mix of genuine historic charm and Yorkshire hospitality with high standards of cuisine. All bedrooms en suite with modern facilities. The hotel has three bars and a large restaurant and has a local reputation for good food and fine ales.

Bedrooms: 14 double/
twin
Bathrooms: 14 en suite

Lunch available
Evening meal available
CC: Delta, Mastercard,
Switch, Visa

Please enquire about any special offers at time of booking.

COUNTRY CODE Always follow the Country Code 🐾 Enjoy the countryside and respect its life and work 🐾 Guard against all risk of fire 🐾 Fasten all gates 🐾 Keep your dogs under close control 🐾 Keep to public paths across farmland 🐾 Use gates and stiles to cross fences, hedges and walls 🐾 Leave livestock, crops and machinery alone 🐾 Take your litter home 🐾 Help to keep all water clean 🐾 Protect wildlife, plants and trees 🐾 Take special care on country roads 🐾 Make no unnecessary noise

HELMSLEY continued

Rating
Applied For

FEVERSHAM ARMS HOTEL

1 High Street, Helmsley, York YO62 5AG
T: (01439) 770766
F: (01439) 770346
E: fevershamarms@hotmail.com

B&B per night:
S £70.00–£90.00
D £90.00–£110.00

HB per person:
DY £65.00–£75.00

OPEN All year round

Traditional inn meets contemporary design. Accommodation comprising 17 en suite bedrooms, of which 7 are suites, the choice to dine in either The Dining Room, 'Brasserie at the Fev' or poolside and garden terrace. Offering a traditional and contemporary menu, comfortable lounges and the new Feversham Arms Health & Fitness Club, heated outdoor swimming pool and tennis court.

Bedrooms: 10 double/
twin, 7 triple/multiple;
suites available
Bathrooms: 17 en suite

Please enquire at time of booking.

Lunch available
Evening meal available
CC: Amex, Delta,
Mastercard, Switch, Visa

★★★

PHEASANT HOTEL
Harome, Helmsley, York YO62 5JG
T: (01439) 771241
F: (01439) 771744

Bedrooms: 1 single,
11 double/twin
Bathrooms: 12 en suite

Lunch available
Evening meal available
CC: Amex, Delta,
Mastercard, Switch, Visa

B&B per night:
S £45.00–£48.00
D £90.00–£95.00

HB per person:
DY £65.00–£72.00

In a quiet rural village, with terrace and gardens overlooking village pond. Oak-beamed bar in a former blacksmith's shop, English food, log fires. New orangery.

HOWDEN, East Riding of Yorkshire Map ref 4C1

★★

WELLINGTON HOTEL

31 Bridgegate, Howden, Goole DN14 7JG
T: (01430) 430258 & (01763) 287773
F: (01430) 432139

B&B per night:
S £25.00–£32.00
D £35.00–£47.50

OPEN All year round

An original coaching inn, dating from the 16thC, situated in an old market town. Character and style now combine with modern amenities and comfortable en suite rooms. A wide selection of freshly-prepared dishes is available from the bar menu or you can dine in the Bowmans Bar and Grill.

Bedrooms: 3 single,
7 double/twin
Bathrooms: 8 en suite,
2 private

Lunch available
Evening meal available
CC: Amex, Delta,
Mastercard, Switch, Visa

AT-A-GLANCE SYMBOLS

Symbols at the end of each accommodation entry give useful information about services and facilities. A key to symbols can be found inside the back cover flap. Keep this open for easy reference.

HUDDERSFIELD, West Yorkshire Map ref 4B1 *Tourist Information Centre Tel: (01484) 223200*

★★★

BRIAR COURT HOTEL

Halifax Road, Birchencliffe, Huddersfield
HD3 3NT
T: (01484) 519902 & 519978
F: (01484) 431812
E: briarcourthotel@btconnect.com
I: www.briaracourthotel.co.uk

Modern hotel, refurbished throughout, with 48 bedrooms, Zanzibar wine and coffee lounge, conference and wedding facilities. Home of Da Sandro Ristorante – authentic Italian cuisine served in an unrivalled atmosphere. Easily accessible from M62, convenient for Leeds and Manchester.

Bedrooms: 46 double/twin, 2 triple/multiple; suites available
Bathrooms: 48 en suite

Lunch available
Evening meal available
CC: Amex, Delta, Diners, Mastercard, Switch, Visa

B&B per night:
S £45.00–£65.00
D £55.00–£75.00

HB per person:
DY £60.00–£100.00

OPEN All year round

★★★

HUDDERSFIELD HOTEL AND ROSEMARY LANE BISTRO

33-47 Kirkgate, Huddersfield
HD1 1QT
T: (01484) 512111
F: (01484) 435262
E: enquiries@huddersfieldhotel.com
I: www.huddersfieldhotel.com

Bedrooms: 14 single, 34 double/twin, 3 triple/multiple
Bathrooms: 51 en suite

Lunch available
Evening meal available
CC: Amex, Delta, Diners, Mastercard, Switch, Visa

B&B per night:
S £39.00–£59.00
D £49.00–£79.00

HB per person:
DY £49.00–£69.00

OPEN All year round

Past winner of 'Yorkshire In Bloom'. Free secure car park. Continental-style brasserie, traditional pub and nightclub within the complex. Renowned for friendliness.

ILKLEY, West Yorkshire Map ref 4B1

★★★
Silver
Award

ROMBALDS HOTEL AND RESTAURANT

West View, Wells Road, Ilkley LS29 9JG
T: (01943) 603201
F: (01943) 816586
E: reception@rombalds.demon.co.uk
I: www.rombalds.co.uk

On the face of Ilkley Moor, 600 yards from town centre, this elegantly furnished hotel provides very comfortable accommodation. Enjoy well-produced food based on local produce in our award-winning restaurant. An ideal centre to tour England's North Country. Finalist of Yorkshire Tourist Board's White Rose Award for Best Small Hotel.

Bedrooms: 2 single, 12 double/twin, 1 triple/multiple; suites available
Bathrooms: 15 en suite

Lunch available
Evening meal available
CC: Amex, Delta, Diners, Mastercard, Switch, Visa

B&B per night:
S £55.00–£99.00

OPEN All year round

Best Western Hotels

KIRKBYMOORSIDE, North Yorkshire Map ref 5C3

★★

GEORGE & DRAGON HOTEL

Market Place, Kirkbymoorside, York
YO62 6AA
T: (01751) 433334
F: (01751) 432933

Bedrooms: 3 single, 13 double/twin, 2 triple/multiple
Bathrooms: 18 en suite

Lunch available
Evening meal available
CC: Delta, Mastercard, Switch, Visa

B&B per night:
S £49.00
D £79.00–£90.00

HB per person:
DY £100.00–£115.00

OPEN All year round

Inn of character adjacent to the North Yorkshire moors. Extensively modernised bedrooms, all with colour TV, en suite bathrooms. Ideal touring location. Good Pub Guide 'Newcomer of the Year Award 1995'.

HALF BOARD PRICES Half board prices are given per person, but in some cases these may be based on double/twin occupancy.

★★

ARAGON HOTEL
250 Stainbeck Lane, Meanwood, Leeds
LS7 2PS
T: (0113) 275 9306
F: (0113) 275 7166
E: aragon@onmail.co.uk
I: www.aragonhotel.co.uk

B&B per night:
S £39.90–£46.90
D £49.90–£64.90

HB per person:
DY £53.90–£60.00

OPEN All year round

A quiet and peaceful late Victorian hotel, recently refurbished, set in an acre of garden. A non-smoking hotel with 'Gold Award for Clean Air'. All bedrooms en suite with TV, radio, telephone, hairdryer and hospitality tray. Two miles from city centre, Headingley, Boddington Hall and the university.

Bedrooms: 2 single,
9 double/twin, 1 triple/
multiple
Bathrooms: 12 en suite

Evening meal available
CC: Amex, Delta, Diners,
Mastercard, Switch, Visa

Reduced prices for weekend stays. Phone for prices.

®
The Independents

★★

ASCOT GRANGE HOTEL
126-130 Otley Road, Headingley,
Leeds LS16 5JX
T: (0113) 293 4444
F: (0113) 293 5555
E: ascotgrangehotel@aol.com

Bedrooms: 7 single,
9 double/twin, 6 triple/
multiple
Bathrooms: 22 en suite

Lunch available
Evening meal available
CC: Delta, Mastercard,
Switch, Visa

B&B per night:
S £42.00–£45.00
D £51.00–£53.00

HB per person:
DY £49.00–£55.00

OPEN All year round

Refurbished throughout. In the heart of Far Headingley, 2 miles from city centre, close to amenities, public transport, golf, Beckets Park and Headingley cricket ground. Warm welcome from friendly staff.

★★★★★
Silver
Award

DE VERE OULTON HALL
Rothwell Lane, Oulton, Woodlesford, Leeds
LS26 8HN
T: (0113) 282 1000
F: (0113) 282 8066
E: oulton.hall@devere-hotels.com
I: www.devereonline.co.uk

B&B per night:
S £70.00–£150.00
D £80.00–£160.00

OPEN All year round

Fully renovated hall in the heart of Yorkshire, south-east of Leeds. Adjacent to a golf-course. Full leisure club including swimming pool, aerobics studio, beauty salon. Fine dining and informal restaurants available. Close to M62, M1 intersection and A1/M1 link road. Attractions include Royal Armouries, Harvey Nichols, York, Yorkshire Dales.

Bedrooms: 152 double/
twin; suites available
Bathrooms: 152 en suite

Lunch available
Evening meal available
CC: Amex, Diners,
Mastercard, Switch, Visa

QUALITY ASSURANCE SCHEME
For an explanation of the quality and facilities represented by the Stars please refer to the front of this guide. A more detailed explanation can be found in the information pages at the back.

LEEDS continued

★★★

RAMADA JARVIS LEEDS
Otley Road, Leeds LS16 8AG
T: (0113) 269 9000
F: (0113) 267 4410
E: jileeds.rs@jarvis.co.uk
I: www.jarvis.co.uk

B&B per night:
S £64.00–£104.00
D £79.00–£119.00

HB per person:
DY £42.00–£67.00

OPEN All year round

You're assured of a consistently warm Yorkshire welcome at this Tudor hotel, set in 5 acres of grounds next to Golden Acre Park and Nature Reserve. This recently refurbished first class hotel has a Sebastian Coe Health Club, tennis courts, leisure bar with a relaxed, friendly restaurant serving English food.

Bedrooms: 5 single, 113 double/twin
Bathrooms: 118 en suite

Lunch available
Evening meal available
CC: Amex, Delta, Diners, Mastercard, Switch, Visa

Jarvis Hotels/Utell International

★★★★

WEETWOOD HALL CONFERENCE CENTRE & HOTEL
Otley Road, Leeds LS16 5PS
T: (0113) 230 6000
F: (0113) 230 6095
E: sales@weetwood.co.uk
I: www.weetwood.co.uk

Bedrooms: 41 single, 67 double/twin; suites available
Bathrooms: 106 en suite

Lunch available
Evening meal available
CC: Amex, Delta, Diners, Mastercard, Switch, Visa

B&B per night:
S £42.50–£123.75
D £80.00–£152.50

HB per person:
DY £58.00–£109.50

OPEN All year round

Built around a Grade II Listed building. In 9.5 acres of beautiful wooded grounds, just 3.5 miles from Leeds city centre.

LEEDS/BRADFORD AIRPORT

See under Bradford, Leeds

LEYBURN, North Yorkshire Map ref 5B3 *Tourist Information Centre Tel: (01969) 623069*

★

GOLDEN LION HOTEL & LICENSED RESTAURANT
Market Place, Leyburn DL8 5AS
T: (01969) 622161
F: (01969) 623836
E: annegoldenlion@aol.com
I: www.thegoldenlion.co.uk

Bedrooms: 2 single, 9 double/twin, 4 triple/multiple
Bathrooms: 14 en suite, 1 private

Lunch available
Evening meal available
CC: Amex, Delta, Diners, Mastercard, Switch, Visa

B&B per night:
S £25.00–£32.00
D £50.00–£64.00

HB per person:
DY Min £40.00

OPEN All year round

Small family-run hotel in the market place of a busy dales town. A good base for touring the surrounding countryside. Special diets. Children/pets welcome.

LIVERSEDGE, West Yorkshire Map ref 4B1

★★

HEALDS HALL HOTEL
Leeds Road, Liversedge WF15 6JA
T: (01924) 409112
F: (01924) 401895
E: healdshall@ndirect.co.uk

B&B per night:
S £45.00–£60.00
D £55.00–£80.00

HB per person:
DY £45.00–£80.00

OPEN All year round

18thC family-run hotel with nationally acclaimed award-winning restaurant, set in large established gardens. Ideal venue for wedding receptions and conferences. On A62, near M1 and M62. Special weekend breaks available, from £90 per person, including meals. New and exciting bistro open.

Bedrooms: 5 single, 16 double/twin, 3 triple/multiple
Bathrooms: 24 en suite

Lunch available
Evening meal available
CC: Amex, Delta, Diners, Mastercard, Switch, Visa

Succesful bistro is a great attraction. Weddings are our speciality.

IDEAS For ideas on places to visit refer to the introduction at the beginning of this section.

MARKINGTON, North Yorkshire Map ref 5C3

★★★ **HOB GREEN**
Markington, Harrogate HG3 3PJ
T: (01423) 770031
F: (01423) 771589
E: info@hobgreen.com
I: www.hobgreen.com

Bedrooms: 3 single,
9 double/twin; suites
available
Bathrooms: 12 en suite

Lunch available
Evening meal available
CC: Amex, Delta, Diners,
Mastercard, Switch, Visa

B&B per night:
S £80.00–£90.00
D £95.00–£105.00

HB per person:
DY £119.00–£145.00

OPEN All year round

(CR)

Best Western Hotels

A country house in 870 acres, with magnificent scenic views of rolling Yorkshire countryside.

MORLEY, West Yorkshire Map ref 4B1

★★ **THE OLD VICARAGE**
Bruntcliffe Road, Morley, Leeds
LS27 0JZ
T: (0113) 253 2174
F: (0113) 253 3549
E: oldvicarage@btinternet.com
I: www.oldvicaragehotel.co.uk

Bedrooms: 11 single,
9 double/twin
Bathrooms: 20 en suite

Evening meal available
CC: Amex, Delta, Diners,
Mastercard, Switch, Visa

B&B per night:
S £34.00–£48.00
D £55.00–£62.00

OPEN All year round

Within minutes of motorways, the Old Vicarage is a friendly, family-run hotel featuring beautiful antiques and Victoriana in an authentic setting. 75% no smoking.

NEWBY WISKE, North Yorkshire Map ref 5C3

★★★ **SOLBERGE HALL**
Newby Wiske, Northallerton
DL7 9ER
T: (01609) 779191
F: (01609) 780472
E: hotel@solberge.freeserve.co.uk
I: www.smoothhound.com

Bedrooms: 4 single,
20 double/twin; suites
available
Bathrooms: 24 en suite

Lunch available
Evening meal available
CC: Amex, Delta, Diners,
Mastercard, Switch, Visa

B&B per night:
S £75.00–£85.00
D £100.00–£120.00

HB per person:
DY £60.00–£65.00

OPEN All year round

(CR)

Best Western Hotels

Georgian country house in the heart of Herriot Country, convenient for the moors and dales. Daily half-board prices based on 2-night stay.

PONTEFRACT, West Yorkshire Map ref 4C1

★★★

ROGERTHORPE MANOR COUNTRY HOTEL
Thorpe Lane, Badsworth, Pontefract
WF9 1AB
T: (01977) 643839
F: (01977) 641571
E: ops@rogerthorpemanor.co.uk
I: www.rogerthorpemanor.co.uk

Bedrooms: 4 single,
19 double/twin, 1 triple/
multiple
Bathrooms: 24 en suite

Lunch available
Evening meal available
CC: Amex, Diners,
Mastercard, Switch, Visa

B&B per night:
S £65.00–£120.00
D £65.00–£120.00

HB per person:
DY £80.00–£150.00

OPEN All year round

(CR)

Best Western Hotels

Set in glorious countryside, yet only minutes from the A1/M62 road links, this impressive Grade II Jacobean manor boasts an oak panelled restaurant, large banqueting suite and conference rooms. The Manor is a perfect venue for dinner parties, functions, conferences, weddings or just a quiet drink. Traditional pub on site.

CHECK THE MAPS
The colour maps at the front of this guide show all the cities, towns and villages for which you will find accommodation entries. Refer to the town index to find the page on which they are listed.

ROSEDALE ABBEY, North Yorkshire Map ref 5C3

★★★

Family-owned country hotel in beautiful forest and moorland setting. Tastefully decorated restaurant with special emphasis on traditional English food and good wine. Quality en suite bedrooms, some ground floor. Cosy bars and lounges, log fires, period furniture and careful restoration combine to provide a hotel of exceptional character.

BLACKSMITHS COUNTRY INN

Hartoft End, Rosedale Abbey, Pickering
YO18 8EN
T: (01751) 417331
F: (01751) 417167
E: blacksmiths.rosedale@virgin.net
I: www.blacksmithsinn-rosedale.co.uk

Bedrooms: 1 single,
17 double/twin, 1 triple/
multiple
Bathrooms: 19 en suite

Lunch available
Evening meal available
CC: Delta, Mastercard,
Switch, Visa

B&B per night:
S £43.50–£49.50
D £67.00–£79.00

HB per person:
DY £45.00–£55.00

OPEN All year round

★★

MILBURN ARMS HOTEL
Rosedale Abbey, Pickering
YO18 8RA
T: (01751) 417312
F: (01751) 417541
E: info@milburnarms.com
I: www.milburnarms.com

Bedrooms: 11 double/
twin
Bathrooms: 11 en suite

Lunch available
Evening meal available
CC: Delta, Mastercard,
Switch, Visa

B&B per night:
S £41.50–£47.00
D £64.00–£80.00

OPEN All year round

Historic inn, in a picturesque conservation area village, central to national park and 15 miles from Yorkshire Heritage Coast. Restaurant noted for enjoyable, well-prepared food.

ROTHERHAM, South Yorkshire Map ref 4B2

★★★

BEST WESTERN CONSORT HOTEL
Brampton Road, Thurcroft,
Rotherham S66 9JA
T: (01709) 530022
F: (01709) 531529
E: info@consorthotel.com
I: www.consorthotel.com

Bedrooms: 25 double/
twin, 2 triple/multiple;
suites available
Bathrooms: 27 en suite

Lunch available
Evening meal available
CC: Amex, Delta, Diners,
Mastercard, Switch, Visa

B&B per night:
S £42.00–£72.00
D £62.00–£82.00

HB per person:
DY £58.00–£88.00

OPEN All year round

ⓒⓡ
Best Western Hotels

Modern hotel, fully air-conditioned and decorated to a high standard throughout, at the junction of M1 and M18 (access exits 31 and 33 off M1 and exit 1 off M18).

★★★

BEST WESTERN ELTON HOTEL
Main Street, Bramley, Rotherham
S66 2SF
T: (01709) 545681
F: (01709) 549100
E: bestwestern.eltonhotel@
btinternet.com
I: www.bestwestern.co.uk

Bedrooms: 9 single,
20 double/twin
Bathrooms: 29 en suite

Lunch available
Evening meal available
CC: Amex, Delta, Diners,
Mastercard, Switch, Visa

B&B per night:
S £49.00–£80.00
D £68.00–£98.00

HB per person:
DY £65.00–£100.00

OPEN All year round

ⓒⓡ
Best Western Hotels

200-year-old, stone-built house with modern extension and restaurant. Half mile from M18, 2 miles M1. Minimum prices for one-day stays apply weekends only.

TOWN INDEX
This can be found at the back of this guide. If you know where you want to stay, the index will give you the page number listing accommodation in your chosen town, city or village.

SCARBOROUGH, North Yorkshire Map ref 5D3 *Tourist Information Centre Tel: (01723) 373333*

★★★

BEIDERBECKE'S HOTEL AND RESTAURANT

1-3 The Crescent, Scarborough YO11 2PW
T: (01723) 365766
F: (01723) 367433
E: info@beiderbeckes.com
I: www.beiderbeckes.com

Property of historic interest in a beautiful Georgian terrace. Fully refurbished in 2000. Central to all amenities, theatre, shops, sea and spa. Own car park. Marmalade's, the hotel's restaurant (2 Rosettes) features live jazz on Friday, Saturday and Monday evenings. Lively Russian-themed flair bar with bar menu.

Bedrooms: 4 single, 23 double/twin; suites available
Bathrooms: 27 en suite

Lunch available
Evening meal available
CC: Mastercard, Switch, Visa

B&B per night:
S £40.00–£70.00
D £70.00–£120.00

HB per person:
DY £50.00–£70.00

OPEN All year round

★★★

ESPLANADE HOTEL
Belmont Road, Scarborough
YO11 2AA
T: (01723) 360382
F: (01723) 376137

Bedrooms: 17 single, 45 double/twin, 10 triple/multiple
Bathrooms: 72 en suite

Evening meal available
CC: Amex, Delta, Diners, Mastercard, Switch, Visa

Welcoming period-style hotel in good position on Scarborough's South Cliff. Close to beach, spa and town centre. Landau restaurant, parlour bar and roof terrace.

B&B per night:
S £47.00
D £89.00–£99.00

HB per person:
DY £53.00–£58.00

OPEN All year round

ⓒ
The Independents

★★

MANOR HEATH HOTEL

67 Northstead Manor Drive, Scarborough
YO12 6AF
T: (01723) 365720
F: (01723) 365720
E: enquiries@manorheath.co.uk
I: www.manorheath.co.uk

Detached hotel offering five-course dinner with choice of menu. Overlooking Peasholm Park and the sea. All rooms en suite with colour TV, radio alarm, tea making facilities. Double glazed and centrally heated. Private car park and garden. Children's reductions. OAP reductions in early/late season. Close to beach. A warm welcome awaits.

Bedrooms: 1 single, 6 double/twin, 7 triple/ multiple
Bathrooms: 14 en suite

Evening meal available
CC: Delta, Mastercard, Switch, Visa

B&B per night:
S £20.00–£24.00
D £40.00–£48.00

HB per person:
DY £28.00–£32.00

OPEN All year round

★★

RED LEA HOTEL
Prince of Wales Terrace, Scarborough YO11 2AJ
T: (01723) 362431
F: (01723) 371230
E: redlea@globalnet.co.uk
I: www.redleahotel.co.uk

Bedrooms: 19 single, 36 double/twin, 13 triple/multiple
Bathrooms: 68 en suite

Lunch available
Evening meal available
CC: Amex, Delta, Mastercard, Switch, Visa

Traditional hotel with sea views, close to the Spa Centre. Restaurant, bar, lounges, lift and colour TVs. Solarium and indoor heated swimming pool.

B&B per night:
S £35.00–£40.00
D £70.00–£80.00

HB per person:
DY £47.00–£52.00

OPEN All year round

PRICES

Please check prices and other details at the time of booking.

SCARBOROUGH continued

★★

RYNDLE COURT PRIVATE HOTEL

47 Northstead Manor Drive, Scarborough
YO12 6AF
T: (01723) 375188 & 07860 711517
F: (01723) 375188
E: enquiries@ryndlecourt.co.uk
I: www.ryndlecourt.co.uk

B&B per night:
S £29.00–£40.00
D £58.00–£62.00

HB per person:
DY £37.00–£41.00

Delightfully situated overlooking Peasholm Park near the sea and North Bay Leisure Parks. The Ryndle Court is a superbly appointed, detached 2 star hotel. All 14 bedrooms are en suite and comfortably furnished to a high standard. There is a relaxing coffee lounge, a residents' licensed bar and car park.

Bedrooms: 1 single,
10 double/twin, 3 triple/
multiple
Bathrooms: 14 en suite

Lunch available
Evening meal available
CC: Delta, Diners,
Mastercard, Switch, Visa

Please enquire about our 4 day Christmas programme inclusive of full board and entertainment.

SCISSETT, West Yorkshire Map ref 4B1

★★★

BAGDEN HALL
Wakefield Road, Scissett,
Huddersfield HD8 9LE
T: (01484) 865330
F: (01484) 861001
E: info@bagdenhall.demon.co.uk
I: www.bagdenhall.demon.co.uk

Bedrooms: 6 single,
11 double/twin
Bathrooms: 17 en suite

Lunch available
Evening meal available
CC: Amex, Delta, Diners,
Mastercard, Switch, Visa

B&B per night:
S £60.00
D £80.00–£100.00

HB per person:
DY £69.00–£79.00

OPEN All year round

Set in 40 acres of beautiful parkland and situated in the heart of 'Summer Wine' country yet only 10 minutes' drive from junctions 38 and 39 of M1.

SCUNTHORPE, North Lincolnshire Map ref 4C1

★★★★
Silver
Award

FOREST PINES HOTEL, GOLF COURSE AND SPA

Ermine Street, Broughton, Brigg DN20 0AQ
T: (01652) 650770 & 650756
F: (01652) 650495
E: enquiries@forestpines.co.uk
I: www.forestpines.co.uk

B&B per night:
S £70.00–£90.00
D £90.00–£100.00

OPEN All year round

CR

Best Western Hotels

Close to junction 4 M180, within easy reach Lincoln, Hull, York. This beautifully-appointed hotel, set in 190 acres of mature woodland with its own 27-hole championship golf course and health club, combined with the choice of exquisite food in the elegant restaurant or real ales in the cosy bars, offers the discerning guest unrivalled quality.

Bedrooms: 84 double/
twin; suites available
Bathrooms: 84 en suite

Lunch available
Evening meal available
CC: Amex, Delta, Diners,
Mastercard, Switch, Visa

USE YOUR *i*s

There are more than 550 Tourist Information Centres throughout England offering friendly help with accommodation and holiday ideas as well as suggestions of places to visit and things to do. You'll find TIC addresses in the local Phone Book.

★★★
Silver
Award

LOFTSOME BRIDGE COACHING HOUSE LTD

Loftsome Bridge, Wressle, Selby YO8 6EN
T: (01757) 630070
F: (01757) 633900
E: reception@loftsomebridge-hotel.co.uk
I: www.loftsomebridge-hotel.co.uk

B&B per night:
S £42.00–£47.00
D £52.00–£57.00

HB per person:
DY £61.95–£66.95

OPEN All year round

Nestling alongside the tranquil River Derwent, 5 minutes from the M62, 20 minutes' drive from York. Dating back to 1782, this family-run country house boasts superb French/ English restaurant, lounges, bar, open fires, large satellite TVs, Chippendale 4-poster room, country views, small lake with wildfowl, riverside walks.

Bedrooms: 12 double/ twin, 5 triple/multiple; suites available
Bathrooms: 17 en suite

Lunch available
Evening meal available
CC: Amex, Delta, Mastercard, Switch, Visa

★★

CUTLERS HOTEL
George Street, Sheffield S1 2PF
T: (0114) 273 9939
F: (0114) 276 8332
E: enquiries@cutlershotel.co.uk
I: www.cutlershotel.co.uk

Bedrooms: 10 single,
40 double/twin
Bathrooms: 50 en suite

Evening meal available
CC: Delta, Mastercard,
Switch, Visa

B&B per night:
S £48.50–£53.50
D £59.50–£64.50

OPEN All year round

Modern hotel superbly positioned in the city centre. Ideal location, friendly atmosphere. Recently refurbished, offering first class accommodation and a wide range of services.

★★★
Silver
Award

WHITLEY HALL HOTEL
Elliott Lane, Grenoside, Sheffield S35 8NR
T: (0114) 245 4444
F: (0114) 245 5414
E: reservations@whitleyhall.com
I: www.whitleyhall.com

Bedrooms: 2 single,
16 double/twin, 1 triple/
multiple; suites available
Bathrooms: 19 en suite

Lunch available
Evening meal available
CC: Amex, Delta, Diners,
Mastercard, Switch, Visa

B&B per night:
S £62.00–£88.00
D £78.00–£108.00

HB per person:
DY £63.00–£112.00

OPEN All year round

Elizabethan mansion with 30 acres of gardens, lakes and woodlands, a few miles from the centres of Sheffield, Rotherham and Barnsley. Food a speciality. Open to non-residents.

★★★
Silver
Award

CONISTON HALL LODGE AND RESTAURANT

Coniston Cold, Skipton BD23 4EB
T: (01756) 748080
F: (01756) 749487
E: conistonhall@clara.net
I: www.conistonhall.co.uk

B&B per night:
S £76.00–£85.00
D £87.00–£96.00

OPEN All year round

Delightful hotel, set in 1,200 acres of private Yorkshire Dales parkland, centred on a 24-acre lake. Ideal for walking and fishing holidays and as a base for exploring the dales. Public bar with log fire serving tapas dishes. En suite rooms, all with satellite TV. Superb cuisine and warm welcome guaranteed.

Bedrooms: 38 double/
twin, 2 triple/multiple
Bathrooms: 40 en suite

Lunch available
Evening meal available
CC: Amex, Delta, Diners,
Mastercard, Switch, Visa

On occasions we offer room only from just £30pppn based on 2 people sharing.

MAP REFERENCES
The map references refer to the colour maps at the front of this guide. The first figure is the map number; the letter and figure which follow indicate the grid reference on the map.

STOKESLEY, North Yorkshire Map ref 5C3

★★★
Silver
Award

WAINSTONES HOTEL
High Street, Great Broughton,
Stokesley, Middlesbrough TS9 7EW
T: (01642) 712268
F: (01642) 711560
E: wstones@netcomuk.co.uk
I: www.wainstoneshotel.co.uk

Bedrooms: 4 single,
19 double/twin, 1 triple/
multiple
Bathrooms: 24 en suite

Lunch available
Evening meal available
CC: Amex, Delta, Diners,
Mastercard, Switch, Visa

B&B per night:
S £55.00–£64.50
D £70.00–£82.50

OPEN All year round

Family-run hotel in the picturesque village of Great Broughton, ideally situated for visiting North Yorkshire coast, moors and dales.

THIRSK, North Yorkshire Map ref 5C3 *Tourist Information Centre Tel: (01845) 522755*

★★

ANGEL INN
Long Street, Topcliffe, Thirsk
YO7 3RW
T: (01845) 577237
F: (01845) 578000

Bedrooms: 2 single,
12 double/twin, 1 triple/
multiple
Bathrooms: 15 en suite

Lunch available
Evening meal available
CC: Delta, Mastercard,
Switch, Visa

B&B per night:
S £45.00
D £54.00–£60.00

OPEN All year round

Well-appointed, attractive village inn, renowned for good food and traditional ales. Ideal centre for touring York and Herriot Country.

★★
Silver
Award

GOLDEN FLEECE
Market Place, Thirsk YO7 1LL
T: (01845) 523108
F: (01845) 523996
I: www.bestwestern.co.uk

B&B per night:
S £55.00–£75.00
D £85.00–£110.00

HB per person:
DY £55.00–£75.00

OPEN All year round

Ⓒⓡ
Best Western Hotels

This historic coaching inn has attractive newly refurbished bedrooms, including some superior and antique 4-poster rooms. The bar and restaurant serve good food and fine wines as well as locally brewed ales. Ideally placed between dales and moors, and within walking distance of the 'World of James Herriot' visitor centre.

Bedrooms: 1 single,
16 double/twin, 1 triple/
multiple
Bathrooms: 18 en suite

Lunch available
Evening meal available
CC: Amex, Delta,
Mastercard, Switch, Visa

Seasonal offers for racing breaks and Herriot breaks.

THORNTON WATLASS, North Yorkshire Map ref 5C3

★

THE BUCK INN
Thornton Watlass, Ripon HG4 4AH
T: (01677) 422461
F: (01677) 422447
E: buckwatlass@btconnect.com

B&B per night:
S Min £40.00
D Min £60.00

HB per person:
DY Min £44.00

OPEN All year round

Friendly village inn overlooking delightful cricket green in quiet village. Just 5 minutes from A1. Relax in our comfortable bedrooms. Enjoy our superb home cooked food and drink from our selection of real ales. Large secluded garden with children's play area. Private river fly fishing. Ideal centre for exploring.

Bedrooms: 1 single,
5 double/twin, 1 triple/
multiple
Bathrooms: 5 en suite

Lunch available
Evening meal available
CC: Amex, Delta, Diners,
Mastercard, Switch, Visa

Golfing breaks arranged with special rates at several local courses.

IMPORTANT NOTE Information on accommodation listed in this guide has been supplied by the proprietors. As changes may occur you are advised to check details at the time of booking.

★★

BANK HOUSE HOTEL
11 Bank Street, Westgate,
Wakefield WF1 1EH
T: (01924) 368248
F: (01924) 363724
E: BankHouseHotel@amserve.net

Bedrooms: 5 single,
6 double/twin, 1 triple/
multiple
Bathrooms: 12 en suite

Lunch available
Evening meal available
CC: Amex, Delta, Diners,
Mastercard, Switch, Visa

B&B per night:
S £35.00–£38.00
D £38.00–£44.00

OPEN All year round

City centre licensed hotel run by professional staff. All rooms have en suite facilities, Sky Digital, telephones, tea/coffee facilities, restaurant facilities and room service.

★★

PARKLANDS HOTEL
143 Horbury Road, Wakefield WF2 8TY
T: (01924) 377407
F: (01924) 290348
E: steve@parklands23.fsnet.co.uk
I: www.parklandshotel.co.uk

B&B per night:
S £32.50–£44.50
D £46.50–£52.50

HB per person:
DY £34.75–£52.45

OPEN All year round

Old friends and new are always welcome at the Parklands Hotel and St Michael's Restaurant. Elegant Victorian former vicarage overlooking 680 acres of beautiful parkland. Family-run for over 35 years, providing a high standard of service and cuisine and well-appointed en suite bedrooms. Self-catering cottages also available.

Bedrooms: 8 single,
4 double/twin, 1 triple/
multiple
Bathrooms: 12 en suite,
1 private

Lunch available
Evening meal available
CC: Amex, Delta,
Mastercard, Switch, Visa

★★★
Silver
Award

WENTBRIDGE HOUSE HOTEL
Wentbridge, Pontefract WF8 3JJ
T: (01977) 620444
F: (01977) 620148
E: info@wentbridgehouse.co.uk
I: www.wentbridgehouse.co.uk

B&B per night:
S £65.00–£100.00
D £80.00–£110.00

OPEN All year round

Dating from 1700, 11 miles from Doncaster and situated in 20 acres of the beautiful Went Valley among century-old trees, Wentbridge House is famous for its special hospitality. Delicious, award-winning food and wines, first-rate service and individually furnished bedrooms combine to guarantee a truly memorable stay.

Bedrooms: 18 double/
twin
Bathrooms: 18 en suite

Lunch available
Evening meal available
CC: Amex, Delta, Diners,
Mastercard, Switch, Visa

Weekend breaks available. Please telephone for further information.

TOWN INDEX
This can be found at the back of this guide. If you know where you want to stay, the index will give you the page number listing accommodation in your chosen town, city or village.

WHITBY, North Yorkshire Map ref 5D3 *Tourist Information Centre Tel: (01947) 602674*

★★★

SAXONVILLE HOTEL
Ladysmith Avenue, Whitby YO21 3HX
T: (01947) 602631 & 0800 019 1147
F: (01947) 820523
E: newtons@saxonville.co.uk
I: www.saxonville.co.uk

B&B per night:
S £42.50–£47.50
D £85.00–£95.00

HB per person:
DY £53.50–£56.50

OPEN Apr–Oct

Family-owned and run since 1946. The hotel is situated on the West Cliff just a short stroll from Whitby's narrow streets and winding alleys. Guests are assured of a warm, friendly welcome and a high standard of service. Private car park. No supplement on single rooms.

Bedrooms: 4 single, 16 double/twin, 2 triple/ multiple
Bathrooms: 22 en suite

Lunch available
Evening meal available
CC: Delta, Mastercard, Switch, Visa

2-night spring weekend break £90. 3-day Feb half-term break £130. 3-day break any night during 2002 season £145.

★★

SNEATON HALL
Sneaton, Nr Whitby YO22 5HP
T: (01947) 605929
F: (01947) 820177
E: sneatonhall@supanet.com

Bedrooms: 5 double/ twin, 3 triple/multiple
Bathrooms: 8 en suite

Lunch available
Evening meal available
CC: Delta, Mastercard, Switch, Visa

B&B per night:
S £41.00–£58.00
D £52.00–£86.00

HB per person:
DY £36.00–£68.00

OPEN All year round

Family-owned and run, small, country house hotel in its own grounds with superb views, close to the sea and moors.

★★
Silver Award

STAKESBY MANOR
Manor Close, High Stakesby, Whitby YO21 1HL
T: (01947) 602773
F: (01947) 602140
E: relax@stakesby-manor.co.uk
I: www.stakesby-manor.co.uk

B&B per night:
S £57.00
D £78.00–£84.00

HB per person:
DY £52.00–£56.00

OPEN All year round

®
Minotel

Georgian house dating back to 1710, in its own grounds, on the outskirts of Whitby in the North York Moors National Park. Atmospheric oak panelled dining room serving freshly prepared food. Some non-smoking rooms. Open fires in winter. Views over moors or the roof tops of Whitby.

Bedrooms: 13 double/ twin
Bathrooms: 13 en suite

Lunch available
Evening meal available
CC: Amex, Delta, Mastercard, Switch, Visa

★★

WHITE HOUSE HOTEL
Upgang Lane, West Cliff, Whitby YO21 3JJ
T: (01947) 600469
F: (01947) 821600
E: Thomas.campbell1@btinternet. com
I: www.s-h-systems.co.uk/hotels/ whitehse.html

Bedrooms: 2 single, 5 double/twin, 3 triple/ multiple
Bathrooms: 10 en suite

Lunch available
Evening meal available
CC: Delta, Mastercard, Switch, Visa

B&B per night:
S £28.00–£33.50
D £56.00–£67.00

HB per person:
DY £38.00–£43.50

OPEN All year round

Family-run hotel in a unique position with panoramic views, overlooking Sandsend Bay, adjoining a golf-course. Emphasis on food.

CENTRAL RESERVATIONS OFFICES
The symbol ® and a group name in an entry indicate that bookings can be made through a central reservations office. These are listed in a separate section towards the back of this guide.

★★

Friendly, family-run 18thC inn with views across Ribble Valley to Pen-y-ghent and Ingleborough. Ideal base for touring and walking in Yorkshire Dales/ Forest of Bowland/ Lakes. Conservatory restaurant, oak-panelled dinning room, homemade food, real ales, fine wines and open fires.

PLOUGH INN AT WIGGLESWORTH

Wigglesworth, Skipton, Nr Settle BD23 4RJ
T: (01729) 840243 & 840638
F: (01729) 840638
E: steve@the-plough-wigglesworth.freeserve.co.uk
I: www.the-plough-wigglesworth.freeserve.co.uk

Bedrooms: 9 double/ twin, 3 triple/multiple
Bathrooms: 12 en suite

Lunch available
Evening meal available
CC: Mastercard, Switch, Visa

Spring, winter and autumn breaks; Christmas and New Year breaks (call for information); reduced rates 2 nights or more.

B&B per night:
S £42.00–£48.00
D £60.00–£80.00

HB per person:
DY £46.50–£58.50

OPEN All year round

 P

★★★
Silver
Award

Superbly appointed hotel with unrivalled location opposite York Minster. All the historic attractions of York are within easy walking distance. All bedrooms and public areas have been tastefully refurbished 2000/2001 and include 4 de-luxe rooms. Enjoy the award-winning food in the restaurant or cosy cafe conservatory. Secure car park and valet parking service.

DEAN COURT HOTEL

Duncombe Place, York YO1 7EF
T: (01904) 625082
F: (01904) 620305
E: info@deancourt-york.co.uk
I: www.deancourt-york.co.uk

Bedrooms: 9 single, 26 double/twin, 4 triple/ multiple; suites available
Bathrooms: 39 en suite

Lunch available
Evening meal available
CC: Amex, Delta, Diners, Mastercard, Switch, Visa

2 night mid-week Literary Breaks with top authors.
2 night mid-week wine and food breaks with top wine producers.

B&B per night:
S £75.00–£95.00
D £105.00–£130.00

HB per person:
DY £70.00–£82.50

OPEN All year round

Best Western Hotels

P

★★★
Silver
Award

Superior Regency townhouse of great charm and character just minutes from York Minster and city centre. Furnished in classic country house style, this beautifully restored Grade II Listed building has 30 luxurious en suite bedrooms, 3 superb restaurants, award-winning food and first class service. Excellent private dining facilities and free car park. YTB White Rose Award 2001.

THE GRANGE HOTEL

1 Clifton, York YO30 6AA
T: (01904) 644744
F: (01904) 612453
E: info@grangehotel.co.uk
I: www.grangehotel.co.uk

Bedrooms: 3 single, 26 double/twin, 1 suite
Bathrooms: 30 en suite

Lunch available
Evening meal available
CC: Amex, Delta, Diners, Mastercard, Switch, Visa

2 night breaks from £65pppn (2 sharing) including full English breakfast, table d'hote dinner and VAT. Christmas and New Year packages.

B&B per night:
S £100.00 £116.00
D £118.00–£220.00

OPEN All year round

P

SYMBOLS
The symbols in each entry give information about services and facilities. A key to these symbols appears at the back of this guide.

★★

HEDLEY HOUSE
3-4 Bootham Terrace, York YO30 7DH
T: (01904) 637404
F: (01904) 639774
E: h.h@mcmail.com
I: www.hedleyhouse.com

B&B per night:
S £30.00–£50.00
D £52.00–£90.00

HB per person:
DY £38.00–£70.00

OPEN All year round

Family-run hotel in a quiet residential area within 10 minutes' walk of the city centre. All rooms have private bathroom, remote colour TV, telephone and hospitality tray. Vegetarian and special diets catered for. Off-street car park and lock-up garages available.

Bedrooms: 2 single, 10 double/twin, 4 triple/ multiple
Bathrooms: 16 en suite

Lunch available
Evening meal available
CC: Amex, Delta, Mastercard, Switch, Visa

2-day mid-week break DB&B winter and spring.

♦♦♦♦♦♦♦♦♦♦♦♦♦♦P

★★★★

HILTON YORK
1 Tower Street, York YO1 9WD
T: (01904) 648111
F: (01904) 610317
E: reservations@york.stakis.co.uk
I: www.york.hilton.com

B&B per night:
S £124.00–£144.00
D £124.00–£144.00

OPEN All year round

The most centrally located 4 star hotel overlooking the medieval Clifford's Tower within easy walking distance of the Shambles, York Minster and other local attractions. Try our exciting new restaurant and bar, Tower's. If more casual is your style try our American-style diner, Henry J Beans.

Bedrooms: 130 double/ twin; suites available
Bathrooms: 130 en suite

Lunch available
Evening meal available
CC: Amex, Delta, Diners, Mastercard, Switch, Visa

♦♦♦♦♦♦♦♦♦♦♦♦♦♦♦♦♦P

★★

KILIMA HOTEL
129 Holgate Road, York YO24 4AZ
T: (01904) 625787
F: (01904) 612083
E: sales@kilima.co.uk
I: www.kilima.co.uk

B&B per night:
S £58.00–£75.00
D £86.00–£110.00

HB per person:
DY £63.00–£95.00

OPEN All year round

Ⓒ®
Best Western Hotels

Completely refurbished hotel with leisure centre including indoor swimming pool, Turkish steam room and fitness centre. Conference facility for 14 delegates, boardroom-style. Private car park. Within walking distance to city centre and historic attractions.

Bedrooms: 2 single, 19 double/twin, 5 triple/ multiple; suites available
Bathrooms: 26 en suite

Lunch available
Evening meal available
CC: Amex, Delta, Diners, Mastercard, Switch, Visa

♦♦♦♦♦♦♦♦♦♦♦♦♦♦♦♦P

★★

KNAVESMIRE MANOR HOTEL
302 Tadcaster Road, York YO24 1HE
T: (01904) 702941
F: (01904) 709274
E: enquire@knavesmire.co.uk
I: www.knavesmire.co.uk

Bedrooms: 1 single, 16 double/twin, 3 triple/ multiple
Bathrooms: 20 en suite

Evening meal available
CC: Amex, Delta, Diners, Mastercard, Switch, Visa

B&B per night:
S £49.00–£65.00
D £55.00–£75.00

HB per person:
DY £44.50–£49.50

OPEN All year round

The Circle

Once a Rowntree family home, overlooking York Racecourse whilst close to the city centre. Award-winning Brasserie restaurant. Walled gardens and car park. Private tropical pool and spa.

♦♦♦♦♦♦♦♦♦♦♦♦♦♦♦♦♦♦♦♦P

★★

LADY ANNE MIDDLETON'S HOTEL

Skeldergate, York YO1 6DS
T: (01904) 611570
F: (01904) 613043
E: bookings@ladyannes.co.uk
I: www.ladyannes.co.uk

B&B per night:
S £60.00–£80.00
D £80.00–£110.00

HB per person:
DY £48.00–£64.00

OPEN All year round

Collection of historic buildings in English courtyard gardens, close to the river and within city walls. Free car parking, short walk to all main attractions. Conservatory restaurant serves predominantly English dishes. Health club with fitness pool (not suitable for under 16s).

Bedrooms: 3 single, 46 double/twin, 3 triple/ multiple
Bathrooms: 52 en suite

Lunch available
Evening meal available
CC: Amex, Delta, Mastercard, Switch, Visa

★★

NEWINGTON HOTEL

147-157 Mount Vale, York
YO24 1DJ
T: (01904) 625173 & 623090
F: (01904) 679937
E: info@thenewington.co.uk
I: www.ladyannes.co.uk

Bedrooms: 6 single, 28 double/twin, 8 triple/ multiple
Bathrooms: 42 en suite

Lunch available
Evening meal available
CC: Amex, Delta, Mastercard, Switch, Visa

B&B per night:
S £50.00–£60.00
D £80.00–£110.00

HB per person:
DY £43.00–£67.00

OPEN All year round

Hotel in a fine Georgian terrace, next to York's famous racecourse and within walking distance of city centre. Car park, indoor swimming pool, sauna.

★★★

RAMADA JARVIS ABBEY PARK

The Mount, York YO24 1BN
T: (01904) 658301
F: (01904) 621224
I: www.jarvis.co.uk

Bedrooms: 4 single, 67 double/twin, 14 triple/multiple
Bathrooms: 85 en suite

Lunch available
Evening meal available
CC: Amex, Delta, Diners, Mastercard, Switch, Visa

B&B per night:
S £24.99–£99.00
D £49.98–£129.00

HB per person:
DY £47.50–£59.50

OPEN All year round

CR
Jarvis Hotels/Utell International

Explore York from this centrally located yet quiet hotel. Friendly service with a full bar and English restaurant. All rooms en-suite and 33 rooms refurbished in 1997.

★★

SAVAGES HOTEL

15 St Peter's Grove, Clifton, York YO30 6AQ
T: (01904) 610818
F: (01904) 627729

B&B per night:
S £25.00–£37.50
D £50.00–£75.00

HB per person:
DY £35.00–£47.50

OPEN All year round

A Victorian hotel, close to the city centre in peaceful tree-lined St Peter's Grove, Savages Hotel offers the comforts and services to make your stay a relaxing and memorable occasion. Comfortable, well-equipped bedrooms (some ground floor) and traditional restaurant serving fine food.

Bedrooms: 3 single, 14 double/twin, 4 triple/ multiple
Bathrooms: 21 en suite

Evening meal available
CC: Amex, Delta, Diners, Mastercard, Switch, Visa

CREDIT CARD BOOKINGS
If you book by telephone and are asked for your credit card number it is advisable to check the proprietor's policy should you cancel your reservation.

A brief guide to the main Towns and Villages offering accommodation in Yorkshire

A AYSGARTH, NORTH YORKSHIRE - Famous for its beautiful Falls - a series of 3 cascades extending for half a mile on the River Ure in Wensleydale. There is a coach and carriage museum at Yore Mill and a National Park Centre. A single-arched Elizabethan bridge spans the River Ure.

B BARNSLEY, SOUTH YORKSHIRE - Barnsley became rich through coal and glass. It has Norman origins and the ruins of Monk Bretton Priory include 13th C chapter house and church. Attractions are Cooper Art Gallery, Cannon Hall and Worsbrough Mill.

- **BEDALE, NORTH YORKSHIRE** - Ancient church of St Gregory and Georgian Bedale Hall occupy commanding positions over this market town situated in good hunting country. The hall, which contains interesting architectural features including great ballroom and flying-type staircase, now houses a library and museum.

- **BEVERLEY, EAST RIDING OF YORKSHIRE** - Beverley's most famous landmark is its beautiful medieval Minster dating from 1220, with Percy family tomb. Many attractive squares and streets, notably Wednesday and Saturday Market and North Bar Gateway. Famous racecourse. Market cross dates from 1714.

- **BOROUGHBRIDGE, NORTH YORKSHIRE** - On the River Ure, Boroughbridge was once an important coaching centre with 22 inns and in the 18th C a port for Knaresborough's linens. It has fine old houses, many trees and a cobbled square with market cross. Nearby stand 3 megaliths known as the Devil's Arrows.

- **BRADFORD, WEST YORKSHIRE** - City founded on wool, with fine Victorian and modern buildings. Attractions include the cathedral, city hall, Cartwright Hall, Lister Park, Moorside Mills Industrial Museum and National Museum of Photography, Film and Television.

- **BRANDESBURTON, EAST RIDING OF YORKSHIRE** - The village church retains work from the Norman period through to the 15th C, and the shaft of a medieval cross stands on the village green.

- **BRIDLINGTON, EAST RIDING OF YORKSHIRE** - Lively seaside resort with long sandy beaches, Leisure World and busy harbour with fishing trips in cobles. Priory church of St Mary whose Bayle Gate is now a museum. Mementoes of flying pioneer, Amy Johnson, in Sewerby Hall. Harbour Museum and Aquarium.

D DEWSBURY, WEST YORKSHIRE - Town most famous for woollen products, with history going back to Saxon times. Robin Hood is reputed to have died and been buried in the Cistercian convent in Kirklees Park nearby. Old custom of tolling the Devil's Knell on Christmas Eve to remind the devil of his defeat.

- **DONCASTER, SOUTH YORKSHIRE** - Ancient Roman town famous for its heavy industries, butterscotch and racecourse (St Leger), also centre of agricultural area. Attractions include 18th C Mansion House, Cusworth Hall Museum, Doncaster Museum, St George's Church, The Dome and Doncaster Leisure Park.

F FILEY, NORTH YORKSHIRE - Resort with elegant Regency buildings along the front and 6 miles of sandy beaches bounded by natural breakwater, Filey Brigg. Starting point of the Cleveland Way. St Oswald's church, overlooking a ravine, belonged to Augustinian canons until the Dissolution.

G GILLAMOOR, NORTH YORKSHIRE - Village much admired by photographers for its views of Farndale, including 'Surprise View' from the churchyard.

- **GOOLE, EAST RIDING OF YORKSHIRE** - Busy port on the River Ouse developed with the opening of the Aire and Calder Canal in 1826 and reminiscent of the Netherlands with its red brick buildings and flat, watery landscape. Goole Museum houses Garside Local History Collection.

H HALIFAX, WEST YORKSHIRE - Founded on the cloth trade, and famous for its building society, textiles, carpets and toffee. Most notable landmark is Piece Hall where wool merchants traded, now restored to house shops, museums and art gallery. Home also to Eureka! The Museum for Children.

- **HARROGATE, NORTH YORKSHIRE** - Major conference, exhibition and shopping centre, renowned for its spa heritage and award-winning floral displays, spacious parks and gardens. Famous for antiques, toffee, fine shopping and excellent tea shops, also its Royal Pump Rooms and Baths. Annual Great Yorkshire Show in July.

- **HAWES, NORTH YORKSHIRE** - The capital of Upper Wensleydale on the famous Pennine Way, Yorkshire's highest market town and renowned for great cheeses. Popular with walkers. Dales National Park Information Centre and Folk Museum. Nearby is spectacular Hardraw Force waterfall.

- **HAWORTH, WEST YORKSHIRE** - Famous since 1820 as home of the Bronte family. The Parsonage is now a Bronte Museum where furniture and possessions of the family are displayed. Moors and Bronte waterfalls nearby and steam trains on the Keighley and Worth Valley Railway pass through.

- **HELMSLEY, NORTH YORKSHIRE** - Delightful small market town with red roofs, warm stone buildings and cobbled market square, on the River Rye at the entrance to Ryedale and the North York Moors. Remains of 12th C castle, several inns and All Saints' Church.

- **HOWDEN, EAST RIDING OF YORKSHIRE** - Small town near the River Ouse, dominated by partly-ruined medieval church of St Peter's which has ancient origins but has been rebuilt in a range of architectural styles over the centuries. The ruined choir and chapter house are best seen from the picturesque market place.

CONFIRM YOUR BOOKING
You are advised to confirm your booking in writing.

- **HUDDERSFIELD, WEST YORKSHIRE** - Founded on wool and cloth, has a famous choral society. Town centre redeveloped, but several good Victorian buildings remain, including railway station, St Peter's Church, Tolson Memorial Museum, art gallery and nearby Colne Valley Museum.

ILKLEY, WEST YORKSHIRE - Former spa with an elegant shopping centre and famous for its ballad. The 16th C manor house, now a museum, displays local prehistoric and Roman relics. Popular walk leads up Heber's Ghyll to Ilkley Moor, with the mysterious Swastika Stone and White Wells, 18th C plunge baths.

KIRKBYMOORSIDE, NORTH YORKSHIRE - Attractive market town with remains of Norman castle. Good centre for exploring moors. Nearby are wild daffodils of Farndale.

LEEDS, WEST YORKSHIRE - Large city with excellent modern shopping centre and splendid Victorian architecture. Museums and galleries including Temple Newsam House (the Hampton Court of the North), Tetley's Brewery Wharf and the Royal Armouries Museum; also home of Opera North.

- **LEYBURN, NORTH YORKSHIRE** - Attractive Dales market town where Mary Queen of Scots was reputedly captured after her escape from Bolton Castle. Fine views over Wensleydale from nearby.

- **LIVERSEDGE, WEST YORKSHIRE** - Typical West Yorkshire town 3 miles north-west of Dewsbury.

MARKINGTON, NORTH YORKSHIRE - This pastoral village lies close to Fountains Abbey and was surrounded by a stone wall, still visible in places and formed by the Cistercian monks. Markington Hall was bequeathed to the Wilberforce family and houses mementoes of William Wilberforce.

- **MORLEY, WEST YORKSHIRE** On the outskirts of Leeds, just off the M62 and close to the M1. The Town Hall dominates the town. Textiles, engineering and coal-mining area.

NEWBY WISKE, NORTH YORKSHIRE - Village on the River Wiske in the Vale of Mowbray.

PONTEFRACT, WEST YORKSHIRE - Close to the A1, this town has a long history, being one of the oldest boroughs in the country. Famous for its castle and locally-processed liquorice, used for sweets and medicines. Also well-known for its racecourse.

ROSEDALE ABBEY, NORTH YORKSHIRE - Sturdy hamlet built around Cistercian nunnery in the reign of Henry II, in the middle of Rosedale, largest of the moorland valleys. Remains of 12th C priory. Disused lead mines on the surrounding moors.

- **ROTHERHAM, SOUTH YORKSHIRE** - In the Don Valley, Rotherham became an important industrial town in the 19th C with discovery of coal and development of iron and steel industry by Joshua Walker who built Clifton House, now the town's museum. Magnificent 15th C All Saints Church is town's showpiece.

SCARBOROUGH, NORTH YORKSHIRE - Large, popular East Coast seaside resort, formerly a spa town. Beautiful gardens and two splendid sandy beaches. Castle ruins date from 1100; fine Georgian and Victorian houses. Scarborough Millennium depicts 1,000 years of town's history. Sea Life Centre.

- **SCISSETT, WEST YORKSHIRE** - Pretty West Yorkshire village near Denby Dale.

- **SCUNTHORPE, NORTH LINCOLNSHIRE** - Consisted of 5 small villages until 1860 when extensive ironstone beds were discovered. Today an industrial 'garden town' with some interesting modern buildings. Nearby Normanby Hall contains fine examples of Regency furniture.

- **SELBY, NORTH YORKSHIRE** - Small market town on the River Ouse, believed to have been birthplace of Henry I, with a magnificent abbey containing much fine Norman and Early English architecture.

- **SHEFFIELD, SOUTH YORKSHIRE** - Local iron ore and coal gave Sheffield its prosperous steel and cutlery industries. The modern city centre has many interesting buildings - Cathedral, Cutlers' Hall, Crucible Theatre, Graves and Mappin Art Galleries. Meadowhall Shopping Centre nearby.

- **SKIPTON, NORTH YORKSHIRE** - Pleasant market town at gateway to Dales, with farming community atmosphere, a Palladian Town Hall, parish church and fully roofed castle at the top of the High Street. The Clifford family motto, 'Desoramis' is sculpted in huge letters on the parapet over the castle gateway.

- **STOKESLEY, NORTH YORKSHIRE** - Handsome market town midway between the North York Moors and the Cleveland border. Famous for its annual show in September.

THIRSK, NORTH YORKSHIRE - Thriving market town with cobbled square surrounded by old shops and inns. St Mary's Church is probably the best example of Perpendicular work in Yorkshire. House of Thomas Lord founder of Lord's Cricket Ground - is now a folk museum.

- **THORNTON WATLASS, NORTH YORKSHIRE** - Picturesque village in Lower Wensleydale.

WAKEFIELD, WEST YORKSHIRE - Thriving city with cathedral church of All Saints boasting 247-ft spire. Old Bridge, a 9-arched structure, has fine medieval chantry chapels of St Mary's. Fine Georgian architecture and good shopping centre (The Ridings). National Coal Mining Museum for England nearby.

- **WENTBRIDGE, WEST YORKSHIRE** - Village on the River Went, just off the A1 on the borders of North and West Yorkshire.

- **WHITBY, NORTH YORKSHIRE** - Quaint holiday town with narrow streets and steep alleys at the mouth of the River Esk. Captain James Cook, the famous navigator, lived in Grape Lane. 199 steps lead to St Mary's Church and St Hilda's Abbey overlooking harbour. Dracula connections. Gothic weekend every April.

YORK, NORTH YORKSHIRE - Ancient walled city nearly 2000 years old, containing many well-preserved medieval buildings. Its Minster has over 100 stained glass windows and is the largest Gothic cathedral in England. Attractions include Castle Museum, National Railway Museum, Jorvik Viking Centre and York Dungeon.

HEART of England

The home of Shakespeare, fine china and the grandest palaces in Britain, the region is full of surprises, from the thriving multicultural cities of Birmingham and Nottingham to countryside both dramatic and picturesque.

classic sights

Hardwick Hall – probably Britain's greatest Elizabethan house
Pottery & porcelain – factory tours of Royal Crown Derby, Wedgewood, Spode and more
Ironbridge Gorge – the world's first cast-iron bridge

country

The Cotswolds – picturebook England
The Peak District – moorland, limestone gorges and ancient woodlands

literary links

Stratford-upon-Avon – Royal Shakespeare Company; the homes of Shakespeare and his family
Nottingham – DH Lawrence Birthplace Museum

arts for all

Walsall – The New Art Gallery
Wightwick Manor – arts & crafts masterpiece
Arts Festivals – Bromsgrove, Malvern and Cheltenham

distinctively different

Cadbury World – Chocaholic heaven

The counties of Derbyshire, Gloucestershire, Herefordshire, Leicestershire, Lincolnshire, Northamptonshire, Nottinghamshire, Rutland, Shropshire, Staffordshire, Warwickshire, Worcestershire and West Midlands

FOR MORE INFORMATION CONTACT:

Heart of England Tourist Board
Larkhill Road, Worcester WR5 2EZ
Tel: (01905) 761100 Fax: (01905) 763450
Internet: www.visitheartofengland.com

The Pictures:
1 South Shropshire Hills
2 Brindley Place, Birmingham
3 Stratford-upon-Avon

Places to Visit - see pages 126-130
Where to Stay - see pages 131-162

125

PLACES to visit

You will find hundreds of interesting places to visit during your stay, just some of which are listed in these pages. Contact any Tourist Information Centre in the region for more ideas on days out.

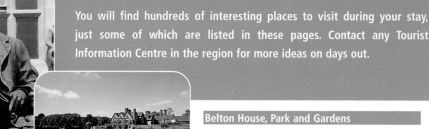

Belton House, Park and Gardens

Belton, Grantham, Lincolnshire NG32 2LS
Tel: (01476) 566116
The crowning achievement of restoration country house architecture, built in 1685-88 for Sir John Brownlow with alterations by James Wyatt in 1777.

Acton Scott Historic Working Farm

Wenlock Lodge, Acton Scott, Church Stretton, Shropshire SY6 6QN
Tel: (01694) 781306 www.actonscotmuseum.co.uk
Acton Scott Historic Working Farm demonstrates farming and rural life in south Shropshire at the close of the 19thC.

Alton Towers Theme Park

Alton, Stoke-on-Trent, Staffordshire ST10 4DB
Tel: (0870) 520 4060 www.alton-towers.co.uk
Theme Park with over 125 rides and attractions including Oblivion, Nemesis, Haunted House, Runaway Mine Train, Congo River Rapids, Log Flume and many children's rides.

The American Adventure

Ilkeston, Derbyshire DE7 5SX
Tel: (01773) 531521 www.americanadventure.co.uk
The American Adventure has action and entertainment for all ages including the Missile white-knuckle rollercoaster, Europe's tallest skycoaster and the world's wettest log flume.

Belvoir Castle Estate Office

Belvoir, Grantham, Lincolnshire NG32 1PD
Tel: (01476) 870262 www.belvoircastle.com
The present castle is the fourth to be built on this site and dates from 1816. Art treasures include works by Poussin, Rubens, Holbein and Reynolds. Queen's Royal Lancers display.

Birmingham Botanical Gardens and Glasshouses

Westbourne Road, Edgbaston, Birmingham, West Midlands B15 3TR
Tel: (0121) 454 1860
www.bham-bot-gdns.demon.co.uk
15 acres (6 ha) of ornamental gardens and glasshouses. Widest range of plants in the Midlands from tropical rainforest to arid desert. Aviaries with exotic birds, children's play area.

Black Country Living Museum

Tipton Road, Dudley, West Midlands DY1 4SQ
Tel: (0121) 557 9643 www.bclm.co.uk
A warm welcome awaits you at Britain's friendliest open-air museum. Wander around original shops and houses, or ride on fair attractions and take a look down the mine.

Blenheim Palace

Woodstock, Oxford, Oxfordshire OX7 1PX
Tel: (01993) 811325
Home of the 11th Duke of Marlborough, birthplace of Sir Winston Churchill. Designed by Vanbrugh in the English Baroque style. Park landscaped by 'Capability' Brown.

Butlins Family Entertainment Resort

Roman Bank, Skegness, Lincolnshire PE25 1NJ
Tel: (01754) 762311
Butlins Family Entertainment Resort has a skyline pavilion, toyland, sub-tropical waterworld, tenpin bowling and entertainments' centre with live shows.

Cadbury World

Linden Road, Bournville, Birmingham, West Midlands B30 2LD
Tel: (0121) 451 4180 www.cadburyworld.co.uk
Story of Cabdury's chocolate includes chocolate-making demonstration and attractions for all ages.

Chatsworth House and Garden

Bakewell, Derbyshire DE45 1PP
Tel: (01246) 582204 www.chatsworth-house.co.uk
Built in 1687-1707 with a collection of fine pictures, books, drawings and furniture. Garden laid out by 'Capability' Brown with fountains, cascades, a farmyard and playground.

Cotswold Farm Park

Guiting Power, Cheltenham, Gloucestershire GL54 5UG
Tel: (01451) 850307
Collection of rare breeds of British farm animals. Pets' corner, adventure playground, Tractor School, picnic area, gift shop, cafe and seasonal farming displays.

Drayton Manor Family Theme Park

Tamworth, Staffordshire B78 3TW
Tel: (01827) 287979 www.draytonmanor.co.uk
A major theme park with over 100 rides and attractions, plus children's rides, Zoo, farm, museums and the new, live 'Popeye Show'.

The Elgar Birthplace Museum

Crown East Lane, Lower Broadheath, Worcester, Worcestershire WR2 6RH
Tel: (01905) 333224 www.elgar.org
Country cottage birthplace displaying Elgar's desk and family possessions, complemented by new Elgar Centre. Memorabilia, sounds and special events illustrate his life.

The Galleries of Justice

Shire Hall, High Pavement, Lace Market, Nottingham, Nottinghamshire NG1 1HN
Tel: (0115) 952 0555 www.galleriesofjustice.org.uk
A museum of law located in and around a 19thC courthouse and county gaol, brought to life by costumed interpreters.

The Heights of Abraham Cable Cars, Caverns and Country Park

Matlock Bath, Matlock, Derbyshire DE4 3PD
Tel: (01629) 582365 www.heights-of-abraham.co.uk
A spectacular cable car ride takes you to the summit where, within the grounds, there is a wide variety of attractions for young and old alike. Gift shop and coffee shop.

Ikon Gallery

1 Oozells Square, Brindleyplace, Birmingham, West Midlands B1 2HS
Tel: (0121) 248 0708 www.ikongallery.co.uk
Ikon Gallery is one of Europe's foremost galleries for presenting the work of living artists within an innovative educational framework.

The Pictures:
1 Cottage Gardens, River Arrow, Herefordshire
2 Darwin Statue, Shrewsbury
3 Packwood House, Warwickshire
4 Rutland Water
5 Rockingham Castle, Northamptonshire

Ironbridge Gorge Museum

Ironbridge, Telford, Shropshire TF8 7AW
Tel: (01952) 433522 www.ironbridge.org.uk
World's first cast-iron bridge, Museum of the Gorge
Visitor Centre, Tar Tunnel, Jackfield Tile Museum, Coalport
China Museum, Rosehill House, Blists Hill Museum and
Museum of Iron.

Lincoln Castle

Castle Hill, Lincoln, Lincolnshire LN1 3AA
Tel: (01522) 511068
A medieval castle, including towers and ramparts, with a
Magna Carta exhibition, a prison chapel experience,
reconstructed Westgate and popular events throughout
the summer.

Museum of British Road Transport

Hales Street, Coventry, West Midlands CV1 1PN
Tel: (024) 7683 2425 www.mbrt.co.uk
200 cars and commercial vehicles from 1896 to date, 200
cycles from 1818 to date, 90 motorcycles from 1920 to
date and the 'Thrust 2' land speed story.

National Sea Life Centre

The Water's Edge, Brindleyplace, Birmingham,
West Midlands B1 2HL
Tel: (0121) 633 4700 www.sealife.co.uk
Over 55 fascinating displays. The opportunity to come
face-to-face with literally hundreds of fascinating sea
creatures, from sharks to shrimps.

The National Tramway Museum

Crich, Matlock, Derbyshire DE4 5DP
Tel: (01773) 852565 www.tramway.co.uk
A collection of over 70 trams from Britain and overseas
from 1873-1969 with tram rides on a 1-mile route, a
period street scene, depots, a power station, workshops
and exhibitions.

Nottingham Industrial Museum

Courtyard Buildings, Wollaton Park, Nottingham,
Nottinghamshire NG8 2AE
Tel: (0115) 915 3910 www.nottinghamcity.gov.uk
An 18thC stables presenting the history of Nottingham's
industries: printing, pharmacy, hosiery and lace. There is
also a Victorian beam engine, a horse gin and transport.

Peak District Mining Museum

The Pavilion, Matlock Bath, Matlock, Derbyshire DE4 3NR
Tel: (01629) 583834 www.peakmines.co.uk
A large exhibition on 3,500 years of lead mining with
displays on geology, mines and miners, tools and
engines. The climbing shafts make it suitable for children
as well.

Rockingham Castle

Rockingham, Market Harborough, Leicestershire LE16 8TH
Tel: (01536) 770240 www.rockinghamcastle.com
An Elizabethan house within the walls of a Norman
castle with fine pictures, extensive views, gardens with
roses and an ancient yew hedge.

Rugby School Museum

10 Little Church Street, Rugby, Warwickshire CV21 3AW
Tel: (01788) 556109
Rugby School Museum tells the story of the school, scene
of 'Tom Brown's Schooldays', and contains the earlier
memorabilia of the game invented on the school close.

Severn Valley Railway

The Railway Station, Bewdley, Worcestershire DY12 1BG
Tel: (01299) 403816 www.svr.co.uk
Preserved standard gauge steam railway running 16
miles between Kidderminster, Bewdley and Bridgnorth.
Collection of locomotives and passenger coaches.

Shakespeare's Birthplace

Henley Street, Stratford-upon-Avon, Warwickshire CV37 6QW
Tel: (01789) 204016 www.shakespeare.org.uk
The world-famous house where William Shakespeare was
born in 1564 and where he grew up. See the highly
acclaimed Shakespeare Exhibition.

The Shrewsbury Quest

193 Abbey Foregate, Shrewsbury, Shropshire SY2 6AH
Tel: (01743) 243324 www.shrewsburyquest.com
12thC medieval visitor attraction. Solve mysteries, create
illuminated manuscripts, play medieval games and relax
in unique herb gardens. Gift shop and cafe.

Shugborough Estate

Shugborough, Milford, Stafford, Staffordshire ST17 0XB
Tel: (01889) 881388 www.staffordshire.gov.uk
18thC mansion house with fine collection of furniture.
Gardens and park contain beautiful neo-classical
monuments.

Skegness Natureland Seal Sanctuary

North Parade, The Promenade, Skegness,
Lincolnshire PE25 1DB
Tel: (01754) 764345 www.skegnessnatureland.co.uk
Collection of performing seals, baby seals, penguins,
aquarium, crocodiles, snakes, terrapins, scorpions, tropical
birds, butterflies (April-October) and pets.

Snibston Discovery Park

Ashby Road, Coalville, Leicester, Leicestershire LE67 3LN
Tel: (01530) 278444 www.leics.gov.uk/museums
An all-weather and award-winning science and
industrial heritage museum.

Spode Visitor Centre

Spode, Church Street, Stoke-on-Trent,
Staffordshire ST4 1BX
Tel: (01782) 744011 www.spode.co.uk
Visitors are shown the various processes in the making of
bone china. Samples can be bought at the Spode Shop.

The Tales of Robin Hood

30-38 Maid Marian Way, Nottingham,
Nottinghamshire NG1 6GF
Tel: (0115) 948 3284
Join the world's greatest medieval adventure. Ride
through the magical green wood and play the Silver
Arrow game, in the search for Robin Hood.

Twycross Zoo

Twycross, Atherstone, Warwickshire CV9 3PX
Tel: (01827) 880250 www.twycrosszoo.com
A zoo with gorillas, orang-utans, chimpanzees, a modern
gibbon complex, elephants, lions, giraffes, a reptile
house, pets' corner and rides.

Walsall Arboretum

Lichfield Street, Walsall, West Midlands WS1 1TJ
Tel: (01922) 653148 www.walsallarboretum.co.uk
Picturesque Victorian park with over 79 acres (32 ha) of
gardens, lakes and parkland.

Warwick Castle

Warwick, Warwickshire CV34 4QU
Tel: (01926) 406600 www.warwick-castle.co.uk
Set in 60 acres (24 ha) of grounds with state rooms,
armoury, dungeon, torture chamber, clock tower, A Royal
Weekend Party 1898, Kingmaker – a preparation for
battle attractions.

The Wedgwood Story Visitor Centre

Barlaston, Stoke-on-Trent, Staffordshire ST12 9ES
Tel: (01782) 204218 www.thewedgwoodstory.com
New £4.5 million visitor centre. It exhibits centuries of
craftsmanship on a plate. Audio guided tour includes
exhibition and demonstration areas. Shop and
restaurants.

The Wildfowl and Wetlands Trust

The Wildfowl and Wetlands Trust
Slimbridge, Gloucester, Gloucestershire GL2 7BT
Tel: (01453) 890333 www.wwt.org.uk
Tropical house, hides, heated observatory, exhibits, shop,
restaurant, children's playground, pond zone.

Worcester Cathedral

10A College Green, Worcester,
Worcestershire WR1 2LH
Tel: (01905) 611002
Norman crypt and chapter house, King John's Tomb,
Prince Arthur's Chantry, medieval cloisters and buildings.
Touch and hearing control visually impaired facilities
available.

The Pictures:
1 Alford Craft Market, Lincolnshire
2 Chatsworth House, Derbyshire

Find out more about
HEART of England

Further information about holidays and attractions in Heart of England is available from:

HEART OF ENGLAND TOURIST BOARD
Larkhill Road, Worcester WR5 2EZ.
Tel: (01905) 761100 Fax: (01905) 763450
Internet: www.visitheartofengland.com

The following publications are available free from the Heart of England Tourist Board:

Heart of England - The Official Guide 2002
Bed & Breakfast Touring Map including Caravan and Camping

Getting to the
HEART of England

BY ROAD: Britain's main motorways (M1/M6/M5) meet in the Heart of England; the M40 links with the M42 south of Birmingham while the M4 provides fast access from London to the south of the region. These road links ensure that the Heart of England is more accessible by road than any other region in the UK.

BY RAIL: The Heart of England lies at the centre of the country's rail network. There are direct trains from London and other major cities to many towns and cities within the region.

The Pictures:
1 River Avon, Evesham
2 Black Country Museum, Dudley

Heart of England

Accommodation entries in this region are listed in alphabetical order of place name, and then in alphabetical order of establishment. As West Oxfordshire and Cherwell are promoted in both Heart of England and South of England, places in these areas with accommodation are listed in this section. See South of England for full West Oxfordshire and Cherwell entries.

Map references refer to the colour location maps at front of this guide. The first number indicates the map to use; the letter and number which follow refer to the grid reference on the map.

At-a-glance symbols at the end of each accommodation entry give useful information about services and facilities. A key to symbols can be found inside the back cover flap. Keep this open for easy reference.

A brief description of the towns and villages offering accommodation in the entries which follow, can be found at the end of this section.

A complete listing of all the English Tourism Council assessed accommodation covered by this guide appears at the back of the guide.

ABBOTS SALFORD, Warwickshire Map ref 2B1

★★★
Silver
Award

SALFORD HALL HOTEL
Abbots Salford, Evesham WR11 5UT
T: (01386) 871300 & 0800 212671
F: (01386) 871301
E: reception@salfordhall.co.uk
I: www.salfordhall.co.uk

Bedrooms: 2 single,
31 double/twin
Bathrooms: 33 en suite

Lunch available
Evening meal available
CC: Amex, Delta, Diners,
Mastercard, Switch, Visa

B&B per night:
S £75.00–£150.00
D £118.00–£150.00

HB per person:
DY £72.50–£97.50

OPEN All year round

Historic, noble manor house, lovingly restored, situated 8 miles west of Stratford-upon-Avon. Atmospheric charm and character of times past, combined with modern comfort.

🄒

Best Western Hotels

Ⓜ🐎⛱🛏&☎🖥📠↓🍷⑤⇙🎿💿🍴🐟🦢🔍↻⟂✳🦢🏮P

ALCESTER, Warwickshire Map ref 2B1

★★★

KINGS COURT HOTEL
Kings Coughton, Alcester B49 5QQ
T: (01789) 763111
F: (01789) 400242
E: info@kingscourthotel.co.uk
I: www.kingscourthotel.co.uk

Bedrooms: 6 single,
35 double/twin, 1 triple/
multiple
Bathrooms: 42 en suite

Lunch available
Evening meal available
CC: Amex, Delta,
Mastercard, Switch, Visa

B&B per night:
S Min £59.00
D Min £86.00

OPEN All year round

Delightful bedrooms set around main part of the hotel, which is a listed Tudor farmhouse. Excellent home-cooked bar and restaurant meals. Close to Stratford-upon-Avon and the Cotswolds.

Ⓜ🐎⛱&☎🖥📠↓🍷⑤⇙🎿📖🍴✳🐎🦢🏮P

---

www.travelengland.org.uk
Log on for information and inspiration. The latest information on places to visit, events and quality assessed accommodation.

ALREWAS, Staffordshire Map ref 4B3

★★

CLAYMAR HOTEL AND RESTAURANT
118a Main Street, Alrewas,
Burton upon Trent DE13 7AE
T: (01283) 790202 & 791281
F: (01283) 791465

Bedrooms: 2 single,
14 double/twin, 4 triple/
multiple
Bathrooms: 20 en suite

Lunch available
Evening meal available
CC: Delta, Mastercard,
Visa

B&B per night:
S Min £42.00
D Min £52.00

OPEN All year round

Privately-run hotel and restaurant. Interesting menu at realistic prices. Bar and children's menu available. Reservations required for Sunday lunch. Convenient for all Staffordshire attractions.

ASHBOURNE, Derbyshire Map ref 4B2 *Tourist Information Centre Tel: (01335) 343666*

★

THE BENTLEY BROOK INN AND FENNY'S RESTAURANT

Fenny Bentley, Ashbourne DE6 1LF
T: (01335) 350278
F: (01335) 350422
E: all@bentleybrookinn.co.uk
I: www.bentleybrookinn.co.uk

B&B per night:
S £35.00–£45.00
D £50.00–£65.00

HB per person:
DY £37.50–£50.00

OPEN All year round

A great place to eat, drink and stay for holidays or business; a traditional, family-run, busy country inn with large garden. Open all day. Close to Tissington Trail, Carsington Water, Dovedale, Chatsworth, Alton Towers. Good home-cooked food served in both bar and restaurant. Real ales from our on-site brewery.

Bedrooms: 1 single,
8 double/twin
Bathrooms: 6 en suite,
1 private

Lunch available
Evening meal available
CC: Amex, Delta, Diners,
Mastercard, Switch, Visa

Medieval banquets; Burns Night suppers; St Georges Day celebrations; beer festival.

BERKELEY, Gloucestershire Map ref 2B1

★★

NEWPORT TOWERS HOTEL
Newport, Berkeley GL13 9PX
T: (01453) 810575
F: (01453) 511062

Bedrooms: 1 single,
53 double/twin, 2 triple/
multiple
Bathrooms: 56 en suite

Lunch available
Evening meal available
CC: Amex, Delta, Diners,
Mastercard, Switch, Visa

B&B per night:
S £40.00
D £45.00

OPEN All year round

Budget hotel within a short drive of the picturesque villages of the Cotswolds. Other local attractions include Berkeley Castle and Slimbridge Wildfowl Trust.

BIGGIN-BY-HARTINGTON, Derbyshire Map ref 4B2

★★

BIGGIN HALL

Biggin-by-Hartington, Buxton SK17 0DH
T: (01298) 84451
F: (01298) 84681
E: bigginhall@compuserve.com
I: www.bigginhall.co.uk

B&B per night:
S £50.00–£80.00
D £60.00–£94.00

HB per person:
DY £37.00–£60.00

OPEN All year round

17thC hall, Grade II* Listed, 1,000 feet up in tranquil countryside in Peak District National Park. Sympathetically modernised. Fresh home cooking and comforts. Beautiful, uncrowded walks from the grounds. Close to Chatsworth, Haddon Hall, Dovedale, etc.

Bedrooms: 1 single,
14 double/twin, 5 triple/
multiple
Bathrooms: 20 en suite

Lunch available
Evening meal available
CC: Amex, Delta,
Mastercard, Switch, Visa

Icebreaker specials Nov–Mar for stays of 2 or more nights. Full English breakfast, packed lunch, and mulled wine before dinner incl.

ACCESSIBILITY

Look for the symbols which indicate accessibility for wheelchair users. A list of establishments is at the front of this guide.

BIRMINGHAM, West Midlands Map ref 4B3 *Tourist Information Centre Tel: (0121) 643 2514 (City Arcade)*

★★★ **ARDEN HOTEL AND LEISURE CLUB**
Coventry Road, Bickenhill, Solihull
B92 0EH
T: (01675) 443221
F: (01675) 445604
E: enquires@ardenhotel.co.uk
I: www.ardenhotel.co.uk

Bedrooms: 28 single,
182 double/twin,
6 triple/multiple
Bathrooms: 216 en suite

Lunch available
Evening meal available
CC: Amex, Delta, Diners,
Mastercard, Switch, Visa

B&B per night:
S £65.00–£109.75
D £75.00–£149.50

HB per person:
DY £55.00–£125.00

Perfect location next to NEC, railway, airport and motorway network. Privately owned and managed. Leisure complex includes swimming pool, sauna and jacuzzi. Free car parking.

OPEN All year round

BIRMINGHAM AIRPORT

See under Birmingham, Coventry, Solihull

BOURTON-ON-THE-WATER, Gloucestershire Map ref 2B1 *Tourist Information Centre Tel: (01451) 820211*

★★★ **APPLE PIE HOUSE HOTEL**
Whiteshoots Hill, Bourton-on-the-
Water, Cheltenham GL54 2LE
T: (01451) 820387
F: (01451) 812821
E: hotel@bourton.com
I: www.bourton.com

Bedrooms: 7 double/
twin, 2 triple/multiple
Bathrooms: 9 en suite

Lunch available
Evening meal available
CC: Amex, Delta,
Mastercard, Switch, Visa

B&B per night:
S £35.00–£50.00
D £40.00–£105.00

HB per person:
DY £37.95–£70.45

Family-run hotel with friendly atmosphere and traditional home cooking. Panoramic views from most bedrooms. Bourton-on-the-Water close by. Within easy driving distance of Cirencester, Cheltenham, Stratford.

OPEN All year round

★★
Silver
Award

THE DIAL HOUSE HOTEL
The Chestnuts, Bourton-on-the-Water,
Cheltenham GL54 2AN
T: (01451) 822244
F: (01451) 810126
E: info@dialhousehotel.com
I: www.dialhousehotel.com

B&B per night:
S £40.00–£57.00
D £90.00–£114.00

HB per person:
DY £60.00–£75.00

OPEN All year round

Built in 1698 of Cotswold stone, the hotel nestles peacefully in village centre within 1.5 acres of walled gardens. All rooms are individually decorated, some with 4-posters. The Inglenook Restaurant has been awarded 2 rosettes for excellent cuisine. Comfortable lounge with log fire.

Bedrooms: 1 single,
11 double/twin, 1 triple/
multiple
Bathrooms: 12 en suite,
1 private

Lunch available
Evening meal available
CC: Amex, Delta,
Mastercard, Switch, Visa

Bargain breaks available all year.

BRIDGNORTH, Shropshire Map ref 4A3 *Tourist Information Centre Tel: (01746) 763257*

★ **THE CROFT HOTEL**
St. Mary's Street, Bridgnorth
WV16 4DW
T: (01746) 762416 & 767155
F: (01746) 767431

Bedrooms: 3 single,
5 double/twin, 4 triple/
multiple
Bathrooms: 10 en suite

Lunch available
Evening meal available
CC: Amex, Mastercard,
Visa

B&B per night:
S £25.00–£41.50
D £46.00–£52.00

HB per person:
DY £35.50–£58.60

Listed building with a wealth of oak beams, in an old street. Family-run and an ideal centre for exploring the delightful Shropshire countryside.

OPEN All year round

QUALITY ASSURANCE SCHEME
Star ratings and awards were correct at the time of going to press but are subject to change. Please check at the time of booking.

BRIDGNORTH continued

★★★
Gold
Award

Luxury country house hotel in the peaceful hamlet of Worfield. The restaurant boasts many awards with menus sourcing fresh local ingredients. Ideal location for business or pleasure. Within easy reach of motorway routes. Local attractions include Severn Valley Railway and Ironbridge Gorge. HB prices based on two-night stay.

THE OLD VICARAGE HOTEL

Worfield, Bridgnorth WV15 5JZ
T: (01746) 716497 & 0800 0968010
F: (01746) 716552
E: admin@the-old-vicarage.demon.co.uk
I: www.oldvicarageworfield.com

Bedrooms: 13 double/ twin, 1 triple/multiple; suites available
Bathrooms: 14 en suite

Lunch available
Evening meal available
CC: Amex, Delta, Diners, Mastercard, Switch, Visa

Leisure break rates for 2 nights or more including dinner, bed and breakfast, third night free bed and breakfast. Subject to availablility.

B&B per night:
S £80.00–£120.00
D £120.00–£185.00

HB per person:
DY £160.00–£225.00

OPEN All year round

Pride of Britain

BROADWAY, Worcestershire Map ref 2B1

★★★
Silver
Award

BROADWAY HOTEL
The Green, Broadway WR12 7AA
T: (01386) 852401
F: (01386) 853879
E: Bookings@
cotswold-inns-hotels.co.uk
I: www.cotswold-inns-hotel.co.uk

Bedrooms: 3 single, 17 double/twin
Bathrooms: 20 en suite

Lunch available
Evening meal available
CC: Amex, Delta, Diners, Mastercard, Switch, Visa

Grade II Listed 17thC hotel in the heart of picturesque village. Newly refurbished, combining stylish modern fabrics and decoration with antique furniture.

B&B per night:
S £75.00–£80.00
D £118.00–£140.00

HB per person:
DY £96.95–£101.95

OPEN All year round

Grand Heritage Hotels

BURFORD, Oxfordshire

See South of England region

CASTLE DONINGTON, Leicestershire Map ref 4C3

★★★

This 18thC coaching inn retains many of its original features and all of its relaxed Regency elegance. The hotel has been considerably extended, achieving a harmonious blend of old and new. Excellent restaurant with classic Anglo-French cuisine. Two miles from the M1, junction 24, and close to Donington Park motor circuit and East Midlands Airport.

DONINGTON MANOR HOTEL

High Street, Castle Donington, Derby
DE74 2PP
T: (01332) 810253
F: (01332) 850330
E: cngrist@dmhgrist.demon.co.uk
I: www.doningtonmanorhotel.co.uk

Bedrooms: 2 single, 25 double/twin, 1 triple/ multiple
Bathrooms: 28 en suite

Lunch available
Evening meal available
CC: Amex, Delta, Diners, Mastercard, Switch, Visa

Off-peak weekends: 4-poster, 3-course dinner and bottle of French house wine £90 per couple per night. £80 if 2nd night booked.

B&B per night:
S £68.00–£85.00
D £82.00–£105.00

OPEN All year round

SPECIAL BREAKS
Many establishments offer special promotions and themed breaks. These are highlighted in red. (All such offers are subject to availability.)

★★★
Gold
Award

BROCKENCOTE HALL
Chaddesley Corbett, Kidderminster
DY10 4PY
T: (01562) 777876
F: (01562) 777872
E: info@brockencotehall.com
I: www.brockencotehall.com

B&B per night:
S £110.00–£130.00
D £135.00–£170.00

HB per person:
DY £87.50–£157.50

OPEN All year round

Country house hotel set in 70 acres of parkland, offering traditional French cooking in an elegant and relaxed atmosphere. Heart of England Tourist Board Independent Hotel of the Year 1998.

Bedrooms: 15 double/
twin, 2 triple/multiple
Bathrooms: 17 en suite

Lunch available
Evening meal available
CC: Amex, Diners,
Mastercard, Switch, Visa

CR
Grand Heritage Hotels

Special mid-week offers.

★★★

CARLTON HOTEL
Parabola Road, Cheltenham GL50 3AQ
T: (01242) 514453
F: (01242) 226487
E: enquires@thecarltonhotel.co.uk
I: www.thecarltonhotel.co.uk

B&B per night:
S £36.50–£65.00
D £73.00–£87.00

HB per person:
DY £40.00–£47.00

OPEN All year round

Conveniently situated in the centre of Cheltenham in a quiet road. Excellently-appointed bedrooms in professional, family-run hotel. Excellent bar and restaurant facilities. Ideal for business, leisure and group bookings.

Bedrooms: 16 single,
59 double/twin
Bathrooms: 75 en suite

Lunch available
Evening meal available
CC: Amex, Delta, Diners,
Mastercard, Switch, Visa

Special weekend breaks and group rates available.

★★★

CHARLTON KINGS HOTEL
London Road, Charlton Kings, Cheltenham
GL52 6UU
T: (01242) 231061
F: (01242) 241900
E: enquiries@charltonkingshotel.co.uk
I: www.charltonkingshotel.co.uk

B&B per night:
S £50.00–£81.00
D £92.00–£105.00

HB per person:
DY £65.95–£89.95

OPEN All year round

A pretty Victorian property, set in an acre of award-winning gardens, situated on the outskirts of Cheltenham. All rooms are beautifully furnished, with en suite bath/shower room. The restaurant provides interesting and varied menus. Light snacks can be enjoyed in the conservatory. Informally run but with high standards throughout.

Bedrooms: 2 single,
9 double/twin, 3 triple/
multiple
Bathrooms: 14 en suite

Lunch available
Evening meal available
CC: Amex, Delta,
Mastercard, Switch, Visa

Sun evenings only: singles £30, doubles £50 for 2. Includes full English breakfast. Excl Bank Hol weekends, Christmas and New Year.

CHECK THE MAPS
The colour maps at the front of this guide show all the cities, towns and villages for which you will find accommodation entries. Refer to the town index to find the page on which they are listed.

★★★

300-year-old country manor house hotel, set in 5 acres of secluded grounds only 1 mile from the centre of Regency Cheltenham. Acclaimed restaurant, en suite character bedrooms, 4-posters, log fires. Excellent walking. Ideal base for Warwick, Bath and Oxford. Special Cotswold Breaks offer.

THE PRESTBURY HOUSE HOTEL AND RESTAURANT

The Burgage, Prestbury, Cheltenham
GL52 3DN
T: (01242) 529533
F: (01242) 227076
E: sandjw@freenetname.co.uk
I: www.prestburyhouse.co.uk

Bedrooms: 1 single,
16 double/twin
Bathrooms: 17 en suite

Lunch available
Evening meal available
CC: Amex, Diners,
Mastercard, Switch, Visa

Fri/Sat/Sun: 2 consecutive nights for 2 sharing en suite bedroom plus breakfast £160 inclusive. (£20 supplement for 4-poster).

B&B per night:
S £60.00–£78.00
D £80.00–£92.00

OPEN All year round

CHESTERFIELD, Derbyshire Map ref 4B2 *Tourist Information Centre Tel: (01246) 345777*

★★

A comfortable hotel in a quiet location near town centre and only 10 minutes' drive from the famous Peak District. We have private car parking, small bar and lounge. In our restaurant we serve dinner every night apart from Sunday; all food served is made from fresh local produce.

ABBEYDALE HOTEL

Cross Street, Chesterfield S40 4TD
T: (01246) 277849
F: (01246) 558223
E: Abbeydale1ef@cs.com
I: www.abbeydalehotel.co.uk

Bedrooms: 4 single,
6 double/twin, 1 triple/
multiple
Bathrooms: 11 en suite

Lunch available
Evening meal available
CC: Delta, Mastercard,
Switch, Visa

Fri-Sun, incl B&B plus dinner Sat night, £125 for 2 people sharing a double room.

B&B per night:
S £40.00–£50.00
D £55.00–£65.00

OPEN All year round

★★★

Country house hotel, c1804, in extensive grounds. Excellent restaurant, popular bar. Easy to find and plenty of parking. Situated at the gateway to 29 acres of gardens and parkland. Sensitively refurbished during the year 2000. Leisure facilities planned in late 2001.

RINGWOOD HALL HOTEL

Brimington, Chesterfield S43 1DQ
T: (01246) 280077
F: (01246) 472241
E: reception@ringwoodhall.fsnet.co.uk
I: www.lyrichotels.co.uk

Bedrooms: 1 single,
30 double/twin
Bathrooms: 31 en suite

Lunch available
Evening meal available
CC: Amex, Delta, Diners,
Mastercard, Switch, Visa

Special event evenings through the year, predominantly on Fridays and Sundays incl live band, performing songs from the West End and Broadway.

B&B per night:
S £45.00–£70.00
D £60.00–£88.00

HB per person:
DY £35.00–£55.00

OPEN All year round

REGIONAL TOURIST BOARD The **M** symbol in an establishment entry indicates that it is a Regional Tourist Board member.

CHIPPING CAMPDEN, Gloucestershire Map ref 2B1

★★★ **NOEL ARMS HOTEL**
High Street, Chipping Campden
GL55 6AT
T: (01386) 840317
F: (01386) 841136
E: bookings@cotswold-inns-hotels.
co.uk
I: www.cotswold-inns-hotels.co.uk

14thC coaching inn set in beautiful Cotswold countryside. Oak-panelled restaurant. Traditional ales and meals served in Dovers Bar.

Bedrooms: 25 double/
twin, 1 triple/multiple
Bathrooms: 26 en suite

Lunch available
Evening meal available
CC: Amex, Delta, Diners,
Mastercard, Switch, Visa

B&B per night:
S Min £80.00
D £115.00–£135.00

HB per person:
DY Min £101.95

OPEN All year round

ⒸⓇ
Grand Heritage Hotels

★★★

THREE WAYS HOUSE
Chapel Lane, Mickleton, Chipping Campden
GL55 6SB
T: (01386) 438429
F: (01386) 438118
E: threeways@puddingclub.com
I: www.puddingclub.com

Cotswold village hotel close to Chipping Campden, Broadway and Stratford-upon-Avon. Comfortable bedrooms, some with pudding themes, cosy bar, good food and attentive service. Seen many times on TV as 'Home of the Pudding Club' where meetings of pudding lovers occur regularly. New, stylish and air conditioned restaurant.

Bedrooms: 3 single,
33 double/twin, 5 triple/
multiple
Bathrooms: 41 en suite

Lunch available
Evening meal available
CC: Amex, Delta, Diners,
Mastercard, Switch, Visa

Pudding Club breaks, walking weekend and chocoholic breaks are all available throughout the year.

B&B per night:
S £66.00–£76.00
D £98.00–£128.00

OPEN All year round

ⒸⓇ
The Circle

CHURCH STRETTON, Shropshire Map ref 4A3

★★ **LONGMYND HOTEL**
Cunnery Road, Church Stretton
SY6 6AG
T: (01694) 722244
F: (01694) 722718
E: reservations@longmynd.co.uk
I: www.longmynd.co.uk

Family-run country hotel commanding panoramic views of the south Shropshire highlands. Situated in an Area of Outstanding Natural Beauty. Self-catering lodges available.

Bedrooms: 6 single,
35 double/twin, 9 triple/
multiple; suites available
Bathrooms: 50 en suite

Lunch available
Evening meal available
CC: Amex, Delta, Diners,
Mastercard, Switch, Visa

B&B per night:
S £58.00–£68.00
D £105.00–£136.00

HB per person:
DY £52.50–£79.00

OPEN All year round

CIRENCESTER, Gloucestershire Map ref 2B1 *Tourist Information Centre Tel: (01285) 654180*

★★★

CROWN OF CRUCIS
Ampney Crucis, Cirencester GL7 5RS
T: (01285) 851806
F: (01285) 851735
E: info@thecrownofcrucis.co.uk
I: www.thecrownofcrucis.co.uk

Delightful, privately owned 16thC Cotswold hotel and coaching inn with elegant fully en suite bedrooms overlooking continental-style courtyard and village cricket pitch. Excellent local reputation for quality food and friendly service. Award-winning restaurant and traditional Cotswold bar both with extensive and varied menu. Quiet riverside location 2.5 miles east of Cirencester.

Bedrooms: 25 double/
twin
Bathrooms: 25 en suite

Lunch available
Evening meal available
CC: Amex, Delta, Diners,
Mastercard, Switch, Visa

Special summer breaks from £45–£50pppn incl 3 course dinner and full English breakfast min 2 night stay.

B&B per night:
S £46.00–£64.00
D £66.00–£92.00

HB per person:
DY Min £80.00

OPEN All year round

CIRENCESTER continued

★★ FLEECE HOTEL

Market Place, Cirencester GL7 2NZ
T: (01285) 658507
F: (01285) 651017
E: relax@fleecehotel.co.uk
I: www.fleecehotel.co.uk

Bedrooms: 5 single,
21 double/twin, 4 triple/
multiple; suites available
Bathrooms: 25 en suite,
4 private

Lunch available
Evening meal available
CC: Amex, Delta,
Mastercard, Switch, Visa

B&B per night:
S £39.50–£107.95
D £79.00–£129.90

HB per person:
DY £49.50–£78.90

OPEN All year round

Set in the gateway to the Cotswolds, this charming Tudor coaching inn has 25 en suite bedrooms. Its restaurant and brasserie have earned it an enviable reputation for good food.

Utell International

★★★ STRATTON HOUSE HOTEL

Gloucester Road, Cirencester
GL7 2LE
T: (01285) 651761
F: (01285) 640024
E: stratton.house@forestdale.com
I: www.forestdale.com

Bedrooms: 4 single,
40 double/twin
Bathrooms: 44 en suite

Lunch available
Evening meal available
CC: Amex, Delta, Diners,
Mastercard, Switch, Visa

B&B per night:
S £85.00–£95.00
D £105.00–£125.00

OPEN All year round

Delightful country house set in private grounds with beautiful walled garden. Renowned for good food and hospitality.

COTSWOLDS

See under Berkeley, Bourton-on-the-Water, Broadway, Cheltenham, Chipping Campden, Cirencester, Fairford, Gloucester, Lower Slaughter, Moreton-in-Marsh, Painswick, Stow-on-the-Wold, Stroud

See also Cotswolds in South of England region

COVENTRY, West Midlands Map ref 4B3 *Tourist Information Centre Tel: (024) 7622 7264*

★★ MERRICK LODGE HOTEL

80-82 St Nicholas Street, Coventry
CV1 4BP
T: (024) 7655 3940
F: (024) 7655 0112
I: www.merricklodge.co.uk

Bedrooms: 8 single,
23 double/twin, 9 triple/
multiple
Bathrooms: 39 en suite,
1 private

Lunch available
Evening meal available
CC: Amex, Delta, Diners,
Mastercard, Switch, Visa

B&B per night:
S £39.50–£59.50
D £49.50–£90.00

HB per person:
DY £42.50–£77.00

OPEN All year round

Former manor house, 5 minutes' walk from city centre. Table d'hote and a la carte restaurant, 3 bars. Comfortable, well-equipped bedrooms. Superb base for visiting the area. Disabled facilities in public areas.

DERBY, Derbyshire Map ref 4B2 *Tourist Information Centre Tel: (01332) 255802*

★★ MUNDY ARMS HOTEL

Ashbourne Road, Mackworth, Derby
DE22 4LZ
T: (01332) 824254 & 824664
F: (01332) 824519
I: www.derbyhotel.com

Bedrooms: 29 double/
twin, 1 triple/multiple;
suites available
Bathrooms: 30 en suite

Lunch available
Evening meal available
CC: Amex, Delta,
Mastercard, Switch, Visa

B&B per night:
S Max £38.00
D £35.00–£50.00

OPEN All year round

Privately-owned hotel 1 mile north of Derby on the A52, close to Peak District and Alton Towers. All rooms en suite with Sky TV and all facilities.

COUNTRY CODE Always follow the Country Code 🐾 Enjoy the countryside and respect its life and work 🐾 Guard against all risk of fire 🐾 Fasten all gates 🐾 Keep your dogs under close control 🐾 Keep to public paths across farmland 🐾 Use gates and stiles to cross fences, hedges and walls 🐾 Leave livestock, crops and machinery alone 🐾 Take your litter home 🐾 Help to keep all water clean 🐾 Protect wildlife, plants and trees 🐾 Take special care on country roads 🐾 Make no unnecessary noise

EVESHAM, Worcestershire Map ref 2B1 *Tourist Information Centre Tel: (01386) 446944*

★★
Silver
Award

THE MILL AT HARVINGTON

Anchor Lane, Harvington, Evesham
WR11 5NR
T: (01386) 870688
F: (01386) 870688
E: millatharvington@aol.com

Peaceful, owner-run, riverside hotel tastefully converted from beautiful house and mill. In acres of gardens, quarter mile Evesham to Stratford road. Old world hospitality and young, friendly staff who care, fresh local ingredients to create and serve meals you will remember. Half board prices based on minimum 2-night stay.

Bedrooms: 21 double/ twin
Bathrooms: 21 en suite

Lunch available
Evening meal available
CC: Amex, Delta, Diners, Mastercard, Switch, Visa

B&B per night:
S £63.00–£85.00
D £85.00–£125.00

HB per person:
DY £55.00–£87.00

OPEN All year round

★★★★
Gold
Award

WOOD NORTON HALL AND CONFERENCE CENTRE

Evesham WR11 4YB
T: (01386) 420007 & 420000
F: (01386) 420190
E: woodnortonhall@bbc.co.uk
I: www.woodnortonhall.co.uk

Formerly home to French royalty, lovingly restored, this Victorian mansion offers stunning views over the Vale of Evesham. Le Duc's restaurant boasts rosettes for fine food. The cuisine is classical French in style, with modern influences and is complemented by an extensive wine cellar. Full range of leisure breaks available.

Bedrooms: 45 double/ twin; suites available
Bathrooms: 45 en suite

Lunch available
Evening meal available
CC: Amex, Diners, Mastercard, Switch, Visa

An excellent range of leisure breaks are available incl Classic Car break, Royal Worcester Porcelain breaks and National Trust experience.

B&B per night:
S £85.00–£145.00
D £130.00–£220.00

OPEN All year round

Grand Heritage Hotels

FAIRFORD, Gloucestershire Map ref 2B1

★★

BULL HOTEL

Market Place, Fairford GL7 4AA
T: (01285) 712535 & 712217
F: (01285) 713785
E: info@thebullhotelfairford.co.uk
I: www.thebullhotelfairford.co.uk

Historic 15thC family-run hotel in Fairford's famous market square. Restaurant offers full a la carte menu and fresh local produce. Home-cooked bar food and range of good beers. Good base for Cotswolds. Wedding and conference facilities. Enjoy the charm of this ancient Cotswold inn. 1.5 miles of private fishing on River Coln.

Bedrooms: 5 single, 16 double/twin, 1 triple/ multiple
Bathrooms: 20 en suite, 2 private

Lunch available
Evening meal available
CC: Amex, Delta, Mastercard, Switch, Visa

Cotswold Breaks available all year, B&B or DB&B from £56.50pp, minimum 2 nights.

B&B per night:
S £47.50–£69.50
D £69.50–£89.50

HB per person:
DY £39.50–£57.50

OPEN All year round

MAP REFERENCES
Map references apply to the colour maps at the front of this guide.

★★

TUDOR GATE HOTEL

35 High Street, Finedon, Wellingborough
NN9 5JN
T: (01933) 680408
F: (01933) 680745
E: info@tudorgate-hotel.co.uk
I: www.tudorgate-hotel.co.uk

B&B per night:
S £45.00–£72.00
D £60.00–£120.00

HB per person:
DY £50.00–£90.00

OPEN All year round

Converted from a 17thC farmhouse, with three 4-poster beds. Close to new A1/M1 link. 30 antique businesses within walking distance, wide range of leisure activities locally. Our head chef leads a kitchen brigade of 6 with emphasis on quality, locally sourced fresh ingredients. Investor in People. View our website!

Bedrooms: 13 single, 14 double/twin
Bathrooms: 27 en suite

Lunch available
Evening meal available
CC: Amex, Delta, Diners, Mastercard, Switch, Visa

2 nights for the price of one year-round, weekends and all Bank Holiday weekends. Horse racing and motor racing themed events.

See under Lydney

★★

GREEN MAN INN
Fownhope, Hereford HR1 4PE
T: (01432) 860243
F: (01432) 860207
I: www.smoothhound.co.uk/Hotels/Greenman.html

Bedrooms: 1 single, 14 double/twin, 5 triple/ multiple; suites available
Bathrooms: 20 en suite

Lunch available
Evening meal available
CC: Amex, Delta, Diners, Mastercard, Switch, Visa

B&B per night:
S £38.50–£39.50
D £65.00–£67.00

HB per person:
DY £45.00–£46.25

OPEN All year round

15thC black and white coaching inn, midway between Ross-on-Wye and Hereford, in picturesque village of Fownhope. On B4224, close to River Wye. Indoor leisure complex.

★

WHITE HART HOTEL
49 Lord Street, Gainsborough
DN21 2DD
T: (01427) 612018
F: (01427) 811756
E: white.hart@tesco.net

Bedrooms: 5 single, 8 double/twin, 1 triple/ multiple
Bathrooms: 14 en suite

Lunch available
Evening meal available
CC: Delta, Mastercard, Switch, Visa

B&B per night:
S £30.00–£40.00
D £50.00–£60.00

OPEN All year round

Family-run hotel within town centre pedestrianisation. Restaurant, bars, room for weddings and seminars. Bar snacks, table d'hote menus. Lively weekends. Two minutes from Old Hall.

★★
Silver
Award

WIND IN THE WILLOWS HOTEL
Derbyshire Level, (A57), Glossop
SK13 7PT
T: (01457) 868001
F: (01457) 853354
E: info@windinthewillows.co.uk
I: www.windinthewillows.co.uk

Bedrooms: 12 double/ twin
Bathrooms: 12 en suite

Evening meal available
CC: Amex, Delta, Diners, Mastercard, Switch, Visa

B&B per night:
S £75.00–£95.00
D £99.00–£123.00

HB per person:
DY £74.50–£120.00

OPEN All year round

Friendly country house hotel with log fires, home cooking, peace and relaxation. Views over the Peak District National Park. Adjacent golf-course, in excellent walking country.

CHECK THE MAPS

The colour maps at the front of this guide show all the cities, towns and villages for which you will find accommodation entries. Refer to the town index to find the page on which they are listed.

★★

EDWARD HOTEL

88 London Road, Gloucester GL1 3PG

T: (01452) 525865

F: (01452) 302165

B&B per night:
S £35.00–£55.00
D £50.00–£70.00

OPEN All year round

A Grade II Victorian, terraced town house hotel with the luxury of a 20-space walled car park. A 500-metre stroll takes you to city shopping, restaurants and on to the Cathedral, Guildhall and museums. We're sure that you'll leave us 'pleased to return' having had a memorable stay.

Bedrooms: 3 single, 15 double/twin, 2 triple/ multiple Bathrooms. 18 en suite

Evening meal available
CC: Delta, Mastercard, Switch, Visa

On selected weekends we offer double/twins at £126 per stay (Fri, Sat, Sun £21pppn).

★★★
Silver
Award

HATTON COURT HOTEL

Upton Hill, Upton St Leonards,
Nr Cheltenham GL4 8DE

T: (01452) 617412

F: (01452) 612945

E: res@hatton-court.co.uk

I: www.hatton-hotels.co.uk

B&B per night:
S £89.00–£155.00
D £100.00–£180.00

OPEN All year round

Nestling in the rolling Gloucestershire countryside, Hatton Court is ideally located for exploring the many unspoilt villages of the Cotswolds. It retains the heritage and charm of the 17thC while providing all the luxury and service expected from a quality hotel in the country. We look forward to welcoming you.

Bedrooms: 45 double/ twin Bathrooms: 45 en suite

Lunch available
Evening meal available
CC: Amex, Delta, Diners, Mastercard, Switch, Visa

Scenechanger breaks (min 2-night stay)-incl twin/ double accommodation, breakfast, dinner, newspaper and VAT. Prices from £145.

★★★

NEW COUNTY HOTEL

44 Southgate Street, Gloucester, GL1 2DU

T: (01452) 307000

F: (01452) 500487

E: newcountry@meridianleisure.com

I: www.meridianleisure.com

B&B per night:
S £42.50–£60.00
D £60.00–£70.00

HB per person:
DY £55.00–£72.50

OPEN All year round

Ideally situated in the heart of Gloucester City, this 19thC hotel combines many original features with all modern amenities to create a fine, modern day hotel. All bedrooms are en suite and decorated to the highest standards. Free car parking adjacent. Ideal base for exploring the Cotswolds and nearby Cheltenham.

Bedrooms: 18 single, 12 double, 3 twin, 6 triple Bathrooms: 39 en suite

Lunch available
EM 1900 (LO 2130)
Parking for 50
CC: Amex, Barclaycard, Delta, Diners, Mastercard, Switch, Visa

TOWN INDEX

This can be found at the back of this guide. If you know where you want to stay, the index will give you the page number listing accommodation in your chosen town, city or village.

GOODRICH, Herefordshire Map ref 2A1

★★

YE HOSTELRIE HOTEL
Goodrich, Ross-on-Wye HR9 6HX
T: (01600) 890241
F: (01600) 890838
E: ye-hostelrie@lineone.net
I: www.ye-hostelrie.8k.com

B&B per night:
S £32.50–£33.00
D £50.00–£52.00

HB per person:
DY £32.25–£33.25

OPEN All year round

Picturesque family-run hotel, in the heart of the Wye Valley, close to Goodrich Castle and the Forest of Dean, Ye Hostelrie offers very comfortable en suite accommodation, excellent home-cooked food and real ales. Attractive patio and garden, secure parking. Pets are welcome in the bedrooms at no charge.

Bedrooms: 5 double/twin, 1 triple/multiple
Bathrooms: 6 en suite

Lunch available
Evening meal available
CC: Amex, Delta, Mastercard, Switch, Visa

GRINDLEFORD, Derbyshire Map ref 4B2

★★★
Silver
Award

MAYNARD ARMS HOTEL
Main Road, Grindleford,
Hope Valley S32 2HE
T: (01433) 630321
F: (01433) 630445
E: info@maynardarms.co.uk
I: www.maynardarms.co.uk

Bedrooms: 10 double/twin; suites available
Bathrooms: 10 en suite

Lunch available
Evening meal available
CC: Amex, Delta, Mastercard, Switch, Visa

B&B per night:
S £69.00–£89.00
D £79.00–£99.00

HB per person:
DY £49.50–£59.50

OPEN All year round

Established hotel with a relaxed, friendly atmosphere and extensive facilities. Picturesque gardens with lovely views of Hope Valley and Peak Park. Excellent walking country.

HEREFORD, Herefordshire Map ref 2A1 *Tourist Information Centre Tel: (01432) 268430*

★★★

BELMONT LODGE AND GOLF COURSE
Belmont, Hereford HR2 9SA
T: (01432) 352666
F: (01432) 358090
E: info@belmontlodge.co.uk
I: www.belmontlodge.co.uk

Bedrooms: 26 double/twin, 4 triple/multiple
Bathrooms: 30 en suite

Lunch available
Evening meal available
CC: Amex, Delta, Diners, Mastercard, Switch, Visa

B&B per night:
S £47.50–£52.00
D £67.50–£72.00

HB per person:
DY Min £65.00

OPEN All year round

Comfortable hotel situated off the A465, 2 miles south of Hereford city centre. Overlooking the River Wye and Herefordshire countryside, offering beautiful views.

★★★
Gold
Award

CASTLE HOUSE
Castle Street, Hereford HR1 2NW
T: (01432) 356321
F. (01432) 365909
E: info@castlehse.co.uk
I: www.castlehse.co.uk

B&B per night:
S Min £90.00
D £155.00–£210.00

OPEN All year round

Pride of Britain

Dr and Mrs A Heijn have created a gracious and hospitable town mansion, where guests enjoy a very high standard of service, comfort and cuisine. Although situated in the centre of Hereford, 100 metres from the Cathedral, nothing should disturb the privacy and perfect tranquillity of your stay.

Bedrooms: 4 single, 11 double/twin
Bathrooms: 15 en suite

Lunch available
Evening meal available
CC: Amex, Delta, Mastercard, Switch, Visa

Two nights for £380.00 inclusive of dinner, bed and full English breakfast.

MAP REFERENCES
The map references refer to the colour maps at the front of this guide. The first figure is the map number; the letter and figure which follow indicate the grid reference on the map.

HEREFORD continued

★ **THE NEW PRIORY HOTEL**
Stretton Sugwas, Hereford
HR4 7AR
T: (01432) 760264 & 760183
F: (01432) 761809
E: newprioryhotel@ukonline.co.uk

Bedrooms: 2 single,
5 double/twin, 1 triple/
multiple
Bathrooms: 7 en suite,
1 private

Lunch available
Evening meal available
CC: Delta, Mastercard,
Switch, Visa

B&B per night:
S £35.00–£45.00
D £55.00–£75.00

HB per person:
DY £30.00–£40.00

OPEN All year round

Friendly family hotel in pleasant, peaceful surroundings, 2 miles from centre of Hereford. Good home-cooked food. En suite 4-poster rooms. Former monastery with lots of historic interest.

★★★ **THREE COUNTIES HOTEL**
Belmont Road, Hereford HR2 7BP
T: (01432) 299955
F: (01432) 275114
E: enquiries@threecountieshotel.co.uk
I: www.threecountieshotel.co.uk

Bedrooms: 60 double/
twin
Bathrooms: 60 en suite

Lunch available
Evening meal available
CC: Amex, Delta, Diners,
Mastercard, Switch, Visa

B&B per night:
S £38.50–£61.50
D £57.00–£80.00

OPEN All year round

Excellently appointed hotel set in 3.5 acres. Emphasis on traditional, friendly service. Tasteful bedrooms, restaurant and bar offer today's guests all modern comforts. Town centre 1 mile.

HOCKLEY HEATH, West Midlands Map ref 4B3

★★★
Gold
Award

NUTHURST GRANGE COUNTRY HOUSE HOTEL AND RESTAURANT
Nuthurst Grange Lane, Hockley Heath,
Solihull B94 5NL
T: (01564) 783972
F: (01564) 783919
E: info@nuthurst-grange.com
I: www.theaa.co.uk/hotels

B&B per night:
S Min £135.00
D £155.00–£185.00

HB per person:
DY Min £79.50

OPEN All year round

Nuthurst Grange nestles in 7.5 acres of landscaped gardens and woodlands. Relax and be pampered in one of our 15 luxurious bedrooms, enjoy a superb meal in our award-winning restaurant. We are perfectly placed in the heart of England close to National Trust attractions and market towns. Also an ideal venue for parties, wedding receptions, meetings and conferences.

Bedrooms: 15 double/
twin; suites available
Bathrooms: 15 en suite

Lunch available
Evening meal available
CC: Amex, Delta, Diners,
Mastercard, Switch, Visa

Special 20% off for guests mentioning our internet offer when booking.

HORNCASTLE, Lincolnshire Map ref 4D2

★★ **ADMIRAL RODNEY HOTEL**
North Street, Horncastle LN9 5DX
T: (01507) 523131
F: (01507) 523104
E: reception@admiralrodney.com
I: www.admiralrodney.com

Bedrooms: 28 double/
twin, 3 triple/multiple
Bathrooms: 31 en suite

Lunch available
Evening meal available
CC: Amex, Delta, Diners,
Mastercard, Switch, Visa

B&B per night:
S £45.00–£55.00
D £60.00–£79.00

HB per person:
DY £40.00–£65.00

OPEN All year round

ⓒⓡ
Best Western Hotels

Located in pleasant market town just off main Lincoln to Skegness road – ideal touring base. Large car park, en suite bedrooms, fine restaurant.

IRONBRIDGE, Shropshire Map ref 4A3 *Tourist Information Centre Tel: (01952) 432166*

★★★ **THE BEST WESTERN VALLEY HOTEL**
Ironbridge, Telford TF8 7DW
T: (01952) 432247
F: (01952) 432308
E: valley.hotel@ironbridge.fsnet.co.uk
I: www.bestwestern.co.uk

Bedrooms: 9 single,
26 double/twin
Bathrooms: 35 en suite

Lunch available
Evening meal available
CC: Amex, Diners,
Mastercard, Switch, Visa

B&B per night:
S £95.00–£110.00
D £105.00–£120.00

HB per person:
DY £62.50–£70.00

OPEN All year round

ⓒⓡ
Best Western Hotels

Georgian Listed building situated in World Heritage Site of Ironbridge. Riverside location with large car park. All Ironbridge Gorge Museum attractions within walking distance.

★★

CLARENDON HOUSE HOTEL
Old High Street, Kenilworth
CV8 1LZ
T: (01926) 857668
F: (01926) 850669
E: info@clarendonhousehotel.com
I: www.clarendonhousehotel.com

Bedrooms: 13 single,
14 double/twin, 1 triple/
multiple
Bathrooms: 28 en suite

Lunch available
Evening meal available
CC: Amex, Delta, Diners,
Mastercard, Switch, Visa

B&B per night:
S £57.50–£69.50
D £79.50–£89.50

HB per person:
DY £45.00–£70.00

Unique, historic inn dating from 1430, still supported by the old oak tree around which the former 'Castle Tavern' was built. Own 16thC well from which they drew water is still open in the bar.

OPEN All year round

★★★

THE PEACOCK HOTEL
149 Warwick Road, Kenilworth CV8 1HY
T: (01926) 851156 & 864500
F: (01926) 864644
E: peacock@rafflesmalaysian.com
I: www.peacockhotel.com

B&B per night:
S £39.00–£90.00
D £49.00–£110.00

HB per person:
DY £52.00–£79.00

OPEN All year round

Small and luxurious hotel committed to providing outstanding quality and first class service at reasonable prices. Ideally located for meetings and conferences. Choice of 3 elegant restaurants, contemporary bar, gardens and ample parking. Optional tours and an 'in-house' coach service available.

Bedrooms: 5 single,
10 double/twin; suites
available
Bathrooms: 15 en suite

Lunch available
Evening meal available
CC: Amex, Delta, Diners,
Mastercard, Switch, Visa

Weekend leisure break-stay Fri and Sat night and get Sun night free, £49pppn incl dinner based on 2 sharing.

★★★

EATON COURT HOTEL
1-7 St Marks Road, Leamington Spa
CV32 6DL
T: (01926) 885848
F: (01926) 885848
E: info@eatoncourt.co.uk
I: www.eatoncourt.co.uk

Bedrooms: 10 single,
22 double/twin, 4 triple/
multiple
Bathrooms: 36 en suite

Lunch available
Evening meal available
CC: Amex, Delta, Diners,
Mastercard, Switch, Visa

B&B per night:
S £40.00–£60.00
D £60.00–£80.00

OPEN All year round

Friendly privately owned and run hotel near town and Warwick Castle. Spacious en suite rooms with comfortable facilities, function rooms, licensed restaurant and secluded garden.

★★
Silver
Award

LEADON HOUSE HOTEL
Ross Road, Ledbury HR8 2LP
T: (01531) 631199
F: (01531) 631476
E: leadon.house@amserve.net
I: www.leadonhouse.co.uk

B&B per night:
S £35.00–£55.00
D £53.00–£68.00

HB per person:
DY £40.00–£50.00

OPEN All year round

Graceful Edwardian family-run hotel. Recent quality refurbishment with period decor and furnishings. Set in open countryside about a mile from town centre. A warm welcome, good food, spacious and comfortable accommodation – the ideal base to explore the many attractions of 'England's most rural county' and Heart of England. All areas non-smoking.

Bedrooms: 1 single,
3 double/twin, 2 triple/
multiple
Bathrooms: 6 en suite

Evening meal available
CC: Amex, Delta,
Mastercard, Switch, Visa

Stay 2 nights or more Nov-Mar and get 2 course evening meal free (excl Christmas and New Year).

LEEK, Staffordshire Map ref 4B2 *Tourist Information Centre Tel: (01538) 483741*

★★ **THREE HORSESHOES INN AND RESTAURANT**

Buxton Road, Blackshaw Moor, Leek
ST13 8TW
T: (01538) 300296
F: (01538) 300320

Bedrooms: 6 double/
twin
Bathrooms: 6 en suite

Lunch available
Evening meal available
CC: Amex, Delta,
Mastercard, Switch, Visa

B&B per night:
S £45.00–£55.00
D £55.00–£85.00

HB per person:
DY £40.00–£60.00

OPEN All year round

Traditional country inn with oak and pine beams, excellent restaurant with fine cuisine and a traditional bar carvery. 240 wines. Log fire.

LEOMINSTER, Herefordshire Map ref 2A1 *Tourist Information Centre Tel: (01568) 616460*

★★★ **TALBOT HOTEL**

West Street, Leominster HR6 8EP
T: (01568) 616347
F: (01568) 614880

Bedrooms: 2 single,
15 double/twin, 3 triple/
multiple
Bathrooms: 20 en suite

Lunch available
Evening meal available
CC: Amex, Delta, Diners,
Mastercard, Switch, Visa

B&B per night:
S £47.00–£56.00
D £68.00–£86.00

HB per person:
DY £61.00–£74.00

OPEN All year round

15thC coaching inn with oak beams and log fire, now offering 20thC facilities. Ideal location for touring Mid-Wales, Shropshire and Herefordshire.

Ⓒℝ
Best Western Hotels

LICHFIELD, Staffordshire Map ref 4B3 *Tourist Information Centre Tel: (01543) 308209*

★★

OAKLEIGH HOUSE HOTEL

25 St. Chad's Road, Lichfield WS13 7LZ
T: (01543) 262688 & 255573
F: (01543) 418556
E: info@oakleighhouse.co.uk
I: www.oakleighhouse.co.uk

B&B per night:
S £45.00–£55.00
D £50.00–£75.00

HB per person:
DY £35.00–£65.00

OPEN All year round

Family-run, friendly, comfortable, licensed hotel. Edwardian house with garden overlooking a lake, 5 minutes' walk from city centre and cathedral. Restaurant, open to non-residents, has good reputation for serving delicious food using fresh local ingredients. Specialises in rare breed meat.

Bedrooms: 5 single,
6 double/twin
Bathrooms: 11 en suite

Lunch available
Evening meal available
CC: Delta, Mastercard,
Switch, Visa

Special weekend breaks available covering either Fri and Sat or Sat and Sun nights.

LINCOLN, Lincolnshire Map ref 4C2 *Tourist Information Centre Tel: (01522) 873213 & 873256*

★★★ **THE BENTLEY HOTEL & LEISURE CLUB**

Newark Road, South Hykeham,
Lincoln LN6 9NH
T: (01522) 878000
F: (01522) 878001
E: info@thebentleyhotel.uk.com
I: www.thebentleyhotel.uk.com

Bedrooms: 53 double/
twin; suites available
Bathrooms: 53 en suite

Lunch available
Evening meal available
CC: Amex, Delta, Diners,
Mastercard, Switch, Visa

B&B per night:
S £62.00–£78.00
D £77.00–£87.00

HB per person:
DY £57.00–£62.00

OPEN All year round

Ⓒℝ
Best Western Hotels

Lincoln's newest and most modern hotel with leisure club. Beauty salon, conference centre, restaurant and bars.

AT-A-GLANCE SYMBOLS

Symbols at the end of each accommodation entry give useful information about services and facilities. A key to symbols can be found inside the back cover flap. Keep this open for easy reference.

LINCOLN continued

★★★

BRANSTON HALL HOTEL

Lincoln Road, Branston, Grantham
LN4 1PD
T: (01522) 793305
F: (01522) 790549
E: brahal@enterprise.net
I: www.scoot.co.uk/branston-hall

B&B per night:
S Min £59.50
D Min £79.50

HB per person:
DY Min £73.50

OPEN All year round

Elegant country house in beautiful grounds yet only 5 minutes from Lincoln city centre. All rooms are en suite and beautifully furnished. Our new leisure facilities include heated indoor pool, fully-equipped gymnasium, sauna and jacuzzi.

Bedrooms: 4 single, 39 double/twin, 2 triple/ multiple; suites available
Bathrooms: 45 en suite

Lunch available
Evening meal available
CC: Mastercard, Switch, Visa

Midweek breaks/weekend £99.50 DB&B per room per night.

★★
Silver
Award

CASTLE HOTEL
Westgate, Lincoln LN1 3AS
T: (01522) 538801
F: (01522) 575457
E: wts@castlehotel.net
I: www.castlehotel.net

Bedrooms: 1 single, 17 double/twin, 1 triple/ multiple; 1 suite
Bathrooms: 19 en suite

Evening meal available
CC: Delta, Diners, Mastercard, Switch, Visa

B&B per night:
S £62.00–£84.00
D £84.00–£150.00

HB per person:
DY £57.00–£77.00

OPEN All year round

Located amid Lincoln's historic heart, a very comfortable traditional English hotel offering hospitality at its best. Also featuring 'Knights', an award-winning seafood and game restaurant.

★★★

GRAND HOTEL
St Mary's Street, Lincoln LN5 7EP
T: (01522) 524211
F: (01522) 537661
E: reception@thegrandhotel.uk.com
I: www.thegrandhotel.uk.com

Bedrooms: 14 single, 30 double/twin, 2 triple/ multiple
Bathrooms: 46 en suite

Lunch available
Evening meal available
CC: Amex, Delta, Diners, Mastercard, Switch, Visa

B&B per night:
S £53.00–£69.00
D £69.00–£78.00

OPEN All year round

The Independents/Best Western Hotels

Family-owned hotel, in the centre of beautiful historic city. Getaway breaks available throughout the year. Half board prices are based on a minimum 2-night stay.

★★

HILLCREST HOTEL

15 Lindum Terrace, Lincoln LN2 5RT
T: (01522) 510182
F: (01522) 510182
E: reservations@hillcrest-hotel.com
I: www.hillcrest-hotel.com

B&B per night:
S £54.00–£60.00
D £81.00–£83.00

HB per person:
DY £58.00–£77.00

OPEN All year round

CR
The Circle

Hillcrest Hotel is a Victorian former rectory overlooking gardens and a Victorian tree park. Great views and a quiet location with parking, and only 7 minutes' walk to the cathedral and city. For you a warm welcome and a smile, full bar and restaurant with candlelit dining.

Bedrooms: 3 single, 8 double/twin, 4 triple/ multiple
Bathrooms: 15 en suite

Lunch available
Evening meal available
CC: Amex, Delta, Mastercard, Switch, Visa

Min 2 nights DB&B sharing twin or double, £110pp for 2 nights.

NB

IMPORTANT NOTE Information on accommodation listed
in this guide has been supplied by the proprietors. As changes may occur you are advised to check details at the time of booking.

LOUTH, Lincolnshire Map ref 4D2 *Tourist Information Centre Tel: (01507) 609289*

★★★

BRACKENBOROUGH ARMS HOTEL & RESTAURANT

Cordeaux Corner, Brackenborough, Louth LN11 0SZ

T: (01507) 609169
F: (01507) 609413
E: info@brackenborough.co.uk
I: www.brackenborough.co.uk

Country house hotel, set in 7 acres of lovely mature gardens, with each bedroom individually styled. Privately-owned and run, this very popular hotel and restaurant also offers friendly service and relaxed dining in the lounge bar. Set back off the A16 Louth to Grimsby road; Louth approximately 2 miles.

Bedrooms: 2 single, 21 double/twin, 1 triple/ multiple
Bathrooms: 24 en suite

Lunch available
Evening meal available
CC: Amex, Delta, Diners, Mastercard, Switch, Visa

B&B per night:
S £58.95–£62.00
D £70.00–£75.00

HB per person:
DY £42.50–£47.50

OPEN All year round

LOWER SLAUGHTER, Gloucestershire Map ref 2B1

★★★
Silver Award

WASHBOURNE COURT HOTEL

Lower Slaughter, Cheltenham GL54 2HS

T: (01451) 822143
F: (01451) 821045
E: washbourne@msn.com
I: www.washbournecourt.co.uk

If you are in search of peace, tranquillity and the epitome of English country life, you need look no further than Washbourne Court. Set in the heart of the beautiful Cotswold countryside on the banks of the River Eye in the enchanting village of Lower Slaughter.

Bedrooms: 24 double/ twin, 4 triple/multiple; suites available
Bathrooms: 28 en suite

Lunch available
Evening meal available
CC: Amex, Delta, Diners, Mastercard, Switch, Visa

B&B per night:
S £105.00–£215.00
D £155.00–£225.00

HB per person:
DY £87.50–£135.00

OPEN All year round

LYDNEY, Gloucestershire Map ref 2B1

★★

PARKEND HOUSE HOTEL

Parkend, Lydney GL15 4HH

T: (01594) 563666
F: (01594) 564631
E: andrewjohnlee@netscapeonline.co.uk
I: www.parkendhousehotel.co.uk

Small country house hotel set in its own grounds in the heart of the Forest of Dean. An ideal centre for exploring the Wye Valley and further afield to Cheltenham, Gloucester and Bath. Our dinner menu changes daily and specialises in fresh local produce.

Bedrooms: 6 double/ twin, 2 triple/multiple
Bathrooms: 8 en suite

Lunch available
Evening meal available
CC: Amex, Delta, Mastercard, Switch, Visa

2 and 3 night special bargain breaks available.

B&B per night:
S £23.00–£37.50
D £46.00–£55.00

HB per person:
DY £33.00–£42.00

OPEN All year round

CENTRAL RESERVATIONS OFFICES

The symbol ⓒⓡ and a group name in an entry indicate that bookings can be made through a central reservations office. These are listed in a separate section towards the back of this guide.

MALVERN, Worcestershire Map ref 2B1 *Tourist Information Centre Tel: (01684) 892289*

★★★
Silver
Award

COLWALL PARK
Walwyn Road, Colwall, Malvern
WR13 6QG
T: (01684) 540000
F: (01684) 540847
E: hotel@colwall.com
I: www.colwall.com

Bedrooms: 3 single,
16 double/twin, 3 triple/
multiple; suites available
Bathrooms: 22 en suite

Lunch available
Evening meal available
CC: Amex, Mastercard,
Switch, Visa

B&B per night:
S £65.00–£80.00
D £110.00–£150.00

OPEN All year round

Charming country house hotel on the sunny western side of the Malvern Hills. Good views of the hills. Award-winning cuisine in relaxing, comfortable surroundings.

★★

COTFORD HOTEL
Graham Road, Malvern WR14 2HU
T: (01684) 572427
F: (01684) 572952
E: reservations@cotfordhotel.co.uk
I: www.cotfordhotel.co.uk

B&B per night:
S £50.00–£60.00
D £70.00–£80.00

HB per person:
DY £55.00–£70.00

OPEN All year round

Beautiful Victorian hotel, built in 1851 reputedly for the Bishop of Worcester. All rooms en suite with satellite TV, telephone, radio and tea-making facilities. Complimentary use of Malvern Splash swimming pool and sauna. Close to town centre, theatre and hills but set in its own mature gardens to add peace and tranquillity to your stay.

Bedrooms: 9 single,
5 double/twin, 3 triple/
multiple
Bathrooms: 17 en suite

Lunch available
Evening meal available
CC: Amex, Delta, Diners,
Mastercard, Switch, Visa

Special breaks available for DB&B for 2 nights or more.

★★★
Silver
Award

THE COTTAGE IN THE WOOD HOTEL
Holywell Road, Malvern Wells, Malvern
WR14 4LG
T: (01684) 575859
F: (01684) 560662
E: reception@cottageinthewood.co.uk
I: www.cottageinthewood.co.uk

B&B per night:
S £76.00–£86.00
D £95.00–£150.00

HB per person:
DY £63.00–£98.00

OPEN All year round

Set high on the Malvern Hills with 30-mile views to the Cotswolds. 'The best view in England' – Daily Mail. All en suite. Family owned and run. Exceptional food. Daily half board prices based on minimum 2-night stay. Weekly is 7 nights for price of 6. Breaks available all week, all year. From the grounds, direct access to Malvern Hills.

Bedrooms: 20 double/
twin
Bathrooms: 20 en suite

Lunch available
Evening meal available
CC: Amex, Delta,
Mastercard, Switch, Visa

DB&B rates include a full 3-course choice from the a la carte menu.

QUALITY ASSURANCE SCHEME

For an explanation of the quality and facilities represented by the Stars please refer to the front of this guide. A more detailed explanation can be found in the information pages at the back.

★★
Silver
Award

HOLDFAST COTTAGE HOTEL

Marlbank Road, Little Malvern, Malvern
WR13 6NA
T: (01684) 310288
F: (01684) 311117
E: holdcothot@aol.com
I: www.holdfast-cottage.co.uk

Enchanting wisteria-covered country house hotel nestling into the foot of the Malvern Hills. Award-winning restaurant, pretty en suite bedrooms, log fires, personal care and service and a wonderfully warm and relaxing atmosphere. Away breaks available all week, all year. Children and pets welcome.

Bedrooms: 1 single,
7 double/twin
Bathrooms: 8 en suite

Evening meal available
CC: Delta, Mastercard,
Switch, Visa

Relaxing 2-night away breaks available all year. Reduction of 10% on 3rd and subsequent nights. 7 nights for the price of 6.

B&B per night:
S £50.00–£64.00
D £84.00–£92.00

HB per person:
DY £60.00–£66.00

OPEN All year round

★★

MALVERN HILLS HOTEL

Wynds Point, British Camp, Malvern
WR13 6DW
T: (01684) 540690
F: (01684) 540327
E: malhilhotl@aol.com
I: www.malvernhillshotel.co.uk

Straddling the Herefordshire/ Worcestershire county border at British Camp (the Herefordshire Beacon) on the A449 midway between Malvern and Ledbury, the site of the hotel has provided a hostelry for travellers for more than 500 years. Walks with breathtaking views, excellent bar food, real ales, elegant restaurant and extensive wine list. Pets welcome.

Bedrooms: 1 single,
10 double/twin, 3 triple/
multiple
Bathrooms: 14 en suite

Lunch available
Evening meal available
CC: Amex, Delta, Diners,
Mastercard, Switch, Visa

Christmas and New Year breaks.

B&B per night:
S £30.00–£45.00
D £65.00–£85.00

HB per person:
DY £104.00–£124.00

OPEN All year round

★★

MOUNT PLEASANT HOTEL

Belle Vue Terrace, Malvern WR14 4PZ
T: (01684) 561837
F: (01684) 569968
E: mountpleasanthotel@btinternet.com
I: www.mountpleasanthotel.co.uk

An attractive early Georgian building with garden and magnificent views across the Severn Valley. Close to the theatre and shops yet with direct access to walking on the Malvern Hills. Ideal for touring. Emphasis is on relaxation, friendly attention and good food. Excellent centre for touring.

Bedrooms: 3 single,
12 double/twin
Bathrooms: 14 en suite,
1 private

Lunch available
Evening meal available
CC: Amex, Delta, Diners,
Mastercard, Switch, Visa

Walking on the Malvern Hills: ask for our group rates.

B&B per night:
S £47.50–£60.00
D £69.00–£92.00

HB per person:
DY £41.00–£56.25

OPEN All year round

The Circle/The
Independents

CREDIT CARD BOOKINGS If you book by telephone and are asked for your credit card number it is advisable to check the proprietor's policy should you cancel your reservation.

MARKET DRAYTON, Shropshire Map ref 4A2 *Tourist Information Centre Tel: (01630) 652139*

★★ **THE BEAR HOTEL**
Hodnet, Market Drayton TF9 3NH
T: (01630) 685214 & 685788
F: (01630) 685787
E: info@bearhotel.org.uk

Bedrooms: 1 single,
5 double/twin, 2 triple/
multiple
Bathrooms: 8 en suite

Lunch available
Evening meal available
CC: Amex, Delta,
Mastercard, Switch, Visa

B&B per night:
S £42.50–£45.00
D £62.50–£70.00

HB per person:
DY £45.00–£65.00

OPEN All year round

Privately owned 16thC inn, with the character of a bygone age but 20thC comfort, and a warm and friendly atmosphere. Oak-beamed, open fires.

MATLOCK, Derbyshire Map ref 4B2 *Tourist Information Centre Tel: (01629) 583388*

★★★
Silver
Award

RIBER HALL
Riber, Matlock DE4 5JU
T: (01629) 582795
F: (01629) 580475
E: info@riber-hall.co.uk
I: www.riber-hall.co.uk

Bedrooms: 14 double/
twin
Bathrooms: 14 en suite

Lunch available
Evening meal available
CC: Amex, Delta, Diners,
Mastercard, Switch, Visa

B&B per night:
S £97.00–£112.00
D £127.00–£170.00

HB per person:
DY £92.00–£125.00

OPEN All year round

Renowned historic and tranquil country manor house set in peaceful, rolling Derbyshire hills. Rosettes and ribbons awarded for gourmet cuisine. Privately owned.

MELTON MOWBRAY, Leicestershire Map ref 4C3 *Tourist Information Centre Tel: (01664) 480992*

★★★

QUORN LODGE HOTEL
46 Asfordby Road, Melton Mowbray
LE13 0HR
T: (01664) 566660 & 562590
F: (01664) 480660
E: quornlodge@aol.com
I: www.quornlodge.co.uk

B&B per night:
S £46.00–£53.50
D £62.00–£80.00

HB per person:
DY £46.75–£56.00

OPEN All year round

Family-owned and personally run by Julie Sturt and her professional friendly staff. An original hunting lodge situated on the edge of a busy market town. Excellent food and wine are served in our delightful restaurant overlooking the garden. Luxury at affordable prices. Individually designed en suite rooms. Ground floor and 4-poster rooms. Special weekend breaks.

Bedrooms: 6 single,
11 double/twin, 2 triple/
multiple; suites available
Bathrooms: 19 en suite

Lunch available
Evening meal available
CC: Amex, Delta,
Mastercard, Switch, Visa

Weekend breaks DB&B min 2 nights Thurs-Sun double/twin £89 per night per room. Single £59.50 per night per room.

★★★

SYSONBY KNOLL HOTEL
Asfordby Road, Melton Mowbray LE13 0HP
T: (01664) 563563
F: (01664) 410364
E: sysonby.knoll@btinternet.com
I: www.sysonby.knoll.btinternet.co.uk

B&B per night:
S £47.00–£65.00
D £63.00–£81.00

OPEN All year round

Privately owned hotel within walking distance of town centre, standing in 4-acre grounds with river frontage. Lively restaurant is locally popular and our reputation for good food and exceptional hospitality gives us a loyal following of regular guests. Weekend breaks and 4-posters available. Pets welcome. Half board prices are for a minimum 2-night weekend stay.

Bedrooms: 7 single,
16 double/twin, 1 triple/
multiple
Bathrooms: 24 en suite

Lunch available
Evening meal available
CC: Amex, Delta, Diners,
Mastercard, Switch, Visa

'Let's Go' weekend breaks-discount for 2-night stay, Thu-Sun when guests dine both nights.

QUALITY ASSURANCE SCHEME
Star ratings and awards are explained at the back of this guide.

MORETON-IN-MARSH, Gloucestershire Map ref 2B1

★★★

MANOR HOUSE HOTEL

High Street, Moreton-in-Marsh
GL56 0LJ
T: (01608) 650501
F: (01608) 651481
E: bookings@cotswold-inns-hotels.co.uk
I: www.cotswold-inns-hotels.co.uk

16thC privately-owned manor house with original features. Some four-poster beds, indoor pool, sauna and jacuzzi. Walled garden.

Bedrooms: 1 single,
37 double/twin; suites available
Bathrooms: 38 en suite

Lunch available
Evening meal available
CC: Amex, Delta, Diners, Mastercard, Switch, Visa

B&B per night:
S £90.00–£99.00
D £115.00–£160.00

HB per person:
DY £120.00–£129.00

OPEN All year round

Grand Heritage Hotels

NOTTINGHAM, Nottinghamshire Map ref 4C2 *Tourist Information Centre Tel: (0115) 915 5330*

★★★

THE NOTTINGHAM GATEWAY HOTEL

Nuthall Road, Nottingham NG8 6AZ
T: (0115) 979 4949
F: (0115) 979 4744
E: nottmgateway@btconnect.com

Modern and conveniently located hotel enjoying a large and impressive glass architectural reception area, which permits you to relax in natural daylight all year round whatever the weather outside. Free on-site car parking. Carvery restaurant offering traditional English food, a la carte and Thai food cooked by our own Thai chef Lec.

Bedrooms: 81 double/twin, 26 triple/multiple
Bathrooms: 107 en suite

Lunch available
Evening meal available
CC: Amex, Delta, Diners, Mastercard, Switch, Visa

B&B per night:
S £40.00–£90.00
D £55.00–£105.00

HB per person:
DY £40.00–£80.00

OPEN All year round

★★★

SWANS HOTEL AND RESTAURANT

84-90 Radcliffe Road,
West Bridgford, Nottingham
NG2 5HH
T: (0115) 981 4042
F: (0115) 945 5745
E: enquiries@swanshotel.co.uk
I: www.swanshotel.co.uk

Ideally placed for all Nottingham's major sporting and tourist attractions. Good value, excellent service, wonderful food.

Bedrooms: 9 single,
19 double/twin, 2 triple/multiple; suites available
Bathrooms: 30 en suite

Lunch available
Evening meal available
CC: Amex, Delta, Diners, Mastercard, Switch, Visa

B&B per night:
S £45.00–£58.00
D £60.00–£63.00

HB per person:
DY £40.00–£71.00

OPEN All year round

OAKHAM, Leicestershire Map ref 4C3 *Tourist Information Centre Tel: (01572) 724329*

★★★
Silver Award

BARNSDALE LODGE HOTEL

The Avenue, Rutland Water, Exton,
Oakham LE15 8AH
T: (01572) 724678
F: (01572) 724961

Enjoy panoramic views across Rutland Water and relax in this ideal retreat, take a theatre, garden or golfing break. Traditional English fare in Edwardian-style dining rooms.

Bedrooms: 8 single,
35 double/twin, 2 triple/multiple; suites available
Bathrooms: 45 en suite

Lunch available
Evening meal available
CC: Amex, Delta, Diners, Mastercard, Switch, Visa

B&B per night:
S £69.00–£75.00
D £89.00–£95.00

HB per person:
DY £69.00–£80.00

OPEN All year round

USE YOUR *i*s

There are more than 550 Tourist Information Centres throughout England offering friendly help with accommodation and holiday ideas as well as suggestions of places to visit and things to do. You'll find TIC addresses in the local Phone Book.

★★★

THE OLD WISTERIA HOTEL

4 Catmos Street, Oakham LE15 6HW
T: (01572) 722844
F: (01572) 724473
E: enquiries@wisteriahotel.co.uk
I: www.wisteriahotel.co.uk

B&B per night:
S £35.00–£65.00
D £65.00–£85.00

HB per person:
DY £50.00–£60.00

OPEN All year round

In Rutland, the heart of the English shires. Ideal base for touring with rolling countryside, picturesque villages and a variety of attractions, including Barnsdale Gardens and Rutland Water. A welcoming country house ambience and 'The Cottage' (circa 1604) lounge bar and restaurant provide an intimate setting for relaxation.

Bedrooms: 7 single,
18 double/twin
Bathrooms: 25 en suite

Lunch available
Evening meal available
CC: Amex, Delta, Diners,
Mastercard, Switch, Visa

For special offers incl short and themed breaks please visit our website.

OSWESTRY, Shropshire Map ref 4A3 *Tourist Information Centre Tel: (01691) 662488 (Mile End)*

★★★
Silver
Award

PEN-Y-DYFFRYN COUNTRY HOTEL

Rhyd-y-Croesau, Oswestry
SY10 7JD
T: (01691) 653700
F: (01691) 650066
E: stay@peny.co.uk
I: www.peny.co.uk

Bedrooms: 1 single,
8 double/twin, 1 triple/
multiple
Bathrooms: 10 en suite

Evening meal available
CC: Amex, Delta,
Mastercard, Switch, Visa

B&B per night:
S £63.00–£68.00
D £88.00–£104.00

HB per person:
DY £63.00–£72.00

Peaceful, Georgian former rectory in 5 acres of grounds in Shropshire/Welsh border hills. Fully licensed, noted restaurant. Informal atmosphere, pets welcome. 30 minutes Shrewsbury and Chester.

PAINSWICK, Gloucestershire Map ref 2B1

★★

THE FALCON HOTEL

New Street, Painswick, Stroud
GL6 6UN
T: (01452) 814222 & 812228
F: (01452) 813377
E: bleninns@clara.net
I: www.falconinn.com

Bedrooms: 8 double/
twin, 4 triple/multiple
Bathrooms: 12 en suite

Lunch available
Evening meal available
CC: Amex, Delta, Diners,
Mastercard, Switch, Visa

B&B per night:
S £42.50–£49.50
D £67.50–£79.50

OPEN All year round

Famous old coaching inn dating from 1554, in the heart of Painswick. Refurbished to very high standards, with antique furniture and original oil paintings. Renowned restaurant.

★★★
Silver
Award

PAINSWICK HOTEL

Kemps Lane, Painswick, Stroud
GL6 6YB
T: (01452) 812160
F: (01452) 814059
E: reservations@painswickhotel.com
I: www.painswickhotel.com

Bedrooms: 2 single,
15 double/twin, 2 triple/
multiple
Bathrooms: 19 en suite

Lunch available
Evening meal available
CC: Amex, Delta,
Mastercard, Switch, Visa

B&B per night:
S £85.00–£145.00
D £125.00–£185.00

OPEN All year round

Situated in the beautiful Cotswold village of Painswick, the hotel is renowned for friendly service, award-winning cuisine and luxurious bedrooms filled with antiques and objets d'art.

PEAK DISTRICT

See under Ashbourne, Biggin-by-Hartington, Calver, Glossop, Grindleford

www.travelengland.org.uk

Log on for information and inspiration. The latest information on places to visit, events and quality assessed accommodation.

★★★
Silver
Award

RISLEY HALL HOTEL LIMITED

Derby Road, Risley, Draycott DE72 3SS
T: (0115) 939 9000
F: (0115) 939 7766
E: enquiries@risleyhallhotel.co.uk
I: www.risleyhallhotel.co.uk

Risley Hall dates from the 16thC to the 20thC. A haven of comfort and luxury, in elegant surroundings. Individually appointed bedrooms, wedding, banqueting, conference facilities. Licensed to conduct civil wedding ceremonies. Modern English and French cuisine. Menu du jour lunch and dinner. The Orangery is open for light snacks.

Bedrooms: 16 double/
twin
Bathrooms: 16 en suite

Lunch available
Evening meal available
CC: Amex, Delta,
Mastercard, Switch, Visa

B&B per night:
S £95.00–£135.00
D £125.00–£145.00

HB per person:
DY £118.45–£138.45

OPEN All year round

★★★
Silver
Award

THE CHASE HOTEL
Gloucester Road, Ross-on-Wye
HR9 5LH
T: (01989) 763161
F: (01989) 768330
E: info@chasehotel.co.uk
I: www.chasehotel.co.uk

A Georgian country house located near the town centre, set in 11 acres of grounds. Excellent cuisine, professional and friendly service. Close to major road and motorway links.

Bedrooms: 35 double/
twin, 1 triple/multiple
Bathrooms: 36 en suite

Lunch available
Evening meal available
CC: Amex, Delta,
Mastercard, Switch, Visa

B&B per night:
S £70.00–£110.00
D £90.00–£150.00

HB per person:
DY £60.00–£90.00

OPEN All year round

★★

ORLES BARN HOTEL & RESTAURANT

Wilton, Ross-on-Wye HR9 6AE
T: (01989) 562155
F: (01989) 768470
E: orles.barn@clara.net
I: www.orles.barn.clara.net

A converted 16thC barn with original oak beams, set in large gardens with outdoor heated pool and barbecue. Privately owned by Rob and Samantha from South Africa, this friendly establishment offers all modern comforts and excellent cuisine. The extensive menu varies from local salmon and beef to African crocodile and springbok.

Bedrooms: 1 single,
6 double/twin, 2 triple/
multiple
Bathrooms: 8 en suite,
1 private

25% off accommodation for 2 or 3 days; 50% off accommodation for 4 days or more; special golfing group rates.

Evening meal available
CC: Amex, Delta,
Mastercard, Switch, Visa

B&B per night:
S £46.00–£48.00
D £58.00–£68.00

HB per person:
DY £40.00–£44.00

OPEN All year round

The Circle

TOWN INDEX

This can be found at the back of this guide. If you know where you want to stay, the index will give you the page number listing accommodation in your chosen town, city or village.

★★★

THE ROYAL

Palace Pound, Ross-on-Wye HR9 5HZ
T: (01989) 565105
F: (01989) 768058

B&B per night:
S £50.00–£75.00
D £80.00–£135.00

HB per person:
DY £45.00–£79.00

OPEN All year round

This magnificent recently refurbished Victorian hotel, with superb views over the Wye Valley, is ideally located close to A40/M50 yet just a minute's walk to the centre of Ross-on-Wye. With modern amenities and superb cuisine, the Royal provides an ideal base from which to tour this stunning region.

Bedrooms: 6 single, 35 double/twin, 1 triple/ multiple
Bathrooms: 42 en suite

Gardening weekends are held twice yearly and include a visit to local gardens as well as illustrated talks from a professional.

Lunch available
Evening meal available
CC: Amex, Delta,
Mastercard, Switch, Visa

RUGBY, Warwickshire Map ref 4C3 *Tourist Information Centre Tel: (01788) 534970*

★★

THE GROSVENOR HOTEL
81-87 Clifton Road, Rugby
CV21 3QQ
T: (01788) 535686
F: (01788) 541297
E: therugbygrosvenorhotel@
freeserve.co.uk

Bedrooms: 9 single,
17 double/twin; suites available
Bathrooms: 26 en suite

Lunch available
Evening meal available
CC: Amex, Delta, Diners,
Mastercard, Switch, Visa

B&B per night:
S Min £81.00
D Min £97.50

HB per person:
DY Min £99.95

OPEN All year round

Privately-owned hotel, sympathetically renovated and restored and ideally situated close to the town centre and main station. Indoor swimming pool and sauna.

RUTLAND WATER

See under Oakham

SHREWSBURY, Shropshire Map ref 4A3 *Tourist Information Centre Tel: (01743) 281200*

★★★
Silver
Award

ALBRIGHT HUSSEY HOTEL AND RESTAURANT
Ellesmere Road, Shrewsbury
SY4 3AF
T: (01939) 290571 & 290523
F: (01939) 291143
E: abhhotel@aol.com
I: www.albrighthussey.co.uk

Bedrooms: 14 double/
twin; suites available
Bathrooms: 14 en suite

Lunch available
Evening meal available
CC: Amex, Delta, Diners,
Mastercard, Switch, Visa

B&B per night:
S £79.00–£93.50
D £110.00–£148.50

HB per person:
DY £70.50–£89.00

OPEN All year round

Historic 16thC moated manor house, only 2 miles from Shrewsbury town centre. Renowned for fine food, fine wines and impeccable and friendly service. In the heart of Shropshire countryside yet only 5 minutes from M54 motorway link.

SLEAFORD, Lincolnshire Map ref 3A1

★★★

THE LINCOLNSHIRE OAK HOTEL

East Road, Sleaford NG34 7EH
T: (01529) 413807
F: (01529) 413710
E: reception@lincolnshire-oak.co.uk
I: www.sleaford.co.uk/lincolnshire-oak

B&B per night:
S Min £57.50
D £72.50–£87.50

HB per person:
DY £37.50–£49.50

OPEN All year round

Sleaford's highest graded hotel. Renowned locally for its character, service, value and the quality of its food. Bar, restaurant, lounge. Surrounded by over 1.5 acres of grounds and gardens. Ample parking. Easy access from A15 and A17, ideally situated for business or pleasure in southern Lincolnshire.

Bedrooms: 5 single,
12 double/twin
Bathrooms: 17 en suite

Lunch available
Evening meal available
CC: Amex, Delta,
Mastercard, Switch, Visa

Weekend and holiday breaks from only £27.50 B&B and £37.50pppn DB&B.

SOLIHULL, West Midlands Map ref 4B3 *Tourist Information Centre Tel: (0121) 704 6130*

★★★★
Silver Award

SWALLOW ST JOHN'S HOTEL

651 Warwick Road, Solihull
B91 1AT
T: (0121) 711 3000
F: (0121) 711 3963

Bedrooms: 10 single,
164 double/twin,
5 triple/multiple; suites
available
Bathrooms: 179 en suite

Lunch available
Evening meal available
CC: Amex, Delta, Diners,
Mastercard, Switch, Visa

B&B per night:
S £55.00–£190.00
D £70.00–£200.00

OPEN All year round

A large, elegant 4 Star hotel with full leisure facilities, 5 miles from Birmingham International Airport and NEC. Ideal for visiting Stratford, Warwick and Cadbury World.

SPALDING, Lincolnshire Map ref 3A1 *Tourist Information Centre Tel: (01775) 725468*

★★

CLEY HALL HOTEL

22 High Street, Spalding PE11 1TX
T: (01775) 725157
F: (01775) 710785
E: cleyhall@enterprise.net
I: homepages.enterprise.net/cleyhall

Bedrooms: 6 single,
6 double/twin
Bathrooms: 12 en suite

Lunch available
Evening meal available
CC: Amex, Delta, Diners,
Mastercard, Switch, Visa

B&B per night:
S £50.00–£90.00
D £65.00–£120.00

HB per person:
DY £68.50–£82.00

OPEN All year round

18thC Georgian manor-house by the River Welland, 500 metres from town centre, with two award-winning restaurants.

STAFFORD, Staffordshire Map ref 4B3 *Tourist Information Centre Tel: (01785) 619619*

★

ALBRIDGE PRIVATE HOTEL

73 Wolverhampton Road, Stafford
ST17 4AW
T: (01785) 254100
F: (01785) 223895

Bedrooms: 2 single,
3 double/twin, 3 triple/
multiple
Bathrooms: 7 en suite,
1 private

Lunch available
Evening meal available
CC: Amex, Delta, Diners,
Mastercard, Switch, Visa

B&B per night:
S £22.95–£28.95
D £32.00–£40.00

HB per person:
DY £32.95–£40.00

OPEN All year round

Privately-owned 2-storey late Victorian building, conveniently set beside the A449 in the suburbs. Home cooking. 2.75 miles from the M6 junction 13.

STAMFORD, Lincolnshire Map ref 3A1 *Tourist Information Centre Tel: (01780) 755611*

★★★

GARDEN HOUSE HOTEL

St Martins, Stamford PE9 2LP
T: (01780) 763359
F: (01780) 763339
E: gardenhousehotel@stamford60.
freeserve.co.uk
I: www.gardenhousehotel.com

Bedrooms: 2 single,
17 double/twin, 1 triple/
multiple
Bathrooms: 20 en suite

Lunch available
Evening meal available
CC: Amex, Mastercard,
Switch, Visa

B&B per night:
S £50.00–£65.00
D £80.00–£90.00

HB per person:
DY £55.00–£65.00

OPEN All year round

Minotel

Charming 18thC townhouse converted to a hotel, where guests are treated as such by their hosts. Features a conservatory full of floral extravaganza and a meandering garden of 1 acre.

★★★
Silver Award

GEORGE OF STAMFORD

71 St Martins, Stamford PE9 2LB
T: (01780) 750750 & 750700
F: (01780) 750701
E: reservations@
georgehotelofstamford.com
I: www.georgehotelofstamford.com

Bedrooms: 10 single,
26 double/twin,
11 triple/multiple; suites
available
Bathrooms: 47 en suite

Lunch available
Evening meal available
CC: Amex, Delta, Diners,
Mastercard, Switch, Visa

B&B per night:
S £80.00
D £115.00–£225.00

OPEN All year round

Full of antique furniture, oak panelling and log fires, this historic inn is one of England's most famous resting places. Popular restaurant, more informal garden lounge.

STOKE-ON-TRENT, Staffordshire Map ref 4B2 *Tourist Information Centre Tel: (01782) 236000*

★★★
Silver Award

GEORGE HOTEL

Swan Square, Burslem, Stoke-on-
Trent ST6 2AE
T: (01782) 577544
F: (01782) 837496
E: georgestoke@btinternet.com
I: www.georgehotelstoke.cwc.net

Bedrooms: 9 single,
26 double/twin, 4 triple/
multiple
Bathrooms: 39 en suite

Lunch available
Evening meal available
CC: Amex, Delta, Diners,
Mastercard, Switch, Visa

B&B per night:
S £40.00–£80.00
D £50.00–£95.00

HB per person:
DY £50.00–£70.00

OPEN All year round

Attractive neo-Georgian building. Conveniently situated between the Midlands, Liverpool and Manchester. Award-winning restaurant. Good centre for exploring the multitude of pottery outlets.

★★★

THE NORTH STAFFORD
Station Road, Stoke-on-Trent
ST4 2AE
T: (01782) 744477
F: (01782) 744580
E: claire.portas@principalhotels.co.uk
I: www.principalhotels.co.uk

Classical and spacious, the North Stafford is situated opposite Stoke railway station and 10 miles from junction 16 of M6. Alton Towers 14 miles away.

Bedrooms: 27 single, 50 double/twin, 3 triple/multiple
Bathrooms: 80 en suite

Lunch available
Evening meal available
CC: Amex, Delta, Mastercard, Switch, Visa

B&B per night:
S £40.00–£95.00
D £60.00–£110.00

HB per person:
DY £39.00–£60.00

OPEN All year round

Principal Hotels/Utell International

★★

Independently owned and recently refurbished motel. Family bedrooms; all rooms en suite. Excellent restaurant offering varied and affordable selection. Open to residents and non-residents. Situated in the heart of the Potteries. Ideal starting point for Alton Towers and Staffordshire Moorlands. Special short breaks. Limousine hire. Warm welcome.

PLOUGH MOTEL AND RESTAURANT
Campbell Road, Stoke-on-Trent ST4 4EN
T: (01782) 414685
F: (01782) 414669
E: info@ploughmotel.co.uk
I: www.ploughmotel.co.uk

Bedrooms: 14 double/twin, 6 triple/multiple
Bathrooms: 20 en suite

Lunch available
Evening meal available
CC: Amex, Delta, Mastercard, Switch, Visa

B&B per night:
S £38.50–£48.50
D £48.50–£58.50

OPEN All year round

★★

AULD STOCKS HOTEL
The Square, Stow-on-the-Wold, Cheltenham GL54 1AF
T: (01451) 830666
F: (01451) 870014

17thC Grade II Listed hotel facing village green. Refurbished to combine modern comforts with original charm and character. Ideal base for exploring the Cotswolds.

Bedrooms: 1 single, 16 double/twin, 1 triple/multiple
Bathrooms: 18 en suite

Lunch available
Evening meal available
CC: Delta, Mastercard, Switch, Visa

B&B per night:
S Min £40.00
D Min £80.00

HB per person:
DY Min £59.50

OPEN All year round

The Independents

★★★
Silver Award

'The Grapevine should be National Treasure'. This unpretentious 17thC market town hotel, exuding warmth and hospitality, has a magnificent historic vine crowning its romantic conservatory restaurant. Beautiful furnishings and fine food are complemented by caring staff for whom nothing is too much trouble. Explore Oxford, Stratford and picturesque villages in mellow Cotswold stone.

BEST WESTERN GRAPEVINE HOTEL
Sheep Street, Stow-on-the-Wold, Cheltenham GL54 1AU
T: (01451) 830344
F: (01451) 832278
E: wts@vines.co.uk
I: www.vines.co.uk

Bedrooms: 20 double/twin, 2 triple/multiple
Bathrooms: 22 en suite

Lunch available
Evening meal available
CC: Amex, Delta, Diners, Mastercard, Switch, Visa

B&B per night:
S £85.00–£99.00
D £140.00–£180.00

HB per person:
DY £95.00–£115.00

OPEN All year round

Best Western Hotels

STOW-ON-THE-WOLD continued

Rating Applied For		

THE ROMAN COURT HOTEL & RESTAURANT

Fosse Way, Stow-on-the-Wold,
Cheltenham GL54 1JX
T: (01451) 870539
F: (01451) 870639
E: logozz@ad.com
I: www.theromancourthotel.co.uk

B&B per night:
S £45.00–£55.00
D £65.00–£85.00

HB per person:
DY £50.00–£70.00

OPEN All year round

Ideally situated in the heart of the Cotswolds. Offering quality accommodation with traditional Italian and English food featuring local produce. An entirely sybaritic base from which to discover the delights of an Area of Outstanding Natural Beauty or be centrally and comfortably placed for Birmingham, Bristol and Oxford's business centres.

Bedrooms: 13 double/ twin, 4 triple/multiple; suites available
Bathrooms: 17 en suite

Lunch available
Evening meal available
CC: Amex, Diners, Mastercard, Switch, Visa

Leisure break-3 days or more 15% off mid-week break-minimum 2-night stay 10% off.

♒🛍️📞🖥️🖨️♿🗝️📺💻🖥️🛏️⛵🅿️🎠🐾🅿️

★★★
Silver
Award

THE ROYALIST HOTEL
Digbeth Street, Stow-on-the-Wold,
Cheltenham GL54 1BN
T: (01451) 830670
F: (01451) 870048
E: info@theroyalisthotel.co.uk
I: www.theroyalisthotel.co.uk

Bedrooms: 8 double/ twin; suites available
Bathrooms: 8 en suite

Lunch available
Evening meal available
CC: Amex, Delta, Mastercard, Switch, Visa

B&B per night:
S £50.00–£65.00
D £90.00–£170.00

OPEN All year round

The oldest inn in England (947 AD) with all the inherent charm and character of the past, yet every modern day facility as well.

♒🐾8♿🏨📞🖥️🖨️♿🗝️📺💻🛏️⛵🐾🅿️

★★★

STOW LODGE HOTEL

The Square, Stow-on-the-Wold,
Cheltenham GL54 1AB
T: (01451) 830485
F: (01451) 831671
E: chris@stowlodge.com
I: www.stowlodge.com

B&B per night:
S £50.00–£100.00
D £65.00–£130.00

OPEN All year round

Stow Lodge Hotel is situated in its own picturesque grounds overlooking the market square of the historic town of Stow-on-the-Wold. The hotel has been family owned and run for over forty years and has built up a fine reputation for its friendly hospitality and excellent service.

Bedrooms: 1 single, 19 double/twin, 1 triple/ multiple
Bathrooms: 21 en suite

Evening meal available
CC: Delta, Mastercard, Switch, Visa

We offer special half board rates if staying two or more nights.

♒🐾5♿🏨📞🖥️🖨️♿🗝️🌙🛏️🅿️

★★★

THE UNICORN INN
Sheep Street, Stow-on-the-Wold,
Cheltenham GL54 1HQ
T: (01451) 830257
F: (01451) 831090
E: bookings@cotswold-inns-hotels.co.uk
I: www.cotswold-inns-hotels.co.uk

Bedrooms: 2 single, 18 double/twin
Bathrooms: 20 en suite

Lunch available
Evening meal available
CC: Amex, Delta, Diners, Mastercard, Switch, Visa

B&B per night:
S £60.00–£70.00
D £90.00–£125.00

HB per person:
DY £82.95–£92.95

OPEN All year round

Ⓖⓡ
Grand Heritage Hotels

17thC coaching inn, well placed for touring Cotswolds. Recently refurbished. Its honey-stoned walls and flower boxes are as typical of the Cotswolds as the warm welcome inside.

♒🐾🏨📞🖥️🖨️♿🗝️📺💻🛏️⛵🐾🅿️

ACCESSIBILITY

Look for the 🦽🦼🚶 symbols which indicate accessibility for wheelchair users. A list of establishments is at the front of this guide.

STRATFORD–UPON–AVON, Warwickshire Map ref 2B1 *Tourist Information Centre Tel: (01789) 293127*

★★★ **FALCON HOTEL**

Chapel Street, Stratford-upon-Avon CV37 6HA
T: (01789) 279953
F: (01789) 414260
E: thefalcon@corushotels.com
I: www.regalhotels.co.uk/thefalcon

Bedrooms: 4 single, 70 double/twin, 10 triple/multiple; suites available
Bathrooms: 84 en suite

Lunch available
Evening meal available
CC: Amex, Delta, Diners, Mastercard, Switch, Visa

B&B per night:
S £57.00–£99.00
D £115.00–£155.00

HB per person:
DY £62.00–£93.00

OPEN All year round

A magnificently preserved 16thC timbered inn, with a skilfully blended modern extension, large enclosed garden and ample car parking, situated in the heart of Stratford.

Corus & Regal Hotels/ Utell International

★★★★ **STRATFORD MANOR HOTEL**

Warwick Road, Stratford-upon-Avon CV37 0PY
T: (01789) 731173
F: (01789) 731131
E: stratfordmanor@marstonhotels.co.uk
I: www.marstonhotels.co.uk

Bedrooms: 104 double/twin
Bathrooms: 104 en suite

Lunch available
Evening meal available
CC: Amex, Delta, Diners, Mastercard, Switch, Visa

B&B per night:
S £105.00–£145.00
D £125.00–£185.00

HB per person:
DY £79.50–£105.00

OPEN All year round

A warm welcome awaits you. Superb leisure facilities. Ideal base for exploring Cotswolds and Stratford-upon-Avon. Half-board rate based on minimum 2-night stay.

Marston Hotels

★★★★ Silver Award **STRATFORD VICTORIA**

Arden Street, Stratford-upon-Avon CV37 6QQ
T: (01789) 271000
F: (01789) 271001
I: www.stratfordvictoria@marstonhotels.com

Bedrooms: 10 single, 39 double/twin, 51 triple/multiple; suites available
Bathrooms: 100 en suite

Lunch available
Evening meal available
CC: Amex, Delta, Diners, Mastercard, Switch, Visa

B&B per night:
S £92.50–£135.00
D £109.00–£175.00

HB per person:
DY £69.50–£95.00

OPEN All year round

Modern, Victorian-style hotel close to town centre. Restaurant, bar, gym, beauty salon, whirlpool spa and conference facilities. Half-board rate based on minimum 2 nights.

Marston Hotels

STROUD, Gloucestershire Map ref 2B1 *Tourist Information Centre Tel: (01453) 760960*

★★★ **BEAR OF RODBOROUGH HOTEL**

Rodborough Common, Stroud GL5 5DE
T: (01453) 878522
F: (01453) 872523
E: bookings@cotswold-inns-hotels.co.uk
I: www.cotswold-inns-hotels.co.uk

Bedrooms: 6 single, 40 double/twin
Bathrooms: 46 en suite

Lunch available
Evening meal available
CC: Amex, Delta, Diners, Mastercard, Switch, Visa

B&B per night:
S £75.00–£95.00
D £120.00–£130.00

HB per person:
DY £99.95–£119.95

OPEN All year round

Newly refurbished 17thC country hotel with log fires and oak beams set in 600 acres of National Trust land. Between Stroud and Minchinhampton.

Grand Heritage Hotels

SYMONDS YAT, Herefordshire Map ref 2A1

★★

ROYAL HOTEL

Symonds Yat East, Nr Ross-on-Wye HR9 6JL
T: (01600) 890238
F: (01600) 890777
E: info@royalhotel-symondsyat.com
I: www.royalhotel-symondsyat.com

B&B per night:
S £33.00–£48.00
D £66.00–£86.00

OPEN All year round

This family-run 1876 hunting lodge is set majestically on the edge of the River Wye and Royal Forest of Dean. Fantastic location for outdoor activities, walking and touring the Wye Valley. The river view restaurant offers excellent and innovative cuisine. Groups welcome. Just off A40 between Ross and Monmouth.

Bedrooms: 2 single, 19 double/twin
Bathrooms: 21 en suite

Lunch available
Evening meal available
CC: Amex, Delta, Diners, Mastercard, Switch, Visa

Stay 2 nights or more, mid-week or weekend, and receive a complimentary starter or dessert when ordering a main restaurant meal.

TELFORD, Shropshire Map ref 4A3 *Tourist Information Centre Tel: (01952) 238008*

★★★
Silver
Award

HADLEY PARK HOUSE HOTEL AND BISTRO

Hadley Park, Telford TF1 6QJ
T: (01952) 677269
F: (01952) 676938
E: hadley.park@btclick.com

Bedrooms: 2 single,
8 double/twin
Bathrooms: 10 en suite

Lunch available
Evening meal available
CC: Amex, Delta, Diners,
Mastercard, Switch, Visa

B&B per night:
S £60.00–£80.00
D £60.00–£100.00

OPEN All year round

*Enjoy the comforts of this 200-year-old manor house, set in 3 acres of gardens.
Conservatory Bistro offering friendly welcome and value for money cuisine.*

★★★

LEA MANOR HOTEL

Holyhead Road, Albrighton,
Wolverhampton WV7 3BX
T: (01902) 373266
F: (01902) 372853
E: hotel@leamanor.co.uk
I: www.leamanor.co.uk

Bedrooms: 6 single,
9 double/twin, 1 triple/
multiple
Bathrooms: 15 en suite

Lunch available
Evening meal available
CC: Amex, Delta,
Mastercard, Switch, Visa

B&B per night:
S £49.50–£65.00
D £55.50–£75.00

OPEN All year round

Ⓒⓡ
Minotel

*On the A464, convenient for Wolverhampton, Ironbridge Gorge Museum, Weston Park and
RAF Museum at Cosford. Well placed for touring the glorious Shropshire countryside.*

TUTBURY, Staffordshire Map ref 4B3

★★★

YE OLDE DOG & PARTRIDGE HOTEL

High Street, Tutbury, Burton upon Trent
DE13 9LS
T: (01283) 813030
F: (01283) 813178
E: info@dogandpartridge.net
I: www.dogandpartridge.net

B&B per night:
S £60.00–£75.00
D £75.00–£85.00

HB per person:
DY Min £72.00

OPEN All year round

*One of England's oldest and finest
15thC coaching inns, situated in the
historic village of Tutbury. This warm
and friendly hotel offers luxury
accommodation and excellent dining
facilities in both the carvery and
award-winning brasserie
restaurants. The bedrooms are all
individually designed and furnished
to the highest standards.*

Bedrooms: 3 single,
16 double/twin, 1 triple/
multiple
Bathrooms: 20 en suite

Lunch available
Evening meal available
CC: Amex, Mastercard,
Switch, Visa

2-night Border Break £100pp including dinner and
house wine. For an extra £30 dine in our brasserie
restaurant.

UPTON-UPON-SEVERN, Worcestershire Map ref 2B1 *Tourist Information Centre Tel: (01684) 594200*

★★★

WHITE LION HOTEL

21 High Street, Upton-upon-Severn,
Nr Malvern WR8 0HJ
T: (01684) 592551
F: (01684) 59333
E: info@whitelionhotel.demon.co.uk
I: www.whitelion.demon.co.uk

B&B per night:
S £53.00–£66.00
D £77.00–£88.00

HB per person:
DY £52.50–£55.00

OPEN All year round

Minotel

*Upton's premier dining venue is
home of Henry Fielding's 'Tom Jones'.
Sample our homemade bread with a
snack, or book into the restaurant
and indulge in our creative cuisine.
Enjoy a drink in our CAMRA
approved bar, or take a break in one
of our individually decorated en suite
bedrooms.*

Bedrooms: 10 double/
twin
Bathrooms: 10 en suite

Lunch available
Evening meal available
CC: Amex, Delta,
Mastercard, Switch, Visa

Discounts usually available for block bookings or
multiple night stays.

QUALITY ASSURANCE SCHEME

Star ratings and awards were correct at the time of going to press but are
subject to change. Please check at the time of booking.

★★★ **CHESFORD GRANGE HOTEL**

Chesford Bridge, Kenilworth
CV8 2LD
T: (01926) 859331
F: (01926) 859075
E: samanthabrown@
principalhotels
I: www.principalhotels.co.uk

Bedrooms: 11 single,
130 double/twin,
13 triple/multiple; suites
available
Bathrooms: 154 en suite

Lunch available
Evening meal available
CC: Amex, Mastercard,
Visa

B&B per night:
S £70.00–£145.00
D £40.00–£165.00

HB per person:
DY £85.00–£160.00

OPEN All year round

Elegant Tudor-style hotel in the glorious Warwickshire countryside. Full leisure facilities and superb grounds.

♒⛄♿&🖥⛺☎️🚭Ⓢ⚲🅗Ⓞ🔄⛏️🛏️🍽️📺☆🍷∪♪▶🎿🐴🐕🏠P

Ⓒ️
Principal Hotels/Utell
International

★★★

THE LORD LEYCESTER HOTEL

17 Jury Street, Warwick CV34 4EJ
T: (01926) 491481
F: (01926) 491561
E: reception@lord-leycester.co.uk
I: www.lord-leycester.co.uk

The Lord Leycester Hotel offers a unique blend of service, character, convenience, history and value. Grade II Listed Georgian building, close to castle. Renowned cuisine, all-day dining, bar, meeting rooms. Fifty bedrooms, car parking. Easy drive NEC and Stratford.

Bedrooms: 12 single,
32 double/twin, 6 triple/
multiple
Bathrooms: 50 en suite

Lunch available
Evening meal available
CC: Amex, Delta, Diners,
Mastercard, Switch, Visa

Weekend and holiday breaks from only £27.50 B&B
and £37.50pppn DB&B .

B&B per night:
S Min £57.50
D £72.50–£87.50

HB per person:
DY £37.50–£49.50

OPEN All year round

♒⛄🖥&🖥⛺☎️🚭Ⓢ⚲🅗Ⓞ🔄⛏️🛏️🍽️▶🎿🐕🏠P

★★ **THE OLD FOURPENNY SHOP HOTEL**

27-29 Crompton Street, Warwick
CV34 6HJ
T: (01926) 491360
F: (01926) 411892

Bedrooms: 2 single,
8 double/twin, 1 triple/
multiple
Bathrooms: 11 en suite

Lunch available
Evening meal available
CC: Amex, Delta, Diners,
Mastercard, Switch, Visa

B&B per night:
S £43.50–£54.50
D £75.00–£85.00

OPEN All year round

Recently refurbished, offering real ale, real food and friendly hospitality. Situated in a quiet side street, close to town centre.

♒⛄10♿&🖥⛺☎️🚭Ⓢ⚲🅗🛏️🍷▶🎿🐴🐕🐎🏠P

★★ **HIGH VIEW HOTEL**

156 Midland Road, Wellingborough
NN8 1NG
T: (01933) 278733
F: (01933) 225948
E: hotelhighview@hotmail.com

Bedrooms: 5 single,
6 double/twin, 3 triple/
multiple
Bathrooms: 14 en suite

Evening meal available
CC: Amex, Delta, Diners,
Mastercard, Switch, Visa

B&B per night:
S £34.00–£45.00
D £45.00–£56.00

HB per person:
DY £29.50–£40.00

OPEN All year round

Large, detached, modernised building with pleasant gardens. In quiet tree-lined area near town centre and railway station. All rooms en suite.

♒⛄3♿&🖥⛺☎️🚭Ⓢ⚲🅗🛏️🍷P

CHECK THE MAPS

The colour maps at the front of this guide show all the cities, towns and villages for which you will find accommodation entries. Refer to the town index to find the page on which they are listed.

WOLVERHAMPTON, West Midlands Map ref 4B3 *Tourist Information Centre Tel: (01902) 556110*

★★★

PATSHULL PARK HOTEL, GOLF AND COUNTRY CLUB

Patshull Park, Pattingham, Wolverhampton WV6 7HR
T: (01902) 700100
F: (01902) 700874
E: sales@patshull-park.co.uk
I: www.patshull-park.co.uk

Modern hotel nestling sympathetically in the midst of this beautiful Capability Brown designed country estate. Own golf course, fishing lakes and extensive leisure complex.

Bedrooms: 45 double/ twin, 4 triple/multiple; suites available
Bathrooms: 49 en suite

Lunch available
Evening meal available
CC: Amex, Delta, Diners, Mastercard, Switch, Visa

For the latest offers visit our website.

B&B per night:
S £44.50–£107.50
D £49.00–£117.50

HB per person:
DY £39.50–£92.25

WOODHALL SPA, Lincolnshire Map ref 4D2

★★

EAGLE LODGE HOTEL
The Broadway, Woodhall Spa
LN10 6ST
T: (01526) 353231
F: (01526) 352797
E: enquiries@eaglelodgehotel.co.uk
I: www.eaglelodgehotel.co.uk

Bedrooms: 4 single, 17 double/twin, 3 triple/ multiple
Bathrooms: 23 en suite, 1 private

Lunch available
Evening meal available
CC: Amex, Diners, Mastercard, Switch, Visa

Mock-Tudor country house hotel in centre of Victorian spa village. Close to both Woodhall Spa golf-courses. Excellent food, real ales, friendly atmosphere.

B&B per night:
S £32.00–£45.00
D £64.00–£70.00

HB per person:
DY £45.00–£48.00

OPEN All year round

★★★

THE GOLF HOTEL
The Broadway, Woodhall Spa LN10 6SG
T: (01526) 353535
F: (01526) 353096
I: www.principalhotels.co.uk

19thC country house hotel, set in 7 acres of gardens in the beautiful village of Woodhall Spa, with trolley access to the famous Woodhall Spa Golf Course. The historic city of Lincoln with its magnificent cathedral, castle and cobbled streets, is a short drive away for shopping and sightseeing.

Bedrooms: 6 single, 44 double/twin
Bathrooms: 50 en suite

Lunch available
Evening meal available
CC: Amex, Delta, Diners, Mastercard, Switch, Visa

B&B per night:
S £30.00–£65.00
D £60.00–£85.00

HB per person:
DY £42.00–£77.00

OPEN All year round

Principal Hotels/Utell International

★★★

PETWOOD HOTEL
Stixwould Road, Woodhall Spa
LN10 6QF
T: (01526) 352411
F: (01526) 353473
E: reception@petwood.co.uk
I: www.petwood.co.uk

Bedrooms: 6 single, 44 double/twin; suites available
Bathrooms: 50 en suite

Lunch available
Evening meal available
CC: Amex, Delta, Diners, Mastercard, Switch, Visa

Country house with superb restaurant, set in 30 acres of formal gardens and woodland. Putting green, croquet, snooker room. Former officers' mess of the famous Dambusters Squadron.

B&B per night:
S £63.00
D £126.00

HB per person:
DY £54.00–£80.00

OPEN All year round

WOODSTOCK, Oxfordshire

See South of England region

★★ **YE OLDE TALBOT HOTEL**
Friar Street, Worcester WR1 2NA
T: (01905) 23573
F: (01905) 612760

Bedrooms: 8 single,
21 double/twin;
Bathrooms: 29 en suite

Lunch available
Evening meal available
CC: Amex, Delta, Diners,
Mastercard, Switch, Visa

B&B per night:
S £36.00–£59.50
D £52.00–£69.50

OPEN All year round

Originally an old courtroom, located close to the town centre and the cathedral, to which it once belonged. Only minutes from the M5 motorway.

WYE VALLEY

See under Fownhope, Goodrich, Hereford, Ross-on-Wye

USE YOUR *i*s

There are more than 550 Tourist Information Centres throughout England offering friendly help with accommodation and holiday ideas as well as suggestions of places to visit and things to do. There may well be a centre in your home town which can help you before you set out. You'll find addresses in the local Phone Book.

A brief guide to the main Towns and Villages offering accommodation in the

Heart of England

A ABBOTS SALFORD, WARWICKSHIRE - This hamlet gets its name from the place where the Salt Way forded the River Avon and from the Abbots of Evesham who owned Salford Hall.

ALCESTER, WARWICKSHIRE - Town has Roman origins and many old buildings around the High Street. It is close to Ragley Hall, the 18th C Palladian mansion with its magnificent baroque Great Hall.

ALREWAS, STAFFORDSHIRE - Delightful village of black and white cottages, past which the willow-fringed Trent runs. The Trent and Mersey Canal enhances the scene and Fradley Junction, a mile away, is one of the most charming inland waterway locations in the country.

ASHBOURNE, DERBYSHIRE - Market town on the edge of the Peak District National Park and an excellent centre for walking. Its impressive church with 212-ft spire stands in an unspoilt old street. Ashbourne is well-known for gingerbread and its Shrovetide football match.

B BERKELEY, GLOUCESTERSHIRE - Town dominated by the castle where Edward II was murdered. Dating from Norman times, it is still the home of the Berkeley family and is open to the public April to September Tuesday to Sunday and October Sundays. The Jenner Museum is here and Slimbridge Wildfowl Trust is nearby.

BIGGIN-BY-HARTINGTON, DERBYSHIRE - Tiny village high in the Peak District above the River Dove approx. 6 miles equidistant from Bakewell and Matlock. Excellent area for walking and exploring attractions nearby.

BIRMINGHAM, WEST MIDLANDS - Britain's second city, whose attractions include Centenary Square and the ICC with Symphony Hall, the NEC, the City Art Gallery, Barber Institute of Fine Arts, 17th C Aston Hall, science and railway museums, Jewellery Quarter, Cadbury World, 2 cathedrals and Botanical Gardens.

BOURTON-ON-THE-WATER, GLOUCESTERSHIRE - The River Windrush flows through this famous Cotswold village which has a green, and cottages and houses of Cotswold stone. Its many attractions include a model village, Birdland, a Motor Museum and the Cotswold Perfumery.

BRIDGNORTH, SHROPSHIRE - Red sandstone riverside town in 2 parts - High and Low - linked by a cliff railway. Much of interest including a ruined Norman keep, half-timbered 16th C houses, Midland Motor Museum and Severn Valley Railway.

BROADWAY, WORCESTERSHIRE - Beautiful Cotswold village called the 'Show village of England', with 16th C stone houses and cottages. Near the village is Broadway Tower with magnificent views over 12 counties and a country park with nature trails and adventure playground.

C CASTLE DONINGTON, LEICESTERSHIRE - A Norman castle once stood here. The world's largest collection of single-seater racing cars is displayed at Donington Park alongside the racing circuit, and an Aeropark Visitor Centre can be seen at nearby East Midlands International Airport.

CHADDESLEY CORBETT, WORCESTERSHIRE - An attractive village with a blend of Georgian and timber framed buildings. One mile west is the moated Harvington Hall and 4 miles, the carpet town of Kidderminster.

CHELTENHAM, GLOUCESTERSHIRE - Cheltenham was developed as a spa town in the 18th C and has some beautiful Regency architecture, in particular the Pittville Pump Room. It holds international music and literature festivals and is also famous for its race meetings and cricket.

CHESTERFIELD, DERBYSHIRE - Famous for the twisted spire of its parish church, Chesterfield has some fine modern buildings and excellent shopping facilities, including a large, traditional open-air market. Hardwick Hall and Bolsover Castle are nearby.

CHIPPING CAMPDEN, GLOUCESTERSHIRE - Outstanding Cotswold wool town with many old stone gabled houses, a splendid church and 17th C almshouses. Nearby are Kiftsgate Court Gardens and Hidcote Manor Gardens (National Trust).

CHURCH STRETTON, SHROPSHIRE - Church Stretton lies under the eastern slope of the Longmynd surrounded by hills. It is ideal for walkers, with marvellous views, golf and gliding. Wenlock Edge is not far away.

CIRENCESTER, GLOUCESTERSHIRE - 'Capital of the Cotswolds', Cirencester was Britain's second most important Roman town with many finds housed in the Corinium Museum. It has a very fine Perpendicular church and old houses around the market place.

COVENTRY, WEST MIDLANDS - Modern city with a long history. It has many places of interest including the post-war and ruined medieval cathedrals, art gallery and museums, some 16th C almshouses, St Mary's Guildhall, Lunt Roman fort and the Belgrade Theatre.

D DERBY, DERBYSHIRE - Modern industrial city but with ancient origins. There is a wide range of attractions including several museums (notably Royal Crown Derby), a theatre, a concert hall, and the cathedral with fine ironwork and Bess of Hardwick's tomb.

E EVESHAM, WORCESTERSHIRE - Market town in the centre of a fruit-growing area. There are pleasant walks along the River Avon and many old houses and inns. A fine 16th C bell tower stands between 2 churches near the medieval Almonry Museum.

F FAIRFORD, GLOUCESTERSHIRE - Small town with a 15th C wool church famous for its complete 15th C stained glass windows, interesting carvings and original wall paintings. It is an excellent touring centre and the Cotswolds Wildlife Park is nearby.

FINEDON, NORTHAMPTONSHIRE - Large ironstone village with interesting Victorian houses and cottages and an ironstone 14th C church. The inn claims to be the oldest in England.

FOWNHOPE, HEREFORDSHIRE - Attractive village close to the River Wye with black and white cottages and other interesting houses. It has a large church with a Norman tower and a 14th C spire.

G GAINSBOROUGH, LINCOLNSHIRE - Britain's most inland port has strong connections with the Pilgrim Fathers. Gainsborough Old Hall, where they worshipped, boasts a 15th C manor house with complete kitchens.

- **GLOSSOP, DERBYSHIRE** - Town in dramatic moorland surroundings with views over the High Peak. The settlement can be traced back to Roman times but expanded during the Industrial Revolution.

- **GLOUCESTER, GLOUCESTERSHIRE** - A Roman city and inland port, its cathedral is one of the most beautiful in Britain. Gloucester's many attractions include museums and the restored warehouses in the Victorian docks containing the National Waterways Museum, Robert Opie Packaging Collection and other attractions.

- **GOODRICH, HEREFORDSHIRE** - Village standing above the River Wye with the magnificent ruins of a red sandstone castle high above it, now in the care of English Heritage.

- **GRINDLEFORD, DERBYSHIRE** - Good centre for walking, at the eastern end of the Hope Valley. Longshaw Estate is nearby with 1500 acres of moorland and woodland.

- **H HEREFORD, HEREFORDSHIRE** - Agricultural county town, its cathedral containing much Norman work, a large chained library and the world-famous Mappa Mundi exhibition. Among the city's varied attractions are several museums including the Cider Museum and the Old House.

- **HOCKLEY HEATH, WEST MIDLANDS** - Village near the National Trust property of Packwood House, with its well-known yew garden, and Kenilworth.

- **HORNCASTLE, LINCOLNSHIRE** - Pleasant market town near the Lincolnshire Wolds, which was once a walled Roman settlement. It was the scene of a decisive Civil War battle, relics of which can be seen in the church. Tennyson's bride lived here.

- **I IRONBRIDGE, SHROPSHIRE** - Small town on the Severn where the Industrial Revolution began. It has the world's first iron bridge built in 1779. The Ironbridge Gorge Museum, of exceptional interest, comprises a rebuilt turn-of-the-century town and sites spread over 6 square miles.

- **K KENILWORTH, WARWICKSHIRE** - The main feature of the town is the ruined 12th C castle. It has many royal associations but was damaged by Cromwell. A good base for visiting Coventry, Leamington Spa and Warwick.

- **L LEAMINGTON SPA, WARWICKSHIRE** - 18th C spa town with many fine Georgian and Regency houses. The refurbished 19th C Pump Rooms with Heritage Centre. The attractive Jephson Gardens are laid out alongside the river.

- **LEDBURY, HEREFORDSHIRE** - Town with cobbled streets and many black and white timbered houses, including the 17th C market house and old inns. In attractive countryside nearby is Eastnor Castle, a venue for many events, with an interesting collection of tapestries and armour.

- **LEEK, STAFFORDSHIRE** - Old silk and textile town, with some interesting buildings and a number of inns dating from the 17th C. Its art gallery has displays of embroidery. Brindley Mill, designed by James Brindley, has been restored as a museum.

- **LEOMINSTER, HEREFORDSHIRE** - The town owed its prosperity to wool and has many interesting buildings, notably the timber-framed Grange Court, a former town hall. The impressive Norman priory church has 3 naves and a ducking stool. Berrington Hall (National Trust) is nearby.

- **LICHFIELD, STAFFORDSHIRE** - Lichfield is Dr Samuel Johnson's birthplace and commemorates him with a museum and statue. The 13th C cathedral has 3 spires and the west front is full of statues. Among the attractive town buildings is the Heritage Centre. The Regimental Museum is in Whittington Barracks.

- **LINCOLN, LINCOLNSHIRE** - Ancient city dominated by the magnificent 11th C cathedral with its triple towers. A Roman gateway is still used and there are medieval houses lining narrow, cobbled streets. Other attractions include the Norman castle, several museums and the Usher Gallery.

- **LOUTH, LINCOLNSHIRE** - Attractive old market town set on the eastern edge of the Lincolnshire Wolds. St James's Church has an impressive tower and spire and there are the remains of a Cistercian abbey. The museum contains an interesting collection of local material.

- **LOWER SLAUGHTER, GLOUCESTERSHIRE** - Pretty Cotswold village of stone cottages with a river running through the main street.

- **LYDNEY, GLOUCESTERSHIRE** - Small town in the Forest of Dean close to the River Severn, where Roman remains have been found. It has a steam centre with engines, coaches and wagons.

- **M MALVERN, WORCESTERSHIRE** - Spa town in Victorian times, its water is today bottled and sold worldwide. 6 resorts, set on the slopes of the Hills, form part of Malvern. Great Malvern Priory has splendid 15th C windows. It is an excellent walking centre.

- **MARKET DRAYTON, SHROPSHIRE** - Old market town with black and white buildings and 17th C houses, also acclaimed for its gingerbread. Hodnet Hall is in the vicinity with its beautiful landscaped gardens covering 60 acres.

- **MATLOCK, DERBYSHIRE** - The town lies beside the narrow valley of the River Derwent surrounded by steep wooded hills. Good centre for exploring Derbyshire's best scenery.

- **MELTON MOWBRAY, LEICESTERSHIRE** - Close to the attractive Vale of Belvoir and famous for its pork pies and Stilton cheese which are the subjects of special displays in the museum. It has a beautiful church with a tower 100ft high.

- **MORETON-IN-MARSH, GLOUCESTERSHIRE** - Attractive town of Cotswold stone with 17th C houses, an ideal base for touring the Cotswolds. Some of the local attractions include Batsford Park Arboretum, the Jacobean Chastleton House and Sezincote Garden.

- **N NOTTINGHAM, NOTTINGHAMSHIRE** - Attractive modern city with a rich history. Outside its castle, now a museum, is Robin Hood's statue. Attractions include 'The Tales of Robin Hood'; the Lace Hall; Wollaton Hall; museums and excellent facilities for shopping, sports and entertainment.

- **O OAKHAM, LEICESTERSHIRE** - Pleasant former county town of Rutland. Fine 12th C Great Hall, part of its castle, with a historic collection of horseshoes. An octagonal Butter Cross stands in the market-place and Rutland County Museum, Rutland Farm Park and Rutland Water are of interest.

- **OSWESTRY, SHROPSHIRE** - Town close to the Welsh border, the scene of many battles. To the north are the remains of a large Iron Age hill fort. An excellent centre for exploring Shropshire and Offa's Dyke.

- **P PAINSWICK, GLOUCESTERSHIRE** - Picturesque wool town with inns and houses dating from the 14th C. Painswick Rococo Garden is open to visitors from January to November, and the house is a Palladian mansion. The churchyard is famous for its yew trees.

- **R ROSS-ON-WYE, HEREFORDSHIRE** - Attractive market town with a 17th C market hall, set above the River Wye. There are lovely views over the surrounding countryside from the Prospect and the town is close to Goodrich Castle and the Welsh border.

- **RUGBY, WARWICKSHIRE** - Town famous for its public school which gave its name to Rugby Union football and which featured in 'Tom Brown's Schooldays'.

S SHREWSBURY, SHROPSHIRE - Beautiful historic town on the River Severn retaining many fine old timber-framed houses. Its attractions include Rowley's Museum with Roman finds, remains of a castle, Clive House Museum, St Chad's 18th C round church, rowing on the river and the Shrewsbury Flower Show in August.

• **SLEAFORD, LINCOLNSHIRE** - Market town whose parish church has one of the oldest stone spires in England and particularly fine tracery round the windows.

• **SOLIHULL, WEST MIDLANDS** - On the outskirts of Birmingham. Some Tudor houses and a 13th C church remain amongst the new public buildings and shopping centre. The 16th C Malvern Hall is now a school and the 15th C Chester House at Knowle is now a library.

• **SPALDING, LINCOLNSHIRE** - Fenland town famous for its bulbfields. A spectaclular Flower Parade takes place at the beginning of May each year and the tulips at Springfields show gardens are followed by displays of roses and bedding plants in summer. Interesting local museum.

• **STAFFORD, STAFFORDSHIRE** - The town has a long history and some half-timbered buildings still remain, notably the 16th C High House. There are several museums in the town and Shugborough Hall and the famous angler Izaak Walton's cottage, now a museum, are nearby.

• **STAMFORD, LINCOLNSHIRE** - Exceptionally beautiful and historic town with many houses of architectural interest, several notable churches and other public buildings all in the local stone. Burghley House, built by William Cecil, is a magnificent Tudor mansion on the edge of the town.

• **STOKE-ON-TRENT, STAFFORDSHIRE** - Famous for its pottery. Factories of several famous makers, including Josiah Wedgwood, can be visited. The City Museum has one of the finest pottery and porcelain collections in the world.

• **STOW-ON-THE-WOLD, GLOUCESTERSHIRE** - Attractive Cotswold wool town with a large market-place and some fine houses, especially the old grammar school. There is an interesting church dating from Norman times. Stow-on-the-Wold is surrounded by lovely countryside and Cotswold villages.

• **STRATFORD-UPON-AVON, WARWICKSHIRE** - Famous as Shakespeare's home town, Stratford's many attractions include his birthplace, New Place where he died, the Royal Shakespeare Theatre and Gallery and Hall's Croft (his daughter's house).

• **STROUD, GLOUCESTERSHIRE** - This old town, surrounded by attractive hilly country, has been producing broadcloth for centuries, the local museum has an interesting display on the subject. Many of the mills have been converted into craft centres and for other uses.

T TELFORD, SHROPSHIRE - New Town named after Thomas Telford, the famous engineer who designed many of the country's canals, bridges and viaducts. It is close to Ironbridge with its monuments and museums to the Industrial Revolution, including restored 18th C buildings.

• **TUTBURY, STAFFORDSHIRE** - Small town on the River Dove with an attractive High Street, old houses and the remains of the castle where Mary Queen of Scots was imprisoned.

U UPTON-UPON-SEVERN, WORCESTERSHIRE - Attractive country town on the banks of the Severn and a good river cruising centre. It has many pleasant old houses and inns, and the pepperpot landmark is now the Heritage Centre.

W WARWICK, WARWICKSHIRE - Castle rising above the River Avon, 15th C Beauchamp Chapel attached to St Mary's Church, medieval Lord Leycester's Hospital almshouses and several museums. Nearby is Ashorne Hall Nickelodeon and the National Heritage museum at Gaydon.

• **WELLINGBOROUGH, NORTHAMPTONSHIRE** - Manufacturing town, mentioned in the Domesday Book, with some old buildings and inns, in one of which Cromwell stayed on his way to Naseby. It has attractive gardens in the centre of the town and 2 interesting churches.

• **WOLVERHAMPTON, WEST MIDLANDS** - Modern industrial town with a long history, a fine parish church and an excellent art gallery. There are several places of interest in the vicinity including Moseley Old Hall and Wightwick Manor with its William Morris influence.

• **WOODHALL SPA, LINCOLNSHIRE** - Attractive town which was formerly a spa. It has excellent sporting facilities with a championship golf-course and is surrounded by pine woods.

• **WORCESTER, WORCESTERSHIRE** - Lovely riverside city dominated by its Norman and Early English cathedral, King John's burial place. Many old buildings including the 15th C Commandery and the 18th C Guildhall. There are several museums and the Royal Worcester porcelain factory.

Ratings
you can trust

English Tourism Council

★ ★ ★

HOTEL

When you're looking for a place to stay, you need a rating system you can trust. The English Tourism Council's ratings are your clear guide to what to expect, in an easy-to-understand form. Properties are visited annually by our trained, impartial assessors, so you can have confidence that your accommodation has been thoroughly checked and rated for quality before you make a booking.

Based on the internationally recognised rating of One to Five Stars, the system puts great emphasis on quality and is based on research which shows exactly what consumers are looking for when choosing an hotel.

Ratings are awarded from One to Five Stars - the more Stars, the higher the quality and the greater the range of facilities and level of services provided.

Look out, too, for the English Tourism Council's Gold and Silver Awards, which are awarded to properties achieving the highest levels of quality within their Star rating. While the overall rating is based on a combination of facilities and quality, the Gold and Silver Awards are based solely on quality.

The ratings are your sign of quality assurance, giving you the confidence to book the accommodation that meets your expectations.

EAST of England

A region of remote and wild beauty, with vast expanses of open country, unspoilt coastline, sweeping views and big skies. It's renowned for its charming half-timbered towns and villages, ancient sites, historic country houses and nature reserves.

classic sights
Blickling Hall – one of England's great Jacobean houses
Sutton Hoo – important Anglo-Saxon burial site

coast & country
Blakeney Point – good for seal and bird watching
Hatfield Forest – medieval royal hunting forest
Norfolk Broads – miles of waterways through glorious countryside

arts for all
Aldeburgh Festival – classical music in a picturesque setting
Dedham Vale – the landscapes of John Constable; his home and early studio are at East Bergholt. Also the home of Sir Alfred Munnings, famous for his paintings of horses
Sudbury – Gainsborough's house, with fine collection of paintings

delightfully different
Whipsnade Tree Cathedral – unique, 26 acres (10.5ha) cathedral made of trees

The counties of Bedfordshire, Cambridgeshire, Essex, Hertfordshire, Norfolk and Suffolk

FOR MORE INFORMATION CONTACT:
East of England Tourist Board
Toppesfield Hall, Hadleigh, Suffolk IP7 5DN
Tel: (01473) 822922 Fax: (01473) 823063
Email: eastofenglandtouristboard@compuserve.com
Internet: www.eastofenglandtouristboard.com

The Pictures:
1 Horsey Mere, Norfolk
2 King's College, Cambridge
3 Norwich

Places to Visit - see pages 168-172
Where to Stay - see pages 173-193

167

PLACES to visit

You will find hundreds of interesting places to visit during your stay, just some of which are listed in these pages. Contact any Tourist Information Centre in the region for more ideas on days out.

Blickling Hall

Blickling, Norwich, Norfolk NR11 6NF
Tel: (01263) 738030 www.nationaltrust.org.uk
A Jacobean redbrick mansion with garden, orangery, parkland and lake. There is also a display of fine tapestries and furniture.

Audley End House and Park

Audley End, Saffron Walden, Essex CB11 4JF
Tel: (01799) 522399
A palatial Jacobean house remodelled in the 18thC-19thC with a magnificent Great Hall with 17thC plaster ceilings. Rooms and furniture by Robert Adam and park by 'Capability' Brown.

Bressingham Steam Experience and Gardens

Bressingham, Diss, Norfolk IP22 2AB
Tel: (01379) 687386 www.bressingham.co.uk
Steam rides through five miles of woodland. Six acres (2 ha) of the Island Beds plant centre. Mainline locomotives, the Victorian Gallopers and over 50 steam engines.

Banham Zoo

The Grove, Banham, Norwich, Norfolk NR16 2HE
Tel: (01953) 887771 www.banhamzoo.co.uk
Wildlife spectacular which will take you on a journey to experience tigers, leopards and zebra and some of the world's most exotic, rare and endangered animals.

Bure Valley Railway

Aylsham Station, Norwich Road, Aylsham, Norwich, Norfolk NR11 6BW
Tel: (01263) 733858 www.bvrw.co.uk
A 15-inch narrow-gauge steam railway covering nine miles of track from Wroxham, in the heart of the Norfolk Broads, to Aylsham, a bustling market town.

Barleylands Farm

Barleylands Road, Billericay, Essex CM11 2UD
Tel: (01268) 290229
Visitor centre with a rural museum, animal centre, craft studios, blacksmith's shop, glass-blowing studio with a viewing gallery, miniature steam railway and a restaurant.

Colchester Castle

Colchester, Essex CO1 1TJ
Tel: (01206) 282931
www.colchestermuseums.org.uk
A Norman keep on the foundations of a Roman temple. The archaeological material includes much on Roman Colchester (Camulodunum).

Colchester Zoo

Maldon Road, Stanway, Colchester, Essex CO3 5SL
Tel: (01206) 331292 www.colchester-zoo.co.uk
Zoo with 200 species and some of the best cat and
primate collections in the UK, 60 acres (27 ha) of gardens
and lakes, award-winning animal enclosures and picnic
areas.

Ely Cathedral

Chapter House, The College, Ely, Cambridgeshire CB7 4DL
Tel: (01353) 667735
One of England's finest cathedrals with guided tours and
tours of the Octagon and West Tower, monastic precincts
and also a brass-rubbing centre and Stained Glass
Museum.

Fritton Lake Country World

Fritton, Great Yarmouth, Norfolk NR31 9HA
Tel: (01493) 488208
A 250-acre (101-ha) centre with a children's assault
course, putting, an adventure playground, golf, fishing,
boating, wildfowl, heavy horses, cart rides, falconry and
flying displays.

The Gardens of the Rose

The Royal National Rose Society, Chiswell Green,
St Albans, Hertfordshire AL2 3NR
Tel: (01727) 850461 www.roses.co.uk
The Royal National Rose Society's Garden with 27 acres
(11 ha) of garden and trial grounds for new varieties of
rose. Roses of all types displayed with 1,700 different
varieties.

Hatfield House, Park and Gardens

Hatfield, Hertfordshire AL9 5NQ
Tel: (01707) 287010 www.hatfield-house.co.uk
Magnificent Jacobean house, home of the Marquess of
Salisbury. Exquisite gardens, model soldiers and park
trails. Childhood home of Queen Elizabeth I.

Hedingham Castle

Castle Hedingham, Halstead, Essex C09 3DJ
Tel: (01787) 460261
www.hedinghamcastle@aspects.net
The finest Norman keep in England, built in 1140 by the
deVeres, Earls of Oxford. Visited by Kings Henry VII and
VIII and Queen Elizabeth I and besieged by King John.

Holkham Hall

Wells-next-the-Sea, Norfolk NR23 1AB
Tel: (01328) 710227 www.holkham.co.uk
A classic 18thC Palladian-style mansion. Part of a great
agricultural estate and a living treasure house of artistic
and architectural history along with a bygones collection.

Ickworth House, Park and Gardens

The Rotunda, Horringer, Bury St Edmunds, Suffolk IP29 5QE
Tel: (01284) 735270 www.nationaltrust.org.uk
An extraordinary oval house with flanking wings, begun
in 1795. Fine paintings, a beautiful collection of Georgian
silver, an Italian garden and stunning parkland.

Imperial War Museum

Duxford, Cambridge, Cambridgeshire CB2 4QR
Tel: (01223) 835000 www.iwm.org.uk
Over 180 aircraft on display with tanks, vehicles and
guns, an adventure playground, shops and a restaurant.

The Pictures:
1 River Wensum, Norfolk
2 Punting on the River Cam, Cambridge
3 Globe Inn, Linslade, Bedfordshire
4 Thorpeness, Suffolk
5 Tulip fields

Kentwell Hall

Long Melford, Sudbury, Suffolk CO10 9BA
Tel: (01787) 310207 www.kentwell.co.uk
A mellow redbrick Tudor manor surrounded by a moat, this family home has been interestingly restored with Tudor costume displays, a 16thC house and mosaic Tudor rose maze.

Knebworth House, Gardens and Park

Knebworth, Stevenage, Hertfordshire SG3 6PY
Tel: (01438) 812661 www.knebworthhouse.com
Tudor manor house, re-fashioned in the 19thC, housing a collection of manuscripts, portraits and Jacobean banquet hall. Formal gardens and adventure playground.

Leighton Buzzard Railway

Page's Park Station, Billington Road, Leighton Buzzard, Bedfordshire LU7 4TN
Tel: (01525) 373888 www.buzzrail.co.uk
An authentic narrow-gauge light railway, built in 1919, offering a 65-minute return journey into the Bedfordshire countryside.

Marsh Farm Country Park

Marsh Farm Road, South Woodham Ferrers, Chelmsford, Essex CM3 5WP
Tel: (01245) 321552
www.marshfarmcountrypark.co.uk
A farm centre with sheep, a pig unit, free-range chickens, milking demonstrations, indoor and outdoor adventure play areas, nature reserve, walks, picnic area and pets' corner.

Melford Hall

Long Melford, Sudbury, Suffolk CO10 9AA
Tel: (01787) 880286
www.nationaltrust.org.uk/eastanglia
Turreted brick Tudor mansion with 18thC and Regency interiors. Collection of Chinese porcelain, gardens and a walk in the grounds. Dogs on leads, where permitted.

Minsmere Nature Reserve

Westleton, Saxmundham, Suffolk IP17 3BY
Tel: (01728) 648281 www.rspb.org.uk
RSPB reserve on the Suffolk coast with bird-watching hides and trails, year-round events, guided walk and visitor centre with large shop and welcoming tearooms.

National Horseracing Museum and Tours

99 High Street, Newmarket, Suffolk CB8 8JL
Tel: (01638) 667333 www.nhrm.co.uk
Award-winning display of the people and horses involved in racing's amazing history. Minibus tours to gallops, stables and equine pool. Hands-on gallery with horse simulator.

National Stud

Newmarket, Suffolk CB8 0XE
Tel: (01638) 663464 www.nationalstud.co.uk
A visit to the National Stud consists of a conducted tour which will include top thoroughbred stallions, mares and foals.

Norfolk Lavender Limited

Caley Mill, Heacham, King's Lynn, Norfolk PE31 7JE
Tel: (01485) 570384 www.norfolk-lavender.co.uk
Lavender is distilled from the flowers and the oil made into a wide range of gifts. There is a slide show when the distillery is not working.

Norwich Cathedral

The Close, Norwich, Norfolk NR1 4EH
Tel: (01603) 218321 www.cathedral.org.uk
A Norman cathedral from 1096 with 14thC roof bosses depicting bible scenes from Adam and Eve to the Day of Judgement. Cloisters, cathedral close, shop and restaurant.

Oliver Cromwell's House

29 St Marys Street, Ely, Cambridgeshire CB7 4HF
Tel: (01353) 662062 www.elyeastcambs.co.uk
The family home of Oliver Cromwell with a 17thC kitchen, parlour, a haunted bedroom, a Tourist Information Centre, souvenirs and craft shop.

Peter Beales Roses

London Road, Attleborough, Norfolk NR17 1AY
Tel: (01953) 454707 www.classicroses.co.uk
Two and a half acres (1 ha) of display rose garden set in rural surroundings.

Pleasure Beach

South Beach Parade, Great Yarmouth, Norfolk NR30 3EH
Tel: (01493) 844585
Rollercoaster, Terminator, log flume, Twister, monorail, galloping horses, caterpillar, ghost train and fun house. Height restrictions are in force on some rides.

Pleasurewood Hills Theme Park

Leisure Way, Corton, Lowestoft, Suffolk NR32 5DZ
Tel: (01502) 586000 pleasurewoodhills.co.uk
(zy coaster, tidal wave watercoaster, log flume, chairlift, two railways, pirate ship, Aladdin's cave, parrot and sea-lion shows, the cannonball express and rattlesnake rides.

Sainsbury Centre for Visual Arts

University of East Anglia, Norwich, Norfolk NR4 7TJ
Tel: (01603) 456060 www.uea.ac.uk/scva
Housing the Sainsbury collection of works by Picasso, Bacon and Henry Moore alongside many objects of pottery and art. Also a cafe and an art bookshop with activities monthly.

Sandringham

Sandringham, King's Lynn, Norfolk PE35 6EN
Tel: (01553) 772675 www.sandringhamestate.co.uk
The country retreat of HM The Queen. A delightful house and 60 acres (24 ha) of grounds and lakes. There is also a museum of royal vehicles and royal memorabilia.

Shuttleworth Collection

Old Warden Aerodrome, Biggleswade, Bedfordshire SG18 9EP
Tel: (01767) 627288 www.shuttleworth.org
A unique historical collection of aircraft, from a 1909 Bleriot to a 1942 Spitfire (in flying condition), and cars, dating from an 1898 Panhard (in running order).

Somerleyton Hall and Gardens

Somerleyton, Lowestoft, Suffolk NR32 5QQ
Tel: (01502) 730224 www.somerleyton.co.uk
Anglo Italian-style mansion with state rooms, a maze, 12-acre (5-ha) gardens with azaleas and rhododendrons, miniature railway, shop and tearooms.

Stondon Museum

Station Road, Lower Stondon, Henlow Camp, Henlow, Bedfordshire SG16 6JN
Tel: (01462) 850339 www.transportmuseum.co.uk
A museum with transport exhibits from the early 1900s to the 1980s. The largest private collection in England of bygone vehicles from the beginning of the century.

Thursford Collection

Thursford Green, Thursford, Fakenham, Norfolk NR21 0AS
Tel: (01328) 878477
Musical evenings some Tuesdays from mid-July to the end of September. A live musical show with nine mechanical organs and a Wurlitzer show starring Robert Wolfe (daily 29 March-mid October).

Whipsnade Wild Animal Park

Dunstable, Bedfordshire LU6 2LF
Tel: (01582) 872171 www.whipsnade.co.uk
Whipsnade Wild Animal Park has over 2,500 animals and is set in 600 acres (243 ha) of beautiful parkland. The Great Whipsnade Railway and free animal demonstrations.

Wimpole Hall and Home Farm

Arrington, Royston, Hertfordshire SG8 0BW
Tel: (01223) 207257 www.wimpole.org
An 18thC house in a landscaped park with a folly, Chinese bridge. Plunge bath and yellow drawing room in the house, the work of John Soane. Home Farm has a rare breeds centre.

Woburn Abbey

Woburn, Milton Keynes, Bedfordshire MK17 9WA
Tel: (01525) 290666 www.woburnabbey.co.uk
An 18thC Palladian mansion, altered by Henry Holland, the Prince Regent's architect, containing a collection of English silver, French and English furniture and art.

Woburn Safari Park

Woburn, Milton Keynes, Bedfordshire MK17 9QN
Tel: (01525) 290407 www.woburnsafari.co.uk
Drive through the safari park with 30 species of animals in natural groups just a windscreen's width away, plus the action-packed Wild World Leisure Area with shows for all.

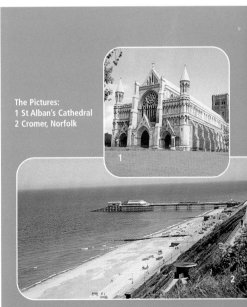

The Pictures:
1 St Alban's Cathedral
2 Cromer, Norfolk

Find out more about the
East of England

Further information about holidays and attractions in the East of England is available from:

EAST OF ENGLAND TOURIST BOARD

Toppesfield Hall, Hadleigh, Suffolk IP7 5DN

Tel: (01473) 822922 Fax: (01473) 823063

Email: eastofenglandtouristboard@compuserve.com

Internet: www.eastofenglandtouristboard.com

The following publications are available from The East of England Tourist Board:

East of England - The Official Guide 2002

an information packed A5 guide featuring all you need to know about places to visit and things to see and do in the East of England. From historic houses to garden centres, from animal collections to craft centres - the Guide has it all, including film and TV locations, city, town and village information, events, shopping, car tours plus lots more! Price £3.99 (excl. p&p)

England's Cycling Country

the East of England offers perfect cycling country - from quiet country lanes to ancient trackways. This free publication promotes the many Cycling Discovery Maps that are available to buy (£1.50 excl. p&p), as well as providing useful information for anyone planning a cycling tour of the region

Getting to the
East of England

BY ROAD: The region is easily accessible. From London and the south via the A1, M11, M25, A10, M1, A46 and A12. From the north via the A17, A1, A15, A5, M1 and A6. From the west via the A14, A47, A421, A428, A418, A41 and A427.

BY RAIL: Regular fast trains run to all major cities and towns in the region. London stations which serve the region are Liverpool Street, Kings Cross, Fenchurch Street, Moorgate, St Pancras, London Marylebone and London Euston. Bedford, Luton and St Albans are on the Thameslink line which runs to Kings Cross and onto London Gatwick Airport. There is also a direct link between London Stansted Airport and Liverpool Street. Through the Channel Tunnel, there are trains direct from Paris and Brussels to Waterloo Station, London. A short journey on the Underground will bring passengers to those stations operating services into the East of England. Further information on rail journeys in the East of England can be obtained on (0845) 748 4950.

Where to stay in the East of England

Accommodation entries in this region are listed in alphabetical order of place name, and then in alphabetical order of establishment.

Map references refer to the colour location maps at front of this guide. The first number indicates the map to use; the letter and number which follow refer to the grid reference on the map.

At-a-glance symbols at the end of each accommodation entry give useful information about services and facilities. A key to symbols can be found inside the back cover flap. Keep this open for easy reference.

A brief description of the towns and villages offering accommodation in the entries which follow, can be found at the end of this section.

A complete listing of all the English Tourism Council assessed accommodation covered by this guide appears at the back of the guide.

ALDEBURGH, Suffolk Map ref 3C2 *Tourist Information Centre Tel: (01728) 453637*

★★★ **THE BRUDENELL HOTEL**
The Parade, Aldeburgh IP15 5BU
T: (01728) 452071
F: (01728) 454082
E: info@brudenellhotel.co.uk
I: www.brudenellhotel.co.uk

Bedrooms: 7 single, 40 double/twin
Bathrooms: 47 en suite

Lunch available
Evening meal available
CC: Amex, Delta, Mastercard, Switch, Visa

B&B per night:
S £63.00–£70.00
D £101.00–£115.00

HB per person:
DY £45.00–£65.00

OPEN All year round

Situated directly on the seafront of Aldeburgh, a totally unspoilt fishing town of great charm. You can enjoy some fantastic views over the sea and the River Alde.

★★★ Silver Award **WHITE LION HOTEL**
Market Cross Place, Aldeburgh IP15 5BJ
T: (01728) 452720
F: (01728) 452986
E: whitelionaldeburgh@btinternet.com
I: www.whitelion.co.uk

Bedrooms: 4 single, 33 double/twin, 1 triple/multiple
Bathrooms: 38 en suite

Lunch available
Evening meal available
CC: Amex, Delta, Mastercard, Switch, Visa

B&B per night:
S £70.00–£80.00
D £108.00–£120.00

HB per person:
DY £50.00–£70.00

OPEN All year round

Best Western Hotels

This imposing hotel set directly on the seafront has the distinction of being the oldest in Aldeburgh, with its own beamed restaurant dating back to 1563.

 SPECIAL BREAKS
Many establishments offer special promotions and themed breaks. These are highlighted in red. (All such offers are subject to availability.)

BASILDON, Essex Map ref 3B3

TRAVEL ACCOMMODATION

CAMPANILE HOTEL
A127 Southend Arterial Road,
Pipps Hill, Basildon SS14 3AE
T: (01268) 530810
F: (01268) 286710

Bedrooms: 84 double/
twin, 13 triple/multiple
Bathrooms: 97 en suite

Lunch available
Evening meal available
CC: Amex, Delta, Diners,
Mastercard, Switch, Visa

B&B per night:
S £39.90–£48.45
D £44.85–£54.40

HB per person:
DY Min £51.00

OPEN All year round

Campanile Basildon is only 30 minutes from the city of London by train or by car. Alternatively, explore some of the country's prettiest villages nearby. Municipal golf course close to the hotel.

★★★

THE CHICHESTER HOTEL
Old London Road, Wickford SS11 8UE
T: (01268) 560555
F: (01268) 560580

B&B per night:
S Min £72.00
D Min £95.00

OPEN All year round

Picturesque family-run hotel surrounded by rural farmland in the Basildon, Chelmsford, Southend triangle. Try our beautiful gallery restaurant (open to non-residents) – fully air conditioned, it overlooks the hotel's charming courtyard garden. Special mini-break packages available at weekends.

Bedrooms: 17 single,
18 double/twin
Bathrooms: 35 en suite

Lunch available
Evening meal available
CC: Amex, Delta, Diners,
Mastercard, Switch, Visa

Mini break for couples Friday or Sunday. Afternoon cream tea, evening dinner, en suite bedroom, full English breakfast. Only £78 per couple.

BLAKENEY, Norfolk Map ref 3B1

★★
Gold
Award

MORSTON HALL
Morston, Holt NR25 7AA
T: (01263) 741041
F: (01263) 740419
E: reception@morstonhall.com
I: www.morstonhall.com

Bedrooms: 6 double/
twin; suites available
Bathrooms: 6 en suite

Evening meal available
CC: Amex, Delta, Diners,
Mastercard, Switch, Visa

HB per person:
DY £100.00–£110.00

Peaceful 17thC country house hotel with delightful gardens, 2 miles from Blakeney. Fine restaurant, large, attractive bedrooms, caring staff, efficient and friendly.

★★

THE PHEASANT HOTEL
The Coast Road, Kelling, Holt
NR25 7EG
T: (01263) 588382
F: (01263) 588101
E: enquiries@
pheasanthotelnorfolk.co.uk
I: www.pheasanthotelnorfolk.co.uk

Bedrooms: 1 single,
29 double/twin
Bathrooms: 30 en suite

Lunch available
Evening meal available
CC: Delta, Mastercard,
Switch, Visa

B&B per night:
S £49.00–£59.00
D £78.00–£88.00

HB per person:
DY £51.00–£65.95

OPEN All year round

North Norfolk's 'Top Hotel 1998'. Country house with facilities for disabled. Brasserie serving home-made food. Three acres of grounds. Midway between Blakeney and Sheringham.

AT-A-GLANCE SYMBOLS
Symbols at the end of each accommodation entry give useful information about services and facilities. A key to symbols can be found inside the back cover flap. Keep this open for easy reference.

BRENTWOOD, Essex Map ref 2D2 *Tourist Information Centre Tel: (01277) 200300*

★★★★
Silver
Award

MARYGREEN MANOR HOTEL

London Road, Brentwood CM14 4NR

T: (01277) 225252

F: (01277) 262809

E: info@marygreenmanor.co.uk

I: www.marygreenmanor.co.uk

B&B per night:
S £124.00–£129.00
D £138.00–£142.00

HB per person:
DY £166.00–£189.00

OPEN All year round

Genuine 4-star 16thC Tudor house situated 2 minutes from M25 with direct motorway links to Channel Tunnel, Stansted, Gatwick and Heathrow Airports. Guests can enjoy creative international cuisine accompanied by an award-winning wine list, 4-poster or courtyard bedrooms, tranquil garden and ample parking.

Bedrooms: 43 double/ twin; suites available
Bathrooms: 43 en suite

Lunch available
Evening meal available
CC: Amex, Delta, Diners, Mastercard, Switch, Visa

Special B&B rates on Fri, Sat and Sun for guests dining in the restaurant.

♒🐎🛏🔥✆🗐🖵♨🥂⑤🗝🖳☺🍴🌸🚗🐕🌿🏤 P

BURY ST EDMUNDS, Suffolk Map ref 3B2 *Tourist Information Centre Tel: (01284) 764667*

★★★

BUTTERFLY HOTEL

A14 Bury East Exit, Moreton Hall,
Bury St Edmunds IP32 7BW
T: (01284) 760884
F: (01284) 755476
E: burybutterfly@lineone.net
I: www.butterflyhotels.co.uk

Bedrooms: 32 single,
33 double/twin
Bathrooms: 65 en suite

Lunch available
Evening meal available
CC: Amex, Delta, Diners, Mastercard, Switch, Visa

B&B per night:
S £65.50–£96.50
D £72.00–£105.00

OPEN All year round

ⒸⓇ
Butterfly Hotels

Situated on the edge of this charming old town at the 'Crossroads of East Anglia'. Leisure travellers will appreciate the close proximity of Cambridge, Ely and Newmarket. Special Weekend Break rates available.

♒🐎🛏✆🗐🖵♨🥂⑤🗝🖳🗝☺🖳🍴🌸🐕 P

★★

THE GRANGE HOTEL

Barton Road, Thurston, Bury St Edmunds IP31 3PQ

T: (01359) 231260

F: (01359) 231387

E: info@thegrangehotel.uk.com

I: www.thegrangehotel.uk.com

B&B per night:
S £48.00–£60.00
D £64.00–£85.00

OPEN All year round

Family-owned country house hotel with chef/proprietor, 4 miles from Bury St Edmunds. Individually decorated rooms all with en suite. Set in secluded grounds, perfect for a relaxing break.

Bedrooms: 2 single,
10 double/twin, 1 triple/
multiple; suites available
Bathrooms: 13 en suite

Lunch available
Evening meal available
CC: Amex, Delta, Mastercard, Switch, Visa

2 nights DB&B £95 per person, available Fri-Sun all year.

♒🐎✆🖵♨🥂⑤🗝🖳☺🍴🌸🐕🚗 P

★★★

PRIORY HOTEL AND RESTAURANT

Fornham Road, Tollgate,
Bury St Edmunds IP32 6EH
T: (01284) 766181
F: (01284) 767604
E: reservations@prioryhotel.co.uk
I: www.prioryhotel.co.uk

Bedrooms: 4 single,
34 double/twin, 1 triple/
multiple
Bathrooms: 39 en suite

Lunch available
Evening meal available
CC: Amex, Delta, Diners, Mastercard, Switch, Visa

B&B per night:
S £75.00–£95.00
D £95.00–£115.00

OPEN All year round

ⒸⓇ
Best Western Hotels

Exceptional 39 bedroom hotel with outstanding food and service. Set in 2 acres of landscaped gardens, yet only minutes from the town.

♒🐎🛏🔥✆🗐🖵♨🥂⑤🗝🖳☺🍴Uℓ🌸🐕🌿🏤 P

CHECK THE MAPS

The colour maps at the front of this guide show all the cities, towns and villages for which you will find accommodation entries. Refer to the town index to find the page on which they are listed.

CAMBRIDGE, Cambridgeshire Map ref 2D1 *Tourist Information Centre Tel: (01223) 322640*

★★

ARUNDEL HOUSE HOTEL
Chesterton Road, Cambridge CB4 3AN
T: (01223) 367701
F: (01223) 367721
E: info@arundelhousehotels.co.uk
I: www.arundelhousehotels.co.uk

B&B per night:
S £65.00–£89.50
D £85.00–£115.00

OPEN All year round

Elegant, privately-owned 19thC terraced hotel, beautifully located overlooking the River Cam and open parkland, close to the city centre and famous historic colleges. The hotel has a reputation for providing some of the best food in the area in both its restaurant and all-day conservatory. Small secluded garden.

Bedrooms: 38 single, 58 double/twin, 6 triple/ multiple
Bathrooms: 102 en suite

Lunch available
Evening meal available
CC: Amex, Delta, Diners, Mastercard, Switch, Visa

★★★
Gold
Award

DUXFORD LODGE HOTEL AND LE PARADIS RESTAURANT
Ickleton Road, Duxford, Cambridge CB2 4RU
T: (01223) 836444
F: (01223) 832271
E: duxford@btclick.com
I: www.touristnetuk.com/em/duxford

B&B per night:
S £57.50–£87.50
D £99.00–£120.00

HB per person:
DY £82.50–£112.50

OPEN All year round

Country house hotel in beautiful grounds. Ten minutes south of Cambridge off J10 M11, ideal when visiting Duxford Air Museum. Near to colleges, Newmarket races and 20 minutes from Stansted Airport. Private dining available. Car parking. Ground floor rooms available leading on to gardens. Minimum rates are for Friday, Saturday and Sunday nights.

Bedrooms: 2 single, 13 double/twin
Bathrooms: 15 en suite

Lunch available
Evening meal available
CC: Amex, Delta, Diners, Mastercard, Switch, Visa

TOWN INDEX
This can be found at the back of this guide. If you know where you want to stay, the index will give you the page number listing accommodation in your chosen town, city or village.

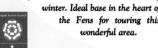

★★★ **GONVILLE HOTEL**

Gonville Place, Cambridge CB1 1LY	Bedrooms: 23 single,	Lunch available
T: (01223) 366611 & 221111	40 double/twin, 1 triple/	Evening meal available
F: (01223) 315470	multiple	CC: Amex, Delta, Diners,
E: info@gonvillehotel.co.uk	Bathrooms: 64 en suite	Mastercard, Switch, Visa
I: www.gonvillehotel.co.uk		

Occupies one of the most favoured positions in Cambridge, overlooking Parkers Piece and close to most of the colleges and shopping areas.

B&B per night:
S £99.50–£115.00
D £120.00–£150.00

HB per person:
DY Min £80.00

OPEN All year round

Ⓒ®
Best Western Hotels

★★

SORRENTO HOTEL
190-196 Cherry Hinton Road, Cambridge CB1 7AN

T: (01223) 243533
F: (01223) 213463
E: sorrento-hotel@cb17an.freeserve.co.uk
I: www.sorrentohotel.com

B&B per night:
S £69.50–£79.50
D £99.00–£150.00

HB per person:
DY £84.50–£104.50

OPEN All year round

Family-managed hotel in a quiet residential area, close to town centre, railway station, Addenbrookes Hospital. High standard of room facilities and service. Bridal suite with jacuzzi, sauna and 4-poster bed. Superb Italian restaurant in romantic setting. Special diets and children's meals available. Weddings, functions, conferences. Free private car park.	Bedrooms: 8 single, 12 double/twin, 3 triple/ multiple Bathrooms: 23 en suite	Lunch available Evening meal available CC: Amex, Delta, Diners, Mastercard, Switch, Visa Special events for: Valentine's Day, Mother's Day, Christmas Day, Graduation Day.

★
Ad on opposite page

CROSS KEYS INN HOTEL
12-16 Market Hill, Chatteris PE16 6BA

T: (01354) 693036 & 692644
F: (01354) 694454
E: thefens@crosskeyshotel.fsnet.co.uk

B&B per night:
S £21.00–£48.00
D £32.50–£68.00

HB per person:
DY £45.00–£49.00

OPEN All year round

This delightful Elizabethan coaching inn, built around 1540, Grade II Listed, sits in the town centre opposite the parish church of St Peter and St Paul. A la carte menu and bar meals 7 days a week. Friendly atmosphere, oak-beamed lounge with log fires to welcome the traveller during winter. Ideal base in the heart of the Fens for touring this wonderful area.	Bedrooms: 11 double/ twin, 1 triple/multiple Bathrooms: 10 en suite	Lunch available Evening meal available CC: Delta, Mastercard, Switch, Visa Weekend breaks: 10% off accommodation only. Stay Fri and Sat and get Sun free. Meal must be taken in the hotel.

QUALITY ASSURANCE SCHEME
For an explanation of the quality and facilities represented by the Stars please refer to the front of this guide. A more detailed explanation can be found in the information pages at the back.

CHELMSFORD, Essex Map ref 3B3 *Tourist Information Centre Tel: (01245) 283400*

★★★

ATLANTIC HOTEL
Brook Street, Off New Street, Chelmsford
CM1 1PP
T: (01245) 268168
F: (01245) 268169
E: info@atlantichotel.co.uk
I: www.atlantichotel.co.uk

B&B per night:
S £59.00–£87.95
D £69.00–£106.90

OPEN All year round

Best Western Hotels

Opened in May 1999, the Atlantic is a contemporary and individual hotel designed with you in mind. Our aim is to provide an efficient and reliable professional service, in smart and stylish surroundings. Ideal for business or pleasure, the hotel is situated close to the town centre and railway station. All rooms are air-conditioned. Free pass to Fitness First Club next door.

Bedrooms: 59 double/ twin
Bathrooms: 59 en suite

Lunch available
Evening meal available
CC: Amex, Delta, Diners, Mastercard, Switch, Visa

⌚ ⬟ ♿ ☎ ▣ 🖵 ♨ ⚓ ⑤ ⚡ ◉ 🖥 ⬟ ⚑ ❄ P

★★★
Silver
Award

COUNTY HOTEL
Rainsford Road, Chelmsford CM1 2PZ
T: (01245) 455700
F: (01245) 492762
E: sales@countyhotel-essex.co.uk
I: www.countyhotel.co.uk

B&B per night:
S £55.00–£79.00
D £66.00–£95.00

HB per person:
DY £55.00–£104.00

OPEN All year round

Minotel

Friendly welcome and excellent customer care. 10 minutes' walk from parks, rivers and town centre. Families welcome – free cots and extra beds. Artista Brasserie open 10am to 10pm. Light meals, snacks, lunch and dinner menus. Children's menu available. Minimum rates are for Friday, Saturday and Sunday nights. Saturday night dinner discos.

Bedrooms: 18 single, 18 double/twin; suites available
Bathrooms: 36 en suite

Lunch available
Evening meal available
CC: Amex, Delta, Diners, Mastercard, Switch, Visa

Ⓜ ⌚ ♿ ☎ ▣ 🖵 ♨ ⚓ ⑤ ⚡ ⒩ ◉ 🖥 ⬟ ⚑ ⑂ ⬟ ❄ P

★★

MIAMI HOTEL
Princes Road, Chelmsford CM2 9AJ
T: (01245) 264848 & 269603
F: (01245) 259860
E: miamihotel@hotmail.com
I: www.miamihotel.co.uk

Bedrooms: 22 single, 33 double/twin
Bathrooms: 55 en suite

Lunch available
Evening meal available
CC: Amex, Delta, Diners, Mastercard, Switch, Visa

B&B per night:
S £55.00–£90.00
D £65.00–£90.00

OPEN All year round

The Independents

Family-run hotel, 1 mile from town centre. All rooms are twin/double size (let as singles when required). Refurbished in 2001.

Ⓜ ⌚ ♿ ☎ ▣ 🖵 ♨ ⚓ ⑤ ⚡ ⒩ ◉ 🖥 ⬟ ⚑ ⑂ ⑤ ⚑ P

★

SNOWS HOTEL
240 Springfield Road, Chelmsford CM2 6BP
T: (01245) 352004
F: (01245) 356675
E: sales@snowshotel.com
I: www.snowshotel.com

Bedrooms: 2 single, 9 double/twin, 2 triple/ multiple
Bathrooms: 11 en suite, 2 private

Lunch available
Evening meal available
CC: Amex, Delta, Mastercard, Switch, Visa

B&B per night:
S £48.00–£68.00
D £58.00–£78.00

OPEN All year round

Neo-Georgian mansion set in its own grounds of nearly three quarters of an acre. Hotel facilities include restaurant, lounge bar, beautiful peaceful garden and conservatory.

⌚ ♿ ☎ ▣ 🖵 ♨ ⚓ ⑤ ⚡ ⒩ 🖥 ⬟ ⚑ ❄ ⑂ ⬟ ⑱ P

MAP REFERENCES The map references refer to the colour maps at the front of this guide. The first figure is the map number; the letter and figure which follow indicate the grid reference on the map.

CLACTON-ON-SEA, Essex Map ref 3B3 *Tourist Information Centre Tel: (01255) 423400*

★

CHUDLEIGH HOTEL

Agate Road, Marine Parade West, Clacton-on-Sea CO15 1RA
T: (01255) 425407
F: (01255) 470280

B&B per night:
S £38.00
D £50.00–£55.00

HB per person:
DY £40.00–£43.00

OPEN All year round

An oasis in a town centre location, 200 metres from the central seafront gardens, near pier and main shops. Ideal for the business visitor, the tourist and for overnight stays. Free parking. Assurance of comfort and efficiency combined with informality. Fluent Italian and French spoken by the proprietor.

Bedrooms: 2 single, 5 double/twin, 3 triple/ multiple
Bathrooms: 10 en suite

Reduced terms by negotion Oct-Mar (excl Christmas and Bank Hols).

Evening meal available
CC: Amex, Delta, Diners, Mastercard, Switch, Visa

COLCHESTER, Essex Map ref 3B2 *Tourist Information Centre Tel: (01206) 282920*

★★★

BUTTERFLY HOTEL
A12-A120 Ardleigh Junction, Old Ipswich Road, Colchester CO7 7QY
T: (01206) 230900
F: (01206) 231095
E: colbutterfly@lineone.net
I: www.butterflyhotels.co.uk

Bedrooms: 22 single, 24 double/twin, 4 triple/ multiple; suites available
Bathrooms: 50 en suite

Lunch available
Evening meal available
CC: Amex, Delta, Diners, Mastercard, Switch, Visa

B&B per night:
S £65.50–£83.50
D £72.00–£92.00

OPEN All year round

Ⓒ
Butterfly Hotels

Leisure travellers will find us the perfect base for exploring Constable country and the East Anglian coastline. Just minutes away from major routes to the port of Harwich. Special Weekend Break rates available.

★★★

ROSE & CROWN

East Street, Colchester CO1 2TZ
T: (01206) 866677
F: (01206) 866616
E: info@rose-and-crown.com
I: www.rose-and-crown.com

B&B per night:
S £59.00–£85.00
D £69.00–£110.00

OPEN All year round

Ⓒ
Best Western Hotels

The oldest inn, in England's oldest recorded town. En suite rooms, a beauty salon, Tudor bar with open log fires and noted restaurant. With a friendly, relaxed atmosphere, it is one of Colchester's finest hotels and restaurants. Located on the Ipswich road, 2 miles off the A12 and half a mile from town centre.

Bedrooms: 1 single, 25 double/twin, 3 triple/ multiple; suites available
Bathrooms: 29 en suite

Lunch available
Evening meal available
CC: Amex, Delta, Diners, Mastercard, Switch, Visa

★★★

WIVENHOE HOUSE HOTEL AND CONFERENCE CENTRE
Wivenhoe Park, Colchester CO4 3SQ
T: (01206) 863666
F: (01206) 868532
E: wivsales@essex.ac.uk
I: www.wivenhoehousehotel.co.uk

Bedrooms: 6 single, 40 double/twin, 1 triple/ multiple
Bathrooms: 47 en suite

Lunch available
Evening meal available
CC: Amex, Delta, Diners, Mastercard, Switch, Visa

B&B per night:
S £64.50–£81.50
D £74.00–£91.00

HB per person:
DY £77.25–£98.25

OPEN All year round

Georgian mansion in 200 acres of parkland on the outskirts of Colchester. Well furnished bedrooms with en suite bathroom and TV with Sky channels.

IMPORTANT NOTE Information on accommodation listed in this guide has been supplied by the proprietors. As changes may occur you are advised to check details at the time of booking.

EAST DEREHAM, Norfolk Map ref 3B1

★★

THE PHOENIX HOTEL

Church Street, East Dereham NR19 1DL
T: (01362) 692276
F: (01362) 691752
E: enquiries@phoenixhotel.org.uk
I: www.phoenixhotel.org.uk

B&B per night:
S £47.50–£55.00
D £57.50–£65.00

OPEN All year round

A small town centre hotel with modern amenities. Recently refurbished bedrooms. Excellent reputation for home-cooked food. Warm, friendly atmosphere. Ideally situated to explore the Norfolk Broads, the Norfolk coast and Thetford Forest. The cathedral city of Norwich is 15 miles away.

Bedrooms: 22 double/ twin
Bathrooms: 22 en suite

Lunch available
Evening meal available
CC: Amex, Delta, Diners, Mastercard, Switch, Visa

FAKENHAM, Norfolk Map ref 3B1

★★

WENSUM LODGE HOTEL

Bridge Street, Fakenham NR21 9AY
T: (01328) 862100
F: (01328) 863365
I: www.scoot.co.uk/
wensum_lodge_hotel/

Bedrooms: 2 single, 15 double/twin
Bathrooms: 17 en suite

Lunch available
Evening meal available
CC: Delta, Mastercard, Switch, Visa

B&B per night:
S £50.00–£55.00
D £65.00–£70.00

HB per person:
DY £45.00–£65.00

OPEN All year round

Riverside location. Private gardens, freshly prepared a la carte menu. All bedrooms en suite with colour satellite TV, hot beverages. Quality civil weddings and receptions.

FELIXSTOWE, Suffolk Map ref 3C2 *Tourist Information Centre Tel: (01394) 276770*

★★

MARLBOROUGH HOTEL

Sea Front, Felixstowe IP11 2BJ
T: (01394) 285621
F: (01394) 670724
E: hsm@marlborough-hotel-felix.
com
I: www.marlborough-hotel-felix.
com

Bedrooms: 4 single, 42 double/twin, 3 triple/ multiple; suites available
Bathrooms: 49 en suite

Lunch available
Evening meal available
CC: Amex, Delta, Diners, Mastercard, Switch, Visa

B&B per night:
S £45.00–£55.00
D £54.00–£70.00

HB per person:
DY £37.00–£55.00

OPEN All year round

Fine Edwardian seafront hotel offering comfort and attentive service to the holidaymaker and business person. Many rooms face the sea. Five executive rooms.

GREAT YARMOUTH, Norfolk Map ref 3C1

★★

BURLINGTON PALM COURT HOTEL

North Drive, Great Yarmouth NR30 1EG
T: (01493) 844568
F: (01493) 331848
E: enquiries@burlington-hotel.co.uk
I: www.burlington-hotel.co.uk

B&B per night:
S £50.00–£70.00
D £74.00–£88.00

HB per person:
DY £47.00–£55.00

OPEN Feb–Dec

Run by the same family for over 20 years. We pride ourselves on our food and our friendly, caring service. The hotel overlooks the sea and golden sands. We have our own car parks, lifts, indoor heated pool. All rooms private facilities.

Bedrooms: 9 single, 45 double/twin, 16 triple/multiple
Bathrooms: 70 en suite

Lunch available
Evening meal available
CC: Amex, Delta, Diners, Mastercard, Switch, Visa

CENTRAL RESERVATIONS OFFICES

The symbol **CR** and a group name in an entry indicate that bookings can be made through a central reservations office. These are listed in a separate section towards the back of this guide.

★★

HORSE & GROOM MOTEL
Rollesby, Great Yarmouth NR29 5ER
T: (01493) 740624
F: (01493) 740022
E: bookings@horsegroommotel.co.uk
I: www.horsegroommotel.co.uk

Renowned for its steak and seafood restaurants, The Horse and Groom Motel is 10 minutes away from Great Yarmouth. All en suite rooms have satellite and terrestrial TV, telephones, fridges, safe and tea/coffee facilities. A bar menu offers a choice of at least 15 different dishes daily.

Bedrooms: 16 double/ twin, 4 triple/multiple
Bathrooms: 16 en suite

Lunch available
Evening meal available
CC: Delta, Mastercard, Switch, Visa

Special offer: 28 Sep 2002-12 Apr 2003 (excl Bank Hols), stay Fri and Sat night, Sun accommodation is free.

B&B per night:
S £44.00
D £52.50–£58.95

HB per person:
DY £75.00–£85.00

OPEN All year round

ⓒ
The Independents

★★★
Silver Award

IMPERIAL HOTEL
North Drive, Great Yarmouth NR30 1EQ
T: (01493) 842000
F: (01493) 852229
E: imperial@scs-datacom.co.uk
I: www.imperialhotel.co.uk

Bedrooms: 4 single, 32 double/twin, 3 triple/ multiple
Bathrooms: 39 en suite

Lunch available
Evening meal available
CC: Amex, Delta, Diners, Mastercard, Switch, Visa

Modern, comfortable accommodation is offered in this family-run seafront hotel, locally renowned for fine food, wine and service. Overnight half-board prices are for mini-breaks.

B&B per night:
S £50.00–£75.00
D £60.00–£86.00

HB per person:
DY £48.00–£60.00

OPEN All year round

★★★

REGENCY DOLPHIN HOTEL
Albert Square, Great Yarmouth NR30 3JH
T: (01493) 855070
F: (01493) 853798
E: regency@meridianleisure.com
I: www.meridianleisure.com

Great Yarmouth's premier and unique venue, ideally located within walking distance of Central Beach. En suite bedrooms with satellite channels and all modern amenities. Weddings, conferences and special occasion dining successfully catered for. Licensed to perform marriages. Heated swimming pool, landscaped garden and complimentary parking.

Bedrooms: 6 single, 38 double/twin, 4 triple/ multiple
Bathrooms: 48 en suite

Lunch available
Evening meal available
CC: Amex, Delta, Diners, Mastercard, Switch, Visa

B&B per night:
S £45.00–£65.00
D £60.00–£75.00

HB per person:
DY £58.50–£78.50

OPEN All year round

★★★

HANOVER INTERNATIONAL HOTEL
Luton Road, Harpenden AL5 2PX
T: (01582) 760271 & 464513
F: (01582) 460819
E: david.hunter9@virgin.net
I: www.hanover.international.com

Bedrooms: 8 single, 52 double/twin; suites available
Bathrooms: 60 en suite

Lunch available
Evening meal available
CC: Amex, Delta, Diners, Mastercard, Switch, Visa

Just off M1, junction 9 or 10, this pleasant country-town hotel offers comfortable facilities for businessmen and tourists. Prices shown are for room only.

B&B per night:
S £69.50–£180.95
D £75.00–£191.90

HB per person:
DY £69.50–£209.00

OPEN All year round

CREDIT CARD BOOKINGS If you book by telephone and are asked for your credit card number it is advisable to check the proprietor's policy should you cancel your reservation.

★★ **CLIFF HOTEL**

Marine Parade, Dovercourt,
Harwich CO12 3RE
T: (01255) 503345 & 507373
F: (01255) 240358
E: johnwade@fsbusinessharwich.co.uk
I: www.cliffhotelharwich.co.uk

Bedrooms: 2 single,
21 double/twin, 3 triple/
multiple; suites available
Bathrooms: 24 en suite,
2 private

Lunch available
Evening meal available
CC: Amex, Delta, Diners,
Mastercard, Switch, Visa

B&B per night:
S £50.00–£60.00
D £60.00–£70.00

HB per person:
DY £66.50–£76.50

OPEN All year round

CR
The Independents

Hotel overlooking sea. Bars, function room, restaurant, car parking. Ideal for cruise ships or North Sea ferries and touring Constable Country.

★★

THE HOTEL CONTINENTAL

28-29 Marine Parade, Dovercourt, Harwich
CO12 3RG
T: (01255) 551298 & 07770 308976
F: (01255) 551698
E: hotconti@aol.com
I: www.hotelcontinental-harwich.co.uk

B&B per night:
S £30.00–£50.00
D £60.00–£85.00

HB per person:
DY £40.00–£75.00

OPEN All year round

CR
The Independents

Hotel overlooking European Blue Flag beach and ever-changing seascape which is busy with shipping activity. Only minutes from Harwich International port. All rooms en suite, all different. Quality food with organically grown ingredients extensively used. Well-stocked bar, restaurant and pavement cafe open to the public. Value for money.

Bedrooms: 5 single,
6 double/twin, 2 triple/
multiple
Bathrooms: 13 en suite

Lunch available
Evening meal available
CC: Amex, Delta, Diners,
Mastercard, Switch, Visa

Perfect for ship-spotters; special 3-day breaks. Fishing trips at sea combined with accommodation and dinner.

★★★★

DOWN HALL COUNTRY HOUSE HOTEL

Hatfield Heath, Bishop's Stortford
CM22 7AS
T: (01279) 731441
F: (01279) 730416
E: reservations@downhall.demon.co.uk
I: www.downhall.co.uk

B&B per night:
S £128.00–£168.00
D £148.00–£188.00

OPEN All year round

CR
Utell International/
Grand Heritage Hotels

Historic country house hotel located on the Hertfordshire/Essex border within easy reach of London and Stansted Airport. Set in 100 acres of grounds, you will discover a Victorian mansion brimming with charm and elegance. Good choice of meeting rooms and bedrooms for training courses, meetings and company incentives.

Bedrooms: 16 single,
83 double/twin; suites
available
Bathrooms: 99 en suite

Lunch available
Evening meal available
CC: Amex, Delta, Diners,
Mastercard, Switch, Visa

Celebration package available incl champagne, flowers and chocolates. Please call for further information.

USE YOUR *i*s

There are more than 550 Tourist Information Centres throughout England offering friendly help with accommodation and holiday ideas as well as suggestions of places to visit and things to do. You'll find TIC addresses in the local Phone Book.

HERTFORD, Hertfordshire Map ref 2D1 *Tourist Information Centre Tel: (01992) 584322*

★★★★

Main house, built in 1876, boasts superb function facilities, offering tradition and comfort with all modern facilities. Set in landscaped gardens with 9-hole golf course, outdoor heated pool, 5 all-weather tennis courts. All bedrooms offer private bath/shower, colour TV, direct-dial phone, hair dryer, drinks-making facilities and memorable views.

THE PONSBOURNE PARK HOTEL

Newgate Street Village, Hertford SG13 8QZ
T: (01707) 876191 & 879300
F: (01707) 875190
E: ponsbournepark@lineone.net
I: www.ponsbournepark.com

Bedrooms: 52 double/ twin; suites available	Lunch available
Bathrooms: 52 en suite	Evening meal available
	CC: Delta, Mastercard, Switch, Visa

Weekend breaks 2 nights DB&B from £135 per couple. Romantic breaks from £80 per couple per night incl a la carte DB&B (suite).

B&B per night:
S £60.00–£105.00
D £90.00–£120.00

OPEN All year round

HUNTINGDON, Cambridgeshire Map ref 3A2 *Tourist Information Centre Tel: (01480) 388588*

★★★
Silver
Award

OLD BRIDGE HOTEL

1 High Street, Huntingdon PE29 3TQ	Bedrooms: 6 single, 18 double/twin	Lunch available	B&B per night:
T: (01480) 424300	Bathrooms: 24 en suite	Evening meal available	S £80.00–£110.00
F: (01480) 411017		CC: Amex, Delta, Diners,	D £100.00–£140.00
E: oldbridge@huntsbridge.co.uk		Mastercard, Switch, Visa	

OPEN All year round

Beautifully decorated Georgian town hotel by River Ouse. Oak-panelled dining room, terrace brasserie with award-winning wine list, real ales and log fires. All rooms air-conditioned, most with CD stereo systems.

IPSWICH, Suffolk Map ref 3B2 *Tourist Information Centre Tel: (01473) 258070*

★★★
Silver
Award

THE MARLBOROUGH AT IPSWICH

Henley Road, Ipswich IP1 3SP	Bedrooms: 4 single,	Lunch available	B&B per night:
T: (01473) 257677	18 double/twin; suites	Evening meal available	S £30.00–£81.00
F: (01473) 226927	available	CC: Amex, Delta, Diners,	D £59.00–£135.00
E: reception@themarlborough.co. uk	Bathrooms: 22 en suite	Mastercard, Switch, Visa	
I: www.the marlborough.co.uk			HB per person: DY £60.00–£80.00

OPEN All year round

Small family-owned hotel close to town centre and Christchurch Park. Tastefully furnished en suite bedrooms. Comfortable restaurant (rosettes for food) overlooking the floodlit garden.

★★★
Silver
Award

Set in 8 acres of landscaped gardens and woodlands, with a fine reputation for quality food. This 16thC former country home also has a fabulous leisure club. Rates shown are Breakaway rates, based on a minimum 2-night stay and subject to availability. Call, quoting EN900, to request a Breakaway brochure full of great deals.

SWALLOW BELSTEAD BROOK HOTEL

Belstead Road, Ipswich IP2 9HB
T: (01473) 684241
F: (01473) 681249
E: sales@belsteadbrook.co.uk
I: www.belsteadbrook.co.uk

Bedrooms: 16 single, 72 double/twin; suites available	Lunch available
Bathrooms: 88 en suite	Evening meal available
	CC: Amex, Delta, Diners, Mastercard, Switch, Visa

Extend your Fri/Sat stay to include Sun night for only an extra £40pppn.

B&B per night:
D £111.20–£139.00

OPEN All year round

KING'S LYNN, Norfolk Map ref 3B1 *Tourist Information Centre Tel: (01553) 763044*

★★★ **BUTTERFLY HOTEL**
A10-A47 Roundabout,
Hardwick Narrows, King's Lynn
PE30 4NB
T: (01553) 771707
F: (01553) 768027
E: kingsbutterfly@lineone.net
I: www.butterflyhotels.co.uk

Bedrooms: 23 single,
27 double/twin
Bathrooms: 50 en suite

Lunch available
Evening meal available
CC: Amex, Delta, Diners,
Mastercard, Switch, Visa

B&B per night:
S £65.50–£83.50
D £72.00–£92.00

OPEN All year round

CR
Butterfly Hotels

Easy access to Sandringham and the picturesque north Norfolk coast. This modern hotel maintains all the traditional values of design and comfort. Special Weekend Break rates available.

LEISTON, Suffolk Map ref 3C2

★ **WHITE HORSE HOTEL**
Station Road, Leiston IP16 4HD
T: (01728) 830694
F: (01728) 833105
E: whihorse@globalnet.co.uk
I: www.whitehorsehotel.co.uk

Bedrooms: 3 single,
8 double/twin, 2 triple/
multiple
Bathrooms: 13 en suite

Lunch available
Evening meal available
CC: Amex, Delta, Diners,
Mastercard, Switch, Visa

B&B per night:
S Min £35.00
D Min £55.00

OPEN All year round

18thC Georgian hotel with a relaxed and informal atmosphere, only 2 miles from the sea, in the heart of bird-watching country.

LOWESTOFT, Suffolk Map ref 3C1

★★★

HOTEL HATFIELD
The Esplanade, Lowestoft NR33 0QG
T: (01502) 565337
F: (01502) 511885

B&B per night:
S £42.00–£62.00
D £72.00–£85.00

OPEN All year round

CR
Best Western Hotels

Superior hotel situated on the seafront at Lowestoft offering superb views and a varied and comprehensive range of facilities. Ideally situated to explore the Norfolk Broads and Suffolk heritage coastline, the bustling resort of Great Yarmouth and the cathedral city of Norwich.

Bedrooms: 10 single,
22 double/twin, 1 triple/
multiple; suites available
Bathrooms: 33 en suite

Lunch available
Evening meal available
CC: Amex, Delta, Diners,
Mastercard, Switch, Visa

★★★
Silver
Award

IVY HOUSE FARM HOTEL
Ivy Lane, Oulton Broad, Lowestoft
NR33 8HY
T: (01502) 501353 & 588144
F: (01502) 501539
E: admin@ivyhousefarm.co.uk
I: www.ivyhousefarm.co.uk

B&B per night:
S £73.00–£95.00
D £95.00–£130.00

HB per person:
DY £49.00–£80.00

OPEN Mar–Dec

On the south-western shores of Oulton Broad with country gardens and lily ponds bordered by 40 acres of meadows. Standard and executive garden bedrooms are spacious and individually decorated. Some are beamed, most have views of the garden or surrounding countryside. Imaginative cuisine is served in the candlelit, thatched Crooked Barn.

Bedrooms: 1 single,
17 double/twin, 1 triple/
multiple
Bathrooms: 19 en suite

Lunch available
Evening meal available
CC: Amex, Delta, Diners,
Mastercard, Switch, Visa

Dine and unwind-en suite accommodation, breakfast, £20 dinner allowance from £49pp double occupancy. (Not available July-Sep 2002).

COLOUR MAPS Colour maps at the front of this guide pinpoint all places under which you will find accommodation listed.

MALDON, Essex Map ref 3B3 *Tourist Information Centre Tel: (01621) 856503*

★★★★
Silver
Award

FIVE LAKES HOTEL, GOLF, COUNTRY CLUB & SPA
Colchester Road,
Tolleshunt Knights, Maldon
CM9 8HX
T: (01621) 868888
F: (01621) 869696
E: enquiries@fivelakes.co.uk
I: www.fivelakes.co.uk

Bedrooms: 114 double/
twin; suites available
Bathrooms: 114 en suite

Lunch available
Evening meal available
CC: Amex, Delta, Diners,
Mastercard, Switch, Visa

B&B per night:
D Min £136.00

HB per person:
DY Min £159.00

OPEN All year round

Ⓒ
Best Western Hotels

Unparalleled sporting and leisure activities including two 18-hole golf courses, indoor/ outdoor tennis and health spa complemented by quality accommodation, bars and 2 restaurants.

⚙🛏🏠🍴🖥💻♿🖧☎🅢🔄●🛗🖥🍴🎱🎳🍺✕🔍👁👟🐎🐴🅿

NEWMARKET, Suffolk Map ref 3B2 *Tourist Information Centre Tel: (01638) 667200*

★★★

♿

HEATH COURT HOTEL
Moulton Road, Newmarket
CB8 8DY
T: (01638) 667171
F: (01638) 666533
E: quality@heathcourt-hotel.co.uk
I: www.heathcourt-hotel.co.uk

Bedrooms: 20 single,
19 double/twin, 2 triple/
multiple; suites available
Bathrooms: 41 en suite

Lunch available
Evening meal available
CC: Amex, Delta, Diners,
Mastercard, Switch, Visa

B&B per night:
S £72.00–£85.00
D £92.00–£150.00

HB per person:
DY £58.00–£60.00

OPEN All year round

Ⓒ
Best Western Hotels

Hotel of high standards in a quiet central position. Ideal location for touring, horseracing and local countryside.

⚙🛏☎🖧☎♿🅢🔄●🛗🖥🍴👟🐴🅿

★★★

THE RUTLAND ARMS HOTEL
High Street, Newmarket CB8 8NB
T: (01638) 664251
F: (01638) 666298
E: rutlandarms.co.uk
I: www.rutlandarms.com

B&B per night:
S £76.25–£103.25
D £95.00–£121.50

HB per person:
DY £63.00–£76.25

OPEN All year round

As the home of racing, Newmarket has attracted the great and good since the time of Charles II. Few have left the town without a visit to the historic Rutland Arms, one of the High Street's most striking buildings and one of Newmarket's finest establishments.

Bedrooms: 12 single,
32 double/twin, 2 triple/
multiple
Bathrooms: 46 en suite

Lunch available
Evening meal available
CC: Amex, Delta, Diners,
Mastercard, Switch, Visa

Short-break weekends (excl racing and sales dates).

⚙🛏☎🖧☎♿🅢🔄●🖥🍴👟❄🐎🅿

NORFOLK BROADS

See under Great Yarmouth, Lowestoft, North Walsham, Norwich

NORTH WALSHAM, Norfolk Map ref 3C1

★★

ELDERTON LODGE HOTEL AND LANGTRY RESTAURANT
Gunton Park, Thorpe Market,
Norwich NR11 8TZ
T: (01263) 833547
F: (01263) 834673
E: enquiries@eldertonlodge.co.uk
I: www.eldertonlodge.co.uk

Bedrooms: 11 double/
twin
Bathrooms: 11 en suite

Lunch available
Evening meal available
CC: Amex, Delta,
Mastercard, Switch, Visa

B&B per night:
S £60.00–£70.00
D £95.00–£115.00

HB per person:
DY £110.00–£145.00

OPEN All year round

Secluded Georgian shooting lodge with historical royal connections, set in 6 acres with spectacular views across the Deer Park. Elegant rooms, quality food.

🛏10🍴☎🖧☎♿🅢🔄🖥💻🍴♿⟳🎣☂❄🐴🛏🐎🅿

www.travelengland.org.uk
Log on for information and inspiration. The latest information on places to visit, events and quality assessed accommodation.

★★
Silver
Award

BEECHES HOTEL

2-6 Earlham Road, Norwich NR2 3DB
T: (01603) 621167 & 667357
F: (01603) 620151
E: reception@beeches.co.uk
I: www.beeches.co.uk

B&B per night:
S £59.00–£69.00
D £76.00–£94.00

HB per person:
DY £51.00–£60.00

OPEN All year round

'An oasis in the heart of Norwich'. Three separate Grade II Listed Victorian houses and modern extension create a welcoming and individual hotel, complemented by a tranquil English Heritage Victorian garden, yet only a 10-minute stroll to city centre. Tastefully refurbished, comfortable accommodation in a relaxed, informal atmosphere.

Bedrooms: 8 single,
28 double/twin
Bathrooms: 36 en suite

Evening meal available
CC: Amex, Delta, Diners,
Mastercard, Switch, Visa

The Independents

★★★★
Silver
Award

MARRIOTT SPROWSTON MANOR HOTEL & COUNTRY CLUB

Sprowston Park, Wroxham Road, Norwich NR7 8RP
T: (01603) 410871
F: (01603) 423911
I: www.marriotthotels.co.uk

B&B per night:
D £130.00–£180.00

HB per person:
DY £80.00–£100.00

OPEN All year round

Lies in 10 acres of parkland with 18-hole golf course close to the Norfolk Broads and cathedral city of Norwich. The hotel has a fabulous leisure club plus health spa and a rosette for good food. Rates based on a minimum of 2 nights, quote WTS2002 when booking.

Bedrooms: 94 double/
twin; suites available
Bathrooms: 94 en suite

Lunch available
Evening meal available
CC: Amex, Delta, Diners,
Mastercard, Switch, Visa

★★

OLD RECTORY

North Walsham Road, Crostwick, Norwich NR12 7BG
T: (01603) 738513
F: (01603) 738712
E: info@therectoryhotel.fsnet.co.uk
I: www.oldrectorycrostwick.com

B&B per night:
S £42.00–£44.00
D £57.50–£60.00

HB per person:
DY £45.00–£51.50

OPEN All year round

Old Victorian rectory set amidst 3.5 acres of beautiful gardens, 5 miles north of Norwich. Outdoor heated pool. Luxurious en suite rooms all ground floor level. Large conservatory restaurant, fully air conditioned, for full English breakfast or evening meals. Close to Broads and Norwich Airport/train station.

Bedrooms: 11 double/
twin, 2 triple/multiple;
suites available
Bathrooms: 13 en suite

Evening meal available
CC: Amex, Delta,
Mastercard, Switch, Visa

ACCESSIBILITY

Look for the ⬛⬛⬛ symbols which indicate accessibility for wheelchair users. A list of establishments is at the front of this guide.

★★★

PARK FARM COUNTRY HOTEL & LEISURE

Hethersett, Norwich NR9 3DL
T: (01603) 810264
F: (01603) 812104
E: enq@parkfarm-hotel.co.uk
I: www.parkfarm-hotel.co.uk

B&B per night:
S £80.00–£105.00
D £110.00–£140.00

HB per person:
DY £100.50–£125.50

OPEN All year round

Located in beautiful landscaped gardens, Park Farm offers 47 en suite bedrooms, many with 4-poster beds and whirlpool baths. Dining in the Georgian Restaurant, informally in the lounge bar or just relaxing in the superb leisure centre means that Park Farm is the perfect choice for a relaxing break.

Bedrooms: 2 single,
33 double/twin,
12 triple/multiple
Bathrooms: 47 en suite

Lunch available
Evening meal available
CC: Amex, Delta, Diners,
Mastercard, Switch, Visa

Weekend breaks from £55pppn DB&B 2 people sharing. Sunday night specials DB&B from £40pp 2 people sharing.

★★★

SWALLOW NELSON HOTEL

Prince of Wales Road, Norwich NR1 1DX
T: (01603) 760260
F: (01603) 620008
I: www.swallowhotels.com

B&B per night:
D £110.00–£130.00

HB per person:
DY £70.00–£90.00

OPEN All year round

Modern, purpose-built hotel on riverside, close to railway station and city centre. Easy access Broads, coast. Leisure club with indoor swimming pool. Rates shown are Breakaway rates, based on a minimum 2-night stay and subject to availability. Call, quoting EN900, to request a Breakaway brochure full of great deals.

Bedrooms: 27 single,
105 double/twin
Bathrooms: 132 en suite

Lunch available
Evening meal available
CC: Amex, Delta, Diners,
Mastercard, Switch, Visa

OVERSTRAND, Norfolk Map ref 3C1

★★★
Silver
Award

SEA MARGE HOTEL

16 High Street, Overstrand, Cromer
NR27 0AB
T: (01263) 579579
F: (01263) 579524
I: www.mackenziehotels.com

B&B per night:
S £50.00–£60.00
D £80.00–£102.00

HB per person:
DY £57.00–£79.00

OPEN All year round

Discover Sea Marge, set in an Area of Outstanding Natural Beauty in the quaint unspoilt fishing village of Overstrand. All 17 en suite rooms are luxuriously furnished, some with spectacular sea views across the terraced gardens. Our high standards of food and service have made us one of north Norfolk's finest hotels.

Bedrooms: 16 double/
twin, 1 triple/multiple
Bathrooms: 17 en suite

Lunch available
Evening meal available
CC: Delta, Mastercard,
Switch, Visa

Christmas 4-night break. New Year 2-night break. Murder Mystery weekend. Romantic Valentine 2-night escape.

QUALITY ASSURANCE SCHEME

Star ratings and awards were correct at the time of going to press but are subject to change. Please check at the time of booking.

PETERBOROUGH, Cambridgeshire Map ref 3A1 *Tourist Information Centre Tel: (01733) 452336*

★★★
Silver Award

THE BELL INN HOTEL

Great North Road, Stilton, Peterborough
PE7 3RA
T: (01733) 241066
F: (01733) 245173
E: reception@thebellstilton.co.uk
I: www.thebellstilton.co.uk

The Bell Inn, 'Birthplace of Stilton Cheese', offers today's demanding traveller modern first class accommodation and conference facilities in the unique setting of this ancient inn. Sited just off the A1 on the Great Old North Road, with easy access to all main transport routes and the thriving city of Peterborough.

Bedrooms: 2 single, 16 double/twin, 1 triple/ multiple
Bathrooms: 19 en suite

Lunch available
Evening meal available
CC: Amex, Delta, Diners, Mastercard, Switch, Visa

B&B per night:
S £69.50–£89.50
D £89.50–£109.50

OPEN All year round

★★★

BUTTERFLY HOTEL
Thorpe Meadows,
Off Longthorpe Parkway,
Peterborough PE3 6GA
T: (01733) 564240
F: (01733) 565538
E: peterbutterfly@lineone.net
I: www.butterflyhotels.co.uk

By the water's edge, overlooking Peterborough's International Rowing Course, this modern hotel maintains all the traditional values of design and comfort. Special Weekend Break rates available.

Bedrooms: 33 single, 33 double/twin, 4 triple/ multiple; suites available
Bathrooms: 70 en suite

Lunch available
Evening meal available
CC: Amex, Delta, Diners, Mastercard, Switch, Visa

B&B per night:
S £65.50–£96.50
D £72.00–£105.00

OPEN All year round

CR
Butterfly Hotels

★★★

ORTON HALL HOTEL

The Village, Orton Longueville,
Peterborough PE2 7DN
T: (01733) 391111
F: (01733) 231912
E: reception@ortonhall.co.uk
I: www.abacushotels.co.uk

17thC manor house in 20 acres of mature parkland 2.5 miles from city centre. Fully equipped en suite bedrooms, some with 4-posters. Choice of dining in either the Huntly Restaurant or Rumblewood Inn traditional country pub. Adjacent to Nene Park and two 18-hole golf courses. Picturesque Stamford is nearby. Half board price shown is special break rate.

Bedrooms: 9 single, 54 double/twin, 2 triple/ multiple
Bathrooms: 65 en suite

Lunch available
Evening meal available
CC: Amex, Delta, Diners, Mastercard, Switch, Visa

B&B per night:
S £84.35–£98.85
D £107.90–£149.90

HB per person:
DY £59.50–£97.45

OPEN All year round

CR
Best Western Hotels

★★

THOMAS COOK LEISURE CENTRE
P O Box 36, Thorpe Wood,
Peterborough PE3 6SB
T: (01733) 502555 & 503008
F: (01733) 502020
E: leisurecentre.general@trauelex.
com

Friendly, efficient service is provided at this modern hotel. All rooms en suite. Complimentary use of extensive leisure facilities during stay. Bar and restaurant.

Bedrooms: 11 double/ twin, 2 triple/multiple
Bathrooms: 13 en suite

Lunch available
Evening meal available
CC: Delta, Mastercard, Switch, Visa

B&B per night:
S £30.00–£55.23
D £40.00–£70.50

OPEN All year round

CONFIRM YOUR BOOKING
You are advised to confirm your booking in writing.

ST IVES, Cambridgeshire Map ref 3A2

★★★

OLIVERS LODGE HOTEL
Needingworth Road, St Ives, Huntingdon
PE27 5JP
T: (01480) 463252
F: (01480) 461150
E: reception@oliverslodge.co.uk
I: www.oliverslodge.co.uk

B&B per night:
S £70.00–£85.00
D £70.00–£110.00

HB per person:
DY £48.00–£62.00

OPEN All year round

Victorian house of character with attractive patio garden. Real ale bar, conservatory restaurant, extensive a la carte and bar snacks. Fresh fish and game specialities. Independently owned and operated. Just 20 minutes' drive from centre of Cambridge in the picturesque riverside town of St Ives. Half board price includes half bottle wine per person, on Sunday nights.

Bedrooms: 1 single,
13 double/twin, 3 triple/
multiple; suites available
Bathrooms: 17 en suite

Lunch available
Evening meal available
CC: Amex, Delta,
Mastercard, Switch, Visa

Free 1 hour trip on hotel cruiser during Aug and Apr, subject to weather and availability.

★★★

SLEPE HALL HOTEL
Ramsey Road, St Ives, Huntingdon
PE27 5RB
T: (01480) 463122
F: (01480) 300706
E: mail@slepehall.co.uk
I: www.slepehall.co.uk

Bedrooms: 2 single,
14 double/twin
Bathrooms: 16 en suite

Lunch available
Evening meal available
CC: Amex, Delta, Diners,
Mastercard, Switch, Visa

B&B per night:
S £50.00–£85.00
D £65.00–£110.00

OPEN All year round

Former private Victorian girls' school converted in 1966. Now a Grade II Listed building, 5 minutes' walk from the River Great Ouse and historic town centre. Extensive bar and restaurant menus.

ST NEOTS, Cambridgeshire Map ref 2D1 *Tourist Information Centre Tel: (01480) 388788*

★★

ABBOTSLEY GOLF HOTEL & COUNTRY CLUB
Eynesbury Hardwicke, St Neots,
Huntingdon PE19 6XN
T: (01480) 474000
F: (01480) 471018
E: abbotsley@americangolf.uk.com

Bedrooms: 10 single,
31 double/twin, 1 triple/
multiple
Bathrooms: 42 en suite

Lunch available
Evening meal available
CC: Delta, Diners,
Mastercard, Switch, Visa

B&B per night:
S £49.00–£59.00
D £75.00–£85.00

HB per person:
DY £65.00–£75.00

OPEN All year round

Charming country hotel amidst its own 2 excellent 18-hole golf-courses. Golf Monthly: 'The design is a revelation, the presentation superb'. Non-golfers just as welcome!

SHERINGHAM, Norfolk Map ref 3B1

★★

BEAUMARIS HOTEL
15 South Street, Sheringham
NR26 8LL
T: (01263) 822370
F: (01263) 821421
E: beauhotel@aol.com.
I: www.ecn.co.uk/beaumaris/

Bedrooms: 5 single,
16 double/twin
Bathrooms: 21 en suite

Lunch available
Evening meal available
CC: Amex, Delta, Diners,
Mastercard, Switch, Visa

B&B per night:
S £40.00–£45.00
D £80.00–£90.00

HB per person:
DY £55.00–£60.00

OPEN Mar–mid Dec

Family-run hotel established in 1947, with a reputation for personal service and English cuisine. Quietly located close to beach, shops and golf club.

★★

SOUTHLANDS HOTEL
South Street, Sheringham NR26 8LL
T: (01263) 822679
F: (01263) 822679

Bedrooms: 2 single,
14 double/twin, 1 triple/
multiple
Bathrooms: 17 en suite

Lunch available
Evening meal available
CC: Mastercard, Visa

B&B per night:
S £34.00–£35.00
D £68.00–£70.00

HB per person:
DY £45.00–£46.00

Privately owned hotel ideally situated close to town, seafront and golf-courses.

RATING
All accommodation in this guide has been rated, or is awaiting a rating, by a trained English Tourism Council assessor.

★★★

THE ESSEX COUNTY HOTEL
Aviation Way, Southend-on-Sea
SS2 6UN
T: (01702) 279955
F: (01702) 541961
E: mail@essexcountyhotel.fsnet.co.uk

Bedrooms: 23 double/ twin, 53 triple/multiple; suites available	Lunch available Evening meal available CC: Amex, Delta, Diners, Mastercard, Switch, Visa
Bathrooms: 76 en suite	

B&B per night:
S £50.00–£62.00
D £65.00–£80.00

OPEN All year round

®
Corus & Regal Hotels/
Utell International

Modern hotel situated close to Southend Airport. Benefits from recent refurbishment. Excellent restaurant and bar facilities, also has nightclub (weekends).

ᴀⴸ👤♿🛎⬜↻🍴ⓢ🔑✉⓪🏧🍴🍽✂🐕P

★★★

ROSLIN HOTEL

Thorpe Esplanade, Thorpe Bay, Southend-on-Sea SS1 3BG
T: (01702) 586375
F: (01702) 586663
E: frontoffice@roslinhotel.demon.co.uk
I: www.roslinhotel.com

B&B per night:
S £38.00–£67.00
D £68.00–£86.00

OPEN All year round

On seafront in residential Thorpe Bay within easy reach of main town centre. Terrace, public rooms and many bedrooms overlook Estuary. First class restaurant open to non-residents. All rooms have full facilities, including tea/coffee-making, hairdryers, telephone, Sky TV.

Bedrooms: 14 single,
20 double/twin, 5 triple/
multiple
Bathrooms: 39 en suite

Lunch available
Evening meal available
CC: Amex, Delta, Diners,
Mastercard, Switch, Visa

Weekend break from £85-£110pp 2 nights minimum.

ᴀⴸ👤♿🛎⬜↻🍴ⓢ🔑✉⓪🏧🍴✂🐕P

★★★

THE VINTAGE COURT HOTEL

Puckeridge, Ware SG11 1SA
T: (01920) 822722
F: (01920) 822877

B&B per night:
S £68.00–£90.00
D £77.00–£99.00

HB per person:
DY £86.85–£118.00

OPEN All year round

Quiet, modern traditional style hotel in picturesque village of Puckeridge, close to the junction of the A10 and A120. Fifteen miles from Stansted Airport. All bedrooms are en suite. Attractive, welcoming restaurant.

Bedrooms: 30 double/
twin
Bathrooms: 30 en suite

Lunch available
Evening meal available
CC: Amex, Delta, Diners,
Mastercard, Switch, Visa

ⴸ👤♿🛎⬜↻🍴ⓢ🔑🏧🍴☎✂🐕P

★★

THE LIFEBOAT INN

Ship Lane, Thornham PE36 6LT
T: (01485) 512236
F: (01485) 512323
E: reception@lifeboatinn.co.uk
I: www.lifeboatinn.co.uk

B&B per night:
S £40.00–£71.00
D £84.00–£92.00

HB per person:
DY £54.00–£70.00

OPEN All year round

This 16thC ale house combines historic charm with 20thC comforts. The relaxing views over the open meadows lead to the distant horizon of Thornham Harbour and the sea. All the attractive bedrooms are well-equipped and tastefully furnished. Both bar and restaurant provide a wide range of tempting meals.

Bedrooms: 10 double/
twin, 3 triple/multiple
Bathrooms: 13 en suite

Lunch available
Evening meal available
CC: Delta, Mastercard,
Switch, Visa

Stay 3 nights and get 3rd night at half price B&B.
Exceptional mid-week discounts Jan, Feb, Nov, Dec.

ⴸ👤♿🛎⬜↻🍴ⓢ🏧🍴✂🐕🐾P

THORPENESS

See display advertisement below

TITCHWELL, Norfolk Map ref 3B1

★★

BRIARFIELDS HOTEL
Main Street, Titchwell, King's Lynn
PE31 8BB
T: (01485) 210742
F: (01485) 210933
E: briarfields@norfolk-hotels.co.uk

Bedrooms: 15 double/
twin, 4 triple/multiple;
suites available
Bathrooms: 19 en suite

Lunch available
Evening meal available
CC: Delta, Diners,
Mastercard, Switch, Visa

B&B per night:
S Max £47.50
D Max £75.00

HB per person:
DY Max £59.50

OPEN All year round

Traditional, privately owned hotel, overlooking Titchwell RSPB Reserve, salt marshes and beaches. Renowned for comfort and excellent menus. Ideal birdwatching, golf, places of local interest.

TIVETSHALL ST MARY, Norfolk Map ref 3B2

★★
Silver
Award

A warm welcome awaits you at this delightful 17thC coaching inn (15 miles south of Norwich). Recent refurbishments give the inn superb bedrooms, many with oak beams. Well known for its quality food. The public rooms are full of character with exposed beams and open log fires. A sheltered, flower-filled terrace restaurant is open for al fresco dining in summer.

THE OLD RAM COACHING INN

Ipswich Road, Tivetshall St Mary, Norwich
NR15 2DE
T: (01379) 676794
F: (01379) 608399
E: theoldram@btinternet.com
I: www.theoldram.com

Bedrooms: 10 double/
twin, 1 triple/multiple
Bathrooms: 11 en suite

Lunch available
Evening meal available
CC: Delta, Mastercard,
Switch, Visa

Short breaks available on application.

B&B per night:
S £51.95–£56.95
D £70.90–£78.90

HB per person:
DY £63.90–£71.90

OPEN All year round

TOWN INDEX

This can be found at the back of this guide. If you know where you want to stay, the index will give you the page number listing accommodation in your chosen town, city or village.

★★★

THE VINTAGE COURT HOTEL

Puckeridge, Ware SG11 1SA
T: (01920) 822722
F: (01920) 822877

B&B per night:
S £68.00–£90.00
D £77.00–£99.00

HB per person:
DY £86.85–£118.00

OPEN All year round

Quiet, modern traditional style hotel in picturesque village of Puckeridge, close to the junction of the A10 and A120. Fifteen miles from Stansted Airport. All bedrooms are en suite. Attractive, welcoming restaurant.

Bedrooms: 30 double/ twin
Bathrooms: 30 en suite

Lunch available
Evening meal available
CC: Amex, Delta, Diners, Mastercard, Switch, Visa

★★

CROWN LODGE HOTEL

Downham Road, Outwell, Wisbech
PE14 8SE
T: (01945) 773391 & 772206
F: (01945) 772668
E: crownlodgehotel@hotmail.com
I: www.smoothhound.co.uk/hotels/crownl.
html

B&B per night:
S £50.00–£55.00
D £65.00–£70.00

HB per person:
DY £55.00–£75.00

OPEN All year round

The Independents

Situated on the A1101/A1122 Downham Market to Wisbech road on the banks of the Welle Creek. Enjoy a meal in our bar, patio garden or the more formal surroundings of the Crown Room. We combine the freshest of local produce with more exotic ingredients to prepare dishes of flair and imagination.

Bedrooms: 10 double/ twin
Bathrooms: 10 en suite

Lunch available
Evening meal available
CC: Amex, Delta, Diners, Mastercard, Switch, Visa

Weekend breaks-2 nights 10% discount, 3 nights for the price of 2.

★★★
Silver Award

SECKFORD HALL HOTEL

Woodbridge IP13 6NU
T: (01394) 385678
F: (01394) 380610
E: reception@seckford.co.uk
I: www.seckford.co.uk

Bedrooms: 3 single, 24 double/twin, 5 triple/ multiple; suites available
Bathrooms: 32 en suite

Lunch available
Evening meal available
CC: Amex, Delta, Diners, Mastercard, Switch, Visa

B&B per night:
S £79.00–£130.00
D £120.00–£170.00

OPEN All year round

Elizabethan country house hotel with 4-poster beds, spa baths, indoor heated swimming pool, gym, beauty salon and 18 hole golf course. Excellent cuisine in 2 restaurants

★★★

UFFORD PARK HOTEL GOLF & LEISURE

Yarmouth Road, Ufford,
Woodbridge IP12 1QW
T: (01394) 383555
F: (01394) 383582
E: uffordparkltd@btinternet.com
I: www.uffordpark.co.uk

Bedrooms: 2 single, 29 double/twin, 19 triple/multiple
Bathrooms: 50 en suite

Lunch available
Evening meal available
CC: Amex, Delta, Diners, Mastercard, Switch, Visa

B&B per night:
S £74.00–£85.00
D £190.00–£258.00

OPEN All year round

Best Western Hotels

Set in 120 acres of historic parkland. Extensive leisure facilities including indoor pool, sauna etc. and 18-hole, par 71 golf course, hair and beauty academy.

SPECIAL BREAKS

Many establishments offer special promotions and themed breaks. These are highlighted in red. (All such offers are subject to availability.)

★★

HOTEL WROXHAM

The Bridge, Wroxham, Norwich NR12 8AJ
T: (01603) 782061
F: (01603) 784279
I: www.hotelwroxham.co.uk

B&B per night:
S £42.50–£62.50
D £65.00–£85.00

HB per person:
DY £37.50–£47.50

OPEN All year round

On the banks of the River Bure in the capital of Broadland, only 7 miles from Norwich, this is a riverside oasis catering for both leisure and business visitors. Unique waterside terrace bar and restaurant, excellent wedding and conference facilities, riverside suites with balconies, private boat moorings, car parking.

Bedrooms: 1 single,
17 double/twin
Bathrooms: 18 en suite

Rail breaks and Christmas programmes are available.

Lunch available
Evening meal available
CC: Amex, Delta, Diners,
Mastercard, Switch, Visa

Minotel

CHECK THE MAPS

The colour maps at the front of this guide show all the cities, towns and villages for which you will find accommodation entries. Refer to the town index to find the page on which they are listed.

A brief guide to the main Towns and Villages offering accommodation in the

East of England

A ALDEBURGH, SUFFOLK - A prosperous port in the 16th C, now famous for the Aldeburgh Music Festival held annually in June. The 16th C Moot Hall, now a museum, is a timber-framed building once used as an open market.

B BASILDON, ESSEX - One of the New Towns planned after World War II. It overlooks the estuary of the River Thames and is set in undulating countryside. The main feature is the town square with a traffic-free pedestrian concourse.

• **BLAKENEY, NORFOLK** - Picturesque village on the north coast of Norfolk and a former port and fishing village. 15th C Guildhall. Marshy creeks extend towards Blakeney Point (National Trust) and are a paradise for naturalists, with trips to the reserve and to see the seals from Blakeney Quay.

• **BRENTWOOD, ESSEX** - The town grew up in the late 12th C and then developed as a staging post, being strategically placed close to the London to Chelmsford road. Deer roam by the lakes in the 428 acre park at South Weald, part of Brentwood's attractive Green Belt.

• **BURY ST EDMUNDS, SUFFOLK** - Ancient market and cathedral town which takes its name from the martyred Saxon King, St Edmund. Bury St Edmunds has many fine buildings including the Athenaeum and Moyses Hall, reputed to be the oldest Norman house in the county.

C CAMBRIDGE, CAMBRIDGESHIRE - A most important and beautiful city on the River Cam with 31 colleges forming one of the oldest universities in the world. Numerous museums, good shopping centre, restaurants, theatres, cinema and fine bookshops.

• **CHATTERIS, CAMBRIDGESHIRE** - A small market town in the heart of the Fens.

• **CHELMSFORD, ESSEX** - The county town of Essex, originally a Roman settlement, Caesaromagus, thought to have been destroyed by Boudicca. Growth of the town's industry can be traced in the excellent museum in Oaklands Park. 15th C parish church has been Chelmsford Cathedral since 1914.

• **CLACTON-ON-SEA, ESSEX** - Developed in the 1870s into a popular holiday resort with pier, pavilion, funfair, theatres and traditional amusements. The Martello Towers on the seafront were built like many others in the early 19th C to defend Britain against Napoleon.

• **COLCHESTER, ESSEX** - Britain's oldest recorded town standing on the River Colne and famous for its oysters. Numerous historic buildings, ancient remains and museums. Plenty of parks and gardens, extensive shopping centre, theatre and zoo.

F FAKENHAM, NORFOLK - Attractive, small market town dates from Saxon times and was a Royal Manor until the 17th C. Its market place has 2 old coaching inns, both showing traces of earlier work behind Georgian facades, and the parish church has a commanding 15th C tower.

• **FELIXSTOWE, SUFFOLK** - Seaside resort that developed at the end of the 19th C. Lying in a gently curving bay with a 2-mile-long beach and backed by a wide promenade of lawns and floral gardens.

G GREAT YARMOUTH, NORFOLK - One of Britain's major seaside resorts with 5 miles of seafront and every possible amenity including an award winning leisure complex offering a huge variety of all-weather facilities. Busy harbour and fishing centre.

H HARPENDEN, HERTFORDSHIRE - Delightful country town with many scenic walks through surrounding woods and fields. Harpenden train station provides a fast service into London.

• **HARWICH, ESSEX** - Port where the Rivers Orwell and Stour converge and enter the North Sea. The old town still has a medieval atmosphere with its narrow streets. To the south is the seaside resort of Dovercourt with long sandy beaches.

• **HERTFORD, HERTFORDSHIRE** - Old county town with attractive cottages and houses and fine public buildings. The remains of the ancient castle, childhood home of Elizabeth I, now form the council offices and the grounds are open to the public.

• **HUNTINGDON, CAMBRIDGESHIRE** - Attractive, interesting town which abounds in associations with the Cromwell family. The town is connected to Godmanchester by a beautiful 14th C bridge over the River Great Ouse.

I IPSWICH, SUFFOLK - Interesting county town and major port on the River Orwell. Birthplace of Cardinal Wolsey. Christchurch Mansion, set in a fine park, contains a good collection of furniture and pictures, with works by Gainsborough, Constable and Munnings.

K KING'S LYNN, NORFOLK - A busy town with many outstanding buildings. The Guildhall and Town Hall are both built of flint in a striking chequer design. Behind the Guildhall in the Old Gaol House the sounds and smells of prison life 2 centuries ago are recreated.

L LEISTON, SUFFOLK - Centrally placed for visiting the Suffolk Heritage Coast, Leiston is a bustling, working town in a rural setting famous for Leiston Abbey and the award winning Long Shop Museum.

• **LOWESTOFT, SUFFOLK** - Seaside town with wide sandy beaches. Important fishing port with picturesque fishing quarter. Home of the famous Lowestoft porcelain and birthplace of Benjamin Britten. East Point Pavilion's exhibition describes the Lowestoft story.

M MALDON, ESSEX - The Blackwater Estuary has made Maldon a natural base for yachtsmen. Boat-building is also an important industry. Numerous buildings of interest. The 13th C church of All Saints has the only triangular church tower in Britain. Also a museum and maritime centre.

N NEWMARKET, SUFFOLK - Centre of the English horse-racing world and the headquarters of the Jockey Club and National Stud. Racecourse and horse sales. The National Horse Racing Museum traces the history and development of the Sport of Kings.

• **NORTH WALSHAM, NORFOLK** - Weekly market has been held here for 700 years. 1 mile south of town is a cross commemorating the Peasants' Revolt of 1381. Nelson attended the local Paston Grammar School, founded in 1606 and still flourishing.

- **NORWICH, NORFOLK** - Beautiful cathedral city and county town on the River Wensum with many fine museums and medieval churches. Norman castle, Guildhall and interesting medieval streets. Good shopping centre and market.

- **OVERSTRAND, NORFOLK** - Village with extensive sandy beach. Church of St Martin, built in 14th C but much rebuilt since, has a round tower and ancient oven for baking the sacrament.

- **PETERBOROUGH, CAMBRIDGESHIRE** - Prosperous and rapidly expanding cathedral city on the edge of the Fens on the River Nene. Catherine of Aragon is buried in the cathedral. City Museum and Art Gallery. Ferry Meadows Country Park has numerous leisure facilities.

- **SHERINGHAM, NORFOLK** - Holiday resort with Victorian and Edwardian hotels and a sand and shingle beach where the fishing boats are hauled up. The North Norfolk Railway operates from Sheringham station during the summer. Other attractions include museums, theatre and Splash Fun Pool.

- **SOUTHEND-ON-SEA, ESSEX** - On the Thames Estuary and the nearest seaside resort to London. Famous for its pier and unique pier trains. Other attractions include Peter Pan's Playground, indoor swimming pools, indoor rollerskating and ten pin bowling.

- **ST IVES, CAMBRIDGESHIRE** - Picturesque market town with a narrow 6-arched bridge spanning the River Ouse on which stands a bridge chapel. There are numerous Georgian and Victorian buildings and the Norris Museum has a good local collection.

- **ST NEOTS, CAMBRIDGESHIRE** - Pleasant market town on the River Ouse with a large square which grew up around a 10th C priory. There are many interesting buildings and St Mary's is one of the largest medieval churches in the country.

- **TIVETSHALL ST MARY, NORFOLK** - Conveniently located on the A140 for access to Norwich.

- **WISBECH, CAMBRIDGESHIRE** - The town is the centre of the agricultural and flower-growing industries of Fenland. Peckover House (National Trust) is an important example of domestic architecture.

- **WOODBRIDGE, SUFFOLK** - Once a busy seaport, the town is now a sailing centre on the River Deben. There are many buildings of architectural merit including the Bell and Angel Inns. The 18th C Tide Mill is now restored and open to the public.

- **WROXHAM, NORFOLK** - Yachting centre on the River Bure which houses the headquarters of the Norfolk Broads Yacht Club. The church of St Mary has a famous doorway and the manor house nearby dates back to 1623.

www.travelengland.org.uk

Log on to travelengland.org.uk and discover something different around every corner. Meander through pages for ideas of places to visit and things to do. Spend time in each region and discover the diversity – from busy vibrant cities to rural village greens; rugged peaks to gentle rolling hills; dramatic coastline to idyllic sandy beaches. England might be a small country but it is brimming with choice and opportunity. Visit www.travelengland.org.uk and see for yourself.

England

Finding
accommodation
is as easy as 1 2 3

Where to Stay makes it quick and easy to find a place to stay.
There are several ways to use this guide.

1

Town Index
The town index, starting on page 366, lists all the places with accommodation featured in the regional sections. The index gives a page number where you can find full accommodation and contact details.

2

Colour Maps
All the place names in black on the colour maps at the front have an entry in the regional sections. Refer to the town index for the page number where you will find one or more establishments offering accommodation in your chosen town or village.

3

Accommodation listing
Contact details for **all** English Tourism Council assessed accommodation throughout England, together with their national Star rating are given in the listing section of this guide. Establishments with a full entry in the regional sections are shown in blue. Look in the town index for the page number on which their full entry appears.

SOUTH WEST

A land of myths and legends – and beautiful beaches. The region has cathedral cities, Georgian Bath and maritime Bristol, mysterious castles, evocative country houses and sub-tropical gardens to discover too.

classic sights
Newquay – surfers' paradise
English Riviera – family-friendly beaches
Dartmoor – wild open moorland and rocky tors

coast & country
Runnymede – riverside meadows and woodland
Pegwell Bay & Goodwin Sands – a haven for birds and seals

glorious gardens
Stourhead – 18th century landscape garden
Lost Gardens of Heligan – 19th century gardens

art for all
Tate Gallery St Ives – modern art and the St Ives School
Arnolfini Gallery, Bristol – contemporary arts

distinctively different
Daphne du Maurier – Cornwall inspired many of her novels
Agatha Christie – follow the trail in Torquay

The counties of Bath, Bristol, Cornwall, Devon, Dorset (Western),Isles of Scilly, Somerset, South Gloucestershire and Wiltshire

FOR MORE INFORMATION CONTACT:
South West Tourism
Admail 3186, Exeter EX2 7WH
Tel: (0870) 442 0880 Fax: (0870) 442 0881
Email: info@westcountryholidays.com
Internet: www.westcountryholidays.com

The Pictures:
1 Weston-super-Mare
2 Bath

Places to Visit - see pages 198-202
Where to Stay - see pages 203-237

197

PLACES to visit

You will find hundreds of interesting places to visit during your stay, just some of which are listed in these pages. Contact any Tourist Information Centre in the region for more ideas on days out.

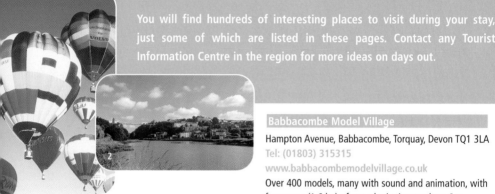

At Bristol Harbourside

Bristol, Avon BS1 5DB
Tel: (0117) 915 5000 www.at-bristol.org.uk
A £97 million Millennium Landmark project on Bristol's revitalised harbourside. It consists of 3 world-class visitor attractions.

Atwell-Wilson Motor Museum Trust

Downside, Stockley Lane, Calne, Wiltshire SN11 0NF
Tel: (01249) 813119 www.atwell-wilson.org
Motor museum with vintage, post-vintage and classic cars, including American models. Classic motorbikes. A 17thC water meadow walk. Car clubs welcome for rallies. Play area.

Avebury Manor and Garden

Avebury, Marlborough, Wiltshire SN8 1RF
Tel: (01672) 539250
Manor house, regularly altered and of monastic origins. Present buildings date from the early 16thC with Queen Anne alterations and Edwardian renovations. Gardens.

Babbacombe Model Village

Hampton Avenue, Babbacombe, Torquay, Devon TQ1 3LA
Tel: (01803) 315315
www.babbacombemodelvillage.co.uk
Over 400 models, many with sound and animation, with four acres (1.6 ha) of award-winning gardens. See modern towns, villages and rural areas. Stunning illuminations.

Bristol City Museum & Art Gallery

Queen's Road, Bristol, Avon BS8 1RL
Tel: (0117) 922 3571
www.bristol-city.gov.uk/museums
Collection representing applied, oriental and fine art, archaeology, geology, natural history, ethnography and Egyptology.

Bristol Zoo Gardens

Clifton, Bristol, Avon BS8 3HA
Tel: (0117) 973 8951 www.bristolzoo.org.uk
Enjoy an exciting, real life experience and see over 300 species of wildlife in beautiful gardens.

Buckland Abbey

Yelverton, Devon PL20 6EY
Tel: (01822) 853607
Originally a Cistercian monastery, then home of Sir Francis Drake. Ancient buildings, exhibitions, herb garden, craft workshops and estate walks.

Cheddar Caves and Gorge

Cheddar, Somerset BS27 3QF
Tel: (01934) 742343 www.cheddarcaves.co.uk
Beautiful caves located in Cheddar Gorge. Gough's Cave with its cathedral-like caverns, and Cox's Cave with stalagmites and stalactites. Also 'The Crystal Quest' fantasy adventure.

The Combe Martin Motor Cycle Collection

Cross Street, Combe Martin, Ilfracombe, Devon EX34 0DH
Tel: (01271) 882346
www.motorcycle-collection.co.uk
Collection of motorcycles, scooters and invalid carriages, displayed against a background of old petrol pumps, signs and garage equipment. Motoring nostalgia.

Combe Martin Wildlife and Dinosaur Park

Jurassic Hotel, Combe Martin, Ilfracombe,
Devon EX34 0NG
Tel: (01271) 882486
Wildlife park and life-size models of dinosaurs.

Crealy Park

Sidmouth Road, Clyst St Mary, Exeter, Devon EX5 1DR
Tel: (01395) 233200 www.crealy.co.uk
One of Devon's largest animal farms. Milk a cow, feed a lamb and pick up a piglet. Adventure playgrounds. Dragonfly Lake and farm trails.

Dairyland Farm World

Newquay, Cornwall TR8 5AA
Tel: (01872) 510246 www.dairylandfarmworld.com
One hundred and seventy cows milked in rotary parlour. Heritage centre. Farm nature trail. Farm park with animals, pets and wildfowl. Daily events. Also conservation area.

Eden Project

Watering Lane Nursery, Pentewan, St Austell,
Cornwall PL26 6EN
Tel: (01726) 222900
A 37-acre (15-ha) china clay pit has been dramatically transformed to accommodate the planthouses, visitor centre and temperate parkland.

Exmoor Falconry & Animal Farm

West Lynch Farm, Allerford, Minehead, Somerset TA24 8HJ
Tel: (01643) 862816 www.exmoorfalconry.co.uk
Farm animals, rare breeds, pets' corner, birds of prey and owls. Flying displays daily. Historic farm buildings.

Flambards Village

Culdrose Manor, Helston, Cornwall TR13 0QA
Tel: (01326) 573404 www.flambards.co.uk
Life-size Victorian village with fully stocked shops, plus carriages and fashions. 'Britain in the Blitz' life-size wartime street, historic aircraft, exploratorium.

Heale Garden & Plant Centre

Middle Woodford, Salisbury, Wiltshire SP4 6NT
Tel: (01722) 782504
Mature, traditional-type garden with shrubs, musk and other roses, and kitchen garden. Authentic Japanese teahouse in water garden. Magnolias. Snowdrops and aconites in winter.

International Animal Rescue Animal Tracks

Ash Mill, South Molton, Devon EX36 4QW
Tel: (01769) 550277 www.iar.org.uk
A 60-acre (24-ha) animal sanctuary with a wide range of rescued animals, from monkeys to chinchillas and shire horses to other horses and ponies. Also rare plant nursery.

The Pictures:
1 Lands End, Cornwall
2 Clifton Suspension Bridge, Bristol
3 Stonehenge
4 Interior of Salisbury Cathedral
5 Shaftesbury Hill, Dorset

Jamaica Inn Museums (Potters Museum of Curiosity)

Jamaica Inn Courtyard, Bolventor, Launceston,
Cornwall PL15 7TS
Tel: (01566) 86838
Museums contain lifetime work of Walter Potter, a
Victorian taxidermist. Exhibits include Kittens' Wedding,
Death of Cock Robin and The Story of Smuggling.

Longleat

The Estate Office, Warminster, Wiltshire BA12 7NW
Tel: (01985) 844400 www.longleat.co.uk
Elizabethan stately home, safari park, plus a wonderland
of family attractions. 'World's Longest Hedge Maze',
Safari Boats, Pets' Corner, Longleat railway.

The Lost Gardens of Heligan

Heligan, Pentewan, St Austell, Cornwall PL26 6EN
Tel: (01726) 845100 www.heligan.com
Heligan Gardens is the scene of the largest garden
restoration project undertaken since the war. Public
access to parts of 'Home Farm'.

Lyme Regis Philpot Museum

Bridge Street, Lyme Regis, Dorset DT7 3QA
Tel: (01297) 443370 www.lymeregismuseum.co.uk
Fossils, geology, local history and lace exhibitions.
Museum shop.

National Marine Aquarium

Rope Walk, Coxside, Plymouth, Devon PL4 0LF
Tel: (01752) 600301 www.national-aquarium.co.uk
The United Kingdom's only world-class aquarium, located
in the heart of Plymouth. Visitor experiences will include
a mountain stream and Caribbean reef complete with
sharks.

Newquay Zoo

Trenance Park, Newquay, Cornwall TR7 2LZ
Tel: (01637) 873342 www.newquayzoo.co.uk
A modern, award-winning zoo where you can have fun
and learn at the same time. A varied collection of
animals, from Acouchi to Zebra.

Paignton Zoo Environmental Park

Totnes Road, Paignton, Devon TQ4 7EU
Tel: (01803) 557479 www.paigntonzoo.org.uk
One of England's largest zoos with over 1,200 animals in
the beautiful setting of 75 acres (30 ha) of botanical
gardens. The zoo is one of Devon's most popular family
days out.

Plant World

St Marychurch Road, Newton Abbot, Devon TQ12 4SE
Tel: (01803) 872939
Four acres (1.6 ha) of gardens including the unique 'map
of the world' gardens. Cottage garden. Panoramic views.
Comprehensive nursery of rare and more unusual plants.

Powderham Castle

The Estate Office, Kenton, Exeter, Devon EX6 8JQ
Tel: (01626) 890243 www.powderham.co.uk
Built c1390, restored in the 18thC. Georgian interiors,
china, furnishings and paintings. Family home of the
Courtenays for over 600 years. Fine views across deer
park and River Exe.

Plymouth Dome

The Hoe, Plymouth, Devon PL1 2NZ
Tel: (01752) 603300
Purpose-built visitor interpretation centre showing the
history of Plymouth and its people from Stone Age
beginnings to satellite technology. Situated on
Plymouth Hoe.

Railway Village Museum

34 Faringdon Road, Swindon, Wiltshire SN1 5BJ
Tel: (01793) 466553 www.swindon.gov.uk
Foreman's house in original Great Western Railway
village. Furnished to re-create a Victorian
working-class home.

Roman Baths

Pump Room, Abbey Church Yard, Bath BA1 1LZ
Tel: (01225) 477785 www.romanbaths.co.uk
Roman baths and temple precinct, hot springs and
Roman temple. Jewellery, coins, curses and votive
offerings from the sacred spring.

St Michael's Mount

Marazion, Cornwall TR17 0HT
Tel: (01736) 710507
Originally the site of a Benedictine chapel, the castle on
its rock dates from the14thC. Fine views towards Land's
End and the Lizard. Reached by foot, or ferry at high tide
in summer.

Steam – Museum of the Great Western Railway

Kemble Drive, Churchward, Swindon, Wiltshire SN2 2TA
Tel: (01793) 466646 www.steam-museum.org.uk
Historic Great Western Railway locomotives, wide range
of nameplates, models, illustrations, posters and tickets.

Stonehenge

Amesbury, Salisbury, Wiltshire SP4 7DE
Tel: (01980) 623108
www.stonehengemasterplan.org
World-famous prehistoric monument built as a
ceremonial centre. Started 5,000 years ago and
remodelled several times in next 1,500 years.

Stourhead House and Garden

The Estate Office, Stourton, Warminster, Wiltshire BA12 6QD
Tel: (01747) 841152 www.nationaltrust.org.uk
Landscaped garden, laid out c1741-80, with lakes,
temples, rare trees and plants. House, begun in c1721 by
Colen Campbell, contains fine paintings and Chippendale
furniture.

Tate Gallery St Ives

Porthmeor Beach, St Ives, Cornwall TR26 1TG
Tel: (01736) 796226 www.tate.org.uk
Opened in 1993 and offering a unique introduction to
modern art. Changing displays focus on the modern
movement St Ives is famous for. Also an extensive
education programme.

Teignmouth Museum

29 French Street, Teignmouth, Devon TQ14 8ST
Tel: (01626) 777041
Exhibits include a16thC cannon and artefacts from the
Armada wreck, local history, c1920s pier machines and
c1877 cannon.

Tintagel Castle

Tintagel, Cornwall PL34 0HE
Tel: (01840) 770328 www.english-heritage.org.uk
Medieval ruined castle on wild, wind-swept coast.
Famous for associations with Arthurian legend. Built
largely in the 13thC by Richard, Earl of Cornwall.
Used as a prison in the 14thC.

Tithe Barn Children's Farm

New Barn Road, Abbotsbury, Weymouth, Dorset DT3 4JF
Tel: (01305) 871817
Extensive children's farm for children under 11 years.
Activities include hand-feeding (with bottles) milk to
lambs and kids. Replicas of Terracotta Warriors on display
in barn.

Totnes Costume Museum – Devonshire Collection of Period Costume

Bogan House, 43 High Street, Totnes, Devon TQ9 5NP
Tel: (01803) 863821
New exhibition of costumes and accessories each season,
displayed in one of the historic merchant's houses of
Totnes. Bogan House recently restored by Mitchell Trust.

Woodlands Leisure Park

Blackawton, Totnes, Devon TQ9 7DQ
Tel: (01803) 712598
www.woodlands-leisure-park.co.uk
All-weather fun guaranteed with unique combination of
indoor and outdoor attractions: 3 watercoasters,
toboggan run, massive indoor adventure centre with
rides. Falconry and animals.

Wookey Hole Caves and Papermill

Wookey Hole, Wells, Somerset BA5 1BB
Tel: (01749) 672243 www.wookey.co.uk
Spectacular caves and legendary home of the Witch of
Wookey. Working Victorian papermill including Old Penny
Arcade, Magical Mirror Maze and Cave Diving Museum.

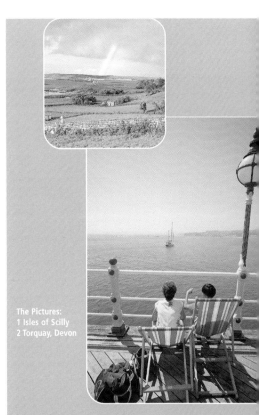

The Pictures:
1 Isles of Scilly
2 Torquay, Devon

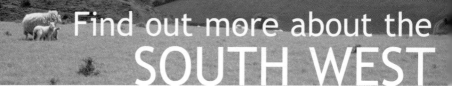

Find out more about the
SOUTH WEST

Further information about holidays and attractions in the South West is available from:

SOUTH WEST TOURISM
Admail 3186, Exeter EX2 7WH.
Tel: (0870) 442 0880
Fax: (0870) 442 0881
Email: info@westcountryholidays.com
Internet: www.westcountryholidays.com

The following publications are available free from South West Tourism:
Bed & Breakfast Touring Map
West Country Holiday Homes & Apartments
West Country Hotels and Guesthouses
Glorious Gardens of the West Country
Camping and Caravan Touring Map
Tourist Attractions Touring Map
Trencherman's West Country, Restaurant Guide

Getting to the
SOUTH WEST

BY ROAD: Somerset, Devon and Cornwall are well served from the North and Midlands by the M6/M5 which extends just beyond Exeter, where it links in with the dual carriageways of the A38 to Plymouth, A380 to Torbay and the A30 into Cornwall. The North Devon Link Road A361 joins Junction 37 with the coast of north Devon and A39, which then becomes the Atlantic Highway into Cornwall.

BY RAIL: The main towns in the South West are served throughout the year by fast, direct and frequent rail services from all over the country. InterCity 125 trains operate from London (Paddington) to Chippenham, Swindon, Bath, Bristol, Weston-super-Mare, Taunton, Exeter, Plymouth and Penzance, and also from Scotland, the North East and the Midlands to the South West. A service runs from London (Waterloo) to Exeter, via Salisbury, Yeovil and Crewkerne. Sleeper services operate between Devon and Cornwall and London as well as between Bristol and Glasgow and Edinburgh. Motorail services operate from strategic points to key South West locations.

Where to stay in the South West

Accommodation entries in this region are listed in alphabetical order of place name, and then in alphabetical order of establishment.

Map references refer to the colour location maps at front of this guide. The first number indicates the map to use; the letter and number which follow refer to the grid reference on the map.

At-a-glance symbols at the end of each accommodation entry give useful information about services and facilities. A key to symbols can be found inside the back cover flap. Keep this open for easy reference.

A brief description of the towns and villages offering accommodation in the entries which follow, can be found at the end of this section.

A complete listing of all the English Tourism Council assessed accommodation covered by this guide appears at the back of the guide.

BABBACOMBE, Devon Map ref 1D2

★★

EXMOUTH VIEW HOTEL
St Albans Road, Babbacombe, Torquay
TQ1 3LG
T: 0800 781 7817 & (01803) 327307
F: (01803) 329967
E: relax@exmouth-view.co.uk
I: www.exmouth-view.co.uk

B&B per night:
S £19.00–£32.00
D £38.00–£64.00

HB per person:
DY Min £29.50

OPEN All year round

A warm welcome awaits guests from the resident family owners. Only a few metres from Babbacombe Downs and close to all local attractions. 27 luxury en suite rooms, colour TV, tea/coffee facilities, central heating. Coastal facing restaurant with freshly prepared home-cooked food. Licensed bar, TV lounge, private car park.

Bedrooms: 3 single, 16 double/twin, 8 triple/ multiple
Bathrooms: 27 en suite

Evening meal available
CC: Amex, Delta, Mastercard, Switch, Visa

Please call for details of Christmas and New Year breaks. Mid-week/weekend breaks available out of high season.

CHECK THE MAPS
The colour maps at the front of this guide show all the cities, towns and villages for which you will find accommodation entries. Refer to the town index to find the page on which they are listed.

BARWICK, Somerset Map ref 2A3

★
Gold
Award

LITTLE BARWICK HOUSE
Barwick, Yeovil BA22 9TD
T: (01935) 423902
F: (01935) 420908

B&B per night:
S £60.00–£70.00
D £95.00–£105.00

HB per person:
DY £69.50–£76.50

OPEN All year round

A charming and comfortable listed Georgian dower house with a delightful garden. The restaurant, locally popular and nationally renowned, serves delicious food complemented by an interesting and extensive wine list. Situated on the Somerset/Dorset border it makes an ideal base to explore both counties with many gardens and historic houses nearby.

Bedrooms: 6 double/ twin
Bathrooms: 6 en suite

Lunch available
Evening meal available
CC: Amex, Delta, Diners, Mastercard, Switch, Visa

Special breaks available for 2 nights stays or longer all year round.

BATH, Bath and North East Somerset Map ref 2B2 *Tourist Information Centre Tel: (01225) 477101*

★★★
Silver
Award

THE LANSDOWN GROVE HOTEL
Lansdown Road, Bath BA1 5EH
T: (01225) 483888
F: (01225) 483838
E: lansdown@marstonhotels.com
I: www.marstonhotels.com

Bedrooms: 7 single, 37 double/twin, 4 triple/ multiple; suites available
Bathrooms: 48 en suite

Lunch available
Evening meal available
CC: Amex, Delta, Diners, Mastercard, Switch, Visa

B&B per night:
S £89.00–£105.00
D £105.00–£140.00

HB per person:
DY £69.50–£75.00

OPEN All year round

Marston Hotels

18thC, Grade II Listed building, recently restored to its original splendour. Breathtaking views over the city of Bath. Half-board rate based on minimum 2-night stay.

★★★★
Gold
Award

LUCKNAM PARK
Colerne, Chippenham SN14 8AZ
T: (01225) 742777
F: (01225) 743536
E: reservations@lucknampark.co.uk
I: www.lucknampark.co.uk

Bedrooms: 1 single, 40 double/twin; suites available
Bathrooms: 41 en suite

Lunch available
Evening meal available
CC: Amex, Delta, Diners, Mastercard, Switch, Visa

B&B per night:
S Min £173.00
D £231.00–£706.00

HB per person:
DY £145.00–£375.00

OPEN All year round

Award-winning hotel in 500 acres of gardens and parkland, 6 miles from Bath. Extensive leisure including spa and equestrian centre.

★★

OLD MALT HOUSE HOTEL
Radford, Timsbury, Bath BA2 0QF
T: (01761) 470106
F: (01761) 472726
E: hotel@oldmalthouse.co.uk
I: www.oldmalthouse.co.uk

B&B per night:
S Max £10.00
D Max £80.00

HB per person:
DY £56.00–£58.00

OPEN All year round

Minotel

Between Bath and Wells in beautiful countryside. Ideally situated for exploring Bath, Wells, Bristol, Mendips, Somerset. Built in 1835 as a malt house, now a hotel with comfort and character. Owned and run by same family for over 25 years. Log fires, extensive menus, bar. Well appointed bedrooms (ground floor rooms available).

Bedrooms: 1 single, 9 double/twin, 2 triple/ multiple
Bathrooms: 12 en suite

Evening meal available
CC: Amex, Diners, Mastercard, Switch, Visa

Country Breaks–minimum 2 nights stay. Rates per person from £32 for B&B. £48 for DB&B.

WHERE TO STAY
Please mention this guide when making your booking.

BATH continued

★★
Silver
Award

THE OLD MILL HOTEL

Tollbridge Road, Batheaston, Bath BA1 7DE
T: (01225) 858476
F: (01225) 852600
E: info@oldmillbath.co.uk
I: www.oldmillbath.co.uk

B&B per night:
S £49.00–£69.00
D £65.00–£125.00

HB per person:
DY £41.00–£74.00

OPEN All year round

Riverside hotel with breathtaking
views, 1.5 miles from centre of Bath.
Unique water wheel restaurant. Most
rooms have river views and all were
recently delightfully refurbished.
Silver Award for quality. Specialises
in short breaks throughout the year.
Own fishing rights, local golfing
arrangements. Free car parking. Free
taxi service from station.

Bedrooms: 1 single,
23 double/twin, 3 triple/
multiple
Bathrooms: 27 private

Lunch available
Evening meal available
CC: Amex, Delta,
Mastercard, Switch, Visa

Nov, Dec, Jan, Feb DB&B rate from £29pppn with
minimum of 2 night stay excl 24, 25, 26 and 31 Dec
and 1st Jan.

♠♫♨♿✆▢↓🔽⑤◎🗐🛏♟🎵♪▶☀🐾♦P

★★

ROYAL HOTEL

Manvers Street, Bath BA1 1JP
T: (01225) 463134
F: (01225) 442931
E: royal@rhotel.freeserve.co.uk
I: www.royalhotelbath.co.uk

B&B per night:
S £47.00
D £70.00–£80.00

HB per person:
DY £35.00–£49.00

OPEN All year round

The Independents

An attractive Georgian-style building
designed by Brunel over 150 years
ago. Wonderful central position,
close to all attractions and the
railway station. All rooms recently
redecorated and en suite. Air-
conditioned restaurant and bar.
Excellent freshly prepared food
served in intimate atmosphere.
Set-price menus. Friendly and
informal.

Bedrooms: 4 single,
22 double/twin, 4 triple/
multiple
Bathrooms: 30 en suite

Lunch available
Evening meal available
CC: Amex, Delta, Diners,
Mastercard, Switch, Visa

Nov/Dec/Jan/Feb DB&B from £29pppn, (minimum
2-night stay) excl 24, 25, 26, 31 Dec and 1st Jan.

♠♫✆🖥▢↓🔽⑤✂◎☒🛏♦♢🎦P

BIGBURY-ON-SEA, Devon Map ref 1C3

★★
Silver
Award

THE HENLEY HOTEL

Folly Hill, Bigbury-on-Sea,
Kingsbridge TQ7 4AR
T: (01548) 810240
F: (01548) 810240

Bedrooms: 5 double/
twin, 1 triple/multiple
Bathrooms: 6 en suite

Lunch available
Evening meal available
CC: Amex, Delta, Diners,
Mastercard, Switch, Visa

B&B per night:
S £47.00–£52.00
D £74.00–£84.00

HB per person:
DY £55.00–£57.00

Small, comfortable hotel on the edge of the sea. Spectacular views with private steps
through garden down to lovely beach. A non-smoking establishment.

♠♫✆🖥▢↓🔽⑤✂🎦◎🗐🛏▶☀🐾🎠🚲P

BILBROOK, Somerset Map ref 1D1

★★

THE DRAGON HOUSE HOTEL & RESTAURANT

Dragon's Cross, Bilbrook, Minehead
TA24 6HQ
T: (01984) 640215
F: (01984) 641340
E: info@dragonhouse.co.uk
I: www.dragonhouse.co.uk

Bedrooms: 1 single,
6 double/twin, 2 triple/
multiple
Bathrooms: 9 en suite

Lunch available
Evening meal available
CC: Amex, Delta, Diners,
Mastercard, Switch, Visa

B&B per night:
S £44.00–£54.00
D £64.00–£84.00

HB per person:
DY £47.00–£57.00

OPEN All year round

Charming, family-run, country house c1700, excellent wine, fine food, in panelled
restaurant or cosy bar. Comfortable and friendly.

♠♫♨✆▢↓🔽⑤✂🎦🗐🛏♟🍽∪▶☀🐾🎠🚲🎦P

HALF BOARD PRICES Half board prices are given per person, but
in some cases these may be based on double/twin occupancy.

BOVEY TRACEY, Devon Map ref 1D2

★★★
Silver
Award

EDGEMOOR HOTEL

Haytor Road, Lowerdown Cross,
Bovey Tracey, Newton Abbot TQ13 9LE
T: (01626) 832466
F: (01626) 834760
E: edgemoor@btinternet.com
I: www.edgemoor.co.uk

B&B per night:
S £55.50–£58.50
D £90.00–£96.50

OPEN All year round

Situated in a wonderful position for touring the area, being literally adjacent to Dartmoor National Park, yet only 2 miles from the A38. Many National Trust properties and places of interest are within easy driving distance. All rooms en suite. Good food. Elegance without pretension.

Bedrooms: 3 single,
13 double/twin
Bathrooms: 16 en suite

Lunch available
Evening meal available
CC: Amex, Delta,
Mastercard, Switch, Visa

Special bargain breaks available for any 2 days or more from £57.50pppn.

BRANSCOMBE, Devon Map ref 1D2

Rating
Applied For

THE BULSTONE HOTEL
Higher Bulstone, Branscombe,
Seaton EX12 3BL
T: (01297) 680446
F: (01297) 680446
E: kevinmon@aol.com
I: www.best-hotel.co.uk/bulstone/
index.html

Bedrooms: 1 double/
twin, 9 triple/multiple
Bathrooms: 7 en suite

Lunch available
Evening meal available

B&B per night:
D £51.00–£81.00

HB per person:
DY £41.25–£56.25

OPEN All year round

Small, friendly, family-run establishment offering personal service. Catering especially for those with young children. Bed and breakfast price includes 2 adults and up to 2 children under 11 years.

BRIDGWATER

See display advertisement below

COUNTRY CODE Always follow the Country Code ✿ Enjoy the countryside and respect its life and work ✿ Guard against all risk of fire ✿ Fasten all gates ✿ Keep your dogs under close control ✿ Keep to public paths across farmland ✿ Use gates and stiles to cross fences, hedges and walls ✿ Leave livestock, crops and machinery alone ✿ Take your litter home ✿ Help to keep all water clean ✿ Protect wildlife, plants and trees ✿ Take special care on country roads ✿ Make no unnecessary noise

★★
Silver
Award

An Edwardian country-house hotel set in an acre of cultivated gardens on elevated ground overlooking the rolling West Dorset hills, the majestic coastline and the sea. Many awards for quality and cuisine. Spacious en suite bedrooms with glorious views, 10 minutes' walk to the sea.

ROUNDHAM HOUSE HOTEL
Roundham Gardens, West Bay Road,
Bridport DT6 4BD
T: (01308) 422753
F: (01308) 421500
E: cyprencom@compuserve.com
I: www.roundhamhouse.co.uk

Bedrooms: 1 single,
5 double/twin, 2 triple/
multiple
Bathrooms: 7 en suite,
1 private

Evening meal available
CC: Delta, Mastercard,
Switch, Visa

B&B per night:
S £35.00–£38.00
D £60.00–£80.00

HB per person:
DY £47.00–£57.00

🐎🔥🛎️📞🖥️🌂🕯️⑤🔢🖥️🛏️🚶❄️🐴🖊️P

★★

COURTLANDS HOTEL
1 Redland Court Road, Redland, Bristol
BS6 7EE
T: (0117) 9424432
F: (0117) 9232432

B&B per night:
S Min £52.00
D Min £62.00

OPEN All year round

This very comfortable family-run hotel is centrally located in a quiet residential area, overlooking tree-lined Victorian gardens. All bedrooms are well appointed and are decorated to a high standard. Our private restaurant offers freshly prepared dishes in a friendly atmosphere and has won a 'Food Hygiene Award' every year since 1985.

Bedrooms: 5 single,
15 double/twin, 5 triple/
multiple
Bathrooms: 25 en suite

Lunch available
Evening meal available
CC: Amex, Delta, Diners,
Mastercard, Switch, Visa

🐎🔥🛎️📞🖥️🌂🕯️⑤🔢🖥️🛏️🚶❄️🐴🚐🏨P

★★

GLENROY HOTEL
Victoria Square, Clifton, Bristol
BS8 4EW
T: (0117) 9739058
F: (0117) 9739058
E: admin@glenroyhotel.demon.co.
uk
I: www.glenroy@bestwest.co.uk

Bedrooms: 14 single,
22 double/twin, 6 triple/
multiple
Bathrooms: 42 en suite

Evening meal available
CC: Amex, Delta, Diners,
Mastercard, Switch, Visa

B&B per night:
S £62.00–£82.00
D £82.00–£92.00

HB per person:
DY £51.00–£56.00

OPEN All year round

CR

Best Western Hotels

Large early Victorian houses, in one of Bristol's most attractive squares. Restaurant open Monday-Friday and for Sunday lunch. Restricted menu on Saturday/Sunday evenings.

🐎🔥🛎️📞🖥️🌂🕯️⑤🔢🖥️☀️🛏️🏨P

★★★

HENBURY LODGE HOTEL
Station Road, Henbury, Bristol
BS10 7QQ
T: (0117) 950 2615
F: (0117) 950 9532
E: enquiries@henburylodge.com
I: www.henburylodge.com

Bedrooms: 1 single,
16 double/twin, 4 triple/
multiple
Bathrooms: 21 en suite

Lunch available
Evening meal available
CC: Amex, Delta, Diners,
Mastercard, Switch, Visa

B&B per night:
S £53.00–£103.50
D £86.00–£113.50

OPEN All year round

One mile from junction 17 off M5, 15 minutes' drive from city centre. Local interest includes Blaise Castle and Blaise Hamlet. Various special diets catered for.

🐎🔥🛎️📞🖥️🌂🕯️⑤🔢🖥️🛏️🚶☀️🐴🏨P

TOWN INDEX
This can be found at the back of this guide. If you know where you want to stay, the index will give you the page number listing accommodation in your chosen town, city or village.

BRISTOL continued

★★

THE OLD BOWL INN AND LILIES RESTAURANT

16 Church Road, Lower Almondsbury,
Almondsbury, Bristol BS32 4DT
T: (01454) 612757
F: (01454) 619910
E: reception@theoldbowlinn.co.uk
I: www.theoldbowlinn.co.uk

We invite you to enjoy the best of the past and the present in this historic and well established village inn. Whether travelling on business or just taking a leisurely break, you will find all the comforts of modern life housed in 12thC surroundings. Five minutes from M4/M5 interchange.

Bedrooms: 13 double/twin
Bathrooms: 13 en suite

Lunch available
Evening meal available
CC: Amex, Delta, Diners, Mastercard, Switch, Visa

Fri, Sat, Sun inclusive weekend break-single 3 nights £119.80, double 3 nights £185.

B&B per night:
S £41.50–£100.50
D £67.50–£118.00

OPEN All year round

★★★

THE TOWN AND COUNTRY LODGE

A38 Bridgwater Road, Bristol BS13 8AG
T: (01275) 392441
F: (01275) 393362
E: reservations@tclodge.co.uk
I: www.tclodge.co.uk

Highly comfortable hotel offering genuine value for money. Splendid rural location on the A38 but only 3 miles central Bristol and handy for airport, Bath, Weston and all major local attractions. Excellent restaurant offering international cuisine with a la carte and set menus. Ideal for functions, wedding receptions and conferences.

Bedrooms: 10 single, 22 double/twin, 4 triple/multiple; suites available
Bathrooms: 36 en suite

Lunch available
Evening meal available
CC: Amex, Delta, Diners, Mastercard, Switch, Visa

Fri, Sat and Sun £150pp sharing, bed and full English breakfast.

B&B per night:
S £49.00–£64.50
D £59.00–£84.50

HB per person:
DY £55.00–£74.50

OPEN All year round

CR
The Independents

BRIXHAM, Devon Map ref 1D2 *Tourist Information Centre Tel: 0906 680 1268 (Premium rate number)*

★★★ **THE BERRY HEAD HOTEL**

Berry Head Road, Brixham TQ5 9AJ
T. (01803) 853225
F: (01803) 882084
E: berryhd@aol.com
I: www.marine-hotel-leisure.com

Bedrooms: 3 single, 22 double/twin, 7 triple/multiple
Bathrooms: 32 en suite

Lunch available
Evening meal available
CC: Amex, Delta, Mastercard, Switch, Visa

B&B per night:
S £42.00–£68.00
D £84.00–£136.00

HB per person:
DY £52.00–£78.00

OPEN All year round

Steeped in history, nestling on water's edge in 6 acres of grounds and in an Area of Outstanding Natural Beauty. Heated indoor swimming pool.

AT-A-GLANCE SYMBOLS

Symbols at the end of each accommodation entry give useful information about services and facilities. A key to symbols can be found inside the back cover flap. Keep this open for easy reference.

BUDE, Cornwall Map ref 1C2 *Tourist Information Centre Tel: (01288) 354240*

★★

BARREL ROCK HOTEL
41-43 Killerton Road, Bude EX23 8EN
T: (01288) 352252
F: (01288) 353122
E: petergoa4u@supanet.com

B&B per night:
D £48.00–£55.00

OPEN All year round

Comfortable, spacious hotel in a peaceful area only minutes' walk to town shops, historic canal, Links Golf Course, glorious surfing beaches and dramatic coastline. Large, well-appointed en suite bedrooms, restaurant serving fresh produce, cosy bar and 3 lounge areas make a perfect choice – whether on holiday or business.

Bedrooms: 7 double/ twin, 2 triple/multiple
Bathrooms: 7 en suite, 2 private

Golfing breaks, including 2 for 1 green fees, at many West Country courses.

Evening meal available
CC: Amex, Delta, Mastercard, Switch, Visa

★★★
Silver
Award

THE FALCON HOTEL
Breakwater Road, Bude EX23 8SD
T: (01288) 352005
F: (01288) 356359

B&B per night:
S £42.00–£44.00
D £84.00–£88.00

HB per person:
DY £56.00–£58.00

OPEN All year round

In beautiful position overlooking the historic Bude Canal. Surrounded by many scenic walks and 2 minutes from the shops and sandy beaches. Well-appointed bedrooms with luxurious bathrooms, and televisions with Teletext and Sky. Superb a la carte restaurant and excellent bar meals. Private walled gardens.

Bedrooms: 6 single, 20 double/twin; suites available
Bathrooms: 26 en suite

Special 2-day breaks available all year, excl Christmas and Bank Hols. Must be booked in advance and incl DB&B.

Lunch available
Evening meal available
CC: Amex, Delta, Diners, Mastercard, Switch, Visa

★★

MAER LODGE HOTEL
Maer Down Road, Crooklets Beach, Bude EX23 8NG
T: (01288) 353306
F: (01288) 354005
E: maerlodgehotel@btinternet.com
I: www.westcountry-hotels.co.uk/maerlodge

B&B per night:
S £32.50–£37.50
D £60.00–£70.00

HB per person:
DY £40.00–£50.00

OPEN All year round

Minotel/The Circle

Peacefully situated in 2 acres of gardens near beach and overlooking the golf course, with rear view across open countryside to distant hills. Large restaurant with fine food and personal service. Nineteen bedrooms all with full facilities. Residents' bar and lounge. Suntrap lawns with seating and umbrellas and private parking.

Bedrooms: 2 single, 13 double/twin, 4 triple/ multiple
Bathrooms: 19 en suite

3 nights for the price of 2, Oct-Mar (excl Christmas).

Evening meal available
CC: Amex, Delta, Diners, Mastercard, Switch, Visa

MAP REFERENCES
The map references refer to the colour maps at the front of this guide. The first figure is the map number; the letter and figure which follow indicate the grid reference on the map.

★★★

LORDLEAZE HOTEL

Henderson Drive, Off Forton Road, Chard
TA20 2HW

T: (01460) 61066
F: (01460) 66468
E: lordleaze@fsbdial.co.uk
I: www.lordleazehotel.co.uk

B&B per night:
S £52.50–£57.50
D £75.00–£85.00

OPEN All year round

Delightfully converted 18thC farmhouse with 16 en suite bedrooms. Three Star accommodation with fine food and friendly, efficient service. Ideal for Dorset/Devon coastline and splendid houses and gardens. Family-owned and run. Surrounded by fields but just 3 minutes from centre of Chard.

Bedrooms: 1 single,
14 double/twin, 1 triple/
multiple
Bathrooms: 16 en suite

Lunch available
Evening meal available
CC: Amex, Delta,
Mastercard, Switch, Visa

★★★

STANTON MANOR HOTEL & BURGHLEYS RESTAURANT

Stanton St Quintin, Chippenham SN14 6DQ

T: (01666) 837552
F: (01666) 837022
E: reception@stantonmanor.co.uk
I: www.stantonmanor.co.uk

B&B per night:
S £75.00–£85.00
D £85.00–£125.00

OPEN All year round

Just 1 mile from junction 17 of M4, set in 7 tranquil acres, the hotel offers graciously appointed accommodation in the traditional style of a fine English country home. Spacious en suite bedrooms. Burghley's Restaurant enjoys a very high reputation for the quality of its cuisine and wine cellar. Ideal for exploring Cotswolds, Bath, Swindon and Bristol.

Bedrooms: 2 single,
22 double/twin, 1 triple/
multiple
Bathrooms: 25 en suite

Lunch available
Evening meal available
CC: Amex, Delta,
Mastercard, Switch, Visa

Short breaks DB&B, offer applies to 2 nights weekends only.

★★

THE NEW INN

High Street, Clovelly, Bideford EX39 5TQ
T: (01237) 431303
F: (01237) 431036
E: newinn@clovelly.co.uk

B&B per night:
S £35.25–£58.00
D £70.50–£86.00

HB per person:
DY £55.00–£76.00

OPEN All year round

Fascinating 17thC inn nestling amongst the flower-strewn cottages which line the cobbled street as it tumbles down the hill to the little harbour. The street is traffic-free, so your luggage is portered by sledge or donkey. Recently refurbished bedrooms with sea or village views. Restaurant serves regional dishes.

Bedrooms: 1 single,
6 double/twin, 1 triple/
multiple
Bathrooms: 8 en suite

Lunch available
Evening meal available
CC: Amex, Delta,
Mastercard, Switch, Visa

Seasonal short breaks and holidays priced from £37.50pppn for DB&B. Christmas and New Year packages (subject to minimum stays and availablity).

IMPORTANT NOTE Information on accommodation listed in this guide has been supplied by the proprietors. As changes may occur you are advised to check details at the time of booking.

CLOVELLY continued

★★

RED LION HOTEL

The Quay, Clovelly, Bideford EX39 5TF
T: (01237) 431237
F: (01237) 431044
E: redlion@clovelly.co.uk

B&B per night:
S £41.75–£67.25
D £83.50–£104.50

HB per person:
DY £63.25–£90.25

OPEN All year round

Ancient inn enjoying a dramatic quayside setting in unique heritage village. Beautifully comfortable bedrooms all with wonderful sea views and the sound of the sea to lull you to sleep. Characterful bars and an intimate lounge. The restaurant specialises in seafood and has a rosette. Staying here is a special experience.

Bedrooms: 9 double/ twin, 2 triple/multiple
Bathrooms: 11 en suite

Lunch available
Evening meal available
CC: Amex, Delta, Mastercard, Switch, Visa

Seasonal short breaks and holidays priced from £44.25pppn for DB&B. Christmas and New Year packages (subject to minimum stays and availability).

🏨🐎♨🌡🖥🕎♿🅿🔇♥⛰️🍴🛖♨🚾🅿

DARTMOOR

See under Bovey Tracey, Lydford, Moretonhampstead, Okehampton

---

DARTMOUTH, Devon Map ref 1D3 *Tourist Information Centre Tel: (01803) 834224*

★★★
Silver
Award

ROYAL CASTLE HOTEL

11 The Quay, Dartmouth TQ6 9PS
T: (01803) 833033
F: (01803) 835445
E: enquiry@royalcastle.co.uk
I: www.royalcastle.co.uk

B&B per night:
S £55.00–£70.00
D £93.90–£152.90

HB per person:
DY £67.95–£88.95

OPEN All year round

Historic 17thC quayside inn, with two beamed bars with open fires on cooler days, cask beers, welcoming staff. Fine restaurant overlooking the river. Individually decorated rooms, many with spa baths, 4-poster beds and brass beds. Fine river views and a warm welcoming atmosphere. 'Eco-Hotel' of the year 1999.

Bedrooms: 22 double/ twin, 3 triple/multiple
Bathrooms: 25 en suite

Lunch available
Evening meal available
CC: Amex, Delta, Mastercard, Switch, Visa

🏨🐎🛏️♨🌡🖥🕎♿🅿⛱🍴🛖♨🚾🅿

★★★

STOKE LODGE HOTEL

Stoke Fleming, Dartmouth TQ6 0RA
T: (01803) 770523
F: (01803) 770851
E: mail@stokelodge.co.uk
I: www.stokelodge.co.uk

B&B per night:
S £47.00–£55.00
D £76.00–£99.00

HB per person:
DY £50.00–£65.00

OPEN All year round

Family-run country-house hotel set in 3 acres of attractive gardens with sea and village views. En suite bedrooms, indoor and outdoor swimming pools, sauna, jacuzzi, tennis court and full-size snooker table. Reduced green fees at Dartmouth Golf Club. Excellent food and fine wines. Open all year.

Bedrooms: 2 single, 16 double/twin, 7 triple/ multiple
Bathrooms: 25 en suite

Lunch available
Evening meal available
CC: Amex, Delta, Mastercard, Switch, Visa

Bargain breaks and special offers-please phone for details.

🏨🐎🛏️♨🌡🖥🕎♿🅿⛱🍴🛖♨🚾🅿

IDEAS For ideas on places to visit refer to the introduction at the beginning of this section.

DARTMOUTH continued

★★ **TOWNSTAL FARMHOUSE**

Townstal Road, Dartmouth TQ6 9HY T: (01803) 832300 F: (01803) 835428	Bedrooms: 1 single, 10 double/twin, 5 triple/ multiple Bathrooms: 16 en suite	Evening meal available CC: Amex, Delta, Mastercard, Switch, Visa

B&B per night:
D £50.00–£75.00

HB per person:
DY £40.00–£50.00

OPEN All year round

Charming 16thC Listed building within a 10-minute walk of town centre. Home-cooked meals in friendly atmosphere. Pets welcome. Rooms suitable for disabled available. Special breaks.

DUNSTER, Somerset Map ref 1D1

★★★

YARN MARKET HOTEL (EXMOOR)

25 High Street, Dunster, Minehead
TA24 6SF
T: (01643) 821425
F: (01643) 821475
E: yarnmarket.hotel@virgin.net
I: www.s-h-systems.co.uk/hotels/yarnmkt

B&B per night:
S £35.00
D £60.00–£90.00

HB per person:
DY £45.00–£60.00

OPEN All year round

Central and accessible hotel, an ideal location for walking and exploring Exmoor National Park. Family-run with a friendly, relaxed atmosphere. En suite rooms with colour TV and tea-making facilities. Non-smoking. Pets by arrangement. Special 2 and 3-night breaks – please enquire for details. Quote WTS01 for restaurant discount during your visit (cash only).

Bedrooms: 12 double/
twin, 2 triple/multiple
Bathrooms: 14 en suite

Evening meal available
CC: Delta, Mastercard,
Switch, Visa

Ring to request a copy of our newsletter giving up-to-date information on special offers and themed breaks.

EXETER, Devon Map ref 1D2 *Tourist Information Centre Tel: (01392) 265700*

★★ **FAIRWINDS VILLAGE HOUSE HOTEL**

Kennford, Exeter EX6 7UD T: (01392) 832911	Bedrooms: 5 double/ twin, 1 triple/multiple Bathrooms: 6 en suite	Evening meal available CC: Mastercard, Visa

B&B per night:
S £37.00–£39.00
D £52.00–£56.00

HB per person:
DY £39.00–£43.00

Friendly little hotel, south of Exeter. Exclusively for non-smokers. Beautiful rural surroundings. Delightful en suite bedrooms (some on ground floor). Delicious homemade food. Bargain breaks available.

★★

GLOBE HOTEL

Fore Street, Topsham, Exeter EX3 0HR
T: (01392) 873471
F: (01392) 873879
E: sales@globehotel.com
I: www.globehotel.com

B&B per night:
S £40.00–£50.00
D £58.00–£65.00

OPEN All year round

Enjoy the atmosphere of a traditional coaching inn and sample the delights of Topsham – Exeter's historic estuary town. Bedrooms with individual character from 4-poster rooms to ground floor bedrooms. Elizabethan restaurant – open Monday to Saturday. Inn bar, real ales, great house wines. Visit our website for a better view.

Bedrooms: 1 single,
13 double/twin, 3 triple/
multiple
Bathrooms: 17 en suite

Lunch available
Evening meal available
CC: Amex, Delta,
Mastercard, Switch, Visa

EXMOOR

See under Dunster, Lynmouth, Lynton, Minehead, Porlock, Parracombe

PRICES

Please check prices and other details at the time of booking.

EXMOUTH, Devon Map ref 1D2 *Tourist Information Centre Tel: (01395) 222299*

★★★

THE ROYAL BEACON HOTEL

The Beacon, Exmouth EX8 2AF
T: (01395) 264886
F: (01395) 268890
E: reception@royalbeaconhotel.co.uk
I: www.royalbeaconhotel.co.uk

B&B per night:
S £45.00–£65.00
D £85.00–£105.00

HB per person:
DY £60.00–£90.00

OPEN All year round

An elegant Georgian former posting house. All rooms have been recently refurbished, most overlooking the River Exe estuary and the sea. The restaurant offers charming ambience and superb cuisine. The hotel is conveniently located, a short walk to the beach and is within easy reach of the city centre.

Bedrooms: 3 single,
25 double/twin
Bathrooms: 28 en suite

Lunch available
Evening meal available
CC: Amex, Delta, Diners,
Mastercard, Switch, Visa

⋔ 🏇 ⛪ ☏ 🖃 ☐ ↓ ♨ Ⓢ ✂ 🏠 🖽 🏢 ⚓ 🍽 Ʊ ► ✲ 🐎 🦯 🐴 P

QUALITY ASSURANCE SCHEME

For an explanation of the quality and facilities represented by the Stars please refer to the front of this guide. A more detailed explanation can be found in the information pages at the back.

WOODBURY PARK

Hotel, Golf and Country Club

Set in 500 acres of idyllic Devonshire countryside, this luxurious hotel is one of the top sporting retreats in the British Isles. Offering the very best in accommodation, cuisine and leisure facilities you can also experience Nigel Mansell's World of Racing situated on site. And the service comes with all with the renowned warmth and hospitality of the West Country.

WP28

Woodbury Castle, Woodbury, Exeter Devon EX5 1JJ.
General Enquiries 01395 233382
Facsimile 01395 233384 Email events@woodbury-park.co.uk

FALMOUTH, Cornwall Map ref 1B3 *Tourist Information Centre Tel: (01326) 312300*

★★★★

BUDOCK VEAN–THE HOTEL ON THE RIVER

Mawnan Smith, Falmouth TR11 5LG
T: (01326) 250288 & 252100
F: (01326) 250892
E: relax@budockvean.co.uk
I: www.budockvean.co.uk

Nestled in 65 acres of subtropical gardens and parkland with private foreshore on the tranquil Helford River, this friendly hotel provides golf course, large pool with log fire, tennis courts, health spa, boating, pampering and relaxation in comfortable lounges and our award-winning restaurant where fresh local seafood is a speciality.

Bedrooms: 7 single,
50 double/twin, 1 triple/
multiple; suites available
Bathrooms: 58 en suite

Lunch available
Evening meal available
CC: Delta, Diners,
Mastercard, Switch, Visa

B&B per night:
S £52.00–£79.00
D £104.00–£178.00

HB per person:
DY £62.00–£99.00

OPEN Feb–Dec

CR
Grand Heritage Hotels

★★★
Silver
Award

GREEN LAWNS HOTEL

Western Terrace, Falmouth TR11 4QJ
T: (01326) 312734 & 312007
F: (01326) 211427
E: info@greenlawnshotel.com
I: www.greenlawnshotel.com

Elegant chateau-style hotel beautifully situated in prize-winning gardens with views across Falmouth Bay. Distinguished by its ivy exterior, the hotel is centrally positioned between the main beaches and town centre. The Green Lawns offers the perfect holiday setting or business retreat at any time of the year.

Bedrooms: 6 single,
25 double/twin, 8 triple/
multiple
Bathrooms: 39 en suite

Lunch available
Evening meal available
CC: Amex, Delta, Diners,
Mastercard, Switch, Visa

B&B per night:
S £55.00–£105.00
D £110.00–£180.00

HB per person:
DY £72.50–£125.00

OPEN All year round

CR
The Independents

★★★

PENMORVAH MANOR HOTEL

Budock Water, Falmouth TR11 5ED
T: (01326) 250277
F: (01326) 250509
E: reception@penmorvah.co.uk
I: www.penmorvah.co.uk

Peaceful and secluded country house set in 6 acres of mature gardens and woodland. 27 beautifully appointed bedrooms, some with ground floor access. All bedrooms are non-smoking. Elegant dining room serving fresh local produce in a friendly, relaxed atmosphere. Ideally situated for visiting Cornwall's superb gardens. Close to busy harbour of Falmouth.

Bedrooms: 1 single,
26 double/twin, 1 triple/
multiple
Bathrooms: 28 en suite

Lunch available
Evening meal available
CC: Amex, Delta, Diners,
Mastercard, Switch, Visa

Special 2/3 night breaks. Christmas and New Year
breaks. Luxury honeymoon breaks.

B&B per night:
S Max £55.00
D £77.50–£120.00

HB per person:
DY £59.75–£81.00

OPEN All year round

CR
Minotel

CENTRAL RESERVATIONS OFFICES

The symbol CR and a group name in an entry indicate that bookings can be made through a central reservations office. These are listed in a separate section towards the back of this guide.

HOLFORD, Somerset Map ref 1D1

★★
Silver
Award

COMBE HOUSE HOTEL
Holford, Bridgwater TA5 1RZ
T: (01278) 741382
F: (01278) 741322
E: enquiries@combehouse.co.uk
I: www.combehouse.co.uk

Bedrooms: 4 single,
12 double/twin
Bathrooms: 16 en suite

Lunch available
Evening meal available
CC: Amex, Delta,
Mastercard, Switch, Visa

B&B per night:
S £33.00–£41.00
D £66.00–£93.00

HB per person:
DY £47.00–£66.50

OPEN All year round

17thC country hotel in beautiful Butterfly Combe in the heart of the Quantock Hills. Traditional hospitality in rural peace and quiet.

♠♥♦♣ ☎ ▢ ♨ ⌧ ▦ 🖥 ♦ ♛ ⌘ ❄ ⛺ 🐎 🐕 ♿ P

HOLSWORTHY, Devon Map ref 1C2

★★

COURT BARN COUNTRY HOUSE HOTEL
Clawton, Holsworthy EX22 6PS
T: (01409) 271219
F: (01409) 271309
E: courtbarnhotel@talk21.com
I: www.hotels-devon.com

B&B per night:
S £38.00–£50.00
D £60.00–£85.00

HB per person:
DY £50.00–£60.00

OPEN All year round

Charming country house set in park-like grounds. Origins in 15thC and partly rebuilt in 1853. With elegant roooms, intimate bar, 2 lounges, dining room and new restaurant. Ideally situated between 3 moors, Atlantic coast, National Trust gardens and nature trails. Enjoy crackling log fires and award-winning food and wines.

Bedrooms: 1 single,
5 double/twin, 2 triple/
multiple
Bathrooms: 8 en suite

Lunch available
Evening meal available
CC: Amex, Delta, Diners,
Mastercard, Switch, Visa

Court Barn's many famous themed breaks include: Romantic Weekend, Cycle Trails, Water Colour Art Course. Golf (reduced rates), food and wine, croquet and cream teas.

♠♥♦♣ ☎ ▦ ▢ ♨ ⌧ ▦ ◉ 🖥 ♦ ♛ ⌘ 🎾 ♪ ❄ 🐎 🐕 ♿ P

HONITON, Devon Map ref 1D2 *Tourist Information Centre Tel: (01404) 43716*

★★
Silver
Award

HOME FARM HOTEL AND RESTAURANT
Wilmington, Honiton EX14 9JR
T: (01404) 831278 & 831246
F: (01404) 831411
E: homefarmhotel@breathemail.net
I: www.homefarmhotel.co.uk

Bedrooms: 3 single,
6 double/twin, 4 triple/
multiple; suites available
Bathrooms: 13 en suite

Lunch available
Evening meal available
CC: Delta, Mastercard,
Switch, Visa

B&B per night:
S £39.50–£49.50
D £65.00–£85.00

HB per person:
DY £49.50–£66.50

OPEN All year round

Thatched 16thC farmhouse hotel in lovely countryside. Restaurant uses local produce to serve food of high standard. Bar with light meals. Log fires. Six miles from sea.

♠♥♦♣ ☎ ▦ ▢ ♨ ⌧ ▦ 🖥 ♦ ♛ ❄ ⛺ 🐕 P

ILFRACOMBE, Devon Map ref 1C1 *Tourist Information Centre Tel: 0845 458 3630*

★★

ELMFIELD HOTEL
Torrs Park, Ilfracombe EX34 8AZ
T: (01271) 863377
F: (01271) 866828
E: elmfieldhotel@aol.com
I: www.elmfieldhotelilfracombe.co.uk

B&B per night:
S £40.00–£45.00
D £80.00–£90.00

HB per person:
DY £45.00–£90.00

The hotel stands in its own acre of gardens, with heated indoor swimming pool, jacuzzi, sauna, solarium. For that special occasion two rooms have 4-poster beds. We have achieved an excellent reputation for our cuisine, using fresh local produce. Book from any day and for any number of days.

Bedrooms: 2 single,
11 double/twin
Bathrooms: 13 en suite

Lunch available
Evening meal available
CC: Delta, Mastercard,
Switch, Visa

♠♥8♦♣ ▦ ▢ ♨ ⌧ ▦ 🖥 ♦ 🔍 ☂ ♛ ❄ 🐎 🐕 ♿ P

SYMBOLS
The symbols in each entry give information about services and facilities. A key to these symbols appears at the back of this guide.

★★

THE ILFRACOMBE CARLTON HOTEL

Runnacleave Road, Ilfracombe EX34 8AR
T: (01271) 862446 & 863711
F: (01271) 865379
E: enquiries@ilfracombecarlton.co.uk

B&B per night:
S £25.00–£29.50
D £45.00–£55.00

HB per person:
DY £36.00–£41.00

OPEN All year round

Premier resort hotel in central location adjacent to beach, seafront and Tarka Trail. Comfortable rooms with good facilities. Buttery, dancing. One non-smoking lounge, non-smoking bedrooms. Special breaks all year. A warm welcome from the 'Hotel with a Smile'.

Bedrooms: 9 single, 31 double/twin, 8 triple/ multiple
Bathrooms: 48 en suite

Evening meal available
CC: Amex, Delta, Mastercard, Switch, Visa

Short breaks from £32.50pppn DB&B weekend specials.

★

THE TORRS HOTEL

Torrs Park, Ilfracombe EX34 8AY
T: (01271) 862334
F: (01271) 862334
I: www.thetorrshotel.co.uk

Bedrooms: 9 double/ twin, 5 triple/multiple
Bathrooms: 14 en suite

Evening meal available
CC: Delta, Mastercard, Switch, Visa

B&B per night:
S £22.50–£27.50
D £45.00–£55.00

HB per person:
DY £32.50–£37.50

Victorian mansion with fine views. Quiet location beside the National Trust Torrs Coastal Walk. Close to seafront and town centre.

★

WESTWELL HALL HOTEL

Torrs Park, Ilfracombe EX34 8AZ
T: (01271) 862792
F: (01271) 862792
E: westwellh@ll.fsnet.co.uk
I: www.westwellhall.co.uk

B&B per night:
S £22.00–£25.00
D £44.00–£50.00

HB per person:
DY £35.00–£38.00

OPEN Easter to end Oct

Elegant early Victorian house set in 2 acres of mature gardens, adjacent to National Trust walks. Overlooking the sea and town in quiet location. An ideal base for exploring the beautiful, rugged coastline of North Devon.

Bedrooms: 1 single, 7 double/twin, 2 triple/ multiple
Bathrooms: 10 en suite

Evening meal available
CC: Amex, Delta, Diners, Mastercard, Switch, Visa

★★
Silver Award

AVIARY COURT HOTEL

Marys Well, Illogan, Redruth TR16 4QZ
T: (01209) 842256
F: (01209) 843744
E: aviarycourt@connexions.co.uk
I: www.connexions.co.uk/aviarycourt/index.htm

B&B per night:
S £42.00–£45.00
D £62.00–£65.00

HB per person:
DY £45.00–£46.50

OPEN All year round

Charming country house in 2 acres of secluded, well-kept gardens with tennis court. Family-run, personal service, good food. Superior en suite bedrooms with TV, telephone, tea/ coffee, fresh fruit. Ideal touring location (coast 5 minutes). St Ives, Tate, Heligan, Eden Project all within easy reach.

Bedrooms: 5 double/ twin, 1 triple/multiple
Bathrooms: 6 en suite

Evening meal available
CC: Delta, Mastercard, Switch, Visa

REGIONAL TOURIST BOARD The ⋀ symbol in an establishment entry indicates that it is a Regional Tourist Board member.

LANDS END, Cornwall Map ref 1A3

★★★

THE LAND'S END HOTEL

Lands End TR19 7AA
T: (01736) 871844
F: (01736) 871599
E: info@landsend-landmark.co.uk
I: www.landsend-landmark.co.uk

B&B per night:
S £39.00–£55.00
D £78.00–£110.00

HB per person:
DY £49.00–£68.00

OPEN All year round

The Land's End Hotel stands on the 200ft cliffs where Cornwall ends. This historic building, solidly built to withstand the strongest buffeting from the ocean winds, is warm, welcoming and comfortable. Many of the rooms command spectacular views across the Atlantic towards the Isles of Scilly and the Longships Lighthouse.

Bedrooms: 4 single, 26 double/twin, 3 triple/ multiple
Bathrooms: 33 en suite

Lunch available
Evening meal available
CC: Amex, Delta, Mastercard, Switch, Visa

Breaks of 2 or more nights available during opening period of Mar-Oct.

LOOE, Cornwall Map ref 1C3

★★
Silver
Award
Ad on this page

FIELDHEAD HOTEL

Portuan Road, Hannafore, West Looe, Looe
PL13 2DR
T: (01503) 262689
F: (01503) 264114
E: field.head@virgin.net
I: www.fieldheadhotel.co.uk

B&B per night:
S £30.00–£55.00
D £60.00–£90.00

HB per person:
DY £45.00–£65.00

OPEN All year round

Minotel

Built as a private house in the grand style in 1896 and now a true country house hotel by the sea. Most bedrooms and all public rooms have wonderful panoramic views over Looe Bay. Lovely tropical gardens with heated pool and patios. Restaurant with daily changing menus and seafood specialities.

Bedrooms: 1 single, 11 double/twin, 3 triple/ multiple
Bathrooms: 15 en suite

Evening meal available
CC: Amex, Mastercard, Switch, Visa

Garden and Eden Project weekends from £120pp DB&B incl tickets, 2 nights. Golf weekends from £105pp DB&B, 2 nights, plus green fees.

CREDIT CARD BOOKINGS If you book by telephone and are asked for your credit card number it is advisable to check the proprietor's policy should you cancel your reservation.

LOOE continued

★★★ HANNAFORE POINT

Marine Drive, West Looe, Looe
PL13 2DG
T: (01503) 263273
F: (01503) 263272
E: hannafore@aol.com
I: www.hannaforepointhotel.com

Bedrooms: 4 single,
25 double/twin, 8 triple/
multiple
Bathrooms: 37 en suite

Lunch available
Evening meal available
CC: Amex, Diners,
Mastercard, Switch, Visa

HB per person:
DY £50.00–£78.00

OPEN All year round

Seafront hotel set in picturesque Cornish fishing village. Hotel facilities include extensive leisure centre, conference room and car park.

★★ RIVERCROFT HOTEL AND APARTMENTS

Station Road, East Looe, Looe PL13 1HL
T: (01503) 262251
F: (01503) 265494
E: rivercroft.hotel@virgin.net
I: www.rivercrofthotel.co.uk

Family-run hotel with friendly atmosphere, occupying a prime position overlooking beautiful Looe River, bridge and wooded valley. Enjoy a drink in the bar then sample fresh seafood, steaks and fresh local produce in the Croft Restaurant, prepared by our resident chef. An ideal base for touring, walking, fishing and golf. 30 mins from Eden Project.

Bedrooms: 1 single,
7 double/twin, 3 triple/
multiple
Bathrooms: 11 en suite

Lunch available
Evening meal available
CC: Delta, Diners,
Mastercard, Switch, Visa

3 nights for the price of 2, Nov-Mar (excl Christmas and New Year).

B&B per night:
S £25.00–£35.00
D £50.00–£70.00

HB per person:
DY £40.00–£50.00

OPEN All year round

LOSTWITHIEL, Cornwall Map ref 1B2

★★★ LOSTWITHIEL HOTEL GOLF & COUNTRY CLUB

Lower Polscoe, Lostwithiel
PL22 0HQ
T: (01208) 873550
F: (01208) 873479
E: reception@golf-hotel.co.uk
I: www.golf-hotel.co.uk

Bedrooms: 2 single,
16 double/twin, 1 triple/
multiple
Bathrooms: 19 en suite

Lunch available
Evening meal available
CC: Amex, Delta, Diners,
Mastercard, Switch, Visa

B&B per night:
S £42.00–£46.0O
D £84.00–£92.00

HB per person:
DY £56.00–£61.00

OPEN All year round

Overlooking the beautiful River Fowey valley in idyllic setting. Charm, character and high levels of comfort and service. Bedrooms are converted from Cornish-stone farm buildings.

LYDFORD, Devon Map ref 1C2

★★ LYDFORD HOUSE HOTEL

Lydford, Okehampton EX20 4AU
T: (01822) 820347 & 820321
F: (01822) 820442
E: relax@lydfordhouse.co.uk
I: www.lydfordhouse.co.uk

Bedrooms: 2 single,
6 double/twin, 4 triple/
multiple; suites available
Bathrooms: 11 en suite,
1 private

Lunch available
Evening meal available
CC: Delta, Mastercard,
Switch, Visa

B&B per night:
S £31.00–£40.00
D £61.00–£79.00

HB per person:
DY £45.00–£55.00

OPEN All year round

Minotel

Delightful, family-run country house hotel in Dartmoor National Park. Own riding stables. Variety of accommodation including family rooms and 4-poster. A real 'home from home' with added pampering.

LYNMOUTH, Devon Map ref 1C1

★★ BATH HOTEL

Lynmouth EX35 6EL
T: (01598) 752238
F: (01598) 752544
E: bathhotel@torslynmouth.co.uk
I: www.torslynmouth.co.uk

Bedrooms: 1 single,
20 double/twin, 3 triple/
multiple
Bathrooms: 24 en suite

Lunch available
Evening meal available
CC: Amex, Delta, Diners,
Mastercard, Switch, Visa

B&B per night:
S £27.00–£46.00
D £54.00–£84.00

HB per person:
DY £37.00–£54.00

OPEN Feb–Nov

Friendly, family-run hotel by picturesque Lynmouth harbour. Ideal centre for exploring Exmoor National Park. Special offers and discounts available throughout the year.

LYNMOUTH continued

★★★ **THE TORS HOTEL**
Lynmouth EX35 6NA
T: (01598) 753236
F: (01598) 752544
E: torshotel@torslynmouth.co.uk
I: www.torslynmouth.co.uk

Bedrooms: 28 double/
twin, 7 triple/multiple
Bathrooms: 35 en suite

Lunch available
Evening meal available
CC: Amex, Delta, Diners,
Mastercard, Switch, Visa

B&B per night:
S £35.00–£55.00
D £70.00–£110.00

HB per person:
DY £50.00–£90.00

Unrivalled position 200 feet above sea level, with splendid views over Lynmouth and the sea. Children and dogs welcome. Christmas and New Year packages.

LYNTON, Devon Map ref 1C1 *Tourist Information Centre Tel: 0845 458 3775*

★★

SANDROCK HOTEL
Longmead, Lynton EX35 6DH
T: (01598) 753307
F: (01598) 752665

B&B per night:
S £23.50–£24.50
D £48.00–£54.00

HB per person:
DY £39.00–£52.00

Relaxing Edwardian hotel with modern comforts, in delightful sunny spot amid Exmoor's superb coastal scenery and beauty spots. En suite double rooms, own car park.

Bedrooms: 1 single,
7 double/twin
Bathrooms: 7 en suite,
1 private

Evening meal available
CC: Amex, Delta,
Mastercard, Switch, Visa

MALMESBURY, Wiltshire Map ref 2B2 *Tourist Information Centre Tel: (01666) 823748*

★★★

KNOLL HOUSE HOTEL
Swindon Road, Malmesbury SN16 9LU
T: (01666) 823114
F: (01666) 823897
E: knollhotel@malmesbury64.freeserve.co.uk
I: www.knoll-house.com

B&B per night:
S Min £75.00
D Min £95.00

HB per person:
DY Min £65.00

OPEN All year round

Ⓒ
Minotel/The
Independents

Ideally located with easy access to M4, Bath, Cheltenham and Cotswolds. Visit Avebury Stone Circles, Westonbirt Arboretum or Castle Combe. Country hotel with award-winning food, outdoor heated pool and croquet lawn. All en suite with tea/coffee facilities. Relaxed and informal atmosphere. Friendly and attentive staff.

Bedrooms: 3 single,
13 double/twin
Bathrooms: 16 en suite

Lunch available
Evening meal available
CC: Amex, Delta,
Mastercard, Switch, Visa

Stay for 3 or more nights DB&B and receive 15% discount.

Rating Applied For

THE OLD RECTORY
Crudwell, Malmesbury SN16 9EP
T: (01666) 577194
F: (01666) 577853
E: office@oldrectorycrudwell.co.uk
I: www.oldrectorycrudwell.co.uk

B&B per night:
S £65.00–£85.00
D £88.00–£120.00

OPEN All year round

Elegant and welcoming 17thC rectory, situated in 3 acres of landscaped gardens. Ideal base for touring the Cotswolds and Bath. Twelve luxuriously furnished bedrooms, with larger rooms offering 4-poster, half-tester, king-size beds and spa baths. Award-winning restaurant renowned for superb cuisine and unpretentious service.

Bedrooms: 12 double/
twin, 1 triple/multiple;
suites available
Bathrooms: 13 en suite

Lunch available
Evening meal available
CC: Amex, Delta, Diners,
Mastercard, Switch, Visa

Short breaks-2-night stay from £110pp, 3-night stay from £155pp, includes B&B and 3-course dinner.

MANACCAN, Cornwall Map ref 1B3

★★
Silver
Award

TREGILDRY HOTEL
Gillan, Manaccan, Helston
TR12 6HG
T: (01326) 231378
F: (01326) 231561
E: trgildry@globalnet.co.uk
I: www.tregildryhotel.co.uk

Bedrooms: 1 single,
9 double/twin
Bathrooms: 10 en suite

Evening meal available
CC: Delta, Mastercard,
Switch, Visa

HB per person:
DY £65.00–£85.00

Elegant, small, beautifully appointed hotel in unspoilt area, with stunning sea views. Welcoming, relaxed atmosphere. Award-winning modern British cuisine. Peaceful coastal walks. No children.

MAWGAN PORTH, Cornwall Map ref 1B2

★★

TREDRAGON HOTEL
Mawgan Porth, Padstow TR8 4DQ
T: (01637) 860213
F: (01637) 860269
E: tredragon@btinternet.com
I: www.tredragon.co.uk

B&B per night:
S £28.00–£51.00
D £56.00–£102.00

HB per person:
DY £45.00–£70.00

OPEN All year round

Grounds lead directly to sandy cove. Magnificent coastal walks and views. Relax in our indoor pool complex. Excellent food and wine. Now under new management. Open all year. Ideal for short breaks. Special interest breaks brochure available.

Bedrooms: 2 single,
14 double/twin,
13 triple/multiple
Bathrooms: 29 en suite

Lunch available
Evening meal available
CC: Mastercard, Visa

MELKSHAM, Wiltshire Map ref 2B2 *Tourist Information Centre Tel: (01225) 707424*

★★

SHAW COUNTRY HOTEL
Bath Road, Shaw, Melksham
SN12 8EF
T: (01225) 702836 & 790321
F: (01225) 790275
E: info@shawcountryhotel.fsnet.
co.uk
I: www.shawcountryhotel.fsnet.
co.uk

Bedrooms: 3 single,
10 double/twin
Bathrooms: 13 en suite

Lunch available
Evening meal available
CC: Amex, Delta, Diners,
Mastercard, Switch, Visa

B&B per night:
S Min £46.00
D £66.00–£90.00

HB per person:
DY £46.00–£52.00

OPEN All year round

400-year-old farmhouse in own grounds, 9 miles from Bath. Licensed bar and restaurant, with table d'hote and a la carte menus. Rosette for good food. All rooms en suite.

MEVAGISSEY, Cornwall Map ref 1B3

★★

TREMARNE HOTEL
Mevagissey, St Austell PL26 6UY
T: (01726) 842213
F: (01726) 843420
E: tremarne@talk21.com
I: www.tremarne-hotel.co.uk

B&B per night:
S £33.00–£39.00
D £32.00–£37.50

HB per person:
DY £49.00–£55.00

OPEN All year round

Charming, licensed hotel and restaurant. Quiet elevated position in Area of Outstanding Natural Beauty. Views over sea and countryside, near harbour and beach. On Cornish Coastal Path, close to Lost Gardens of Heligan and Eden Project. Excellent reputation for service, hospitality and cuisine. Vegetarians catered for. Outdoor heated pool and gardens.

Bedrooms: 2 single,
10 double/twin, 2 triple/
multiple
Bathrooms: 14 en suite

Lunch available
Evening meal available
CC: Amex, Delta, Diners,
Mastercard, Switch, Visa

Murder Mystery weekends; garden breaks; winter breaks Nov-Mar; 5-day Christmas break; 4-day New Year break.

★★
Gold Award

CHANNEL HOUSE HOTEL

Church Path, Off Northfield Road,
Minehead TA24 5QG
T: (01643) 703229
F: (01643) 708925
E: channel.house@virgin.net
I: www.channelhouse.co.uk

First class award-winning hotel specialising in superb cuisine and comfort. Nestling on the lower slopes of Exmoor's picturesque North Hill, it sits within 2 acres of peaceful and secluded gardens. All well-appointed bedrooms enjoy lovely views. The hotel will best suit those who appreciate quality and the delights of Exmoor. Non-smoking hotel.

Bedrooms: 7 double/ twin, 1 triple/multiple
Bathrooms: 8 en suite

Evening meal available
CC: Amex, Delta, Diners, Mastercard, Switch, Visa

Gourmet weekends 1 and 2 Nov and 8 and 9 Nov 2002. Early booking essential.

B&B per night:
S £64.00–£74.00
D £92.00–£118.00

HB per person:
DY £56.00–£69.00

★★★★
Silver Award

MANOR HOUSE HOTEL AND GOLF COURSE

Moretonhampstead, Newton Abbot
TQ13 8RE
T: (01647) 445000
F: (01647) 440961
I: www.principalhotels.co.uk

Bedrooms: 16 single, 66 double/twin, 3 triple/ multiple; suites available
Bathrooms: 85 en suite

Lunch available
Evening meal available
CC: Amex, Delta, Diners, Mastercard, Switch, Visa

Set in majestic rolling countryside, this stunning Jacobean hotel with an exceptional level of style and comfort offers championship golf and various outdoor pursuits.

B&B per night:
S Min £95.00
D Min £170.00

HB per person:
DY Min £79.00

OPEN All year round

®
Principal Hotels/Utell International

★★

PHILEMA HOTEL

1 Esplanade Road, Pentire,
Newquay TR7 1PY
T: (01637) 872571
F: (01637) 873188
E: info@philema.demon.co.uk
I: www.smoothhound.co.uk/hotels/ philema.html

Bedrooms: 9 double/ twin, 24 triple/multiple; suites available
Bathrooms: 33 en suite

Lunch available
Evening meal available
CC: Delta, Mastercard, Switch, Visa

Furnished to a high standard with magnificent views overlooking Fistral Beach and golf-course. Friendly informal hotel with good facilities, including indoor pool, leisure complex and apartments.

B&B per night:
S £25.00–£40.00
D £50.00–£80.00

HB per person:
DY £27.00–£45.00

★★★

TREBARWITH HOTEL

Newquay TR7 1BZ
T: (01637) 872288
F: (01637) 875431
E: enquiry@trebarwith-hotel.co.uk
I: www.trebarwith-hotel.co.uk

'Probably the best views in Newquay'. There's more too! Gardens, sun terraces, private beach entrance, large indoor pool. All complemented by relaxing, comfortable, friendly atmosphere, high standards of housekeeping, excellent food and caring hospitality. Extensive indoor leisure facilities, entertainment, secure parking. Quiet, central location, an oasis in the heart of Newquay.

Bedrooms: 3 single, 32 double/twin, 6 triple/ multiple
Bathrooms: 41 en suite

Lunch available
Evening meal available
CC: Delta, Mastercard, Switch, Visa

B&B per night:
S £29.00–£65.00
D £55.00–£130.00

HB per person:
DY £58.00–£140.00

OPEN Mar–Oct

★

TREGURRIAN HOTEL

Watergate Bay, Newquay TR8 4AB
T: (01637) 860280
F: (01637) 860540
E: tregurrian.hotel@virgin.net
I: www.holidaysincornwall.net

B&B per night:
S £19.00–£34.00
D £38.00–£68.00

HB per person:
DY £29.00–£41.00

In tiny hamlet between Newquay and Padstow just 100 yards from the superb sandy beach, this family-run hotel offers a friendly, informal atmosphere and attentive service. Just 4 miles from Newquay and an ideal base for touring Cornwall...or simply relax around the pool and sun patio.

Bedrooms: 4 single, 15 double/twin, 8 triple/ multiple
Bathrooms: 22 en suite

Lunch available
Evening meal available
CC: Delta, Mastercard, Switch, Visa

Stay 4 nights pay for only 3, excl 21 Jul–6 Sep. Plus special golf and garden breaks.

OKEHAMPTON, Devon Map ref 1C2

★★

OXENHAM ARMS

South Zeal, Okehampton EX20 2JT
T: (01837) 840244
F: (01837) 840791
E: jhenry1928@aol.com
I: www.hoteldevon.net

Bedrooms: 5 double/ twin, 3 triple/multiple
Bathrooms: 7 en suite, 1 private

Lunch available
Evening meal available
CC: Amex, Delta, Diners, Mastercard, Switch, Visa

B&B per night:
S £40.00–£50.00
D £60.00–£70.00

HB per person:
DY £45.00–£55.00

OPEN All year round

12thC inn in Dartmoor National Park. En suite rooms with direct-dial phones with modems. Colour TV. International bar and dining room menus. Walkers' paradise.

★★

WHITE HART HOTEL

Fore Street, Okehampton EX20 1HD
T: (01837) 52730 & 54514
F: (01837) 53979

Bedrooms: 2 single, 17 double/twin
Bathrooms: 19 en suite

Lunch available
Evening meal available
CC: Delta, Mastercard, Switch, Visa

B&B per night:
S £40.00–£50.00
D £60.00–£70.00

HB per person:
DY £55.00–£65.00

OPEN All year round

Family-run, town centre 17thC coaching inn. Fully licensed freehouse with bars, restaurant, function suites and car parking.

PAIGNTON, Devon Map ref 1D2 *Tourist Information Centre Tel: 0906 680 1268 (Premium rate number)*

★★

HARWIN HOTEL AND APARTMENTS

Alta Vista Road, Goodrington Sands,
Paignton TQ4 6DA
T: (01803) 558771
F: 0870 8313998
E: enquiries@hotel-harwin.co.uk
I: www.hotel-harwin.co.uk

B&B per night:
S £24.00–£35.00
D £48.00–£56.00

HB per person:
DY £33.00–£45.00

The Harwin has for over 40 years been a family-run hotel, specialising in friendly, personal service. Panoramic sea views from restaurant, bar, patio, and most bedrooms. Idyllic location, just 60 metres by footpath to safe, sandy beaches of Goodrington, with Water Park and harbour close by.

Bedrooms: 1 single, 12 double/twin, 9 triple/ multiple
Bathrooms: 20 en suite, 2 private

Lunch available
Evening meal available
CC: Delta, Mastercard, Switch, Visa

Special mini-break rates early and late season. Please ask for details.

www.travelengland.org.uk

Log on for information and inspiration. The latest information on places to visit, events and quality assessed accommodation.

★★★

THE QUEENS HOTEL

The Promenade, Penzance TR18 4HG
T: (01736) 362371
F: (01736) 350033
E: enquiries@queens-hotel.com
I: www.queens-hotel.com

B&B per night:
S £45.00–£61.00
D £86.00–£130.00

HB per person:
DY £60.00–£76.00

OPEN All year round

Discover Britain's Hotel of The Year 2000. Elegant Victorian hotel on the seafront promenade of Penzance with majestic views across Mounts Bay from Mousehole Point to Lizard Peninsula and St Michael's Mount. Our award-winning dining room which overlooks the bay offers a table d'hote menu including local fresh fish and produce.

Bedrooms: 15 single,
45 double/twin,
10 triple/multiple
Bathrooms: 70 en suite

Lunch available
Evening meal available
CC: Amex, Delta, Diners,
Mastercard, Switch, Visa

★★★

THE GRAND HOTEL

Elliot Street, The Hoe, Plymouth PL1 2PT
T: (01752) 661195
F: (01752) 600653
E: info@plymouthgrand.com
I: www.plymouthgrand.com

B&B per night:
S £85.00–£148.00
D £95.00–£158.00

HB per person:
DY £39.50–£49.50

OPEN All year round

Ⓒ
Utell International

Victorian hotel on the Hoe with magnificent sea views (see picture) over the Sound. Close to Theatre Royal, Aquarium, historic Barbican. Range of bedrooms from standard to sea view with open balcony and suites. Free car parking. Leisure breaks all year – minimum 2-night stay. Live entertainment/dancing most Saturdays.

Bedrooms: 72 double/
twin, 5 triple/multiple;
suites available
Bathrooms: 77 en suite

Lunch available
Evening meal available
CC: Amex, Delta,
Mastercard, Switch, Visa

Burns Night Scottish speciality dinner. Valentines romantic breaks. Thanksgiving dinner. Ring for more details.

★★

INVICTA HOTEL
11/12 Osborne Place,
Lockyer Street, The Hoe, Plymouth
PL1 2PU
T: (01752) 664997
F: (01752) 664994
E: info@invicta-hotel.co.uk
I: www.invictahotel.co.uk

Bedrooms: 5 single,
12 double/twin, 6 triple/
multiple; suites available
Bathrooms: 23 en suite

Evening meal available
CC: Amex, Delta,
Mastercard, Switch, Visa

B&B per night:
S £42.00–£52.00
D £52.00–£62.00

HB per person:
DY Max £41.00

OPEN All year round

Elegant Victorian hotel opposite the famous Plymouth Hoe, close to all amenities. Well-appointed bedrooms, warm and personal service. Lock-up car park.

USE YOUR *i*s

There are more than 550 Tourist Information Centres throughout England offering friendly help with accommodation and holiday ideas as well as suggestions of places to visit and things to do. You'll find TIC addresses in the local Phone Book.

PLYMOUTH continued

★★★

KITLEY HOUSE HOTEL AND RESTAURANT

Kitley Estate, Yealmpton, Plymouth
PL8 2NW
T: (01752) 881555
F: (01752) 881667
E: sales@kitleyhousehotel.com
I: www.kitleyhousehotel.com

Unique country house hotel, set in own valley and overlooking a trout lake. Luxury suites and standard bedrooms feature contemporary facilities with magnificent views. Restaurant is popular with local residents and is open for lunch and dinner. Grade I Listed building, originally a Tudor Revival house and remodelled by George Repton in 1820s.

Bedrooms: 4 single, 16 double/twin; suites available
Bathrooms: 20 en suite

Lunch available
Evening meal available
CC: Amex, Delta, Diners, Mastercard, Switch, Visa

Christmas, New Year and Easter seasonal packages. Mid-week and weekend short breaks available all year.

B&B per night:
S £49.50–£115.00
D £79.00–£130.00

HB per person:
DY £110.00–£160.00

OPEN All year round

★★★

NEW CONTINENTAL HOTEL

Millbay Road, Plymouth PL1 3LD
T: (01752) 220782
F: (01752) 227013
E: newconti@aol.com
I: www.newcontinental.co.uk

Victorian Grade II Listed building, Plymouth's largest independent hotel, in the city centre adjacent to conference and leisure centre and close to Theatre Royal, Barbican and Plymouth Hoe. Beautifully appointed bedrooms offering some of the finest accommodation available in Plymouth today. Half board prices for minimum 2-night break.

Bedrooms: 22 single, 49 double/twin, 28 triple/multiple; suites available
Bathrooms: 99 en suite

Lunch available
Evening meal available
CC: Amex, Delta, Mastercard, Switch, Visa

B&B per night:
S £65.00–£93.00
D £80.00–£170.00

OPEN All year round

★★★

NOVOTEL PLYMOUTH

Marsh Mills, Plymouth PL6 8NH
T: (01752) 221422
F: (01752) 223922
E: h0508@accor-hotels.com
I: www.novotel.com

Ideally situated at the gateway to Plymouth adjacent to the A38. Easy access to both Devon and Cornwall. Modern hotel with outdoor heated pool, easy to find with ample parking. All rooms en suite, hairdryer, Playstation, colour TV/radio, in-house movies and tea/coffee facilities, restaurant and bar open 6.00am to midnight.

Bedrooms: 100 triple/ multiple
Bathrooms: 100 en suite

Lunch available
Evening meal available
CC: Amex, Delta, Diners, Mastercard, Switch, Visa

Visit the Eden Project and stay at Novotel Plymouth for just £60 per room per night. Minimum 2 night stay.

B&B per night:
S £67.95–£69.00
D £81.90–£85.00

HB per person:
DY £56.90–£85.00

OPEN All year round

★★★

STRATHMORE HOTEL
Elliot Street, The Hoe, Plymouth
PL1 2PR
T: (01752) 662101
F: (01752) 223690

Bedrooms: 19 single, 30 double/twin, 6 triple/ multiple
Bathrooms: 55 en suite

Evening meal available
CC: Amex, Delta, Mastercard, Switch, Visa

B&B per night:
S £20.00–£37.00
D £35.00–£49.00

OPEN All year round

A warm and friendly welcome awaits you at this ideally situated hotel – close to city centre.

PORLOCK, Somerset Map ref 1D1

★★★

Attractive, quiet, comfortable hotel at water's edge. Picturesque harbour – amidst Exmoor's magnificent scenery and coastline. Wildlife everywhere – red deer, buzzards with 5ft wing spans. Ancient villages, medieval castles, smugglers' caves. The hotel concentrates on excellent food and attentive service.

ANCHOR AND SHIP HOTEL

Porlock Harbour, Porlock, Minehead TA24 8PB

T: (01643) 862753
F: (01643) 862843
E: anchorhotel@clara.net

Bedrooms: 1 single,	Lunch available
17 double/twin, 2 triple/	Evening meal available
multiple	CC: Amex, Delta,
Bathrooms: 20 en suite	Mastercard, Switch, Visa

B&B per night:
S £49.00–£69.00
D £88.00–£131.50

HB per person:
DY £68.75–£92.75

OPEN Feb–Dec

★★
Silver
Award

Formerly a hunting lodge, now a small, friendly hotel where you can enjoy good food and wines and roaring log fires – perfect for a short break at any time of year. Its situation could hardly be bettered, nestling where Exmoor meets the sea, with spectacular views across Porlock Bay.

PORLOCK VALE HOUSE

Porlock Weir, Minehead TA24 8NY

T: (01643) 862338
F: (01643) 863338
E: info@porlockvale.co.uk
I: www.porlockvale.co.uk

Bedrooms: 15 double/	Lunch available
twin; suites available	Evening meal available
Bathrooms: 15 en suite	CC: Amex, Delta,
	Mastercard, Switch, Visa

B&B per night:
S £30.00–£55.00
D £60.00–£120.00

HB per person:
DY £50.00–£75.00

OPEN All year round

RUAN HIGH LANES, Cornwall Map ref 1B3

★★
Silver
Award

Peaceful 19thC Cornish country house in 3-acre garden, near St Mawes, Fal Estuary and 12 miles from Truro. Beautifully furnished with antiques, pictures and fresh flowers. Pretty en suite bedrooms. Log fire, delicious candlelit dinners using fresh West Country produce. Ideal for walking coastal path, exploring Cornish gardens and visiting Eden Project.

THE HUNDRED HOUSE HOTEL

Ruan High Lanes, Truro TR2 5JR

T: (01872) 501336
F: (01872) 501151
E: eccles@hundredhousehotel.co.uk
I: www.hundredhousehotel.co.uk

Bedrooms: 2 single,	Evening meal available
8 double/twin	CC: Amex, Delta,
Bathrooms: 10 en suite	Mastercard, Switch, Visa

Spring breaks: 'A Mad March Hare' 1–31 Mar –
3 nights DB&B £159pp.
A Gardener's Delight 1 Apr–mid May –
3 nights DB&B £180pp.

B&B per night:
S £46.00–£50.00
D £92.00–£100.00

HB per person:
DY £65.00–£75.00

OPEN Mar–Oct

ACCESSIBILITY

Look for the 🚶 symbols which indicate accessibility for wheelchair users. A list of establishments is at the front of this guide.

ST AGNES, Cornwall Map ref 1B3

Rating
Applied For

SUNHOLME HOTEL

Goonvrea Road, St Agnes TR5 0NW
T: (01872) 552318
E: jefferies@sunholme.co.uk
I: www.sunholme.co.uk

B&B per night:
S £25.00–£36.00
D £50.00–£72.00

HB per person:
DY £36.00–£48.00

OPEN All year round

Wonderful countryside and coastal views and a warm welcome await you at this country house hotel. Situated in extensive grounds with ample parking on the southern slope of St Agnes Beacon. Excellent home-cooked meals and bespoke wine list. Children and pets welcome. Open all year.

Bedrooms: 1 single, 6 double/twin, 3 triple/ multiple
Bathrooms: 10 en suite

All inclusive Christmas and New Year breaks-three nights £295pp.

Evening meal available
CC: Delta, Mastercard, Switch, Visa

ST AUSTELL, Cornwall Map ref 1B3

★★★
Silver
Award

CLIFF HEAD HOTEL LIMITED

Sea Road, Carlyon Bay, St Austell PL24 3RB
T: (01726) 812345
F: (01726) 815511
E: cliffheadhotel@btconnect.com
I: www.cornishriviera.co.uk/cliffhead

B&B per night:
S £50.00–£52.00
D £84.00–£88.00

HB per person:
DY £58.00–£65.00

OPEN All year round

South-facing hotel, close to the beach with fine sea views and cliff walks. Standing in its own grounds. Situated in the centre of the Cornish Riviera, it is ideally positioned for exploring Cornwall and visiting the new Eden Project.

Bedrooms: 19 single, 32 double/twin, 8 triple/ multiple
Bathrooms: 59 en suite

Lunch available
Evening meal available
CC: Delta, Mastercard, Switch, Visa

SALISBURY, Wiltshire Map ref 2B3 *Tourist Information Centre Tel: (01722) 334956*

★★★

ROSE AND CROWN HOTEL

Harnham Road, Salisbury SP2 8JQ
T: (01722) 399955
F: (01722) 339816
E: reservations@corushotels.com
I: www.corushotels.com

B&B per night:
S Max £120.00
D £95.00–£160.00

HB per person:
DY £69.00–£72.00

OPEN All year round

ⓒⓡ
Corus & Regal Hotels

13thC hotel on the banks of the River Avon overlooking the cathedral. The Pavilions Restaurant is virtually on the water's edge. Serving a large selection of traditional fayre. Public areas are very attractively furnished with 2 roaring log fires in winter.

Bedrooms: 25 double/ twin, 3 triple/multiple; suites available
Bathrooms: 28 en suite

Lunch available
Evening meal available
CC: Amex, Delta, Diners, Mastercard, Switch, Visa

Please phone for promotions or look on our website.

SALISBURY PLAIN

See under Hindon, Salisbury

QUALITY ASSURANCE SCHEME

Star ratings and awards were correct at the time of going to press but are subject to change. Please check at the time of booking.

SHALDON, Devon Map ref 1D2

★★
Silver
Award

NESS HOUSE HOTEL

Marine Parade, Shaldon, Teignmouth
TQ14 0HP
T: (01626) 873480
F: (01626) 873486
E: nesshouse@talk21.com
I: www.nesshouse.co.uk

B&B per night:
S £45.00–£69.00
D £79.00–£99.00

HB per person:
DY £60.00–£84.00

OPEN All year round

A charming Grade II Listed Colonial Georgian building overlooking the Teign Estuary and beautiful Devon coastline. Parkland setting in pretty Shaldon fishing village. You will be welcomed by friendly and attentive staff in this comfortable hotel.

Bedrooms: 2 single,
8 double/twin, 2 triple/
multiple
Bathrooms: 12 en suite

Lunch available
Evening meal available
CC: Amex, Mastercard,
Switch, Visa

Special prices for short breaks Oct–Apr.

SHEPTON MALLET, Somerset Map ref 2A2 *Tourist Information Centre Tel: (01749) 345258*

★★
THE SHRUBBERY HOTEL
17 Commercial Road,
Shepton Mallet BA4 5BU
T: (01749) 346671
F: (01749) 346581

Bedrooms: 1 single,
10 double/twin, 3 triple/
multiple
Bathrooms: 13 en suite,
1 private

Lunch available
Evening meal available
CC: Amex, Delta, Diners,
Mastercard, Switch, Visa

B&B per night:
S £52.50–£55.00
D £75.00–£79.50

OPEN All year round

A small in-town oasis. Privately owned hotel set in delightful gardens, offering customer comfort, a quality restaurant and lounge with light eating facilities. Ideal stopping-off point for the West Country.

SIDMOUTH, Devon Map ref 1D2 *Tourist Information Centre Tel: (01395) 516441*

★★
Silver
Award

DEVORAN HOTEL
The Esplanade, Sidmouth EX10 8AU
T: (01395) 513151 & 0800 317171
F: (01395) 579929
E: devoran@cosmic.org.uk
I: www.devoran.com

Bedrooms: 5 single,
14 double/twin, 4 triple/
multiple
Bathrooms: 23 en suite

Evening meal available
CC: Delta, Mastercard,
Switch, Visa

B&B per night:
S £32.00–£45.00
D £64.00–£90.00

HB per person:
DY £32.00–£56.00

Family-run hotel overlooking beach, very close to town centre and amenities. Relaxed, happy atmosphere, with traditional home-cooked food using local produce.

★★★
FORTFIELD HOTEL
Sidmouth EX10 8NU
T: (01395) 512403
F: (01395) 512403
E: reservations@fortfield-hotel.
demon.co.uk
I: www.fortfield-hotel.demon.co.uk

Bedrooms: 5 single,
38 double/twin, 7 triple/
multiple
Bathrooms: 50 en suite

Lunch available
Evening meal available
CC: Amex, Delta, Diners,
Mastercard, Switch, Visa

B&B per night:
S £40.00–£45.00
D £70.00–£100.00

HB per person:
DY £46.00–£65.00

OPEN All year round

Country house style hotel overlooking sea, with swimming pool and solarium. Spacious lounges, attractive gardens and free parking. Warm welcome assured.

TOWN INDEX

This can be found at the back of this guide. If you know where you want to stay, the index will give you the page number listing accommodation in your chosen town, city or village.

SIDMOUTH continued

★★★★
Gold
Award

HOTEL RIVIERA

The Esplanade, Sidmouth EX10 8AY
T: (01395) 515201
F: (01395) 577775
E: enquiries@hotelriviera.co.uk
I: www.hotelriviera.co.uk

B&B per night:
S £79.00–£107.00
D £138.00–£194.00

HB per person:
DY £80.00–£118.00

OPEN All year round

The hotel has a long tradition of hospitality and is perfect for unforgettable holidays, long weekends, unwinding breaks and all the spirit of the glorious festive season... you will be treated to the kind of friendly personal attention that can only be found in a private hotel of this quality.

Bedrooms: 7 single, 20 double/twin; suites available
Bathrooms: 27 en suite

Lunch available
Evening meal available
CC: Amex, Diners, Mastercard, Visa

Luxury 3-day breaks and carefree weekend breaks at certain times of year. Christmas and New Year programme also available.

★★
Silver
Award

ROYAL YORK AND FAULKNER HOTEL

Esplanade, Sidmouth EX10 8AZ
T: 0800 220714 & (01395) 513043
F: (01395) 577472
E: yorkhotel@eclipse.co.uk
I: www.royalyorkhotel.net

B&B per night:
S £30.00–£48.00
D £60.00–£96.00

HB per person:
DY £38.00–£60.00

OPEN Feb–Dec

Charming Regency hotel, centre of the Esplanade and adjacent picturesque town centre. The Hook family, who have run the hotel for more than 60 years, pay great attention to detail and offer friendly, personal service coupled with very well-appointed amenities and extensive indoor leisure facilities. A perfect base for exploring the area.

Bedrooms: 22 single, 38 double/twin, 8 triple/ multiple
Bathrooms: 66 en suite, 2 private

Lunch available
Evening meal available
CC: Delta, Mastercard, Switch, Visa

Special offers available throughout the year. Freephone 0800 220714 for details.

★★

WOODLANDS HOTEL

Cotmaton Cross, Station Road, Sidmouth EX10 8HG
T: (01395) 513120 & 513166
F: (01395) 513348
E: info@woodlands-hotel.com
I: www.woodlands-hotel.com

B&B per night:
S £32.00–£79.00
D £56.00–£80.00

HD per person:
DY £38.00–£49.95

OPEN All year round

Listed Georgian building set in peaceful gardens, just 5 minutes' easy walk from seafront and shops. The hotel is family-run and we use local produce in our traditional home cooking. All bedrooms are en suite and individually decorated, some rooms are on the ground floor.

Bedrooms: 6 single, 14 double/twin; suites available
Bathrooms: 20 en suite

Evening meal available
CC: Delta, Diners, Mastercard, Switch, Visa

Murder and ballroom dancing weekends are run occasionally throughout the year. Special breaks year round. Available for functions.

SPECIAL BREAKS

Many establishments offer special promotions and themed breaks. These are highlighted in red. (All such offers are subject to availability.)

SOURTON, Devon Map ref 1C2

★★
Silver
Award

COLLAVEN MANOR HOTEL

Sourton, Okehampton EX20 4HH
T: (01837) 861522
F: (01837) 861614
I: www.collavenmanor.co.uk

B&B per night:
S £48.00–£53.00
D £74.00–£112.00

HB per person:
DY £56.00–£74.00

OPEN All year round

Historic 15thC manor, edge of Dartmoor. Characterful bedrooms, some with 4-posters, glorious views. Delicious home-cooked, home grown food including vegetarian specialities. Ideal touring centre, 3 minutes from A30 yet peacefully located in 4-acre grounds and surrounded by open countryside. Riding, fishing, golf nearby.

Bedrooms: 2 single, 6 double/twin, 1 triple/ multiple
Bathrooms: 9 en suite

Lunch available
Evening meal available
CC: Amex, Delta, Mastercard, Switch, Visa

Off-season breaks: 25% discount for 2 nights or more DB&B.

STREET, Somerset Map ref 2A2 *Tourist Information Centre Tel: (01458) 447384*

★★★

WESSEX HOTEL

High Street, Street BA16 0EF
T: (01458) 443383 & 442227
F: (01458) 446589
E: wessex@hotel-street.freeserve.
co.uk
I: www.wessexhotel.com

Bedrooms: 46 double/ twin, 4 triple/multiple
Bathrooms: 50 en suite

Lunch available
Evening meal available
CC: Amex, Delta, Diners, Mastercard, Switch, Visa

B&B per night:
S £56.50
D £73.50

HB per person:
DY £67.50–£70.00

OPEN All year round

In the heart of Somerset, legendary country of King Arthur. Nearby attractions include Bath, Glastonbury Abbey, Cheddar Gorge, Wookey Hole Caves and Wells Cathedral.

SWINDON, Wiltshire Map ref 2B2 *Tourist Information Centre Tel: (01793) 530328*

Rating
Applied For

THE ROYSTON HOTEL

34 Victoria Road, Oldtown, Swindon SN1 3AS
T: (01793) 522990
F: (01793) 522991
E: info@roystonhotel.co.uk
I: www.roystonhotel.co.uk

Bedrooms: 4 single, 8 double/twin, 2 triple/ multiple
Bathrooms: 8 en suite

CC: Amex, Delta, Diners, Mastercard, Switch, Visa

B&B per night:
S £25.00–£45.00
D £35.00–£60.00

OPEN All year round

An ivy-clad Victorian townhouse in town centre. Recently refurbished. All rooms have telephones, complimentary cable television and refreshments. Most rooms en suite. Car parking.

TINTAGEL, Cornwall Map ref 1B2

★★

WILLAPARK MANOR HOTEL

Bossiney, Tintagel PL34 0BA
T: (01840) 770782

B&B per night:
S £29.50–£35.00
D £59.00–£70.00

HB per person:
DY £43.00–£49.00

OPEN All year round

'One of the most beautifully situated hotels in Cornwall'. Set in 14 acres of garden and woodland overlooking picturesque bay and with direct access to coastal path and beach. Our unique situation, well appointed rooms, excellent cuisine and friendly, informal atmosphere bring our guests back year after year.

Bedrooms: 2 single, 9 double/twin, 2 triple/ multiple
Bathrooms: 13 en suite

Lunch available
Evening meal available

MAP REFERENCES

Map references apply to the colour maps at the front of this guide.

TINTAGEL continued

★★ **THE WOOTONS COUNTRY HOTEL**

Fore Street, Tintagel PL34 0DQ
T: (01840) 770170
F: (01840) 770170

Bedrooms: 1 single,
10 double/twin
Bathrooms: 11 en suite

Lunch available
Evening meal available
CC: Amex, Delta, Diners,
Mastercard, Switch, Visa

B&B per night:
S Min £25.00
D Min £50.00

HB per person:
DY Min £32.50

OPEN All year round

Family-managed hotel offering highest standard en suite accommodation, excellent cuisine and homely atmosphere. Five golf courses within easy reach and numerous local recreational activities.

TORPOINT, Cornwall Map ref 1C2

★★ **WHITSAND BAY HOTEL**

Portwrinkle, Torpoint PL11 3BU
T: (01503) 230276
F: (01503) 230329

Bedrooms: 2 single,
28 double/twin,
13 triple/multiple; suites
available
Bathrooms: 43 en suite

Lunch available
Evening meal available
CC: Delta, Diners,
Mastercard, Switch, Visa

B&B per night:
S £25.00–£50.00
D £30.00–£100.00

OPEN All year round

Spectacularly sited elegant country mansion with sea views. Own 18-hole golf-course. Indoor heated pools and leisure complex. Self-catering units also available.

TORQUAY, Devon Map ref 1D2 *Tourist Information Centre Tel: 0906 680 1268 (Premium rate number)*

★★★ **BELGRAVE HOTEL**

Belgrave Road, Torquay TQ2 5HE
T: (01803) 296666
F: (01803) 211308
E: info@belgrave-hotel.co.uk
I: www.belgrave-hotel.co.uk

Bedrooms: 8 single,
47 double/twin,
16 triple/multiple
Bathrooms: 71 en suite

Lunch available
Evening meal available
CC: Amex, Delta, Diners,
Mastercard, Switch, Visa

B&B per night:
S £39.00–£62.00
D £78.00–£124.00

HB per person:
DY £54.00–£70.00

OPEN All year round

Traditional 3 Star hotel, superbly located at the centre of Torquay seafront. Adjacent to Torre Abbey gardens and the Riviera Centre.

★★
Silver
Award
THE BERBURRY HOTEL

64 Bampfylde Road, Torquay
TQ2 5AY
T: (01803) 297494
F: (01803) 215902
E: bsellick@berburry.co.uk
I: www.berburry.co.uk

Bedrooms: 2 single,
11 double/twin, 2 triple/
multiple
Bathrooms: 15 en suite

Lunch available
Evening meal available
CC: Mastercard, Visa

B&B per night:
S £25.00–£35.00
D £50.00–£70.00

HB per person:
DY £35.00–£50.00

OPEN All year round

Totally non-smoking, this small, detached Victorian hotel near the sea offers a memorable West Country experience. Exceptional food and personal consideration in quality surroundings.

★★

BUTE COURT HOTEL

Belgrave Road, Torquay TQ2 5HQ
T: (01803) 213055
F: (01803) 213429
E: bute-court-hotel@talk21.com
I: www.bute-court-hotel.co.uk

B&B per night:
S £24.00–£40.00
D £48.00–£80.00

HB per person:
DY £29.00–£45.00

OPEN All year round

Run by the same family for 50 years, the hotel is situated in its own grounds with garden, swimming pool and car park, overlooking Torbay. All 45 bedrooms are en suite. Lift, bar, spacious lounges and games rooms. Off-season mini-breaks. Entertainment in season. Pets welcome.

Bedrooms: 10 single,
25 double/twin,
10 triple/multiple
Bathrooms: 45 en suite

Winter breaks available.

Lunch available
Evening meal available
CC: Amex, Delta, Diners,
Mastercard, Switch, Visa

QUALITY ASSURANCE SCHEME

Star ratings and awards are explained at the back of this guide.

★★

CARLTON COURT HOTEL

18 Cleveland Road, Torquay TQ2 5BE
T: (01803) 297318
F: (01803) 290069
E: carltoncourt@onetel.net.uk
I: www.carlton-court.co.uk

B&B per night:
S £25.00–£30.00
D £38.00–£54.00

HB per person:
DY £27.00–£35.00

OPEN All year round

Lovely detached Victorian villa set in a peaceful part of Torquay with private garden and car park, yet only a short walk to the beach, Torre Park, town and Riviera Conference and Sport Centre. All rooms are en suite and enjoy a bright, open aspect. Fluent Spanish spoken.

Bedrooms: 7 double/
twin, 2 triple/multiple
Bathrooms: 9 en suite

Evening meal available
CC: Mastercard, Switch,
Visa

4 nights for price of 3 during low season. Christmas package. Honeymoon and anniversary specials arranged.

★★

FROGNEL HALL

Higher Woodfield Road, Torquay TQ1 2LD
T: (01803) 298339
F: (01803) 215115
E: mail@frognel.co.uk
I: www.frognel.co.uk

B&B per night:
S £24.00–£31.00
D £48.00–£62.00

HB per person:
DY £32.00–£40.00

OPEN All year round

Beautiful Victorian mansion set in large, peaceful gardens near harbour, beaches and Torquay centre. With a wide choice of freshly prepared food and good wine, fine views, parking and lift, this is the ideal base from which to explore Devon, Cornwall, Dartmoor National Park and the South Coastal path.

Bedrooms: 4 single,
15 double/twin, 9 triple/
multiple
Bathrooms: 27 en suite,
1 private

Lunch available
Evening meal available
CC: Amex, Delta, Diners,
Mastercard, Switch, Visa

Informal and entertaining Murder Mystery evenings, selected weekends Dec-Mar. Also Christmas and New Year special breaks.

★★★

LIVERMEAD HOUSE HOTEL

Sea Front, Torquay TQ2 6QJ
T: (01803) 294361
F: (01803) 200758
E: rewhotels@aol.com
I: www.livermead.com

B&B per night:
S £40.00–£55.00
D £80.00–£110.00

HB per person:
DY £45.00–£120.00

OPEN All year round

Built in 1820 on the edge of the Cockington Valley lies the Livermead House. This privately owned picturesque country house hotel is situated by the sea in 3 acres of award-winning grounds and offers outstanding cuisine, luxurious surroundings and service synonymous with one of Torbay's leading hotels.

Bedrooms: 6 single,
56 double/twin, 5 triple/
multiple
Bathrooms: 67 en suite

Lunch available
Evening meal available
CC: Amex, Delta, Diners,
Mastercard, Switch, Visa

Special breaks offered throughout the year. Please enquire by quoting Special Breaks 2002 when telephoning reservations.

CHECK THE MAPS

The colour maps at the front of this guide show all the cities, towns and villages for which you will find accommodation entries. Refer to the town index to find the page on which they are listed.

★★★★

PALACE HOTEL

Babbacombe Road, Torquay TQ1 3TG
T: (01803) 200200
F: (01803) 299899
E: info@palacetorquay.co.uk
I: www.palacetorquay.co.uk

HB per person:
DY £59.00–£79.00

OPEN All year round

A fine independent hotel, beautifully set in 25 acres of magnificent grounds, overlooking the charming Anstey's Cove. The unrivalled leisure facilities include a 9-hole short golf course, indoor and outdoor swimming pools and tennis courts. The hotel offers exceptionally high standards of service and excellent cuisine.

Bedrooms: 36 single, 85 double/twin, 20 triple/multiple; suites available
Bathrooms: 141 en suite
3-night special breaks available at most times, prices from £55pppn DB&B.

Lunch available
Evening meal available
CC: Amex, Delta, Diners, Mastercard, Switch, Visa

★★

RED HOUSE HOTEL
Rousdown Road, Chelston, Torquay TQ2 6PB
T: (01803) 607811
F: (01803) 200592
E: stay@redhouse-hotel.co.uk
I: www.redhouse-hotel.co.uk

Bedrooms: 1 single, 4 double/twin, 5 triple/multiple
Bathrooms: 10 en suite

Lunch available
Evening meal available
CC: Delta, Mastercard, Switch, Visa

B&B per night:
S £22.00–£34.00
D £44.00–£68.00

HB per person:
DY £27.00–£40.00

OPEN All year round

Small friendly hotel offering indoor/outdoor pools, spa, sauna, gym and beauty salon. Adjoining self-catering or serviced apartments. Convenient for seafront and other amenities.

★★

SHEDDEN HALL HOTEL

Shedden Hill, Torquay TQ2 5TX
T: (01803) 292964
F: (01803) 295306
E: sheddenhtl@aol.com
I: www.sheddenhallhotel.co.uk

B&B per night:
S £27.00–£35.00
D £54.00–£70.00

HB per person:
DY £32.00–£43.00

Situated in one of the most enviable postions in Torquay with magnificent panoramic sea views, this quality family-run hotel is within easy walking distance of Torre Abbey sands, the town, theatre and leisure centre. Heated outdoor swimming pool set in own gardens, entertainment, superb cuisine, car park.

Bedrooms: 2 single, 15 double/twin, 7 triple/multiple
Bathrooms: 24 en suite

Evening meal available
CC: Amex, Delta, Diners, Mastercard, Switch, Visa

TOTNES, Devon Map ref 1D2 *Tourist Information Centre Tel: (01803) 863168*

★★

ROYAL SEVEN STARS HOTEL
The Plains, Totnes TQ9 5DD
T: (01803) 862125 & 863241
F: (01803) 867925
I: www.smoothhound.co.uk/hotels/royal7.html

Bedrooms: 1 single, 13 double/twin, 2 triple/multiple
Bathrooms: 14 en suite, 2 private

Lunch available
Evening meal available
CC: Amex, Delta, Diners, Mastercard, Switch, Visa

B&B per night:
S £54.00–£60.00
D £67.00–£74.00

HB per person:
DY £70.00–£76.00

OPEN All year round

Old coaching inn in the centre of Totnes, near River Dart. Short drive to coast and Dartmoor. Brochures available on request. Weekend breaks available.

COLOUR MAPS Colour maps at the front of this guide pinpoint all places under which you will find accommodation listed.

★★★

ALVERTON MANOR

Tregolls Road, Truro TR1 1ZQ
T: (01872) 276633
F: (01872) 222989
E: reception@alvertonmanor.demon.co.uk

B&B per night:
S £72.00
D £109.00–£165.00

HB per person:
DY £66.50–£94.50

OPEN All year round

The Alverton Manor is an impressive sight on its hillside setting, providing luxurious and relaxing accommodation, superb award-winning cuisine and the highest standard of service. Alverton also boasts its own 18-hole golf course located in over 400 acres of rolling parkland within the historic Killiow Estate.

Bedrooms: 6 single, 28 double/twin; suites available
Bathrooms: 34 en suite

Lunch available
Evening meal available
CC: Amex, Delta, Diners, Mastercard, Switch, Visa

★★★

BROOKDALE HOTEL

Tregolls Road, Truro TR1 1JZ
T: (01872) 273513
F: (01872) 272400
E: brookdale@hotelstruro.com
I: hotelstruro.com

B&B per night:
S £40.00–£52.00
D £60.00–£70.00

OPEN All year round

The Brookdale Hotel has a fine, traditional restaurant featuring locally sourced produce. It is a popular venue for business conferences and family celebrations. Truro is a fine city, well positioned to tour anywhere in Cornwall as most destinations are within a 30-minute drive.

Bedrooms: 7 single, 14 double/twin
Bathrooms: 21 en suite

Lunch available
Evening meal available
CC: Amex, Delta, Mastercard, Switch, Visa

£85 DB&B in a double/twin room, 14 Sep–1 Apr.

★★

CARLTON HOTEL
Falmouth Road, Truro TR1 2HL
T: (01872) 272450
F: (01872) 223938
E: reception@carltonhotel.co.uk
I: www.carltonhotel.co.uk

Bedrooms: 3 single, 22 double/twin, 4 triple/multiple
Bathrooms: 29 en suite

Evening meal available
CC: Amex, Delta, Diners, Mastercard, Switch, Visa

B&B per night:
S £35.00–£40.00
D £49.00–£53.00

HB per person:
DY £34.50–£50.00

OPEN All year round

Within easy walking distance of city centre. 29 en suite bedrooms, all with TV, telephone, tea/coffee facilities. Sauna/spa bath. Restaurant and residential license.

★★
Silver
Award

DOWNFIELD HOUSE HOTEL
16 St Decuman's Road, Watchet
TA23 0HR
T: (01984) 631267
F: (01984) 634369
I: www.smoothhound.co.uk/hotels/downf

Bedrooms: 6 double/twin, 1 triple/multiple
Bathrooms: 7 en suite

Evening meal available
CC: Amex, Delta, Mastercard, Switch, Visa

B&B per night:
S £36.00–£45.00
D £48.00–£66.00

HB per person:
DY £57.00–£69.00

OPEN All year round

Attractive Victorian country house, set in secluded grounds with views over harbour and town. Comfortable lounge, chandeliered dining room. Close to Quantocks and Exmoor.

TOWN INDEX

This can be found at the back of this guide. If you know where you want to stay, the index will give you the page number listing accommodation in your chosen town, city or village.

★★★

WATERGATE BAY HOTEL

Watergate Bay, Newquay TR8 4AA
T: (01637) 860543
F: (01637) 860333
E: hotel@watergate.co.uk
I: www.watergate.co.uk

B&B per night:
S £30.00–£60.00
D £55.00–£110.00

HB per person:
DY £35.00–£65.00

OPEN All year round

Beside its own spectacular beach. The hotel is stylish and comfortable, perfect for exploring Cornwall and the Eden Project. Facilities include 2 swimming pools, sports hall, tennis court, massage, sauna, spa pool. Good coastal walking. The food is excellent Cornish cuisine and the service is very friendly. Dogs welcome. Open all year.

Bedrooms: 7 single,
26 double/twin,
29 triple/multiple
Bathrooms: 62 en suite

Lunch available
Evening meal available
CC: Delta, Mastercard,
Switch, Visa

There are themed breaks and special offers spring, autumn and winter, from Eden Breaks to Murder Mystery Weekends. Child free offers.

★★

THE CROWN AT WELLS

Market Place, Wells BA5 2RP
T: (01749) 673457
F: (01749) 679792
E: reception@crownatwells.co.uk
I: www.crownatwells.co.uk

B&B per night:
S £50.00–£55.00
D £65.00–£80.00

HB per person:
DY £55.00–£65.00

OPEN All year round

The 2-star, 15thC Crown is situated in the market place in the heart of Wells, close to Wells Cathedral and Bishop's Palace. The Crown serves a variety of delicious meals, snacks and refreshments in the Penn Bar and Anton's Bistro throughout the day. Warm welcome and friendly service.

Bedrooms: 2 single,
13 double/twin
Bathrooms: 15 en suite

Lunch available
Evening meal available
CC: Amex, Delta,
Mastercard, Switch, Visa

★★★

SWAN HOTEL
Sadler Street, Wells BA5 2RX
T: (01749) 836300
F: (01749) 836301
E: swan@bhere.co.uk
I: www.bhere.co.uk

Bedrooms: 2 single,
33 double/twin
Bathrooms: 35 en suite

Lunch available
Evening meal available
CC: Amex, Delta, Diners,
Mastercard, Switch, Visa

B&B per night:
S £79.50–£84.50
D £87.50–£126.00

OPEN All year round

Ⓡ
Best Western Hotels

Privately-owned 15thC hotel with views of the cathedral's west front. Oak-panelled restaurant, log fires. Four-poster beds available.

★★

THE WHITE HART HOTEL
19-21 Sadler Street, Wells BA5 2RR
T: (01749) 672056
F: (01749) 671074
E: info@whitehart-wells.co.uk
I: www.whitehart-wells.co.uk

Bedrooms: 1 single,
11 double/twin, 1 triple/
multiple
Bathrooms: 13 en suite

Lunch available
Evening meal available
CC: Amex, Delta,
Mastercard, Switch, Visa

B&B per night:
S £63.00–£68.00
D £80.00–£90.00

HB per person:
DY £57.50–£75.00

OPEN All year round

15thC coaching hotel in city centre, opposite Wells Cathedral, offering comfortable accommodation and fine English food. Ideally located, family-run business.

QUALITY ASSURANCE SCHEME

Star ratings and awards were correct at the time of going to press but are subject to change. Please check at the time of booking.

WEST BEXINGTON, Dorset Map ref 2A3

★★ **THE MANOR HOTEL**

West Bexington, Dorchester
DT2 9DF
T: (01308) 897616 & 897785
F: (01308) 897035
E: themanorhotel@btconnect.com
I: www.themanorhotel.com

Bedrooms: 1 single,
11 double/twin, 1 triple/
multiple
Bathrooms: 13 en suite

Lunch available
Evening meal available
CC: Amex, Mastercard,
Switch, Visa

B&B per night:
S Max £60.00
D Max £100.00

HB per person:
DY Max £73.50

OPEN All year round

16thC manor house, 500 yards from Chesil Beach. Panoramic views from most bedrooms. Three real ales and character cellar bar.

WESTBURY, Wiltshire Map ref 2B2 *Tourist Information Centre Tel: (01373) 827158*

★★ **THE CEDAR HOTEL**

Warminster Road, Westbury
BA13 3PR
T: (01373) 822753
F: (01373) 858423
E: cedarwestbury@aol.com
I: www.cedarhotel.co.uk

Bedrooms: 1 single,
15 double/twin
Bathrooms: 16 en suite

Lunch available
Evening meal available
CC: Amex, Delta, Diners,
Mastercard, Switch, Visa

B&B per night:
S £55.00–£65.00
D £70.00–£85.00

HB per person:
DY £50.00–£60.00

OPEN All year round

CR
The Independents

18thC country house hotel with a friendly and relaxed atmosphere. Offering comfortable, well-appointed accommodation and good cuisine.

WESTON-SUPER-MARE, North Somerset Map ref 1D1 *Tourist Information Centre Tel: (01934) 888800*

★★ **AROSFA HOTEL**

Lower Church Road, Weston-super-
Mare BS23 2AG
T: (01934) 419523
F: (01934) 636084
E: info@arosfahotel.co.uk
I: www.arosfahotel.co.uk

Bedrooms: 14 single,
27 double/twin, 5 triple/
multiple
Bathrooms: 46 en suite

Lunch available
Evening meal available
CC: Amex, Delta, Diners,
Mastercard, Switch, Visa

B&B per night:
S £45.00–£55.00
D £65.00

HB per person:
DY £45.00–£70.00

OPEN All year round

Family hotel with 3 lounges, bars, dining room and comfortable bedrooms. Situated on level ground 100 yards from the town centre and seafront.

WEYMOUTH, Dorset Map ref 2B3 *Tourist Information Centre Tel: (01305) 785747*

★★

THE GLENBURN HOTEL

42 Preston Road, Weymouth DT3 6PZ
T: (01305) 832353
F: (01305) 835610
E: info@glenburnhotel.com
I: www.glenburnhotel.com

B&B per night:
S £33.00–£48.00
D £55.00–£75.00

HB per person:
DY £39.45–£49.45

OPEN All year round

Home from home. Very comfortable, family-run small hotel, refurbished, large garden. Quieter side of Weymouth. Excellent home-cooked fresh food, all diets catered for. Fully licensed, open to non-residents, outdoor spa pool, large free car park. All rooms en suite. Five minutes' walk to beach.

Bedrooms: 3 single,
8 double/twin, 2 triple/
multiple
Bathrooms: 13 en suite

Evening meal available
CC: Delta, Mastercard,
Switch, Visa

3 nights for the price of 2 half board Oct-Mar (excl Christmas and New Year).

CHECK THE MAPS

The colour maps at the front of this guide show all the cities, towns and villages for which you will find accommodation entries. Refer to the town index to find the page on which they are listed.

★★★

HOTEL REX

29 The Esplanade, Weymouth DT4 8DN
T: (01305) 760400
F: (01305) 760500
E: rex@kingshotels.f9.co.uk
I: www.kingshotel.co.uk

B&B per night:
S £50.00–£59.00
D £75.00–£102.00

OPEN All year round

Georgian townhouse situated on the Esplanade overlooking Weymouth Bay, adjacent to the harbour and town centre and close to the Pavilion. Easy access to beautiful Thomas Hardy Country. Portland and Chesil Beach with its Jurassic coastline is close by.

Bedrooms: 11 single, 15 double/twin, 5 triple/ multiple
Bathrooms: 31 en suite

Lunch available
Evening meal available
CC: Amex, Delta, Diners, Mastercard, Switch, Visa

★
Silver
Award

CROSSWAYS HOTEL

The Esplanade, Woolacombe EX34 7DJ
T: (01271) 870395
F: (01271) 870395
I: www.smoothhound.co.uk/hotels/ crossway.html

B&B per night:
S £25.00–£32.00
D £50.00–£64.00

HB per person:
DY £30.00–£37.00

Friendly, award-winning family-run hotel in quiet seafront position with superb views of Combesgate beach, Morte Point and Lundy Island. Surfing and swimming from the hotel which is surrounded by National Trust land. Personal service, menu choice, children and pets welcome. Why not find out why guests return year after year?

Bedrooms: 1 single, 5 double/twin, 3 triple/ multiple
Bathrooms: 6 en suite, 1 private

Lunch available
Evening meal available

★★★
Silver
Award

WATERSMEET HOTEL

Mortehoe, Woolacombe EX34 7EB
T: (01271) 870333
F: (01271) 870890
E: Info@watersmeethotel.co.uk
I: www.watersmeethotel.co.uk

B&B per night:
S £73.00–£112.00
D £116.00–£197.00

HB per person:
DY £01.00 £120.00

OPEN All year round

Watersmeet personifies the comfortable luxury of a country-house hotel. Gardens reach down to the sea and coast path, with nearby steps leading directly to the beach. All the bedrooms have sea views towards Hartland Point and Lundy Island. Tempting English and international dishes are served in the award-winning restaurant.

Bedrooms: 1 single, 19 double/twin, 2 triple/ multiple
Bathrooms: 22 en suite

Lunch available
Evening meal available
CC: Amex, Delta, Mastercard, Switch, Visa

IMPORTANT NOTE Information on accommodation listed in this guide has been supplied by the proprietors. As changes may occur you are advised to check details at the time of booking.

WOOLACOMBE continued

★★★
Silver
Award

WOOLACOMBE BAY HOTEL
South Street, Woolacombe
EX34 7BN
T: (01271) 870388
F: (01271) 870613
E: woolacombe.bayhotel@
btinternet.com
I: www.woolacombe-bay-hotel.co.
uk

Bedrooms: 38 double/
twin, 26 triple/multiple
Bathrooms: 64 en suite

Lunch available
Evening meal available
CC: Amex, Delta, Diners,
Mastercard, Switch, Visa

B&B per night:
S £35.00–£87.00
D £70.00–£174.00

HB per person:
DY £50.00–£113.00

OPEN mid Feb–Dec

Gracious hotel in 6 acres of gardens leading to the sea. With heated pools, squash, tennis, solarium, sauna, pitch and putt, short-mat bowling. Self-catering also available.

USE YOUR *i*s

There are more than 550 Tourist Information Centres throughout England offering friendly help with accommodation and holiday ideas as well as suggestions of places to visit and things to do. There may well be a centre in your home town which can help you before you set out. You'll find addresses in the local Phone Book.

A brief guide to the main Towns and Villages offering accommodation in the South West

BARWICK, SOMERSET - Village 2 miles south of Yeovil, with 13th C church. Four early 19th C follies in the surrounding area of Barwick Park.

BATH, BATH AND NORTH EAST SOMERSET - Georgian spa city beside the River Avon. Important Roman site with impressive reconstructed baths, uncovered in 19th C. Bath Abbey built on site of monastery where first king of England was crowned (AD 973). Fine architecture in mellow local stone. Pump Room and museums.

BIGBURY-ON-SEA, DEVON - Small resort on Bigbury Bay at the mouth of the River Avon. Wide sands, rugged cliffs. Burgh Island can be reached on foot at low tide.

BOVEY TRACEY, DEVON - Standing by the river just east of Dartmoor National Park, this old town has good moorland views. Its church, with a 14th C tower, holds one of Devon's finest medieval rood screens.

BRANSCOMBE, DEVON - Scattered village of unusual character. Houses of cob and thatch are sited irregularly on the steep wooded slopes of a combe, which widens towards the sea. Much of Branscombe Estate is National Trust property.

BRIDPORT, DORSET - Market town and chief producer of nets and ropes just inland of dramatic Dorset coast. Old, broad streets built for drying and twisting and long gardens for rope-walks. Grand arcaded Town Hall and Georgian buildings. Local history museum has Roman relics.

BRISTOL - Famous for maritime links, historic harbour, Georgian terraces and Brunel's Clifton suspension bridge. Many attractions including SS Great Britain, Bristol Zoo, museums and art galleries and top name entertainments. Events include Balloon Fiesta and Regatta.

BRIXHAM, DEVON - Famous for its trawling fleet in the 19th C, a steeply-built fishing port overlooking the harbour and fish market. A statue of William of Orange recalls his landing here before deposing James II. There is an aquarium and museum. Good cliff views and walks.

BUDE, CORNWALL - Resort on dramatic Atlantic coast. High cliffs give spectacular sea and inland views. Golf-course, cricket pitch, folly, surfing, coarse-fishing and boating. Mother-town Stratton was base of Royalist Sir Bevil Grenville.

CHARD, SOMERSET - Market town in hilly countryside. The wide main street has some handsome buildings, among them the Guildhall, court house and almshouses. Modern light industry and dairy produce have replaced 19th C lace making which came at decline of cloth trade.

CHIPPENHAM, WILTSHIRE - Ancient market town with modern industry. Notable early buildings include the medieval Town Hall and the gabled 15th C Yelde Hall, now a local history museum. On the outskirts Hardenhuish has a charming hilltop church by the Georgian architect John Wood of Bath.

CLOVELLY, DEVON - Clinging to wooded cliffs, fishing village with steep cobbled street zigzagging, or cut in steps, to harbour. Carrying sledges stand beside whitewashed flower-decked cottages. Charles Kingsley's father was rector of the church set high up near the Hamlyn family's Clovelly Court.

DARTMOUTH, DEVON - Ancient port at mouth of Dart. Has fine period buildings, notably town houses near Quay and Butterwalk of 1635. Harbour castle ruin. In 12th C Crusader fleets assembled here. Royal Naval College dominates from Hill. Carnival, June; Regatta, August.

DUNSTER, SOMERSET - Ancient town with views of Exmoor. The hilltop castle has been continuously occupied since 1070. Medieval prosperity from cloth built 16th C octagonal Yarn Market and the church. A riverside mill, packhorse bridge and 18th C hilltop folly occupy other interesting corners in the town.

EXETER, DEVON - University city rebuilt after the 1940s around its cathedral. Attractions include 13th C cathedral with fine west front; notable waterfront buildings; Guildhall; Royal Albert Memorial Museum; underground passages; Northcott Theatre.

EXMOUTH, DEVON - Developed as a seaside resort in George III's reign, set against the woods of the Exe Estuary and red cliffs of Orcombe Point. Extensive sands, small harbour, chapel and almshouses, a model railway and A la Ronde, a 16-sided house.

FALMOUTH, CORNWALL - Busy port and fishing harbour, popular resort on the balmy Cornish Riviera. Henry VIII's Pendennis Castle faces St Mawes Castle across the broad natural harbour and yacht basin Carrick Roads, which receives 7 rivers.

HOLFORD, SOMERSET - Sheltered in a wooded combe on the edge of the Quantocks, small village near Alfoxden House where William Wordsworth and his sister Dorothy lived in the late 1790s. Samuel Coleridge occupied a cottage at Nether Stowey during the same period. Nearby Quantock Forest has nature trails.

HOLSWORTHY, DEVON - Busy rural town and centre of a large farming community. Market day attracts many visitors.

HONITON, DEVON - Old coaching town in undulating farmland. Formerly famous for lace-making, it is now an antiques trade centre and market town. Small museum.

ILFRACOMBE, DEVON - Resort of Victorian grandeur set on hillside between cliffs with sandy coves. At the mouth of the harbour stands an 18th C lighthouse, built over a medieval chapel. There are fine formal gardens and a museum. Chambercombe Manor, an interesting old house, is nearby.

ILLOGAN, CORNWALL - Former mining village 2 miles north-west of Redruth and close to the coast. The Victorian engineer and benefactor, Sir Richard Tangye, was born here in 1833.

LANDS END, CORNWALL - The most westerly point of the English mainland, 8 miles south-west of Penzance. Spectacular cliffs with marvellous views. Exhibitions and multi-sensory Last Labyrinth Show.

MAP REFERENCES
Map references apply to the colour maps at the front of this guide.

LOOE, CORNWALL - Small resort developed around former fishing and smuggling ports occupying the deep estuary of the East and West Looe Rivers. Narrow winding streets, with old inns; museum and art gallery are housed in interesting old buildings. Shark fishing centre, boat trips; busy harbour.

LOSTWITHIEL, CORNWALL - Cornwall's ancient capital which gained its Royal Charter in 1189. Tin from the mines around the town was smelted and coined in the Duchy Palace. Norman Restormel Castle, with its circular keep and deep moat, overlooks the town.

LYDFORD, DEVON - Former important tin mining centre, a small village on edge of West Dartmoor. Remains of Norman castle where all falling foul of tinners' notorious 'Lydford Law' were incarcerated. Bridge crosses River Lyd where it rushes through a mile-long gorge of boulders and trees.

LYNMOUTH, DEVON - Resort set beneath bracken-covered cliffs and pinewood gorges where 2 rivers meet, and cascade between boulders to the town. Lynton, set on cliffs above, can be reached by water-operated cliff railway from the Victorian esplanade. Valley of the Rocks, to the west, gives dramatic walks.

LYNTON, DEVON - Hilltop resort on Exmoor coast linked to its seaside twin, Lynmouth, by a water-operated cliff railway which descends from the town hall. Spectacular surroundings of moorland cliffs with steep chasms of conifer and rocks through which rivers cascade.

M MALMESBURY, WILTSHIRE - Overlooking the River Avon, an old town dominated by its great church, once a Benedictine abbey. The surviving Norman nave and porch are noted for fine sculptures, 12th C arches and musicians' gallery.

MANACCAN, CORNWALL - Village 7 miles east of Helston at the inner end of Gillan Harbour. The Norman church is largely built of Cornish granite.

MAWGAN PORTH, CORNWALL - Holiday village occupying a steep valley on the popular coastal route to Newquay. Golden sands, rugged cliffs and coves. Nearby Bedruthan Steps offers exhilarating cliff walks and views. The chapel of a Carmelite nunnery, once the home of the Arundells, may be visited.

MELKSHAM, WILTSHIRE - Small industrial town standing on the banks of the River Avon. Old weavers' cottages and Regency houses are grouped around the attractive church which has traces of Norman work. The 18th C Round House, once used for dyeing fleeces, is now a craft centre.

MEVAGISSEY, CORNWALL - Small fishing town, a favourite with holidaymakers. Earlier prosperity came from pilchard fisheries, boat-building and smuggling. By the harbour are fish cellars, some converted, and a local history museum is housed in an old boat-building shed. Handsome Methodist chapel; shark fishing, sailing.

MINEHEAD, SOMERSET - Victorian resort with spreading sands developed around old fishing port on the coast below Exmoor. Former fishermen's cottages stand beside the 17th C harbour; cobbled streets climb the hill in steps to the church. Boat trips, steam railway. Hobby Horse festival 1 May.

MORETONHAMPSTEAD, DEVON - Small market town with a row of 17th C almshouses standing on the Exeter road. Surrounding moorland is scattered with ancient farmhouses, prehistoric sites.

N NEWQUAY, CORNWALL - Popular resort spread over dramatic cliffs around its old fishing port. Many beaches with abundant sands, caves and rock pools; excellent surf. Pilots' gigs are still raced from the harbour and on the headland stands the stone Huer's House from the pilchard-fishing days.

O OKEHAMPTON, DEVON - Busy market town near the high tors of northern Dartmoor. The Victorian church, with William Morris windows and a 15th C tower, stands on the site of a Saxon church. A Norman castle ruin overlooks the river to the west of the town. Museum of Dartmoor Life in a restored mill.

P PAIGNTON, DEVON - Lively seaside resort with a pretty harbour on Torbay. Bronze Age and Saxon sites are occupied by the 15th C church, which has a Norman door and font. The beautiful Chantry Chapel was built by local landowners, the Kirkhams.

PENZANCE, CORNWALL - Resort and fishing port on Mount's Bay with mainly Victorian promenade and some fine Regency terraces. Former prosperity came from tin trade and pilchard fishing. Grand Georgian style church by harbour. Georgian Egyptian building at head of Chapel Street and Morrab Gardens.

PLYMOUTH, DEVON - Devon's largest city, major port and naval base. Old houses on the Barbican and ambitious architecture in modern centre, with new National Marine Aquarium, museum and art gallery, the Dome - a heritage centre on the Hoe. Superb coastal views over Plymouth Sound from the Hoe.

PORLOCK, SOMERSET - Village set between steep Exmoor hills and the sea at the head of beautiful Porlock Vale. The narrow street shows a medley of building styles. South-westward is Porlock Weir with its old houses and tiny harbour and further along the shore at Culbone is England's smallest church.

R RUAN HIGH LANES, CORNWALL - Village at the northern end of the Roseland Peninsula.

S SALISBURY, WILTSHIRE - Beautiful city and ancient regional capital set amid water meadows. Buildings of all periods are dominated by the cathedral whose spire is the tallest in England. Built between 1220 and 1258, it is one of the purest examples of Early English architecture.

SHALDON, DEVON - Pretty resort facing Teignmouth from the south bank of the Teign Estuary. Regency houses harmonise with others of later periods; there are old cottages and narrow lanes. On the Ness, a sandstone promontory nearby, a tunnel built in the 19th C leads to a beach revealed at low tide.

SHEPTON MALLET, SOMERSET - Historic town in the Mendip foothills, important in Roman times and site of many significant archaeological finds. Cloth industry reached its peak in the 17th C, and many fine examples of cloth merchants' houses remain. Beautiful parish church, market cross, local history museum, Collett Park.

SIDMOUTH, DEVON - Charming resort set amid lofty red cliffs where the River Sid meets the sea. The wealth of ornate Regency and Victorian villas recalls the time when this was one of the south coast's most exclusive resorts. Museum; August International Festival of Folk Arts.

SOURTON, DEVON - Village on the edge of Dartmoor National Park, on A386 between Okehampton and Tavistock. Acclaimed village pub.

ST AGNES, CORNWALL - Small town in a once-rich mining area on the north coast. Terraced cottages and granite houses slope to the church. Some old mine workings remain, but the attraction must be the magnificent coastal scenery and superb walks. St Agnes Beacon offers one of Cornwall's most extensive views.

ST AUSTELL, CORNWALL - Leading market town, the meeting point of old and new Cornwall. One mile from St Austell Bay with its sandy beaches, old fishing villages and attractive countryside. Ancient narrow streets, pedestrian shopping precincts. Fine church of Pentewan stone and Italiante Town Hall.

SYMBOLS The symbols in each entry give information about services and facilities. A key to these symbols appears at the back of this guide.

STREET, SOMERSET - Busy shoe-making town set beneath the Polden Hills. A museum at the factory, which was developed with the rest of the town in the 19th C, can be visited. Just south, the National Trust has care of woodland on Ivythorn Hill which gives wide views northward. Factory shopping village.

SWINDON, WILTSHIRE - Wiltshire's industrial and commercial centre, an important railway town in the 19th C, situated just north of the Marlborough Downs. The railway village created in the mid-19th C has been preserved. Railway museum, art gallery, theatre and leisure centre. Designer shopping village.

TINTAGEL, CORNWALL - Coastal village near the legendary home of King Arthur. There is a lofty headland with the ruin of a Norman castle and traces of a Celtic monastery are still visible in the turf.

TORPOINT, CORNWALL - Town beside the part of the Tamar Estuary known as the Hamoaze, linked by car ferry to Devonport. The fine 18th C Anthony House (National Trust) is noted for its 19th C portico.

TORQUAY, DEVON - Devon's grandest resort, developed from a fishing village. Smart apartments and terraces rise from the seafront and Marine Drive, along the headland, gives views of beaches and colourful cliffs.

TOTNES, DEVON - Old market town steeply built near the head of the Dart Estuary. Remains of motte and bailey castle, medieval gateways, a noble church, 16th C Guildhall and medley of period houses recall former wealth from cloth and shipping, continued in rural and water industries.

TRURO, CORNWALL - Cornwall's administrative centre and cathedral city, set at the head of Truro River on the Fal Estuary. A medieval stannary town, it handled mineral ore from west Cornwall; fine Georgian buildings recall its heyday as a society haunt in the second mining boom.

WATCHET, SOMERSET - Small port on Bridgwater Bay, sheltered by the Quantocks and the Brendon Hills. A thriving paper industry keeps the harbour busy; in the 19th C it handled iron from the Brendon Hills. Cleeve Abbey, a ruined Cistercian monastery, is 3 miles to the south-west.

WATERGATE BAY, CORNWALL - Beautiful long board-riders' beach backed by tall cliffs, north-west of Newquay. A small holiday village nestles in a steep river valley making a cleft in the cliffs.

WELLS, SOMERSET - Small city set beneath the southern slopes of the Mendips. Built between 1180 and 1424, the magnificent cathedral is preserved in much of its original glory and with its ancient precincts forms one of our loveliest and most unified groups of medieval buildings.

WEST BEXINGTON, DORSET - Village on the stretch of Dorset coast known as Chesil Beach. Close to the famous Abbotsbury Sub-tropical Gardens and Swannery.

WESTBURY, WILTSHIRE - Wiltshire's best-known white horse looks down on the town with its Georgian houses around the Market Place. Handsome Perpendicular church with fine carved chancel screen and stone reredos. Above the white horse are the prehistoric earthworks of Bratton Castle.

WESTON-SUPER-MARE, NORTH SOMERSET - Large, friendly resort developed in the 19th C. Traditional seaside attractions include theatres and a dance hall. The museum has a Victorian seaside gallery and Iron Age finds from a hill fort on Worlebury Hill in Weston Woods.

WEYMOUTH, DORSET - Ancient port and one of the south's earliest resorts. Curving beside a long, sandy beach, the elegant Georgian esplanade is graced with a statue of George III and a cheerful Victorian Jubilee clock tower. Museum, Sea-Life Centre.

WOOLACOMBE, DEVON - Between Morte Point and Baggy Point, Woolacombe and Mortehoe offer 3 miles of the finest sand and surf on this outstanding coastline. Much of the area is owned by the National Trust.

Welcome Host

Welcome Host is a nationally recognised customer care initiative, sponsored in England by the English Tourism Council. When visiting accommodation in this guide you may find this sign on display. It demonstrates commitment to courtesy and service and an aim to provide high standards of service and a warm welcome for all visitors.

SOUTH of England

A seafaring region with 800 years of nautical heritage to enjoy in its busy harbours and family resorts. For landlubbers there's gentle countryside, Georgian towns, modern cities and outstanding historic houses too.

classic sights

Blenheim Palace – a gilded Italian palace in an English park
Oxford – University town with ancient colleges
Claydon House – unusual interiors in the Rococo, Gothick and Chinoiserie styles

coast & country

Chiltern Hills – tranquil country walks
New Forest – historic wood and heathland
Studland Bay – glorious sweeping beach

glorious gardens

Cliveden – a series of distinctive and delightful gardens
Mottisfont Abbey – the perfect English rose garden

maritime history

Portsmouth Historic Dockyard – Henry VIII's Mary Rose, HMS Victory and HMS Warrior

distinctively different

Sandham Memorial Chapel – houses Stanley Spencer's WW1 murals

The counties of Berkshire, Buckinghamshire, Dorset (Eastern), Hampshire, Isle of Wight and Oxfordshire

FOR MORE INFORMATION CONTACT:
Southern Tourist Board
40 Chamberlayne Road, Eastleigh,
Hampshire SO50 5JH
Tel: (023) 8062 5505 Fax: (023) 8062 0010
Email: info@southerntb.co.uk
Internet: www.visitbritain.com

The Pictures:
1 Freshwater Bay, Isle of Wight
2 Radcliffe Camera, Oxford
3 Lulworth Cove, Dorset

Places to Visit - see pages 242-245
Where to Stay - see pages 246-268

PLACES to visit

You will find hundreds of interesting places to visit during your stay, just some of which are listed in these pages. Contact any Tourist Information Centre in the region for more ideas on days out.

Beaulieu National Motor Museum

Beaulieu, Brockenhurst, Hampshire SO42 7ZN
Tel: (01590) 612345 www.beaulieu.co.uk
Motor museum with over 250 exhibits showing the history of motoring from 1896. Also Palace House, Wheels Experience, Beaulieu Abbey ruins and a display of monastic life.

Bekonscot Model Village

Warwick Road, Beaconsfield, Buckinghamshire HP9 2PL
Tel: (01494) 672919 www.bekonscot.org.uk
The oldest model village in the world, Bekonscot depicts rural England in the 1930s, where time has stood still for 70 years.

Blenheim Palace

Woodstock, Oxfordshire OX20 1PX
Tel: (01993) 811325 www.blenheimpalace.com
Home of the 11th Duke of Marlborough. Birthplace of Sir Winston Churchill. Designed by Vanbrugh in the English baroque style. Landscaped by `Capability' Brown.

Breamore House

Breamore, Fordingbridge, Hampshire SP6 2DF
Tel: (01725) 512233
Elizabethan manor house of 1583, with fine collection of works of art. Furniture, tapestries, needlework, paintings mainly 17thC and 18thC Dutch School.

Broughton Castle

Banbury, Oxfordshire OX15 5EB
Tel: (01295) 276070
Medieval moated house built in 1300 and enlarged between 1550 and 1600. The home of Lord and Lady Saye and Sele and family home for 600 years. Has Civil War connections.

Buckinghamshire County Museum

Church Street, Aylesbury, Buckinghamshire HP20 2QP
Tel: (01296) 331441
www.buckscc.gov.uk/tourism/museum
Lively hands-on, innovative museum complex consisting of county heritage displays, regional art gallery and Roald Dahl Children's Gallery in lovely garden setting.

Carisbrooke Castle

Newport, Isle of Wight PO30 1XY
Tel: (01983) 522107 www.english-heritage.org.uk
A splendid Norman castle where Charles I was imprisoned. The governor's lodge houses the county museum. Wheelhouse with wheel operated by donkeys.

Compton Acres

Canford Cliffs Road, Canford Cliffs,
Poole, Dorset BH13 7ES
Tel: (01202) 700778 www.comptonacres.co.uk
Ten separate and distinct gardens of the world. The gardens include Italian, Japanese, Indian glen and Spanish water garden. Country crafts and 'Off the Beaten Track Trail'.

Cotswold Wildlife Park

Bradwell Grove, Burford, Oxford, Oxfordshire OX18 4JW
Tel: (01993) 823006
Wildlife park in 200 acres (81 ha) of gardens and woodland with a variety of animals from all over the world.

The D Day Museum and Overlord Embroidery

Clarence Esplanade, Portsmouth, Hampshire PO5 3NT
Tel: (023) 9282 7261
www.portsmouthmuseums.co.uk
The magnificent 272 ft- (83 m-) long 'Overlord Embroidery' depicts the allied invasion of Normandy on 6 June 1944. Sound guides available in 4 languages.

Dicot Railway Centre

Great Western Society, Didcot, Oxfordshire OX11 7NJ
Tel: (01235) 817200
www.didcotrailwaycentre.org.uk
Living museum recreating the golden age of the Great Western Railway. Steam locomotives and trains, engine shed and small relics museum.

Exbury Gardens

Exbury Estate Office, Exbury, Southampton, Hampshire SO45 1AZ
Tel: (023) 8089 1203 www.exbury.co.uk.
Over 200 acres (81 ha) of woodland garden, including the Rothschild collection of rhododendrons, azaleas, camellias and magnolias.

Flagship Portsmouth

Porter's Lodge, 1/7 College Road, HM Naval Base, Portsmouth, Hampshire PO1 3LJ
Tel: (023) 9286 1533 www.flagship.org.uk
The world's greatest historic ships: Mary Rose, HMS Victory, HMS Warrior 1860. Royal Naval Museum, 'Warships by Water' tours, Dockyard Apprentice exhibition.

Gilbert White's House and Garden and The Oats Museum

The Wakes, High Street, Selborne, Alton, Hampshire GU34 3JH
Tel: (01420) 511275
Historic house and garden, home of Gilbert White, author of 'The Natural History of Selborne'. Exhibition on Frank Oates, explorer, and Captain Lawrence Oates of Antarctica fame.

The Hawk Conservancy and Country Park

Andover, Hampshire SP11 8DY
Tel: (01264) 772252 www.hawk-conservancy.org
Unique to Great Britain – `Valley of the Eagles' held here daily at 1400.

Jane Austen's House

Chawton, Alton, Hampshire GU34 1SD
Tel: (01420) 83262
A 17thC house where Jane Austen lived from 1809-1817 and wrote or revised her six great novels. Letters, pictures, memorabilia, garden with old-fashioned flowers.

Kingston Lacy

Wimborne Minster, Dorset BH21 4EA
Tel: (01202) 883402 www.nationaltrust.org.uk
A 17thC house designed for Sir Ralph Bankes by Sir Roger Pratt, altered by Sir Charles Barry in the19thC. Collection of paintings, 250-acre (101-ha) wooded park, herd of Devon cattle.

Legoland Windsor

Winkfield Road, Windsor, Berkshire SL4 4AY
Tel: (0870) 504 0404 www.legoland.co.uk
A family park with hands-on activities, rides, themed playscapes and more Lego bricks than you ever dreamed possible!

The Pictures:
1 Blenheim Palace, Oxfordshire
2 HMS Victory, Portsmouth
3 Deer at Bolderwood, New Forest
4 Poole, Dorset
5 Oxford
6 Swan Green, New Forest

The Living Rainforest

Hampstead Norreys, Newbury, Berkshire RG18 0TN
Tel: (01635) 202444 www.livingrainforest.org
Two tropical rainforests, all under cover, approximately 20,000 sq ft (1,858 sq m). Collection of rare and exotic tropical plants together with small representation of wildlife in rainforest.

Manor Farm (Farm and Museum)

Manor Farm Country Park, Pylands Lane, Bursledon, Southampton, Hampshire SO30 2ER
Tel: (01489) 787055
www.hants.gov.uk/countryside/manorfarm
Traditional Hampshire farmstead with range of buildings, farm animals, machinery and equipment, pre-1950s farmhouse and 13thC church set for 1900.
Living history site.

Marwell Zoological Park

Colden Common, Winchester, Hampshire SO21 1JH
Tel: (01962) 777407
Set in 100 acres (40.5 ha) of parkland surrounding Marwell Hall. Venue suitable for all age groups including disabled.

Oceanarium

Pier Approach, West Beach, Bournemouth, Dorset BH2 5AA
Tel: (01202) 311993 www.oceanarium.co.uk
Situated in the heart of Bournemouth next to the pier, the Oceanarium will take you on a fascinating voyage of the undersea world with creatures such as elegant seahorses and sinister sharks.

Osborne House

Yorke Avenue, East Cowes, Isle of Wight PO32 6JY
Tel: (01983) 200022 www.english-heritage.com
Queen Victoria and Prince Albert's seaside holiday home. Swiss Cottage where royal children learnt cooking and gardening. Victorian carriage service to Swiss Cottage.

The Oxford Story

6 Broad Street, Oxford, Oxfordshire OX1 3AJ
Tel: (01865) 728822 www.heritageattractions.co.uk
An excellent introduction to Oxford – experience 900 years of University history in one hour. From scientists to poets, astronomers to comedians.

Paultons Park

Ower, Romsey, Hampshire SO51 6AL
Tel: (023) 8081 4442
A full day out for all the family with over 40 attractions. Rides, play areas, entertainments, museums, birds and animals, beautiful gardens and lots more.

River and Rowing Museum

Mill Meadows, Henley-on-Thames, Oxfordshire RG9 1BF
Tel: (01491) 415600 www.rrm.co.uk
A unique, award-winning museum with galleries dedicated to rowing, the River Thames and the town of Henley. Special exhibitions run throughout the year.

Royal Navy Submarine Museum and HMS Alliance

Haslar Jetty Road, Gosport, Hampshire PO12 2AS
Tel: (023) 9252 9217 www.rnsubmus.co.uk
HM Submarine Alliance, HM Submarine No 1 (Holland 1), midget submarines and models of every type of submarine from earliest days to present nuclear age.

Swanage Railway

Station House, Swanage, Dorset BH19 1HB
Tel: (01929) 425800 www.swanrail.demon.co.uk
Enjoy a nostalgic steam train ride on the Purbeck line. Steam trains run every weekend throughout the year with daily running from April to October.

The Vyne

Sherborne St John, Basingstoke, Hampshire RG24 9HL
Tel: (01256) 881337 www.nationaltrust.org.uk
Original house dating back to Henry VIII's time. Extensively altered in the mid 17thC. Tudor chapel, beautiful gardens and lake.

Waterperry Gardens

Waterperry, Oxford, Oxfordshire OX33 1JZ
Tel: (01844) 339254 www.waterperrygardens.co.uk
Ornamental gardens covering six acres (2 ha) of the 83-acre (33.5-ha) 18thC Waterperry House estate. Saxon village church, garden shop, teashop and art and craft gallery.

Whitchurch Silk Mill

28 Winchester Street, Whitchurch, Hampshire RG28 7AL
Tel: (01256) 892065
Unique Georgian silk-weaving watermill, now a working museum producing fine silk fabrics on Victorian machinery. Riverside garden, tearooms for light meals, silk gift shop.

Windsor Castle

Windsor, Berkshire SL4 1NJ
Tel: (01753) 869898 www.royal.gov.uk
Official residence of HM The Queen and royal residence for 9 centuries. State apartments, Queen Mary's Doll's House.

Find out more about the
SOUTH of England

Further information about holidays and attractions in the South of England is available from:

SOUTHERN TOURIST BOARD
40 Chamberlayne Road, Eastleigh, Hampshire SO50 5JH.
Tel: (023) 8062 5505 Fax: (023) 8062 0010
Email: info@southerntb.co.uk
Internet: www.visitbritain.com

Getting to the
SOUTH of England

BY ROAD: A good road network links London and the rest of the UK with major Southern destinations. The M27 provides a near continuous motorway route along the south coast and the M25/M3/A33 provides a direct route from London to Winchester and Southampton. The scenic A31 stretches from London, through Hampshire and to mid Dorset, whilst the M40/A34 have considerably cut travelling times from the West Midlands to the South. The M25 has speeded up access to Berkshire on the M4, Buckinghamshire and Oxfordshire on the M40.

BY RAIL: From London's Waterloo, trains travel to Portsmouth, Southampton and Bournemouth approximately three times an hour. From these stations, frequent trains go to Poole, Salisbury and Winchester. Further information on rail journeys in the South of England can be obtained from 08457 484950.

The Pictures:
1 River Isis, Oxford
2 Alum Bay, Isle of Wight

Where to stay in the South of England

Accommodation entries in this region are listed in alphabetical order of place name, and then in alphabetical order of establishment.

Map references refer to the colour location maps at front of this guide. The first number indicates the map to use; the letter and number which follow refer to the grid reference on the map.

At-a-glance symbols at the end of each accommodation entry give useful information about services and facilities. A key to symbols can be found inside the back cover flap. Keep this open for easy reference.

A brief description of the towns and villages offering accommodation in the entries which follow, can be found at the end of this section.

A complete listing of all the English Tourism Council assessed accommodation covered by this guide appears at the back of the guide.

ALTON, Hampshire Map ref 2C2 *Tourist Information Centre Tel: (01420) 88448*

★★★ **ALTON GRANGE HOTEL & RESTAURANT**
London Road, Alton GU34 4EG
T: (01420) 86565
F: (01420) 541346
E: info@altongrange.co.uk
I: www.altongrange.co.uk

Bedrooms: 10 single, 17 double/twin, 2 triple/ multiple; suites available
Bathrooms: 29 en suite

Lunch available
Evening meal available
CC: Amex, Delta, Diners, Mastercard, Switch, Visa

B&B per night:
S £79.00–£97.00
D £97.00–£160.00

HB per person:
DY £76.00–£106.50

OPEN All year round

Privately-run country house-style hotel, set in 2 acres, with 'Truffles' restaurant for award-winning cuisine and fine wines. Executive rooms to the highest luxury standard.

AYLESBURY, Buckinghamshire Map ref 2C1 *Tourist Information Centre Tel: (01296) 330559*

★★ **WEST LODGE HOTEL**
45 London Road, Aston Clinton,
Aylesbury HP22 5HL
T: (01296) 630331 & 630362
F: (01296) 630151
E: jb@westlodge.co.uk
I: www.westlodge.co.uk

Bedrooms: 2 single, 4 double/twin
Bathrooms: 6 en suite

Evening meal available
CC: Amex, Delta, Mastercard, Switch, Visa

B&B per night:
S £50.00–£55.00
D £70.00

OPEN All year round

Victorian elegance in individually styled bedrooms with all modern comforts. Picturesque water garden, indoor pool, sauna, hot-air balloon trips. Fifty minutes London/Heathrow.

CENTRAL RESERVATIONS OFFICES
The symbol **CR** and a group name in an entry indicate that bookings can be made through a central reservations office. These are listed in a separate section towards the back of this guide.

BASINGSTOKE, Hampshire Map ref 2C2 *Tourist Information Centre Tel: (01256) 817618*

★★★
Silver Award

HAMPSHIRE CENTRECOURT
Centre Drive, Chineham,
Basingstoke RG24 8FY
T: (01256) 816664
F: (01256) 816727
E: hampshirec@marstonhotels.com
I: www.marstonhotels.com

Bedrooms: 50 double/twin
Bathrooms: 50 en suite

Lunch available
Evening meal available
CC: Amex, Delta, Diners, Mastercard, Switch, Visa

B&B per night:
S £115.00–£135.00
D £125.00–£155.00

HB per person:
DY £59.50–£85.00

OPEN All year round

(CR)
Marston Hotels

Superb purpose-built tennis centre, including 5 indoor and 5 outdoor tennis courts, indoor pool, spa bath, steam room, sauna and gym. Half-board rate based on minimum 2 nights.

★★★

RED LION HOTEL
24 London Street, Basingstoke RG21 7NY
T: (01256) 328525
F: (01256) 844056
E: redlion@msihotels.co.uk
I: www.msihotels.co.uk

B&B per night:
S £47.50–£105.00
D £65.00–£120.00

OPEN All year round

The Red Lion Hotel is in the heart of Basingstoke town centre. The hotel offers high levels of service and comfort in settings full of character and charm, making it the ideal venue for a relaxing stay, either for business or leisure guests. With friendly staff and a first class service, who could ask for more?

Bedrooms: 18 single, 39 double/twin, 2 triple/multiple; suites available
Bathrooms: 59 en suite

Lunch available
Evening meal available
CC: Amex, Diners, Mastercard, Switch, Visa

BEMBRIDGE, Isle of Wight Map ref 2C3

★★★

BEMBRIDGE COAST HOTEL
Fishermans Walk, Bembridge
PO35 5TH
T: (01983) 873931
F: (01983) 874693
I: www.warnerholidays.co.uk

Bedrooms: 17 single, 217 double/twin; suites available
Bathrooms: 234 en suite

Lunch available
Evening meal available
CC: Delta, Mastercard, Switch, Visa

B&B per night:
S £50.00–£95.00
D £100.00–£145.00

OPEN All year round

Bembridge Coast hotel is set in 23 acres of colourful grounds and gardens edged by superb views over the Solent. Part of Warner Holidays that offer leisure breaks just for adults.

BLANDFORD FORUM, Dorset Map ref 2B3 *Tourist Information Centre Tel: (01258) 454770*

★★

ANVIL HOTEL & RESTAURANT
Salisbury Road, Pimperne,
Blandford Forum DT11 8UQ
T: (01258) 453431 & 480182
F: (01258) 480182
E: theanvil@euphony.net

Bedrooms: 1 single, 9 double/twin, 1 triple/multiple
Bathrooms: 11 en suite

Lunch available
Evening meal available
CC: Amex, Delta, Diners, Mastercard, Switch, Visa

B&B per night:
S £50.00–£55.00
D £75.00–£90.00

OPEN All year round

Picturesque 16thC thatched hotel. Beamed a la carte restaurant, log fire, mouth-watering menu, delicious desserts. Tasty bar meals and specials cooked from fresh, fine food.

BOURNEMOUTH, Dorset Map ref 2B3

★★★

BELVEDERE HOTEL
Bath Road, Bournemouth BH1 2EU
T: (01202) 297556 & 293336
F: (01202) 294699
E: Belvedere_Hotel@msn.com
I: www.belvedere-hotel.co.uk

Bedrooms: 11 single, 38 double/twin, 12 triple/multiple
Bathrooms: 61 en suite

Lunch available
Evening meal available
CC: Amex, Delta, Diners, Mastercard, Switch, Visa

B&B per night:
S £43.00–£69.00
D £68.00–£104.00

HB per person:
DY £47.00–£52.00

OPEN All year round

Centrally located with a large car park. Superb food and friendly service. Ideal for both business and holidays, offering high standards all round. Group rates available on request.

CONFIRM YOUR BOOKING
You are advised to confirm your booking in writing.

BOURNEMOUTH continued

★★★

CLIFFESIDE HOTEL
East Overcliff Drive, Bournemouth
BH1 3AQ
T: (01202) 555724
F: (01202) 314534
I: www.arthuryoung.co.uk

Bedrooms: 7 single,
50 double/twin, 4 triple/
multiple
Bathrooms: 61 en suite

Lunch available
Evening meal available
CC: Amex, Delta, Diners,
Mastercard, Switch, Visa

B&B per night:
S £49.00–£64.00
D £98.00–£128.00

HB per person:
DY £57.50–£72.50

OPEN All year round

On East Cliff with views to the Isle of Wight and the Purbeck Hills. Within easy reach of the town centre.

🅰🐕♿&🖼🖥📞♨🎱🚻◐❄📶🖥💻🍴♻️🍽☓🔍⛵▶🏇🐾🅿

★★★
Silver
Award

THE CONNAUGHT HOTEL
West Hill Road, West Cliff, Bournemouth
BH2 5PH
T: (01202) 298020
F: (01202) 298028
E: sales@theconnaught.co.uk
I: www.theconnaught.co.uk

Superbly presented hotel, centrally located to town centre, BIC, pier and sandy beaches. Magnificent indoor leisure centre with large swimming pool, spa, saunas, steam rooms, gym and games room. Attractive en suite bedrooms, some with balconies. Good food and wine. Unique blend of traditional good service and modern facilities.

Bedrooms: 9 single,
37 double/twin,
11 triple/multiple; suites
available
Bathrooms: 57 en suite

Lunch available
Evening meal available
CC: Amex, Delta, Diners,
Mastercard, Switch, Visa

Three nights for price of 2–Oct–Mar.

B&B per night:
S £40.00–£59.00
D £80.00–£118.00

HB per person:
DY £46.00–£69.00

OPEN All year round

🆑
Best Western Hotels

🅰🐕♿&🖼🖥📞♨🎱🚻◐❄📶🖥💻⊖♻️🍽☓🔍⛵▶❄🏇🐾🅿

★★

THE COTTAGE PRIVATE HOTEL
12 Southern Road, Southbourne,
Bournemouth BH6 3SR
T: (01202) 422764
F: (01202) 381442
E: ron+val@rjvhalliwell.force9.co.uk
I: www.smoothound.co.uk/hotels/cottage3.html

Charming, character, family-run licensed private hotel in restful location near Blue Flag beach yet convenient for the New Forest and Dorset countryside. Noted for home-prepared fresh cooking, cleanliness and tastefully furnished accommodation. Totally non-smoking. Minimum age children 12 years. Acclaimed for award-winning floral displays.

Bedrooms: 4 double/
twin, 2 triple/multiple
Bathrooms: 4 en suite,
2 private

Evening meal available

Stay for a week, pay for 6 days. Also senior citizens 5% discount on spring and autumn 2-week stays.

B&B per night:
S £25.50–£38.50
D £45.00–£59.00

HB per person:
DY £35.00–£48.00

🅰🐕12♿&🖼🖥📞♨🎱🚻◐📶🖥💻♻️❄🚗🅿

★★★

CUMBERLAND HOTEL
East Overcliff Drive, Bournemouth
BH1 3AF
T: (01202) 290722
F: (01202) 311394
E: cumberland@arthuryoung.co.uk
I: www.arthuryoung.co.uk

Bedrooms: 12 single,
78 double/twin,
12 triple/multiple; suites
available
Bathrooms: 102 en suite

Lunch available
Evening meal available
CC: Delta, Mastercard,
Switch, Visa

B&B per night:
S £39.50–£64.00
D £75.00–£128.00

HB per person:
DY £49.50–£75.00

OPEN All year round

Family hotel on East Cliff overlooking the bay and offering a high standard of service and cuisine for all ages. Complimentary use of nearby indoor leisure facility.

🅰🐕♿&🖼🖥📞♨🎱🚻◐❄📶🖥💻♻️🍴⛵▶❄🏇🐾🎰🅿

CREDIT CARD BOOKINGS
If you book by telephone and are asked for your credit card number it is advisable to check the proprietor's policy should you cancel your reservation.

★★★

Childhood home of comedian Tony Hancock, and flagship of privately owned Seaviews Hotel Group. Friendly, proficient staff provide all the personal touches to make your stay memorable. 55 tastefully decorated en suite bedrooms complete with tea/coffee-making facilities and remote controlled TV. Lounges, restaurant, pool, small health suite including jacuzzi and sauna.

DURLSTON COURT HOTEL

47 Gervis Road, East Cliff, Bournemouth
BH1 3DD
T: (01202) 316316
F: (01202) 316999
E: dch@seaviews.co.uk
I: www.seaviews.co.uk

Bedrooms: 8 single, 37 double/twin, 11 triple/multiple Bathrooms: 56 en suite	Lunch available Evening meal available CC: Delta, Mastercard, Switch, Visa

All year special discounted rates for 3 nights or more.

B&B per night:
S £26.50–£41.00
D £53.00–£82.00

HB per person:
DY £37.00–£51.50

OPEN All year round

★★

FIRCROFT HOTEL
Owls Road, Bournemouth BH5 1AE
T: (01202) 309771
F: (01202) 395644
E: info@fircroft.co.uk
I: www.fircrofthotel.co.uk

Bedrooms: 6 single, 27 double/twin, 19 triple/multiple Bathrooms: 52 en suite	Lunch available Evening meal available CC: Amex, Delta, Diners, Mastercard, Switch, Visa

Long-established family hotel, close to sea and comprehensive shopping. Free entry to hotel-owned sports and leisure club 9am – 6pm. Licensed, entertainment in season.

B&B per night:
S £25.00–£31.00
D £50.00–£62.00

HB per person:
DY £36.00–£40.00

OPEN All year round

★★

KENSINGTON HOTEL
18 Durley Chine Road, West Cliff,
Bournemouth BH2 5LE
T: (01202) 557434
F: (01202) 290562
E: kensington18@aol.com
I: www.plu44.com/o/kensington/

Bedrooms: 4 single, 12 double/twin, 10 triple/multiple Bathrooms: 26 en suite	Lunch available Evening meal available CC: Delta, Mastercard, Switch, Visa

Family-owned hotel on Westcliff. Close to beach and shops. High standard of food and cleanliness, car park. Warm welcome awaits.

B&B per night:
S £26.00–£31.00
D £52.00–£62.00

HB per person:
DY £30.00–£35.00

OPEN All year round

★★

KIWI HOTEL
West Hill Road, Bournemouth
BH2 5EG
T: (01202) 555889
F: (01202) 789567
E: kiwihotel@aol.com
I: www.kiwihotel.co.uk

Bedrooms: 7 single, 22 double/twin, 17 triple/multiple Bathrooms: 46 en suite	Evening meal available CC: Amex, Delta, Mastercard, Switch, Visa

Family-run hotel, 100 metres from seafront and a few minutes from town centre. Excellent service and menus. Children welcome. Licensed. Parking.

B&B per night:
S £22.00–£35.00
D £44.00–£70.00

HB per person:
DY £27.00–£39.00

OPEN All year round

AT-A-GLANCE SYMBOLS

Symbols at the end of each accommodation entry give useful information about services and facilities. A key to symbols can be found inside the back cover flap. Keep this open for easy reference.

BOURNEMOUTH continued

★★★

MARSHAM COURT HOTEL

Russell-Cotes Road, East Cliff,
Bournemouth BH1 3AB
T: (01202) 552111
F: (01202) 294744
E: reservations@marshamcourt.co.uk
I: www.marshamcourt.com

B&B per night:
S £45.00–£65.00
D £80.00–£110.00

HB per person:
DY £40.00–£70.00

OPEN All year round

Located in a central yet secluded position with magnificent bay views. Heated outdoor swimming pool, sun terraces. Beautifully decorated bedrooms with all amenities. Our restaurant offers superb cuisine. Summer entertainment. Free parking. Professional and friendly staff with an attention to detail that ensures the enjoyment of your stay.

Bedrooms: 8 single,
63 double/twin,
15 triple/multiple; suites available
Bathrooms: 86 en suite

Lunch available
Evening meal available
CC: Amex, Delta, Diners, Mastercard, Switch, Visa

Special offers available all year round. Festive programmes with entertainment at Easter, Christmas and New Year. Summer holiday packages.

★★★

QUEEN'S HOTEL

Meyrick Road, East Cliff,
Bournemouth BH1 3DL
T: (01202) 554415
F: (01202) 294810
E: hotels@arthuryoung.co.uk
I: www.arthuryoung.co.uk

Bedrooms: 12 single,
89 double/twin, 8 triple/multiple
Bathrooms: 109 en suite

Lunch available
Evening meal available
CC: Mastercard, Switch, Visa

B&B per night:
S £51.50–£62.50
D £99.00–£125.00

HB per person:
DY £61.50–£72.50

OPEN All year round

Modern, family-run hotel near the beach, ideal for family holidays and with facilities for business conventions. Leisure club. Award-winning cuisine. Special breaks.

★★

RUSSELL COURT HOTEL

Bath Road, Bournemouth BH1 2EP
T: (01202) 295819
F: (01202) 293457
E: russelcrt@aol.com
I: www.enterprisehotel.co.uk

Bedrooms: 9 single,
42 double/twin, 5 triple/multiple
Bathrooms: 56 en suite

Lunch available
Evening meal available
CC: Amex, Delta, Diners, Mastercard, Switch, Visa

B&B per night:
S £35.00–£63.50
D £50.00–£107.00

HB per person:
DY £62.00–£119.00

OPEN All year round

Good location in town centre, sea views, large car park and varied menu. Regular entertainment and dancing. Attractive bedrooms, all en suite with TV and telephones.

★★★

TROUVILLE HOTEL

Priory Road, West Cliff,
Bournemouth BH2 5DH
T: (01202) 552262
F: (01202) 293324
E: reservations@trouvillehotel.com
I: www.arthuryoung.co.uk

Bedrooms: 8 single,
63 double/twin, 6 triple/multiple
Bathrooms: 77 en suite

Lunch available
Evening meal available
CC: Amex, Delta, Diners, Mastercard, Switch, Visa

B&B per night:
S £53.00–£60.00
D £106.00–£120.00

HB per person:
DY £67.00–£73.50

OPEN All year round

Centrally located close to all amenities, the Trouville boasts a leisure centre and has a fine reputation for friendly service and superb food.

QUALITY ASSURANCE SCHEME

For an explanation of the quality and facilities represented by the Stars please refer to the front of this guide. A more detailed explanation can be found in the information pages at the back.

BOURNEMOUTH continued

★★

ULLSWATER HOTEL

Westcliff Gardens, Bournemouth BH2 5HW
T: (01202) 555181
F: (01202) 317896
E: enq@ullswater.uk.com
I: www.ullswater.uk.com

B&B per night:
S £25.00–£33.00
D £50.00–£66.00

HB per person:
DY £30.00–£39.00

OPEN All year round

The Ullswater is situated within sight of the sea in the most favoured position on the West Cliff and within a few minutes' walking distance of the beach, town centre and Bournemouth International Centre. The Ullswater offers a high degree of comfort in tasteful surroundings, with good food and personal service.

Bedrooms: 9 single, 26 double/twin, 7 triple/ multiple
Bathrooms: 42 en suite

Lunch available
Evening meal available
CC: Amex, Mastercard, Switch, Visa

Regular Murder Mystery weekends, Turkey and Tinsel breaks and party weekends.

BRACKNELL, Berkshire Map ref 2C2

★★★★
Silver Award

COPPID BEECH HOTEL

John Nike Way, Bracknell RG12 8TF
T: (01344) 303333
F: (01344) 301200
E: reservations@coppid-beech-hotel.co.uk
I: www.coppidbeech.com

B&B per night:
S £85.00–£175.00
D £114.00–£205.00

HB per person:
DY £104.00–£238.00

OPEN All year round

Unusual Alpine-style hotel with exceptional facilities, including our rosette fine dining Rowans Restaurant, next door to a dry ski slope and ice rink. Located only 20 minutes from the charms of Windsor, Eton and Ascot for wonderful sightseeing. Legoland is closer, only 15 minutes away, for a magical family experience.

Bedrooms: 44 single, 155 double/twin, 6 triple/multiple; suites available
Bathrooms: 205 en suite

Lunch available
Evening meal available
CC: Amex, Delta, Diners, Mastercard, Switch, Visa

Leisure breaks inlcuding Windsor, Legoland, Savill Gardens, Chessington, Thorpe, golf, ski tuition, racing at Newbury, Epsom, Ascot, Windsor, Sandown, Kempton.

★★

DIAL HOUSE HOTEL
62 Dukes Ride, Crowthorne RG45 6DL
T: (01344) 776941
F: (01344) 777191
E: dhh@fardellhotels.com
I: www.fardellhotels.com

Bedrooms: 8 single, 11 double/twin, 2 triple/ multiple
Bathrooms: 21 en suite

Evening meal available
CC: Amex, Delta, Mastercard, Switch, Visa

B&B per night:
S £45.00–£89.00
D £65.00–£103.00

HB per person:
DY £59.00–£103.00

OPEN All year round

Family-run hotel in quiet village of Crowthorne close to Bracknell, Camberley, Ascot and Windsor. Licensed restaurant and bar. Ample parking.

BROCKENHURST, Hampshire Map ref 2C3

★★

THE WATERSPLASH HOTEL
The Rise, Brockenhurst SO42 7ZP
T: (01590) 622344
F: (01590) 624047
E: bookings@watersplash.co.uk
I: www.watersplash.co.uk

Bedrooms: 3 single, 17 double/twin, 3 triple/ multiple
Bathrooms: 20 en suite, 3 private

Lunch available
Evening meal available
CC: Amex, Delta, Mastercard, Switch, Visa

B&B per night:
S £55.00–£75.00
D £76.00–£116.00

HB per person:
DY £60.00–£80.00

OPEN All year round

Quiet Victorian country house hotel, set in beautiful gardens. Renowned for its family-run atmosphere, good food, service and accommodation.

www.travelengland.org.uk
Log on for information and inspiration. The latest information on places to visit, events and quality assessed accommodation.

BUCKINGHAM, Buckinghamshire Map ref 2C1 *Tourist Information Centre Tel: (01280) 823020*

★★★
Silver
Award

VILLIERS HOTEL
3 Castle Street, Buckingham
MK18 1BS
T: (01280) 822444
F: (01280) 822113
E: villiers@villiers-hotels.demon.co.uk

Bedrooms: 3 single,
43 double/twin; suites
available
Bathrooms: 46 en suite

Lunch available
Evening meal available
CC: Amex, Delta, Diners,
Mastercard, Switch, Visa

B&B per night:
S £85.00–£105.00
D £110.00–£160.00

OPEN All year round

400-year-old coaching inn with individually designed bedrooms and suites set around an old cobbled courtyard, incorporating English restaurant and Jacobean pub.

BURFORD, Oxfordshire Map ref 2B1 *Tourist Information Centre Tel: (01993) 823558*

★★★

THE BAY TREE
Sheep Street, Burford, Oxford
OX18 4LW
T: (01993) 822791
F: (01993) 823008
E: bookings@cotswold-inns-hotels.co.uk
I: www.cotswold-inns-hotels.co.uk

Bedrooms: 1 single,
20 double/twin; suites
available
Bathrooms: 21 en suite

Lunch available
Evening meal available
CC: Amex, Delta, Diners,
Mastercard, Switch, Visa

B&B per night:
S £99.00
D £145.00–£220.00

HB per person:
DY Min £123.95

OPEN All year round

Ⓒ®
Grand Heritage Hotels

16thC Cotswold-stone building with exposed beams, flagstone floors and open log fires. Decorated throughout with antique furniture.

BURLEY, Hampshire Map ref 2B3

★★★

MOORHILL HOUSE HOTEL
Burley, Ringwood BH24 4AG
T: (01425) 403285
F: (01425) 403715
E: moorhill@carehotels.co.uk
I: www.carehotels.co.uk

Bedrooms: 2 single,
15 double/twin, 7 triple/
multiple
Bathrooms: 24 en suite

Lunch available
Evening meal available
CC: Amex, Diners,
Mastercard, Switch, Visa

B&B per night:
S £57.50–£72.50
D £115.00–£145.00

HB per person:
DY £79.00–£94.00

OPEN All year round

Quiet country house hotel in secluded two and a half acres, in picturesque village of Burley. All bedrooms en suite, indoor leisure facilities.

CHALE, Isle of Wight Map ref 2C3

★★

CLARENDON HOTEL & WIGHT MOUSE INN
Nr Blackgang, Chale, Ventnor
PO38 2HA
T: (01983) 730431
F: (01983) 730431
E: info@wightmouseinns.co.uk
I: www.wightmouseinns.co.uk

Bedrooms: 2 double/
twin, 10 triple/multiple;
suites available
Bathrooms: 12 en suite

Lunch available
Evening meal available
CC: Delta, Mastercard,
Switch, Visa

B&B per night:
D £78.00–£98.00

HB per person:
DY £56.00–£84.00

OPEN All year round

17thC coaching hotel overlooking Freshwater Bay and the Needles. Children most welcome. Six real ales, 365 whiskies and live entertainment nightly, all year round. Well-appointed bedrooms, good food, service and hospitality.

CORFE CASTLE, Dorset Map ref 2B3

★★★
Silver
Award

MORTONS HOUSE HOTEL
East Street, Corfe Castle, Wareham
BH20 5EE
T: (01929) 480988
F: (01929) 480820
E: stay@mortonshouse.co.uk
I: www.mortonshouse.co.uk

B&B per night:
S £75.00–£150.00
D £84.00–£116.00

HB per person:
DY £58.00–£101.00

OPEN All year round

Built in the shape of an 'E' to commemorate Elizabeth I, with stone taken from the 'sleighted' castle, this original manor house boasts a fine reputation for service and standards in the award-winning rosette restaurant. All bedrooms tastefully decorated and furnished. Suites, superior rooms, and those with castle views available.

Bedrooms: 16 double/
twin, 1 triple/multiple;
suites available
Bathrooms: 17 en suite

Lunch available
Evening meal available
CC: Amex, Delta, Diners,
Mastercard, Switch, Visa

Hibernation breaks-Nov-Mar, Summer breaks-Apr-Oct.

COTSWOLDS

See under Burford, Woodstock

See also Cotswolds in Heart of England region

EASTLEIGH, Hampshire Map ref 2C3

★★★

Ellington Lodge is in a woodland setting across the charming Monks Brook in the grounds of the Concorde Club. The comfortable bedrooms are en suite, air conditioned, have TVs, trouser press, tea and coffee facilities. You can choose from either the Wine Bar or the Main Restaurant to dine, with fine wines and excellent food.

THE CONCORDE CLUB & HOTEL

Ellington Lodge, Stoneham Lane, Eastleigh
SO50 9HQ
T: (023) 8065 1478
F: (023) 8065 1479
E: info@theconcordeclub.com
I: www.theconcordeclub.com

Bedrooms: 35 double/ twin
Bathrooms: 35 en suite

Lunch available
Evening meal available
CC: Amex, Delta, Diners, Mastercard, Switch, Visa

Stay any Fri and Sat and get Sun half price (excl Christmas and New Year). Subject to availability.

B&B per night:
S £45.00–£115.00
D £65.00–£115.00

HB per person:
DY £40.00–£55.00

OPEN All year round

Ａ♦♪℡■▯♦◨Ⓢ◉⊞▥．⊙♨♈☼☂♞♔❀▥P

FAREHAM, Hampshire Map ref 2C3 *Tourist Information Centre Tel: (01329) 221342*

★★

Family-run hotel set in 10 acres of landscaped gardens in the Meon Valley, with a private lake adjoining the Meon River. Well situated for touring Southern England – only 6 miles from the M27 and at the foot of South Downs Way. Welcoming staff and award-winning restaurant.

UPLAND PARK HOTEL

Garrison Hill (A32), Droxford, Southampton
SO32 3QL
T: (01489) 878507
F: (01489) 877853
E: reservations@uplandparkhotel.co.uk
I: www.uplandparkhotel.co.uk

Bedrooms: 3 single, 12 double/twin, 2 triple/ multiple
Bathrooms: 17 en suite

Lunch available
Evening meal available
CC: Amex, Delta, Diners, Mastercard, Switch, Visa

Mon-Fri £85 DB&B for 2 people. Quote 'Madness deal'.

B&B per night:
S £44.00–£46.00
D £60.00–£64.00

HB per person:
DY £52.00–£56.00

OPEN All year round

Ａ♨☎⚷℡■▯♦◨Ⓢ⚓▥．♨♈☂☽♪♈☼☂♞▥P

FARINGDON, Oxfordshire Map ref 2B2 *Tourist Information Centre Tel: (01367) 242191*

★★

FARINGDON HOTEL
Market Place, Faringdon SN7 7HL
T: (01367) 240536
F: (01367) 243250

Bedrooms: 3 single, 14 double/twin, 3 triple/ multiple
Bathrooms: 20 en suite

Lunch available
Evening meal available
CC: Amex, Delta, Diners, Mastercard, Switch, Visa

B&B per night:
S £55.00–£60.00
D £70.00–£75.00

OPEN All year round

Situated near the 12thC parish church. The hotel's tradition of hospitality dates from before the coaching age. The hotel offers authentic Thai cuisine.

Ａ♨☎⚷℡■▯♦◨Ⓢ☙▥．♨♈☂♞☂P

FENNY STRATFORD, Buckinghamshire Map ref 2C1

TRAVEL ACCOMMODATION

CAMPANILE MILTON KEYNES HOTEL
40 Penn Road, Fenny Stratford, Milton Keynes MK2 2AU
T: (01908) 649819
F: (01908) 649818

Bedrooms: 35 double/ twin, 43 triple/multiple
Bathrooms: 78 en suite

Lunch available
Evening meal available
CC: Amex, Delta, Diners, Mastercard, Switch, Visa

B&B per night:
S £41.95–£50.00
D £41.95–£50.00

HB per person:
DY £60.00–£70.00

OPEN All year round

Hotel located on the outskirts of Milton Keynes in Bletchley.

☙♨☎■▯♦Ⓢ▥．♨♈☂♞▥P

RATING
All accommodation in this guide has been rated, or is awaiting a rating, by a trained English Tourism Council assessor.

GOSPORT, Hampshire Map ref 2C3 *Tourist Information Centre Tel: (023) 9252 2944*

★★ **THE MANOR HOTEL**
Brewers Lane, Gosport PO13 0JY
T: (01329) 232946
F: (01329) 220392
E: tony_lid@msn.com
I: www.smoothhounds.co.uk/hotels/manorhtml

Bedrooms: 1 single,
8 double/twin, 3 triple/multiple
Bathrooms: 12 en suite

Lunch available
Evening meal available
CC: Amex, Delta,
Mastercard, Switch, Visa

B&B per night:
S £40.00–£47.50
D £55.00–£65.00

OPEN All year round

Very popular private hotel and public house. Close to Portsmouth's naval history. Midway between Fareham and Gosport.

HECKFIELD, Hampshire Map ref 2C2

★★ **THE NEW INN**
Heckfield, Hook RG27 0LE
T: (0118) 932 6374
F: (0118) 932 6550

Bedrooms: 15 double/twin, 1 triple/multiple
Bathrooms: 16 en suite

Lunch available
Evening meal available
CC: Amex, Delta, Diners,
Mastercard, Switch, Visa

B&B per night:
S £55.00–£80.00
D £70.00–£90.00

OPEN All year round

15thC inn set in the picturesque countryside of North Hampshire, recently extended but retaining its unique character. Conference facilities and restaurant.

ISLE OF WIGHT

See under Bembridge, Chale, Shanklin, Totland Bay, Ventnor

LIPHOOK, Hampshire Map ref 2C3

★★★ **OLD THORNS HOTEL, GOLF & COUNTRY CLUB**
Griggs Green, Liphook GU30 7PE
T: (01428) 724555
F: (01428) 725036
E: info@oldthorns.com
I: www.oldthorns.com

Bedrooms: 32 double/twin, 1 triple/multiple;
suites available
Bathrooms: 33 en suite

Lunch available
Evening meal available
CC: Amex, Delta, Diners,
Mastercard, Switch, Visa

B&B per night:
S £125.00–£135.00
D £145.00–£160.00

HB per person:
DY £82.50–£100.00

OPEN All year round

Set in 400 acres of Hampshire parkland with an 18-hole golf course, hotel, Japanese and European restaurants and leisure complex. One hour's drive from London, Heathrow and Gatwick airports.

LULWORTH COVE, Dorset Map ref 2B3

★★

CROMWELL HOUSE HOTEL

Lulworth Cove, West Lulworth, Wareham BH20 5RJ
T: (01929) 400253 & 400332
F: (01929) 400566
E: catriona@lulworthcove.co.uk
I: www.lulworthcove.co.uk

B&B per night:
S £30.00–£42.50
D £60.00–£80.00

HB per person:
DY £45.00–£51.50

OPEN All year round

Family hotel on the Dorset Heritage Coast footpath. Outstanding sea views over Lulworth Cove. Secluded garden. Good walking country. Swimming pool (May-October). Restaurant, wine list, bar. Fish specialities including local lobsters and scallops. Group bookings welcome. Midweek/weekend breaks available. Private business parties catered for.

Bedrooms: 2 single,
12 double/twin, 3 triple/multiple
Bathrooms: 17 en suite

Evening meal available
CC: Amex, Delta, Diners,
Mastercard, Switch, Visa

Art and photography courses.

ACCESSIBILITY

Look for the [🦽][🦽][🧍] symbols which indicate accessibility for wheelchair users. A list of establishments is at the front of this guide.

LYMINGTON, Hampshire Map ref 2C3

★★★
Silver
Award

SOUTH LAWN HOTEL

Lymington Road, Milford-on-Sea,
Lymington SO41 0RF
T: (01590) 643911
F: (01590) 644820
E: enquiries@southlawn.co.uk
I: www.southlawn.co.uk

B&B per night:
S £50.00–£70.00
D £90.00–£120.00

HB per person:
DY £77.00–£87.00

OPEN All year round

A beautiful former dower house, set in own grounds. The chef/proprietor's award-winning restaurant is well supported locally, offering homely elegance with professional, friendly staff. Individually furnished rooms decorated to a high standard with all facilities for the discerning traveller. Special breaks and golf concessions.

Bedrooms: 24 double/ twin
Bathrooms: 24 en suite

Lunch available
Evening meal available
CC: Delta, Mastercard, Switch, Visa

★★★
Silver
Award

STANWELL HOUSE HOTEL

Jane McIntyre Hotels Ltd, 15 High Street,
Lymington SO41 9AA
T: (01590) 677123
F: (01590) 677756
E: sales@stanwellhousehotel.co.uk
I: www.stanwellhousehotel.co.uk

B&B per night:
S £85.00–£160.00
D £110.00–£160.00

HB per person:
DY £80.00–£105.00

OPEN All year round

Privately-owned Georgian townhouse with award-winning accommodation and dining. Four-poster suites, lovely bedrooms, candlelit dining and dramatic decor. Huge, lofty conservatory with big, squashy cushions, charming flower-filled terrace and walled garden for al fresco dining. Friendly and relaxed, close to the marinas and New Forest, utterly irresistible!

Bedrooms: 28 double/ twin, 1 triple/multiple; suites available
Bathrooms: 29 en suite

Lunch available
Evening meal available
CC: Amex, Delta, Diners, Mastercard, Switch, Visa

Stay Fri and Sat or Mon and Tues and get Sun free (excl Bank Hols).

LYNDHURST, Hampshire Map ref 2C3

★★★

WOODLANDS LODGE HOTEL

Bartley Road, Woodlands, Southampton
SO40 7GN
T: (023) 8029 2257
F: (023) 8029 3090
E: woodlands@nortels.ltd.uk
I: www.nortels.ltd.uk

B&B per night:
S £70.00–£90.00
D £126.00–£186.00

HB per person:
DY £89.00–£119.00

OPEN All year round

Georgian country house hotel set in 3 acres of gardens, within the beautiful New Forest. Well-equipped en suite rooms with whirlpool baths and king size beds. The restaurant has an award for excellent cuisine, making use of fresh local produce. Many local attractions to visit or just enjoy the peace and tranquillity.

Bedrooms: 13 double/ twin, 2 triple/multiple; suites available
Bathrooms: 15 en suite

Lunch available
Evening meal available
CC: Delta, Mastercard, Switch, Visa

Christmas, New Year, Easter and Valentine packages available. Low season discounts also available.

QUALITY ASSURANCE SCHEME

Star ratings and awards were correct at the time of going to press but are subject to change. Please check at the time of booking.

MAIDENHEAD, Berkshire Map ref 2C2

★

ELVA LODGE HOTEL
Castle Hill, Maidenhead SL6 4AD
T: (01628) 622948
F: (01628) 778954
E: reservations@elvalodgehotel.
demon.co.uk
I: www.elvalodgehotel.demon.co.uk

Bedrooms: 10 single,
14 double/twin, 2 triple/
multiple
Bathrooms: 19 en suite,
3 private

Evening meal available
CC: Amex, Delta, Diners,
Mastercard, Switch, Visa

B&B per night:
S £50.00–£100.00
D £65.00–£110.00

OPEN All year round

*Family-run hotel in central Maidenhead. Friendly atmosphere and personal attention.
Ideal for Heathrow, Windsor, Henley and Ascot. M4 5 minutes, M40 and M25 10 minutes.*

MARLOW, Buckinghamshire Map ref 2C2 *Tourist Information Centre Tel: (01628) 483597*

★★★★
**Silver
Award**

DANESFIELD HOUSE HOTEL AND SPA
Henley Road, Marlow-on-Thames,
Marlow SL7 2EY
T: (01628) 891010
F: (01628) 890408
E: sales@danesfieldhouse.co.uk
I: www.danesfieldhouse.co.uk

Bedrooms: 9 single,
75 double/twin, 3 triple/
multiple; suites available
Bathrooms: 87 en suite

Lunch available
Evening meal available
CC: Amex, Delta, Diners,
Mastercard, Switch, Visa

B&B per night:
S £175.00–£275.00
D £205.00–£300.00

OPEN All year round

CR
Small Luxury Hotels

*Country house hotel set within 65 acres of outstanding gardens, overlooking the River
Thames between Marlow and Henley. Luxurious spa opening October 2001.*

MILFORD-ON-SEA, Hampshire Map ref 2C3

★★★
**Gold
Award**

WESTOVER HALL HOTEL
Park Lane, Milford-on-Sea, Lymington
SO41 0PT
T: (01590) 643044
F: (01590) 644490
E: westoverhallhotel@barclays.net
I: www.westoverhallhotel.com

B&B per night:
S £70.00–£90.00
D £120.00–£160.00

HB per person:
DY £80.00–£110.00

OPEN All year round

*Victorian mansion in the New Forest
with uninterrupted sea views.
Magnificent oak panelling and
dramatic stained glass windows are
complemented by family antiques
and contemporary art. Luxury
bathrooms and stylish bedrooms
complete a relaxed 'home from
home' atmosphere. Award-winning
restaurant, candlelit and with sea
views. Unique!*

Bedrooms: 1 single,
11 double/twin, 1 triple/
multiple
Bathrooms: 13 en suite

Lunch available
Evening meal available
CC: Amex, Delta, Diners,
Mastercard, Switch, Visa

MILTON COMMON, Oxfordshire Map ref 2C1

★★★★

THE OXFORD BELFRY
Milton Common, Oxford OX9 2JW
T: (01844) 279381
F: (01844) 279624
E: oxfordbelfry@marstonhotels.
com
I: www.marstonhotels.com

Bedrooms: 130 double/
twin; suites available
Bathrooms: 130 en suite

Lunch available
Evening meal available
CC: Amex, Delta, Diners,
Mastercard, Switch, Visa

B&B per night:
S £105.00–£145.00
D £125.00–£185.00

HB per person:
DY Min £69.50

OPEN All year round

CR
Marston Hotels

*Delightful hotel with stunning views of the Cotswold countryside, yet convenient M40.
Minutes from the centre of Oxford. Award-winning restaurant. Leisure facilities including
heated indoor pool.*

SPECIAL BREAKS
**Many establishments offer special promotions and themed breaks.
These are highlighted in red. (All such offers are subject to availability.)**

MILTON KEYNES, Buckinghamshire Map ref 2C1

★★★

PARKSIDE HOTEL

Newport Road, Woughton on the Green,
Milton Keynes MK6 3LR
T: (01908) 661919
F: (01908) 676186
E: rooms@parkside-hotel.co.uk
I: www.parkside-hotel.co.uk

B&B per night:
S £48.00–£110.00
D £58.00–£125.00

HB per person:
DY £75.00–£130.00

OPEN All year round

Nestled in the tranquil village of Woughton on the Green, the Parkside Hotel is in stark contrast to the hustle and bustle of central Milton Keynes just 5 minutes away. Five acres of landscaped gardens provide a perfect location. Within easy reach of the M1 motorway, junctions 13 and 14.

Bedrooms: 10 single, 39 double/twin; suites available
Bathrooms: 49 en suite

Lunch available
Evening meal available
CC: Amex, Delta, Diners, Mastercard, Switch, Visa

Wedding venue. See our website for events and special offers and to join our mailing list.

★★

SWAN REVIVED HOTEL

High Street, Newport Pagnell MK16 8AR
T: (01908) 610565
F: (01908) 210995
E: swanrevived@btinternet.com
I: www.swanrevived.co.uk

B&B per night:
S £48.00–£76.00
D £64.00–£84.00

HB per person:
DY Min £90.00

OPEN All year round

ⓒⓡ
The Independents

Extensively modernised coaching inn boasting comfortable guest rooms, 2 bars, a la carte restaurant, conference and banqueting facilities. Close to Silverstone, Woburn and 50 miles from London. Licensed for civil wedding ceremonies.

Bedrooms: 17 single, 23 double/twin, 2 triple/ multiple; suites available
Bathrooms: 42 en suite

Lunch available
Evening meal available
CC: Amex, Delta, Diners, Mastercard, Switch, Visa

NEW FOREST

See under Brockenhurst, Burley, Lymington, Lyndhurst, Milford-on-Sea, Sway, Woodlands

NEWBURY, Berkshire Map ref 2C2 *Tourist Information Centre Tel: (01635) 30267*

★★★★
Silver
Award

DONNINGTON VALLEY HOTEL & GOLF COURSE
Old Oxford Road, Donnington,
Newbury RG14 3AG
T: (01635) 551199
F: (01635) 551123
E: general@donningtonvalley.co.uk
I: www.donningtonvalley.co.uk

Bedrooms: 58 double/ twin; suites available
Bathrooms: 58 en suite

Lunch available
Evening meal available
CC: Amex, Delta, Diners, Mastercard, Switch, Visa

B&B per night:
D Min £160.00

HB per person:
DY Min £72.00

OPEN All year round

Stylish country house hotel set in Berkshire countryside. 18-hole golf-course, award-winning restaurant. Excellent touring base for southern England.

USE YOUR *i*s

There are more than 550 Tourist Information Centres throughout England offering friendly help with accommodation and holiday ideas as well as suggestions of places to visit and things to do. You'll find TIC addresses in the local Phone Book.

NEWBURY continued

★★★★
Silver
Award

REGENCY PARK HOTEL

Bowling Green Road, Thatcham RG18 3RP
T: (01635) 871555
F: (01635) 871571
E: info@regencypark.co.uk
I: www.regencyparkhotel.co.uk

B&B per night:
S £69.00–£320.00
D £83.00–£341.00

HB per person:
DY £89.00–£340.00

OPEN All year round

Set in 5 acres of Berkshire countryside, 7 minutes from junction 13, M4 this recently refurbished luxury hotel is renowned for its high standards of service. Extensive indoor leisure facilities with pool, gymnasium and health & beauty treatment rooms. Executive standard bedrooms and award-winning restaurant, The Watermark.

Bedrooms: 3 single, 79 double/twin; suites available
Bathrooms: 82 en suite

Lunch available
Evening meal available
CC: Amex, Delta, Diners, Mastercard, Switch, Visa

Best Western Hotels

★★★★★
Gold
Award

THE VINEYARD AT STOCKCROSS

Stockcross, Newbury RG20 8JU
T: (01635) 528770
F: (01635) 528398
E: general@the-vineyard.co.uk
I: www.the-vineyard.co.uk

Bedrooms: 6 single, 25 double/twin; suites available
Bathrooms: 31 en suite

Lunch available
Evening meal available
CC: Amex, Delta, Diners, Mastercard, Switch, Visa

B&B per night:
S Min £190.00
D Min £266.00

HB per person:
DY Min £163.00

OPEN All year round

Elegant country hotel in tranquil setting. 31 luxury rooms and suites and award-winning restaurant. Leisure facilities include spa, gymnasium, pool and treatment suites.

ODIHAM, Hampshire Map ref 2C2

★★

GEORGE HOTEL

High Street, Odiham, Hook RG29 1LP
T: (01256) 702081
F: (01256) 704213

B&B per night:
S £65.00–£90.00
D £85.00–£95.00

OPEN All year round

15thC coaching inn with many fine beams and original wattle and daub visible. Oak-panelled restaurant with flagstone floor and fireplace said to have come from Basing House. Traditionally restored bedrooms in the old building, some with 4-poster beds, and newer rooms designed with every modern comfort in mind for today's traveller.

Bedrooms: 8 single, 20 double/twin
Bathrooms: 28 en suite

Lunch available
Evening meal available
CC: Amex, Delta, Diners, Mastercard, Switch, Visa

£40pppn sharing a twin or double room to incl B&B each day and dinner on Fri evening only.

TOWN INDEX

This can be found at the back of this guide. If you know where you want to stay, the index will give you the page number listing accommodation in your chosen town, city or village.

OXFORD, Oxfordshire Map ref 2C1 *Tourist Information Centre Tel: (01865) 726871*

★★★★

COTSWOLD LODGE HOTEL

66A Banbury Road, Oxford OX2 6JP
T: (01865) 512121
F: (01865) 512490

B&B per night:
S £125.00–£145.00
D £175.00–£455.00

HB per person:
DY £150.00–£225.00

OPEN All year round

The Independents

An elegant retreat set in a peaceful conservation area 0.5 miles from the centre of Oxford. The 10 individually designed suites boast carefully selected handmade furniture and furnishings. The hotel is known for its excellent level of service and its award-winning 'Fellows Restaurant' creates dishes with a traditional influence.

Bedrooms: 6 single, 43 double/twin; suites available
Bathrooms: 49 en suite

Lunch available
Evening meal available
CC: Amex, Delta, Diners, Mastercard, Switch, Visa

★★

MOUNT PLEASANT

76 London Road, Headington, Oxford OX3 9AJ
T: (01865) 762749
F: (01865) 762749
E: mount.pleasant@ukonline.co.uk

Bedrooms: 7 double/twin, 1 triple/multiple
Bathrooms: 8 en suite

Lunch available
Evening meal available
CC: Amex, Diners, Mastercard, Visa

B&B per night:
S £45.00–£65.00
D £65.00–£75.00

HB per person:
DY £57.50–£60.00

OPEN All year round

Small, no smoking, family-run hotel offering full facilities. On the A40 and convenient for Oxford shopping, hospitals, colleges, visiting the Chilterns and the Cotswolds.

★★★★
Gold
Award

OLD BANK HOTEL

92-94 High Street, Oxford OX1 4BN
T: (01865) 799599
F: (01865) 799598
E: info@oldbank-hotel.co.uk
I: www.oxford-hotels-restaurants.co.uk

B&B per night:
S £143.00–£203.00
D £171.00–£316.00

OPEN All year round

These beautiful old buildings, formerly a bank, have been superbly converted into a contemporary 42-bedroom luxury hotel. Central location with stunning views of Oxford skyline. All rooms are air conditioned, CD players, satellite TV and 24-hour room service. Restaurant and bar serving Italian-style food. Private parking.

Bedrooms: 35 double/twin, 7 triple/multiple; suites available
Bathrooms: 42 en suite

Lunch available
Evening meal available
CC: Amex, Delta, Diners, Mastercard, Switch, Visa

CHECK THE MAPS

The colour maps at the front of this guide show all the cities, towns and villages for which you will find accommodation entries. Refer to the town index to find the page on which they are listed.

OXFORD continued

★★★★
Silver
Award

TOWNHOUSE

17thC wisteria-clad building in
central Oxford. Thirty beautiful en
suite bedrooms with marble
bathrooms. Informal restaurant and
bar serving excellent food. Meals
taken on the front terrace in
summer. Private car park, 24-hour
room service, roof terrace. A warm
welcome from efficient, friendly
young staff.

THE OLD PARSONAGE HOTEL

1 Banbury Road, Oxford OX2 6NN
T: (01865) 811022
F: (01865) 811016
E: jwj@mogford.co.uk
I: www.oxford-hotels-restaurants.co.uk

Bedrooms: 1 single, | Lunch available
25 double/twin, 4 triple/ | Evening meal available
multiple; suites available | CC: Amex, Delta, Diners,
Bathrooms: 30 en suite | Mastercard, Switch, Visa

Sun and Mon night special-£132.50 per room with
breakfast.

B&B per night:
S £130.00–£170.00
D £155.00–£200.00

OPEN All year round

★★★
Silver
Award

Converted Elizabethan manor house
in a rural setting north east of
Oxford, with a restaurant that
specialises in modern English
cooking.

STUDLEY PRIORY HOTEL

Horton cum Studley, Oxford OX33 1AZ
T: (01865) 351203
F: (01865) 351613
E: res@studley-priory.co.uk
I: www.studley-priory.co.uk

Bedrooms: 3 single, | Lunch available
15 double/twin; suites | Evening meal available
available | CC: Amex, Delta, Diners,
Bathrooms: 18 en suite | Mastercard, Switch, Visa

B&B per night:
S £125.00
D £165.00–£300.00

HB per person:
DY Min £180.00

OPEN All year round

®
Small Luxury Hotels

PORTSMOUTH & SOUTHSEA, Hampshire Map ref 2C3

★★

OCEAN HOTEL & APARTMENTS

8-10 St Helens Parade, Southsea
PO4 0RW
T: (023) 92734233 & 92734342
F: (023) 92297046
E: feris@oceanhotel.freeserve.co.uk
I: www.oceanhotel.freeserve.co.uk

Bedrooms: 1 single, | Evening meal available
7 double/twin, 8 triple/ | CC: Amex, Mastercard,
multiple; suites available | Switch, Visa
Bathrooms: 13 en suite,
2 private

Imposing building in foremost seafront position between South Parade Pier and Canoe
Lake with magnificent sea views. Choice of hotel rooms, suites, or self-contained
apartments.

B&B per night:
S £25.00–£40.00
D £50.00–£60.00

HB per person:
DY £35.00–£45.00

OPEN All year round

★

SALISBURY HOTEL

57-59 Festing Road, Southsea
PO4 0NQ
T: (023) 9282 3606 & 9273 4233
F: (023) 9282 0955
E: feris@oceanhotel.freeserve.co.uk
I: www.oceanhotel.freeserve.co.uk

Bedrooms: 5 single, | Evening meal available
7 double/twin, 6 triple/ | CC: Mastercard, Visa
multiple; suites available
Bathrooms: 13 en suite,
1 private

Friendly hotel with character. Two minutes' walk from sea and other attractions. En suite
rooms. Private car park. The hotel you will confidently come back to.

B&B per night:
S £25.00–£35.00
D £40.00–£60.00

HB per person:
DY £35.00–£45.00

OPEN All year round

ACCESSIBILITY

Look for the ♿ symbols which indicate accessibility for
wheelchair users. A list of establishments is at the front of this guide.

READING, Berkshire Map ref 2C2 *Tourist Information Centre Tel: (0118) 956 6226*

★★★

THE GREAT HOUSE AT SONNING

Thames Street, Sonning-on-Thames,
Reading RG4 6UT
T: (0118) 969 2277
F: (0118) 944 1296
E: greathouse@btconnect.com
I: www.greathouseatsonning.com

Situated in the beautiful conservation village of Sonning, parts of the Great House date back to pre-Elizabethan times. In a 4-acre estate, the elegant Moorings Restaurant overlooks the gardens and offers a wide choice of dishes at luncheon and dinner. Al fresco dining during summer months. Weekend rates shown.

Bedrooms: 7 single,
41 double/twin, 1 triple
multiple; suites available
Bathrooms: 49 en suite

Lunch available
Evening meal available
CC: Amex, Diners,
Mastercard, Switch, Visa

Tickets for The Mill at Sonning's Theatre productions may be booked in conjunction with your reservation.

B&B per night:
S £59.50–£64.50
D £99.00–£129.00

HB per person:
DY Min £129.00

OPEN All year round

★★

RAINBOW CORNER HOTEL

132-138 Caversham Road, Reading
RG1 8AY
T: (0118) 958 8140
F: (0118) 958 6500
E: info@rainbowhotel.co.uk
I: www.rainbowhotel.co.uk

Bedrooms: 10 single,
21 double/twin, 1 triple/
multiple
Bathrooms: 32 en suite

Evening meal available
CC: Amex, Delta, Diners,
Mastercard, Switch, Visa

B&B per night:
S £41.50–£81.50
D £58.00–£108.00

OPEN All year round

Victorian hotel. All rooms fully en suite, bar and restaurant. Ten minutes from station and town centre, 100 yards from River Thames. Car parking at rear.

★★★

UPCROSS HOTEL

68 Berkeley Avenue, Reading RG1 6HY
T: (0118) 959 0796
F: (0118) 957 6517
E: reservations@upcrosshotel.co.uk

B&B per night:
S Max £80.00
D Max £98.00

OPEN All year round

Privately-owned country house hotel of character and warmth, reputed to have one of the best restaurants in Berkshire. Our conference facilities overlook beautifully kept gardens. Large car park. Town centre/railway station 10 minutes away. Easy access M4, junctions 11 and 12. Awards for food.

Bedrooms: 7 single,
14 double/twin, 2 triple/
multiple
Bathrooms: 23 en suite

Lunch available
Evening meal available
CC: Amex, Delta, Diners,
Mastercard, Switch, Visa

Fri and Sat nights single room £38.50, double room £56.50 for 2 people. Incl full English breakfast.

COUNTRY CODE Always follow the Country Code ✿ Enjoy the countryside and respect its life and work ✿ Guard against all risk of fire ✿ Fasten all gates ✿ Keep your dogs under close control ✿ Keep to public paths across farmland ✿ Use gates and stiles to cross fences, hedges and walls ✿ Leave livestock, crops and machinery alone ✿ Take your litter home ✿ Help to keep all water clean ✿ Protect wildlife, plants and trees ✿ Take special care on country roads ✿ Make no unnecessary noise

SHAFTESBURY, Dorset Map ref 2B3 *Tourist Information Centre Tel: (01747) 853514*

★★★

THE ROYAL CHASE HOTEL

Salisbury Road, Shaftesbury SP7 8DB
T: (01747) 853355
F: (01747) 851969
E: royalchasehotel@btinternet.com
I: www.theroyalchase.co.uk

Welcome to one of Wessex's most friendly hotels. Enjoy award-winning cuisine in our Byzant Restaurant, a welcoming log fire in the bar, comfortable standard or upgraded accommodation and our excellent heated indoor pool. Ideal as a touring base for Devon, Somerset, Wiltshire and Dorset.

Bedrooms: 3 single, 22 double/twin, 10 triple/multiple
Bathrooms: 35 en suite

Lunch available
Evening meal available
CC: Amex, Diners, Mastercard, Switch, Visa

B&B per night:
S £93.00–£114.00
D £117.00–£132.00

HB per person:
DY £79.50–£94.50

OPEN All year round

Ⓒ®
Best Western Hotels

ὁ ♿ 🛏 ☏ 📠 ❑ ♨ ♦ 🖥 ⑤ ⚲ ⅀ ⓘ ▥ ⊿ ↑ ⚘ ❀ 🏇 ⚑ ⚁ P

SHANKLIN, Isle of Wight Map ref 2C3 *Tourist Information Centre Tel: (01983) 862942*

★★

HAMBLEDON HOTEL

11 Queens Road, Shanklin
PO37 6AW
T: (01983) 862403
F: (01983) 867894
E: Enquiries@Hambledon-hotel.co.uk
I: www.Hambledon-hotel.co.uk

Bedrooms: 1 single, 6 double/twin, 4 triple/multiple
Bathrooms: 11 en suite

Evening meal available
CC: Delta, Mastercard, Switch, Visa

B&B per night:
S £23.00–£27.00
D £46.00–£54.00

HB per person:
DY £33.00–£38.00

OPEN All year round

Small, family-run hotel close to beach and shops, providing varied food, comfort and friendly service. All rooms en suite. Free use of leisure centre.

ὁ ♿ 🛏 ❑ ♦ 🖥 ⑤ ⚲ ▥ ⊿ ❀ 🐎 P

SOUTHAMPTON, Hampshire Map ref 2C3

★★★★

BOTLEIGH GRANGE HOTEL

Grange Road, Hedge End, Southampton SO30 2GA
T: (01489) 787700
F: (01489) 788535
E: enquiries@botleighgrangehotel.co.uk
I: www.botleighgrangehotel.co.uk

Bedrooms: 48 double/twin, 8 triple/multiple; suites available
Bathrooms: 56 en suite

Lunch available
Evening meal available
CC: Amex, Delta, Diners, Mastercard, Switch, Visa

B&B per night:
S £90.00–£100.00
D £120.00–£180.00

HB per person:
DY £112.00–£122.00

OPEN All year round

Ⓒ®
Best Western Hotels

𝔐 ὁ ♿ 🛏 ☏ 📠 ❑ ♦ 🖥 ⑤ ⚲ ⅀ ⓘ ⊞ ▥ ⊿ ⅃ ↑ ❀ ⚑ 🏵 P

SOUTHSEA

See under Portsmouth & Southsea

STONOR, Oxfordshire Map ref 2C2

★★★
Silver
Award

🚶

THE STONOR ARMS HOTEL

Stonor, Henley-on-Thames
RG9 6HE
T: (01491) 638866
F: (01491) 638863
E: stonorarms.hotel@virgin.net
I: www.stonor-arms.co.uk

Bedrooms: 10 double/twin
Bathrooms: 10 en suite

Lunch available
Evening meal available
CC: Amex, Delta, Mastercard, Switch, Visa

B&B per night:
S £120.00–£155.00
D £145.00–£175.00

OPEN All year round

The Stonor Arms Hotel, nestled in the Chiltern Valley in the village of Stonor, is the perfect setting for a short break or special occasion.

𝔐 ὁ ♿ ☏ ❑ ♦ 🖥 ⑤ ⚲ ▥ ⊿ ⅃ ❀ ↑ ⚑ 🏵 P

TOWN INDEX

This can be found at the back of this guide. If you know where you want to stay, the index will give you the page number listing accommodation in your chosen town, city or village.

STRATFIELD TURGIS, Hampshire Map ref 2C2

★★★

THE WELLINGTON ARMS

Stratfield Turgis, Hook RG27 0AS
T: (01256) 882214
F: (01256) 882934
E: wellington.arms@virgin.net

Bedrooms: 7 single,
22 double/twin, 2 triple/
multiple
Bathrooms: 31 en suite

Lunch available
Evening meal available
CC: Amex, Delta, Diners,
Mastercard, Switch, Visa

B&B per night:
S £70.00–£125.00
D £80.00–£135.00

OPEN All year round

Traditional coaching inn on the Duke of Wellington's estate, midway between Basingstoke and Reading on the A33. Motorway access from junction 6 of M3, junction 11 of M4.

STUDLAND, Dorset Map ref 2B3

★★

THE MANOR HOUSE HOTEL

Manor Road, Studland, Swanage
BH19 3AU
T: (01929) 450288
F: (01929) 450288
E: themanorhousehotel@lineone.net
I: themanorhousehotel.com

B&B per night:
S £60.00–£82.00
D £80.00–£144.00

HB per person:
DY £58.00–£90.00

OPEN All year round

Romantic 18thC manor house in 20 acres of secluded grounds overlooking the sea. Residential and restaurant licence. All rooms en suite with central heating, TV, telephone, radio, hairdryer, tea/coffee-making facilities. Four-poster beds. Menus feature fresh local seafood. Oak-panelled bar and dining room with conservatory. 2 hard tennis courts. Riding and golf nearby.

Bedrooms: 12 double/
twin, 6 triple/multiple;
suites available
Bathrooms: 18 en suite

Lunch available
Evening meal available
CC: Delta, Mastercard,
Switch, Visa

Good discounts on stays of 3 nights or more.
Christmas 3-day package and New Year 2 day
package available.

SWANAGE, Dorset Map ref 2B3 *Tourist Information Centre Tel: (01929) 422885*

★★★

THE PINES HOTEL

Burlington Road, Swanage BH19 1LT
T: (01929) 425211
F: (01929) 422075
E: reservations@pineshotel.co.uk
I: www.pineshotel.co.uk

B&B per night:
S £47.00–£59.50
D £94.00–£128.00

HB per person:
DY £59.50–£74.50

OPEN All year round

Modern family-run hotel set around the Purbeck countryside at the quiet end of Swanage Bay. The hotel has its own access to the beach and marvellous coastal views. The Pines prides itself on the friendliness of its staff, the comfort of its sea-facing lounges and especially its reputation for cuisine.

Bedrooms: 2 single,
21 double/twin,
24 triple/multiple; suites
available
Bathrooms: 47 en suite

Lunch available
Evening meal available
CC: Delta, Mastercard,
Switch, Visa

Details of bargain breaks / special weekends /
Christmas and New Year available on request.

AT-A-GLANCE SYMBOLS

Symbols at the end of each accommodation entry give useful information about services and facilities. A key to symbols can be found inside the back cover flap. Keep this open for easy reference.

★★★

Unique, secluded hotel in quiet New Forest country lane. Relaxed atmosphere with service, cuisine and accommodation of the highest standard. Luxurious bedrooms with en suite jacuzzis, 4-posters and sauna. Heated pool in peaceful gardens plus new steam and sauna. Excellent candlelit award-winning French restaurant. Regretfully no children, pets or smoking.

STRING OF HORSES COUNTRY HOUSE HOTEL

Mead End Road, Sway, Lymington
SO41 6EH
T: (01590) 682631
F: (01590) 682911
E: relax@stringofhorses.co.uk
I: www.stringofhorses.co.uk

Bedrooms: 8 double/	Lunch available
twin	Evening meal available
Bathrooms: 8 en suite	CC: Amex, Delta,
	Mastercard, Switch, Visa

Valentine's Break with special menu, champagne, roses and live entertainment. Christmas and New Year breaks-2 or 3 night stays.

B&B per night:
S Min £73.00
D £104.00–£124.00

HB per person:
DY £77.00–£87.00

OPEN All year round

★★★

Caringly converted coaching inn, centre of interesting country market town. Comfortable accommodation, plenty of parking. Restaurant and bar meals with wide choice of dishes including vegetarian options. Good centre for touring Oxfordshire and the Vale of Aylesbury. Easy access M40 junction 6 from the south and junction 8 from the north.

THE SPREAD EAGLE HOTEL

Cornmarket, Thame OX9 2BW
T: (01844) 213661
F: (01844) 261380
E: enquiries@spreadeaglethame.co.uk
I: www.spreadeaglethame.co.uk

Bedrooms: 5 single,	Lunch available
27 double/twin, 1 triple/	Evening meal available
multiple; suites available	CC: Amex, Diners,
Bathrooms: 33 en suite	Mastercard, Visa

B&B per night:
S £95.00–£115.00
D £112.00–£135.00

HB per person:
DY £70.00–£86.00

OPEN All year round

★★★

Delightful, personable, boutique hotel set in beautiful grounds in tranquil west Wight. Lovely strolls/ hikes to the Solent, Needles and Tennyson Downs. Golf and sports centre nearby. En suite garden, sea views and ground floor rooms available. Lounge, bar, locally popular pleasant dining room with great cuisine. Ferry inclusive offer October-April.

COUNTRY GARDEN HOTEL

Church Hill, Totland Bay PO39 0ET
T: (01983) 754521
F: (01983) 754521
E: countrygardeniow@cs.com
I: www.thecountrygardenhotel.co.uk

Bedrooms: 3 single,	Evening meal available
13 double/twin; suites	CC: Delta, Mastercard,
available	Switch, Visa
Bathrooms: 16 en suite	

Ferry inclusive for double room 2 nights or more Oct-Apr.

B&B per night:
S £40.00–£59.00
D £72.00–£118.00

HB per person:
DY £51.00–£70.00

OPEN Feb–Dec

WHERE TO STAY
Please mention this guide when making your booking.

VENTNOR, Isle of Wight Map ref 2C3

★★★
Silver
Award

BURLINGTON HOTEL
Bellevue Road, Ventnor PO38 1DB
T: (01983) 852113
F: (01983) 853862

Bedrooms: 3 single,
14 double/twin, 7 triple/
multiple
Bathrooms: 24 en suite

Evening meal available
CC: Delta, Mastercard,
Switch, Visa

B&B per night:
S £30.00–£38.00
D £60.00–£76.00

HB per person:
DY £40.00–£48.00

Friendly family-run hotel with heated swimming pool, commanding wonderful sea views. Central, yet affords peace and quiet. Car park.

★★
Silver
Award

LECONFIELD HOTEL
85 Leeson Road, Upper Bonchurch,
Bonchurch, Ventnor PO38 1PU
T: (01983) 852196
F: (01983) 856525
E: admin@leconfieldhotel.co.uk
I: www.leconfieldhotel.co.uk

Bedrooms: 2 single,
8 double/twin, 4 triple/
multiple
Bathrooms: 13 en suite,
1 private

Evening meal available
CC: Delta, Mastercard,
Switch, Visa

B&B per night:
S £30.00–£35.00
D £60.00–£70.00

HB per person:
DY £40.00–£48.00

OPEN Mar–Oct

Victorian hotel set in award-winning gardens with superb sea views. Seasonal heated outdoor pool. Very comfortable lounge/library. Completely non-smoking, no children or pets.

WAREHAM, Dorset Map ref 2B3 *Tourist Information Centre Tel: (01929) 552740*

★★

KEMPS COUNTRY HOUSE HOTEL
East Stoke, Wareham BH20 6AL
T: (01929) 462563
F: (01929) 405287
E: kemps.hotel@lineone.net
I: www.smooothound.co.uk/hotels/kemps.html

B&B per night:
S £57.00–£77.00
D £84.00–£134.00

HB per person:
DY £63.95–£88.95

OPEN All year round

Personally run Victorian former rectory, set in its own grounds facing the Purbeck Hills. Lovely views. Daily changing menu plus a la carte. Spacious en suite rooms, 4-poster, whirlpool baths. Real value and bargain breaks all year. Rosette for food.

Bedrooms: 10 double/
twin, 4 triple/multiple
Bathrooms: 14 en suite

Lunch available
Evening meal available
CC: Amex, Delta, Diners,
Mastercard, Switch, Visa

Bargain breaks available all year from £49pp DB&B,
minimum 2 nights.

★★★

SPRINGFIELD COUNTRY HOTEL & LEISURE CLUB
Grange Road, Wareham BH20 5AL
T: (01929) 552177
F: (01929) 551862

B&B per night:
S £74.00–£84.00
D £230.00–£250.00

HB per person:
DY £135.00–£155.00

OPEN All year round

Family-owned country hotel set in 6 acres of beautifully landscaped gardens at foot of Purbeck Hills. 48 en suite rooms, executive rooms with bath, shower and balcony. Ground floor rooms for disabled guests available. Luxurious leisure club, indoor and outdoor swimming pools. Restaurant, bar and oak-beamed lounge with views of gardens. Beaches and golf nearby.

Bedrooms: 1 single,
42 double/twin, 5 triple/
multiple
Bathrooms: 48 en suite

Lunch available
Evening meal available
CC: Amex, Delta, Diners,
Mastercard, Switch, Visa

Special breaks 2 nights or more: double/twin
£50pppn B&B, £60pppn DB&B; executive double/
twin £60pppn B&B, £70pppn DB&B.

HALF BOARD PRICES Half board prices are given per person, but in some cases these may be based on double/twin occupancy.

WIMBORNE MINSTER, Dorset Map ref 2B3 *Tourist Information Centre Tel: (01202) 886116*

★★
Silver
Award

BEECHLEAS HOTEL & RESTAURANT

17 Poole Road, Wimborne Minster
BH21 1QA
T: (01202) 841684
F: (01202) 849344
E: beechleas@hotmail.com
I: www.beechleas.com

Beautifully restored Grade II Listed Georgian house. Awards for food and dining. Log fires in autumn/winter, delightful conservatory and garden, own car park. Award-winning restaurant. Recognised for hospitality and service. Sailing in Poole Harbour. Visit Wimborne Minster, Kingston Lacey, Corfe Castle, New Forest, Thomas Hardy Country.

Bedrooms: 9 double/twin
Bathrooms: 9 en suite

Evening meal available
CC: Amex, Delta, Diners, Mastercard, Switch, Visa

Weekend breaks from £59pppn.

B&B per night:
S £69.00–£99.00
D £79.00–£119.00

HB per person:
DY £57.00–£76.00

OPEN All year round

WINCHESTER, Hampshire Map ref 2C3 *Tourist Information Centre Tel: (01962) 840500*

★★★

HARESTOCK LODGE HOTEL

Harestock Road, Winchester SO22 6NX
T: (01962) 881870 & 880038
F: (01962) 886959
I: www.harestocklodgehotel.com

Peacefully situated on the outskirts of Winchester, a short distance from all major road links. A family-run hotel with well-appointed, finely furnished en suite bedrooms. Views over open countryside, large secluded garden and ample parking. Professionally run to a high standard, offering good food and friendly service in a relaxed atmosphere.

Bedrooms: 4 single, 12 double/twin, 1 triple/multiple
Bathrooms: 17 en suite

Lunch available
Evening meal available
CC: Amex, Delta, Diners, Mastercard, Switch, Visa

Special 2-day breaks DB&B or longer. Special rates all year.

B&B per night:
S £63.00–£68.00
D £85.00–£95.00

HB per person:
DY £57.00–£62.00

OPEN All year round

⊕
The Independents

★★★★
Silver
Award

THE WESSEX HOTEL

Paternoster Row, Winchester
SO23 9LQ
T. 0870 400 8120
F: (01962) 841503
E: heritagehotels_winchester@forte-hotels.com
I: www.wessexhotel.co.uk

Bedrooms: 15 single, 79 double/twin; suites available
Bathrooms: 94 en suite

Lunch available
Evening meal available
CC: Amex, Delta, Diners, Mastercard, Switch, Visa

Spacious modern hotel overlooking the magnificent cathedral. Ideal for strolling around this historic city, former home of Jane Austen, Trollope, Keats and ancient kings of England.

B&B per night:
S £67.50–£77.50
D £75.00–£115.00

OPEN All year round

⊕
Utell International

★★★

THE WINCHESTER ROYAL HOTEL

Marston Hotels Ltd,
St Peters Street, Winchester
SO23 8BS
T: (01962) 840840
F: (01962) 841582
E: royal@marstonhotels.com
I: www.marstonhotels.com

Bedrooms: 75 double/twin; suites available
Bathrooms: 75 en suite

Lunch available
Evening meal available
CC: Amex, Delta, Diners, Mastercard, Switch, Visa

Historic hotel in peaceful location close to cathedral, shops and attractions. Large private garden, car park, award-winning food. Half-board rate based on minimum 2 nights.

B&B per night:
S £99.00–£120.00
D £109.00–£159.00

HB per person:
DY £65.00–£79.00

OPEN All year round

⊕
Best Western Hotels/
Marston Hotels

WINDSOR, Berkshire Map ref 2D2 *Tourist Information Centre Tel: (01753) 743900*

★★ **FAIRLIGHT LODGE ROYAL WINDSOR HOTEL**

41 Frances Road, Windsor SL4 3AQ
T: (01753) 861207
F: (01753) 865963
E: fairlightlodge@hotmail.com
I: www.fairlightlodge.webjump.com

Bedrooms: 2 single,
7 double/twin, 1 triple/
multiple
Bathrooms: 10 en suite

Evening meal available
CC: Amex, Delta, Diners,
Mastercard, Switch, Visa

B&B per night:
S £55.00–£86.00
D £69.00–£110.00

HB per person:
DY £69.00–£110.00

OPEN All year round

Comfortable Victorian property, once the mayoral residence, a few minutes' walk to the town centre, River Thames, historic Eton and Windsor Castle. Fully licensed bar, restaurant.

★★★

ROYAL ADELAIDE HOTEL

46 Kings Road, Windsor SL4 2AG
T: (01753) 863916
F: (01753) 830682
E: royaladelaide@meridianleisure.com
I: www.meridianleisure.com

B&B per night:
S £69.00–£99.00
D £79.00–£115.00

HB per person:
DY £50.00–£75.00

OPEN All year round

Ideally situated in the heart of Windsor town centre, within walking distance of the castle. This beautiful Georgian property offers 42 fully refurbished en suite bedrooms with TV, courtesy tray, modem telephone, ironing board, hairdryer and bedroom safe. A perfect venue for weddings, anniversaries and conferences. Car parking. Full English breakfast.

Bedrooms: 19 single,
18 double/twin, 5 triple/
multiple
Bathrooms: 42 en suite

Lunch available
Evening meal available
CC: Amex, Delta, Diners,
Mastercard, Switch, Visa

Legoland packages including overnight accommodation, full English breakfast, dinner (optional) and Legoland tickets. (Kids under 12 stay free). Licensed for registry marriages.

★★★★
Silver
Award

RUNNYMEDE HOTEL AND SPA

Windsor Road, Egham TW20 0AG
T: (01784) 436171
F: (01784) 436340
E: Info@runnymedehotel.com
I: www.runnymedehotel.com

B&B per night:
S £85.00–£95.00
D £135.00–£170.00

HB per person:
DY £176.00–£196.00

OPEN All year round

Delightfully situated overlooking Thames at Bell-Weir Lock, privately owned modern hotel in 12 acres of landscaped gardens. Extensive state-of-the-art spa and beauty facilities including 18m indoor pool and 5 outdoor tennis courts. Ideally located for the wealth of tourist attractions in the area. On A308, off M25 junction 13. Prices quoted are weekend rates.

Bedrooms: 80 single,
90 double/twin,
10 triple/multiple
Bathrooms: 180 en suite

Lunch available
Evening meal available
CC: Amex, Delta, Diners,
Mastercard, Switch, Visa

Please call for details of health breaks, Legoland packages and other special promotions.

QUALITY ASSURANCE SCHEME

For an explanation of the quality and facilities represented by the Stars please refer to the front of this guide. A more detailed explanation can be found in the information pages at the back.

WINDSOR continued

★★★
Silver
Award

STIRRUPS COUNTRY HOUSE HOTEL

Maidens Green, Bracknell RG42 6LD
T: (01344) 882284
F: (01344) 882300
E: reception@stirrupshotel.co.uk
I: www.stirrupshotel.co.uk

B&B per night:
S £100.00–£140.00
D £110.00–£160.00

HB per person:
DY £65.00–£95.00

OPEN All year round

Stirrups, with its Tudor origins, is located between Bracknell, Ascot and Windsor and is the perfect venue for visits to Legoland Windsor (3 miles). Round off your day by relaxing in the oak-beamed bar by the inglenook fire prior to dinner.

Bedrooms: 24 double/ twin, 5 triple/multiple; suites available
Bathrooms: 29 en suite

Lunch available
Evening meal available
CC: Amex, Delta, Diners, Mastercard, Switch, Visa

WOODLANDS, Hampshire Map ref 2C3

★★

BUSKETTS LAWN HOTEL

174 Woodlands Road, Woodlands, New Forest, Nr Southampton SO40 7GL
T: (023) 8029 2272 & 8029 2077
F: (023) 8029 2487
E: enquiries@buskettslawnhotel.co.uk
I: www.buskettslawnhotel.co.uk

B&B per night:
S £42.00–£75.00
D £70.00–£85.00

HB per person:
DY £53.50–£60.00

OPEN All year round

Warm hospitality offered in this delightful family-run country house hotel in quiet forest surroundings, 8 miles west of Southampton. Seasonal heated swimming pool. Every amenity. All rooms en suite, colour TV, telephone, hairdryer, fridge, beautiful garden. Excellent generous menus served by friendly and helpful staff.

Bedrooms: 4 single, 8 double/twin, 2 triple/ multiple
Bathrooms: 14 en suite

Lunch available
Evening meal available
CC: Amex, Diners, Mastercard, Switch, Visa

2, 3 and 4 day breaks off-season, includes a free night.

WOODSTOCK, Oxfordshire Map ref 2C1 *Tourist Information Centre Tel: (01993) 813276*

★★

THE KINGS ARMS HOTEL

19 Market Street, Woodstock, Oxford OX20 1SU
T: (01993) 813636
F: (01993) 813737
E: enquiries@kings-woodstock. fsnet.co.uk

Bedrooms: 1 single, 8 double/twin
Bathrooms: 9 en suite

Lunch available
Evening meal available
CC: Amex, Delta, Mastercard, Switch, Visa

B&B per night:
S £50.00–£60.00
D £75.00–£90.00

HB per person:
DY £70.00–£85.00

OPEN All year round

Late-Georgian building in the heart of historic Woodstock, an ideal base for Oxford and the Cotswolds. Gates to Blenheim Palace a few minutes' walk.

USE YOUR *i*s

There are more than 550 Tourist Information Centres throughout England offering friendly help with accommodation and holiday ideas as well as suggestions of places to visit and things to do. You'll find TIC addresses in the local Phone Book.

A brief guide to the main Towns and Villages offering accommodation in the

South of England

A **ALTON, HAMPSHIRE** - Pleasant old market town standing on the Pilgrim's Way, with some attractive Georgian buildings. The parish church still bears the scars of bullet marks, evidence of a bitter struggle between the Roundheads and the Royalists.

- **AYLESBURY, BUCKINGHAMSHIRE** - Historic county town in the Vale of Aylesbury. The cobbled market square has a Victorian clock tower and the 15th C King's Head Inn (National Trust). Interesting county museum and 13th C parish church.

B **BASINGSTOKE, HAMPSHIRE** - Rapidly developing commercial and industrial centre. The town is surrounded by charming villages and places to visit.

- **BEMBRIDGE, ISLE OF WIGHT** - Village with harbour and bay below Bembridge Down - the most easterly village on the island. Bembridge Sailing Club is one of the most important in southern England.

- **BLANDFORD FORUM, DORSET** - Almost completely destroyed by fire in 1731, the town was rebuilt in a handsome Georgian style. The church is large and grand and the town is the hub of a rich farming area.

- **BOURNEMOUTH, DORSET** - Seaside town set among the pines with a mild climate, sandy beaches and fine coastal views. The town has wide streets with excellent shops, a pier, a pavilion, museums and conference centre.

- **BRACKNELL, BERKSHIRE** - Designated a New Town in 1949, the town has ancient origins. Set in heathlands, it is an excellent centre for golf and walking. South Hill Park, an 18th C mansion, houses an art centre.

- **BROCKENHURST, HAMPSHIRE** - Attractive village with thatched cottages and a ford in its main street. Well placed for visiting the New Forest.

- **BUCKINGHAM, BUCKINGHAMSHIRE** - Interesting old market town surrounded by rich farmland. It has many Georgian buildings, including the Town Hall and Old Jail and many old almshouses and inns. Stowe School nearby has magnificent 18th C landscaped gardens.

- **BURFORD, OXFORDSHIRE** - One of the most beautiful Cotswold wool towns with Georgian and Tudor houses, many antique shops and a picturesque High Street sloping to the River Windrush.

- **BURLEY, HAMPSHIRE** - Attractive centre from which to explore the south-west part of the New Forest. There is an ancient earthwork on Castle Hill nearby, which also offers good views.

C **CHALE, ISLE OF WIGHT** - Village overlooking Chale Bay and near Blackgang Chine which has a children's maze, a water garden and a museum displaying many objects from shipwrecks.

- **CORFE CASTLE, DORSET** - One of the most spectacular ruined castles in Britain. Norman in origin, the castle was a Royalist stronghold during the Civil War and held out until 1645. The village had a considerable marble-carving industry in the Middle Ages.

E **EASTLEIGH, HAMPSHIRE** - Town developed around the railway engineering works built there in 1889. The borough stretches from Southampton Water to the Test Valley in the north. Yachting centres at Hamble and Bursledon.

F **FAREHAM, HAMPSHIRE** - Lies on a quiet backwater of Portsmouth Harbour. The High Street is lined with fine Georgian buildings.

G **GOSPORT, HAMPSHIRE** - From a tiny fishing hamlet, Gosport has grown into an important centre with many naval establishments, including HMS Dolphin, the submarine base, with the Naval Submarine Museum which preserves HMS Alliance and Holland.

L **LIPHOOK, HAMPSHIRE** - Large village astride the A3 and close to the West Sussex border.

- **LYMINGTON, HAMPSHIRE** - Small, pleasant town with bright cottages and attractive Georgian houses, lying on the edge of the New Forest with a ferry service to the Isle of Wight. A sheltered harbour makes it a busy yachting centre.

- **LYNDHURST, HAMPSHIRE** - The 'capital' of the New Forest, surrounded by attractive woodland scenery and delightful villages. The town is dominated by the Victorian Gothic-style church where the original Alice in Wonderland is buried.

M **MAIDENHEAD, BERKSHIRE** - Attractive town on the River Thames which is crossed by an elegant 18th C bridge and by Brunel's well-known railway bridge. It is a popular place for boating with delightful riverside walks. The Courage Shire Horse Centre is nearby.

- **MARLOW, BUCKINGHAMSHIRE** - Attractive Georgian town on the River Thames, famous for its 19th C suspension bridge. The High Street contains many old houses and there are connections with writers including Shelley and T S Eliot.

- **MILFORD-ON-SEA, HAMPSHIRE** - Victorian seaside resort with shingle beach and good bathing, set in pleasant countryside and looking out over the Isle of Wight. Nearby is Hurst Castle, built by Henry VIII. The school chapel, former abbey church, can be visited.

- **MILTON KEYNES, BUCKINGHAMSHIRE** - Designated a New Town in 1967, Milton Keynes offers a wide range of housing and is abundantly planted with trees. It has excellent shopping facilities and 3 centres for leisure and sporting activities. The Open University is based here.

N **NEWBURY, BERKSHIRE** - Ancient town surrounded by the Downs and on the Kennet and Avon Canal. It has many buildings of interest, including the 17th C Cloth Hall, which is now a museum. The famous racecourse is nearby.

RATING All accommodation in this guide has been rated, or is awaiting a rating, by a trained English Tourism Council assessor.

O ODIHAM, HAMPSHIRE - Situated close to the Hampshire/Surrey border. Village retains a sense of historical identity. Convenient for RAF base.

• **OXFORD, OXFORDSHIRE** - Beautiful university town with many ancient colleges, some dating from the 13th C, and numerous buildings of historic and architectural interest. The Ashmolean Museum has outstanding collections. Lovely gardens and meadows with punting on the Cherwell.

P PORTSMOUTH & SOUTHSEA, HAMPSHIRE - There have been connections with the Navy since early times and the first dock was built in 1194. HMS Victory, Nelson's flagship, is here and Charles Dickens' former home is open to the public. Neighbouring Southsea has a promenade with magnificent views of Spithead.

R READING, BERKSHIRE - Busy, modern county town with large shopping centre and many leisure and recreation facilities. There are several interesting museums and the Duke of Wellington's Stratfield Saye is nearby.

S SHAFTESBURY, DORSET - Hilltop town with a long history. The ancient and cobbled Gold Hill is one of the most attractive in Dorset. There is an excellent small museum containing a collection of buttons for which the town is famous.

• **SHANKLIN, ISLE OF WIGHT** - Set on a cliff with gentle slopes leading down to the beach, esplanade and marine gardens. The picturesque, old thatched village nestles at the end of the wooded chine.

• **SOUTHAMPTON, HAMPSHIRE** - One of Britain's leading seaports with a long history, now a major container port. In the 18th C it became a fashionable resort with the assembly rooms and theatre. The old Guildhall and the Wool House are now museums. Sections of the medieval wall can still be seen.

• **STONOR, OXFORDSHIRE** - The fine manor house of Stonor Park has been a family home for over 800 years and its private chapel has been a centre of Catholicism since Tudor times. The park is one of the most beautiful in southern England.

• **STRATFIELD TURGIS, HAMPSHIRE** - More a collection of 3 hamlets as opposed to a village. Convenient for Basingstoke.

• **STUDLAND, DORSET** - On a beautiful stretch of coast and good for walking, with a National Nature Reserve to the north. The Norman church is the finest in the country, with superb rounded arches and vaulting. Brownsea Island, where the first scout camp was held, lies in Poole Harbour.

• **SWANAGE, DORSET** - Began life as an Anglo-Saxon port, then a quarrying centre of Purbeck marble. Now the safe, sandy beach set in a sweeping bay and flanked by downs is good walking country, making it an ideal resort.

• **SWAY, HAMPSHIRE** - Small village on the south-western edge of the New Forest. It is noted for its 220-ft tower, Peterson's Folly, built in the 1870s by a retired Indian judge to demonstrate the value of concrete as a building material.

T THAME, OXFORDSHIRE - Historic market town on the River Thames. The wide, unspoilt High Street has many styles of architecture with medieval timber-framed cottages, Georgian houses and some famous inns.

• **TOTLAND BAY, ISLE OF WIGHT** - On the Freshwater Peninsula. It is possible to walk from here around to Alum Bay.

V VENTNOR, ISLE OF WIGHT - Town lies at the bottom of an 800-ft hill and has a reputation as a winter holiday and health resort due to its mild climate. The mile-long esplanade reaches the shore of the delightful village of Bonchurch, and in the other direction are the 22-acre Botanical Gardens.

W WAREHAM, DORSET - This site has been occupied since pre-Roman times and has a turbulent history. In 1762 fire destroyed much of the town, so the buildings now are mostly Georgian.

• **WIMBORNE MINSTER, DORSET** - Market town centred on the twin-towered Minster Church of St Cuthberga which gave the town the second part of its name. Good touring base for the surrounding countryside, depicted in the writings of Thomas Hardy.

• **WINCHESTER, HAMPSHIRE** - King Alfred the Great made Winchester the capital of Saxon England. A magnificent Norman cathedral, with one of the longest naves in Europe, dominates the city. Home of Winchester College founded in 1382.

• **WINDSOR, BERKSHIRE** - Town dominated by the spectacular castle, home of the Royal Family for over 900 years. Parts are open to the public. There are many attractions including the Great Park, Eton and trips on the river.

• **WOODLANDS, HAMPSHIRE** - Scattered village on the edge of the New Forest west of Southampton.

• **WOODSTOCK, OXFORDSHIRE** - Small country town clustered around the park gates of Blenheim Palace, the superb 18th C home of the Duke of Marlborough. The town has well-known inns and an interesting museum. Sir Winston Churchill was born and buried nearby.

SOUTH EAST England

The White cliffs of Dover, beach huts and piers, yachts at Chichester – this distinctive coast combines with famous gardens and the apples and hops of Kent to make a quintessentially English region.

classic sights
Battle of Hastings – audio tour brings the battle to life
Hever Castle – romantic moated castle, home of Anne Boleyn

coast & country
Runnymede – riverside meadows and woodland
Pegwell Bay & Goodwin Sands – a haven for birds and seals

gorgeous gardens
Sissinghurst – celebrated garden of Vita Sackville-West
Leonardslee – rhododendrons and azaleas ablaze with colour in May

literary links
Charles Dickens – Rochester; his home Gad's Hill Place
Rudyard Kipling – Bateman's, his momento filled home
Chaucer – The Canterbury Tales

arts for all
Brighton Festival – international performers, artists and writers every May

distinctively different
Royal Pavilion – exotic palace of King George IV

The counties of East Sussex, Kent, Surrey and West Sussex

FOR MORE INFORMATION CONTACT:
South East England Tourist Board
The Old Brew House, Warwick Park,
Tunbridge Wells, Kent TN2 5TU
Tel: (01892) 540766 Fax: (01892) 511008
Email: enquiries@seetb.org.uk
Internet: www.SouthEastEngland.uk.com

The Pictures:
1 Bodiam Castle, East Sussex
2 Southover Grange Gardens,
  Lewes, East Sussex

Places to Visit - see pages 272-275
Where to Stay - see pages 276-289

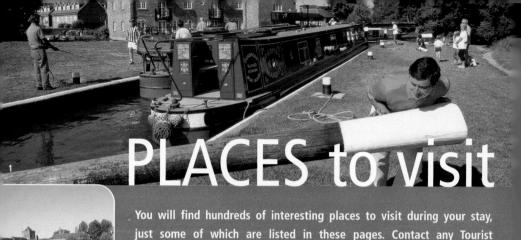

PLACES to visit

You will find hundreds of interesting places to visit during your stay, just some of which are listed in these pages. Contact any Tourist Information Centre in the region for more ideas on days out.

Alfriston Clergy House

The Tye, Alfriston, Polegate, East Sussex BN26 5TL
Tel: (01323) 870001 www.nationaltrust.org.uk
A thatched, half-timbered 14thC building with exhibition on Wealden house-building. It was the first building acquired by The National Trust in 1896. Cottage garden.

Amberley Museum

Houghton Bridge, Amberley, Arundel, West Sussex BN18 9LT
Tel: (01798) 831370 www.amberleymuseum.co.uk
Open-air industrial history centre in chalk quarry. Working craftsmen, narrow-gauge railway, early buses, working machines and other exhibits. Nature trail/visitor centre.

Anne of Cleves House Museum

52 Southover High Street, Lewes, East Sussex BN7 1JA
Tel: (01273) 474610 www.sussexpast.co.uk
A 16thC timber-framed Wealden hall-house which contains collections of Sussex interest. Displays feature Lewes from the 16thC to the present day.

Arundel Castle

Arundel, West Sussex BN18 9AB
Tel: (01903) 883136 www.arundelcastle.org
An impressive Norman stronghold in extensive grounds, much restored in the 18thC and 19thC. 11thC keep, 13thC barbican, barons' hall, armoury, chapel. Van Dyck and Gainsborough paintings.

Basingstoke Canal Visitor Centre

Mytchett Place Road, Mytchett, Camberley, Hampshire GU16 6DD
Tel: (01252) 370073 www.basingstoke-canal.co.uk
A canal interpretation centre with an exhibition displaying the history of canals over the past 200 years. Boat trips and boat hire available. Adventure playground.

Battle Abbey and Battlefield

High Street, Battle, East Sussex TN33 0AD
Tel: (01424) 773792 www.english-heritage.org.uk
An abbey founded by William the Conqueror on the site of the Battle of Hastings. The church altar is on the spot where King Harold was killed. Battlefield views and exhibition.

Beaver Zoological Gardens

Waylands Farm, Approach Road, Tatsfield, Westerham, Kent TN16 2JT
Tel: (01959) 577747 www.beaverwaterworld.com
Visitors to Beaver Zoological Gardens can see reptiles, tropical and cold water fish, Canadian beavers, aviary birds, rabbits and chipmunks. Play area, sandpit and cafe.

Borde Hill Garden

Balcombe Road, Haywards Heath, West Sussex RH16 1XP
Tel: (01444) 450326 www.bordehill.co.uk
Winner of two prestigious awards. A garden of contrasts where botanical interest and garden design play equally important roles. Extended colour throughout the year.

Brooklands Museum

Brooklands Road, Weybridge, Surrey KT13 0QN
Tel: (01932) 857381 www.motor-software.co.uk
Original 1907 motor racing circuit. Features the most
historic and steepest section of the old banked track and
1-in-4 test hill. Motoring village and Grand Prix
exhibition.

The Canterbury Tales Visitor Attraction

St Margaret's Street, Canterbury, Kent CT1 2TG
Tel: (01227) 479227 www.canterburytales.org.uk
An audiovisual recreation of life in medieval England.
Visitors join Chaucer's pilgrims on their journey from
London's Tabard Inn to Thomas Becket's shrine at
Canterbury.

Charleston

Firle, Lewes, East Sussex BN8 6LL
Tel: (01323) 811265 www.charleston.org.uk
A 17thC-18thC farmhouse, home of Vanessa Bell and
Duncan Grant of the Bloomsbury Set. House and contents
decorated by the artists. Traditional walled garden.

Chartwell

Westerham, Kent TN16 1PS
Tel: (01732) 866368 www.nationaltrust.org.uk
The home of Sir Winston Churchill with study, studio,
museum rooms with gifts, uniforms and photos. Garden,
Golden Rose Walk, lakes. 'Years at Chartwell' exhibition.

Chatley Heath Semaphore Tower

Pointers Road, Cobham, Surrey KT11 1PQ
Tel: (01483) 517595
A restored historic semaphore tower, set in woodland,
displaying the history of overland naval communications
in the early 19thC. Working semaphore mast and models.

Drusillas Park

Alfriston, East Sussex BN26 5QS
Tel: (01323) 874100 www.drusillas.co.uk
South East England Tourist Board Visitor Attraction of the
Year. Jungle Adventure Golf, adventure playground,
toddlers' play village, zoolympics and small-gauge
railway.

Eagle Heights

Hulberry Farm, Lullingstone Lane, Eynsford,
Dartford, Kent DA4 0JB
Tel: (01322) 866466 www.eagleheights.co.uk
Bird of prey centre housed undercover where visitors can
see eagles, hawks, falcons, owls and vultures from all
over the world. Reptile centre, play area and sandpit.

English Wine Centre

Alfriston Roundabout, Alfriston, East Sussex BN26 5QS
Tel: (01323) 870164 www.weddingwine.co.uk
The English Wine Centre was established in 1972 and
stocks a large range of English wines, fruit wines and
ciders within the attractive wine shop. Tours and tastings
available.

Goodwood House

Goodwood, Chichester, West Sussex PO18 OPX
Tel: (01243) 755040 www.goodwood.co.uk
A magnificent Regency house, home to the Earl of
March, extensively refurbished in 1997 and set in a large
area of open parkland. Fine furnishings, tapestries and
porcelain.

Kent & East Sussex Railway

Tenterden Town Station, Tenterden, Kent TN30 6HE
Tel: (01580) 765155 www.kesr.org.uk
Full-size steam railway with restored Edwardian stations
at Tenterden and Northiam. 14 steam engines, Victorian
coaches and Pullman carriages. Museum and children's
play area.

Leeds Castle and Gardens

Maidstone, Kent ME17 1PL
Tel: (01622) 765400 www.leeds-castle.co.uk
A castle built on two islands in a lake, dating from the
9thC. Furniture, tapestries, art treasures, dog collar
museum, gardens, duckery, aviaries, maze, grotto,
vineyard and greenhouses.

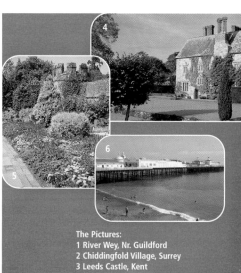

The Pictures:
1 River Wey, Nr. Guildford
2 Chiddingfold Village, Surrey
3 Leeds Castle, Kent
4 Bateman's, East Sussex
5 Chichester Cathedral Gardens, West Sussex
6 Brighton Pier

Port Lympne Wild Animal Park, Mansion and Gardens

Port Lympne, Hythe, Kent CT21 4PD
Tel: (01303) 264647 www.howletts.net
A 300-acre (121-ha) wild animal park specialising in rare breeds including gorillas, deer, rhino, tigers, elephants etc. Mansion with art gallery exhibitions, murals and gardens. Trailer rides.

Rural Life Centre

Old Kiln Museum, Reeds Road, Tilford,
Farnham, Surrey GU10 2DL
Tel: (01252) 792300
www.surreyweb.org.uk/rural-life
A museum with a comprehensive collection of farm machines, implements, wagons, displays on past village life, small arboretum and a woodland walk.

The Savill Garden

Windsor Great Park, Wick Lane, Englefield Green,
Egham, Surrey TW20 0UU
Tel: (01753) 847518 www.savillgarden.co.uk
Woodland garden with formal gardens and herbaceous borders offering much of great interest and beauty in all seasons. Landscaped Queen Elizabeth Temperate House.

Scotney Castle Garden

Lamberhurst, Royal Tunbridge Wells, Kent TN3 8JN
Tel: (01892) 891081 www.nationaltrust.org.uk
Romantic gardens created around the ruins of a 14thC moated castle containing exhibitions. Gardens created by the Hussey family with shrubs, winding paths and good views.

Sculpture at Goodwood

Hat Hill Copse, Goodwood, Chichester, West Sussex PO18 0QP
Tel: (01243) 538449 www.sculpture.org.uk
A changing collection of contemporary British sculpture set in 20 acres (8 ha) of beautiful grounds on the South Downs overlooking Chichester.

St Mary's House and Gardens

Bramber, Steyning, West Sussex BN44 3WE
Tel: (01903) 816205
A medieval, timber-framed Grade I Listed house with rare 16thC wall-leather, fine panelled rooms and a unique painted room. Topiary gardens.

South of England Rare Breeds Centre

Highlands Farm, Woodchurch, Ashford, Kent TN26 3RJ
Tel: (01233) 861493 www.rarebreeds.org.uk
Large collection of rare farm breeds on a working farm with children's play activities. Georgian farmstead under reconstruction. Home to the 'Tamworth Two'. Woodland walks.

Titsey Place and Gardens

Oxted, Surrey RH8 0SD
Tel: (01273) 407056 www.titsey.com
A guided tour of Titsey Place includes the library, old servants' hall, dining room and drawing room. The gardens comprise 10 acres (4 ha) of formal gardens and a walled garden.

Weald and Downland Open Air Museum

Singleton, Chichester, West Sussex PO18 0EU
Tel: (01243) 811348 www.wealddown.co.uk
Over 40 rescued historic buildings from South East England, reconstructed on a downland country park site. Homes and workplaces of the past include a medieval farmstead.

West Dean Gardens

West Dean Estate, West Dean, Chichester,
West Sussex PO18 0QZ
Tel: (01243) 818210 www.westdean.org.uk
Extensive downland garden with specimen trees, 300 ft (91 m) pergola, rustic summerhouses and restored walled kitchen garden. Walk in parkland and 45-acre (18-ha) arboretum.

Wilderness Wood

Hadlow Down, Uckfield, East Sussex TN22 4HJ
Tel: (01825) 830509 www.wildernesswood.co.uk
A family-run working woodland of 60 acres (24 ha), beautiful in all seasons. There are trails, a bluebell walk, a play area, workshop and a timber barn with exhibitions.

The Wildfowl and Wetlands Trust

Mill Road, Arundel, West Sussex BN18 9PB
Tel: (01903) 883355 www.wwt.org.uk
A wildlife paradise and a haven of peace and tranquility for swans, ducks and geese from around the world. Visitor centre and viewing gallery.

Winkworth Arboretum

Hascombe Road, Hascombe, Godalming, Surrey GU8 4AD
Tel: (01483) 208477 www.cornuswwweb.co.uk
One hundred acres (40 ha) of hillside planted with rare trees and shrubs. Good views, lakes, newly restored boathouse, azaleas, bluebells, wild spring flowers and autumn colours.

Find out more about
SOUTH EAST England

Further information about holidays and attractions in South East England is available from:

SOUTH EAST ENGLAND TOURIST BOARD
The Old Brew House, Warwick Park, Tunbridge Wells, Kent TN2 5TU.
Tel: (01892) 540766 Fax: (01892) 511008
Email: enquiries@seetb.org.uk
Internet: www.SouthEastEngland.uk.com

The following publications are available from the South East England Tourist Board:

South East Holiday and Short Breaks Guide
a detailed guide to the region including places to visit and inspected accommodation

Bed and Breakfast Touring map 2002 - including Camping and Caravan Parks in the South East
a useful touring map detailing inspected guest accommodation in the South East and London regions.
Also contains camping and caravan parks

Eating and Drinking at Traditional Inns
in partnership with Whitbread Pubs, a guide to some of the fine inns to be found in the South and South East of England

Churches and Cathedrals of the South of England
a guide detailing some of the region's finest churches and cathedrals, their fascinating history and architecture

Spoilt for Choice - 100s of Places to Visit in South East England
the definitive guide to over 300 places to visit in South East England. Also contains a Web site directory, map and information on the network of Tourist Information Centres

Leisure Map and Gazetteer - South East England
produced in conjunction with Estate Publications Ltd, a colourful tourist map of the South East showing roads, railways, hundreds of places to visit and the topography of the region

The pictures:
1 Guildford Castle

Getting to
SOUTH EAST England

BY ROAD: From the north of England - M1/M25; the west and Wales - M4/M25; the east of England - M25; the south of England M3/M25; London - M20 or M2.

BY RAIL: Regular services from London's Charing Cross, Victoria and Waterloo East stations to all parts of South East England.

Where to stay in South East England

Accommodation entries in this region are listed in alphabetical order of place name, and then in alphabetical order of establishment.

Map references refer to the colour location maps at front of this guide. The first number indicates the map to use; the letter and number which follow refer to the grid reference on the map.

At-a-glance symbols at the end of each accommodation entry give useful information about services and facilities. A key to symbols can be found inside the back cover flap. Keep this open for easy reference.

A brief description of the towns and villages offering accommodation in the entries which follow, can be found at the end of this section.

A complete listing of all the English Tourism Council assessed accommodation covered by this guide appears at the back of the guide.

ASHFORD, Kent Map ref 3B4 *Tourist Information Centre Tel: (01233) 629165*

★★★★
Gold
Award

The finest country house hotel in the South East, boasts 62 bedrooms, restaurant, indoor and outdoor heated 20m swimming pools, tennis court, croquet, petanque, sauna, steam room, jacuzzi, solarium, gymnasium, 12 beauty treatment rooms offering therapy from 4 major product houses, hairdressing salon, bar and brasserie.

EASTWELL MANOR HOTEL

Eastwell Park, Boughton Lees, Ashford
TN25 4HR
T: (01233) 213000
F: (01233) 635530
E: eastwell@btinternet.com
I: www.eastwellmanor.co.uk

Bedrooms: 27 double/
twin, 35 triple/multiple;
suites available
Bathrooms: 62 en suite

Lunch available
Evening meal available
CC: Amex, Delta, Diners,
Mastercard, Switch, Visa

Weekend breaks-1 night, DB&B for 2 people sharing from £230 to £385. Sunday night B&B per person sharing £60.

B&B per night:
S £170.00–£325.00
D £200.00–£355.00

HB per person:
DY £202.00–£357.00

OPEN All year round

Pride of Britain

MAP REFERENCES The map references refer to the colour maps at the front of this guide. The first figure is the map number; the letter and figure which follow indicate the grid reference on the map.

★★★

Attractive, modern hotel near the M20 jct 9 in the Kent countryside. Offering spacious, quality bedrooms and value for money. Superb buffet breakfast. Traditional pub restaurant in hotel grounds. Warm, friendly welcome. Central locaton for sightseeing. Canterbury, Leeds Castle, shopping and many other attractions. Easy access for channel crossings.

HOLIDAY INN GARDEN COURT ASHFORD/KENT

A20 Maidstone Road, Hothfield, Ashford
TN26 1AR
T: (01233) 713333 & 713950
F: (01233) 712082
E: sales@holidayinn-ashford.freeserve.
co.uk
I: www.holiday-inn.com/hotels/asduk

Bedrooms: 89 double/
twin, 11 triple/multiple
Bathrooms: 100 en suite

Lunch available
Evening meal available
CC: Amex, Delta, Diners,
Mastercard, Switch, Visa

B&B per night:
S £49.00–£69.00
D £69.00–£89.00

HB per person:
DY £47.00–£57.00

OPEN All year round

ASHINGTON, West Sussex Map ref 2D3

★★★
Silver
Award

This charming Grade II Listed small country house hotel exudes warmth and character, to form a lasting testiment to its 17thC past. The Mill House combines relaxed elegance with an appealing air of informality, while the dining room offers excellent and imaginative cuisine, complemented by a notably well-chosen wine list.

THE MILL HOUSE HOTEL

Mill Lane, Ashington, Pulborough
RH20 3BX
T: (01903) 892426
F: (01903) 892855
E: mill1@netcomuk.co.uk

Bedrooms: 3 single,
6 double/twin; suites
available
Bathrooms: 9 en suite

Lunch available
Evening meal available
CC: Amex, Delta,
Mastercard, Switch, Visa

B&B per night:
S £49.00–£57.00
D £79.00–£89.00

OPEN All year round

BEXHILL, East Sussex Map ref 3B4 *Tourist Information Centre Tel: (01424) 732208*

★★

Family-managed for 45 years and furnished with antique and reproduction furniture, creating a warm, friendly and homely atmosphere in elegant surroundings. Adjacent to seafront and close to town centre. All rooms en suite. Restaurants and bar open to non-residents. Short breaks, holiday and residential accommodation. Functions up to 50 people.

THE NORTHERN HOTEL

72-82 Sea Road, Bexhill TN40 1JL
T: (01424) 212836
F: (01424) 213036
E: reception@northernhotel.co.uk
I: www.northernhotel.co.uk

Bedrooms: 12 single,
8 double/twin
Bathrooms: 20 en suite

Lunch available
Evening meal available
CC: Amex, Delta,
Mastercard, Switch, Visa

4-day Christmas break.

B&B per night:
S £30.00–£45.00
D £45.00–£80.00

OPEN All year round

IDEAS For ideas on places to visit refer to the introduction at the beginning of this section.

★★★

BEACHCROFT HOTEL

Clyde Road, Felpham, Bognor Regis
PO22 7AH
T: (01243) 827142
F: (01243) 827142
E: reservations@beachcroft-hotel.co.uk
I: www.beachcroft-hotel.co.uk

B&B per night:
S £41.00–£55.00
D £73.00–£90.00

HB per person:
DY £53.00–£59.00

OPEN All year round

Family-run, with south-facing beachside garden, adjoining the promenade (1 mile to Bognor Regis town). Indoor heated pool. All bedrooms en suite, many facing the sea, some ground floor. Spacious restaurant offering extensive menu choices, and comprehensive wine list. Lounge bar with hot and cold snacks. Discounted seasonal breaks.

Bedrooms: 9 single, 28 double/twin
Bathrooms: 37 en suite

Evening meal available
CC: Amex, Delta, Diners, Mastercard, Switch, Visa

Discounts available for 2 or more nights B&B or HB on various dates throughout the year.

★★★★

OLD SHIP HOTEL

King's Road, Brighton BN1 1NR
T: (01273) 329001
F: (01273) 820718
E: oldship@paramount-hotels.co.uk
I: www.paramount-hotels.co.uk

B&B per night:
S £65.00–£85.00
D £130.00–£160.00

HB per person:
DY £75.00–£95.00

OPEN All year round

Located on Brighton's seafront, the Old Ship Hotel is the oldest hotel in Brighton. The Old Ship has been recently refurbished but has retained all of its ambience and charm. Facilities include a stylish new bar/ brasserie with sea views, numerous lounge areas and 152 newly refurbished bedrooms.

Bedrooms: 11 single, 141 double/twin
Bathrooms: 152 en suite

Lunch available
Evening meal available
CC: Amex, Delta, Diners, Mastercard, Switch, Visa

Jul/Aug mid-week breaks-only £39pppn based on 2 people sharing, for a minimum of 2 nights-offer is subject to availability.

★★★

PRINCES MARINE HOTEL

153 Kingsway, Hove, Brighton
BN3 4GR
T: (01273) 207660
F: (01273) 325913
E: princesmarine@bestwestern.co
uk
I: www.brighton.co.uk/hotels/
princes

Bedrooms: 44 double/ twin, 4 triple/multiple
Bathrooms: 48 en suite

Lunch available
Evening meal available
CC: Amex, Delta, Diners, Mastercard, Switch, Visa

B&B per night:
S £40.00–£60.00
D £70.00–£110.00

HB per person:
DY £55.00–£75.00

OPEN All year round

Best Western Hotels

Seafront hotel opposite leisure centre near shops and entertainments, 5 minutes from Brighton, 25 minutes from Gatwick. Seaview restaurant and bar, large free car park.

★★★

ROYAL ALBION HOTEL

35 Old Steine, Brighton BN1 1NT
T: (01273) 329202
F: (01273) 748078
I: www.britanniahotels.com

Bedrooms: 10 single, 166 double/twin, 10 triple/multiple; suites available
Bathrooms: 186 en suite

Lunch available
Evening meal available
CC: Amex, Delta, Diners, Mastercard, Switch, Visa

B&B per night:
S Min £105.00
D Min £135.00

HB per person:
DY Min £117.50

OPEN All year round

Refurbished Regency, Grade II Listed building on sea front opposite Brighton Pier. Close to Lanes and Royal Pavilion. NCP car parking available nearby.

PRICES
Please check prices and other details at the time of booking.

CANTERBURY, Kent Map ref 3B3 *Tourist Information Centre Tel: (01227) 766567*

★★

CANTERBURY HOTEL AND RESTAURANT

71 New Dover Road, Canterbury
CT1 3DZ
T: (01227) 450551
F: (01227) 780145
E: canterbury.hotel@btinternet.
com
I: www.
canterbury-hotel-apartments.co.uk

Bedrooms: 3 single,
19 double/twin, 1 triple/
multiple
Bathrooms: 23 en suite

Lunch available
Evening meal available
CC: Amex, Delta, Diners,
Mastercard, Switch, Visa

B&B per night:
S £55.00–£85.00
D £55.00–£115.00

HB per person:
DY Min £70.00

OPEN All year round

Elegant Georgian-style hotel, 10 minutes from city centre, providing high standards of personal service and comfort. Executive rooms, 4-poster suite. 'La Bonne Cuisine' award-winning restaurant.

★★
Silver
Award

EBURY HOTEL

65-67 New Dover Road, Canterbury
CT1 3DX
T: (01227) 768433 & 811550
F: (01227) 459187
E: info@ebury-hotel.co.uk
I: www.ebury-hotel.co.uk

Bedrooms: 2 single,
11 double/twin, 2 triple/
multiple
Bathrooms: 15 en suite

Evening meal available
CC: Amex, Delta, Diners,
Mastercard, Switch, Visa

B&B per night:
S £50.00–£70.00
D £65.00–£95.00

HB per person:
DY £46.00

OPEN All year round
except Christmas and
New Year

Family-run hotel located within walking distance of Canterbury city centre. Offering well-appointed en suite accommodation, parking, restaurant, large garden and an indoor heated swimming pool.

★★

THE OLD COACH HOUSE

Dover Road (A2), Barham,
Canterbury CT4 6SA
T: (01227) 831218
F: (01227) 831932

Bedrooms: 4 double/
twin, 3 triple/multiple
Bathrooms: 7 en suite

Lunch available
Evening meal available
CC: Amex, Delta,
Mastercard, Switch, Visa

B&B per night:
S £40.00–£44.00
D £48.00–£56.00

HB per person:
DY £40.00–£46.00

OPEN All year round

The Independents

Originally a coaching inn (c1645), run along the lines of a French auberge. Restaurant specialising in local fish. Convenient for Dover, Canterbury, Channel Tunnel.

CHICHESTER, West Sussex Map ref 2C3 *Tourist Information Centre Tel: (01243) 775888*

★★★
Gold
Award

MILLSTREAM HOTEL & RESTAURANT

Bosham Lane, Bosham, Chichester
PO18 8HL
T: (01243) 573234
F: (01243) 573459
E: info@millstream-hotel.co.uk
I: www.millstream-hotel.co.uk

B&B per night:
S £75.00–£80.00
D £120.00–£125.00

HB per person:
DY £60.00–£82.00

OPEN All year round

Period building dating from 1701. All rooms are individually furnished, and are with en suite facilities with shower and bath. Set in a quiet, peaceful quayside location. The Millstream, from which the hotel takes its name, flows through the gardens on its way to the sea just 300 yards away.

Bedrooms: 5 single,
28 double/twin, 2 triple/
multiple; suites available
Bathrooms: 35 en suite

Lunch available
Evening meal available
CC: Amex, Delta, Diners,
Mastercard, Switch, Visa

Hibernation breaks available from Nov-Apr. Sun or Thurs nights half price if they are part of a 3-night break.

IMPORTANT NOTE
Information on accommodation listed in this guide has been supplied by the proprietors. As changes may occur you are advised to check details at the time of booking.

CHICHESTER continued

★★★

SHIP HOTEL

North Street, Chichester PO19 1NH
T: (01243) 778000
F: (01243) 788000
I: www.shiphotel.com

B&B per night:
S £70.00–£78.00
D £95.00–£120.00

HB per person:
DY £77.00–£100.00

OPEN All year round

18thC Georgian hotel in the centre of this lovely city with the Festival Theatre and cathedral within strolling distance. The hotel offers a friendly service and is now fully refurbished in period style.

Bedrooms: 6 single, 28 double/twin, 2 triple/ multiple
Bathrooms: 36 en suite

Lunch available
Evening meal available
CC: Amex, Delta, Diners, Mastercard, Switch, Visa

Christmas residential breaks available with trips to theatre and cathedral included.

CLIFTONVILLE

See under Margate

COPTHORNE, Surrey Map ref 2D2

★★★★
Silver Award

COPTHORNE HOTEL EFFINGHAM PARK

Copthorne Way, Copthorne, Crawley RH10 3PG
T: (01342) 348800
F: (01342) 348833
E: sales.gatwick@mill-cop.com
I: www.millennium-hotels.com

B&B per night:
S £99.00–£153.00
D £109.00–£166.00

HB per person:
DY £129.00–£183.00

OPEN All year round

A 16thC farmhouse is the focal point for this 227 bedroom, 4-star hotel, set amidst 100 acres of beautiful parkland. Guests have a choice of activities – gym, squash, tennis, swimming to name a few. Located in the pleasant village of Copthorne, yet 4 miles from Gatwick Airport (shuttle bus service).

Bedrooms: 5 single, 218 double/twin, 4 triple/multiple; suites available
Bathrooms: 227 en suite

Lunch available
Evening meal available
CC: Amex, Diners, Mastercard, Switch, Visa

Weekend breaks from only £37.50pppn B&B (based on 2 people sharing for 2 nights) Fri-Sun, subject to availability.

CUCKFIELD, West Sussex Map ref 2D3

★★★

HILTON PARK HOTEL

Tylers Green, Cuckfield, Haywards Heath RH17 5EG
T: (01444) 454555
F: (01444) 457222
E: hiltonpark@janus-systems.com
I: www.janus-systems.com/hiltonpark.htm

B&B per night:
S £75.00–£90.00
D £100.00–£125.00

OPEN All year round

Victorian country house in 3 acres of gardens, with magnificent views of South Downs from conservatory bar and bedrooms. An ideal centre for visiting the gardens and stately homes of Sussex.

Bedrooms: 11 double/ twin
Bathrooms: 11 en suite

Lunch available
Evening meal available
CC: Amex, Delta, Diners, Mastercard, Switch, Visa

CENTRAL RESERVATIONS OFFICES

The symbol **CR** and a group name in an entry indicate that bookings can be made through a central reservations office. These are listed in a separate section towards the back of this guide.

DORKING, Surrey Map ref 2D2

★★★

GATTON MANOR HOTEL, GOLF & COUNTRY CLUB

Standon Lane, Ockley, Dorking
RH5 5PQ
T: (01306) 627555
F: (01306) 627713
E: gattonmanor@enterprise.net
I: www.smoothhound.co.uk/hotels/
gatton.html

Bedrooms: 18 double/
twin
Bathrooms: 18 en suite

Lunch available
Evening meal available
CC: Amex, Delta, Diners,
Mastercard, Switch, Visa

B&B per night:
S £67.50
D £105.00

HB per person:
DY £67.00–£82.50

OPEN All year round

18thC manor house on 200-acre estate. Championship-length golf-course, hotel, a la carte restaurants, conference suites, bowls, fishing, tennis, gym and health club. Village is 6 miles south of Dorking.

DOVER, Kent Map ref 3C4 *Tourist Information Centre Tel: (01304) 205108*

★★★
Silver
Award

THE CHURCHILL

Dover Waterfront, Dover CT17 9BP
T: (01304) 203633
F: (01304) 216320
E: enquiries@churchill-hotel.com
I: www.churchill-hotel.com

B&B per night:
S £68.00
D £97.00

OPEN All year round

ⓒⓡ
Best Western Hotels

On Dover's waterfront, the hotel is a Listed building set in a Regency crescent with panoramic views over the English Channel. We offer excellent standards of cuisine and a very warm and friendly service. Guests have use of the hotel's health club, with a choice of activities, and hair/beauty salons.

Bedrooms: 4 single,
58 double/twin, 4 triple/
multiple; suites available
Bathrooms: 66 en suite

Lunch available
Evening meal available
CC: Amex, Delta, Diners,
Mastercard, Switch, Visa

Champagne cruise to France-available at weekends-includes 2 nights' accommodation (subject to availability).

★★★
Silver
Award

WALLETTS COURT COUNTRY HOUSE HOTEL, RESTAURANT AND SPA

West-Cliffe, St-Margarets-at-Cliffe, Dover
CT15 6EW
T: (01304) 852424 & 0800 0351628
F: (01304) 853430
E: wc@wallettscourt.com
I: www.wallettscourt.com

B&B per night:
S £75.00–£115.00
D £90.00–£150.00

HB per person:
DY £80.00–£110.00

OPEN All year round

Set in the heart of White Cliffs country, this 17thC manor house with restaurant and spa is simply beautiful. Relaxed and secluded, yet only 3 miles from Dover. A hotel noted for its setting with distant sea views, for the quality of its cuisine and indoor pool and health spa.

Bedrooms: 13 double/
twin, 3 triple/multiple;
suites available
Bathrooms: 16 en suite

Lunch available
Evening meal available
CC: Amex, Delta, Diners,
Mastercard, Switch, Visa

Stay 2 nights 1 Oct-30 Apr. From £35pppn B&B. Dinner must be taken both evenings.

CREDIT CARD BOOKINGS If you book by telephone and are asked for your credit card number it is advisable to check the proprietor's policy should you cancel your reservation.

EASTBOURNE, East Sussex Map ref 3B4 *Tourist Information Centre Tel: (01323) 411400*

★★★

CHATSWORTH HOTEL

Grand Parade, Eastbourne BN21 3YR
T: (01323) 411016
F: (01323) 643270
E: stay@chatsworth-hotel.com
I: www.chatsworth-hotel.com

B&B per night:
S £43.00–£59.00
D £76.00–£96.00

HB per person:
DY £53.00–£69.00

OPEN All year round

Elegant Victorian detached hotel in a prominent position on seafront, very close to shops, theatres, pier and bandstand. All rooms have been recently refurbished and offer every guest comfort. The Devonshire Restaurant overlooks the sea and provides the very best in English cookery with sensibly priced wines.

Bedrooms: 10 single, 35 double/twin, 2 triple/ multiple; suites available
Bathrooms: 47 en suite

Lunch available
Evening meal available
CC: Amex, Delta, Diners, Mastercard, Switch, Visa

3 night break including 4 course dinner and sea view room £139 per person Oct-Mar (excl Christmas, New Year and some weekends).

★★

CONGRESS HOTEL

31-41 Carlisle Road, Eastbourne BN21 4JS
T: (01323) 732118 & 644605
F: (01323) 720016

Bedrooms: 13 single, 43 double/twin, 5 triple/ multiple
Bathrooms: 61 en suite

Lunch available
Evening meal available
CC: Delta, Mastercard, Switch, Visa

B&B per night:
S £29.00–£38.00
D £58.00–£76.00

HB per person:
DY £35.00–£45.00

OPEN Mar–Nov & Christmas

Family-run hotel in peaceful location. Close to theatres and seafront. Suitable for wheelchair users. Car parking on site.

★★★
Silver
Award

HYDRO HOTEL

Mount Road, Eastbourne BN20 7HZ
T: (01323) 720643
F: (01323) 641167
E: sales@hydrohotel.com
I: www.hydrohotel.com

B&B per night:
S £38.00–£64.00
D £70.00–£122.00

HB per person:
DY £50.00–£75.00

OPEN All year round

Elegant hotel enjoying a fantastic elevated position on the South Cliff. 84 comfortable bedrooms/suites, spacious lounges, conservatory and cocktail bar and picturesque sea view gardens. Fine cuisine and unrivalled hospitality. Ample parking, hair and beauty salon, pool and mini gym. Croquet, putting and entertainment (during season).

Bedrooms: 18 single, 63 double/twin, 2 triple/ multiple
Bathrooms: 83 en suite

Lunch available
Evening meal available
CC: Diners, Mastercard, Switch, Visa

Winter breaks, Nov-Feb from £39.50 DB&B min 2 nights. Christmas and New Year programme.

★★★
Silver
Award

LANSDOWNE HOTEL

King Edward's Parade, Eastbourne BN21 4EE
T: (01323) 725174
F: (01323) 739721
E: the.lansdowne@btinternet.com
I: www.the.lansdowne.btinternet.co.uk

B&B per night:
S £53.00–£65.00
D £86.00–£112.00

HB per person:
DY £43.00–£77.00

OPEN All year round

Best Western Hotels

Traditional privately owned seafront hotel close to theatres and shops. En suite rooms with every modern facility, 9 executive suites. Elegant foyer and lounges facing sea. Attractive Regency bar, 2 lifts. Snooker and games rooms, 22 lock-up garages, 24-hour porterage. Sky Sports TV in public room.

Bedrooms: 36 single, 67 double/twin, 9 triple/ multiple
Bathrooms: 112 en suite

Lunch available
Evening meal available
CC: Amex, Delta, Diners, Mastercard, Switch, Visa

Golfing holidays all year. Specific arrangement with 7 local clubs. Duplicate/social bridge weekends winter and spring with residential hosts.

EASTBOURNE continued

★★★

YORK HOUSE HOTEL
14-22 Royal Parade, Eastbourne
BN22 7AP
T: (01323) 412918
F: (01323) 646238
E: frontdesk@yorkhousehotel.co.uk
I: www.yorkhousehotel.co.uk

Bedrooms: 8 single,
71 double/twin, 7 triple/
multiple
Bathrooms: 86 en suite

Lunch available
Evening meal available
CC: Amex, Delta, Diners,
Mastercard, Switch, Visa

B&B per night:
S £45.00–£50.00
D £90.00–£100.00

HB per person:
DY £61.00–£66.00

OPEN All year round

CR
Best Western Hotels

Comfortable bedrooms, lounges and bars and an unrivalled seafront position. The day begins with a dip in the heated indoor pool, and finishes with good food and wine in the dining room and dancing in the Crumbles Suite.

FARNHAM, Surrey Map ref 2C2 Tourist Information Centre Tel: (01252) 715109

★★★
Silver
Award

This award-winning, charming 18thC country town hotel has easy access to motorways M25 and M3. All rooms are individually decorated, en suite and well equipped. The restaurant has an enviable reputation for fine cuisine. A delightful walled garden is at the rear.

THE BISHOP'S TABLE HOTEL & RESTAURANT
27 West Street, Farnham GU9 7DR
T: (01252) 710222
F: (01252) 733494
E: welcome@bishopstable.com
I: www.bishopstable.com

Bedrooms: 6 single,
11 double/twin
Bathrooms: 17 en suite

Lunch available
Evening meal available
CC: Amex, Diners,
Mastercard, Visa

Weekend breaks available. Many theme nights during the year.

B&B per night:
S £79.50–£111.50
D £132.50–£145.00

HB per person:
DY £109.50–£195.00

OPEN All year round

CR
Best Western Hotels

FOLKESTONE, Kent Map ref 3B4 Tourist Information Centre Tel: (01303) 258594

★★★

THE BURLINGTON HOTEL
Earls Avenue, Folkestone CT20 2HR
T: (01303) 255301
F: (01303) 251301
E: sales@theburlingtonhotel.com
I: www.theburlingtonhotel.com

Bedrooms: 12 single,
49 double/twin, 9 triple/
multiple; suites available
Bathrooms: 70 en suite

Lunch available
Evening meal available
CC: Amex, Delta, Diners,
Mastercard, Switch, Visa

B&B per night:
S £59.00–£80.00
D £80.00–£100.00

HB per person:
DY £51.45–£97.95

OPEN All year round

CR
Minotel

Victorian hotel overlooking English Channel, close to Eurotunnel and Dover port. Ideal for conferences, weddings and weekend breaks. Locally renowned Bay Tree restaurant and bar.

GATWICK AIRPORT

See under Copthorne

HASTINGS, East Sussex Map ref 3B4 Tourist Information Centre Tel: (01424) 781111

★★★

A modern hotel, but with a traditional atmosphere, by wooded area, close to historic town centre. Well appointed en suite bedrooms, elegant lounge, friendly restaurant and bar. Four-poster and family rooms available. Flexible facilities for conferences and banqueting. Ample on-site car parking. Complimentary membership and swimming in adjacent leisure centre.

CINQUE PORTS HOTEL
Summerfields, Bohemia Road, Hastings
TN34 1ET
T: (01424) 439222
F: (01424) 437277
E: enquiries@cinqueports.co.uk
I: www.cinqueports.co.uk

Bedrooms: 36 double/
twin, 4 triple/multiple
Bathrooms: 40 en suite

Lunch available
Evening meal available
CC: Amex, Mastercard,
Switch, Visa

Leisure breaks throughout year (min 2 nights). Easter, Bank Hols, Christmas and New Year packages.

B&B per night:
S £55.00–£65.00
D £70.00–£85.00

HB per person:
DY £47.50–£55.00

OPEN All year round

HASTINGS continued

★★★

HIGH BEECH HOTEL

Battle Road, St Leonards-on-Sea, Hastings
TN37 7BS
T: (01424) 851383
F: (01424) 854265
E: highbeech@barbox.net
I: www.highbeechhotel.com

Privately-owned country house hotel situated in the heart of 1066 countryside. Between the historic towns of Hastings and Battle, 500 yards off A2100. Luxury accommodation. All rooms en suite, some with 4-poster beds and corner baths. Superb French/English cuisine served in elegant Edwardian surroundings.

Bedrooms: 1 single,
16 double/twin
Bathrooms: 17 en suite

Lunch available
Evening meal available
CC: Amex, Delta, Diners,
Mastercard, Switch, Visa

Special breaks mid-week or weekends, £60pp HB.
Further discounts for longer stays.

B&B per night:
S £70.00
D £100.00–£110.00

HB per person:
DY £68.50–£73.50

OPEN All year round

HOVE

See under Brighton & Hove

HYTHE, Kent Map ref 3B4

★★★★
Silver
Award

THE HYTHE IMPERIAL
Princes Parade, Hythe CT21 6AE
T: (01303) 267441
F: (01303) 264610
E: hytheimperial@marstonhotels.com
I: www.marstonhotels.com

Bedrooms: 17 single,
83 double/twin; suites
available
Bathrooms: 100 en suite

Lunch available
Evening meal available
CC: Amex, Delta, Diners,
Mastercard, Switch, Visa

Quality hotel offering leisure and family packages, indoor pool, spa, sauna, steam, childminding, golf-course, squash, hairdressing and beauty. Family suites, four-poster, half tester and jacuzzi suites.

B&B per night:
S £89.00–£155.00
D £125.00–£185.00

HB per person:
DY £79.50–£105.00

OPEN All year round

Ⓒ®
Marston Hotels

★★★

STADE COURT HOTEL
West Parade, Hythe CT21 6DT
T: (01303) 268263
F: (01303) 261803
E: stadecourt@marstonhotels.com
I: www.marstonhotels.com

Bedrooms: 11 single,
28 double/twin, 3 triple/
multiple
Bathrooms: 42 en suite

Lunch available
Evening meal available
CC: Amex, Delta, Diners,
Mastercard, Switch, Visa

Seafront hotel, with well-appointed family suites. Extensive leisure facilities, 600 metres away at our sister hotel. Daily half board price based on minimum 2-night stay.

B&B per night:
S £69.00–£95.00
D £79.00–£109.00

HB per person:
DY £62.50–£69.50

OPEN All year round

Ⓒ®
Marston Hotels

LENHAM, Kent Map ref 3B4

★★★★
Silver
Award

CHILSTON PARK COUNTRY HOUSE HOTEL

Sandway, Lenham, Maidstone ME17 2BE
T: (01622) 859803
F: (01622) 858588
E: chilstonpark@arcadianhotels.co.uk
I: www.chilstonparkhotel.co.uk

Grade I Listed mansion lovingly restored to create the epitome of an English country house. Featuring 53 individually-styled bedrooms, an award-winning restaurant, extensive meeting and private dining rooms, it also boasts a beautiful lake and parkland setting. Ample car parking and easy access to M20, Channel Tunnel and ports.

Bedrooms: 50 double/
twin, 3 triple/multiple;
suites available
Bathrooms: 53 en suite

Lunch available
Evening meal available
CC: Amex, Delta, Diners,
Mastercard, Switch, Visa

Gourmet evenings and Murder Mystery evenings throughout the year. Calendar of events available on request. Pre-booking is essential.

B&B per night:
S £120.00–£220.00
D £140.00–£250.00

HB per person:
DY £85.00–£110.00

OPEN All year round

MAIDSTONE, Kent Map ref 3B3 *Tourist Information Centre Tel: (01622) 602169*

★★

GRANGEMOOR HOTEL
St Michael's Road, Maidstone
ME16 8BS
T: (01622) 677623
F: (01622) 678246
E: reservations@grangemoor.co.uk

Bedrooms: 12 single, 33 double/twin, 5 triple/ multiple	Lunch available
	Evening meal available
	CC: Delta, Mastercard, Switch, Visa
Bathrooms: 50 en suite	

B&B per night:
S £44.00–£48.00
D £52.00–£58.00

OPEN All year round

Friendly family hotel in quiet position near town centre. Tudor-style bar and restaurant. One hour from London and Kent coast.

MARGATE, Kent Map ref 3C3 *Tourist Information Centre Tel: (01843) 220241*

★★

CLINTONS
9 Dalby Square, Cliftonville,
Margate CT9 2ER
T: (01843) 290598 & 299550

Bedrooms: 8 double/ twin, 4 triple/multiple	Evening meal available
	CC: Diners, Mastercard, Visa
Bathrooms: 12 en suite	

B&B per night:
S £28.00–£35.00
D £50.00–£60.00

OPEN All year round

Set in illuminated garden square, this elegant hotel offers comfortable en suite bedrooms, spacious lounge, licensed restaurant, saunas, jacuzzi, gymnasium and solarium.

★★

LONSDALE COURT HOTEL
51-61 Norfolk Road, Cliftonville, Margate
CT9 2HX
T: (01843) 221053
F: (01843) 299993
E: info@courthotels.com
I: www.courthotels.com

B&B per night:
S £43.50–£49.50
D £72.50–£84.50

HB per person:
DY £46.25–£59.50

OPEN All year round

Family-run for over 30 years, the Lonsdale Court is the ideal place to stay. Situated on Kent's coast, it's ideally located to sample the sights and sounds of the Garden of England as well as the continent. The bedrooms are equipped with all mod cons and we boast excellent customer services and leisure facilities.

Bedrooms: 11 single, 32 double/twin, 20 triple/multiple; suites available	Lunch available
	Evening meal available
	CC: Amex, Delta, Diners, Mastercard, Switch, Visa
Bathrooms: 61 en suite, 2 private	

A wide range of themed breaks, from champagne weekends to summer safaris. Seasonal discounts also available.

NEW ROMNEY, Kent Map ref 3B4 *Tourist Information Centre Tel: (01797) 364044*

★★

BROADACRE HOTEL
North Street, New Romney
TN28 8DR
T: (01797) 362381
F: (01797) 362381
E: broadacrehotel@newromney1. fsnet.co.uk
I: www.smoothound.co.uk/hotels/ broadacre.html

Bedrooms: 3 single, 6 double/twin, 1 triple/ multiple	Lunch available
	Evening meal available
	CC: Delta, Mastercard, Switch, Visa
Bathrooms: 10 en suite	

B&B per night:
S £36.00–£50.00
D £52.00–£65.00

OPEN All year round

Small 16thC family-run hotel offering a warm, friendly welcome and personal attention. Some ground floor bedrooms in cottage annexe. Weekend breaks.

TOWN INDEX
This can be found at the back of this guide. If you know where you want to stay, the index will give you the page number listing accommodation in your chosen town, city or village.

★★★

This stylish, modern hotel, overlooking Ramsgate's Royal Harbour, has excellent views from many of its refurbished bedrooms. Close to many of the town's attractions and sandy beaches, with its own leisure club. From Murder Mystery breaks to continental day trips, it's the perfect place to relax and enjoy yourself.

RAMADA JARVIS RAMSGATE

Harbour Parade, Ramsgate CT11 8LZ
T: (01843) 588276 & 572201
F: (01843) 586866
E: jmarina.rs@jarvis.co.uk
I: www.jarvis.co.uk

Bedrooms: 4 single, 47 double/twin, 7 triple/ multiple
Bathrooms: 58 en suite

Lunch available
Evening meal available
CC: Amex, Delta, Diners, Mastercard, Switch, Visa

Murder Mystery breaks, Continental day trips, Cameo Opera weekends, flying breaks.

B&B per night:
S £37.50–£95.00
D £65.00–£105.00

HB per person:
DY £45.00–£67.00

OPEN All year round

Jarvis Hotels/Utell International

★★★

Grade II Listed Victorian cliff top hotel, overlooking sea and sands and near cross-Channel ferry terminals and harbour. Quiet location, easy reach of ample parking. Ten minutes' walk to town centre. All of our prices include full English breakfast and VAT at 17.5%. All rooms have full en suite facilities.

SAN CLU HOTEL

Victoria Parade, East Cliff, Ramsgate CT11 8DT
T: (01843) 592345 & 0800 594 2626
F: (01843) 580157
E: sancluhotel@lineone.net
I: www.ramsgate-hotel.co.uk

Bedrooms: 7 single, 23 double/twin, 14 triple/multiple; suites available
Bathrooms: 44 en suite

Lunch available
Evening meal available
CC: Amex, Delta, Diners, Mastercard, Switch, Visa

Please contact our reservations department to enquire about our special weekend breaks inclusive of DB&B (subject to availability).

B&B per night:
S £50.00–£60.00
D £65.00–£150.00

HB per person:
DY £55.00–£70.00

OPEN All year round

Minotel

★★★★
Silver Award

BRIDGEWOOD MANOR HOTEL

Bridgewood Roundabout, Walderslade Woods, Chatham ME5 9AX
T: (01634) 201333
F: (01634) 201330
E: bridgewoodmanor@marstonhotels.co.uk
I: www.marstonhotels.co.uk

Bedrooms: 100 double/ twin; suites available
Bathrooms: 100 en suite

Lunch available
Evening meal available
CC: Amex, Delta, Diners, Mastercard, Switch, Visa

B&B per night:
S £99.00–£135.00
D £125.00–£185.00

HB per person:
DY £69.50–£89.50

OPEN All year round

Marston Hotels

Modern manor built around a classical courtyard. Superb leisure facilities. Ideal choice for exploring Kent's many attractions. Half-board rate based on minimum 2 nights.

CHECK THE MAPS

The colour maps at the front of this guide show all the cities, towns and villages for which you will find accommodation entries. Refer to the town index to find the page on which they are listed.

ROYAL TUNBRIDGE WELLS, Kent Map ref 2D2 *Tourist Information Centre Tel: (01892) 515675*

★★★

ROYAL WELLS INN

Mount Ephraim, Royal Tunbridge Wells
TN4 8BE
T: (01892) 511188
F: (01892) 511908
E: info@royalwells
I: www.royalwells.co.uk

B&B per night:
S £55.00–£80.00
D £85.00–£120.00

OPEN All year round

Best Western Hotels

Family run, this cosmopolitan hotel proudly boasts the conservatory restaurant (closed Sun/Mon), where high standards of food demonstrate a serious, dedicated approach to cooking. Wells brasserie, also serviced by the same kitchen. Five minutes' walk from shops, in a commanding position overlooking the town, and central to the South East.

Bedrooms: 2 single, 15 double/twin, 1 triple/ multiple
Bathrooms: 18 en suite

Lunch available
Evening meal available
CC: Amex, Delta, Diners, Mastercard, Switch, Visa

Classic car self-drive weekend breaks.

★★★

THE SPA HOTEL
Mount Ephraim,
Royal Tunbridge Wells TN4 8XJ
T: (01892) 520331
F: (01892) 510575
E: info@spahotel.co.uk
I: www.spahotel.co.uk

Bedrooms: 9 single, 55 double/twin, 7 triple/ multiple; suites available
Bathrooms: 71 en suite

Lunch available
Evening meal available
CC: Amex, Delta, Diners, Mastercard, Switch, Visa

B&B per night:
S £95.75–£105.75
D £126.50–£186.50

HB per person:
DY £82.00–£102.00

OPEN All year round

Elegant country mansion overlooking the historic town of Royal Tunbridge Wells. Extensive leisure facilities, fine dining. Ideal for weekend breaks.

RYE, East Sussex Map ref 3B4 *Tourist Information Centre Tel: (01797) 226696*

★★★

FLACKLEY ASH HOTEL & RESTAURANT
London Road, Peasmarsh, Rye
TN31 6YH
T: (01797) 230651
F: (01797) 230510
E: flackleyash@marstonhotels.co.uk
I: www.marstonhotels.co.uk

Bedrooms: 40 double/ twin, 2 triple/multiple; suites available
Bathrooms: 42 en suite

Lunch available
Evening meal available
CC: Amex, Delta, Diners, Mastercard, Switch, Visa

B&B per night:
S £79.00–£108.00
D £119.00–£175.00

HB per person:
DY £76.00–£96.00

OPEN All year round

Best Western Hotels/
Marston Hotels

Georgian country house hotel in 5 acres. Swimming pool and leisure centre. Fresh fish, well-stocked cellar. Half board daily rate based on minimum 2-night stay.

★★★
Silver
Award

RYE LODGE HOTEL

Hilders Cliff, Rye TN31 7LD
T: (01797) 223838 & 226688
F: (01797) 223585
E: info@ryelodge.co.uk
I: www.ryelodge.co.uk

B&B per night:
S £59.50–£95.00
D £90.00–£150.00

HB per person:
DY £60.00–£95.00

OPEN All year round

Stunning estuary views yet adjacent to town centre. Dine by candlelight in the elegant Terrace Restaurant, delicious food and fine wines. Full room service – enjoy breakfast in bed as late as you like! Indoor swimming pool and sauna. Private car park plus all the delights of the medieval Cinque Port of Rye.

Bedrooms: 2 single, 18 double/twin
Bathrooms: 20 en suite

Evening meal available
CC: Amex, Delta, Diners, Mastercard, Switch, Visa

Wine and food breaks: Gourmet meals, wine tastings, talks, visits to vineyards. Historic interludes include special visits to historic stately homes etc.

SYMBOLS The symbols in each entry give information about services and facilities. A key to these symbols appears at the back of this guide.

SANDWICH, Kent Map ref 3C3

★★★

BELL HOTEL
The Quay, Sandwich CT13 9EF
T: (01304) 613388
F: (01304) 615308
E: hotel@princes-leisure.co.uk
I: www.princes-leisure.co.uk

Bedrooms: 7 single,
25 double/twin, 1 triple/
multiple
Bathrooms: 33 en suite

Lunch available
Evening meal available
CC: Amex, Delta, Diners,
Mastercard, Switch, Visa

B&B per night:
S Min £78.75
D Min £105.00

HB per person:
DY Min £94.70

OPEN All year round

17thC riverside inn extended during Victorian times, recently refurbished in traditional manner to provide individual and comfortable accommodation with quality restaurant and cellar. Own golf club, Princes, just a short drive away.

SHEPPERTON, Surrey Map ref 2D2

★★

THE SHIP HOTEL
Russell Road, Shepperton
TW17 9HX
T: (01932) 227320
F: (01932) 226668

Bedrooms: 15 single,
13 double/twin, 3 triple/
multiple
Bathrooms: 31 en suite

Evening meal available
CC: Amex, Delta, Diners,
Mastercard, Switch, Visa

B&B per night:
S £37.50–£72.00
D £60.00–£125.00

OPEN All year round

Character hotel in an attractive and convenient location beside the River Thames. Comfortably refurbished over recent years. All rooms en suite. Fully licensed. Night porter.

STEYNING, West Sussex Map ref 2D3

★★★
**Silver
Award**

THE OLD TOLLGATE RESTAURANT & HOTEL

The Street, Bramber, Steyning BN44 3WE
T: (01903) 879494
F: (01903) 813399
E: otr@fastnet.co.uk
I: www.oldtollgatehotel.com

B&B per night:
S £82.65–£127.65
D £90.30–£135.30

HB per person:
DY £67.10–£149.60

OPEN All year round

Best Western Hotels

Beautifully appointed hotel at the foot of South Downs, opposite Bramber Castle ruins. Stunning award-winning carvery (booking always advisable). Four-poster bedrooms with jacuzzi available. Ideal touring base with many gardens and places of interest nearby. Set in glorious countryside yet with good road links. In short – a perfect spot.

Bedrooms: 31 double/
twin; suites available
Bathrooms: 31 en suite

Lunch available
Evening meal available
CC: Amex, Delta, Diners,
Mastercard, Switch, Visa

Getaway breaks-2 nights minimum. Summer Sparkler, Jul and Aug. Beat the Blues, Jan. Valentine special.

TENTERDEN, Kent Map ref 3B4

★★★
**Silver
Award**

LITTLE SILVER COUNTRY HOTEL

Ashford Road, St Michaels, Tenterden
TN30 6SP
T: (01233) 850321
F: (01233) 850647
E: enquiries@little-silver.co.uk
I: www.little-silver.co.uk

B&B per night:
S £60.00–£75.00
D £85.00–£110.00

HB per person:
DY £60.00–£70.00

OPEN All year round

Tudor-style country hotel set in landscaped gardens, sumptuous comfort, elegant cuisine, delightful restaurant, garden room for light lunches and afternoon tea. Personal service, quality and charm abound. Oak-beamed lounge with log fires adjacent to well-stocked bar. All bedrooms en suite, 4-posters with jacuzzi baths. Family and disabled facilities.

Bedrooms: 8 double/
twin, 2 triple/multiple
Bathrooms: 10 en suite

Lunch available
Evening meal available
CC: Amex, Delta,
Mastercard, Switch, Visa

Take a Break DB&B packages. Christmas and New Year's packages.

REGIONAL TOURIST BOARD The **M** symbol in an establishment entry indicates that it is a Regional Tourist Board member.

TICEHURST, East Sussex Map ref 3B4

★★★★
Silver
Award

DALE HILL HOTEL &
GOLF CLUB

Ticehurst, Wadhurst TN5 7DQ
T: (01580) 200112
F: (01580) 201249
E: info@dalehill.co.uk
I: www.dalehill.co.uk

B&B per night:
S £70.00–£100.00
D £80.00–£140.00

OPEN All year round

Dale Hill is situated in an Area of Outstanding Natural Beauty. Our bedrooms offer comfort and luxury and many have magnificent views overlooking the Kentish Weald. Dale Hill boasts new leisure facilities and two 18-hole golf courses, one of which was designed by Ian Woosnam to USGA championship specifications.

Bedrooms: 6 single,
20 double/twin; suites
available
Bathrooms: 26 en suite

Lunch available
Evening meal available
CC: Amex, Delta,
Mastercard, Switch, Visa

TUNBRIDGE WELLS

See under Royal Tunbridge Wells

WEST CHILTINGTON, West Sussex Map ref 2D3

★★★

ROUNDABOUT HOTEL
Monkmead Lane, West Chiltington,
Pulborough RH20 2PF
T: (01798) 813838
F: (01798) 812962
E: roundabouthotelltd@btinternet.
com
I: www.roundabouthotel.co.uk

Bedrooms: 3 single,
16 double/twin, 4 triple/
multiple
Bathrooms: 23 en suite

Lunch available
Evening meal available
CC: Amex, Delta, Diners,
Mastercard, Switch, Visa

B&B per night:
S £67.95–£72.95
D £100.00–£125.00

HB per person:
DY £87.50–£92.15

OPEN All year round

Best Western Hotels

Tudor-style hotel in the countryside. Nowhere near a roundabout – in fact, a haven of tranquility. Plenty of historic castles to see in the immediate area.

COUNTRY CODE Always follow the Country Code 🌳 Enjoy the countryside and respect its life and work 🌳 Guard against all risk of fire 🌳 Fasten all gates 🌳 Keep your dogs under close control 🌳 Keep to public paths across farmland 🌳 Use gates and stiles to cross fences, hedges and walls 🌳 Leave livestock, crops and machinery alone 🌳 Take your litter home 🌳 Help to keep all water clean 🌳 Protect wildlife, plants and trees 🌳 Take special care on country roads 🌳 Make no unnecessary noise

A brief guide to the main Towns and Villages offering accommodation in the

South East

A ASHFORD, KENT - Once a market centre for the farmers of the Weald of Kent and Romney Marsh. The town centre has a number of Tudor and Georgian houses and a museum. Eurostar trains stop at Ashford International station.

- **ASHINGTON, WEST SUSSEX** - Village 3 miles north of Washington.

B BEXHILL, EAST SUSSEX - Popular resort with beach of shingle and firm sand at low tide. The impressive 1930s designed De la Warr Pavilion has good entertainment facilities. Costume Museum in Manor Gardens.

- **BOGNOR REGIS, WEST SUSSEX** - Five miles of firm, flat sand have made the town a popular family resort. Well supplied with gardens.

- **BRIGHTON & HOVE, EAST SUSSEX** - Brighton's attractions include the Royal Pavilion, Volks Electric Railway, Sea Life Centre and Marina Village, 'The Lanes', Conference Centre and several theatres.

C CANTERBURY, KENT - Place of pilgrimage since the martyrdom of Becket in 1170 and the site of Canterbury Cathedral. Visit St Augustine's Abbey, St Martin's (the oldest church in England), Royal Museum and Art Gallery and the Canterbury Tales. Nearby is Howletts Wild Animal Park. Good shopping centre.

- **CHICHESTER, WEST SUSSEX** - The county town of West Sussex with a beautiful Norman cathedral. Surrounded by places of interest, including Fishbourne Roman Palace, Weald and Downland Open-Air Museum and West Dean Gardens.

- **COPTHORNE, SURREY** - Residential village on the Surrey/West Sussex border, near Crawley and within easy reach of Gatwick Airport.

- **CUCKFIELD, WEST SUSSEX** - The High Street is lined with Elizabethan and Georgian shops, inns and houses and was once part of the London to Brighton coach road. Nearby Nymans (National Trust) is a 30-acre garden with fine topiary work.

D DORKING, SURREY - Ancient market town and a good centre for walking, delightfully set between Box Hill and the Downs. Denbies Wine Estate - England's largest vineyard - is situated here.

- **DOVER, KENT** - A Cinque Port and busiest passenger port in the world. Still a historic town and seaside resort beside the famous White Cliffs. The White Cliffs Experience attraction traces the town's history through the Roman, Saxon, Norman and Victorian periods.

E EASTBOURNE, EAST SUSSEX - One of the finest, most elegant resorts on the south-east coast situated beside Beachy Head. Long promenade, well known Carpet Gardens on the seafront, Devonshire Park tennis and indoor leisure complex, theatres, Towner Art Gallery, 'How We Lived Then' Museum of Shops and Social History.

F FARNHAM, SURREY - Town noted for its Georgian houses. Willmer House (now a museum) has a facade of cut and moulded brick with fine carving and panelling in the interior. The 12th C castle has been occupied by Bishops of both Winchester and Guildford.

- **FOLKESTONE, KENT** - Popular resort. The town has a fine promenade, the Leas, from where orchestral concerts and other entertainments are presented. Horse-racing at Westenhanger Racecourse nearby.

H HASTINGS, EAST SUSSEX - Ancient town which became famous as the base from which William the Conqueror set out to fight the Battle of Hastings. Later became one of the Cinque Ports, now a leading resort. Castle, Hastings Embroidery inspired by the Bayeux Tapestry and Sea Life Centre.

- **HYTHE, KENT** - Once one of the Cinque Ports, the town today stands back from the sea. The Royal Military Canal is the scene of a summer pageant, the Romney, Hythe and Dymchurch Railway terminates here and Port Lympne Wild Animal Park, Mansion and Gardens is nearby.

L LENHAM, KENT - Shops, inns and houses, many displaying timber-work of the late Middle Ages, surround a square which is the centre of the village. The 14th C parish church has one of the best examples of a Kentish tower.

M MAIDSTONE, KENT - Busy county town of Kent on the River Medway has many interesting features and is an excellent centre for excursions. Museum of Carriages, Museum and Art Gallery, Mote Park.

- **MARGATE, KENT** - Oldest and most famous resort in Kent. Many Regency and Victorian buildings survive from the town's early days. There are 9 miles of sandy beach. 'Dreamland' is a 20-acre amusement park and the Winter Gardens offer concert hall entertainment.

N NEW ROMNEY, KENT - Capital of Romney Marsh. Now a mile from the sea, it was one of the original Cinque Ports. Romney, Hythe and Dymchurch Railway's main station is here.

R RAMSGATE, KENT - Popular holiday resort with good sandy beaches. At Pegwell Bay is a replica of a Viking longship.

- **ROCHESTER, KENT** - Ancient cathedral city on the River Medway. Has many places of interest connected with Charles Dickens (who lived nearby) including the fascinating Dickens Centre. Also massive castle overlooking the river and Guildhall Museum.

- **ROYAL TUNBRIDGE WELLS, KENT** - This 'Royal' town became famous as a spa in the 17th C and much of its charm is retained, as in the Pantiles, a shaded walk lined with elegant shops. Heritage attraction 'A Day at the Wells'. Excellent shopping centre.

- **RYE, EAST SUSSEX** - Cobbled, hilly streets and fine old buildings make Rye, once a Cinque Port, a most picturesque town. Noted for its church with ancient clock, potteries and antique shops. Town Model Sound and Light Show gives a good introduction to the town.

S SANDWICH, KENT - Delightful old market town, once a Cinque Port, now 2 miles from the sea. Many interesting old buildings including the 16th C Barbican and the Guildhall which contains the town's treasures. Several excellent golf-courses.

- **SHEPPERTON, SURREY** - Made famous by its connections with the British film industry, this town by the Thames retains an air of detachment from London, despite being only 10 miles from the centre of the capital.

- **STEYNING, WEST SUSSEX** - An important market town and thriving port before the Norman Conquest, lying at the foot of the South Downs. Retains a picturesque charm with fascinating timber-framed and stone buildings.

T TENTERDEN, KENT - Most attractive market town with a broad main street full of 16th C houses and shops. The tower of the 15th C parish church is the finest in Kent. Fine antiques centre.

W WEST CHILTINGTON, WEST SUSSEX - Well-kept village caught in the maze of lanes leading to and from the South Downs.

English Tourism Council
assessed

English Tourism Council

★ ★ ★
HOTEL

Accommodation

On the following pages you will find an exclusive listing of every hotel in England that has been assessed for quality by the English Tourism Council.

The information includes brief contact details for each place to stay, together with its Star rating, and quality award if appropriate. The listing also shows if an establishment has a National Accessible rating (see the front of the guide for further information).

More detailed information on all the places shown in blue can be found in the regional sections (where establishments have paid to have their details included). To find these entries please refer to the appropriate regional section, or look in the town index at the back of this guide.

The list which follows was compiled slightly later than the regional sections. For this reason you may find that, in a few instances, a Star rating and quality award may differ between the two sections. This list contains the most up-to-date information and was correct at the time of going to press.

LONDON

INNER LONDON
E10

Sleeping Beauty Motel
Travel Accommodation
543 Lea Bridge Road, Leyton,
London E10 7EB
T: (020) 8556 8080
F: (020) 8556 8080

N1

Great Northern Hotel ★★★
King's Cross, London N1 9AN
T: (020) 7837 5454
F: (020) 7278 5270
E: gnres@compasshotels.co.uk
I: www.compasshotels.co.uk

Jurys London Inn ★★★
60 Pentonville Road, Islington,
London N1 9LA
T: (020) 7282 5500
F: (020) 7282 5511
E: london_inn@jurysdoyle.com
I: www.jurysdoyle.com

N4

Spring Park Hotel ★
400 Seven Sisters Road, London
N4 2LX
T: (020) 8800 6030
F: (020) 8802 5652
E: sphotel400@aol.com
I: www.smoothhound.
co.uk/hotels/springpa.html

NW1

Melia White House ★★★★
Albany Street, Regent's Park,
London NW1 3UP
T: (020) 7387 1200
F: (020) 7388 0091
E: melia.white.house@solmelia.
es
I: www.solmelia.es

Regents Park Hotel ★★
154-156 Gloucester Place,
London NW1 6DT
T: (020) 7258 1911
F: (020) 7258 0288
E: rph-reservation@usa.net

SE1

**London Marriott Hotel, County
Hall ★★★★★**
The County Hall, London
SE1 7PB
T: (020) 7928 5200
F: (020) 7928 5300
E: catriona.savage@whitbread.
com
I: www.mariott.
com/marriott/lonch

The Mad Hatter ★★
3-7 Stamford Street, London
SE1 9NY
T: (020) 7401 9222
F: (020) 7401 7111
E: madhatter@fullers.co.uk
I: www.fullers.co.uk

SE3

Bardon Lodge Hotel ★★★
15-17 Stratheden Road,
Blackheath, London SE3 7TH
T: (020) 8853 7000
F: (020) 8858 7387
E: bardonlodge@btclick.com
I: www.bardonlodgehotel.com

Clarendon Hotel ★★
8-16 Montpelier Row,
Blackheath, London SE3 0RW
T: (020) 8318 4321
F: (020) 8318 4378
E: relax@clarendonhotel.com
I: www.clarendonhotel.com

SE10

Hamilton House Hotel ★★
14 West Grove, Greenwich,
London SE10 8QT
T: (020) 8694 9899
F: (020) 8694 2370
E: reception@
hamiltonhousehotel.co.uk
I: www.hamiltonhousehotel.
co.uk

SW1

Dolphin Square Hotel ★★★★
Dolphin Square, Chichester
Street, London SW1V 3LX
T: (020) 7834 3800 &
0800 616607
F: (020) 7798 8735
E: reservations@
dolphinsquarehotel.co.uk
I: www.dolphinsquarehotel.
co.uk

The Goring Hotel ★★★★
15 Beeston Place, Grosvenor
Gardens, London SW1W 0JW
T: (020) 7396 9000
F: (020) 7834 4393
E: reception@goringhotel.co.uk
I: www.goringhotel.co.uk

Hyatt Carlton Tower ★★★★★
On Cadogan Place, London
SW1X 9PY
T: (020) 7235 1234
F: (020) 7235 9129

**Sheraton Park Tower
★★★★★**
101 Knightsbridge, London
SW1X 7RN
T: (020) 7235 8050
F: (020) 7235 8231
E: morten.ebbesen@
luxurycollection.com
I: www.luxurycollection.
com/parktowerlondon

SW3

The Basil Street Hotel ★★★
Basil Street, Knightsbridge,
London SW3 1AH
T: (020) 7581 3311
F: (020) 7581 3693
E: info@thebasil.com
I: www.thebasil.com

SW4

**Windmill on the Common
★★★**
Southside, Clapham Common,
London SW4 9DE
T: (020) 8673 4578
F: (020) 8675 1486

SW5

**Barkston Gardens Hotel,
Kensington ★★★**
34-44 Barkston Gardens,
London SW5 0EW
T: (020) 7373 7851
F: (020) 7370 6570
E: info@barkstongardens.com
I: www.cairn.hotels.co.uk

The Burns Hotel ★★★
18-26 Barkston Gardens,
Kensington, London SW5 0EN
T: (020) 7373 3151
F: (020) 7370 4090
E: burnshotel@vienna-group.
co.uk
I: www.vienna-group.co.uk

The Cranley Hotel ★★★★
Townhouse
10-12 Bina Gardens, South
Kensington, London SW5 0LA
T: (020) 7373 0123
F: (020) 7373 9497
E: karendukes@thecranley.com
I: www.thecranley.com

Enterprise Hotel ★★
15-25 Hogarth Road, London
SW5 0QJ
T: (020) 7373 4502 & 7373 4503
F: (020) 7373 5115
E: ehotel@aol.com
I: www.enterprisehotel.com

Hogarth Hotel ★★★
33 Hogarth Road, Kensington,
London SW5 0QQ
T: (020) 7370 6831
F: (020) 7373 6179
E: hogarth@marstonhotels.
co.uk
I: www.marstonhotels.co.uk

**Lord Kensington Hotel
Rating Applied For**
38 Trebovir Road, Earls Court,
London SW5 9NJ
T: (0207) 373 7331 & 373 9248
F: (0207) 460 3524
E: lkh@lgh-hotels.com
I: www.lgh-hotels.com

**Swallow International Hotel
★★★★**
Cromwell Road, London
SW5 0TH
T: (020) 7973 1000
F: (020) 7244 8194
E: international@
swallow-hotels.co.uk
I: www.swallowhotels.com

**Twenty Nevern Square
★★★★**
Townhouse
20 Nevern Square, London
SW5 9PD
I: (020) 7565 9555
F: (020) 7565 9444
E: hotel@twentynevernsquare.
co.uk
I: www.twentynevernsquare.
co.uk

SW7

Forum Hotel London ★★★★
97 Cromwell Road, London
SW7 4DN
T: (020) 7370 5757
F: (020) 7373 1448
E: forumlondon@interconti.
com
I: www.forum-london.interconti.
com

**Ramada Jarvis Kensington
★★★**
31-34 Queen's Gate, South
Kensington, London SW7 5JA
T: (020) 7584 7222
F: (020) 7589 3910
E: jkensington.rs@jarvis.co.uk
I: www.jarvis.co.uk

**Millennium Gloucester London
★★★★**
4-18 Harrington Gardens,
London SW7 4LH
T: (020) 7373 6030
F: (020) 7373 0409
E: sales.gloucester@mill-cop.
com
I: www.millennium-hotels.com

Montana Hotel ★★
67-69 Gloucester Road, London
SW7 4PG
T: (020) 7584 7654
F: (020) 7581 3109
I: www.montanahotel.co.uk

SW8

**Comfort Inn Vauxhall
Rating Applied For**
87 South Lambeth Road,
Vauxhall, London SW8 1RN
T: (020) 7735 9494
F: (020) 7735 1001
E: stay@comfortinnvx.co.uk
I: www.comfortinnvx.co.uk

W1

The Berners Hotel ★★★★
10 Berners Street, London
W1A 3BE
T: (020) 7666 2000
F: (020) 7666 2001
E: berners@berners.co.uk
I: www.thebernershotel.co.uk

The Dorchester ★★★★★
Park Lane, London W1A 2HJ
T: (020) 7629 8888
F: (020) 7409 0114
E: reservations@
dorchesterhotel.com
I: www.dorchesterhotel.com

The Leonard ★★★★
Townhouse
15 Seymour Street, London
W1H 5AA
T: (020) 7935 2010
F: (020) 7935 6700
E: the.leonard@dial.pipex.com
I: www.theleonard.com

London Hilton ★★★★★
22 Park Lane, London W1Y 4BE
T: (020) 7493 8000
F: (020) 7208 4136
E: sales-park_lane@hilton.com
I: www.london-parklane.hilton.
com

**Le Meridien Grosvenor House
★★★★★**
Park Lane, London W1A 3AA
T: 0870 400 8500
F: (020) 7493 3341
E: grosvenor.reservations@
forte-hotels.com
I: www.
lemeridien-grosvenorhouse.com

W2

The Abbey Court ★★★★
20 Pembridge Gardens,
Kensington, London W2 4DU
T: (020) 7221 7518
F: (020) 7792 0858
E: info@abbeycourthotel.co.uk
I: www.abbeycourthotel.co.uk

Establishments printed in blue have a detailed entry in this guide

Albro House Hotel ★★
155 Sussex Gardens, London
W2 2RY
T: (020) 7724 2931 & 7706 8153
F: (020) 7262 2278
E: joe@albrohotel.co.uk
I: www.albrohotel.co.uk

Central Park Hotel ★★★
49-67 Queensborough Terrace,
London W2 3SS
T: (020) 7229 2424
F: (020) 7229 2904
E: cph@centralparklondon.co.uk
I: www.centralparklondon.co.uk

The Delmere Hotel ★★
128-130 Sussex Gardens, Hyde
Park, London W2 1UB
T: (020) 7706 3344
F: (020) 7262 1863
E: delmerehotel@compuserve.
com
I: www.delmerehotels.com

Royal Lancaster Hotel ★★★★
Lancaster Terrace, London
W2 2TY
T: (020) 7262 6737
F: (020) 7724 3191
E: book@royallancaster.com
I: www.royallancaster.com

Westland Hotel ★★
154 Bayswater Road, London
W2 4HP
T: (020) 7229 9191
F: (020) 7727 1054
E: reservations@westlandhotel.
co.uk
I: www.westlandhotel.co.uk
🏃

W4

Chiswick Hotel ★★★
73 High Road, London W4 2LS
T: (020) 8994 1712
F: (020) 8742 2585
E: chishot@clara.net
I: www.chiswick-hotel.co.uk

W5

Jarvis International, Ealing
★★★★
Ealing Common, London
W5 3HN
T: (020) 8896 8400
F: (020) 8992 7082
E: jiealing.rs@jarvis.co.uk
I: www.jarvis.co.uk

W8

Kensington House Hotel
★★★★
Townhouse
15/16 Prince of Wales Terrace,
London W8 5PQ
T: (020) 7937 2345
F: (020) 7368 6700
E: sales@kenhouse.com
I: www.kenhouse.com

London Lodge Hotel ★★★
134-136 Lexham Gardens,
London W8 6JE
T: (020) 7244 8444
F: (020) 7373 6661
E: info@londonlodgehotel.com
I: www.londonlodgehotel.com

**The Milestone Hotel and
Apartments** ★★★★★
Townhouse
1 Kensington Court, London
W8 5DL
T: (020) 7917 1000
F: (020) 7917 1010
E: guestservices@milestone.
redcarnationhotels.com
I: www.themilestone.com

W9

**The Colonnade, The Little
Venice Town House**★★★★
2 Warrington Crescent, Little
Venice, London W9 1ER
T: (020) 7286 1052
F: (020) 7286 1057
E: res_colonnade@
etontownhouse.com
I: www.etontownhouse.com

W14

K West ★★★★
Richmond Way, London
W14 0AX
T: (020) 7674 1000
F: (020) 7674 1050
E: reservations@thekensington.
co.uk
I: www.thekensington.co.uk

WC1

Bloomsbury Park Hotel
Rating Applied For
126 Southampton Row, London
WC1B 5AD
T: (020) 7430 0434
F: (020) 7242 0665
E: bloomsburypark@thistle.
co.uk
I: www.thistlehotels.
com/bloomsbury_park

The Bonnington in Bloomsbury
★★★
92 Southampton Row, London
WC1B 4BH
T: (020) 7242 2828
F: (020) 7831 9170
E: sales@bonnington.com
I: www.bonnington.com
🛇

The Montague on the Gardens
★★★★
15 Montague Street,
Bloomsbury, London WC1B 5BJ
T: (020) 7637 1001
F: (020) 7637 2516
E: sales@montague.
redcarnationhotels.com
I: www.redcarnationhotels.com

myhotel Bloomsbury ★★★★
11-13 Bayley Street, Bedford
Square, London WC1B 3HD
T: (020) 7667 6000
F: (020) 7667 6044
E: guest_services@myhotels.
co.uk
I: www.myhotels.co.uk

Waverley House Hotel ★★★
130-134 Southampton Row,
London WC1B 5AF
T: (020) 7833 3691
F: (020) 7837 3485
E: whhres@aquariushotels.
co.uk
I: www.aquarius-hotels.co.uk

WC2

Le Meridien Waldorf
★★★★★
Aldwych, London WC2B 4DD
T: 0870 400 8484
F: (020) 7836 7244
I: www.lemeridien-waldorf.com

**Radisson Edwardian
Hampshire Hotel** ★★★★
31-36 Leicester Square, London
WC2H 7LH
T: (020) 7839 9399
F: (020) 7930 8122
E: reshamp@radisson.com
I: www.radisson.
com/londonuk_hampshire

The Savoy ★★★★★
The Strand, London WC2R 0EU
T: (020) 7836 4343
F: (020) 7240 6040
E: info@the-savoy.co.uk
I: www.the-savoy.co.uk

OUTER LONDON
Bromley

Bickley Manor Hotel ★★
Thornet Wood Road, Bickley,
Bromley, Kent BR1 2LW
T: (020) 8467 3851 & 8467 3030
F: (020) 8295 1642
E: info@bickleymanor.co.uk
I: www.bickleymanor.co.uk

BEXLEYHEATH

Marriott Hotel ★★★★
1 Broadway, Bexleyheath, Kent
DA6 7JZ
T: (020) 8298 1000
F: (020) 8298 1234
E: bexleyheath@marriotthotels.
co.uk
I: www.marriott.
com/marriott/lonbh
🏃

CROYDON

Coulsdon Manor ★★★★
Coulsdon Court Road, Coulsdon,
Surrey CR5 2LL
T: (020) 8668 0414
F: (020) 8668 3118
E: coulsdonmanor@
marstonhotels.co.uk
I: www.marstonhotels.co.uk

Hayesthorpe Hotel ★★★
48-52 St Augustine's Avenue,
Croydon, CR2 6JJ
T: (020) 8688 8120
F: (020) 8680 1099

**Markington Hotel and
Conference Centre**★★
9 Haling Park Road, South
Croydon, Surrey CR2 6NG
T: (020) 8681 6494
F: (020) 8688 6530
E: rooms@markingtonhotel.
com
I: www.markingtonhotel.com

Selsdon Park Hotel ★★★★
Addington Road, Sanderstead,
South Croydon, Surrey CR2 8YA
T: (020) 8657 8811
F: (020) 8651 6171
E: caroline.chardon@
principalhotels.co.uk
I: www.principalhotels.co.uk

ENFIELD

Enfield Hotel ★★★
52 Rowantree Road, Enfield,
Middlesex EN2 8PW
T: (020) 8366 3511
F: (020) 8366 2432
E: enfield@meridianleisure.com
I: www.meridianleisure.
com/enfield

Oak Lodge Hotel ★★
80 Village Road, Bush Hill Park,
Enfield, Middlesex EN1 2EU
T: (020) 8360 7082 & 83600194
E: oaklodge@FSmail.net
I: www.oaklodgehotel.co.uk

HARROW

Cumberland Hotel ★★★
St John's Road, Harrow,
Middlesex HA1 2EF
T: (020) 8863 4111
F: (020) 8861 5668
E: Reception@cumberlandhotel.
co.uk
I: www.cumberlandhotel.co.uk

HOUNSLOW

Channins Hounslow Hotel ★
41 Hounslow Road, Feltham,
Middlesex TW14 0AU
T: (020) 8890 2358
F: (020) 8751 6103
E: channinshotel@aol.com

Jarvis International Hotel
★★★
Bath Road, Cranford, Hounslow,
Middlesex TW5 9QE
T: (020) 8897 2121 & 8897 3079
F: (020) 8897 7014
E: jiheathrow.rs@jarvis.co.uk
I: www.jarvis.co.uk

KINGSTON UPON THAMES

Hotel Antoinette ★★
Beaufort Road, Kingston upon
Thames, Surrey KT1 2TQ
T: (020) 8546 1044
F: (020) 8547 2595
E: hotelantoinette@btinternet.
com
I: www.hotelantoinette.co.uk

Chase Lodge Hotel ★★
10 Park Road, Hampton Wick,
Kingston upon Thames, Surrey
KT1 4AS
T: (020) 8943 1862
F: (020) 8943 9363
E: info@chaselodgehotel.com
I: www.chaselodgehotel.com

ORPINGTON

The Mary Rose Hotel ★
40-50 High Street, St Mary Cray,
Orpington, Kent BR5 3NJ
T: (01689) 871917 & 875369
F: (01689) 839445
I: www.maryrose.co.uk/

SUTTON

Thatched House Hotel ★★
135-141 Cheam Road, Sutton,
Surrey SM1 2BN
T: (020) 8642 3131
F: (020) 8770 0684

TEDDINGTON

The Park Lodge Hotel ★★★
Park Road, Teddington,
Middlesex TW11 0AB
T: (020) 8614 9700
F: (020) 8614 9701
E: theparklodge@dial.pipex.com

WOODFORD GREEN

Packfords Hotel ★★
16 Snakes Lane West, Woodford
Green, Essex IG8 0BX
T: (020) 8504 2642
F: (020) 8505 5778
E: packfords.hotel@virgin.net
I: www.eppingforest.
co.uk/packford

CUMBRIA

ALSTON
Cumbria

Lovelady Shield Country House Hotel★★★
Nenthead Road, Alston, Cumbria
CA9 3LF
T: (01434) 381203 & 381305
F: (01434) 381515
E: enquiries@lovelady.co.uk
I: www.lovelady.co.uk

Nent Hall Country House Hotel ★★
Nenthall, Alston, Cumbria
CA9 3LQ
T: (01434) 381584
F: (01434) 382668
E: info@nenthallhotel.com
I: www.nenthallcountryhousehotel.co.uk

AMBLESIDE
Cumbria

The Ambleside Salutation Hotel ★★★
Lake Road, Ambleside, Cumbria
LA22 9BX
T: (01539) 432244
F: (01539) 434157
E: reservations@hotelambleside.uk.com
I: www.hotelambleside.uk.com

Crow How Hotel ★★
Rydal Road, Ambleside, Cumbria
LA22 9PN
T: (01539) 432193
F: (01539) 431770
E: patredman200@netscapeonline
I: www.crowhowhotel.co.uk

Fisherbeck Hotel ★★
Lake Road, Ambleside, Cumbria
LA22 0DH
T: (01539) 433215
F: (01539) 433600

Langdale Hotel and Country Club ★★★
Great Langdale, Ambleside, Cumbria LA22 9JD
T: (01539) 437302
F: (01539) 437130
E: itsgreat@langdale.co.uk
I: www.langdale.co.uk

Nanny Brow Hotel ★★★
Clappersgate, Ambleside, Cumbria LA22 9NF
T: (015394) 32036
F: (015394) 32450
E: reservations@nannybrowhotel.demon.co.uk

Queens Hotel ★★
Market Place, Ambleside, Cumbria LA22 9BU
T: (01539) 432206
F: (01539) 432721
E: queenshotel.ambleside@btinternet.com
I: www.smoothhound.co.uk/hotels/quecum.html

The Regent Hotel ★★★
Waterhead Bay, Ambleside, Cumbria LA22 0ES
T: (01539) 432254
F: (01539) 431474
E: lile@regentlakes.co.uk
I: www.regentlakes.co.uk

Rothay Garth Hotel ★★
Rothay Road, Ambleside, Cumbria LA22 0EE
T: (01539) 432217
F: (01539) 434400
E: enquiries@rothay-garth.co.uk
I: www.rothay-garth.co.uk

Rothay Manor ★★★
Rothay Bridge, Ambleside, Cumbria LA22 0EH
T: (01539) 433605
F: (01539) 433607
E: hotel@rothaymanor.co.uk
I: www.rothaymanor.co.uk

Smallwood House Hotel ★★
Compston Road, Ambleside, Cumbria LA22 9DJ
T: (01539) 432330
F: (01539) 433764
E: enq@smallwoodhotel.co.uk
I: www.smallwoodhotel.co.uk

Wateredge Inn ★★★
Waterhead Bay, Ambleside, Cumbria LA22 0EP
T: (01539) 432332
F: (01539) 431878
E: contact@wateredgeinn.co.uk
I: www.wateredgeinn.co.uk

APPLEBY-IN-WESTMORLAND
Cumbria

Royal Oak Inn ★★
Bongate, Appleby-in-Westmorland, Cumbria
CA16 6UN
T: (01768) 351463
F: (01768) 352300
E: royaloakinn@mortalmaninns.fsnet.co.uk
I: www.mortal-man-inns.co.uk/royaloak

BARROW-IN-FURNESS
Cumbria

Abbey House Hotel ★★★
Abbey Road, Barrow-in-Furness, Cumbria LA13 0PA
T: (01229) 838282
F: (01229) 820403
E: enquiries@abbeyhousehotel.com
I: www.abbeyhousehotel.com

Hotel Majestic ★★
Duke Street, Barrow-in-Furness, Cumbria LA14 1HP
T: (01229) 870448
F: (01229) 870448

BASSENTHWAITE
Cumbria

Ouse Bridge Hotel ★★
Dubwath, Bassenthwaite Lake, Cockermouth, Cumbria
CA13 9YD
T: (01768) 776322
E: enquiries@ousebridge.com
I: www.ousebridge.com

The Pheasant ★★★
Bassenthwaite Lake, Cockermouth, Cumbria
CA13 9YE
T: (017687) 76234
F: (017687) 76002
E: thepheasant@easynet.co.uk
I: www.the-pheasant.co.uk

Ravenstone Hotel ★★
Bassenthwaite, Keswick, Cumbria CA12 4QG
T: (01768) 776240
F: (01768) 776733
E: info@ravenstone-hotel.co.uk
I: www.ravenstone-hotel.co.uk

BORROWDALE
Cumbria

Leathes Head Hotel and Restaurant ★★★
Borrowdale, Keswick, Cumbria
CA12 5UY
T: (017687) 77247
F: (017687) 77363
E: enq@leatheshead.co.uk
I: www.leatheshead.co.uk

Mary Mount Hotel ★★
Borrowdale, Keswick, Cumbria
CA12 5UU
T: (01768) 777223 & 777381
E: marymount@bigfoot.com
I: www.marymount.pcrrn.co.uk

BRAITHWAITE
Cumbria

Middle Ruddings Hotel ★★
Braithwaite, Keswick, Cumbria
CA12 5RY
T: (01768) 778436
F: (01768) 778438
E: reception@middleruddings.com
I: www.middleruddings.com

BRAMPTON
Cumbria

Kirby Moor Country House Hotel and Bella Vista Restaurant★★
Longtown Road, Brampton, Cumbria CA8 2AB
T: (01697) 73893
F: (01697) 741847
E: info@kirbymoor-hotel.com
I: www.kirbymoor-hotel.com

Sands House Hotel ★★
The Sands, Brampton, Cumbria
CA8 1UG
T: (016977) 3085
F: (016977) 3297

BUTTERMERE
Cumbria

Bridge Hotel ★★
Buttermere, Cockermouth, Cumbria CA13 9UZ
T: (01768) 770252
F: (01768) 770215
E: enquiries@bridge-hotel.com
I: www.bridge-hotel.com

CALDBECK
Cumbria

Parkend Country Hotel ★★
Parkend, Caldbeck, Wigton, Cumbria CA7 8HH
T: (01697) 478494 & 07976 741005
F: (01697) 478580
E: carol.parkend@tinyworld.co.uk

CARLISLE
Cumbria

Central Plaza Hotel ★★★
Victoria Viaduct, Carlisle, CA3 8AL
T: (01228) 520256
F: (01228) 514657
E: info@centralplazahotel.co.uk
I: www.centralplazahotel.co.uk

County Hotel ★★
9 Botchergate, Carlisle, CA1 1QP
T: (01228) 531316
F: (01228) 401805
E: countyh@hotmail.com
I: www.cairnhotelgroup.com

Crosby Lodge Country House Hotel and Restaurant ★★★
High Crosby, Crosby-on-Eden, Carlisle CA6 4QZ
T: (01228) 573618
F: (01228) 573428
E: crosbylodge@crosby-eden. demon.co.uk
I: www.crosbylodge.co.uk

Pinegrove Hotel ★★
262 London Road, Carlisle, CA1 2QS
T: (01228) 524828
F: (01228) 810941

Swallow Hilltop Hotel Whitbread Hotel Company ★★★
London Road, Carlisle, CA1 2PQ
T: (01228) 529255
F: (01228) 525238
E: carlisle@swallow-hotels. co.uk
I: www.swallowhotels.com

Tarn End House Hotel ★★
Talkin Tarn, Brampton, Cumbria CA8 1LS
T: (016977) 2340
F: (016977) 2089

Wallfoot Hotel and Restaurant ★★
Park Broom, Crosby-on-Eden, Carlisle, CA6 4QH
T: (01228) 573696
F: (01228) 573240
E: frazer@wallfoot.freeserve. co.uk

CARTMEL
Cumbria

Aynsome Manor Hotel ★★
Cartmel, Grange-over-Sands, Cumbria LA11 6HH
T: (01539) 536653
F: (01539) 536016
E: info@aynsomemanorhotel. co.uk
I: www.aynsomemanorhotel. co.uk

CASTLERIGG
Cumbria

The Heights Hotel ★
Rakefoot Lane, Castlerigg, Keswick, Cumbria CA12 4TE
T: (01768) 772251
E: info@theheightshotel.co.uk
I: www.theheightshotel.co.uk

CLEATOR
Cumbria

The Ennerdale Country House Hotel ★★★
Cleator, Cumbria CA23 3DT
T: (01946) 813907
F: (01946) 815260
E: ennerdale@bestwestern.co.uk
I: www.feathers.uk.com

Grove Court ★★
Cleator Gate, Cleator, Cumbria CA23 3DT
T: (01946) 810503
F: (01946) 815412

COCKERMOUTH
Cumbria

Allerdale Court Hotel ★★
Market Square, Cockermouth, Cumbria CA13 9NQ
T: (01900) 823654
F: (01900) 823033
E: john-h-carlin@tinyonline. co.uk
I: www.allerdalecourthotel.co.uk

Manor House Hotel ★★★
Crown Street, Cockermouth, Cumbria CA13 0EH
T: (01900) 828663
F: (01900) 828679

Trout Hotel ★★★
Crown Street, Cockermouth, Cumbria CA13 0EJ
T: (01900) 823591
F: (01900) 827514
E: enquiries@trouthotel.co.uk
I: www.trouthotel.co.uk

CONISTON
Cumbria

Sun Hotel & 16th Century Inn ★★
Coniston, Cumbria LA21 8HQ
T: (01539) 441248
F: (01539) 441219
E: thesun@hotelconiston.com
I: www.smoothhound. co.uk/hotels/sun.html

Waterhead Hotel ★★
Coniston, Cumbria LA21 8AJ
T: (01539) 441244 & 441454
F: (01539) 441193
E: wh@pofr.co.uk

Yewdale Hotel ★★
Yewdale Road, Coniston, Cumbria LA21 8DU
T: (01539) 441280
F: (01539) 441871
E: mail@yewdalehotel.com
I: www.yewdalehotel.com

ENNERDALE
Cumbria

Shepherd's Arms Hotel ★★
Ennerdale Bridge, Cleator, Cumbria CA23 3AR
T: (01946) 861249
F: (01946) 861249
E: enquiries@ shepherdsarmshotel.co.uk
I: shepherdsarmshotel.co.uk

ESKDALE
Cumbria

Bower House Inn ★★
Eskdale, Holmrook, Cumbria CA19 1TD
T: (01946) 723244
F: (01946) 723308
E: info@bowerhouseinn. freeserve.co.uk
I: www.bowerhouseinn.co.uk

Brook House Inn ★★
Boot, Holmrook, Cumbria CA19 1TG
T: (01946) 723288
F: (01946) 723160
E: stay@brookhouseinn.co.uk
I: www.brookhouseinn.co.uk

GRANGE-OVER-SANDS
Cumbria

Clare House ★
Park Road, Grange-over-Sands, Cumbria LA11 7HQ
T: (01539) 533026 & 534253

The Cumbria Grand Hotel ★
Lindale Road, Grange-over-Sands, Cumbria LA11 6EN
T: (015395) 32331
F: (015395) 34534
E: cumbria@cgrandhotel. freeserve.co.uk
I: www.scoot.co.uk/strathmore/

Grange Hotel ★★★
Station Square, Grange-over-Sands, Cumbria LA11 6EJ
T: (01539) 533666
F: (01539) 535064
E: ctbinfo@grange-hotel.co.uk
I: www.grange-hotel.co.uk

Graythwaite Manor Hotel ★★★
Fernhill Road, Grange-over-Sands, Cumbria LA11 7JE
T: (01539) 532001 & 533755
F: (01539) 535549
E: enquiries@ graythwaitemanor.co.uk
I: www.graythwaitemanor.co.uk

Hampsfell House Hotel ★★
Hampsfell Road, Grange-over-Sands, Cumbria LA11 6BG
T: (01539) 532567
F: (01539) 535995
E: hampsfellhotel@email.msn. com
I: www.hampsfellhotel.com

Kents Bank Hotel ★★
96 Kentsford Road, Kents Bank, Grange-over-Sands, Cumbria LA11 7BB
T: (015395) 32054

Netherwood Hotel ★★★
Lindale Road, Grange-over-Sands, Cumbria LA11 6ET
T: (01539) 532552
F: (01539) 534121
E: blawith@aol.com
I: www.netherwood-hotel.co.uk

GRASMERE
Cumbria

Bridge House Hotel ★★
Church Bridge, Grasmere, Ambleside, Cumbria LA22 9SN
T: (01539) 435425
F: (01539) 435523
E: stay@bridgehousegrasmere. co.uk
I: www.bridgehousegrasmere. co.uk

Gold Rill Country House Hotel ★★★
Grasmere, Ambleside, Cumbria LA22 9PU
T: (01539) 435486
F: (01539) 435486
E: enquiries@gold-rill.com
I: www.goldrill.com

The Grasmere Hotel ★★
Broadgate, Grasmere, Ambleside, Cumbria LA22 9TA
T: (01539) 435277
F: (01539) 435277
E: enquiries@grasmerehotel. co.uk
I: www.grasmerehotel.co.uk

Grasmere Red Lion Hotel ★★★
Red Lion Square, Grasmere, Ambleside, Cumbria LA22 9SS
T: (01539) 435456
F: (01539) 435579
E: enquiries@hotelgrasmere. com
I: www.hotelgrasmere.uk.com

Moss Grove Hotel ★★
Grasmere, Ambleside, Cumbria LA22 9SW
T: (01539) 435251
F: (01539) 435691
E: martinw@globalnet.co.uk
I: www.mossgrove.co.uk

Rothay Garden Hotel ★★★
Broadgate, Grasmere, Ambleside, Cumbria LA22 9RJ
T: (01539) 435334
F: (01539) 435723
E: rothay@grasmere.com
I: www.grasmere.com

HAVERTHWAITE
Cumbria

Rusland Pool Hotel and Restaurant ★★★
Haverthwaite, Ulverston, Cumbria LA12 8AA
T: (01229) 861384
F: (01229) 861425
E: enquiries@rusland-pool. ndirect.co.uk
I: www.rusland-pool.ndirect. co.uk

HAWKSHEAD
Cumbria

Queens Head Hotel ★★
Main Street, Hawkshead, Ambleside, Cumbria LA22 0NS
T: (015394) 36271
F: (015394) 36722
E: enquiries@queensheadhotel. co.uk
I: www.queensheadhotel.co.uk

KENDAL
Cumbria

The County Hotel ★★
Station Road, Kendal, Cumbria LA9 6BT
T: (01539) 722461
F: (01539) 732644

Garden House ★★
Fowl-Ing Lane, Kendal, Cumbria LA9 6PH
T: (01539) 731131
F: (01539) 740064
E: gardenhouse.hotel@virgin. net
I: ww.gardenhousehotel.co.uk

Heaves Hotel ★
Kendal, Cumbria LA8 8EF
T: (01539) 560269
F: (01539) 560269
E: hotel@heaves.freeserve.co.uk
I: www.heaveshotel.co.uk

MacDonald Riverside Hotel ★★★
Stramongate Bridge, Kendal, Cumbria LA9 4BZ
T: (01539) 734861
F: (01538) 9734863
E: riverside@macdonald-hotels. co.uk
I: www.macdonaldhotels.co.uk

KESWICK
Cumbria

Borrowdale Gates Country House Hotel and Restaurant ★★★
Grange-in-Borrowdale, Keswick, Cumbria CA12 5UQ
T: (01768) 777204
F: (01768) 777254
E: hotel@borrowdale-gates.com
I: www.borrowdale-gates.com

Borrowdale Hotel ★★★
Borrowdale, Keswick, Cumbria CA12 5UY
T: (01768) 777224
F: (01768) 777338
E: theborrowdalehotel@yahoo. com
I: www.theborrowdalehotel. co.uk

Castle Head House Hotel ★★
Borrowdale Road, Keswick,
Cumbria CA12 5DD
T: (01768) 772082
F: (01768) 774065

Crow Park Hotel ★★
The Heads, Keswick, Cumbria
CA12 5ER
T: (01768) 772208
F: (01768) 774776

Dale Head Hall Lakeside Hotel ★★★
Thirlmere, Keswick, Cumbria
CA12 4TN
T: (017687) 72478
F: (017687) 71070
E: onthelakeside@
dale-head-hall.co.uk
I: www.dale-head-hall.co.uk

Derwentwater Hotel ★★★
Portinscale, Keswick, Cumbria
CA12 5RE
T: (01768) 772538
F: (01768) 771002
E: reservations@
derwentwater-hotel.co.uk
I: www.derwentwater-hotel.
co.uk

George Hotel ★★
St John Street, Keswick, Cumbria
CA12 5AZ
T: (017687) 72076
F: (017687) 75968

Hazeldene Hotel ★
The Heads, Keswick, Cumbria
CA12 5ER
T: (01768) 772106
F: (01768) 775435
E: helen8@supanet.com
I: www.hazeldene-hotel.co.uk

Highfield Hotel ★★
The Heads, Keswick, Cumbria
CA12 5ER
T: (01768) 772508
F: (01768) 780634
E: info@highfieldkeswick.co.uk
I: www.highfieldkeswick.co.uk

The Keswick Country House Hotel ★★★
Station Road, Keswick, Cumbria
CA12 4NQ
T: (017687) 72020
F: (017687) 71300

Keswick Park Hotel ★★
33 Station Road, Keswick,
Cumbria CA12 4NA
T: (017687) 72072 &
07802 762536
F: (017687) 74816
I: www.keswickparkhotel.co.uk

King's Arms Hotel ★★
Main Street, Keswick, Cumbria
CA12 5BL
T: (01768) 772083 & 771108
F: (01768) 775550
E: info@kingsarmshotelkeswick.
co.uk
I: www.kingsarmshotelkeswick.
co.uk

Kings Head Hotel ★★★
Thirlspot, Keswick, Cumbria
CA12 4TN
T: (017687) 72393 & 0870 011
2152
F: (017687) 72309
E: kings@lakelandsheart.demon.
co.uk
I: www.lakelandsheart.co.uk

Ladstock Country House Hotel ★★
Thornthwaite, Keswick, Cumbria
CA12 5RZ
T: (01768) 778210 & 778249
F: (01768) 778088

Lairbeck Hotel ★★
Vicarage Hill, Keswick, Cumbria
CA12 5QB
T: (01768) 773373
F: (01768) 773144
E: WTS@lairbeckhotel-keswick.
co.uk
I: www.lairbeckhotel-keswick.
co.uk

Lyzzick Hall Hotel ★★
Underskiddaw, Keswick, Cumbria
CA12 4PY
T: (01768) 772277
F: (01768) 772278
E: lyzzickhall@netscapeonline.
co.uk
I: www.lyzzickhall.co.uk

Queen's Hotel ★★★
Main Street, Keswick, Cumbria
CA12 5JF
T: (01768) 773333
F: (01768) 771144
E: book@queenshotel.co.uk
I: www.queenshotel.co.uk

Swan Hotel and Country Inn ★★
Thornthwaite, Keswick, Cumbria
CA12 5SQ
T: (01768) 778256
F: (01768) 778080
E: bestswan@aol.com
I: www.swan-hotel-keswick.
co.uk

Swinside Lodge Hotel ★
Grange Road, Newlands,
Keswick, Cumbria CA12 5UE
T: (01768) 772948 &
07887 930998
F: (01768) 772948
E: info@swinsidelodge-hotel.
co.uk
I: www.swinsidelodge-hotel.
co.uk

Thwaite Howe Hotel ★★
Thornthwaite, Keswick, Cumbria
CA12 5SA
T: (017687) 78281
F: (017687) 78529
E: info@thwaitehowe.co.uk
I: www.thwaitehowe.co.uk

Pheasant Inn ★★
Casterton, Kirkby Lonsdale,
Carnforth, Lancashire LA6 2RX
T: (015242) 71230
F: (015242) 71230
E: pheasant.casterton@
eggconnect.net
I: www.pheasantinn.co.uk

Whoop Hall Inn ★★
Burrow with Burrow, Kirkby
Lonsdale, Carnforth, Lancashire
LA6 2HP
T: (01524) 271284
F: (01524) 272154
E: info@whoophall.co.uk
I: www.whoophall.co.uk

The Black Swan Hotel ★★
Ravenstonedale, Kirkby Stephen,
Cumbria CA17 4NG
T: (01539) 623204
F: (01539) 623604
E: reservations@
blackswanhotel.com
I: www.blackswanhotel.com

Britannia Inn ★
Elterwater, Ambleside, Cumbria
LA22 9HP
T: (015394) 37210
F: (015394) 37311
E: info@britinn.co.uk
I: www.britinn.co.uk

Eltermere Country House Hotel ★★
Elterwater, Ambleside, Cumbria
LA22 9HY
T: (015394) 37207
F: (015394) 37540
E: colin@hensington.demon.
co.uk
I: www.eltermere.co.uk

Three Shires Inn ★★
Little Langdale, Ambleside,
Cumbria LA22 9NZ
T: (01539) 437215
F: (01539) 437127
E: ian@threeshiresinn.co.uk
I: www.threeshiresinn.co.uk

Graham Arms Hotel ★★
English Street, Longtown,
Carlisle CA6 5SE
T: (01228) 791213
F: (01228) 791213
E: hotel@cumbria.com
I: www.graham-arms-hotels.
co.uk

The Plough Hotel ★★
Cow Brow, Lupton, Cumbria
LA6 1PJ
T: (015395) 67227
F: (015395) 67848

Newby Bridge Hotel ★★★
Newby Bridge, Ulverston,
Cumbria LA12 8NA
T: (01539) 531222
F: (01539) 531868
E: info@newbybridgehotel.co.uk
I: www.newbybridgehotel.co.uk

Swan Hotel ★★★★
Newby Bridge, Ulverston,
Cumbria LA12 8NB
T: (01539) 531681
F: (01539) 531917
E: swanhotel@aol.com
I: www.swanhotel.com

Whitewater Hotel ★★★
The Lakeland Village, Newby
Bridge, Ulverston, Cumbria
LA12 8PX
T: (01539) 531133
F: (01539) 531881
E: enquiries@whitewater-hotel.
co.uk
I: www.whitewater-hotel.co.uk

Clifton Hill Hotel and Motel ★★
Clifton, Penrith, Cumbria
CA10 2EJ
T: (01768) 862717
F: (01768) 867182

Westmorland Hotel ★★★
Westmorland Place, Orton,
Penrith, Cumbria CA10 3SB
T: (01539) 624351
F: (01539) 624354
E: westmorlandhotel@aol.com
I: www.westmorland.com

The Fat Lamb ★★
Crossbank, Ravenstonedale,
Kirkby Stephen, Cumbria
CA17 4LL
T: (015396) 23242
F: (015396) 23285
E: fatlamb@cumbria.com
I: www.fatlamb.co.uk

Seacote Hotel ★★
Beach Road, St Bees, Cumbria
CA27 0ES
T: (01946) 822777
F: (01946) 824442
E: reception@seacote.com
I: www.seacote.com

Sawrey Hotel ★★
Far Sawrey, Ambleside, Cumbria
LA22 0LQ
T: (01539) 443425
F: (01539) 443425

Shap Wells Hotel ★★★
Shap, Penrith, Cumbria
CA10 3QU
T: (01931) 716628
F: (01931) 716377
E: manager@shapwells.com
I: www.shapwells.com

Skinburness Hotel ★★★
Silloth, Carlisle CA5 4QY
T: (01697) 332332
F: (01697) 332549

Horse and Farrier Inn ★★
Threlkeld, Keswick, Cumbria
CA12 4SQ
T: (01768) 779688
F: (01768) 779824

Mortal Man Hotel ★★
Troutbeck, Windermere, Cumbria
LA23 1PL
T: (01539) 433193
F: (01539) 431261
E: the-mortalman@btinternet.
com
I: www.mortal-man-inns.co.uk

ULLSWATER
Cumbria
Patterdale Hotel ★★
Patterdale, Lake Ullswater,
Penrith, Cumbria CA11 0NN
T: (017684) 82231
F: (017684) 82440

WETHERAL
Cumbria
Killoran Country House Hotel ★★
The Green, Wetheral, Carlisle
CA4 8ET
T: (01228) 560200
F: (01228) 560222
E: killoranhotel@wetheral.
fsbusiness.co.uk

WIGTON
Cumbria
The Kelsey Hotel ★★
Mealsgate, Wigton, Cumbria
CA7 1JP
T: (01697) 371229 & 371372
F: (01697) 371372
E: the kelseyhotel@aol.com
I: www.kelseyhotel.co.uk

WINDERMERE
Cumbria
The Belsfield ★★★
Bowness-on-Windermere,
Windermere, Cumbria LA23 3EL
T: (01539) 442448
F: (01539) 446397
E: belsfield@regalhotels.co.uk
I: www.corushotels.com

Briery Wood Country House ★★
Ambleside Road, Windermere,
Cumbria LA23 1ES
T: (015394) 33316
F: (015394) 34258

Burnside Hotel ★★★
Kendal Road, Bowness-on-
Windermere, Windermere,
Cumbria LA23 3EP
T: (015394) 42211 & 44530
F: (015394) 43824
E: stay@burnsidehotel.com
I: www.burnsidehotel.com
&

Cedar Manor Hotel ★★
Ambleside Road, Windermere,
Cumbria LA23 1AX
T: (01539) 443192
F: (01539) 445970
E: cedarmanor@fsbdial.co.uk
I: www.cedarmanor.co.uk

Crag Brow Cottage Hotel ★★
Helm Road, Bowness-on-
Windermere, Windermere,
Cumbria LA23 3BU
T: (01539) 444080
F: (01539) 446003
E: cragbrow@aol.com

**Cragwood Country House
Hotel and Restaurant ★★★**
Ecclerigg, Windermere, Cumbria
LA23 1LQ
T: (01539) 488177
F: (01539) 447263

Cranleigh Hotel ★★
Kendal Road, Bowness-on-
Windermere, Windermere,
Cumbria LA23 3EW
T: (01539) 443293
F: (01539) 447283
E: mike@thecranleigh.com
I: www.thecranleigh.com

Dalegarth Private Hotel ★★
Lake Road, Windermere,
Cumbria LA23 2EQ
T: (01539) 445052
F: (01539) 446702
E: enquiries@dalegarthe.
demon.co.uk
I: www.dalegarthe.demon.co.uk

Fayrer Garden House Hotel ★★★
Lyth Valley Road, Bowness-on-
Windermere, Windermere,
Cumbria LA23 3JP
T: (015394) 88195
F: (015394) 45986
E: lakescene@fayrergarden.com
I: www.fayrergarden.com

**Gilpin Lodge Country House
Hotel and Restaurant ★★★**
Crook Road, Windermere,
Cumbria LA23 3NE
T: (01539) 488818
F: (01539) 488058
E: hotel@gilpin-lodge.co.uk
I: www.gilpin-lodge.co.uk

Glenburn ★★
New Road, Windermere,
Cumbria LA23 2EE
T: (01539) 442649
F: (01539) 488998
E: glen.burn@virgin.net
I: www.glenburn.uk.com or
www.hotelslakedistrict.uk.com

Grey Walls Hotel ★★
Elleray Road, Windermere,
Cumbria LA23 1AG
T: (015394) 43741
F: (015394) 47546

Hideaway Hotel ★★
Phoenix Way, Windermere,
Cumbria LA23 1DB
T: (01539) 443070
F: (01539) 448664
E: enquiries@hideaway-hotel.
co.uk
I: www.hideaway-hotel.co.uk

Hillthwaite House ★★★
Thornbarrow Road, Windermere,
Cumbria LA23 2DF
T: (01539) 443636 & 446691
F: (01539) 488660
E: reception@hillthwaite.com
I: www.hillthwaite.com

**Holbeck Ghyll Country House
Hotel and Restaurant ★★★**
Holbeck Lane, Windermere,
Cumbria LA23 1LU
T: (01539) 432375
F: (01539) 434743
E: stay@holbeckghyll.com
I: www.holbeckghyll.com

Lakeside Hotel ★★★★
Newby Bridge, Ulverston,
Cumbria LA12 8AT
T: (01539) 530001
F: (01539) 531699
E: sales@lakesidehotel.co.uk
I: www.lakesidehotel.co.uk

**Lindeth Fell Country House
Hotel ★★**
Lyth Valley Road, Bowness-on-
Windermere, Windermere,
Cumbria LA23 3JP
T: (015394) 43286 & 44287
F: (015394) 47455
E: kennedy@lindethfell.co.uk
I: www.lindethfell.co.uk

**Lindeth Howe Country House
Hotel ★★★**
Lindeth Drive, Longtail Hill,
Bowness-on-Windermere,
Windermere, Cumbria LA23 3JF
T: (015394) 45759
F: (015394) 46368
E: hotel@lindeth-howe.co.uk
I: www.lindeth-howe.co.uk
&

Linthwaite House Hotel ★★★
Crook Road, Windermere,
Cumbria LA23 3JA
T: (01539) 488600
F: (01539) 488601
E: admin@linthwaite.com
I: www.linthwaite.com
&

**Merewood Country House
Hotel ★★**
Ecclerigg, Windermere, Cumbria
LA23 1LH
T: (01539) 446484
F: (01539) 442128
E: merewood.hotel@
impact-dtg.com
I: www.
lakedistrictcountryhotels.co.uk

Mountain Ash Hotel ★★★
Ambleside Road, Windermere,
Cumbria LA23 1AT
T: (01539) 443715 &
0500 535383
F: (01539) 488480
E: john_fawbert@msn.com
I: www.mountainashhotel.co.uk

The Old England ★★★
Church Street, Bowness-on-
Windermere, Windermere,
Cumbria LA23 3DF
T: 0870 400 8130
F: (01539) 443432

Ravensworth Hotel ★★
Ambleside Road, Windermere,
Cumbria LA23 1BA
T: (01539) 443747
F: (01539) 443670
E: ravenswth@aol.com
I: www.ravensworthhotel.co.uk

The Willowsmere Hotel ★
Ambleside Road, Windermere,
Cumbria LA23 1ES
T: (01539) 443575 & 444962
F: (01539) 444962
E: willowsmerehotel@hotmail.
com

Windermere Manor ★★
Rayrigg Road, Windermere,
Cumbria LA23 1ES
T: (01539) 445801
F: (01539) 448397
E: windermere@afbp.org
I: www.afbp.org

WITHERSLACK
Cumbria
The Old Vicarage Hotel ★★
Church Road, Witherslack,
Grange-over-Sands, Cumbria
LA11 6RS
T: (01539) 552381
F: (01539) 552373
E: hotels@oldvicarage.com
I: www.oldvicarage.com

WORKINGTON
Cumbria
Hunday Manor Hotel ★★★
Hunday, Workington, Cumbria
CA14 4JF
T: (01900) 61798
F: (01900) 601202

The Washington Central Hotel ★★★
Washington Street, Workington,
Cumbria CA14 3AY
T: (01900) 65772
F: (01900) 68770

ALLENSFORD
Durham

The Royal Derwent Hotel ★★★
Hole Row, Allensford, Newcastle upon Tyne, Northumberland DH8 9BB
T: (01207) 592000
F: (01207) 502472
E: info@royalderwent.macdonald-hotels.co.uk
I: www.macdonaldhotels.co.uk

ALNMOUTH
Northumberland

The Famous Schooner Hotel and Restaurant ★★★
Northumberland Street, Alnmouth, Alnwick, Northumberland NE66 2RS
T: (01665) 830216
F: (01665) 830287
E: ghost@schooner.sagehost.co.uk
I: www.schooner.sagehost.co.uk

Saddle Hotel ★★
24-25 Northumberland Street, Alnmouth, Alnwick, Northumberland NE66 2RA
T: (01665) 830476

BAMBURGH
Northumberland

Lord Crewe Arms Hotel ★★
Front Street, Bamburgh, Northumberland NE69 7BL
T: (01668) 214243 & 214393
F: (01668) 214273
E: lca@tinyonline.co.uk
I: www.lordcrewe.com

The Mizen Head Hotel ★★
Lucker Road, Bamburgh, Northumberland NE69 7BS
T: (01668) 214254 & 07990 900327
F: (01668) 214104
E: mizenheadhtl@aol.co.uk

Sunningdale Hotel ★★
Lucker Road, Bamburgh, Northumberland NE69 7BS
T: (01668) 214334
F: (01668) 214334
I: www.geocities.com/sunningdalehotel

Victoria Hotel ★★
Front Street, Bamburgh, Northumberland NE69 7BP
T: (01668) 214431
F: (01668) 214404
E: enquiries@victoriahotel.net
I: www.victoriahotel.net

Waren House Hotel ★★★
Waren Mill, Belford, Northumberland NE70 7EE
T: (01668) 214581
F: (01668) 214484
E: enquiries@warenhousehotel.co.uk
I: www.warenhousehotel.co.uk

BARNARD CASTLE
Durham

Jersey Farm Hotel ★★★
Darlington Road, Barnard Castle, County Durham DL12 8TA
T: (01833) 638223
F: (01833) 631988
E: enquiries@jerseyfarm.co.uk
I: www.jerseyfarm.co.uk

Rose & Crown Hotel ★★
Romaldkirk, Barnard Castle, County Durham DL12 9EB
T: (01833) 650213
F: (01833) 650828
E: hotel@rose-and-crown.co.uk
I: www.rose-and-crown.co.uk

BELFORD
Northumberland

Blue Bell Hotel ★★★
Market Place, Belford, Northumberland NE70 7NE
T: (01668) 213543
F: (01668) 213787
E: bluebel@globalnet.co.uk

BELLINGHAM
Northumberland

Riverdale Hall Hotel ★★
Bellingham, Hexham, Northumberland NE48 2JT
T: (01434) 220254
F: (01434) 220457
E: iben@riverdalehall.demon.co.uk

BERWICK-UPON-TWEED
Northumberland

Kings Arms Hotel ★★★
43 Hide Hill, Berwick-upon-Tweed, TD15 1EJ
T: (01289) 307454
F: (01289) 308867
E: info@kings-arms-hotel.com
I: www.kings-arms-hotel.com

Queens Head Hotel ★
Sandgate, Berwick-upon-Tweed, Northumberland TD15 1EP
T: (01289) 307852
F: (01289) 307858

BISHOP AUCKLAND
Durham

The Castle Hotel And Health Spa ★★
41 Market Place, Bishop Auckland, County Durham DL14 7PB
T: (01388) 458322
F: (01388) 451626
E: info@castlesinns.fsnet
I: www.castlesinns.com

BLANCHLAND
Northumberland

Lord Crewe Arms Hotel ★★
Blanchland, Consett, County Durham DH8 9SP
T: (01434) 675251
F: (01434) 675337
E: lord@crewearms.freeserve.co.uk
I: stay-at.com/lordcrewe/welcome.html

CHOLLERFORD
Northumberland

Swallow George Hotel ★★★
Chollerford, Hexham, Northumberland NE46 4EW
T: (01434) 681611
F: (01434) 681727
I: www.georgehotel-chollerford.com

CORBRIDGE
Northumberland

Lion of Corbridge Hotel ★★★
Bridge End, Corbridge, Northumberland NE45 5AX
T: (01434) 632504
F: (01434) 632571
E: lionofcorbridge@talk21.com
I: freespace.virgin.net/rodeo.visual/thelion.htm

CORNHILL-ON-TWEED
Northumberland

Tillmouth Park Country House Hotel ★★★
Cornhill-on-Tweed, Northumberland TD12 4UU
T: (01890) 882255
F: (01890) 882540
E: reception@tillmouthpark.f9.co.uk
I: www.tillmouthpark.co.uk

CROOK
Durham

Helme Park Hall Country House and Restaurant Hotel ★★★
Fir Tree, Crook, County Durham DL13 4NW
T: (01388) 730970
F: (01388) 730970

DARLINGTON
Durham

Blackwell Grange Hotel ★★★
Blackwell Grange, Darlington, County Durham DL3 8QH
T: (01325) 509955
F: (01325) 380899
I: www.corushotels.com

Headlam Hall Hotel and Restaurant ★★★
Headlam, Gainford, Darlington, County Durham DL2 3HA
T: (01325) 730238
F: (01325) 730790
E: admin@headlamhall.co.uk
I: www.headlamhall.co.uk

Newbus Arms Hotel and Restaurant ★★
Newbus Arms, Neasham, Darlington, County Durham DL2 1PE
T: (01325) 721071
F: (01325) 721770

Stanwick House Airport Hotel ★
Stanwick House, Teesside International Airport, Darlington, County Durham DL2 1PD
T: (01325) 333353
F: (01325) 334250
E: enquiries@stanwick-house.co.uk
I: www.stanwick-house.co.uk

DURHAM
Durham

Bowburn Hall Hotel ★★★
Bowburn, Durham DH6 5NH
T: (0191) 377 0311
F: (0191) 377 3459

Crossways Hotel ★★
Dunelm Road, Thornley, Durham DH6 3HT
T: (01429) 821248
F: (01429) 820034
E: enquiries@www.crossways.org.uk
I: www.crossways.org.uk

Durham Marriott Hotel Royal County ★★★★
Old Elvet, Durham, DH1 3JN
T: (0191) 386 6821
F: (0191) 386 0704
E: durhamroyal.marriott@whitbread.com
I: www.marriott.com
⟨⟩

Hallgarth Manor Hotel ★★
Pittington, Durham DH6 1AB
T: (0191) 372 1188
F: (0191) 372 1249
E: hmhotel@zoom.co.uk
I: www.sale@hallgarthmanorhotel.com

Kensington Hall Hotel ★★
Kensington Terrace, Willington, Crook, County Durham DL15 0PJ
T: (01388) 745071
F: (01388) 745800
E: kensingtonhall@cs.com
I: ourworld.cs.com/kensingtonhall

Lumley Castle Hotel ★★★
Chester-le-Street, County Durham DH3 4NX
T: (0191) 389 1111
F: (0191) 389 1881
E: lumcastle@netcomuk.co.uk
I: www.lumleycastle.com

Ramside Hall Hotel ★★★
Carrville, Durham DH1 1TD
T: (0191) 386 5282
F: (0191) 386 0399
E: Ramsidehal@aol.com
⟨⟩

Swallow Three Tuns Hotel ★★★
New Elvet, Durham, DH1 3AQ
T: (0191) 386 4326
F: (0191) 386 1406
E: threetuns.reservations@btinternet.com
I: www.swallowthreetuns.ntb.org.uk

EAGLESCLIFFE
Tees Valley

Sunnyside Hotel ★★
580-582 Yarm Road, Eaglescliffe, Stockton-on-Tees, Cleveland TS16 0DF
T: (01642) 780075
F: (01642) 783789

EMBLETON
Northumberland

Dunstanburgh Castle Hotel ★★
Embleton, Alnwick, Northumberland NE66 3UN
T: (01665) 576111
E: stay@dunstanburghcastlehotel.co.uk
I: www.dunstanburghcastlehotel.co.uk

HALTWHISTLE
Northumberland

Centre of Britain Hotel and Restaurant ★★
___ _istle, Northumberland 0BH
_1434) 322422
F: (01434) 322655
E: enquiries@centre-of-britain.org.uk
I: www.centre-of-britain.org.uk

HARTLEPOOL
Tees Valley

Grand Hotel ★★★
Swainson Street, Hartlepool, Cleveland TS24 8AA
T: (01429) 266345
F: (01429) 265217

Ryedale Moor Hotel ★★
3 Beaconsfield Street, Headland, Hartlepool, Cleveland TS24 0NX
T: (01429) 231436 & 288051
F: (01429) 288053
E: ryedalemoore@hotelo.demon.co.uk
I: www.hotel-hartlepool.co.uk

HEXHAM
Northumberland

Beaumont Hotel ★★★
Beaumont Street, Hexham, Northumberland NE46 3LT
T: (01434) 602331
F: (01434) 606184
E: beaumont.hotel@btinternet.com
I: www.beaumont-hotel.co.uk

The Hexham Royal Hotel ★★
Priestpopple, Hexham, Northumberland NE46 1PQ
T: (01434) 602270
F: (01434) 604084
E: service@hexham-royal-hotel.co.uk
I: www.hexham-royal-hotel.co.uk

Langley Castle ★★★
Langley-on-Tyne, Hexham, Northumberland NE47 5LU
T: (01434) 688888
F: (01434) 684019
E: manager@langleycastle.com
I: www.langleycastle.com

HOLY ISLAND
Northumberland

Lindisfarne Hotel ★
Holy Island, Berwick-upon-Tweed TD15 2SQ
T: (01289) 389273
F: (01289) 389284

HOUGHTON-LE-SPRING
Tyne and Wear

Chilton Lodge Country Pub & Hotel ★★
Black Boy Road, Fencehouses, Houghton-le-Spring, Tyne and Wear DH4 6LX
T: (0191) 385 2694
F: (0191) 385 6762

JESMOND
Tyne and Wear

New Northumbria Hotel ★★★
61-69 Osborne Road, Jesmond, Newcastle upon Tyne NE2 2AN
T: (0191) 281 4961
F: (0191) 281 8588
E: reservations@newnorthumbriahotel.co.uk
I: www.newnorthumbriahotel.co.uk

KIRKWHELPINGTON
Northumberland

Knowesgate Inn ★★
Knowesgate, Kirkwhelpington, Newcastle upon Tyne NE19 2SH
T: (01830) 540336
F: (01830) 540449

MATFEN
Northumberland

Matfen Hall ★★★
Matfen, Newcastle upon Tyne NE20 0RH
T: (01661) 886500
F: (01661) 886055
E: info@matfenhall.com
I: www.matfenhall.com

MIDDLESBROUGH
Tees Valley

Baltimore Hotel ★★★
250 Marton Road, Middlesbrough, Cleveland TS4 2EZ
T: (01642) 224111
F: (01642) 226156
E: info@lincoln-group.co.uk

Quality Hotel and Conference Centre ★★★
Ormesby Road, Middlesbrough, Cleveland TS3 7SF
T: (01642) 203000
E: info@tad-centre.co.uk
I: www.tad-centre.co.uk

MIDDLETON–IN–TEESDALE
Durham

The Teesdale Hotel ★★
Market Place, Middleton-in-Teesdale, Barnard Castle, County Durham DL12 0QG
T: (01833) 640264 & 640537
F: (01833) 640651
I: www.teesdalehotels.com

MORPETH
Northumberland

Linden Hall ★★★
Longhorsley, Morpeth, Northumberland NE65 8XF
T: (01670) 500000
F: (01670) 500001
E: stay@lindenhall.co.uk
I: www.lindenhall.co.uk

Longhirst Hall ★★★
Longhirst, Morpeth, Northumberland NE61 3LL
T: (01670) 791348
F: (01670) 791385
E: enquiries@longhirst.co.uk
I: www.longhirst.co.uk

Queens Head Hotel ★★
Bridge Street, Morpeth, Northumberland NE61 1NB
T: (01670) 512083
F: (01670) 517042

NEWCASTLE UPON TYNE
Tyne and Wear

Cairn Hotel ★★
97-103 Osborne Road, Jesmond, Newcastle upon Tyne NE2 2TJ
T: (0191) 281 1358
F: (0191) 281 9031
E: cairn_hotel@hotmail.com
I: www.cairnhotelgroup.com

Caledonian Hotel ★★★
Osborne Road, Jesmond, Newcastle upon Tyne NE2 2AT
T: (0191) 281 7881
F: (0191) 281 6241
E: caledonian.hotel@lineone.net
I: www.peelhotel.com

Comfort Inn Newcastle Upon Tyne ★★
82-86 Osborne Road, Jesmond, Newcastle upon Tyne NE2 2AP
T: (0191) 281 3361
F: (0191) 281 7722

The Copthorne Newcastle ★★★★
The Close, Quayside, Newcastle upon Tyne, Tyne & Wear NE1 3RT
T: (0191) 222 0333
F: (0191) 230 1111
E: sales.newcastle@mill-cop.com
I: www.stay.with-us.com

Dene Hotel ★★
38-42 Grosvenor Road, Jesmond, Newcastle upon Tyne NE2 2RP
T: (0191) 281 1502
F: (0191) 281 8110
E: denehotel@ukonline.co.uk

Ferncourt ★★★
Osborne Road, Jesmond, Newcastle upon Tyne NE2 2AJ
T: (0191) 281 5377 & 281 5418
F: (0191) 212 0783
E: enquiries.ferncourthotel@zoom.co.uk
I: www.ferncourthotel.co.uk

George Hotel ★★
88 Osborne Road, Jesmond, Newcastle upon Tyne NE2 2AP
T: (0191) 281 4442 & 281 2943
F: (0191) 281 8300
E: georgehotel@dial.pipex.com

Grosvenor Hotel ★★
Grosvenor Road, Jesmond, Newcastle upon Tyne NE2 2RR
T: (0191) 281 0543
F: (0191) 281 9217
E: info@grosvenor-hotel.com
I: www.grosvenor-hotel.com

Grove Hotel ★
134 Brighton Grove, Newcastle upon Tyne, NE4 5NT
T: (0191) 273 8248
F: (0191) 272 5649
I: www.grove-hotel.co.uk

Kenilworth Hotel ★★
44 Osborne Road, Jesmond, Newcastle upon Tyne NE2 2AL
T: (0191) 281 8111
F: (0191) 281 9476
E: kenilworth.nc@talk21.com
I: www.hotelnewcastle.co.uk

New Kent Hotel ★★★
127 Osborne Road, Jesmond, Newcastle upon Tyne NE2 2TB
T: (0191) 281 7711
F: (0191) 281 3369

The Newcastle Marriott Hotel ★★★★
High Gosforth Park, Newcastle upon Tyne, NE3 5HN
T: (0191) 236 4111
F: (0191) 236 8192

Novotel Newcastle ★★★
Ponteland Road, Kenton, Newcastle upon Tyne NE3 3HZ
T: (0191) 214 0303
F: (0191) 214 0633
E: h1118@accor-hotels.com
I: www.novotel.com

Osborne Hotel ★★
13-15 Osborne Road, Jesmond, Newcastle upon Tyne NE2 2AE
T: (0191) 281 3385
F: (0191) 281 7717

Royal Station Hotel ★★★
Neville Street, Newcastle upon Tyne, NE1 5DH
T: (0191) 232 0781
F: (0191) 222 0786
E: info@royalstationhotel.com
I: www.royalstationhotel.com

Ryton Park Country House Hotel ★★
Holburn Lane, Ryton, Tyne and Wear NE40 3PF
T: (0191) 413 3535
F: (0191) 413 6582

Springfield Hotel ★★★
Durham Road, Gateshead, Tyne and Wear NE9 5BT
T: (0191) 477 4121
F: (0191) 477 7213
E: reception@springfield_hotel.fsnet.co.uk

Surtees Hotel Ltd ★★★
12-18 Dean Street, Newcastle upon Tyne, NE1 1PG
T: (0191) 261 7771
F: (0191) 230 1322
E: surtees@milburn.net
I: www.surteeshotel.co.uk

Swallow Hotel ★★★
High West Street, Gateshead, Tyne and Wear NE8 1PE
T: (0191) 477 1105
F: (0191) 478 7214
I: www.swallowhotelgateshead.com

Swallow Imperial Hotel ★★★
Jesmond Road, Newcastle upon Tyne, NE2 1PR
T: (0191) 281 5511
F: (0191) 281 8472
E: jesmond@swallow-hotels.co.uk

OTTERBURN
Northumberland

Otterburn Tower Hotel ★★★
Otterburn, Newcastle upon Tyne NE19 1NS
T: (01830) 520620 & (01670) 772287
F: (01830) 521504
E: reservations@otterburntower.co.uk
I: www.otterburntower.co.uk

Percy Arms Hotel ★★
Otterburn, Newcastle upon Tyne NE19 1NR
T: (01830) 520261
F: (01830) 520567
E: percyarms@bestwestern.co.uk
I: www.percyarms.co.uk

RUSHYFORD
Durham

Swallow Eden Arms Hotel ★★★
Rushyford, Ferryhill, County
Durham DL17 0LL
T: (01388) 720541
F: (01388) 721871
E: edenarmsswallow@
whitbread.com
I: www.swallowhotels.co.uk

SALTBURN-BY-THE-SEA
Tees Valley

Grinkle Park Hotel ★★★
Easington-Loftus, Saltburn-by-
the-Sea, Cleveland TS13 4UB
T: (01287) 640515
F: (01287) 641278
E: grinkle.parkhotel@bass.com
I: www.grinklepark.co.uk

SEAHOUSES
Northumberland

Bamburgh Castle Hotel ★★
Seahouses, Northumberland
NE68 7SQ
T: (01665) 720283
F: (01665) 720848
E: bamburghcastlehotel@
talk21.com
I: www.bamburghcastlehotel.
co.uk

Beach House Hotel ★★
Sea Front, Seahouses,
Northumberland NE68 7SR
T: (01665) 720337
F: (01665) 720921
E: enq@beachhousehotel.co.uk
I: www.beachhousehotel.co.uk

Longstone House Hotel ★★
182 Main Street, Seahouses,
Northumberland NE68 7UA
T: (01665) 720212

Olde Ship Hotel ★★
Seahouses, Northumberland
NE68 7RD
T: (01665) 720200
F: (01665) 721383
E: theoldeship@seahouses.co.uk
I: www.seahouses.co.uk

SEATON BURN
Tyne and Wear

Horton Grange ★★
Seaton Burn, Newcastle upon
Tyne NE13 6BU
T: (01661) 860686 &
07889 196637
F: (01661) 860308
E: andrew@norton-grange.
co.uk
I: www.horton-grange.co.uk

SEDGEFIELD
Durham

Hardwick Hall Hotel ★★★
Sedgefield, Stockton-on-Tees,
Cleveland TS21 2EH
T: (01740) 620253
F: (01740) 622771

SLALEY
Northumberland

De Vere Slaley Hall ★★★★
Slaley, Hexham,
Northumberland NE47 0BY
T: (01434) 673350
F: (01434) 673962
E: slaley.hall@devere-hotels.
com
I: www.devereonline.co.uk

SOUTH SHIELDS
Tyne and Wear

Fountain Lodge Hotel ★★
Newcastle Road, South Shields,
Tyne and Wear NE34 9PQ
T: (0191) 456 4631
F: (0191) 456 4444
E: info@fountainlodgehotel.
co.uk
I: www.
info@fountainlodgehotel.co.uk

Little Haven Hotel ★★★
River Drive, Littlehaven, South
Shields, Tyne and Wear
NE33 1LH
T: (0191) 455 4455
F: (0191) 455 4466
I: www.littlehavenhotel.com

Sea Hotel ★★★
Sea Road, South Shields, Tyne
and Wear NE33 2LD
T: (0191) 427 0999
F: (0191) 454 0500
E: sea@bestwestern.co.uk
I: www.theseahotel.co.uk

STOCKTON-ON-TEES
Tees Valley

**Parkmore Hotel and Leisure
Club ★★★**
636 Yarm Road, Eaglescliffe,
Stockton-on-Tees, Cleveland
TS16 0DH
T: (01642) 786815
F: (01642) 790485
E: enquiries@parkmorehotel.
co.uk
I: www.parkmorehotel.co.uk

Swallow Hotel ★★★★
John Walker Square, High Street,
Stockton-on-Tees, Cleveland
TS18 1AQ
T: (01642) 679721
F: (01642) 601714
E: stockton.swallow@
whitbread.com
I: www.swallowhotels.com

SUNDERLAND
Tyne and Wear

**George Washington Golf &
Country Club ★★★**
Stone Cellar Road, High
Usworth, District 12,
Washington, Tyne and Wear
NE37 1PH
T: (0191) 402 9988
F: (0191) 415 1166
E: georgewashington@
corushotels.com
I: www.corushotels.co.uk

Mowbray Park Hotel ★★
Borough Road, Sunderland,
SR1 1PR
T: (0191) 567 8221
F: (0191) 510 2572
E: reception@
mowbray-park-hotel.co.uk
I: mowbray-park-hotel.co.uk

**Quality Hotel Sunderland
★★★**
Junction A19/A184, Witney Way,
Boldon, Sunderland, NE35 9PE
T: (0191) 519 1999
F: (0191) 519 0655
E: admin@gb621.u-net.com
I: www.choicehotelseurope.com

THORNABY
Tees Valley

**Holiday Inn Middlesbrough/
Teesside ★★★**
Low Lane, Stainton Village,
Thornaby, Stockton-on-Tees,
Cleveland TS17 9LW
T: 0870 400 9081
F: (01642) 594989
E: gm1221@forte-hotels.com
I: www.posthouse-hotels.com

TYNEMOUTH
Tyne and Wear

Grand Hotel ★★★
Grand Parade, Tynemouth,
North Shields, Tyne and Wear
NE30 4ER
T: (0191) 293 6666
F: (0191) 293 6665
E: info@grandhotel-uk.com
I: www.grandhotel-uk.com

WARKWORTH
Northumberland

Sun Hotel ★★
6 Castle Terrace, Warkworth,
Alnwick, Northumberland
NE65 0UP
T: (01665) 711259
F: (01665) 711833

Warkworth House Hotel ★★
16 Bridge Street, Warkworth,
Morpeth, Northumberland
NE65 0XB
T: (01665) 711276
F: (01665) 713323
E: welcome@
warkworthhousehotel.co.uk
I: www.warkworthhousehotel.
co.uk

WEST AUCKLAND
Durham

**Manor House Hotel and
Country Club ★★★**
The Green, Front Street, West
Auckland, Bishop Auckland,
County Durham DL14 9HW
T: (01388) 834834
F: (01388) 833566
E: enquiries@manorhousehotel.
net
I: www.manorhousehotel.net

WHICKHAM
Tyne and Wear

Gibside Hotel ★★★
Front Street, Whickham,
Newcastle upon Tyne NE16 4JG
T: (0191) 488 9292
F: (0191) 488 8000
E: reception@gibside-hotel.
co.uk
I: www.gibside-hotel.co.uk

WHITLEY BAY
Tyne and Wear

Avalon Hotel ★★
26 South Parade, Whitley Bay,
Tyne and Wear NE26 2RG
T: (0191) 251 0080
F: (0191) 251 0100
E: reception@avalon-hotel.
freeserve.co.uk
I: www.avalon-hotel.freeserve.
co.uk

The Esplanade Hotel ★★★
The Esplanade, Whitley Bay,
Tyne and Wear NE26 2AW
T: (0191) 252 1111
F: (0191) 252 0101

High Point Hotel ★★
The Promenade, Whitley Bay,
Tyne and Wear NE26 2NJ
T: (0191) 251 7782
F: (0191) 251 6318
E: highpointhotel@aol.com

Park Lodge Hotel ★★
162-164 Park Avenue, Whitley
Bay, Tyne and Wear NE26 1AU
T: (0191) 252 6879 & 253 0288
F: (0191) 297 1006
E: parklodgehotel@hotmail.com
I: www.the-parklodgehotel.co.uk

Rex Hotel ★★★
The Promenade, Whitley Bay,
Tyne and Wear NE26 2RL
T: (0191) 252 3201
F: (0191) 251 4663
E: reception@rex-hotel.com
I: www.rex-hotel.com

Windsor Hotel ★★★
South Parade, Whitley Bay, Tyne
and Wear NE26 2RF
T: (0191) 251 8888
F: (0191) 297 0272
E: info@windsorhotel-uk.com
I: www.windsorhotel-uk.com

WOOLER
Northumberland

Tankerville Arms Hotel ★★
22 Cottage Road, Wooler,
Northumberland NE71 6AD
T: (01668) 281581
F: (01668) 281387
E: enquiries@tankervillehotel.
co.uk
I: www.tankervillehotel.co.uk

NORTH WEST

ALDERLEY EDGE
Cheshire

The Alderley Edge Hotel ★★★
Macclesfield Road, Alderley
Edge, Cheshire SK9 7BJ
T: (01625) 583033
F: (01625) 586343
E: sales@alderley-edge-hotel.
co.uk
I: www.alderley-edge-hotel.
co.uk

ALSAGER
Cheshire

The Manor House Hotel ★★★
Audley Road, Alsager, Stoke-on-
Trent ST7 2QQ
T: (01270) 884000
F: (01270) 882483
E: mhres@compassmotels.co.uk
I: www.compasshotels.co.uk

ALTRINCHAM
Greater Manchester

Cresta Court Hotel ★★★
Church Street, Altrincham,
Cheshire WA14 4DP
T: (0161) 927 7272
F: (0161) 926 9194
E: info@cresta-court.co.uk
I: www.cresta-court.co.uk

Oasis Hotel ★★
46-48 Barrington Road,
Altrincham, Cheshire WA14 1HN
T: (0161) 928 4523
F: (0161) 928 1055
E: Enquiries@oasishotel.co.uk
I: www.oasishotel.co.uk

BIRKENHEAD
Merseyside

Central Hotel ★
Clifton Crescent, Birkenhead,
Merseyside CH41 2QH
T: (0151) 647 6347 &
07812 378565
F: (0151) 647 5476

BLACKBURN
Lancashire

Northcote Manor Hotel ★★★
Northcote Road, Old Langho,
Blackburn BB6 8BE
T: (01254) 240555
F: (01254) 246568
E: admin@northcotemanor.com
I: www.northcotemanor.com

BLACKPOOL
Lancashire

Brabyns Hotel ★★
1-5 Shaftesbury Avenue,
Blackpool, FY2 9QQ
T: (01253) 354263 & 352163
F: (01253) 352915
E: brabynshotel@
netscapeonline.co.uk

Doric Hotel ★★
48-52 Queens Promenade,
Blackpool, FY2 9RP
T: (01253) 352640 & 351751
F: (01253) 596842
E: info@dorichotel-blackpool.
net
I: dorichotel.blackpool.net

The Headlands ★★
611-613 South Promenade,
Blackpool, FY4 1NJ
T: (01253) 341179
F: (01253) 342047
E: headlands@blackpool.net
I: www.theheadlands.blackpool.
net

New Mayfair ★★
673-677 New South Promenade,
Blackpool, FY4 1RN
T: (01253) 347543
F: (01253) 349678
E: new.mayfair@virgin.net

Ruskin Hotel ★★
Albert Road, Blackpool, FY1 4PW
T: (01253) 624063
F: (01253) 623571
E: ruskinhotel@aol.com
I: ruskinhotel.com

St Chads Hotel ★★
317-323 Promenade, Blackpool,
FY1 6BN
T: (01253) 346348 & 344669
F: (01253) 348240

Savoy Hotel ★★★
Queens Promenade, Blackpool,
FY2 9SJ
T: (01253) 352561
F: (01253) 595549

Stretton Hotel ★★
206-214 North Promenade,
Blackpool, FY1 1RU
T: (01253) 625688
F: (01253) 624075
E: strettonhotel@btconnect.
com
I: www.strettonhotel.co.uk

BOLTON
Greater Manchester

Bolton Moat House ★★★
1 Higher Bridge Street, Bolton,
Greater Manchester BL1 2EW
T: (01204) 879988
F: (01204) 380777
E: cbbol@queensmoat.co.uk

**Jarvis International Hotel
★★★**
Manchester Road, Blackrod,
Bolton BL6 5RU
T: (01942) 814598
F: (01942) 816026
I: www.jarvis.co.uk

Melrose Hotel ★★
181-183 Chorley New Road,
Bolton, BL1 4QZ
T: (01204) 525130
F: (01204) 525130

BURNLEY
Lancashire

Alexander Hotel ★★
2 Tarleton Avenue, Todmorden
Road, Burnley, Lancashire
BB11 3ET
T: (01282) 422684
F: (01282) 424094
E: phleisure@aol.com
I: www.thealexanderhotel.co.uk

Sparrowhawk Hotel ★★★
Church Street, Burnley,
Lancashire BB11 2DN
T: (01282) 421551
F: (01282) 456506
I: www.sparrowhawkhotel.co.uk

BURY
Greater Manchester

**Red Hall Hotel & Restaurant
★★★**
Manchester Road, Walmersley,
Bury, Lancashire BL9 5NA
T: (01706) 822476
F: (01706) 828086
I: www.redhall.co.uk

CARNFORTH
Lancashire

**The County Hotel and Lodge
★★**
Lancaster Road, Carnforth,
Lancashire LA5 9LD
T: (01524) 732469
F: (01524) 720142
E: info@thecountyhotel.co.uk
I: www.thecountyhotel.co.uk

Royal Station Hotel ★★
Market Street, Carnforth,
Lancashire LA5 9BT
T: (01524) 732033 & 733636
F: (01524) 720267
E: j.thornber@aol.com

CASTLETON
Greater Manchester

The Royal Toby Hotel ★★★
Manchester Road, Castleton,
Rochdale, Lancashire OL11 3HF
T: (01706) 861861
F: (01706) 869428

CHADDERTON
Greater Manchester

Bower Hotel ★★★
Hollinwood Avenue,
Chadderton, Oldham OL9 8DE
T: (0161) 682 7254
F: (0161) 683 4605
E: bower@macdonald-hotels.
co.uk
I: www.bowerhotel.com

CHESTER
Cheshire

Abbey Court Hotel ★★
Liverpool Road, Chester,
CH2 1AG
T: (01244) 374100
F: (01244) 379240
I: www.macdonaldhotels.
co.uk/abbeycourthotel/

**The Chester Crabwall Manor
Rating Applied For**
Parkgate Road, Mollington,
Chester CH1 6NE
T: (01244) 851666
F: (01244) 851400
E: crabwallmanor@
marstonhotels.com
I: www.marstonhotels.com

**The Chester Grosvenor
★★★★★**
Eastgate, Chester, CH1 1LT
T: (01244) 324024 & 895614
F: (01244) 313246
E: chesgrov@chestergrosvenor.
co.uk
I: www.chestergrosvenor.co.uk

Chester Moat House ★★★★
Trinity Street, Chester, CH1 2BD
T: (01244) 899988
F: (01244) 316118
E: cbchs@queensmoat.co.uk
I: www.moathousehotels.com

Curzon Hotel ★★
52-54 Hough Green, Chester,
CH4 8JQ
T: (01244) 678581
F: (01244) 680866
E: curzon.chester@virgin.net
I: www.chestercurzonhotel.co.uk

**De Vere Carden Park Hotel Golf
Resort & Spa★★★★**
Carden Park, Chester, CH3 9DQ
T: (01829) 731000
F: (01829) 731032
E: reservations.carden@
devere-hotels.com
I: www.cardenpark.com

Dene Hotel ★★
Hoole Road, Chester, CH2 3ND
T: (01244) 321165
F: (01244) 350277
E: denehotel@btconnect.com
I: www.denehotel.com

**Green Bough Hotel and
Restaurant ★★★**
60 Hoole Road, Chester,
CH2 3NL
T: (01244) 326241
F: (01244) 326265
E: greenboughhotel@cwcom.
net
I: www.smoothhound.
co.uk/hotels/greenbo.html

**Grosvenor-Pulford Hotel
★★★**
Wrexham Road, Pulford, Chester
CH4 9DG
T: (01244) 570560
F: (01244) 570809
E: enquiries@
grosvenorpulfordhotel.co.uk
I: www.grosvenorpulfordhotel.
co.uk

Mill Hotel ★★★
Milton Street, Chester, CH1 3NF
T: (01244) 350035
F: (01244) 345635
E: reservations@millhotel.com
I: www.millhotel.com

**Mollington Banastre Hotel
★★★★**
Parkgate Road, Mollington,
Chester CH1 6NN
T: (01244) 851471
F: (01244) 851165
E: mollington@arcadianhotels.
co.uk
I: www.mollingtonbanastre.
co.uk

Queen Hotel ★★★★
City Road, Chester, CH1 3AH
T: (01244) 305000
F: (01244) 318483
E: richard.hopson-cossey@
principalhotels.co.uk
I: www.principalhotels.co.uk

Hotel Romano ★★★
51 Lower Bridge Street, Chester,
CH1 1RS
T: (01244) 325091 & 320841
F: (01244) 315628
E: hotelromano@aol.com
I: www.hotel-romano.co.uk

Rowton Hall Hotel ★★★
Whitchurch Road, Rowton,
Chester CH3 6AD
T: (01244) 335262
F: (01244) 335464
E: rowtonhall@rowtonhall.co.uk
I: rowtonhallhotel.co.uk

Stafford Hotel ★★
City Road, Chester, CH1 3AE
T: (01244) 326052 & 302695
F: (01244) 311403
E: enquiries@staffordhotel.com
I: www.staffordhotel.com

Westminster Hotel ★★
City Road, Chester, CH1 3AF
T: (01244) 317341
F: (01244) 325369
E: westminsterhotel@feathers.
uk.com
I: www.feathers.uk.com

CHIPPING
Lancashire
Gibbon Bridge Hotel ★★★★
Chipping, Preston PR3 2TQ
T: (01995) 61456
F: (01995) 61277
E: reception@gibbon-bridge.
co.uk
I: www.gibbon-bridge.co.uk

CHORLEY
Lancashire
**Park Hall Hotel, Leisure and
Conference Centre★★★★**
Park Hall Road, Charnock
Richard, Chorley, Preston
PR7 5LP
T: (01257) 452090 & 455000
F: (01257) 451838
E: conf@parkhall-hotel.co.uk
I: www.parkhall-hotel.co.uk

CLAYTON–LE–MOORS
Lancashire
Sparth House Hotel ★★★
Whalley Road, Clayton-le-
Moors, Accrington, Lancashire
BB5 5RP
T: (01254) 872263
F: (01254) 872263

CLITHEROE
Lancashire
Shireburn Arms Hotel ★★
Whalley Road, Hurst Green,
Clitheroe, Lancashire BB7 9QJ
T: (01254) 020510
F: (01254) 826208
E: sales@shireburn-hotel.co.uk
I: www.shireburn-hotel.co.uk

DARWEN
Lancashire
Astley Bank ★★★
Bolton Road, Darwen, Blackburn,
Lancashire BB3 2QB
T: (01254) 777700
F: (01254) 777707

**Whitehall Hotel & Country
Club★★★**
Spring Bank, Whitehall, Darwen,
Lancashire BB3 2JU
T: (01254) 701595
F: (01254) 773426
E: hotel@thewhitehallhotel.
freeserve.co.uk

FLEETWOOD
Lancashire
North Euston Hotel ★★★
Esplanade, Fleetwood,
Lancashire FY7 6BN
T: (01253) 876525
F: (01253) 777842
E: admin@northeustonhotel.
co.uk
I: www.northeustonhotel.co.uk

FORMBY
Merseyside
**Tree Tops Restaurant and Hotel
★★★**
Southport Old Road, Formby,
Merseyside L37 0AB
T: (01704) 572430
F: (01704) 572430

FRODSHAM
Cheshire
Forest Hills Hotel ★★★
Overton Hill, Frodsham,
WA6 6HH
T: (01928) 735255
F: (01928) 735517
E: info@foresthillshotel.com
I: www.foresthillshotel.com

GARSTANG
Lancashire
Crofters Hotel ★★★
A6, Cabus, Garstang, Preston
PR3 1PH
T: (01995) 604128
F: (01995) 601646

**Garstang Country Hotel and
Golf Club★★★**
Garstang Road, Bowgreave,
Garstang, Preston PR3 1YE
T: (01995) 600100
F: (01995) 600950
E: reception@
garstanghotelandgolf.co.uk
I: www.garstanghotelandgolf.
co.uk

GISBURN
Lancashire
Stirk House Hotel ★★★
Gisburn, Clitheroe, Lancashire
BB7 4LJ
T: (01200) 445581
F: (01200) 445744
E: stirkhouse@ukhotels.com

KNUTSFORD
Cheshire
**Longview Hotel and
Restaurant★★**
Manchester Road, Knutsford,
Cheshire WA16 0LX
T: (01565) 632119
F: (01565) 652402
E: enquiries@longviewhotel.
com
I: www.longviewhotel.com

Mere Court Hotel ★★★★
Mere, Knutsford, Cheshire
WA16 0RW
T: (01565) 831000
F: (01565) 831001
E: sales@merecourt.co.uk
I: www.merecourt.co.uk

LANCASTER
Lancashire
The Greaves Hotel ★★
Greaves Road, Lancaster,
LA1 4UW
T: (01524) 63943
F: (01524) 382679

Hampson House Hotel ★★
Hampson Lane, Hampson Green,
Lancaster, LA2 0JB
T: (01524) 751158 & 751189
F: (01524) 751779

**Scarthwaite Country House
Hotel ★**
Crook O'Lune, Caton, Lancaster
LA2 9HR
T: (01524) 770267
F: (01524) 770711

Thurnham Mill Hotel ★★
Thurnham, Lancaster LA2 0BD
T: (01524) 752852
F: (01524) 752477
E: stay@thurnham-mill-hotel.
fsnet.co.uk
I: www.thurnham-mill-hotel.
co.uk

LANGHO
Lancashire
**Mytton Fold Hotel and Golf
Complex ★★★**
Whalley Road, Langho,
Blackburn BB6 8AB
T: (01254) 240662
F: (01254) 248119
E: enquiries@myttonfold.co.uk
I: www.myttonfold.co.uk

LEIGH
Greater Manchester
**The Sporting Lodge Greyhound
Hotel ★★**
Warrington Road, Leigh,
Lancashire WN7 3XQ
T: (01942) 671256
F: (01942) 261949
I: www.jarvis.co.uk

LEYLAND
Lancashire
Jarvis Leyland Hotel ★★
Leyland Way, Leyland, Preston
PR5 2JX
T: (01772) 422922
F: (01772) 622282
I: www.jarvis.co.uk

LIVERPOOL
Merseyside
**The Devonshire House Hotel
and Conference Centre★★★**
293-297 Edge Lane, Liverpool,
L7 9LD
T: (0151) 264 6600
F: (0151) 263 2109
E: sales@devonshirehousehotel.
co.uk
I: www.devonshirehousehotel.
co.uk

**Feathers Hotel
Rating Applied For**
117 Mount Pleasant, Liverpool,
L3 5TF
T: (0151) 709 9655
F: (0151) 709 3838
E: feathershotel@feathers.uk.
com
I: www.feathers.uk.com

Gateacre Hall Hotel ★★★
The Nook, Halewood Road,
Liverpool, L25 5PG
T: (0151) 428 6322
F: (0151) 428 4302

Liverpool Moat House ★★★★
Paradise Street, Liverpool, L1 8JD
T: (0151) 471 9988 & 709 1937
F: (0151) 709 2706

Rockland Hotel ★
View Road, Rainhill, Prescot,
Merseyside L35 0LG
T: (0151) 426 4603
F: (0151) 426 0107

Royal Hotel ★★★
Marine Terrace, Waterloo,
Liverpool L22 5PR
T: (0151) 928 2332
F: (0151) 949 0320
E: royalhotel@compuserve.com
I: www.liverpool-royal.hotel.
co.uk

LONGRIDGE
Lancashire
**Ferraris Country House Limited
Hotel & Restaurant★★**
Chipping Road, Thornley,
Longridge, Preston PR3 2TB
T: (01772) 783148
F: (01772) 786174
E: alferrari@compuserve.com

LYMM
Cheshire
Lymm Hotel ★★★
Whitbarrow Road, Lymm,
Cheshire WA13 9AQ
T: (01925) 752233
F: (01925) 756035
E: info@lymm.
macdonald-hotels.co.uk
I: www.macdonaldhotels.co.uk

**Statham Lodge Country House
Hotel ★★★**
Warrington Road, Statham,
Lymm, Cheshire WA13 9BP
T: (01925) 752204
F: (01925) 757406
E: statham_lodge@btconnect.
com
I: www.statham-lodge.com

LYTHAM ST ANNES
Lancashire
Chadwick Hotel ★★★
South Promenade, Lytham St
Annes, Lancashire FY8 1NP
T: (01253) 720061
F: (01253) 714455
E: sales@thechadwickhotel.com
I: www.thechadwickhotel.com

Clifton Arms Hotel ★★★★
West Beach, Lytham St Annes,
Lancashire FY8 5QJ
T: (01253) 739898 & 730657
F: (01253) 730657
E: welcome@cliftonarms.com
I: www.cliftonarms.com

Dalmeny Hotel ★★★
19-33 South Promenade,
Lytham St Annes, Lancashire
FY8 1LX
T: (01253) 712236
F: (01253) 724447
E: info@dalmenyhotel.com
I: www.dalmenyhotel.com

The Grand Hotel ★★★
South Promenade, Lytham St
Annes, Lancashire FY8 1NB
T: (01253) 721288 & 0800 731
2208
F: (01253) 714459
E: book@the-grand.co.uk
I: www.the-grand.co.uk

Langdales Hotel ★★
318-328 Clifton Drive North,
Lytham St Annes, Lancashire
FY8 2PB
T: (01253) 721342
F: (01253) 729517

Lindum Hotel ★★
63-67 South Promenade,
Lytham St Annes, Lancashire
FY8 1LZ
T: (01253) 721534 & 722516
F: (01253) 721364
E: info@lindumhotel.co.uk
I: www.lindumhotel.co.uk

St Ives Hotel ★★
7 South Promenade, Lytham St
Annes, Lancashire FY8 1LS
T: (01253) 720011
F: (01253) 722873
E: book@st-ives-hotel.co.uk
I: www.st-ives-hotel.co.uk

MACCLESFIELD
Cheshire

**Shrigley Hall Hotel Golf and
Country Club**★★★★
Shrigley Park, Pott Shrigley,
Macclesfield, Cheshire SK10 5SB
T: (01625) 575757
F: (01625) 573323
E: shrigleyhall@
paramount-hotels.co.uk
I: www.paramount-hotels.co.uk

MANCHESTER
Greater Manchester

Albany Hotel ★★
21 Albany Road, Chorlton-cum-
Hardy, Manchester, M21 0AY
T: (0161) 881 6774
F: (0161) 862 9405

Castlefield Hotel ★★★
Liverpool Road, Castlefield,
Manchester, M3 4JR
T: (0161) 832 7073
F: (0161) 837 3534
E: info@castlefield-hotel.co.uk
I: www.castlefield-hotel.co.uk

Copthorne Manchester
★★★★
Clippers Quay, Salford Quays,
Manchester, M5 2XP
T: (0161) 873 7321
F: (0161) 873 7318
E: manchester@mill-cop.com
I: www.millennium-hotels.com

**Crowne Plaza Manchester–The
Midland** ★★★★
Peter Street, Manchester,
M60 2DS
T: (0161) 236 3333
F: (0161) 932 4100
E: basshotels-uknorth.co.uk
I: www.manchester-themidland.
crowneplaza.com

Gardens Hotel ★★★
55 Piccadilly, Manchester,
M1 2AP
T: (0161) 236 5155
F: (0161) 228 7287
E: gardensman@hotmail.com
I: www.cairn-hotels.co.uk

Golden Tulip Manchester
★★★
Waters Reach, Trafford Park,
Manchester, M17 1WS
T: (0161) 873 8899
F: (0161) 872 6556
E: info@goldentulipmanchester.
co.uk
I: www.goldentulipmanchester.
co.uk

Holiday Inn Garden Court
★★★
Outwood Lane, Manchester
Airport, Manchester, M90 4HL
T: (0161) 498 0333
F: (0161) 498 0222
E: reservations@mchap.co.uk
I: www.holiday-inn.
com/manchester-apt

Jurys Inn Manchester ★★★
56 Great Bridgewater Street,
Manchester, M1 5LE
T: (0161) 953 8888
F: (0161) 953 9090
I: www.jurysdoyle.com

**Manchester Conference Centre
and Hotel**★★
The Weston Building, Sackville
Street, Manchester, M1 3BB
T: (0161) 955 8000
F: (0161) 955 8050
E: weston@umist.ac.uk
I: www.meeting.co.uk

Novotel Manchester West
★★★
Worsley Brow, Worsley,
Manchester M28 2YA
T: (0161) 799 3535
F: (0161) 703 8207
E: h0907@accor-hotels.com
I: www.novotel.com

The Palace Hotel ★★★★
Oxford Street, Manchester,
M60 7HA
T: (0161) 288 1111
F: (0161) 288 2222
I: www.principalhotels.co.uk

Princess Hotel ★★★
101 Portland Street,
Manchester, M1 6DF
T: (0161) 236 5122
F: (0161) 236 4468
E: admin@princesshotels.co.uk
I: www.princesshotels.co.uk

**Radisson SAS Hotel
Manchester Airport**★★★★
Chicago Avenue, Manchester
Airport, Manchester, M90 3RA
T: (0161) 490 5000
F: (0161) 490 5100
E: sales@manzq.rdsas.com
I: www.radissonsas.com

Village Leisure Hotel ★★★
George Street, Sedgley Park,
Prestwich, Manchester
M25 9WS
T: (0161) 798 8905
F: (0161) 773 5421
E: village.prestwich@
village-hotels.com
I: www.vlh.co.uk

Willow Bank Hotel ★★
340 Wilmslow Road, Fallowfield,
Manchester, M14 6AF
T: (0161) 224 0461
F: (0161) 257 2561
I: www.
willowbankhotel@feathers.uk.
com

MAWDESLEY
Lancashire

**Mawdsleys Eating House and
Hotel**★★★
Hall Lane, Mawdesley, Ormskirk,
Lancashire L40 2QZ
T: (01704) 822552 & 821874
F: (01704) 822096
E: mawdsleyeh@aol.com
I: www.mawdsleyeh.co.uk

MIDDLEWICH
Cheshire

The Kinderton House Hotel
★★
Kinderton Street, Middlewich,
Cheshire CW10 0JE
T: (01606) 834325
F: (01606) 834325

MORECAMBE
Lancashire

The Auckland Hotel ★★
312-315 Marine Road, Central
Promenade, Morecambe,
Lancashire LA4 5AA
T: (01524) 412565
F: (01524) 400862
E: info@aucklandhotel.co.uk
I: www.aucklandhotel.co.uk

Broadway Hotel ★★
East Promenade, Morecambe,
Lancashire LA4 5AR
T: (01524) 410777
F: (01524) 417573
I: www.morecambe.
net/broadwayhotel

Clarendon Hotel ★★★
76 Marine Road West,
Morecambe, Lancashire LA4 4EP
T: (01524) 410180
F: (01524) 421616

Elms Hotel ★★★
Bare Village, Morecambe,
Lancashire LA4 6DD
T: (01524) 411501
F: (01524) 831979

Headway Hotel ★★★
Marine Road, East Promenade,
Morecambe, Lancashire
LA4 5AW
T: (01524) 412525
F: (01524) 832630
E: admin@headway.net1.co.uk
I: www.headwayhotel.co.uk

Lothersdale Hotel ★★
320-323 Marine Road, Central
Promenade, Morecambe,
Lancashire LA4 5AA
T: (01524) 416 404
F: (01524) 416 000
E: info@lothersdale.com
I: www.lothersdale.com

MORETON
Merseyside

Leasowe Castle Hotel ★★★
Leasowe Road, Moreton, Wirral,
Merseyside CH46 3RF
T: (0151) 606 9191 & 6785551
F: (0151) 678 5551
E: reservations@leasowecastle.
com
I: www.leasowecastle.com

NANTWICH
Cheshire

Rookery Hall ★★★
Main Road, Worleston,
Nantwich, Cheshire CW5 6DQ
T: (01270) 610016
F: (01270) 626027
I: www.arcadianhotels.co.uk

NEWTON-LE-WILLOWS
Merseyside

Kirkfield Hotel ★★
2-4 Church Street, Newton-le-
Willows, Merseyside WA12 9SU
T: (01925) 228196
F: (01925) 291540

NORTHWICH
Cheshire

Oaklands Country House Hotel
★★
Millington Lane, Gorstage,
Northwich, Cheshire CW8 2SU
T: (01606) 853249
F: (01606) 852419

Quality Hotel Northwich
★★★
London Road, Northwich,
Cheshire CW9 5HD
T: (01606) 44443
F: (01606) 42596
E: admin@gb618.u-net.com
I: www.choicehotelseurope.com

OLD TRAFFORD
Greater Manchester

Old Trafford Lodge
Travel Accommodation
Lancashire County Cricket Club,
Old Trafford, Manchester
M16 0PX
T: (0161) 874 3333
F: (0161) 874 3399
E: sales.lancs@ecb.co.uk
I: www.lccc.co.uk

OLDHAM
Greater Manchester

Hotel Smokies Park ★★★
Ashton Road, Bardsley, Oldham
OL8 3HX
T: (0161) 785 5000
F: (0161) 785 5010
E: sales@smokies.co.uk
I: www.smokies.co.uk

ORMSKIRK
Lancashire

Beaufort Hotel ★★★
High Lane, Burscough, Ormskirk,
Lancashire L40 7SN
T: (01704) 892655
F: (01704) 895135
E: info@beaufort.uk.com
I: www.beaufort.uk.com

PARKGATE
Cheshire

Ship Hotel ★★
The Parade, Parkgate, South
Wirral CH64 6SA
T: (0151) 336 3931
F: (0151) 336 3931
I: www.the-shiphotel.co.uk

PILLING
Lancashire

Springfield House Hotel and Restaurant ★★★
Wheel Lane, Pilling, Preston
PR3 6HL
T: (01253) 790301
F: (01253) 790907
E: recep@springfieldhouse.uk.com
I: www.springfieldhouse.uk.com

PRESTBURY
Cheshire

The White House Manor ★★★★
Townhouse
The Village, Prestbury,
Macclesfield, Cheshire SK10 4HP
T: (01625) 829376
F: (01625) 828627
E: info@thewhitehouse.uk.com
I: thewhitehouse.uk.com

PRESTON
Lancashire

Novotel Preston ★★★
Reedfield Place, Walton Summit,
Preston, PR5 8AA
T: (01772) 313331
F: (01772) 627868
E: h0838@accor-hotels.com
I: www.novotel.com

Swallow Hotel ★★★
Preston New Road, Samlesbury,
Preston PR5 0UL
T: (01772) 877351 & 872703
F: (01772) 877424
E: swallow.preston@whitbread.com
I: www.swallowhotels.com

Tickled Trout Hotel ★★★
Preston New Road, Samlesbury,
Preston PR5 0UJ
T: (01772) 877671
F: (01772) 877463
E: info@tickledtrout.macdonald.hotels.co.uk
I: www.macdonaldhotels.co.uk

RUFFORD
Lancashire

Rufford Arms Hotel ★★
380 Liverpool Road, Rufford,
Lancashire L40 1SQ
T: (01704) 822040
F: (01704) 821910
E: ruffordarmshotel@hotmail.com

SADDLEWORTH
Greater Manchester

La Pergola Hotel and Restaurant ★★★
Rochdale Road, Denshaw,
Oldham OL3 5UE
T: (01457) 871040
F: (01457) 873804
E: reception@lapergola.freeserve.co.uk
I: www.hotel-restaurant.uk.com

SALE
Greater Manchester

Lennox Lea Hotel ★★
Irlam Road, Sale, Cheshire
M33 2BH
T: (0161) 973 1764
F: (0161) 969 6059
E: info@lennoxlea.co.uk
I: www.lennoxlea.co.uk

SANDBACH
Cheshire

Chimney House Hotel ★★★
Congleton Road, Sandbach,
Cheshire CW11 4ST
T: (01270) 764141 & 769900
F: (01270) 768961
E: chimneyhouse@corushotels.com
I: www.regalhotels.co.uk/chimneyhouse

Saxon Cross Hotel ★★
M6 junction 17, Holmes Chapel
Road, Sandbach, Cheshire
CW11 1SE
T: (01270) 763281
F: (01270) 768723

SOUTHPORT
Merseyside

Crimond Hotel ★★
28-30 Knowsley Road,
Southport, Merseyside PR9 0HN
T: (01704) 536456
F: (01704) 548643
E: dtarl10164@aol.com
I: www.crimondhotel.com

Dukes Folly Hotel ★★
11 Duke Street, Southport,
Merseyside PR8 1LS
T: (01704) 533355
F: (01704) 530065
E: mjatdukesfoll@bluecarrots.co.uk
I: www.dukesfolly.co.uk

Metropole Hotel ★★
3 Portland Street, Southport,
Merseyside PR8 1LL
T: (01704) 536836
F: (01704) 549041
E: metropole.southport@btinternet.com
I: www.btinternet.com/~metropole.southport

Scarisbrick Hotel ★★★
239 Lord Street, Southport,
Merseyside PR8 1NZ
T: (01704) 543000
F: (01704) 533335
E: scarisbrickhotel@talk21.com
I: www.scarisbrickhotel.com

Stutelea Hotel and Leisure Club ★★★
Alexandra Road, Southport,
Merseyside PR9 0NB
T: (01704) 544220
F: (01704) 500232
E: info@stutelea.co.uk
I: www.stutelea.co.uk

STANDISH
Greater Manchester

Wigan/Standish Moat House ★★★
Almond Brook Road, Standish,
Wigan, Lancashire WN6 0SR
T: (01257) 499988
F: (01257) 427327
E: gmwig@queensmoat.co.uk
I: www.moathousehotels.com

SUTTON
Cheshire

Sutton Hall ★★
Bullocks Lane, Sutton,
Macclesfield, Cheshire SK11 0HE
T: (01260) 253211
F: (01260) 252538

TARPORLEY
Cheshire

Willington Hall Hotel ★★★
Willington, Tarporley, Cheshire
CW6 0NB
T: (01829) 752321
F: (01829) 752596
E: enquiries@willingtonhall.co.uk
I: www.willingtonhall.co.uk

THORNTON HOUGH
Merseyside

Thornton Hall Hotel & Country Health Club ★★★
Neston Road, Thornton Hough,
Wirral, Merseyside CH63 1JF
T: (0151) 336 3938
F: (0151) 336 7864
E: thorntonhallhotel@btinternet.com
I: www.thorntonhallhotel.com

WADDINGTON
Lancashire

The Moorcock Inn ★★
Slaidburn Road, Waddington,
Clitheroe, Lancashire BB7 3AA
T: (01200) 422333
F: (01200) 429184

WARRINGTON
Cheshire

Hanover International Hotel and Club ★★★★
Stretton Road, Stretton,
Warrington WA4 4NS
T: (01925) 730706
F: (01925) 730740
E: hotel@park-royal-int.co.uk
I: www.hanover-international.com

WHITTLE-LE-WOODS
Lancashire

Shaw Hill Hotel Golf & Country Club ★★★
Preston Road, Whittle-le-
Woods, Chorley, Lancashire
PR6 7PP
T: (01257) 269221 & 226821
F: (01257) 261223

WIGAN
Greater Manchester

Burridges Hotel and Restaurant ★★★
Standishgate, Wigan, Lancashire
WN1 1XA
T: (01942) 741674
F: (01942) 741683
E: reception@burridges.co.uk
I: www.burridges.co.uk

Quality Hotel Wigan ★★★
Riverway, Wigan, Lancashire
WN1 3SS
T: (01942) 826888
F: (01942) 825800
E: admin@gb058.u-net.com
I: www.choicehotelseurope.com

WILMSLOW
Cheshire

Stanneylands Hotel ★★★
Stanneylands Road, Wilmslow,
Cheshire SK9 4EY
T: (01625) 525225
F: (01625) 537282
E: email@stanneylands.co.uk
I: www.stanneylandshotel.co.uk

WINCHAM
Cheshire

Wincham Hall ★★
Hall Lane, Wincham, Northwich,
Cheshire CW9 6DG
T: (01606) 43453
F: (01606) 40128
E: jane@winchamhall.co.uk
I: www.winchamhall.co.uk

WREA GREEN
Lancashire

Manor House Hotel
Rating Applied For
Ribby Hall Holiday Village, Ribby
Road, Wrea Green, Preston
PR4 2PR
T: (01772) 688000
F: (01772) 688036
E: themanorhousehotel@ribbyhall.co.uk
I: www.mhhotel.co.uk

The Villa ★★★
Moss Side Lane, Wrea Green,
Preston PR4 2PE
T: (01772) 684347
F: (01772) 687647
E: skilshaw@jenningsbrewery.co.uk
I: www.jenningsbrewery.co.uk

YORKSHIRE

APPLETON–LE–MOORS
North Yorkshire

Appleton Hall Country House Hotel ★★
Appleton-le-Moors, York
YO62 6TF
T: (01751) 417227
F: (01751) 417540

ASKERN
South Yorkshire

Owston Hall Hotel ★★★
Owston Hall, Askern, Doncaster,
South Yorkshire DN6 9JF
T: (01302) 722800 & 722231
F: (01302) 728885

ASKRIGG
North Yorkshire

Winville Hotel & Restaurant ★
Main Street, Askrigg, Leyburn,
North Yorkshire DL8 3HG
T: (01969) 650515
F: (01969) 650594

AYSGARTH
North Yorkshire

The George & Dragon Inn ★★
Aysgarth, Leyburn, North
Yorkshire DL8 3AD
T: (01969) 663358
F: (01969) 663773

Palmer Flatt Hotel ★★
Aysgarth, Leyburn, North
Yorkshire DL8 3SR
T: (01969) 663228
F: (01969) 663182
E: stay@palmerflathotel.co.uk

BARNSLEY
South Yorkshire

Ardsley House Hotel and Health Club ★★★
Doncaster Road, Ardsley,
Barnsley, South Yorkshire
S71 5EH
T: (01226) 309955
F: (01226) 205374
E: sales@ardsley-house.co.uk
I: ardsley-house.co.uk

Tankersley Manor Hotel ★★★
Church Lane, Upper Tankersley,
Tankersley, Barnsley, South
Yorkshire S75 3DQ
T: (01226) 744700
F: (01226) 745405
E: tankersley@marstonhotels.com
I: www.marstonhotels.com

BEDALE
North Yorkshire

The Lodge at Leeming Bar
Travel Accommodation
A1/A684 Intersection, Great
North Road, Bedale, North
Yorkshire DL8 1DT
T: (01677) 422122
F: (01677) 424507
E: thelodgeatleemingbar@btinternet.com

White Rose Hotel ★★
Bedale Road, Leeming Bar,
Northallerton, North Yorkshire
DL7 9AY
T: (01677) 422707 & 424941
F: (01677) 425123
E: royston@whiterosehotel.co.uk
I: www.whiterosehotel.co.uk

BEVERLEY
East Riding of Yorkshire

Manor House ★★
Newbald Road, Northlands,
Walkington, Beverley, North
Humberside HU17 8RT
T: (01482) 881645
F: (01482) 866501
E: nicola@the-manor-house.co.uk
I: www.the-manor-house.co.uk

Tickton Grange Hotel & Restaurant ★★★
Tickton Grange, Tickton,
Beverley, North Humberside
HU17 9SH
T: (01964) 543666
F: (01964) 542556
E: maggy@tickton-grange.demon.co.uk
I: www.ticktongrange.co.uk

BINGLEY
West Yorkshire

Jarvis Bankfield Hotel ★★★
Bradford Road, Bingley, West
Yorkshire BD16 1TU
T: (01274) 567123
F: (01274) 551331
E: bankfield@jarvis.co.uk
I: www.jarvis.co.uk

BISHOP THORNTON
North Yorkshire

Chequers Inn Country Hotel and Restaurant★
Fountain's Abbey Road, Bishop
Thornton, Harrogate, North
Yorkshire HG3 3JN
T: (01423) 770173 & 771544
F: (01423) 770049

BOROUGHBRIDGE
North Yorkshire

Crown Hotel ★★★
Horsefair, Boroughbridge, York
YO51 9LB
T: (01423) 322328
F: (01423) 324512
E: sales@crownboroughbridge.co.uk
I: www.crownboroughbridge.co.uk

Rose Manor Hotel ★★★
Horsefair, Boroughbridge, York
YO51 9LL
T: (01423) 322245
F: (01423) 324920
E: rosemanorhotel@ukf.net
I: www.rosemanorhotel.co.uk

BRADFORD
West Yorkshire

Cartwright Hotel ★★
308 Manningham Lane,
Manningham, Bradford, West
Yorkshire BD8 7AX
T: (01274) 499908
F: (01274) 481309
E: info@cartwrighthotel.co.uk
I: www.cartwrighthotel.co.uk

Hanover International Hotel & Club ★★★★
Mayo Avenue (top of the M606),
Off Rooley Lane, Bradford, West
Yorkshire BD5 8HZ
T: (01274) 406606
F: (01274) 406600
E: sales.bradford@hanover-international.com
I: www.hanover-international.com

Hilton Bradford ★★★
Hall Ings, Bradford, West
Yorkshire BD1 5SH
T: (01274) 734734
F: (01274) 306146

Midland Hotel ★★★
Forster Square, Bradford, West
Yorkshire BD1 4HU
T: (01274) 735735
F: (01274) 720003
I: www.peelhotel.com

Novotel Bradford ★★★
6 Roydsdale Way, Euroway
Estate, Bradford, West Yorkshire
BD4 6SA
T: (01274) 653683
F: (01274) 651342
E: h0510@accor-hotels.com
I: www.novotel.com

Park Drive Hotel ★★
12 Park Drive, Heaton, Bradford,
West Yorkshire BD9 4DR
T: (01274) 480194
F: (01274) 484869
E: info@parkdrivehotel.co.uk
I: www.parkdrivehotel.co.uk

Park Grove Hotel and Restaurant ★★
Park Grove, Frizinghall, Bradford,
West Yorkshire BD9 4JY
T: (01274) 543444
F: (01274) 495619
E: enquiries@parkgrovehotel.co.uk
I: www.parkgrovehotel.co.uk

Quality Hotel Bradford ★★★
Bridge Street, Bradford, West
Yorkshire BD1 1JX
T: (01274) 728706
F: (01274) 736358
E: admin@gb654.u-net.com
I: www.choicehotels.com

BRAMLEY
West Yorkshire

Corn Mill Lodge Hotel ★★★
Pudsey Road, Bramley, Leeds
LS13 4JA
T: (0113) 257 9059
F: (0113) 257 6665

BRANDESBURTON
East Riding of Yorkshire

Burton Lodge Hotel ★★
Brandesburton, Driffield, North
Humberside YO25 8RU
T: (01964) 542847
F: (01964) 544771
E: email@burtonlodgefsnet.co.uk

BRIDLINGTON
East Riding of Yorkshire

Expanse Hotel ★★★
North Marine Drive, Bridlington,
East Riding of Yorkshire
YO15 2LS
T: (01262) 675347
F: (01262) 604928
E: expanse@brid.demon.co.uk
I: www.expanse.co.uk

The Ferns Hotel ★★★
Main Street, Carnaby,
Bridlington, East Riding of
Yorkshire YO16 4UJ
T: (01262) 678961
F: (01262) 400712
E: the.ferns_hotel@virgin.net
I: www.fernshotel.co.uk

Manor Court Hotel & Restaurant ★★★
53 Main Street, Carnaby,
Bridlington, East Riding of
Yorkshire YO16 4UJ
T: (01262) 606468
F: (01262) 400217
E: info@manorcourt.co.uk
I: www.manorcourt.co.uk

Strathmore Hotel
Rating Applied For
63-65 Horsforth Avenue,
Bridlington, East Riding of
Yorkshire YO15 3DH
T: (01262) 502828
F: (01262) 602828
E: strathmore_hotel@compuserve.com

BRIERLEY
South Yorkshire

The Owl Lodge Motel at Burntwood Sports Ltd
Travel Accommodation
Common Road, Brierley,
Barnsley, South Yorkshire
S72 9ET
T: (01226) 711123
F: (01226) 711700

BUCKDEN
North Yorkshire

The Buck Inn ★★
Buckden, Skipton, North
Yorkshire BD23 5JA
T: (01756) 760228 & 760416
F: (01756) 760227
E: thebuckinn@buckden.yorks.net
I: www.thebuckinn.yorks.net

BURNSALL
North Yorkshire

The Devonshire Fell Hotel and Restaurant★★
Burnsall, Skipton, North
Yorkshire BD23 6BT
T: (01756) 729000 & 710441
F: (01756) 729009

CASTLEFORD
West Yorkshire

Little Red Lion Premier Lodge
Travel Accommodation
Commerce Park, Off Pioneer
Way, Castleford, West Yorkshire
WF10 5TG
T: (01977) 665400
F: (01977) 667240

CLAPHAM
North Yorkshire

Flying Horseshoe Hotel ★★
Clapham Station, Clapham,
Lancaster LA2 8ES
T: (01524) 251229 &
07773 182584

DARLEY
North Yorkshire

Wellington Inn ★★
Darley, Harrogate, North
Yorkshire HG3 2QQ
T: (01423) 780362 & 781445
F: (01423) 781534

DEWSBURY
West Yorkshire

**Heath Cottage Hotel &
Restaurant ★★★**
Wakefield Road, Dewsbury, West
Yorkshire WF12 8ET
T: (01924) 465399
F: (01924) 459405
E: Bookings@heathcottage.
co.uk
I: www.heathcottage.co.uk

DONCASTER
South Yorkshire

Regent Hotel ★★★
Regent Square, Doncaster,
South Yorkshire DN1 2DS
T: (01302) 364180 & 364336
F: (01302) 322331
E: admin@theregenthotel.co.uk
I: www.theregenthotel.co.uk

DRIFFIELD
East Riding of Yorkshire

The Bell In Driffield ★★★
Market Place, Driffield, North
Humberside YO25 6AN
T: (01377) 256661
F: (01377) 253228
E: bell@bestwestern.co.uk
(symbol)

EASINGWOLD
North Yorkshire

The George at Easingwold ★★
Market Place, Easingwold, York
YO61 3AD
T: (01347) 821698
F: (01347) 823448
E: info@the-george-hotel.co.uk
I: www.the-george-hotel.co.uk

**Old Farmhouse Country Hotel
& Restaurant ★★**
Raskelf, York YO61 3LF
T: (01347) 821971
F: (01347) 822392

FILEY
North Yorkshire

**The Downcliffe House Hotel
★★**
The Beach, Filey, North Yorkshire
YO14 9LA
T: (01723) 513310
F: (01723) 513773
E: downcliffe@2filey.co.uk

Sea Brink Hotel ★★
3 The Beach, Filey, North
Yorkshire YO14 9LA
T: (01723) 513257
F: (01723) 514139
E: seabrink@supanet.com
I: www.seabrink.co.uk

White Lodge Hotel ★★★
The Crescent, Filey, North
Yorkshire YO14 9JX
T: (01723) 514771
F: (01723) 516590
E: white.lodge@lineone.net

FIXBY
West Yorkshire

Huddersfield Premier Lodge
Travel Accommodation
New Hey Road, Ainley Top,
Huddersfield HD2 2EA
T: 0870 700 1408
F: 0870 700 1409
I: www.premierlodge.com

FLAMBOROUGH
East Riding of Yorkshire

Flaneburg Hotel ★★
North Marine Road,
Flamborough, Bridlington, East
Riding of Yorkshire YO15 1LF
T: (01262) 850284
F: (01262) 850284

North Star Hotel ★★
North Marine Road,
Flamborough, Bridlington, East
Riding of Yorkshire YO15 1BL
T: (01262) 850379
F: (01262) 850379
E: info@puffinsatflamborough.
co.uk
I: www.puffinsatflamborough.
co.uk

GIGGLESWICK
North Yorkshire

The Harts Head Hotel ★★
Belle Hill, Giggleswick, Settle,
North Yorkshire BD24 0BA
T: (01729) 822086
F: (01729) 824992
E: hartshead@hotel52.
freeserve.co.uk

GILLING WEST
North Yorkshire

Hartforth Hall Hotel ★★
Gilling West, Richmond, North
Yorkshire DL10 5JU
T: (01748) 825715 & 825781
I: www.hartforthhall.com

GOATHLAND
North Yorkshire

Mallyan Spout Hotel ★★
The Common, Goathland,
Whitby, North Yorkshire
YO22 5AN
T: (01947) 896486 & 896206
F: (01947) 896327
E: mallyan@ukgateway.net
I: www.mywebpage.
net/mallyanspout

Whitfield House Hotel ★★
Darnholm, Goathland, Whitby,
North Yorkshire YO22 5LA
T: (01947) 896215 & 896214

GOMERSAL
West Yorkshire

The Gomersal Lodge Hotel ★★
Spen Lane, Gomersal,
Cleckheaton, West Yorkshire
BD19 4PJ
T: (01274) 861111
F: (01274) 861111

GOOLE
East Riding of Yorkshire

Clifton Hotel ★★
Boothferry Road, Goole, East
Riding of Yorkshire DN14 6AL
T: (01405) 761336
F: (01405) 762350
E: cliftonhotel@telinco.co.uk
I: www.cliftonhotel.cwc.net

GRASSINGTON
North Yorkshire

Black Horse Hotel ★★
Garrs Lane, Grassington,
Skipton, North Yorkshire
BD23 5AT
T: (01756) 752770
F: (01756) 753452
I: www.grassington.net.

**Grassington House Hotel and
Restaurant ★★**
5 The Square, Grassington,
Skipton, North Yorkshire
BD23 5AQ
T: (01756) 752406
F: (01756) 752135

Tennant Arms Hotel ★★
Kilnsey, Skipton, North Yorkshire
BD23 5PS
T: (01756) 752301

GRIMSBY
North East Lincolnshire

Millfields ★★★
53 Bargate, Grimsby, South
Humberside DN34 5AD
T: (01472) 356068
F: (01472) 250286
E: info@millfieldshotel.co.uk
I: www.millfieldshotel.co.uk
(symbol)

HALIFAX
West Yorkshire

The Hobbit Hotel ★★
Hob Lane, Norland, Halifax, West
Yorkshire HX6 3QL
T: (01422) 832202
F: (01422) 835381
E: info@hobbit-hotel
I: www.hobbit-hotel.co.uk

**Milan's Hotel and Conference
Suite ★★**
6-8 Carlton Place, Halifax, West
Yorkshire HX1 2SB
T: (01422) 330539
F: (01422) 381873
I: www.milanshotel.co.uk

**The Rock Inn Hotel & Palmer's
Restaurant ★★★**
Holywell Green, Halifax, West
Yorkshire HX4 9BS
T: (01422) 379721
F: (01422) 379110
E: the.rock@dial.pipex.com
I: www.rockinnhotel.com

White Swan Hotel ★★★
Princess Street, Halifax, West
Yorkshire HX1 1TS
T: (01422) 355541
F: (01422) 357311
E: info@whiteswanhalifax.co.uk
I: www.whiteswanhalifax.co.uk

HARROGATE
North Yorkshire

Ascot House Hotel ★★
53 Kings Road, Harrogate, North
Yorkshire HG1 5HJ
T: (01423) 531005
F: (01423) 503523
E: admin@ascothouse.com
I: www.ascothouse.com

Balmoral Hotel ★★★
Franklin Mount, Harrogate,
North Yorkshire HG1 5EJ
T: (01423) 508208
F: (01423) 530652
E: info@balmoralhotel.co.uk
I: www.balmoralhotel.co.uk

The Boar's Head Hotel ★★★
Ripley Castle Estate, Ripley,
Harrogate, North Yorkshire
HG3 3AY
T: (01423) 771888
F: (01423) 771509
E: reservations@
boarsheadripley.co.uk
I: www.ripleycastle.co.uk
(symbol)

Cairn Hotel ★★★
Ripon Road, Harrogate, North
Yorkshire HG1 2JD
T: (01423) 504005
F: (01423) 500056
E: cairnhot@aol.com

The Crown Hotel ★★★
Crown Place, Harrogate, North
Yorkshire HG1 2RZ
T: (01423) 567755
F: (01423) 502284
E: thecrown@corushotels.com
I: www.regalhotels.
co.uk/thecrown

Cutlers On The Stray ★★★
19 West Park, Harrogate, North
Yorkshire HG1 1BL
T: (01423) 524471
F: (01423) 506728
I: www.cutlers-brasserie.co.uk

Grants Hotel ★★★
Swan Road, Harrogate, North
Yorkshire HG1 2SS
T: (01423) 560666
F: (01423) 502550
E: enquiries@
grantshotel-harrogate.com
I: www.grantshotel-harrogate.
com

Imperial Hotel ★★★
Prospect Place, Harrogate, North
Yorkshire HG1 1LA
T: (01423) 565071
F: (01423) 500082
E: imperial@
british-trust-hotels.com

The Majestic ★★★★
Ripon Road, Harrogate, North
Yorkshire HG1 2HU
T: (01423) 700300
F: (01423) 502283
E: majesticevents@
paramount-hotels.co.uk
I: www.paramount-hotels.co.uk

**Rudding Park Hotel & Golf
★★★★**
Rudding Park, Follifoot,
Harrogate, North Yorkshire
HG3 1JH
T: (01423) 871350
F: (01423) 872286
E: sales@ruddingpark.com
I: www.ruddingpark.com

**Studley Hotel and Orchid
Restaurant ★★★**
Swan Road, Harrogate, North
Yorkshire HG1 2SE
T: (01423) 560425
F: (01423) 530967
E: studleyhotel@faxdoc.net

**Swallow St George Hotel
★★★**
Ripon Road, Harrogate, North
Yorkshire HG1 2SY
T: (01423) 561431
F: (01423) 530037
I: www.swallowhotels.com
(symbol)

White Hart Hotel ★★★
Cold Bath Road, Harrogate,
North Yorkshire HG2 0NF
T: (01423) 505681
F: (01423) 568354
E: pwalker@whitehart.net
I: www.whitehart.net

HAWES
North Yorkshire

Stone House Hotel ★★
Sedbusk, Hawes, North Yorkshire
DL8 3PT
T: (01969) 667571
F: (01969) 667720
E: daleshotel@aol.com
I: www.stonehousehotel.com

HAWORTH
West Yorkshire

Old White Lion Hotel ★★
Main Street, Haworth, Keighley,
West Yorkshire BD22 8DU
T: (01535) 642313
F: (01535) 646222
E: enquiries@oldwhitelionhotel.
com
I: www.oldwhitelionhotel.com

HEBDEN BRIDGE
West Yorkshire

Carlton Hotel ★★★
Albert Street, Hebden Bridge,
West Yorkshire HX7 8ES
T: (01422) 844400
F: (01422) 843117
E: ctonhotel@aol.com
I: www.hebdenbridgecarlton.
co.uk

White Lion Hotel ★★
Bridge Gate, Hebden Bridge,
West Yorkshire HX7 8EX
T: (01422) 842197
F: (01422) 846619
E: les@whitelionhotelhb.co.uk
I: www.whitelionhotelhb.co.uk

HELMSLEY
North Yorkshire

Carlton Lodge ★★
Bondgate, Helmsley, York
YO62 5EY
T: (01439) 770557
F: (01439) 770623
E: enquiries@carlton-lodge.com
I: www.carlton-lodge.com

The Crown Hotel ★★
Market Place, Helmsley, York
YO62 5BJ
T: (01439) 770297
F: (01439) 771595

Feathers Hotel ★★
Market Place, Helmsley, York
YO62 5BH
T: (01439) 770275
F: (01439) 771101
E: feathers@zen.co.uk
I: www.feathershotel.co.uk

Feversham Arms Hotel
Rating Applied For
1 High Street, Helmsley, York
YO62 5AG
T: (01439) 770766
F: (01439) 770346
E: fevershamarms@hotmail.
com

Pheasant Hotel ★★★
Harome, Helmsley, York
YO62 5JG
T: (01439) 771241
F: (01439) 771744

HOLME UPON SPALDING MOOR
East Riding of Yorkshire

Ye Olde Red Lion ★★
Old Road, Holme upon Spalding
Moor, York YO43 4AD
T: (01430) 860220
F: (01430) 861471

HOLMFIRTH
West Yorkshire

Old Bridge Hotel ★★★
Off Victoria Street, Holmfirth,
Huddersfield HD7 1DA
T: (01484) 681212
F: (01484) 687978
E: oldbridgehotel@enterprise.
net
I: www.oldbridgehotel.com

HOVINGHAM
North Yorkshire

Worsley Arms Hotel ★★★
Hovingham, York YO62 4LA
T: (01653) 628234
F: (01653) 628130
E: worsleyarms@aol.com
I: fine-individual-hotels.co.uk

HOWDEN
East Riding of Yorkshire

Wellington Hotel ★★
31 Bridgegate, Howden, Goole,
North Humberside DN14 7JG
T: (01430) 430258 &
(01763) 287773
F: (01430) 432139

HUDDERSFIELD
West Yorkshire

Briar Court Hotel ★★★
Halifax Road, Birchencliffe,
Huddersfield, HD3 3NT
T: (01484) 519902 & 519978
F: (01484) 431812
E: briarcourthotel@btconnect.
com
I: www.briaracourthotel.co.uk

**Hanover International Hotel
Huddersfield ★★★**
Penistone Road, Kirkburton,
Huddersfield HD8 0PE
T: (01484) 607788
F: (01484) 607961
E: steven@hihhuddersfield.ndo.
co.uk
I: www.hanover.international.
com

Hilton Huddersfield ★★★
M62 Exit 24, Ainley Top,
Huddersfield HD3 3RH
T: (01422) 375431
F: (01422) 310067

**Huddersfield Hotel and
Rosemary Lane Bistro ★★★**
33-47 Kirkgate, Huddersfield,
HD1 1QT
T: (01484) 512111
F: (01484) 435262
E: enquiries@huddersfieldhotel.
com
I: www.huddersfieldhotel.com

The Lodge Hotel ★★
48 Birkby Lodge Road, Birkby,
Huddersfield HD2 2BG
T: (01484) 431001
F: (01484) 421590

HULL
East Riding of Yorkshire

Cornmill Hotel ★
Mount Pleasant, Holderness
Road, Hull, HU9 1LA
T: (01482) 589000
F: (01482) 586447
E: ops@cornmill.globalnet.co.uk
I: www.webmarketing.
co.uk/cornmill/html/wedding.
htm.

**Jarvis International Hotel
★★★**
Grange Park Lane, Willerby, Hull
HU10 6EA
T: (01482) 656488
F: (01482) 655848
I: www.jarvis.co.uk

Pearson Park Hotel ★★
Pearson Park, Hull, HU5 2TQ
T: (01482) 343043
F: (01482) 447679
E: manager@pearsonparkhotel.
karoo.co.uk
I: www.pearsonparkhotel.co.uk

ILKLEY
West Yorkshire

The Crescent Hotel ★★★
Brook Street, Ilkley, West
Yorkshire LS29 8DG
T: (01943) 600012
F: (01943) 601513
E: crescenthotel@dialstart.net
I: www.crescenthotelilkley.co.uk

Riverside Hotel ★
Riverside Gardens, Bride Lane,
Ilkley, West Yorkshire LS29 9EU
T: (01943) 607338 & 432021
F: (01943) 607338

**Rombalds Hotel and
Restaurant ★★★**
West View, Wells Road, Ilkley,
West Yorkshire LS29 9JG
T: (01943) 603201
F: (01943) 816586
E: reception@rombalds.demon.
co.uk
I: www.rombalds.co.uk

KIRKBYMOORSIDE
North Yorkshire

George & Dragon Hotel ★★
Market Place, Kirkbymoorside,
York YO62 6AA
T: (01751) 433334
F: (01751) 432933

Kings Head Hotel ★★
Market Place, Kirkbymoorside,
York YO62 6AT
T: (01751) 431340
F: (01751) 431340

KNARESBOROUGH
North Yorkshire

General Tarleton Inn ★★★
Boroughbridge Road, Ferrensby,
Knaresborough, North Yorkshire
HG5 0PZ
T: (01423) 340284
F: (01423) 340288
E: gti@generaltarleton.co.uk
I: www.generaltarleton.co.uk

LEEDS
West Yorkshire

Aragon Hotel ★★
250 Stainbeck Lane, Meanwood,
Leeds, LS7 2PS
T: (0113) 275 9306
F: (0113) 275 7166
E: aragon@onmail.co.uk
I: www.aragonhotel.co.uk

Ascot Grange Hotel ★★
126-130 Otley Road,
Headingley, Leeds LS16 5JX
T: (0113) 293 4444
F: (0113) 293 5555
E: ascotgrangehotel@aol.com

The Butlers Hotel ★★★
Cardigan Road, Headingley,
Leeds LS6 3AG
T: (0113) 274 4755
F: (0113) 274 4755
E: info@butlershotel.co.uk
I: www.butlershotel.co.uk

De Vere Oulton Hall ★★★★★
Rothwell Lane, Oulton,
Woodlesford, Leeds LS26 8HN
T: (0113) 282 1000
F: (0113) 282 8066
E: oulton.hall@devere-hotels.
com
I: www.devereonline.co.uk

The Hotel Metropole ★★★★
King Street, Leeds, LS1 2HQ
T: (0113) 245 0841
F: (0113) 242 5156
I: www.principalhotels.com

Jarvis Leeds North ★★★
Ring Road, Mill Green View,
Seacroft, Leeds LS14 5QF
T: (0113) 273 2323
F: (0113) 232 3018
I: www.jarvis.co.uk

Le Meridien Queens ★★★★
City Square, Leeds, LS1 1PL
T: 0870 400 8696
F: (0113) 242 5154
E: queens.reservations@
forte-hotels.com
I: www.lemeridien-hotels.com

Ramada Jarvis Leeds ★★★
Otley Road, Leeds, LS16 8AG
T: (0113) 269 9000
F: (0113) 267 4410
E: jileeds.rs@jarvis.co.uk
I: www.jarvis.co.uk

Travelodge
Travel Accommodation
Blayds Court, Blayds Yard, Leeds,
LS1 4AG
T: (0113) 244 5793 & 247 0076
I: www.travelodge.co.uk

**Weetwood Hall Conference
Centre & Hotel ★★★**
Otley Road, Leeds, LS16 5PS
T: (0113) 230 6000
F: (0113) 230 6095
E: sales@weetwood.co.uk
I: www.weetwood.co.uk

LEYBURN
North Yorkshire

**Golden Lion Hotel & Licensed
Restaurant ★**
Market Place, Leyburn, North
Yorkshire DL8 5AS
T: (01969) 622161
F: (01969) 623836
E: annegoldenlion@aol.com
I: www.thegoldenlion.co.uk

LITTLE WEIGHTON
East Riding of Yorkshire
Rowley Manor ★★
Rowley Road, Little Weighton,
Cottingham, North Humberside
HU20 3XR
T: (01482) 848248 & 843132
F: (01482) 849900
E: info@rowleymanor.com
I: www.rowleymanor.com

LIVERSEDGE
West Yorkshire
Geordie Pride Lodge Hotel ★★
112 Roberttown Lane,
Roberttown, Liversedge, West
Yorkshire WF15 7LZ
T: (01924) 402069
F: (01924) 410136

Healds Hall Hotel ★★
Leeds Road, Liversedge, West
Yorkshire WF15 6JA
T: (01924) 409112
F: (01924) 401895
E: healdshall@ndirect.co.uk

MALHAM
North Yorkshire
Buck Inn ★★
Malham, Skipton, North
Yorkshire BD23 4DA
T: (01729) 830317
F: (01729) 830670

MALTON
North Yorkshire
The Green Man ★★★
15 Market Street, Malton, North
Yorkshire YO17 7LY
T: (01653) 600370
F: (01653) 696006
E: greenman@
englishhousehotels.co.uk

MARKINGTON
North Yorkshire
Hob Green ★★★
Markington, Harrogate, North
Yorkshire HG3 3PJ
T: (01423) 770031
F: (01423) 771589
E: info@hobgreen.com
I: www.hobgreen.com

MASHAM
North Yorkshire
Swinton Park ★★★★
Masham, Ripon, North Yorkshire
HG4 4JH
T. (01765) 000000 & 680001
E: enquiries@swintonpark.com
I: www.swintonpark.com

MELTHAM
West Yorkshire
Durker Roods Hotel ★★
Bishops Way, Meltham,
Huddersfield HD7 3AG
T: (01484) 851413
F: (01484) 851843
E: spencer@durkerroodshotel.
co.uk
I: www.durkerroodshotel.co.uk

MONK FRYSTON
North Yorkshire
Monk Fryston Hall ★★★
Monk Fryston, Leeds LS25 5DU
T: (01977) 682369
F: (01977) 683544
E: reception@
monkfryston-hotel.com
I: www.monkfryston-hotel.com

MORLEY
West Yorkshire
The Old Vicarage ★★
Bruntcliffe Road, Morley, Leeds
LS27 0JZ
T: (0113) 253 2174
F: (0113) 253 3549
E: oldvicarage@btinternet.com
I: www.oldvicaragehotel.co.uk

NEWBY WISKE
North Yorkshire
Solberge Hall ★★★
Newby Wiske, Northallerton,
North Yorkshire DL7 9ER
T: (01609) 779191
F: (01609) 780472
E: hotel@solberge.freeserve.
co.uk
I: www.smoothhound.com

NIDD
North Yorkshire
Nidd Hall ★★
Nidd, Harrogate, North Yorkshire
HG3 3BN
T: (01423) 771598
F: (01423) 770931

NORTH KILLINGHOLME
North Lincolnshire
**Giovanni's Hotel and
Restaurant ★★**
Vicarage Lane, North
Killingholme, Immingham, North
Lincolnshire DN40 3JQ
T: (01469) 541010
F: (01469) 541020

NUNNINGTON
North Yorkshire
Ryedale Country Lodge ★★
Nunnington, York YO62 5XB
T: (01439) 748246
F: (01439) 748346

OTLEY
West Yorkshire
**Chevin Lodge Country Park
Hotel ★★★**
Yorkgate, Otley, West Yorkshire
LS21 3NU
T: (01943) 467818
F: (01943) 850335
E: reception@chevinlodge.co.uk
I: www.chevinlodge.co.uk

PATELEY BRIDGE
North Yorkshire
**Grassfields Country House
Hotel ★★**
Low Wath Road, Pateley Bridge,
Harrogate, North Yorkshire
HG3 5HL
T: (01423) 711412 & 712844
F: (01423) 712844
E: grassfields@nidderdale.co.uk
I: www.nidderdale.co.uk

Sportsmans Arms Hotel ★★
Wath-in-Nidderdale, Pateley
Bridge, Harrogate, North
Yorkshire HG3 5PP
T: (01423) 711306
F: (01423) 712524

PICKERING
North Yorkshire
Crossways Hotel ★★
Eastgate, Pickering, North
Yorkshire YO18 7DW
T: (01751) 472804
F: (01751) 472804

Forest & Vale Hotel ★★★
Malton Road, Pickering, North
Yorkshire YO18 7DL
T: (01751) 472722
F: (01751) 472972
E: reception@
forestandvalehotel.co.uk

White Swan Hotel ★★
Market Place, Pickering, North
Yorkshire YO18 7AA
T: (01751) 472288
F: (01751) 475554
E: welcome@white-swan.co.uk
I: www.white-swan.co.uk

PONTEFRACT
West Yorkshire
**Rogerthorpe Manor Country
Hotel ★★★**
Thorpe Lane, Badsworth,
Pontefract, West Yorkshire
WF9 1AB
T: (01977) 643839
F: (01977) 641571
E: ops@rogerthorpemanor.
co.uk
I: www.rogerthorpemanor.co.uk

REDBOURNE
North Lincolnshire
The Red Lion Hotel ★★
Main Street, Redbourne,
Gainsborough, Lincolnshire
DN21 4QR
T: (01652) 648302
F: (01652) 648302
E: enquiries@redlion.org
I: www.redlion.org

RICHMOND
North Yorkshire
Bridge House Hotel ★★
Catterick Bridge, Richmond,
North Yorkshire DL10 7PE
T: (01748) 818331
F: (01748) 818331
E: bridgehousehotel@hotmail.
com

Frenchgate Hotel ★★
59-61 Frenchgate, Richmond,
North Yorkshire DL10 7AE
T: (01748) 822087
F: (01748) 823596
I: www.smoothhound.
co.uk/hotels/frenchgate.html

King's Head Hotel ★★
Market Place, Richmond, North
Yorkshire DL10 4HS
T: (01748) 850220
F: (01748) 850635
E: res@kingsheadrichmond.
co.uk
I: www.kingsheadrichmond.
co.uk

RIPON
North Yorkshire
Ripon Spa Hotel ★★★
Park Street, Ripon, North
Yorkshire HG4 2BU
T: (01765) 602172
F: (01765) 690770
E: spahotel@bronco.co.uk
I: www.stemsys.co.uk/spa

Unicorn Hotel ★★
Market Place, Ripon, North
Yorkshire HG4 1BP
T: (01765) 602202
F: (01765) 690734
E: info@unicorn-hotel.co.uk
I: www.unicorn-hotel.co.uk

ROSEDALE ABBEY
North Yorkshire
Blacksmiths Country Inn ★★★
Hartoft End, Rosedale Abbey,
Pickering, North Yorkshire
YO18 8EN
T: (01751) 417331
F: (01751) 417167
E: blacksmiths.rosedale@virgin.
net
I: www.blacksmithsinn-rosedale.
co.uk

Milburn Arms Hotel ★★
Rosedale Abbey, Pickering,
North Yorkshire YO18 8RA
T: (01751) 417312
F: (01751) 417541
E: info@milburnarms.com
I: www.milburnarms.com

White Horse Farm Hotel ★★
Rosedale Abbey, Pickering,
North Yorkshire YO18 8SE
T: (01751) 417239
F: (01751) 417781
E: sales@whitehorsefarmhotel.
co.uk

ROTHERHAM
South Yorkshire
**Best Western Consort Hotel
★★★**
Brampton Road, Thurcroft,
Rotherham, South Yorkshire
S66 9JA
T: (01709) 530022
F: (01709) 531529
E: info@consorthotel.com
I: www.consorthotel.com

**Best Western Elton Hotel
★★★**
Main Street, Bramley,
Rotherham, South Yorkshire
S66 2SF
T: (01709) 545681
F: (01709) 549100
E: bestwestern.eltonhotel@
btinternet.com
I: www.bestwestern.co.uk

Swallow Hotel ★★★
West Bawtry Road, Rotherham,
South Yorkshire S60 4NA
T: (01709) 830630
F: (01709) 830549

RUSWARP
North Yorkshire
**Old Hall Hotel
Rating Applied For**
High Street, Ruswarp, Whitby,
North Yorkshire YO21 1NH
T: (01947) 602801
F: (01947) 602801
E: enquiries@oldhallhotel.co.uk
I: www.oldhallhotel.co.uk

SCARBOROUGH
North Yorkshire
Ambassador Hotel ★★★
Centre of the Esplanade,
Scarborough, North Yorkshire
YO11 2AY
T: (01723) 362841
F: (01723) 366166
I: scarboroughhotel.com

Beiderbecke's Hotel and Restaurant ★★★
1-3 The Crescent, Scarborough,
North Yorkshire YO11 2PW
T: (01723) 365766
F: (01723) 367433
E: info@beiderbeckes.com
I: www.beiderbeckes.com

Brooklands Hotel ★★
7-11 Esplanade Gardens,
Scarborough, North Yorkshire
YO11 2AW
T: (01723) 376576 & 890314
F: (01723) 376576
E: stay@brooklands-hotel.co.uk
I: www.brooklands-hotel.co.uk

The Clifton Hotel ★★★
Queens Parade, North Cliff,
Scarborough, North Yorkshire
YO12 7HX
T: (01723) 375691
F: (01723) 364203
E: cliftonhotel@
englishrosehotels.co.uk
I: www.englishrosehotels.co.uk

Crown Hotel ★★★
The Esplanade, Scarborough,
North Yorkshire YO11 2AG
T: (01723) 357400
F: (01723) 362271
E: crownreservations@
scarboroughhotel.com
I: www.scarboroughhotel.com

Delmont ★★
18-19 Blenheim Terrace,
Scarborough, North Yorkshire
YO12 7HE
T: (01723) 364500
F: (01723) 373606

Esplanade Hotel ★★★
Belmont Road, Scarborough,
North Yorkshire YO11 2AA
T: (01723) 360382
F: (01723) 376137

Gridleys Crescent Hotel ★★
The Crescent, Scarborough,
North Yorkshire YO11 2PP
T: (01723) 360929 & 507507
F: (01723) 354126
E: reception@crescent-hotel.
co.uk
I: www.crescent-hotel.co.uk

Londesborough Arms Hotel ★★
24 Main Street, Seamer,
Scarborough, North Yorkshire
YO12 4PS
T: (01723) 863230
F: (01723) 863230
E: londesborough@
scarborough.co.uk
I: www.londesborough.
scarborough.co.uk

Hotel Majestic ★★
57 Northstead Manor Drive,
Scarborough, North Yorkshire
YO12 6AG
T: (01723) 363806
F: (01723) 363806
E: hotelmajestic@btinternet.
com
I: www.majestichotel.co.uk

Manor Heath Hotel ★★
67 Northstead Manor Drive,
Scarborough, North Yorkshire
YO12 6AF
T: (01723) 365720
F: (01723) 365720
E: enquiries@manorheath.co.uk
I: www.manorheath.co.uk

Mount Hotel ★★
Cliff Bridge Terrace, Saint
Nicholas Cliff, Scarborough,
North Yorkshire YO11 2HA
T: (01723) 360961
F: (01723) 375850

Ox Pasture Hall ★★★
Lady Ediths Drive, Throxenby,
Scarborough, North Yorkshire
YO15 5TD
T: (01723) 365295
F: (01723) 355156

Palm Court Hotel ★★★
St Nicholas Cliff, Scarborough,
North Yorkshire YO11 2ES
T: (01723) 368161
F: (01723) 371547

Red Lea Hotel ★★
Prince of Wales Terrace,
Scarborough, North Yorkshire
YO11 2AJ
T: (01723) 362431
F: (01723) 371230
E: redlea@globalnet.co.uk
I: www.redleahotel.co.uk

Ryndle Court Private Hotel ★★
47 Northstead Manor Drive,
Scarborough, North Yorkshire
YO12 6AF
T: (01723) 375188 &
07860 711517
F: (01723) 375188
E: enquiries@ryndlecourt.co.uk
I: www.ryndlecourt.co.uk

Scarborough Travel and Holiday Lodge
Travel Accommodation
33 Valley Road, Scarborough,
North Yorkshire YO11 2LX
T: (01723) 363537
F: (01723) 501239
E: scarborough.lodge@onyxnet.
co.uk
I: www.scarborough-lodge.co.uk

Selbourne Hotel ★
4 West Street, South Cliff,
Scarborough, North Yorkshire
YO11 2QL
T: (01723) 372822 & 373240
F: (01723) 372822

Southlands Hotel ★★
West Street, South Cliff,
Scarborough, North Yorkshire
YO11 2QW
T: (01723) 361461
F: (01723) 376035
E: sales@southlandshotel.co.uk
I: www.epworth.co.uk

Hotel St Nicholas ★★★
St Nicholas Cliff, Scarborough,
North Yorkshire YO11 2EU
T: (01723) 364101
F: (01723) 500538
I: www.british-trust-hotels.co.uk

Sunningdale Hotel ★★
105 Peasholm Drive,
Scarborough, North Yorkshire
YO12 7NB
T: (01723) 372041
F: (01723) 354691
E: sunningdale@barclay.net
I: www.
sunningdale-scarborough.co.uk

Wrea Head Country House Hotel ★★★
Barmoor Lane, Scalby,
Scarborough, North Yorkshire
YO13 0PB
T: (01723) 378211
F: (01723) 355936

SCARTHO
North East Lincolnshire

The Beeches Hotel ★★★
42 Waltham Road, Scartho,
Grimsby, South Humberside
DN33 2LX
T: (01472) 278830
F: (01472) 752880
E: themanager@
thebeecheshotel.com
I: www.thebeecheshotel.com

SCISSETT
West Yorkshire

Bagden Hall ★★★
Wakefield Road, Scissett,
Huddersfield HD8 9LE
T: (01484) 865330
F: (01484) 861001
E: info@bagdenhall.demon.
co.uk
I: www.bagdenhall.demon.co.uk

SCOTCH CORNER
North Yorkshire

Quality Hotel Scotch Corner ★★★
A1/A66 Junction, Scotch Corner,
Richmond, North Yorkshire
DL10 6NR
T: (01748) 850900
F: (01748) 825417
E: admin@gb609.u-net.com
I: www.choicehotels.com

SCUNTHORPE
North Lincolnshire

The Bridge House Hotel ★
Station Road, Scunthorpe, South
Humberside DN15 6PY
T: (01724) 847590
F: (01724) 861708
I: www.lincs.co.uk/bridge

Forest Pines Hotel, Golf Course and Spa★★★★
Ermine Street, Broughton, Brigg,
South Humberside DN20 0AQ
T: (01652) 650770 & 650756
F: (01652) 650495
E: enquiries@forestpines.co.uk
I: www.forestpines.co.uk

Wortley House Hotel ★★★
Rowland Road, Scunthorpe,
South Humberside DN16 1SU
T: (01724) 842223
F: (01724) 280646
E: wortley.hotel@virgin.net

SELBY
North Yorkshire

Loftsome Bridge Coaching House Ltd ★★★
Loftsome Bridge, Wressle, Selby,
North Yorkshire YO8 6EN
T: (01757) 630070
F: (01757) 633900
E: reception@
loftsomebridge-hotel.co.uk
I: www.loftsomebridge-hotel.
co.uk

SETTLE
North Yorkshire

Bowerley Hotel and Conference Centre★★
Langcliffe, Settle, North
Yorkshire BD24 9LY
T: (01729) 823811
F: (01729) 822317
E: bowerley_hotel@aol.com

Falcon Manor Hotel ★★★
Skipton Road, Settle, North
Yorkshire BD24 9BD
T: (01729) 823814
F: (01729) 822087
E: enquiries@thefalconmanor.
com
I: www.thefalconmanor.com

New Inn Hotel ★★
Clapham, Lancaster LA2 8HH
T: (01524) 251203
F: (01524) 251496
E: info@newinn-clapham.co.uk
I: www.newinn-clapham.co.uk

SHEFFIELD
South Yorkshire

Hotel Bristol ★★★
Blonk Street, Sheffield, S1 2AU
T: (0114) 220 4000
F: (0114) 220 3900
E: sheffield@bhg.co.uk
I: www.bhg.co.uk

Cutlers Hotel ★★
George Street, Sheffield, S1 2PF
T: (0114) 273 9939
F: (0114) 276 8332
E: enquiries@cutlershotel.co.uk
I: www.cutlershotel.co.uk

The Hillsborough Hotel ★★
54-58 Langsett Road,
Hillsborough, Sheffield, S6 2UB
T: (0114) 232 2100
E: reception@hillsboroughhotel.
com
I: www.hillsboroughhotel.com

Novotel Sheffield ★★★
Arundel Gate, Sheffield, S1 2PR
T: (0114) 278 1781
F: (0114) 278 7744
E: h1348@accor-hotels.com
I: www.novotel.com

Swallow Hotel ★★★★
Kenwood Road, Sheffield,
S7 1NQ
T: (0114) 258 3811
F: (0114) 255 4744
I: www.marriotthotels.
com/SZORH

Whitley Hall Hotel ★★★
Elliott Lane, Grenoside, Sheffield
S35 8NR
T: (0114) 245 4444
F: (0114) 245 5414
E: reservations@whitleyhall.
com
I: www.whitleyhall.com

SKIPTON
North Yorkshire

Coniston Hall Lodge and Restaurant ★★★
Coniston Cold, Skipton, North
Yorkshire BD23 4EB
T: (01756) 748080
F: (01756) 749487
E: conistonhall@clara.net
I: www.conistonhall.co.uk

Highfield Hotel ★★
58 Keighley Road, Skipton,
North Yorkshire BD23 2NB
T: (01756) 793182 & 798834
F: (01756) 793182
I: www.highfield-hotel.co.uk

SOUTH MILFORD
North Yorkshire

**Best Western Milford Lodge
Hotel** ★★★
A1 Great North Road, Peckfield,
South Milford, Leeds LS25 5LQ
T: (01977) 681800
F: (01977) 681245
E: enquiries@mlh.co.uk
I: www.mlh.co.uk

STEETON
West Yorkshire

Steeton Hall Hotel ★★
Station Road, Steeton, Keighley,
West Yorkshire BD20 6RY
T: (01535) 655676
F: (01535) 655663
I: www.steetonhallhotel.co.uk

STOKESLEY
North Yorkshire

Wainstones Hotel ★★★
High Street, Great Broughton,
Stokesley, Middlesbrough,
Cleveland TS9 7EW
T: (01642) 712268
F: (01642) 711560
E: wstones@netcomuk.co.uk
I: www.wainstoneshotel.co.uk

TADCASTER
North Yorkshire

Hazlewood Castle ★★★
Paradise Lane, Hazlewood,
Tadcaster, North Yorkshire
LS24 9NJ
T: (01937) 535353 & 535306
F: (01937) 535316
E: info@hazlewood-castle.co.uk
I: www.hazlewood-castle.co.uk

THIRSK
North Yorkshire

Angel Inn ★★
Long Street, Topcliffe, Thirsk,
North Yorkshire YO7 3RW
T: (01845) 577237
F: (01845) 578000

Golden Fleece ★★
Market Place, Thirsk, North
Yorkshire YO7 1LL
T: (01845) 523108
F: (01845) 523996
I: www.bestwestern.co.uk

Three Tuns Hotel ★★
Market Place, Thirsk, North
Yorkshire YO7 1LH
T: (01845) 523124
F: (01845) 526126
E: threetuns@talk21.com

Treetops Hotel ★★
Sutton Road, Thirsk, North
Yorkshire YO7 2ER
T: (01845) 522293
F: (01845) 522579
E: treetops.hotel@virginnet.
co.uk
I: www.treetops-hotel.com

THORNE
South Yorkshire

Belmont Hotel ★★
Horsefair Green, Thorne,
Doncaster, South Yorkshire
DN8 5EE
T: (01405) 812320
F: (01405) 740508
E: belmonthotel@cs.com
I: www.belmonthotel.com

THORNTON WATLASS
North Yorkshire

The Buck Inn ★
Thornton Watlass, Ripon, North
Yorkshire HG4 4AH
T: (01677) 422461
F: (01677) 422447
E: buckwatlass@btconnect.com

WAKEFIELD
West Yorkshire

Bank House Hotel ★★
11 Bank Street, Westgate,
Wakefield, West Yorkshire
WF1 1EH
T: (01924) 368248
F: (01924) 363724
E: BankHouseHotel@amserve.
net

Billy Budd Hotel & Restaurant
★★
10 Drury Lane, Wakefield, West
Yorkshire WF1 2TE
T: (01924) 372069 & 299368
F: (01924) 374787

Cedar Court Hotel ★★★★
Denby Dale Road, Calder Grove,
Wakefield, West Yorkshire
WF4 3QZ
T: (01924) 276310 & 261459
F: (01924) 280221
I: www.cedarcourthotels.co.uk

Dimple Well Lodge Hotel ★★
The Green, Ossett, West
Yorkshire WF5 8JX
T: (01924) 264352
F: (01924) 274024

Parklands Hotel ★★
143 Horbury Road, Wakefield,
West Yorkshire WF2 8TY
T: (01924) 377407
F: (01924) 290348
E: steve@parklands23.fsnet.
co.uk
I: www.parklandshotel.co.uk

Hotel St Pierre ★★★
733 Barnsley Road,
Newmillerdam, Wakefield, West
Yorkshire WF2 6QG
T: (01924) 255596
F: (01924) 252746
E: sales@hotelstpierre.co.uk
I: www.hotelstpierre.co.uk

WALSHFORD
North Yorkshire

Bridge Inn Hotel ★★★
Walshford, Wetherby, West
Yorkshire LS22 5HS
T: (01937) 580115
F: (01937) 580556
E: bridge.walshford@virgin.net
I: www.thebridgeinnhotel.co.uk

WENTBRIDGE
West Yorkshire

Wentbridge House Hotel
★★★
Wentbridge, Pontefract, West
Yorkshire WF8 3JJ
T: (01977) 620444
F: (01977) 620148
E: info@wentbridgehouse.co.uk
I: www.wentbridgehouse.co.uk

WEST WITTON
North Yorkshire

Wensleydale Heifer ★★
West Witton, Leyburn, North
Yorkshire DL8 4LS
T: (01969) 622322
F: (01969) 624183
E: heifer@daelnet.co.uk
I: www.wensleydaleheifer.co.uk

WETHERBY
West Yorkshire

Jarvis Wetherby Hotel ★★★
Leeds Road, Wetherby, West
Yorkshire LS22 5HE
T: (01937) 583881
F: (01937) 580062
E: rs.jwetherby@jarvis.co.uk
I: www.jarvis.co.uk

Wood Hall Hotel ★★★
Trip Lane, Linton, Wetherby,
West Yorkshire LS22 4JA
T: (01937) 587271
F: (01937) 584353
E: events.woodhall@
arcadianhotels.co.uk
I: www.arcadianhotels.co.uk

WHITBY
North Yorkshire

Bagdale Hall & Bagdale Lodge
★★★
1 Bagdale, Whitby, North
Yorkshire YO21 1QL
T: (01947) 602958
F: (01947) 820714
I: www.smoothhound.
co.uk/hotels/bagdale.html

**Dunsley Hall Country House
Hotel and Leisure Club** ★★★
Dunsley, Whitby, North
Yorkshire YO21 3TL
T: (01947) 893437
F: (01947) 893505
E: reception@dunsleyhall.com
I: www.dunsleyhall.com

Saxonville Hotel ★★★
Ladysmith Avenue, Whitby,
North Yorkshire YO21 3HX
T: (01947) 602631 & 0800 019
1147
F: (01947) 820523
E: newtons@saxonville.co.uk
I: www.saxonville.co.uk

Sneaton Hall ★★
Sneaton, Whitby, North
Yorkshire YO22 5HP
T: (01947) 605929
F: (01947) 820177
E: sneatonhall@supanet.com

Stakesby Manor ★★
Manor Close, High Stakesby,
Whitby, North Yorkshire
YO21 1HL
T: (01947) 602773
F: (01947) 602140
E: relax@stakesby-manor.co.uk
I: www.stakesby-manor.co.uk

White House Hotel ★★
Upgang Lane, West Cliff, Whitby,
North Yorkshire YO21 3JJ
T: (01947) 600469
F: (01947) 821600
E: Thomas.campbell1@
btinternet.com
I: www.s-h-systems.
co.uk/hotels/whitehse.html

WHITLEY
West Yorkshire

**The Woolpack Country Inn
Hotel & Restaurant** ★★★
Whitley Road, Whitley,
Dewsbury, West Yorkshire
WF12 0LZ
T: (01924) 499999 &
07930 418311
F: (01924) 495289
I: www.woolpackhotel.co.uk

WIGGLESWORTH
North Yorkshire

Plough Inn at Wigglesworth
★★
Wigglesworth, Skipton, North
Yorkshire BD23 4RJ
T: (01729) 840243 & 840638
F: (01729) 840638
E: steve@
the-plough-wigglesworth.
freeserve.co.uk
I: www.
the-plough-wigglesworth.
freeserve.co.uk

WILLERBY
East Riding of Yorkshire

Willerby Manor Hotel ★★★
Well Lane, Willerby, Hull
HU10 6ER
T: (01482) 652616
F: (01482) 653901
E: info@willerbymanor.co.uk
I: www.willerbymanor.co.uk

YORK
North Yorkshire

Abbots Mews Hotel ★★
6 Marygate Lane, Bootham,
York, YO30 7DE
T: (01904) 634866 & 622395
F: (01904) 612848

**Aldwark Manor Hotel, Golf
and Country Club** ★★★
Aldwark, Alne, York YO61 1UF
T: (01347) 838146
F: (01347) 838867
E: reception@aldwarkmanor.
co.uk
I: www.aldwarkmanor.co.uk

Alhambra Court Hotel ★★
31 St Mary's, Bootham, York,
YO30 7DD
T: (01904) 628474
F: (01904) 610690

Ambassador ★★★
123-125 The Mount, York,
YO24 1DU
T: (01904) 641316
F: (01904) 640259
E: stay@ambassadorhotel.co.uk
I: www.ambassadorhotel.co.uk

Beechwood Close Hotel ★★
19 Shipton Road, Clifton, York
YO30 5RE
T: (01904) 658378
F: (01904) 647124
E: bch@selcom.co.uk
I: www.beechwood-close.co.uk

Black Bull Hotel ★★
Hull Road, York, YO10 3LF
T: (01904) 411856
F: (01904) 430667

The Churchill ★★★
65 Bootham, York, YO30 7DQ
T: (01904) 644456
F: (01904) 652447
E: churchillh@aol.com
I: www.churchillhotel.com

Clifton Bridge Hotel ★★
Water End, Clifton, York
YO30 6LL
T: (01904) 610510
F: (01904) 640208
E: enq@cliftonbridgehotel.co.uk
I: www.cliftonbridgehotel.co.uk

Coach House Hotel ★★
20-22 Marygate, Bootham, York,
YO30 7BH
T: (01904) 652780
F: (01904) 679943
E: coach_house@btclick.com
I: www.coachhousehotel-york.
com

Dean Court Hotel ★★★
Duncombe Place, York, YO1 7EF
T: (01904) 625082
F: (01904) 620305
E: info@deancourt-york.co.uk
I: www.deancourt-york.co.uk

Elmbank ★★★
The Mount, York, YO24 1GE
T: (01904) 610653
F: (01904) 627139
E: elmbank@hotmail.com

Granby Lodge Hotel ★
41-43 Scarcroft Road, York,
YO24 1DB
T: (01904) 653291
F: (01904) 653291

The Grange Hotel ★★★
1 Clifton, York, YO30 6AA
T: (01904) 644744
F: (01904) 612453
E: info@grangehotel.co.uk
I: www.grangehotel.co.uk

Hedley House ★★
3-4 Bootham Terrace, York,
YO30 7DH
T: (01904) 637404
F: (01904) 639774
E: h.h@mcmail.com
I: www.hedleyhouse.com

Hilton York ★★★★
1 Tower Street, York, YO1 9WD
T: (01904) 648111
F: (01904) 610317
E: reservations@york.stakis.
co.uk
I: www.york.hilton.com

Holgate Hill Hotel ★★
124 Holgate Road, York,
YO24 4BB
T: (01904) 653786
F: (01904) 643223
E: info@holgatehillhotel.co.uk

**Jarvis International Hotel
★★★**
Shipton Road, Skelton, York,
YO30 1XW
T: (01904) 670222
F: (01904) 670311
E: jiyork.rs@jarvis.co.uk
I: www.jarvis.co.uk

Jorvik Hotel ★★
50-52 Marygate, Bootham, York,
YO30 7BH
T: (01904) 653511
F: (01904) 627009
I: www.jorvikhotel.co.uk

Judges Lodging ★★★
9 Lendal, York, YO1 8AQ
T: (01904) 623587 & 638733
F: (01904) 679947
E: judgeshotel@aol.com
I: www.judges-lodging.co.uk

Kilima Hotel ★★
129 Holgate Road, York,
YO24 4AZ
T: (01904) 625787
F: (01904) 612083
E: sales@kilima.co.uk
I: www.kilima.co.uk

Knavesmire Manor Hotel ★★
302 Tadcaster Road, York,
YO24 1HE
T: (01904) 702941
F: (01904) 709274
E: enquire@knavesmire.co.uk
I: www.knavesmire.co.uk

**Lady Anne Middleton's Hotel
★★**
Skeldergate, York, YO1 6DS
T: (01904) 611570
F: (01904) 613043
E: bookings@ladyannes.co.uk
I: www.ladyannes.co.uk

Monkbar Hotel ★★★
Monkbar, York, YO31 7JA
T: (01904) 638086
F: (01904) 629195
E: sales@monkbar-hotel.co.uk
I: www.monkbar-hotel.co.uk

Mount Royale Hotel ★★★
The Mount, York, YO24 1GU
T: (01904) 628856
F: (01904) 611171
E: reservations@mountroyale.
co.uk
I: www.mountroyale.co.uk

Newington Hotel ★★
147-157 Mount Vale, York,
YO24 1DJ
T: (01904) 625173 & 623090
F: (01904) 679937
E: info@thenewington.co.uk
I: www.ladyannes.co.uk

Novotel York ★★★
Fishergate, York, YO10 4FD
T: (01904) 611660
F: (01904) 610925
E: h0949@accor-hotels.com
I: www.novotel.com

**The Parsonage Country House
Hotel ★★★**
York Road, Escrick, York
YO19 6LF
T: (01904) 728111
F: (01904) 728151
E: reservations@
parsonagehotel.co.uk
I: www.parsonagehotel.co.uk

Queens Hotel
Travel Accommodation
Queens Staith Road,
Skeldergate, York, YO1 6DH
T: (01904) 611321
F: (01904) 611388
E: sales@queenshotel-york.com
I: www.queenshotel-york.com

**Ramada Jarvis Abbey Park
★★★**
The Mount, York, YO24 1BN
T: (01904) 658301
F: (01904) 621224
I: www.jarvis.co.uk

Royal York Hotel ★★★★
Station Road, York, YO24 1AA
T: (01904) 653681
F: (01904) 623503
E: julia.bodmer@principalhotels.
co.uk
I: www.principalhotels.co.uk

Savages Hotel ★★
15 St Peter's Grove, Clifton, York
YO30 6AQ
T: (01904) 610818
F: (01904) 627729

Wheatlands Lodge Hotel ★★
75-85 Scarcroft Road, York,
YO24 1DB
T: (01904) 654318
F: (01904) 654318
E: wheatlodge@aol.com
I: www.smoothhound.
co.uk/hotels/wheatlan.html

York Marriott Hotel ★★★★
Tadcaster Road, Dringhouses,
York, YO24 2QQ
T: (01904) 701000 & 770600
F: (01904) 702308
E: york@marriotthotels.co.uk
I: www.marriott.com

York Moat House ★★★
North Street, York, YO1 6JF
T: (01904) 459988
F: (01904) 641793
E: cbyrk@queensmoat.co.uk
I: www.moathousehotels.com

York Pavilion Hotel ★★★
Main Street, Fulford, York
YO10 4PJ
T: (01904) 622099
F: (01904) 626939

HEART OF ENGLAND

ABBOTS SALFORD
Warwickshire

Salford Hall Hotel ★★★
Abbots Salford, Evesham,
Worcestershire WR11 5UT
T: (01386) 871300 &
0800 212671
F: (01386) 871301
E: reception@salfordhall.co.uk
I: www.salfordhall.co.uk

ALCESTER
Warwickshire

Kings Court Hotel ★★★
Kings Coughton, Alcester,
Warwickshire B49 5QQ
T: (01789) 763111
F: (01789) 400242
E: info@kingscourthotel.co.uk
I: www.kingscourthotel.co.uk

ALREWAS
Staffordshire

**Claymar Hotel and Restaurant
★★**
118a Main Street, Alrewas,
Burton upon Trent, Staffordshire
DE13 7AE
T: (01283) 790202 & 791281
F: (01283) 791465

ALTON
Staffordshire

Alton Towers Hotel ★★★
Alton Towers, Alton, Stoke-on-
Trent ST10 4DB
T: (01538) 704600
F: (01538) 704657

ASHBOURNE
Derbyshire

**The Bentley Brook Inn and
Fenny's Restaurant★**
Fenny Bentley, Ashbourne,
Derbyshire DE6 1LF
T: (01335) 350278
F: (01335) 350422
E: all@bentleybrookinn.co.uk
I: www.bentleybrookinn.co.uk

**Callow Hall Country House
Hotel & Restaurant★★★**
Mappleton, Ashbourne,
Derbyshire DE6 2AA
T: (01335) 300900 & 300900
F: (01335) 300512
E: reservations@callowhall.
demon.co.uk
I: www.callowhall.co.uk

BAKEWELL
Derbyshire

Ashford Arms ★★
Church Street, Ashford in the
Water, Bakewell, Derbyshire
DE45 1QB
T: (01629) 812725
F: (01629) 814749

**The Croft Country House Hotel
★★**
Great Longstone, Bakewell,
Derbyshire DE45 1TF
T: (01629) 640278
F: (01629) 640369
E: jthursbury@ukonline.co.uk
I: www.croftcountryhouse.co.uk

East Lodge Country House Hotel and Restaurant ★★★
Rowsley, Matlock, Derbyshire
DE4 2EF
T: (01629) 734474
F: (01629) 733949
E: info@eastlodge.com
I: www.eastlodge.com

Rutland Arms Hotel ★★★
The Square, Bakewell, Derbyshire
DE45 1BT
T: (01629) 812812
F: (01629) 812309
E: rutland@bakewell.demon.co.uk
I: www.bakewell.demon.co.uk

BALSALL COMMON
West Midlands

Haigs Hotel ★★
Kenilworth Road, Balsall
Common, Coventry CV7 7EL
T: (01676) 533004
F: (01676) 535132

BAMFORD
Derbyshire

Yorkshire Bridge Inn ★★
Ashopton Road, Bamford, Hope
Valley S33 0AZ
T: (01433) 651361
F: (01433) 651361
E: mr@ybridge.force9.co.uk
I: www.yorkshire-bridge.co.uk

BARNBY MOOR
Nottinghamshire

Ye Olde Bell ★★★
Barnby Moor, Retford,
Nottinghamshire DN22 8QS
T: (01777) 705121
F: (01777) 860424
E: yeoldbell@
british-trust-hotels.com
I: www.british-trust-hotels.com

BASLOW
Derbyshire

Devonshire Arms Hotel ★★
Nether End, Baslow, Bakewell,
Derbyshire DE45 1SR
T: (01246) 582551
F: (01246) 582116
E: devonshirearms@btinternet.com

Fischers Baslow Hall ★★
Calver Road, Baslow, Bakewell,
Derbyshire DE45 1RR
T: (01246) 583259
F: (01246) 583818

BELPER
Derbyshire

The Lion Hotel ★
Bridge Street, Belper, Derbyshire
DE56 1AX
T: (01773) 824033
F: (01773) 828393
E: enquiries@lionhotel.uk.com
I: www.lionhotel.uk.com

BERKELEY
Gloucestershire

The Berkeley Arms Hotel ★★
Canonbury Street, Berkeley,
Gloucestershire GL13 9BG
T: (01453) 810291
F: (01453) 511334

Newport Towers Hotel ★★
Newport, Berkeley,
Gloucestershire GL13 9PX
T: (01453) 810575
F: (01453) 511062

Prince of Wales Hotel ★★★
Berkeley Road, Berkeley,
Gloucestershire GL13 9HD
T: (01453) 810474
F: (01453) 511370

BERKSWELL
West Midlands

Nailcote Hall Hotel and Restaurant ★★★★
Nailcote Lane, Berkswell,
Coventry CV7 7DE
T: (024) 7646 6174
F: (024) 7647 0720
E: info@nailcotehall.co.uk
I: www.nailcotehall.co.uk

BEWDLEY
Worcestershire

Heath Hotel and Country Club and Country Club ★★★
Habberley Road, Bewdley,
Worcestershire DY12 1LJ
T: (01299) 406400
F: (01299) 400921
E: enquiries@jarvisheath.co.uk
I: www.jarvisheath.co.uk

BIBURY
Gloucestershire

The Swan Hotel ★★★
Bibury, Cirencester,
Gloucestershire GL7 5NW
T: (01285) 740695
F: (01285) 740473
E: swanhot1@
swanhotel-cotswolds.co.uk
I: www.swanhotel.co.uk

BIGGIN-BY-HARTINGTON
Derbyshire

Biggin Hall ★★
Biggin-by-Hartington, Buxton,
Derbyshire SK17 0DH
T: (01298) 84451
F: (01298) 84681
E: bigginhall@compuserve.com
I: www.bigginhall.co.uk

BIRMINGHAM
West Midlands

Arden Hotel and Leisure Club ★★★
Coventry Road, Bickenhill,
Solihull, West Midlands B92 0EH
T: (01675) 443221
F: (01675) 445604
E: enquires@ardenhotel.co.uk
I: www.ardenhotel.co.uk

Birmingham Marriott Hotel ★★★★★
12 Hagley Road, Five Ways,
Birmingham, B16 8SJ
T: (0121) 452 1144
F: (0121) 456 3442
E: salesadmin.birmingham@
whitbread.com
I: www.marriotthotels.com/bhxbh

The Burlington Hotel ★★★★
Burlington Arcade, 126 New
Street, Birmingham, B2 4JQ
T: (0121) 643 9191
F: (0121) 643 5075
E: mail@Burlingtonhotel.com
I: www.burlingtonhotel.com

The Copthorne Hotel Birmingham ★★★★
Paradise Circus, Birmingham,
B3 3HJ
T: (0121) 200 2727
F: (0121) 200 1197
E: sales.birmingham@mill-cop.com
I: www.millennium-hotels.com

Fountain Court Hotel ★★
339-343 Hagley Road,
Edgbaston, Birmingham
B17 8NH
T: (0121) 429 1754
F: (0121) 429 1209
E: fountain-court@excite.co.uk

Old Farm Hotel ★★
108 Linden Road, Bournville,
Birmingham B30 1LA
T: (0121) 458 3146
F: (0121) 459 0607
E: oldfarmhotel@voogd.co.uk
I: www.smoothhound.
co.uk/hotels/oldfarm2.html

BLYTH
Nottinghamshire

The Charnwood Hotel ★★★
Sheffield Road, Blyth, Worksop,
Nottinghamshire S81 8HF
T: (01909) 591610
F: (01909) 591429
E: info@charnwoodhotel.com
I: www.charnwoodhotel.com

BOSTON
Lincolnshire

Comfort Inn Boston ★★
Junction A17/A52, Donnington
Road, Bicker Bar Roundabout,
Boston, Lincolnshire PE20 3AN
T: (01205) 820118
F: (01205) 820228
E: admin@gb607.u-net.com
I: www.choicehotels.com

The New England Hotel ★★★
Wide Bargate, Boston,
Lincolnshire PE21 6SH
T: (01205) 365255
F: (01205) 310597

BOURTON-ON-THE-WATER
Gloucestershire

Apple Pie House Hotel ★★★
Whiteshoots Hill, Bourton-on-
the-Water, Cheltenham,
Gloucestershire GL54 2LE
T: (01451) 820387
F: (01451) 812821
E: hotel@bourton.com
I: www.bourton.com

Chester House Hotel ★★
Victoria Street, Bourton-on-the-
Water, Cheltenham,
Gloucestershire GL54 2BU
T: (01451) 820286
F: (01451) 820471
E: juliand@chesterhouse.u-net.com
I: www.chesterhouse.u-net.com

The Dial House Hotel ★★
The Chestnuts, Bourton-on-the-
Water, Cheltenham,
Gloucestershire GL54 2AN
T: (01451) 822244
F: (01451) 810126
E: info@dialhousehotel.com
I: www.dialhousehotel.com

Old Manse Hotel ★★
Victoria Street, Bourton-on-the-
Water, Cheltenham,
Gloucestershire GL54 2BX
T: (01451) 820082
F: (01451) 810381
E: centralreservations@
oldenglish.co.uk
I: www.oldenglish.co.uk

BRETBY
Derbyshire

Stanhope Arms Hotel ★★
Ashby Road East, Bretby, Burton
upon Trent, Staffordshire
DE15 0PU
T: (01283) 217954 & 219 562
F: (01283) 550 106
E: info@stanhopearmshotel.com
I: www.stanhopearmshotel.com

BRIDGNORTH
Shropshire

The Croft Hotel ★
St. Mary's Street, Bridgnorth,
Shropshire WV16 4DW
T: (01746) 762416 & 767155
F: (01746) 767431

Mill Hotel ★★★★
Alveley, Bridgnorth, Shropshire
WV15 6HL
T: (01746) 780437
F: (01746) 780850
I: www.theaa.com/hotels/36837.html

The Old Vicarage Hotel ★★★
Worfield, Bridgnorth, Shropshire
WV15 5JZ
T: (01746) 716497 &
0800 0968010
F: (01746) 716552
E: admin@the-old-vicarage.
demon.co.uk
I: www.oldvicarageworfield.com

BROADWAY
Worcestershire

Broadway Hotel ★★★
The Green, Broadway,
Worcestershire WR12 7AA
T: (01386) 852401
F: (01386) 853879
E: Bookings@
cotswold-inns-hotels.co.uk
I: www.cotswold-inns-hotel.co.uk

Dormy House ★★★
Willersey Hill, Broadway,
Worcestershire WR12 7LF
T: (01386) 852711
F: (01386) 858636
E: reservation@dormyhouse.co.uk

The Lygon Arms ★★★★
Broadway, Worcestershire
WR12 7DU
T: (01386) 852255
F: (01386) 854470
E: info@the-lygon-arms.co.uk
I: www.the-lygon-arms.co.uksavoy-group.co.uk

BROMSGROVE
Worcestershire
Hanover International ★★★★
Kidderminster Road,
Bromsgrove, Worcestershire
B61 9AB
T: (01527) 576600
F: (01527) 878981
E: enquiries.
hanover-bromsgrove@virgin.
net

Hilton Bromsgrove ★★★★
Birmingham Road, Bromsgrove,
Worcestershire B61 0JB
T: (0121) 447 7888
F: (0121) 447 7273
E: reservations@stakis.co.uk
I: www.hilton.com

BUCKLAND
Gloucestershire
Buckland Manor ★★★
Buckland, Broadway,
Worcestershire WR12 7LY
T: (01386) 852626
F: (01386) 853557
E: enquire@bucklandmanor.
com
I: www.bucklandmanor.com

BURTON UPON TRENT
Staffordshire
The Queens Hotel ★★★
One Bridge Street, Burton upon
Trent, Staffordshire DE14 1SY
T: (01283) 523800
F: (01283) 523823

**The Riverside at Branston
★★★**
Riverside Drive, Branston,
Burton upon Trent, Staffordshire
DE14 3EP
T: (01283) 511234
F: (01283) 511441
I: www.oldenglish.co.uk

BUXTON
Derbyshire
Alison Park ★★
3 Temple Road, Buxton,
Derbyshire SK17 9BA
T: (01298) 22473
F: (01298) 72709
E: reservations@
alison-park-hotel.co.uk
I: www.alison-park-hotel.co.uk

Buckingham Hotel ★★★
1 Burlington Road, Buxton,
Derbyshire SK17 9AS
T: (01298) 70481
F: (01298) 72186
E: frontdesk@buckinghamhotel.
co.uk
I: www.buckinghamhotel.co.uk

Old Hall Hotel ★★★
The Square, Buxton, Derbyshire
SK17 6BD
T: (01298) 22841
F: (01298) 72437
E: reception@
oldhallhotelbuxton.co.uk
I: www.oldhallhotelbuxton.co.uk

Palace Hotel ★★★★
Palace Road, Buxton, Derbyshire
SK17 6AG
T: (01298) 22001
F: (01298) 72131
E: palace@paramount-hotels.
co.uk
I: www.paramount-hotels.co.uk

**Portland Hotel and Park
Restaurant ★★**
32 St John's Road, Buxton,
Derbyshire SK17 6XQ
T: (01298) 71493 & 22462
F: (01298) 27464
E: brian@portland-hotel.
freeserve.co.uk
I: www.highpeak.co.uk/portland

CANNOCK
Staffordshire
Oak Farm Hotel ★★★
Watling Street, Hatherton,
Cannock, Staffordshire
WS11 1SB
T: (01543) 462045
F: (01543) 500257
I: n.banford@oakfarmhotel.
fsbusiness.co.uk

CASTLE DONINGTON
Leicestershire
Donington Manor Hotel ★★★
High Street, Castle Donington,
Derby DE74 2PP
T: (01332) 810253
F: (01332) 850330
E: cngrist@dmhgrist.demon.
co.uk
I: www.doningtonmanorhotel.
co.uk

CASTLETON
Derbyshire
Castle Hotel ★★
Castle Street, Castleton, Hope
Valley S33 8WG
T: (01433) 620578 &
07885 952810
F: (01433) 622902
I: www.thecheshirecat.co.uk

CHADDESLEY CORBETT
Worcestershire
Brockencote Hall ★★★
Chaddesley Corbett,
Kidderminster, Worcestershire
DY10 4PY
T: (01562) 777876
F: (01562) 777872
E: info@brockencotehall.com
I: www.brockencotehall.com

CHELTENHAM
Gloucestershire
Carlton Hotel ★★★
Parabola Road, Cheltenham,
Gloucestershire GL50 3AQ
T: (01242) 514453
F: (01242) 226487
E: enquires@thecarltonhotel.
co.uk
I: www.thecarltonhotel.co.uk

Charlton Kings Hotel ★★★
London Road, Charlton Kings,
Cheltenham, Gloucestershire
GL52 6UU
T: (01242) 231061
F: (01242) 241900
E: enquiries@
charltonkingshotel.co.uk
I: www.charltonkingshotel.co.uk

**The Cheltenham Park Hotel
★★★★**
Cirencester Road, Charlton
Kings, Cheltenham,
Gloucestershire GL53 8EA
T: (01242) 222021
F: (01242) 254880
E: cheltenhampark@
paramount-hotels.co.uk
I: www.paramount-hotels.co.uk

**Clarence Court Hotel
Rating Applied For**
Clarence Square, Cheltenham,
Gloucestershire GL50 4JR
T: (01242) 580411
F: (01242) 224609

Dumbleton Hall Hotel ★★★
Dumbleton, Evesham,
Worcestershire WR11 6TS
T: (01386) 881240
F: (01386) 882142
E: dh@pofr.co.uk
I: www.dumbletonhallforce9.
co.uk

North Hall Hotel ★★
Pittville Circus Road,
Cheltenham, Gloucestershire
GL52 2PZ
T: (01242) 520589
F: (01242) 261953
E: northhallhotel@btinternet.
com

Hotel On The Park ★★★
38 Evesham Road, Cheltenham,
Gloucestershire GL52 2AH
T: (01242) 518898
F: (01242) 511526
E: stay@hotelonthepark.co.uk
I: www.hotelonthepark.co.uk

**The Prestbury House Hotel and
Restaurant★★★**
The Burgage, Prestbury,
Cheltenham, Gloucestershire
GL52 3DN
T: (01242) 529533
F: (01242) 227076
E: sandjw@freenetname.co.uk
I: www.prestburyhouse.co.uk
🔥

White House Hotel ★★★
Gloucester Road, Staverton,
Cheltenham, Gloucestershire
GL51 0ST
T: (01452) 713226
F: (01452) 857590
E: stay@white-house-hotel.
co.uk
I: www.white-house-hotel.co.uk

Willoughby House Hotel ★★★
1 Suffolk Square, Cheltenham,
Gloucestershire GL50 2DR
T: (01242) 522798
F: (01242) 256369
E: bookings@willoughbyhouse.
com
I: www.willoughbyhouse.co

CHESTERFIELD
Derbyshire
Abbeydale Hotel ★★
Cross Street, Chesterfield,
Derbyshire S40 4TD
T: (01246) 277849
F: (01246) 558223
E: Abbeydale1ef@cs.com
I: www.abbeydalehotel.co.uk
🔥

Ringwood Hall Hotel ★★★
Brimington, Chesterfield,
Derbyshire S43 1DQ
T: (01246) 280077
F: (01246) 472241
E: reception@ringwoodhall.
fsnet.co.uk
I: www.lyrichotels.co.uk

**The Tullamore Inn
Rating Applied For**
32 Springbank Road,
Chesterfield, Derbyshire S40 1NL
T: (01246) 550542

CHIPPING CAMPDEN
Gloucestershire
Noel Arms Hotel ★★★
High Street, Chipping Campden,
Gloucestershire GL55 6AT
T: (01386) 840317
F: (01386) 841136
E: bookings@
cotswold-inns-hotels.co.uk
I: www.cotswold-inns-hotels.
co.uk

Three Ways House ★★★
Chapel Lane, Mickleton,
Chipping Campden,
Gloucestershire GL55 6SB
T: (01386) 438429
F: (01386) 438118
E: threeways@puddingclub.com
I: www.puddingclub.com

CHURCH STRETTON
Shropshire
Longmynd Hotel ★★
Cunnery Road, Church Stretton,
Shropshire SY6 6AG
T: (01694) 722244
F: (01694) 722718
E: reservations@longmynd.
co.uk
I: www.longmynd.co.uk

Mynd House Hotel ★★
Ludlow Road, Little Stretton,
Church Stretton, Shropshire
SY6 6RB
T: (01694) 722212
F: (01694) 724180
E: info@myndhouse.co.uk
I: www.myndhouse.co.uk

CIRENCESTER
Gloucestershire
Corinium Hotel ★★
12 Gloucester Street,
Cirencester, Gloucestershire
GL7 2DG
T: (01285) 659711 &
07970 372208
F: (01285) 885807
E: info@coriniumhotel.co.uk
I: www.coriniumhotel.co.uk

The Crown of Crucis ★★★
Ampney Crucis, Cirencester,
Gloucestershire GL7 5RS
T: (01285) 851806 & 851403
F: (01285) 851735
E: info@thecrownofcrucis.co.uk
I: www.thecrownofcrucis.co.uk

Fleece Hotel ★★
Market Place, Cirencester,
Gloucestershire GL7 2NZ
T: (01285) 658507
F: (01285) 651017
E: relax@fleecehotel.co.uk
I: www.fleecehotel.co.uk

Stratton House Hotel ★★★
Gloucester Road, Cirencester,
Gloucestershire GL7 2LE
T: (01285) 651761
F: (01285) 640024
E: stratton.house@forestdale.
com
I: www.forestdale.com
🔥

CLEARWELL
Gloucestershire
Wyndham Arms ★★★
Clearwell, Coleford,
Gloucestershire GL16 8JT
T: (01594) 833666
F: (01594) 836450

CLEEVE HILL
Gloucestershire

Rising Sun Hotel ★★★
Cleeve Hill, Cheltenham,
Gloucestershire GL52 3PX
T: (01242) 676281 & 672002
F: (01242) 673069

COALVILLE
Leicestershire

Charnwood Arms ★★
Beveridge Lane, Bardon Hill,
Coalville, Leicester LE67 1TB
T: (01530) 813644
F: (01530) 815425
E: thecharnwoodarms@work.
go.com

COLEFORD
Gloucestershire

**The Lambsquay House Hotel
★★**
Royal Forest of Dean, Coleford,
Gloucestershire GL16 8QB
T: (01594) 833127
F: (01594) 833127

The Speech House ★★★
Forest of Dean, Coleford,
Gloucestershire GL16 7EL
T: (01594) 822607
F: (01594) 823658
E: relax@thespeechhouse.co.uk
I: www.thespeechhouse.co.uk

COLESHILL
Warwickshire

Coleshill Hotel ★★★
152 High Street, Coleshill,
Birmingham B46 3BG
T: (01675) 465527
F: (01675) 464013

**Grimstock Country House
Hotel ★★★**
Gilson Road, Coleshill,
Birmingham B46 1LJ
T: (01675) 462121 & 462161
F: (01675) 467646
E: grimstockhotel@easynet.
co.uk
I: www.grimstockhotel.co.uk

CORLEY
West Midlands

Toffs Country House Hotel ★★
Wall Hill Hall, Wall Hill Road,
Corley, Coventry CV7 8AD
T: (02476) 332030
F: (02476) 332255
E: stay@toffs-hotel.co.uk
I: www.toffs-hotel.co.uk

COVENTRY
West Midlands

Coombe Abbey Hotel ★★★
Brinklow Road, Binley, Coventry
CV3 2AB
T: (024) 7645 0450
F: (024) 7663 5101
I: www.coombeabbey.com

Coventry Holiday Inn Express
Travel Accommodation
Kenpass Highway, Coventry,
CV3 6PB
T: (024) 7641 7555
F: (024) 7641 3388

Merrick Lodge Hotel ★★
80-82 St Nicholas Street,
Coventry, CV1 4BP
T: (024) 7655 3940
F: (024) 7655 0112
I: www.merricklodge.co.uk

DARLEY DALE
Derbyshire

**Dales and Peaks Hotel and
Restaurant★★**
Old Road, Darley Dale, Matlock,
Derbyshire DE4 2ER
T: (01629) 733775
F: (01629) 733775

DERBY
Derbyshire

European Inn
Travel Accommodation
Midland Road, Derby, DE1 2SL
T: (01332) 292000
F: (01332) 293940
E: admin@euro-derby.co.uk
I: www.euro-derby.co.uk

**International Hotel &
Restaurant★★★**
Burton Road (A5250), Derby,
DE23 6AD
T: (01332) 369321
F: (01332) 294430
E: internationalhotel.derby@
virgin.net

**Kedleston Country House
Hotel ★★**
Kedleston Road, Derby,
DE52 2JD
T: (01332) 559202
F: (01332) 558822

Mundy Arms Hotel ★★
Ashbourne Road, Mackworth,
Derby DE22 4LZ
T: (01332) 824254 & 824664
F: (01332) 824519
I: www.derbyhotel.com

DUDLEY
West Midlands

**The Copthorne Merry Hill
★★★★**
The Waterfront, Level Street,
Brierley Hill, Dudley, West
Midlands DY5 1UR
T: (01384) 482882
F: (01384) 482773
E: reservations@mill-cop.com
I: www.mill-cop.com

EDGBASTON
West Midlands

Apollo Hotel ★★★
Hagley Road, Edgbaston,
Birmingham Bl6 9RA
T: (0121) 455 0271
F: (0121) 456 2394
E: info@
apollo-hotel-birmingham.com

ETRURIA
Staffordshire

**Stoke on Trent Moat House
★★★★**
Etruria Hall, Festival Way,
Etruria, Stoke-on-Trent ST1 5BQ
T: (01782) 609988
F: (01782) 284500

EVESHAM
Worcestershire

**Chequers Inn (Fladbury) Ltd
★★**
Chequers Lane, Fladbury,
Pershore, Worcestershire
WR10 2PZ
T: (01386) 860276 & 860527
F: (01386) 861286
E: chequers_inn_fladbury@
hotmail.com

The Mill at Harvington ★★
Anchor Lane, Harvington,
Evesham, Worcestershire
WR11 5NR
T: (01386) 870688
F: (01386) 870688
E: millatharvington@aol.com

Riverside Hotel ★★
The Parks, Offenham Road,
Evesham, Worcestershire
WR11 5JP
T: (01386) 446200
F: (01386) 40021
E: riversidehotel@
theparksoffenham.freeserve.
co.uk
I: www.river-side-hotel.co.uk

The Waterside Hotel ★★★
56 Waterside, Evesham,
Worcestershire WR11 6JZ
T: (01386) 442420
F: (01386) 446272

**Wood Norton Hall and
Conference Centre★★★★**
Evesham, Worcestershire
WR11 4YB
T: (01386) 420007 & 420000
F: (01386) 420190
E: woodnortonhall@bbc.co.uk
I: www.woodnortonhall.co.uk

FAIRFORD
Gloucestershire

Bull Hotel ★★
Market Place, Fairford,
Gloucestershire GL7 4AA
T: (01285) 712535 & 712217
F: (01285) 713785
E: info@thebullhotelfairford.
co.uk
I: www.thebullhotelfairford.
co.uk

FINEDON
Northamptonshire

Tudor Gate Hotel ★★
35 High Street, Finedon,
Wellingborough,
Northamptonshire NN9 5JN
T: (01933) 680408
F: (01933) 680745
E: info@tudorgate-hotel.co.uk
I: www.tudorgate-hotel.co.uk

FOWNHOPE
Herefordshire

Green Man Inn ★★
Fownhope, Hereford HR1 4PE
T: (01432) 860243
F: (01432) 860207
I: www.smoothhound.
co.uk/Hotels/Greenman.html

GAINSBOROUGH
Lincolnshire

White Hart Hotel ★
49 Lord Street, Gainsborough,
Lincolnshire DN21 2DD
T: (01427) 612018
F: (01427) 811756
E: white.hart@tesco.net

GLOSSOP
Derbyshire

Wind in the Willows Hotel ★★
Derbyshire Level, (A57), Glossop,
Derbyshire SK13 7PT
T: (01457) 868001
F: (01457) 853354
E: info@windinthewillows.co.uk
I: www.windinthewillows.co.uk

GLOUCESTER
Gloucestershire

**Bowden Hall Hotel and
Country Club ★★★**
Bondend Lane, Upton St
Leonards, Gloucester GL4 8ED
T: (01452) 614121
F: (01452) 611885
I: www.jarvis.co.uk

Edward Hotel ★★
88 London Road, Gloucester,
GL1 3PG
T: (01452) 525865
F: (01452) 302165

Hatton Court Hotel ★★★
Upton Hill, Upton St Leonards,
Gloucester GL4 8DE
T: (01452) 617412
F: (01452) 612945
E: res@hatton-court.co.uk
I: www.hatton-hotels.co.uk

**Jarvis International Hotel and
Country Club★★★**
Matson Lane, Robinswood Hill,
Gloucester, GL4 6EA
T: (01452) 525653
F: (01452) 307212
I: www.jarvis.co.uk

New County Hotel ★★★
44 Southgate Street, Gloucester,
GL1 2DU
T: (01452) 307000
F: (01452) 500487
E: newcounty@meridianleisure.
com
I: www.meridianleisure.com

**The New Inn Hotel
Rating Applied For**
16 Northgate Street, Gloucester,
GL1 1SF
T: (01452) 522177
F: (01452) 301054
E: newinn@soft-data.net
I: chapmansgroup.com

GOODRICH
Herefordshire

Ye Hostelrie Hotel ★★
Goodrich, Ross-on-Wye,
Herefordshire HR9 6HX
T: (01600) 890241
F: (01600) 890838
E: ye-hostelrie@lineone.net
I: www.ye-hostelrie.8k.com

GRANTHAM
Lincolnshire

**Grantham Marriott Hotel
★★★**
Swingbridge Road, Grantham,
Lincolnshire NG31 7XT
T: (01476) 593000
F: (01476) 592592
E: deborah.wright@whitbread.
com
I: www.swallowhotels.con

Kings Hotel ★★★
North Parade, Grantham,
Lincolnshire NG31 8AU
T: (01476) 590800
F: (01476) 590800
E: kingshotel@compuserve.com

GRINDLEFORD
Derbyshire

Maynard Arms Hotel ★★★
Main Road, Grindleford, Hope
Valley S32 2HE
T: (01433) 630321
F: (01433) 630445
E: info@maynardarms.co.uk
I: www.maynardarms.co.uk

HARTINGTON
Derbyshire

Charles Cotton Hotel ★
The Square, Hartington, Buxton,
Derbyshire SK17 0AL
T: (01298) 84229
F: (01298) 84301
E: dogpart@fsbdial.co.uk
I: www.charlescotton.co.uk

HASSOP
Derbyshire

Hassop Hall Hotel ★★★
Hassop, Bakewell, Derbyshire
DE45 1NS
T: (01629) 640488
F: (01629) 640577
E: hassophallhotel@btinternet.
com

HATTON
Warwickshire

**Haseley House Hotel and
Brasserie ★★★**
Haseley, Hatton, Warwick
CV35 7LS
T: (01926) 484222
F: (01926) 484227
E: info@haseleyhouse.co.uk
I: www.haseleyhouse.co.uk

HENLEY-IN-ARDEN
Warwickshire

Henley Hotel ★★
Tanworth Lane, Henley-in-
Arden, Solihull, West Midlands
B95 5RA
T: (01564) 794551
F: (01564) 795044
E: reception@henleyhotel.co.uk
I: www.henleyhotel.co.uk

HEREFORD
Herefordshire

**Belmont Lodge and Golf
Course ★★★**
Belmont, Hereford, HR2 9SA
T: (01432) 352666
F: (01432) 358090
E: info@belmontlodge.co.uk
I: www.belmontlodge.co.uk

Castle House ★★★
Castle Street, Hereford,
HR1 2NW
T: (01432) 356321
F: (01432) 365909
E: info@castlehse.co.uk
I: www.castlehse.co.uk

Merton Hotel ★★
Commercial Road, Hereford,
HR1 2BD
T: (01432) 265925 &
07860 550288
F: (01432) 354983
E: sales@mertonhotel.co.uk
I: www.mertonhotel.co.uk

The New Priory Hotel ★
Stretton Sugwas, Hereford
HR4 7AR
T: (01432) 760264 & 760183
F: (01432) 761809
E: newprioryhotel@ukonline.
co.uk

Three Counties Hotel ★★★
Belmont Road, Hereford,
HR2 7BP
T: (01432) 299955
F: (01432) 275114
E: enquiries@
threecountieshotel.co.uk
I: www.threecountieshotel.co.uk

HIGHAM
Derbyshire

**Santo's Higham Farm Hotel
★★★**
Main Road, Higham, Alfreton,
Derbyshire DE55 6EH
T: (01773) 833812
F: (01773) 520525
E: reception@
santoshighamfarm.demon.co.uk
I: www.santoshighamfarm.
demon.co.uk

HIMLEY
Staffordshire

**Himley Country Hotel
Rating Applied For**
School Road, Himley, Dudley,
West Midlands DY3 4LG
T: (01902) 896716
F: (01902) 896668
E: himleycountryhotel@
courshotels.co.uk
I: courshotels.co.uk

HINDLIP
Worcestershire

**Pear Tree Inn & Country Hotel
★★★**
Smite, Hindlip, Worcester
WR3 8SY
T: (01905) 756565
F: (01905) 756777
E: thepeartreeuk@aol.com
I: www.thepeartree.co.uk

HOCKLEY HEATH
West Midlands

**Nuthurst Grange Country
House Hotel and Restaurant
★★★**
Nuthurst Grange Lane, Hockley
Heath, Solihull, West Midlands
B94 5NL
T: (01564) 783972
F: (01564) 783919
E: info@nuthurst-grange.com
I: www.theaa.co.uk/hotels

HORNCASTLE
Lincolnshire

Admiral Rodney Hotel ★★
North Street, Horncastle,
Lincolnshire LN9 5DX
T: (01507) 523131
F: (01507) 523104
E: reception@admiralrodney.
com
I: www.admiralrodney.com

IRONBRIDGE
Shropshire

**The Best Western Valley Hotel
★★★**
Ironbridge, Telford, Shropshire
TF8 7DW
T: (01952) 432247
F: (01952) 432308
E: valley.hotel@ironbridge.fsnet.
co.uk
I: www.bestwestern.co.uk

KEGWORTH
Leicestershire

The Kegworth Hotel ★★
Packington Hill, Kegworth,
Derby DE74 2DF
T: (01509) 672427
F: (01509) 674664
E: info@kegworth-hotel.co.uk
I: www.kegworth-hotel.co.uk

KENILWORTH
Warwickshire

Clarendon House Hotel ★★
Old High Street, Kenilworth,
Warwickshire CV8 1LZ
T: (01926) 857668
F: (01926) 850669
E: info@clarendonhousehotel.
com
I: www.clarendonhousehotel.
com

**Macdonald De Montfort
★★★★**
The Square, Kenilworth,
Warwickshire CV8 1ED
T: (01926) 855944
F: (01926) 855952
E: info@demontfort.
macdonald-hotels.co.uk

The Peacock Hotel ★★★
149 Warwick Road, Kenilworth,
Warwickshire CV8 1HY
T: (01926) 851156 & 864500
F: (01926) 864644
E: peacock@rafflesmalaysian.
com
I: www.peacockhotel.com

KIDDERMINSTER
Worcestershire

Cedars Hotel ★★
Mason Road, Kidderminster,
Worcestershire DY11 6AG
T: (01562) 515595
F: (01562) 751103
E: reservations@cedars.hotel.
co.uk

**Gainsborough House Hotel
★★★**
Bewdley Hill, Kidderminster,
Worcestershire DY11 6BS
T: (01562) 820041
F: (01562) 66179
I: www.gainsborough-hotel.
co.uk

**The Granary Hotel and
Restaurant ★★★**
Heath Lane, Shenstone,
Kidderminster, Worcestershire
DY10 4BS
T: (01562) 777535
F: (01562) 777722

KNIGHTWICK
Worcestershire

Talbot ★
Knightwick, Worcester WR6 5PH
T: (01886) 821235
F: (01886) 821060
E: info@the-talbot.co.uk
I: www.the-talbot.co.uk

LANGAR
Nottinghamshire

Langar Hall ★★★
Langar, Nottingham NG13 9HG
T: (01949) 860559
F: (01949) 861045
E: langarhall-hotel@ndirect.
co.uk
I: www.langarhall.com

LEAMINGTON SPA
Warwickshire

Angel Hotel ★★★
143 Regent Street, Leamington
Spa, Warwickshire CV32 4NZ
T: (01926) 881296
F: (01926) 881296
E: angelhotel143@hotmail.com
I: www.the-angel-hotel.co.uk

Eaton Court Hotel ★★★
1-7 St Marks Road, Leamington
Spa, Warwickshire CV32 6DL
T: (01926) 885848
F: (01926) 885848
E: info@eatoncourt.co.uk
I: www.eatoncourt.co.uk

Falstaff Hotel ★★★
16-20 Warwick New Road,
Leamington Spa, Warwickshire
CV32 5JQ
T: (01926) 312044
F: (01926) 450574
E: falstaff@meridianleisure.com
I: meridianleisure.com

LEDBURY
Herefordshire

Feathers Hotel ★★★
High Street, Ledbury,
Herefordshire HR8 1DS
T: (01531) 635266
F: (01531) 638955
E: mary@feathers-ledbury.co.uk
I: www.feathers-ledbury.co.uk

Leadon House Hotel ★★
Ross Road, Ledbury,
Herefordshire HR8 2LP
T: (01531) 631199
F: (01531) 631476
E: Eleadon.house@amserve.net
I: www.leadonhouse.co.uk

The Talbot ★★
New Street, Ledbury,
Herefordshire HR8 2DX
T: (01531) 632963
F: (01531) 633796
E: talbot.ledbury@wadworth.
co.uk
I: www.talbotledbury.co.uk

LEEK
Staffordshire

The Jester Hotel ★★
81-83 Mill Street, Leek,
Staffordshire ST13 8EU
T: (01538) 382880
F: (01538) 398288

**Three Horseshoes Inn and
Restaurant ★★**
Buxton Road, Blackshaw Moor,
Leek, Staffordshire ST13 8TW
T: (01538) 300296
F: (01538) 300320

LEICESTER
Leicestershire

**Chase Hotel and Leisure
Complex ★★**
The Racecourse, Oadby, Leicester
LE2 3QH
T: (0116) 270 3920 & 270 2323
F: (0116) 270 0008
E: thechasehotel@talk21.com
I: www.lookitup.
co.uk/chase/leisure.htm

Holiday Inn Leicester ★★★★
129 St Nicholas Circle, Leicester,
LE1 5LX
T: (0116) 253 1161
F: (0116) 251 3169
I: www.holiday-inn.
com/leicester

Kabalou's Hotel and Restaurant ★★
23-25 Loughborough Road,
Leicester, LE4 5LD
T: (0116) 2682626
F: (0116) 2682641

Mill on the Soar Hotel ★★
Coventry Road, Sutton in the
Elms, LE9 6QD
T: (01455) 282419
F: (01455) 285937

The Red Cow ★★
Hinckley Road, Leicester Forest
East, Leicester LE3 3PG
T: (0116) 238 7878
F: (0116) 238 6539
E: alanjudd@msn.com

LEOMINSTER
Herefordshire

Royal Oak Hotel ★★
South Street, Leominster,
Herefordshire HR6 8JA
T: (01568) 612610
F: (01568) 612710

Talbot Hotel ★★★
West Street, Leominster,
Herefordshire HR6 8EP
T: (01568) 616347
F: (01568) 614880

LICHFIELD
Staffordshire

**The George Hotel Lichfield
Limited ★★★**
Bird Street, Lichfield,
Staffordshire WS13 6PR
T: (01543) 414822
F: (01543) 415817
E: mail@thegeorgelichfield.
co.uk
I: www.thegeorgelichfield.co.uk

Little Barrow Hotel ★★★
Beacon Street, Lichfield,
Staffordshire WS13 7AR
T: (01543) 414500
F: (01543) 415734
E: hinecjp@netscapeonline.
co.uk
I: www.thelittlebarrowhotel.
co.uk

Oakleigh House Hotel ★★
25 St. Chad's Road, Lichfield,
Staffordshire WS13 7LZ
T: (01543) 262688 & 255573
F: (01543) 418556
E: info@oakleighhouse.co.uk
I: www.oakleighhouse.co.uk

**The Olde Corner House Hotel
★★**
Walsall Road, Muckley Corner,
Lichfield, Staffordshire
WS14 0BG
T: (01543) 372182
F: (01543) 372211

Swinfen Hall Hotel ★★★
Swinfen, Lichfield, Staffordshire
WS14 9RS
T: (01543) 481494
F: (01543) 480341
E: swinfen.hall@virgin.net

LINCOLN
Lincolnshire

**The Bentley Hotel & Leisure
Club ★★★**
Newark Road, South Hykeham,
Lincoln, LN6 9NH
T: (01522) 878000
F: (01522) 878001
E: info@thebentleyhotel.uk.com
I: www.thebentleyhotel.uk.com

Branston Hall Hotel ★★★
Lincoln Road, Branston,
Grantham, Lincolnshire LN4 1PD
T: (01522) 793305
F: (01522) 790549
E: brahal@enterprise.net
I: www.scoot.
co.uk/branston-hall

Castle Hotel ★★
Westgate, Lincoln, LN1 3AS
T: (01522) 538801
F: (01522) 575457
E: bta@castlehotel.net
I: www.castlehotel.net

Grand Hotel ★★★
St Mary's Street, Lincoln,
LN5 7EP
T: (01522) 524211
F: (01522) 537661
E: reception@thegrandhotel.
com
I: www.thegrandhotel.uk.com

Hillcrest Hotel ★★
15 Lindum Terrace, Lincoln,
LN2 5RT
T: (01522) 510182
F: (01522) 510182
E: reservations@hillcrest-hotel.
com
I: www.hillcrest-hotel.com

Moor Lodge Hotel ★★
Sleaford Road, Branston,
Grantham, Lincolnshire LN4 1HU
T: (01522) 791366
F: (01522) 794389
E: moorlodge@bestwestern.
co.uk

LONG COMPTON
Warwickshire

The Red Lion Hotel ★★
Main Street, Long Compton,
Shipston-on-Stour,
Warwickshire CV36 5JS
T: (01608) 684221
F: (01608) 684221
E: redlionhot@aol.com

LONG EATON
Derbyshire

**Jarvis Nottingham Hotel
★★★**
Bostock Lane, Long Eaton,
Nottingham NG10 5NL
T: (0115) 946 0000
F: (0115) 946 0726
I: www.jarvis.co.uk

LONG WHATTON
Leicestershire

**The Falcon Inn
Rating Applied For**
Main Street, Long Whatton,
Loughborough, Leicestershire
LE12 5DG
T: (01509) 842416
F: (01509) 646802

LOUGHBOROUGH
Leicestershire

**Jarvis Loughborough Hotel
★★★**
High Street, Loughborough,
Leicestershire LE11 2QL
T: (01509) 233222
F: (01509) 262911
E: 015gm@jarvis.co.uk
I: www.jarvis.co.uk

LOUTH
Lincolnshire

The Beaumont Hotel ★★★
Victoria Road, Louth,
Lincolnshire LN11 0BX
T: (01507) 605005
F: (01507) 607768
E: enquiries @thebeaumont.
freeserve.co.uk
I: www.louthnet.com

**Brackenborough Arms Hotel &
Restaurant★★★**
Cordeaux Corner,
Brackenborough, Louth,
Lincolnshire LN11 0SZ
T: (01507) 609169
F: (01507) 609413
E: info@brackenborough.co.uk
I: www.brackenborough.co.uk

**Kenwick Park Hotel & Leisure
Club ★★★**
Kenwick Park, Kenwick, Louth,
Lincolnshire LN11 8NR
T: (01507) 608806
F: (01507) 608027
E: enquiries@kenwick-park.
co.uk
I: www.kenwick-park.co.uk

LOWER SLAUGHTER
Gloucestershire

**Washbourne Court Hotel
★★★**
Lower Slaughter, Cheltenham,
Gloucestershire GL54 2HS
T: (01451) 822143
F: (01451) 821045
E: washbourne@msn.com
I: www.washbournecourt.co.uk

LUDLOW
Shropshire

**Dinham Hall Hotel and
Restaurant ★★★**
Dinham, By The Castle, Ludlow,
Shropshire SY8 1EJ
T: (01584) 876464
F: (01584) 876019
E: info@dinhamhall.co.uk
I: www.dinhamhall.co.uk

The Feathers at Ludlow ★★★
Bull Ring, Ludlow, Shropshire
SY8 1AA
T: (01584) 875261
F: (01584) 876030
I: www.corushotels.com

Overton Grange Hotel ★★★
Old Hereford Road, Ludlow,
Shropshire SY8 4AD
T: (01584) 873500
F: (01584) 873524
I: www.goz.uk/overtongrange

LYDNEY
Gloucestershire

Parkend House Hotel ★★
Parkend, Lydney, Gloucestershire
GL15 4HH
T: (01594) 563666
F: (01594) 564631
E: andrewjohnlee@
netscapeonline.co.uk
I: www.parkendhousehotel.co.uk

MALVERN
Worcestershire

Colwall Park ★★★
Walwyn Road, Colwall, Malvern,
Worcestershire WR13 6QG
T: (01684) 540000
F: (01684) 540847
E: hotel@colwall.com
I: www.colwall.com

Cotford Hotel ★★
Graham Road, Malvern,
Worcestershire WR14 2HU
T: (01684) 572427
F: (01684) 572952
E: reservations@cotfordhotel.
co.uk

**The Cottage in the Wood Hotel
★★★**
Holywell Road, Malvern Wells,
Malvern, Worcestershire
WR14 4LG
T: (01684) 575859
F: (01684) 560662
E: reception@
cottageinthewood.co.uk
I: www.cottageinthewood.co.uk

Great Malvern Hotel ★★
Graham Road, Malvern,
Worcestershire WR14 2HN
T: (01684) 563411
F: (01684) 560514
E: sutton@great-malvern-hotel.
co.uk
I: www.great-malvern-hotel.
co.uk

Holdfast Cottage Hotel ★★
Marlbank Road, Little Malvern,
Malvern, Worcestershire
WR13 6NA
T: (01684) 310288
F: (01684) 311117
E: holdcothot@aol.com
I: www.holdfast-cottage.co.uk

Malvern Hills Hotel ★★
Wynds Point, British Camp,
Malvern, Worcestershire
WR13 6DW
T: (01684) 540690
F: (01684) 540327
E: malhilhotl@aol.com
I: www.malvernhillshotel.co.uk

Mount Pleasant Hotel ★★
Belle Vue Terrace, Malvern,
Worcestershire WR14 4PZ
T: (01684) 561837
F: (01684) 569968
E: mountpleasanthotel@
btinternet.com
I: www.mountpleasanthotel.
co.uk

Thornbury House Hotel ★★
Avenue Road, Malvern,
Worcestershire WR14 3AR
T: (01684) 572278
F: (01684) 577042
E: thornburyhousehotel@
compuserve.com

MANSFIELD
Nottinghamshire
Pine Lodge Hotel ★★
281-283 Nottingham Road,
Mansfield, Nottinghamshire
NG18 4SE
T: (01623) 622308
F: (01623) 656819
E: reception@pinelodge-hotel.
co.uk
I: www.pinelodge-hotel.co.uk

Portland Hall Hotel ★★
Carr Bank Park, Windmill Lane,
Mansfield, Nottinghamshire
NG18 2AL
T: (01623) 452525
F: (01623) 452550
E: enquiries@portlandhallhotel.
co.uk
I: www.portlandhallhotel.co.uk

MARKET DEEPING
Lincolnshire
The Towngate Inn Motel ★★
3 Towngate East, Market
Deeping, Peterborough PE6 8DP
T: (01778) 348000 & 348000
F: (01778) 347947
E: towngateinn@
marketdeepinglincs.freeserve.
co.uk

MARKET DRAYTON
Shropshire
The Bear Hotel ★★
Hodnet, Market Drayton,
Shropshire TF9 3NH
T: (01630) 685214 & 685788
F: (01630) 685787
E: info@bearhotel.org.uk

**Rosehill Manor Hotel &
Restaurant ★★**
Tern Hill, Market Drayton,
Shropshire TF9 2JF
T: (01630) 638532 & 637000
F: (01630) 637008

MARKFIELD
Leicestershire
Field Head Hotel ★★
Markfield Lane, Markfield,
Leicester LE67 9PS
T: (01530) 245454
F: (01530) 243740
E: fieldhead.hotel@virgin.net

MATLOCK
Derbyshire
Riber Hall ★★★
Riber, Matlock, Derbyshire
DE4 5JU
T: (01629) 582795
F: (01629) 580475
E: info@riber-hall.co.uk
I: www.riber-hall.co.uk

MELTON MOWBRAY
Leicestershire
Quorn Lodge Hotel ★★★
46 Asfordby Road, Melton
Mowbray, Leicestershire
LE13 0HR
T: (01664) 566660 & 562590
F: (01664) 480660
E: quornlodge@aol.com
I: www.quornlodge.co.uk

Sysonby Knoll Hotel ★★★
Asfordby Road, Melton
Mowbray, Leicestershire
LE13 0HP
T: (01664) 563563
F: (01664) 410364
E: sysonby.knoll@btinternet.
com
I: www.sysonby.knoll.btinternet.
co.uk

MERIDEN
West Midlands
**Strawberry Bank Restaurant
and Hotel★★★**
Main Road, Meriden, Coventry
CV7 7NF
T: (01676) 522117
F: (01676) 523804
I: www.strawberrybank.co.uk

MORETON-IN-MARSH
Gloucestershire
Manor House Hotel ★★★
High Street, Moreton-in-Marsh,
Gloucestershire GL56 0LJ
T: (01608) 650501
F: (01608) 651481
E: bookings@
cotswold-inns-hotels.co.uk
I: www.cotswold-inns-hotels.
co.uk

NAILSWORTH
Gloucestershire
Egypt Mill ★★
Nailsworth, Stroud,
Gloucestershire GL6 0AE
T: (01453) 833449
F: (01453) 836098

NEWARK
Nottinghamshire
South Parade Hotel ★★
117 Balderton Gate, Newark,
Nottinghamshire NG24 1RY
T: (01636) 703008 & 703030
F: (01636) 605593
E: enquiries@southparadehotel.
co.uk
I: www.southparadehotel.co.uk

NEWNHAM-ON-SEVERN
Gloucestershire
The Victoria Hotel ★★
High Street, Newnham-on-
Severn, Gloucestershire
GL14 1AD
T: (01594) 516221
F: (01594) 516652
E: victoria-hotel@
newnham-on-severn.fsnet.co.uk
I: victoria-hotel.org

NEWTON SOLNEY
Derbyshire
Newton Park Hotel ★★★
Newton Solney, Burton upon
Trent, Staffordshire DE15 0SS
T: (01283) 703568
F: (01283) 703214
I: www.jarvis.co.uk

NORTHAMPTON
Northamptonshire
Lime Trees Hotel ★★★
8 Langham Place, Barrack Road,
Northampton, NN2 6AA
T: (01604) 632188
F: (01604) 233012
E: info@limetreeshotel.co.uk
I: www.limetreeshotel.co.uk

**Northampton Marriott
★★★★**
Eagle Drive, Northampton,
NN4 7HW
T: (01604) 768700 & 667617
F: (01604) 769011

**Quality Hotel Northampton
★★★**
Ashley Way, Weston Favell,
Northampton NN7 3EA
T: (01604) 739955
F: (01604) 415023
E: admin@gbo70.u-net.com

NOTTINGHAM
Nottinghamshire
**Comfort Hotel Nottingham
★★**
George Street, Nottingham,
NG1 3BP
T: (0115) 947 5641
F: (0115) 948 3292
E: admin@gb620.u-net.com
I: www.choicehotelseurope.com

**The Nottingham Gateway
Hotel ★★★**
Nuthall Road, Nottingham,
NG8 6AZ
T: (0115) 979 4949
F: (0115) 979 4744
E: nottmgateway@btconnect.
com

**Swans Hotel and Restaurant
★★★**
84-90 Radcliffe Road, West
Bridgford, Nottingham
NG2 5HH
T: (0115) 981 4042
F: (0115) 945 5745
E: enquiries@swanshotel.co.uk
I: www.swanshotel.co.uk

OAKHAM
Leicestershire
Barnsdale Lodge Hotel ★★★
The Avenue, Rutland Water,
Exton, Oakham, Leicestershire
LE15 8AH
T: (01572) 724678
F: (01572) 724961

The Old Wisteria Hotel ★★★
4 Catmos Street, Oakham,
Leicestershire LE15 6HW
T: (01572) 722844
F: (01572) 724473
E: enquiries@wisteriahotel.
co.uk
I: www.wisteriahotel.co.uk

OSWESTRY
Shropshire
**Pen-y-Dyffryn Country Hotel
★★★**
Rhyd-y-Croesau, Oswestry,
Shropshire SY10 7JD
T: (01691) 653700
F: (01691) 650066
E: stay@peny.co.uk
I: www.peny.co.uk

Sweeney Hall Hotel ★★
Morda, Oswestry, Shropshire
SY10 9EU
T: (01691) 652450
F: (01691) 668023

PAINSWICK
Gloucestershire
The Falcon Hotel ★★
New Street, Painswick, Stroud,
Gloucestershire GL6 6UN
T: (01452) 814222 & 812228
F: (01452) 813377
E: bleninns@clara.net
I: www.falconinn.com

Painswick Hotel ★★★
Kemps Lane, Painswick, Stroud,
Gloucestershire GL6 6YB
T: (01452) 812160
F: (01452) 814059
E: reservations@painswickhotel.
com
I: www.painswickhotel.com

PENKRIDGE
Staffordshire
Quality Hotel Stafford ★★
Pinfold Lane, Penkridge, Stafford
ST19 5QP
T: (01785) 712459
F: (01785) 715532
E: admin@gb067.u-net.com
I: www.qualityinn.
com/hotel/gb067

PERSHORE
Worcestershire
**Angel Inn & Posting House
★★★**
9 High Street, Pershore,
Worcestershire WR10 1AF
T: (01386) 552046
F: (01386) 552581

QUORN
Leicestershire
**Quorn Grange Hotel and
Restaurant ★★★**
Quorn Grange, 88 Wood Lane,
Quorn, Loughborough,
Leicestershire LE12 8DB
T: (01509) 412167
F: (01509) 415621

REDDITCH
Worcestershire
**Campanile Hotel and
Restaurant**
Travel Accommodation
Far Moor Lane, Winyates Green,
Redditch, Worcestershire
B98 0SD
T: (01527) 510710
F: (01527) 517269
I: www.campanile.fr

Quality Hotel Redditch ★★★
Pool Bank, Southcrest, Redditch,
Worcestershire B97 4JS
T: (01527) 541511
F: (01527) 402600
E: admin@gb646.u-net.com
I: www.choicehotelseurope.com

RISLEY
Derbyshire
**Risley Hall Hotel Limited
★★★**
Derby Road, Risley, Draycott,
Derbyshire DE72 3SS
T: (0115) 939 9000
F: (0115) 939 7766
E: enquiries@risleyhallhotel.
co.uk
I: www.risleyhallhotel.co.uk

ROSS-ON-WYE
Herefordshire

Bridge House Hotel ★★
Wilton, Ross-on-Wye,
Herefordshire HR9 6AA
T: (01989) 562655
F: (01989) 567652
E: alison@bhhotel.fsnet.co.uk

The Chase Hotel ★★★
Gloucester Road, Ross-on-Wye,
Herefordshire HR9 5LH
T: (01989) 763161
F: (01989) 768330
E: info@chasehotel.co.uk
I: www.chasehotel.co.uk

Glewstone Court Hotel ★★
Glewstone, Ross-on-Wye,
Herefordshire HR9 6AW
T: (01989) 770367
F: (01989) 770282
E: glewstone@aol.com
I: www.smoothhound.
co.uk/hotels/glewston.html

Orles Barn Hotel & Restaurant ★★
Wilton, Ross-on-Wye,
Herefordshire HR9 6AE
T: (01989) 562155
F: (01989) 768470
E: orles.barn@clara.net
I: www.orles.barn.clara.net

Pencraig Court Hotel ★★★
Pencraig, Ross-on-Wye,
Herefordshire HR9 6HR
T: (01989) 770306 & 770416
F: (01989) 770040
E: mike@pencraig-court.co.uk
I: www.pencraig-court.co.uk

Rosswyn Hotel ★
17 High Street, Ross-on-Wye,
Herefordshire HR9 5BZ
T: (01989) 562733
F: (01989) 567 115
E: rosswynhotel@talk21.com

The Royal ★★★
Palace Pound, Ross-on-Wye,
Herefordshire HR9 5HZ
T: (01989) 565105
F: (01989) 768058

Wilton Court Hotel ★★
Wilton Lane, Wilton, Ross-on-
Wye, Herefordshire HR9 6AQ
T: (01989) 562569
F: (01989) 768460
E: info@wiltoncourthotel.com
I: www.wiltoncourthotel.com

ROWSLEY
Derbyshire

The Peacock Hotel ★★★
Bakewell Road, Rowsley,
Matlock, Derbyshire DE4 2EB
T: (01629) 733518
F: (01629) 732671
E: j.peacock.gm@jarvis.co.uk
I: www.jarvis.co.uk

RUDYARD
Staffordshire

Hotel Rudyard ★★★
Lake Road, Rudyard, Leek,
Staffordshire ST13 8RN
T: (01538) 306208
F: (01538) 306208

RUGBY
Warwickshire

Brownsover Hall ★★★
Brownsover Lane, Old
Brownsover, Rugby,
Warwickshire CV21 1HU
T: (01788) 546100
F: (01788) 579241
I: www.corushotels.com

The Grosvenor Hotel ★★
81-87 Clifton Road, Rugby,
Warwickshire CV21 3QQ
T: (01788) 535686
F: (01788) 541297
E: therugbygrosvenorhotel@
freeserve.co.uk

ST BRIAVELS
Gloucestershire

The Florence Country Hotel ★★
Bigsweir, St Briavels, Lydney,
Gloucestershire GL15 6QQ
T: (01594) 530830
F: (01594) 531198
E: enquiries@florencehotel.
co.uk
I: www.visitus.co.uk

SHIPSTON-ON-STOUR
Warwickshire

Chavignol at The Old Mill ★★
Mill Street, Shipston-on-Stour,
Warwickshire CV36 4AW
T: (01608) 663888
E: enquiries@old-mill-hotel.
co.uk
I: www.old-mill-hotel.co.uk

SHREWSBURY
Shropshire

Abbot's Mead Hotel ★★
9-10 St. Julian Friars,
Shrewsbury, Shropshire SY1 1XL
T: (01743) 235281
F: (01743) 369133
E: res@abbotsmeadhotel.co.uk
I: www.abbotsmeadhotel.co.uk

Albright Hussey Hotel and Restaurant★★★
Ellesmere Road, Shrewsbury,
SY4 3AF
T: (01939) 290571 & 290523
F: (01939) 291143
E: abhhotel@aol.com
I: www.albrighthussey.co.uk

Hawkstone Park Hotel, Golf and Leisure Centre★★★
Weston-under-Redcastle,
Shrewsbury SY4 5UY
T: (01939) 200611 & 200204
F: (01939) 200311
E: reservations@hawkstone.
co.uk
I: www.hawkstone.co.uk

Lion and Pheasant Hotel ★★
49-50 Wyle Cop, Shrewsbury,
SY1 1XJ
T: (01743) 236288
F: (01743) 244475
E: info@lionandpheasant.co.uk
I: www.lionandpheasant.co.uk

SKEGNESS
Lincolnshire

The Vine ★★★
Vine Road, Seacroft, Skegness,
Lincolnshire PE25 3DB
T: (01754) 610611 & 763018
F: (01754) 769845

SLEAFORD
Lincolnshire

Carre Arms Hotel ★★
Mareham Lane, Sleaford,
Lincolnshire NG34 7JP
T: (01529) 303156
F: (01529) 303139
E: enquiries@carrearmshotel.
co.uk
I: www.carrearmshotel.co.uk

The Lincolnshire Oak Hotel ★★★
East Road, Sleaford, Lincolnshire
NG34 7EH
T: (01529) 413807
F: (01529) 413710
E: reception@lincolnshire-oak.
co.uk
I: www.sleaford.
co.uk/lincolnshire-oak

SOLIHULL
West Midlands

Regency Hotel ★★★
Stratford Road, Shirley, Solihull,
West Midlands B90 4EB
T: (0121) 745 6119 & 745 0400
F: (0121) 733 3801
E: regencyhotel.regalhotel@
pop3.hiway.co.uk
I: www.corushotels.com

Swallow St John's Hotel ★★★★
651 Warwick Road, Solihull,
West Midlands B91 1AT
T: (0121) 711 3000
F: (0121) 711 3963

SOUTH NORMANTON
Derbyshire

Swallow Hotel ★★★★
Carter Lane East, Junction 28 of
M1, South Normanton, Alfreton,
Derbyshire DE55 2EH
T: (01773) 812000
F: (01773) 580032

SPALDING
Lincolnshire

Cley Hall Hotel ★★
22 High Street, Spalding,
Lincolnshire PE11 1TX
T: (01775) 725157
F: (01775) 710785
E: cleyhall@enterprise.net
I: homepages.enterprise.
net/cleyhall

STAFFORD
Staffordshire

Abbey Hotel ★★
65-68 Lichfield Road, Stafford,
Staffordshire ST17 4LW
T: (01785) 258531
F: (01785) 246875

Albridge Private Hotel ★
73 Wolverhampton Road,
Stafford, ST17 4AW
T: (01785) 254100
F: (01785) 223895

STAMFORD
Lincolnshire

Crown Hotel ★★
All Saints Place, Stamford,
Lincolnshire PE9 2AG
T: (01780) 763136
F: (01780) 756111
E: thecrownhotel@excite.com

Garden House Hotel ★★★
St Martins, Stamford,
Lincolnshire PE9 2LP
T: (01780) 763359
F: (01780) 763339
E: gardenhousehotel@
stamford60.freeserve.co.uk
I: www.gardenhousehotel.com

George of Stamford ★★★
71 St Martins, Stamford,
Lincolnshire PE9 2LB
T: (01780) 750750 & 750700
F: (01780) 750701
E: reservations@
georgehotelofstamford.com
I: www.georgehotelofstamford.
com

STAPENHILL
Staffordshire

Redhill Hotel ★
66 Stanton Road, Stapenhill,
Burton upon Trent, Staffordshire
DE15 9RS
T: (01283) 564629 & 565078
F: (01283) 564629

STOKE-ON-TRENT
Staffordshire

George Hotel ★★★
Swan Square, Burslem, Stoke-
on-Trent ST6 2AE
T: (01782) 577544
F: (01782) 837496
E: georgestoke@btinternet.com
I: www.georgehotelstoke.cwc.
net

Jarvis Clayton Lodge Hotel ★★★
Clayton Road, Newcastle-under-
Lyme, Staffordshire ST5 4AF
T: (01782) 613093 & 338 319
F: (01782) 711896
I: www.jarvis.co.uk

The North Stafford ★★★
Station Road, Stoke-on-Trent,
ST4 2AE
T: (01782) 744477
F: (01782) 744580
E: claire.portas@principalhotels.
co.uk
I: www.principalhotels.co.uk

The Plough Motel and Restaurant ★★
Campbell Road, Stoke-on-Trent,
ST4 4EN
T: (01782) 414685
F: (01782) 414669
E: info@ploughmotel.co.uk
I: www.ploughmotel.co.uk

Sneyd Arms Hotel ★★
Tower Square, Tunstall, Stoke-
on-Trent ST6 5AA
T: (01782) 826722
F: (01782) 826722
E: markethesneydarms.co.uk
I: www.thesneydarms.co.uk

Tollgate Hotel and Leisure ★★★
Ripon Road, Blurton, Stoke-on-
Trent, ST3 3BS
T: (01782) 313029
F: (01782) 593959
E: adrian@tollgate.co.uk
I: www.tollgate.co.uk

STONE
Worcestershire

Stone Manor Hotel ★★★★
Stone, Kidderminster,
Worcestershire DY10 4PJ
T: (01562) 777555
F: (01562) 777834
E: enquiries@stonemanorhotel.co.uk
I: www.stonemanorhotel.co.uk

STOW-ON-THE-WOLD
Gloucestershire

Auld Stocks Hotel ★★
The Square, Stow-on-the-Wold,
Cheltenham, Gloucestershire
GL54 1AF
T: (01451) 830666
F: (01451) 870014

Best Western Grapevine Hotel ★★★
Sheep Street, Stow-on-the-Wold, Cheltenham,
Gloucestershire GL54 1AU
T: (01451) 830344
F: (01451) 832278
E: enquiries@vines.co.uk
I: www.vines.co.uk

Fosse Manor Hotel ★★★
Stow-on-the-Wold,
Cheltenham, Gloucestershire
GL54 1JX
T: (01451) 830354
F: (01451) 832486
E: fossemanor@bestwestern.co.uk
I: www.bestwestern.co.uk

The Roman Court Hotel & Restaurant
Rating Applied For
Fosse Way, Stow-on-the-Wold,
Cheltenham, Gloucestershire
GL54 1JX
T: (01451) 870539
F: (01451) 870639
E: logozz@ad.com
I: www.theromancourthotel.co.uk

The Royalist Hotel ★★★
Digbeth Street, Stow-on-the-Wold, Cheltenham,
Gloucestershire GL54 1BN
T: (01451) 830670
F: (01451) 870048
E: info@theroyalisthotel.co.uk
I: www.theroyalisthotel.co.uk

Stow Lodge Hotel ★★★
The Square, Stow-on-the-Wold,
Cheltenham, Gloucestershire
GL54 1AB
T: (01451) 830485
F: (01451) 831671
E: chris@stowlodge.com
I: www.stowlodge.com

The Unicorn Inn ★★★
Sheep Street, Stow-on-the-Wold, Cheltenham,
Gloucestershire GL54 1HQ
T: (01451) 830257
F: (01451) 831090
E: bookings@cotswold-inns-hotels.co.uk
I: www.cotswold-inns-hotels.co.uk

STRATFORD-UPON-AVON
Warwickshire

Charlecote Pheasant Country Hotel ★★★
Charlecote, Warwick CV35 9EW
T: (01789) 279954
F: (01789) 470222
I: www.corushotels.com

Ettington Park ★★★★
Alderminster, Stratford-upon-Avon, Warwickshire CV37 8BU
T: (01789) 450123
F: (01789) 450472

Falcon Hotel ★★★
Chapel Street, Stratford-upon-Avon, Warwickshire CV37 6HA
T: (01789) 279953
F: (01789) 414260
E: thefalcon@corushotels.com
I: www.regalhotels.co.uk/thefalcon

Grosvenor Hotel ★★★
Warwick Road, Stratford-upon-Avon, Warwickshire CV37 6YT
T: (01789) 269213
F: (01789) 266087
E: info@groshotelstratford.co.uk
I: www.groshotelstratford.co.uk
🏃

The New Inn ★★
Clifford Chambers, Stratford-upon-Avon, Warwickshire
CV37 8HR
T: (01789) 293402
F: (01789) 292716
E: thenewinn65@aol.com
I: www.stratford-upon-avon.co.uk

Stratford Court Hotel ★★
20 Avenue Road, Stratford-upon-Avon, Warwickshire
CV37 6UX
T: (01789) 297799
F: (01789) 262449
E: stratfordcourt@easynet.co.uk
I: www.stratford-upon-avon.co.uk/stratcrt.htm

Stratford Manor Hotel ★★★★
Warwick Road, Stratford-upon-Avon, Warwickshire CV37 0PY
T: (01789) 731173
F: (01789) 731131
E: stratfordmanor@marstonhotels.co.uk
I: www.marstonhotels.co.uk

Stratford Victoria ★★★★
Arden Street, Stratford-upon-Avon, Warwickshire CV37 6QQ
T: (01789) 271000
F: (01789) 271001
E: www.stratfordvictoria@marstonhotels.com
I: www.stratfordvictoria@marstonhotels.com

Welcombe Hotel and Golf Course ★★★★
Warwick Road, Stratford-upon-Avon, Warwickshire CV37 0NR
T: (01789) 295252
F: (01789) 414666
E: sales@welcombe.co.uk
I: www.welcombe.co.uk
🏃

The White Swan ★★★
Rother Street, Stratford-upon-Avon, Warwickshire CV37 6NH
T: (01789) 297022
F: (01789) 268773
E: thewhiteswan@work.gb.com

STRENSHAM
Worcestershire

Strensham Travel Inn
Travel Accommodation
Travel Inn, M5 Service Area,
Strensham, Worcester WR8 0BZ
T: (01684) 273931
F: (01684) 273606
I: www.travelinn.co.uk

STRETTON UNDER FOSSE
Warwickshire

Ashton Lodge Country Hotel and Restaurant★★
Stretton under Fosse, Rugby,
Warwickshire CV23 0PJ
T: (01788) 832278
F: (01788) 833497
E: enquiries@ashtonlodgehotel.co.uk
I: www.ashtonlodgehotel.co.uk

STROUD
Gloucestershire

Bear of Rodborough Hotel ★★★
Rodborough Common, Stroud, Gloucestershire GL5 5DE
T: (01453) 878522
F: (01453) 872523
E: bookings@cotswold-inns-hotels.co.uk
I: www.cotswold-inns-hotels.co.uk

Bell Hotel and Restaurant ★★
Wallbridge, Stroud, Gloucestershire GL5 3JS
T: (01453) 763556
F: (01453) 758611
E: reservations@bellhotel.net
I: www.thebellhotel.net

Stonehouse Court Hotel ★★★
Bristol Road, Stonehouse, Gloucestershire GL10 3RA
T: (01453) 825155
F: (01453) 824611
E: stonehouse.court@pageant.co.uk
I: www.pageant.co.uk

SUTTON COLDFIELD
West Midlands

Jarvis Penns Hall Hotel and Country Club★★★
Penns Lane, Walmley, Sutton Coldfield, West Midlands
B76 1LH
T: (0121) 351 3111
F: (0121) 313 1297
E: jpennshall.gm@jarvis.co.uk
I: www.jarvis.co.uk

Marston Farm Hotel ★★★
Bodymoor Heath, Sutton Coldfield, West Midlands
B76 9JD
T: (01827) 872133
F: (01827) 875043
E: marston.farm@lineone.net
I: www.brook-hotels.co.uk

SWINSCOE
Staffordshire

The Dog and Partridge Country Inn with Rooms in the Grounds ★★
Swinscoe, Ashbourne, Derbyshire DE6 2HS
T: (01335) 343183
F: (01335) 342742

SYMONDS YAT
Herefordshire

Forest View Hotel ★★
Symonds Yat East, Ross-on-Wye, Herefordshire HR9 6JL
T: (01600) 890210
F: (01600) 890210

Old Court Hotel ★
Symonds Yat West, Ross-on-Wye, Herefordshire HR9 6DA
T: (01600) 890367
F: (01600) 890964
E: oldcourt@aol.com
I: www.oldcourthotel.com

Royal Hotel ★★
Symonds Yat East, Ross-on-Wye, Herefordshire HR9 6JL
T: (01600) 890238
F: (01600) 890777
E: info@royalhotel-symondsyat.com
I: www.royalhotel-symondsyat.com

Woodlea Country Hotel ★★
Symonds Yat West, Ross-on-Wye, Herefordshire HR9 6BL
T: (01600) 890206
F: (01600) 890206
E: woodlea_hotel@compuserve.com

TELFORD
Shropshire

Arleston Inn Hotel ★★
Arleston Lane, Wellington, Telford, Shropshire TF1 2LA
T: (01952) 501881
F: (01952) 506429

Buckatree Hall Hotel ★★★★
The Wrekin, Wellington, Telford, Shropshire TF6 5AL
T: (01952) 641821
F: (01952) 240564
E: buckatree@macdonald-hotels.co.uk
I: www.macdonaldhotels.co.uk

Hadley Park House Hotel and Bistro ★★★
Hadley Park, Telford, Shropshire TF1 6QJ
T: (01952) 677269
F: (01952) 676938
E: hadley.park@btclick.com

Lea Manor Hotel ★★★
Holyhead Road, Albrighton, Wolverhampton WV7 3BX
T: (01902) 373266
F: (01902) 372853
E: hotel@leamanor.co.uk
I: www.leamanor.co.uk

The Oaks at Redhill ★★
Redhill, St Georges, Telford, Shropshire TF2 9NZ
T: (01952) 620126
F: (01952) 620257
I: www.scoot.oaks/uk.co

TETBURY
Gloucestershire
Calcot Manor ★★★
Beverston, Tetbury,
Gloucestershire GL8 8YJ
T: (01666) 890391
F: (01666) 890394
E: reception@calcotmanor.co.uk
I: www.calcotmanor.co.uk

TETTENHALL WOOD
West Midlands
**Mount Country House Hotel
★★★**
Mount Road, Tettenhall Wood,
Wolverhampton, West Midlands
WV6 8HL
T: (01902) 752055
F: (01902) 745263
I: www.jarvis.co.uk

TEWKESBURY
Gloucestershire
Corse Lawn House Hotel ★★★
Corse Lawn, Gloucester
GL19 4LZ
T: (01452) 780771
F: (01452) 780840
E: hotel@corselawnhouse.
u-net.com
I: www.corselawnhousehotel.
co.uk

**Hilton Puckrup Hall
Tewkesbury ★★★★**
Puckrup, Tewkesbury,
Gloucestershire GL20 6EL
T: (01684) 296200
F: (01684) 850788
E: general.manager@
puckruphall.stakis.co.uk

**Tewkesbury Park Hotel Golf
and Country Club★★★**
Lincoln Green Lane, Tewkesbury,
Gloucestershire GL20 7DN
T: (01684) 295405
F: (01684) 292386
E: tewkesburypark@
corushotels.com
I: www.regalhotels.
co.uk/tewkesburypark

THURLASTON
Warwickshire
**Whitefields Hotel and Golf
Complex Limited★★**
Coventry Road, Thurlaston,
Rugby, Warwickshire CV23 9JR
T: (01788) 521800
F: (01788) 521695
E: mail@whitefields-hotel.co.uk
I: www.whitefield-hotel.co.uk

TUTBURY
Staffordshire
Ye Olde Dog & Partridge Hotel
★★★
High Street, Tutbury, Burton
upon Trent, Staffordshire
DE13 9LS
T: (01283) 813030
F: (01283) 813178
E: info@dogandpartridge.net
I: www.dogandpartridge.net

UPPER SLAUGHTER
Gloucestershire
**Lords of the Manor Hotel
★★★**
Upper Slaughter, Cheltenham,
Gloucestershire GL54 2JD
T: (01451) 820243
F: (01451) 820696
E: lordsofthemanor@btinternet.
com
I: www.lordsofthemanor.com

UPPINGHAM
Rutland
Lake Isle Hotel ★★
16 High Street East, Uppingham,
Oakham, Leicestershire LE15 9PZ
T: (01572) 822951
F: (01572) 822951

UPTON-UPON-SEVERN
Worcestershire
White Lion Hotel ★★★
21 High Street, Upton-upon-
Severn, Worcester WR8 0HJ
T: (01684) 592551
F: (01684) 59333
E: info@whitelionhotel.demon.
co.uk
I: www.whitelion.demon.co.uk

WARWICK
Warwickshire
Chesford Grange Hotel ★★★
Chesford Bridge, Kenilworth,
Warwickshire CV8 2LD
T: (01926) 859331
F: (01926) 859075
E: samanthabrown@
principalhotels
I: www.principalhotels.co.uk

The Glebe at Barford ★★★
Church Street, Barford, Warwick
CV35 8BS
T: (01926) 624218
F: (01926) 624625
E: sales@glebehotel.co.uk
I: www.glebehotel.co.uk

Hilton Warwick ★★★★
A429 Stratford Road, (Junction
15 of M40), Warwick, CV34 6RE
T: (01926) 499555
F: (01926) 410020

The Lord Leycester Hotel
★★★
17 Jury Street, Warwick,
CV34 4EJ
T: (01926) 491481
F: (01926) 491561
E: reception@lord-leycester.
co.uk
I: www.lord-leycester.co.uk

The Old Fourpenny Shop Hotel
★★
27-29 Crompton Street,
Warwick, CV34 6HJ
T: (01926) 491360
F: (01926) 411892

Warwick Arms Hotel ★★
17 High Street, Warwick,
CV34 4AT
T: (01926) 492759
F: (01926) 410587

WATERHOUSES
Staffordshire
**Old Beams Restaurant with
Rooms★★**
Leek Road, Waterhouses, Stoke-
on-Trent ST10 3HW
T: (01538) 308254
F: (01538) 308157
I: www.oldbeamsrestaurant

WELLINGBOROUGH
Northamptonshire
High View Hotel ★★
156 Midland Road,
Wellingborough,
Northamptonshire NN8 1NG
T: (01933) 278733
F: (01933) 225948
E: hotelhighview@hotmail.com

WHATTON
Nottinghamshire
The Haven ★★
Grantham Road, Whatton,
Nottingham NG13 9EU
T: (01949) 850800
F: (01949) 851454

WHITCHURCH
Shropshire
Terrick Hall Hotel & Restaurant
★★★
Terrick Road, Hill Valley,
Whitchurch, Shropshire
SY13 4JZ
T: (01948) 663031
F: (01948) 663020
E: stay@terrickhall.com
I: www.terrickhall.com

WHITNEY-ON-WYE
Worcestershire
The Rhydspence Inn ★★
Whitney-on-Wye, Hereford
HR3 6EU
T: (01497) 831262
F: (01497) 831751

WHITTLEBURY
Northamptonshire
**Whittlebury Hall Hotel,
Management Training Centre,
Hotel and Spa.★★★★**
Whittlebury, Towcester,
Northamptonshire NN12 8QA
T: (01327) 857857
F: (01327) 857867
E: sales@whittleburyhall.co.uk
I: whittleburyhall.co.uk

WISHAW
Warwickshire
The Belfry ★★★★
Wishaw, Sutton Coldfield, West
Midlands B76 9PR
T: (01675) 470301 &
08709 000066
F: (01675) 470256
E: enquiries@thebelfry.com
I: www.thebelfry.com

Moxhull Hall Hotel ★★
Holly Lane, Wishaw, Sutton
Coldfield, West Midlands
B76 9PE
T: (0121) 329 2056
F: (0121) 311 1980
E: john@moxhull-hall.demon.
co.uk

WOLVERHAMPTON
West Midlands
**Novotel Wolverhampton
★★★**
Union Street, Wolverhampton,
WV1 3JN
T: (01902) 871100
F: (01902) 870054
E: h1188@accor-hotels.com
I: www.novotel.com

**Park Hall Hotel and
Conference Centre★★★**
Park Drive, Goldthorn Park,
Wolverhampton WV4 5AJ
T: (01902) 331121
F: (01902) 344760
E: enquiries@parkhallhotel.
co.uk
I: www.parkhallhotel.co.uk

**Patshull Park Hotel, Golf and
Country Club★★★**
Patshull Park, Pattingham,
Wolverhampton, WV6 7HR
T: (01902) 700100
F: (01902) 700874
E: sales@patshull-park.co.uk
I: www.patshull-park.co.uk

WOODHALL SPA
Lincolnshire
Eagle Lodge Hotel ★★
The Broadway, Woodhall Spa,
Lincolnshire LN10 6ST
T: (01526) 353231
F: (01526) 352797
E: enquiries@eaglelodgehotel.
co.uk
I: www.eaglelodgehotel.co.uk

The Golf Hotel ★★★
The Broadway, Woodhall Spa,
Lincolnshire LN10 6SG
T: (01526) 353535
F: (01526) 353096
I: www.principalhotels.co.uk

Petwood Hotel ★★★
Stixwould Road, Woodhall Spa,
Lincolnshire LN10 6QF
T: (01526) 352411
F: (01526) 353473
E: reception@petwood.co.uk
I: www.petwood.co.uk

WORCESTER
Worcestershire
Diglis House Hotel ★★
Riverside, Severn Street,
Worcester, WR1 2NF
T: (01905) 353518
F: (01905) 767772
E: diglishouse@yahoo.com
I: www.diglishousehotel.co.uk

Five Ways Hotel ★★
Angel Place, Worcester,
WR1 3QN
T: (01905) 616980
F: (01905) 616344

**The Hadley Bowling Green Inn
& Country Hotel★★**
Hadley Heath, Droitwich,
Worcestershire WR9 0AR
T: (01905) 620294
F: (01905) 620771
E: hbginn@backissues.freeserve.
co.uk
I: www.english-inns.
co.uk/HadleyBowlingGreen

Severn View Hotel ★★
Newport Street, Worcester,
WR1 3NS
T: (01905) 27600
F: (01905) 612643

Ye Olde Talbot Hotel ★★
Friar Street, Worcester,
WR1 2NA
T: (01905) 23573
F: (01905) 612760

WORKSOP
Nottinghamshire
**Lion Hotel and Restaurant
★★★**
112 Bridge Street, Worksop,
Nottinghamshire S80 1HT
T: (01909) 477925
F: (01909) 479038
E: lionhotel@hotmail.com
I: www.lionhotel.org.uk

EAST OF ENGLAND

ALDEBURGH
Suffolk

The Brudenell Hotel ★★★
The Parade, Aldeburgh, Suffolk
IP15 5BU
T: (01728) 452071
F: (01728) 454082
E: info@brudenellhotel.co.uk
I: www.brudenellhotel.co.uk

Uplands Hotel ★★
Victoria Road, Aldeburgh,
Suffolk IP15 5DX
T: (01728) 452420
F: (01728) 454872
I: www.smoothound.
co.uk/hotels/uplands.html

Wentworth Hotel ★★★
Wentworth Road, Aldeburgh,
Suffolk IP15 5BD
T: (01728) 452312
F: (01728) 454343
E: stay@wentworth-aldeburgh.
co.uk
I: www.wentworth-aldeburgh.
com

White Lion Hotel ★★★
Market Cross Place, Aldeburgh,
Suffolk IP15 5BJ
T: (01728) 452720
F: (01728) 452986
E: whitelionaldeburgh@
btinternet.com
I: www.whitelion.co.uk

AYLMERTON
Norfolk

Roman Camp Inn ★★
Holt Road, Aylmerton, Norwich
NR11 8QD
T: (01263) 838291
F: (01263) 837071

BASILDON
Essex

Campanile Hotel
Travel Accommodation
A127 Southend Arterial Road,
Pipps Hill, Basildon, Essex
SS14 3AE
T: (01268) 530810
F: (01268) 286710

The Chichester Hotel ★★★
Old London Road, Wickford,
Essex SS11 8UE
T: (01268) 560555
F: (01268) 560580

BEDFORD
Bedfordshire

Bedford Swan Hotel ★★★
The Embankment, Bedford,
MK40 1RW
T: (01234) 346565
F: (01234) 212009
E: info@bedfordswanhotel.
co.uk
I: www.bedfordswanhotel.co.uk

BLACK NOTLEY
Essex

Woodlands Manor Hotel ★★
Upper London Road, Black
Notley, Braintree, Essex
CM7 8QN
T: (01245) 361502 & 363201
F: (01245) 363209
I: www.business.thisisessex.
co.uk/woodlands

BLAKENEY
Norfolk

Morston Hall ★★
Morston, Holt, Norfolk
NR25 7AA
T: (01263) 741041
F: (01263) 740419
E: reception@morstonhall.com
I: www.morstonhall.com

The Pheasant Hotel ★★
The Coast Road, Kelling, Holt,
Norfolk NR25 7EG
T: (01263) 588382
F: (01263) 588101
E: enquiries@
pheasanthotelnorfolk.co.uk
I: www.pheasanthotelnorfolk.
co.uk

BRAINTREE
Essex

White Hart Hotel ★★★
Bocking End, Braintree, Essex
CM7 9AB
T: (01376) 321401
F: (01376) 552628
E: geaves@cix.co.uk.
I: www.thewhitehart.
freeserve.co.uk

BRANCASTER STAITHE
Norfolk

The White Horse ★★
Main Road, Brancaster Staithe,
King's Lynn, Norfolk PE31 8BW
T: (01485) 210262
F: (01485) 210930
E: whitehorse.brancaster@
virgin.net
I: www.whitehorsebrancaster.
co.uk

BRENTWOOD
Essex

Marygreen Manor Hotel
★★★★
London Road, Brentwood, Essex
CM14 4NR
T: (01277) 225252
F: (01277) 262809
E: info@marygreenmanor.co.uk
I: www.marygreenmanor.co.uk

New World Hotel ★★
Great Warley Street, Great
Warley, Brentwood, Essex
CM13 3JP
T: (01277) 226418 & 220483
F: (01277) 229795
E: newworldhotel@btinternet.
com
I: www.newworldhotel.co.uk

BUCKDEN
Cambridgeshire

Lion Hotel ★★
High Street, Buckden,
Huntingdon, Cambridgeshire
PE19 5XA
T: (01480) 810313
F: (01480) 811070

BUCKHURST HILL
Essex

**Express By Holiday Inn,
London, Buckhurst Hill**
Travel Accommodation
High Road, Buckhurst Hill, Essex
IG9 5HT
T: (020) 85044450
F: (020) 84980011

BUNGAY
Suffolk

The Kings Head Hotel ★
Market Place, Bungay, Suffolk
NR35 1AF
T: (01986) 893583 & 893582
F: (01986) 893583
E: admin@vintagealecompany.
co.uk
I: www.vintagealecompany.
co.uk

BURNHAM MARKET
Norfolk

The Hoste Arms ★★
The Green, Burnham Market,
King's Lynn, Norfolk PE31 8HD
T: (01328) 738777 & 738257
F: (01328) 730103
E: thehostearms@compuserve.
com
I: www.hostearms.co.uk

BURY ST EDMUNDS
Suffolk

Angel Hotel ★★★
Angel Hill, Bury St Edmunds,
Suffolk IP33 1LT
T: (01284) 714000
F: (01284) 714001
E: sales@theangel.co.uk
I: www.theangel.co.uk

Butterfly Hotel ★★★
A14 Bury East Exit, Moreton
Hall, Bury St Edmunds, Suffolk
IP32 7BW
T: (01284) 760884
F: (01284) 755476
E: burybutterfly@lineone.net
I: www.butterflyhotels.co.uk

The Grange Hotel ★★
Barton Road, Thurston, Bury St
Edmunds, Suffolk IP31 3PQ
T: (01359) 231260
F: (01359) 231387
E: info@thegrangehotel.uk.com
I: www.thegrangehotel.uk.com

**Priory Hotel and Restaurant
★★★**
Fornham Road, Tollgate, Bury St
Edmunds, Suffolk IP32 6EH
T: (01284) 766181
F: (01284) 767604
E: reservations@prioryhotel.
co.uk
I: www.prioryhotel.co.uk

CAMBRIDGE
Cambridgeshire

Arundel House Hotel ★★
Chesterton Road, Cambridge,
CB4 3AN
T: (01223) 367701
F: (01223) 367721
E: info@arundelhousehotels.
co.uk
I: www.arundelhousehotels.
co.uk

Bridge Hotel (Motel) ★
Clayhythe, Waterbeach,
Cambridge CB5 9NZ
T: (01223) 860252
F: (01223) 440448

Centennial Hotel ★★
63-71 Hills Road, Cambridge,
CB2 1PG
T: (01223) 314652
F: (01223) 315443
E: reception@centennialhotel.
co.uk
I: www.centennialhotel.co.uk

**Duxford Lodge Hotel and Le
Paradis Restaurant★★★**
Ickleton Road, Duxford,
Cambridge CB2 4RU
T: (01223) 836444
F: (01223) 832271
E: duxford@btclick.com
I: www.touristnetuk.
com/em/duxford

Gonville Hotel ★★★
Gonville Place, Cambridge,
CB1 1LY
T: (01223) 366611 & 221111
F: (01223) 315470
E: info@gonvillehotel.co.uk
I: www.gonvillehotel.co.uk

Royal Cambridge Hotel ★★★
Trumpington Street, Cambridge,
CB2 1PY
T: (01223) 351631
F: (01223) 352972
E: royalcambridge@
zoffanyhotels.co.uk
I: www.zoffanyhotels.co.uk

Sorrento Hotel ★★
190-196 Cherry Hinton Road,
Cambridge, CB1 7AN
T: (01223) 243533
F: (01223) 213463
E: sorrento-hotel@cb17an.
freeserve.co.uk
I: www.sorrentohotel.com

CHATTERIS
Cambridgeshire

Cross Keys Inn Hotel ★
12-16 Market Hill, Chatteris,
Cambridgeshire PE16 6BA
T: (01354) 693036 & 692644
F: (01354) 694454
E: thefens@crosskeyshotel.
fsnet.co.uk

CHELMSFORD
Essex

Atlantic Hotel ★★★
Brook Street, Off New Street,
Chelmsford, CM1 1PP
T: (01245) 268168
F: (01245) 268169
E: info@atlantichotel.co.uk
I: www.atlantichotel.co.uk

County Hotel ★★★
Rainsford Road, Chelmsford,
CM1 2PZ
T: (01245) 455700
F: (01245) 492762
E: sales@countyhotel-essex.
co.uk
I: www.countyhotel.co.uk

Miami Hotel ★★
Princes Road, Chelmsford,
CM2 9AJ
T: (01245) 264848 & 269603
F: (01245) 259860
E: miamihotel@hotmail.com
I: www.miamihotel.co.uk

Pontlands Park Country Hotel and Conservatory Restaurant ★★★
West Hanningfield Road, Great Baddow, Chelmsford CM2 8HR
T: (01245) 476444 & 478999
F: (01245) 478393
E: sales@pontlandsparkhotel.co.uk
I: www.pontlandsparkhotel.co.uk

Saracens Head Hotel ★★
3-5 High Street, Chelmsford, CM1 1BE
T: (01245) 262368
F: (01245) 262418

Snows Hotel ★
240 Springfield Road, Chelmsford, CM2 6BP
T: (01245) 352004
F: (01245) 356675
E: sales@snowshotel.com
I: www.snowshotel.com

CHESHUNT
Hertfordshire

Cheshunt Marriott Hotel ★★★
Halfhide Lane, Turnford, Broxbourne, Hertfordshire EN10 6NG
T: (01992) 451245
F: (01992) 440120
I: www.marriott.com

CLACTON-ON-SEA
Essex

Chudleigh Hotel ★
Agate Road, Marine Parade West, Clacton-on-Sea, Essex CO15 1RA
T: (01255) 425407
F: (01255) 470280

Esplanade Hotel ★★
27-29 Marine Parade East, Clacton-on-Sea, Essex CO15 1UU
T: (01255) 220450
F: (01255) 221800
E: alex@esplanadehoteluk.com
I: www.esplanadehoteluk.com

COGGESHALL
Essex

The White Hart Hotel ★★
Market End, Coggeshall, Colchester CO6 1NH
T: (01376) 561654
F: (01376) 561789
E: wharthotel@ndirect.co.uk
I: www.whiteharthotelandrestaurant.co.uk

COLCHESTER
Essex

Butterfly Hotel ★★★
A12-A120 Ardleigh Junction, Old Ipswich Road, Colchester, CO7 7QY
T: (01206) 230900
F: (01206) 231095
E: colbutterfly@lineone.net
I: www.butterflyhotels.co.uk

George Hotel ★★★
116 High Street, Colchester, CO1 1TD
T: (01206) 578494
F: (01206) 761732
E: colcgeorge@aol.com
I: www.bestwestern.co.uk

The Lodge ★★
The Essex Golf & Country Club, Earls Colne, Colchester CO6 2NS
T: (01787) 224466
F: (01787) 224410
I: www.clubhaus.com

Quality Hotel Colchester ★★★
East Street, Colchester, CO1 2TS
T: (01206) 865022
F: (01206) 792884
E: qhotel@netscapeonline.co.uk
I: www.qualityhotelcolchester.co.uk

Red Lion Hotel ★★★
43 High Street, Colchester, Essex CO1 1DJ
T: (01206) 577986
F: (01206) 578207
E: redlion@redlionhotel.fsnet.co.uk
I: www.brook-hotels.co.uk

Rose & Crown ★★★
East Street, Colchester, CO1 2TZ
T: (01206) 866677
F: (01206) 866616
E: info@rose-and-crown.com
I: www.rose-and-crown.com

Wivenhoe House Hotel and Conference Centre★★★
Wivenhoe Park, Colchester, CO4 3SQ
T: (01206) 863666
F: (01206) 868532
E: wivsales@essex.ac.uk
I: www.wivenhoehousehotel.co.uk

COLTISHALL
Norfolk

The Norfolk Mead Hotel ★★
Church Loke, Coltishall, Norwich NR12 7DN
T: (01603) 737531
F: (01603) 737521
E: info@norfolkmead.co.uk
I: www.norfolkmead.co.uk

CROMER
Norfolk

Cliftonville Hotel ★★
Seafront, Runton Road, Cromer, Norfolk NR27 9AS
T: (01263) 512543
F: (01263) 515700
E: reservations@cliftonvillehotel.co.uk
I: www.cliftonvillehotel.co.uk

Virginia Court Hotel ★★
Cliff Avenue, Cromer, Norfolk NR27 0AN
T: (01263) 512398
F: (01263) 515529
E: virginiacourt.hotel@virgin.net
I: www.virginiacourt.co.uk

Ye Olde Red Lion Hotel ★★
Brook Street, Cromer, Norfolk NR27 9HD
T: (01263) 514964
F: (01263) 512834

DISS
Norfolk

The Park Hotel ★★
29 Denmark Street, Diss, Norfolk IP22 4LE
T: (01379) 642244
F: (01379) 644218
E: park.hotel@btinternet.com
I: www.eurotrail.com

Scole Inn ★★
Ipswich Road, Scole, Diss, Norfolk IP21 4DR
T: (01379) 740481
F: (01379) 740762

DOVERCOURT
Essex

Tower Hotel ★★
Main Road, Dovercourt, Harwich, Essex CO12 3PJ
T: (01255) 504952
F: (01255) 504952
E: admin@towerharwich.fsnet.co.uk
I: www.a-z-uk.com/towerhotel

DOWNHAM MARKET
Norfolk

Castle Hotel ★★
High Street, Downham Market, Norfolk PE38 9HF
T: (01366) 384311
F: (01366) 384311
E: howard@castle-hotel.com
I: www.castle-hotel.com

DUNSTABLE
Bedfordshire

Old Palace Lodge Hotel ★★★
Church Street, Dunstable, Bedfordshire LU5 4RT
T: (01582) 662201 & 470774
F: (01582) 696422

EAST DEREHAM
Norfolk

The Phoenix Hotel ★★
Church Street, East Dereham, Norfolk NR19 1DL
T: (01362) 692276
F: (01362) 691752
E: enquiries@phoenixhotel.org.uk
I: www.phoenixhotel.org.uk

ELY
Cambridgeshire

Lamb Hotel ★★★
2 Lynn Road, Ely, Cambridgeshire CB7 4EJ
T: (01353) 663574
F: (01353) 662023

EYE
Suffolk

The Cornwallis Country Hotel and Restaurant★★★
Brome, Eye, Suffolk IP23 8AJ
T: (01379) 870326
F: (01379) 870051
E: info@thecornwallis.com
I: www.thecornwallis.com

FAKENHAM
Norfolk

Wensum Lodge Hotel ★★
Bridge Street, Fakenham, Norfolk NR21 9AY
T: (01328) 862100
F: (01328) 863365
I: www.scoot.co.uk/wensum_lodge_hotel/

FELIXSTOWE
Suffolk

Brook Hotel and Carvery ★★
Orwell Road, Felixstowe, Suffolk IP11 7PF
T: (01394) 278441
F: (01394) 670422

Castle Lodge Private Hotel ★
Chevalier Road, Felixstowe, Suffolk IP11 7EY
T: (01394) 282149

Marlborough Hotel ★★
Sea Front, Felixstowe, Suffolk IP11 2BJ
T: (01394) 285621
F: (01394) 670724
E: hsm@marlborough-hotel-felix.com
I: www.marlborough-hotel-felix.com

Waverley Hotel ★★
Wolsey Gardens, Felixstowe, Suffolk IP11 7DF
T: (01394) 282811
F: (01394) 670185

FRINTON-ON-SEA
Essex

The Rock Hotel ★★
The Esplanade, Frinton-on-Sea, Essex CO13 9EQ
T: (01255) 677194 & 0800 0187194
F: (01255) 675173
E: enquiries@therockhotel.co.uk
I: www.therockhotel.co.uk

GORLESTON-ON-SEA
Norfolk

Cliff Hotel ★★★
Cliff Hill, Gorleston-on-Sea, Great Yarmouth, Norfolk NR31 6BN
T: (01493) 662179
F: (01493) 653617

Pier Hotel ★★
Harbour Mouth, Gorleston-on-Sea, Great Yarmouth, Norfolk NR31 6PL
T: (01493) 662631
F: (01493) 440263

GREAT CHESTERFORD
Essex

Crown House ★★
Great Chesterford, Saffron Walden, Essex CB10 1NY
T: (01799) 530515
F: (01799) 530683
I: www.virtualhotels.com/crown-house

GREAT YARMOUTH
Norfolk

Burlington Palm Court Hotel ★★
North Drive, Great Yarmouth, Norfolk NR30 1EG
T: (01493) 844568
F: (01493) 331848
E: enquiries@burlington-hotel.co.uk
I: www.burlington-hotel.co.uk

Hotel Elizabeth ★★
1 Marine Parade, Great Yarmouth, Norfolk NR30 3AG
T: (01493) 855551
F: (01493) 853338
E: enquires@hotelelizabeth.co.uk
I: www.hotelelizabeth.co.uk

Embassy Hotel ★★
38-41 Camperdown, Great Yarmouth, Norfolk NR30 3JB
T: (01493) 843135
F: (01493) 331064
I: www.embassy-hotel.co.uk

Furzedown Private Hotel ★★
19-20 North Drive, Great Yarmouth, Norfolk NR30 4EW
T: (01493) 844138
F: (01493) 844138

Establishments printed in blue have a detailed entry in this guide

Horse & Groom Motel ★★
Rollesby, Great Yarmouth,
Norfolk NR29 5ER
T: (01493) 740624
F: (01493) 740022
E: bookings@horsegroommotel.
co.uk
I: www.horsegroommotel.co.uk

Imperial Hotel ★★★
North Drive, Great Yarmouth,
Norfolk NR30 1EQ
T: (01493) 842000
F: (01493) 852229
E: imperial@scs-datacom.co.uk
I: www.imperialhotel.co.uk

Regency Dolphin Hotel ★★★
Albert Square, Great Yarmouth,
Norfolk NR30 3JH
T: (01493) 855070
F: (01493) 853798
E: regency@meridianleisure.
com
I: www.meridianleisure.com

Regency Private Hotel ★★
5 North Drive, Great Yarmouth,
Norfolk NR30 1ED
T: (01493) 843759
F: (01493) 330411
E: regency35@hotmail.com
I: www.norfolkregency.co.uk

HARPENDEN
Hertfordshire

Hanover International Hotel ★★★
Luton Road, Harpenden,
Hertfordshire AL5 2PX
T: (01582) 760271 & 464513
F: (01582) 460819
E: david.hunter9@virgin.net
I: www.hanover.international.
com

HARWICH
Essex

Cliff Hotel ★★
Marine Parade, Dovercourt,
Harwich, Essex CO12 3RE
T: (01255) 503345 & 507373
F: (01255) 240358
E: johnwade@
fsbusinessharwich.co.uk
I: www.cliffhotelharwich.co.uk

The Hotel Continental ★★
28-29 Marine Parade,
Dovercourt, Harwich, Essex
CO12 3RG
T: (01255) 551298 &
07770 308976
F: (01255) 551698
E: hotconti@aol.com
I: www.
hotelcontinental-harwich.co.uk

The Pier at Harwich ★★★
The Quay, Harwich, Essex
CO12 3HH
T: (01255) 241212
F: (01255) 551922
E: info@thepieratharwich.co.uk
I: www.pieratharwich.com

HATFIELD
Hertfordshire

Hatfield Lodge Hotel ★★★
Comet Way, Hatfield,
Hertfordshire AL10 9NG
T: (01707) 288500
F: (01707) 256282
E: beales-hatfieldlodge@
compuserve.com
I: www.bealeshotels.co.uk

Jarvis International Hotel ★★★
St Albans Road West, Hatfield,
Hertfordshire AL10 9RH
T: (01707) 265411
F: (01707) 264019
E: rs42@jarvis.co.uk
I: www.jarvis.co.uk

Quality Hotel Hatfield ★★★
Roehyde Way, Hatfield,
Hertfordshire AL10 9AF
T: (01707) 275701
F: (01707) 266033
E: admin@q59.u-net.com
I: www.choicehotelseurope.com

HATFIELD HEATH
Essex

Down Hall Country House Hotel ★★★★
Hatfield Heath, Bishop's
Stortford, Hertfordshire
CM22 7AS
T: (01279) 731441
F: (01279) 730416
E: reservations@downhall.
demon.co.uk
I: www.downhall.co.uk

HERTFORD
Hertfordshire

The Ponsbourne Park Hotel ★★★★
Newgate Street Village,
Hertford, SG13 8QZ
T: (01707) 876191 & 879300
F: (01707) 875190
E: ponsbournepark@lineone.net
I: www.ponsbournepark.com

Salisbury Arms Hotel ★★
Fore Street, Hertford, SG14 1BZ
T: (01992) 583091
F: (01992) 552510

HEYBRIDGE
Essex

Benbridge Hotel ★★
The Square, Heybridge, Maldon,
Essex CM9 4LT
T: (01621) 857666
F: (01621) 841966
E: helen@cbn.co.uk
I: www.minotel.com

HILLINGTON
Norfolk

Ffolkes Arms Hotel ★★
Lynn Road, Hillington, King's
Lynn, Norfolk PE31 6BJ
T: (01485) 600210
F: (01485) 601196
E: ffolkespub@aol.com
I: www.ffolkes-arms-hotel.co.uk

HINTLESHAM
Suffolk

Hintlesham Hall ★★★★
Hintlesham, Ipswich IP8 3NS
T: (01473) 652334 & 652268
F: (01473) 652463
E: hintleshamhall.com
I: www.hintleshamhall.com

HITCHIN
Hertfordshire

Firs Hotel ★
83 Bedford Road, Hitchin,
Hertfordshire SG5 2TY
T: (01462) 422322
F: (01462) 432051
E: info@firshotel.co.uk
I: www.firshotel.co.uk

HORNING
Norfolk

Petersfield House Hotel ★★★
Lower Street, Horning, Norwich
NR12 8PF
T: (01692) 630741
F: (01692) 630745
E: reception@petersfieldhotel.
co.uk
I: www.petersfieldhotel.co.uk

HUNSTANTON
Norfolk

Caley Hall Motel and Restaurant ★★
Old Hunstanton, Hunstanton,
Norfolk PE36 6HH
T: (01485) 533486
F: (01485) 533348

The Golden Lion Hotel ★★
The Green, Hunstanton, Norfolk
PE36 6BQ
T: (01485) 532688
F: (01485) 535310
E: enquiries@hunstanton-hotel.
co.uk

Le Strange Arms Hotel ★★★
Golf Course Road, Old
Hunstanton, Hunstanton,
Norfolk PE36 6JJ
T: (01485) 534411
F: (01485) 534724
E: reception@lestrangearms.
co.uk
I: www.abacushotels.co.uk

The Lodge Hotel ★★
Old Hunstanton, Hunstanton,
Norfolk PE36 6HX
T: (01485) 532896
F: (01485) 535007
E: reception@thelodge-hotel.
co.uk
I: www.thelodge-hotel.co.uk

HUNTINGDON
Cambridgeshire

Huntingdon Marriott ★★★★
Kingfisher Way, Hinchingbrooke
Business Park, Huntingdon,
Cambridgeshire PE29 6FL
T: (01480) 446000
F: (01480) 451111
E: huntingdon@marriotthotels.
co.uk
I: www.marriotthotels.
com/cbghd

Old Bridge Hotel ★★★
1 High Street, Huntingdon,
Cambridgeshire PE29 3TQ
T: (01480) 424300
F: (01480) 411017
E: oldbridge@huntsbridge.co.uk

INGATESTONE
Essex

The Heybridge Hotel ★★★
Roman Road, Ingatestone, Essex
CM4 9AB
T: (01277) 355355
F: (01277) 353288

IPSWICH
Suffolk

Claydon Country House Hotel and Restaurant★★
Ipswich Road, Claydon, Ipswich
IP6 0AR
T: (01473) 830382
F: (01473) 832476
E: kayshotels@aol.com
I: www.hotelsipswich.com

Courtyard By Marriott Ipswich ★★★
The Havens, Ransomes Europark,
Ipswich, IP3 9SJ
T: (01473) 272244
F: (01473) 272484
I: www.marriotthotels.com

Ipswich County Hotel ★★★
London Road, Copdock, Ipswich
IP8 3JD
T: (01473) 209988
F: (01473) 730801
E: county.ipswich@corushotels.
com
I: www.
corushotels.com/ipswichcounty

The Marlborough at Ipswich ★★★
Henley Road, Ipswich, IP1 3SP
T: (01473) 257677
F: (01473) 226927
E: reception@themarlborough.
co.uk
I: www.the marlborough.co.uk

Novotel Ipswich ★★★
Greyfriars Road, Ipswich,
IP1 1UP
T: (01473) 232400
F: (01473) 232414
E: h0995@accor-hotels.com
I: www.novotel.com

Swallow Belstead Brook Hotel ★★★
Belstead Road, Ipswich, IP2 9HB
T: (01473) 684241
F: (01473) 681249
E: sales@belsteadbrook.co.uk
I: www.belsteadbrook.co.uk

KING'S LYNN
Norfolk

Butterfly Hotel ★★★
A10-A47 Roundabout, Hardwick
Narrows, King's Lynn, Norfolk
PE30 4NB
T: (01553) 771707
F: (01553) 768027
E: kingsbutterfly@lineone.net
I: www.butterflyhotels.co.uk

Congham Hall Country House Hotel ★★★
Lynn Road, Grimston, King's
Lynn, Norfolk PE32 1AH
T: (01485) 600250
F: (01485) 601191
E: reception@
conghamhall.co.uk
I: www.conghamhallhotel.co.uk

Knights Hill Hotel ★★★
South Wootton, King's Lynn,
Norfolk PE30 3HQ
T: (01553) 675566
F: (01553) 675568
E: reception@knightshill.co.uk
I: www.abacushotels.co.uk

Park View Hotel ★★
Blackfriars Street, King's Lynn,
Norfolk PE30 1NN
T: (01553) 775146
F: (01553) 766957
E: info@hotel-parkview.com
I: www.hotel-parkview.com

Stuart House Hotel ★★
35 Goodwins Road, King's Lynn,
Norfolk PE30 5QX
T: (01553) 772169
F: (01553) 774788
E: stuarthousehotel@btinternet.
com
I: www.
stuart-house-hotel-co.uk

The Tudor Rose Hotel ★★
St Nicholas Street, Off Tuesday
Market Place, King's Lynn,
Norfolk PE30 1LR
T: (01553) 762824
F: (01553) 764894
E: kltudorrose@aol.com
I: www.tudorrose-hotel.co.uk

LEAVENHEATH
Suffolk

**The Stoke by Nayland Club
Hotel ★★★**
Keepers Lane, Leavenheath,
Colchester, Essex CO6 4PZ
T: (01206) 262836
F: (01206) 263356
E: info@golf-club.co.uk
I: www.stokebynaylandclub.
co.uk

LEISTON
Suffolk

White Horse Hotel ★
Station Road, Leiston, Suffolk
IP16 4HD
T: (01728) 830694
F: (01728) 833105
E: whihorse@globalnet.co.uk
I: www.whitehorsehotel.co.uk

LETCHWORTH
Hertfordshire

Letchworth Hall Hotel ★★★
Letchworth Lane, Letchworth,
Hertfordshire SG6 3NP
T: (01462) 683747
F: (01462) 481540
I: www.aquarius-hotels.com

LOWESTOFT
Suffolk

Hotel Hatfield ★★★
The Esplanade, Lowestoft,
Suffolk NR33 0QG
T: (01502) 565337
F: (01502) 511885

Ivy House Farm Hotel ★★★
Ivy Lane, Oulton Broad,
Lowestoft, Suffolk NR33 8HY
T: (01502) 601353 & 588144
F: (01502) 501539
E: admin@ivyhousefarm.co.uk
I: www.ivyhousefarm.co.uk

Hotel Victoria ★★★
Kirkley Cliff, Lowestoft, Suffolk
NR33 0BZ
T: (01502) 574433
F: (01502) 501529
E: info@hotelvictoria.freeserve.
co.uk
I: www.hotelvictoria.freeserve.
co.uk

MALDON
Essex

**Five Lakes Hotel, Golf, Country
Club & Spa ★★★★**
Colchester Road, Tolleshunt
Knights, Maldon, Essex CM9 8HX
T: (01621) 868888
F: (01621) 869696
E: enquiries@fivelakes.co.uk
I: www.fivelakes.co.uk

MARCH
Cambridgeshire

Olde Griffin Hotel Ltd ★★
High Street, March,
Cambridgeshire PE15 9JS
T: (01354) 652517
F: (01354) 650086
E: griffhotel@aol.com

**Oliver Cromwell Hotel
Rating Applied For**
High Street, March,
Cambridgeshire PE15 9LH
T: (01354) 602890
F: (01354) 602891
E: reception@
olivercromwellhotel.fsnet
I: www.olivercromwellhotels.
co.uk

MARKS TEY
Essex

Marks Tey Hotel ★★★
London Road, Marks Tey,
Colchester CO6 1DU
T: (01206) 210001
F: (01206) 212167
E: info@marksteyhotel.co.uk
I: www.marksteyhotel.co.uk

MILDENHALL
Suffolk

Riverside Hotel ★★★
Mill Street, Mildenhall, Bury St
Edmunds, Suffolk IP28 7DP
T: (01638) 717274
F: (01638) 715997
E: bookings@riverside-hotel.net
I: www.riverside-hotel.net

The Smoke House ★★★
Beck Row, Bury St Edmunds,
Suffolk IP28 8DH
T: (01638) 713223
F: (01638) 712202
E: enquiries@smoke-house.
co.uk
I: www.smoke-house.co.uk

NEEDHAM MARKET
Suffolk

The Limes Hotel ★★★
High Street, Needham Market,
Ipswich IP6 8DQ
T: (01449) 720305
F: (01449) 722233
E: limes@enterprise.net

NEWMARKET
Suffolk

Heath Court Hotel ★★★
Moulton Road, Newmarket,
Suffolk CB8 8DY
T: (01638) 667171
F: (01638) 666533
E: quality@heathcourt-hotel.
co.uk
I: www.heathcourt-hotel.co.uk

The Rutland Arms Hotel ★★★
High Street, Newmarket, Suffolk
CB8 8NB
T: (01638) 664251
F: (01638) 666298
E: rutlandarms.co.uk
I: www.rutlandarms.com

**Swynford Paddocks Hotel
★★★**
Six Mile Bottom, Newmarket,
Suffolk CB8 0UE
T: (01638) 570234
F: (01638) 570283
E: sales@swynfordpaddocks.
com
I: www.swynfordpaddocks.com

NORTH WALSHAM
Norfolk

Beechwood Hotel ★★
20 Cromer Road, North
Walsham, Norfolk NR28 0HD
T: (01692) 403231
F: (01692) 407284
E: enquiries@beechwood-hotel.
co.uk
I: beechwood-hotel.co.uk

**Elderton Lodge Hotel and
Langtry Restaurant ★★**
Gunton Park, Thorpe Market,
Norwich NR11 8TZ
T: (01263) 833547
F: (01263) 834673
E: enquiries@eldertonlodge.
co.uk
I: www.eldertonlodge.co.uk

**Scarborough Hill Country
House Hotel ★★**
Old Yarmouth Road, North
Walsham, Norfolk NR28 9NA
T: (01692) 402151
F: (01692) 406686

NORWICH
Norfolk

Annesley House Hotel ★★★
6 Newmarket Road, Norwich,
NR2 2LA
T: (01603) 624553
F: (01603) 621577

**Barnham Broom Hotel, Golf,
Conference & Leisure Centre
★★★**
Honingham Road, Barnham
Broom, Norwich NR9 4DD
T: (01603) 759393 & 759552
F: (01603) 758224
E: enquiry@
barnhambroomhotel.co.uk
I: www.barnham-broom.co.uk

Beeches Hotel ★★★
2-6 Earlham Road, Norwich,
NR2 3DB
T: (01603) 621167 & 667357
F: (01603) 620151
E: reception@beeches.co.uk
I: www.beeches.co.uk

**De Vere Dunston Hall Hotel
★★★★**
Ipswich Road, Norwich,
NR14 8PQ
T: (01508) 470444
F: (01508) 471499
E: dhreception@devere-hotels.
com
I: www.devereonline.co.uk

The Georgian House Hotel ★★
32-34 Unthank Road, Norwich,
NR2 2RB
T: (01603) 615655
F: (01603) 765689
E: reception@georgian-hotel.
co.uk
I: georgian-hotel.co.uk

**Marriott Sprowston Manor
Hotel & Country Club ★★★★**
Sprowston Park, Wroxham Road,
Norwich, NR7 8RP
T: (01603) 410871
F: (01603) 423911
I: www.marriotthotels.co.uk

Old Rectory ★★
North Walsham Road,
Crostwick, Norwich NR12 7BG
T: (01603) 738513
F: (01603) 738712
E: info@therectoryhotel.fsnet.
co.uk
I: www.oldrectorycrostwick.com

The Old Rectory ★★
103 Yarmouth Road, Thorpe St
Andrew, Norwich, NR7 0HF
T: (01603) 700772
F: (01603) 300772
E: enquiries@
oldrectorynorwich.com
I: www.oldrectorynorwich.com

**Park Farm Country Hotel &
Leisure ★★★**
Hethersett, Norwich NR9 3DL
T: (01603) 810264
F: (01603) 812104
E: enq@parkfarm-hotel.co.uk
I: www.parkfarm-hotel.co.uk

Pearl Continental Hotel ★★
116 Thorpe Road, Norwich,
NR1 1RU
T: (01603) 620302
F: (01603) 761706
E: info@pc-hotels.co.uk
I: www.pc-hotels.co.uk

Quality Hotel Norwich ★★★
2 Barnard Road, Bowthorpe,
Norwich, NR5 9JB
T: (01603) 741161
F: (01603) 741500
E: admin@gb619.u-net.com
I: www.qualityinn.
com/hotel/gb619

Swallow Hotel Nelson ★★★
Prince of Wales Road, Norwich,
NR1 1DX
T: (01603) 760260
F: (01603) 620008
I: www.swallowhotels.com

OULTON BROAD
Suffolk

Broadlands Hotel ★★
56-58 Bridge Road, Oulton
Broad, Lowestoft, Suffolk
NR32 3LN
T: (01502) 516031 & 572157
F: (01502) 501454
E: broadlandshotel@
netscapeonline.co.uk

OVERSTRAND
Norfolk

Sea Marge Hotel ★★★
16 High Street, Overstrand,
Cromer, Norfolk NR27 0AB
T: (01263) 579579
F: (01263) 579524
I: www.mackenziehotels.com

PAPWORTH EVERARD
Cambridgeshire

Papworth Hotel ★★
Ermine Street South, Papworth
Everard, Cambridge CB3 8PB
T: (01954) 718851
F: (01954) 718069

PETERBOROUGH
Cambridgeshire

The Bell Inn Hotel ★★★
Great North Road, Stilton,
Peterborough PE7 3RA
T: (01733) 241066
F: (01733) 245173
E: reception@thebellstilton.
co.uk
I: www.thebellstilton.co.uk

Butterfly Hotel ★★★
Thorpe Meadows, Off
Longthorpe Parkway,
Peterborough, PE3 6GA
T: (01733) 564240
F: (01733) 565538
E: peterbutterfly@lineone.net
I: www.butterflyhotels.co.uk

Orton Hall Hotel ★★★
The Village, Orton Longueville,
Peterborough, PE2 7DN
T: (01733) 391111
F: (01733) 231912
E: reception@ortonhall.co.uk
I: www.abacushotels.co.uk

The Peterborough Marriott
★★★★
Peterborough Business Park,
Lynch Wood, Peterborough,
PE2 6GB
T: (01733) 371111
F: (01733) 236725
E: Reservations.Peterborough@
marriotthotels.co.uk
I: www.marriotthotels.co.uk

Peterborough Moat House
★★★
Thorpe Wood, Peterborough,
PE3 6SG
T: (01733) 289988 & 289900
F: (01733) 262737
E: revptb@queensmoat.co.uk
I: www.moathousehotels.com

Queensgate Hotel ★★
5 Fletton Avenue, Peterborough,
PE2 8AX
T: (01733) 562572
F: (01733) 558982
E: reservations@
thequeensgatehotel.co.uk
I: www.thequeensgatehotel.
co.uk

Talbot Hotel ★★★
New Street, Oundle,
Peterborough, PE8 4EA
T: (01832) 273621
F: (01832) 274545

**Thomas Cook Bluebell Lodge
Leisure Centre**★★
P O Box 36, Thorpe Wood,
Peterborough, PE3 6SB
T: (01733) 502555 & 503008
F: (01733) 502020
E: leisurecentre.general@
trauelex.com

ST ALBANS
Hertfordshire

The Apples Hotel ★★
133 London Road, St Albans,
Hertfordshire AL1 1TA
T: (01727) 844111
F: (01727) 861100

Avalon Hotel ★★
260 London Road, St Albans,
Hertfordshire AL1 1TJ
T: (01727) 856757
F: (01727) 856750
E: hotelavalon@aol.com
I: www.avalonhotel.net

Jarvis International Hotel
★★★
Hemel Hempstead Road,
Redbourn, Hemel Hempstead,
Hertfordshire AL3 7AF
T: (01582) 792105
F: (01582) 792001
I: www.jarvis.co.uk

**Saint Michaels Manor St
Michaels Village**★★★
Fishpool Street, St Albans,
Hertfordshire AL3 4RY
T: (01727) 864444
F: (01727) 848909
E: smmanor@globalnet.co.uk
I: www.stmichaelsmanor.com

**Sopwell House Hotel, Country
Club and Spa**★★★★
Cottonmill Lane, Sopwell, St
Albans, Hertfordshire AL1 2HQ
T: (01727) 864477
F: (01727) 844741
E: enquiries@sopwellhouse.
co.uk
I: www.sopwellhouse.co.uk

ST IVES
Cambridgeshire

The Dolphin Hotel ★★★
Bridgefoot, London Road, St
Ives, Huntingdon,
Cambridgeshire PE27 6EP
T: (01480) 466966
F: (01480) 495597
I: www.dolphinhotelcambs.co.uk

Olivers Lodge Hotel ★★★
Needingworth Road, St Ives,
Huntingdon, Cambridgeshire
PE27 5JP
T: (01480) 463252
F: (01480) 461150
E: reception@oliverslodge.co.uk
I: www.oliverslodge.co.uk

Slepe Hall Hotel ★★★
Ramsey Road, St Ives,
Huntingdon, Cambridgeshire
PE27 5RB
T: (01480) 463122
F: (01480) 300706
E: mail@slepehall.co.uk
I: www.slepehall.co.uk

ST NEOTS
Cambridgeshire

**Abbotsley Golf Hotel &
Country Club** ★★
Eynesbury Hardwicke, St Neots,
Huntingdon, Cambridgeshire
PE19 6XN
T: (01480) 474000
F: (01480) 471018
E: abbotsley@americangolf.uk.
com

SAWBRIDGEWORTH
Hertfordshire

**The Manor of Groves Hotel
Golf and Country Club**★★
High Wych, Sawbridgeworth,
Hertfordshire CM21 0LA
T: (01279) 600777 & 722333
F: (01279) 600374
E: info@manorofgroves.com
I: www.manorofgroves.com

SHERINGHAM
Norfolk

Beaumaris Hotel ★★
15 South Street, Sheringham,
Norfolk NR26 8LL
T: (01263) 822370
F: (01263) 821421
E: beauhotel@aol.com
I: www.ecn.co.uk/beaumaris/

Southlands Hotel ★★
South Street, Sheringham,
Norfolk NR26 8LL
T: (01263) 822679
F: (01263) 822679

SHOTTISHAM
Suffolk

**Wood Hall Country House
Hotel** ★★★
Shottisham, Woodbridge,
Suffolk IP12 3EG
T: (01394) 411283
F: (01394) 410007
I: www.woodhall.uk.com

SOUTHEND-ON-SEA
Essex

Camelia Hotel and Restaurant
★★
178 Eastern Esplanade, Thorpe
Bay, Southend-on-Sea, SS1 3AA
T: (01702) 587917
F: (01702) 585704
E: cameliahotel@fsbdial.co.uk
I: www.cameliahotel.co.uk

The Essex County Hotel ★★★
Aviation Way, Southend-on-Sea,
SS2 6UN
T: (01702) 279955
F: (01702) 541961
E: mail@essexcountyhotel.fsnet.
co.uk

Roslin Hotel ★★★
Thorpe Esplanade, Thorpe Bay,
Southend-on-Sea, SS1 3BG
T: (01702) 586375
F: (01702) 586663
E: frontoffice@roslinhotel.
demon.co.uk
I: www.roslinhotel.com

Tower Hotel and Restaurant
★★
146 Alexandra Road, Southend-
on-Sea, SS1 1HE
T: (01702) 348635
F: (01702) 433044

SOUTHWOLD
Suffolk

The Crown ★★
High Street, Southwold, Suffolk
IP18 6DP
T: (01502) 722275
F: (01502) 727263
E: crownreception@adnams.
co.uk

Swan Hotel ★★★
Market Place, Southwold,
Suffolk IP18 6EG
T: (01502) 722186
F: (01502) 724800
E: swan.hotel@adnams.co.uk
I: www.adnams.co.uk

SPROUGHTON
Suffolk

Express By Holiday Inn Ipswich
Travel Accommodation
Old Hadleigh Road, Sproughton,
Ipswich IP8 3AR
T: (01473) 222279
F: (01473) 222297

STALHAM
Norfolk

Wayford Bridge Hotel ★★★
Wayford Bridge, Stalham,
Norwich NR12 9LL
T: (01692) 582414
F: (01692) 581109
E: wayford-bridge-hotel@
fsmail.net
I: wayford-bridge-hotel.co.uk

STANSTED
Essex

The Vintage Court Hotel ★★★
Puckeridge, Ware, Hertfordshire
SG11 1SA
T: (01920) 822722
F: (01920) 822877

STOWMARKET
Suffolk

Cedars Hotel ★★
Needham Road, Stowmarket,
Suffolk IP14 2AJ
T: (01449) 612668
F: (01449) 674704
E: enquiries@cedarshotel.co.uk
I: www.cedarshotel.co.uk

SWAFFHAM
Norfolk

George Hotel ★★★
Station Street, Swaffham,
Norfolk PE37 7LJ
T: (01760) 721238
F: (01760) 725333
E: georgehotel@bestwestern.
co.uk
I: www.bestwestern.co.uk

Lydney House Hotel ★★
Norwich Road, Swaffham,
Norfolk PE37 7QS
T: (01760) 723355
F: (01760) 721410
E: rooms@lydney-house.
demon.co.uk
I: www.lydney-house.demon.
co.uk

TAVERHAM
Norfolk

**Wensum Valley Hotel, Golf &
Country Club**★★
Beech Avenue, Taverham,
Norwich NR8 6HP
T: (01603) 261012
F: (01603) 261664
E: enqs@wensumvalley.co.uk
I: www.wensumvalley.co.uk or
www.wensumvalley.co.uk

THETFORD
Norfolk

The Bell Hotel ★★★
King Street, Thetford, Norfolk
IP24 2AZ
T: (01842) 754455
F: (01842) 755552
E: thetbell@aol.com
I: www.oldenglish.co.uk

The Thomas Paine Hotel ★★
White Hart Street, Thetford,
Norfolk IP24 1AA
T: (01842) 755631
F: (01842) 766505
E: thomaspainehotel@
netscapeonline.co.uk
I: www.ecn.
co.uk/thomaspainehotel./

THORNHAM
Norfolk

The Lifeboat Inn ★★
Ship Lane, Thornham,
Hunstanton, Norfolk PE36 6LT
T: (01485) 512236
F: (01485) 512323
E: reception@lifeboatinn.co.uk
I: www.lifeboatinn.co.uk

THORPENESS
Suffolk

Thorpeness Hotel & Golf Club ★★
Lakeside Avenue, Thorpeness, Leiston, Suffolk IP16 4NH
T: (01728) 452176 & 454926
F: (01728) 453868
E: info@thorpeness.co.uk.
I: www.thorpeness.co.uk

TITCHWELL
Norfolk

Briarfields Hotel ★★
Main Street, Titchwell, King's Lynn, Norfolk PE31 8BB
T: (01485) 210742
F: (01485) 210933
E: briarfields@norfolk-hotels.co.uk

TIVETSHALL ST MARY
Norfolk

The Old Ram Coaching Inn ★★
Ipswich Road, Tivetshall St Mary, Norwich NR15 2DE
T: (01379) 676794
F: (01379) 608399
E: theoldram@btinternet.com
I: www.theoldram.com

UPPER SHERINGHAM
Norfolk

**The Dales Hotel
Rating Applied For**
Lodge Hill, Upper Sheringham, Sheringham, Norfolk NR26 8TJ
T: (01263) 824555
F: (01263) 822647

WALTHAM ABBEY
Essex

Marriott Hotel ★★★★
Old Shire Lane, Waltham Abbey, Essex EN9 3LX
T: (01992) 717170
F: (01992) 711841
E: waltham.abbey@marriott-hotels.co.uk.
I: www.marriott.com

WANSFORD
Cambridgeshire

Haycock Hotel ★★★
Wansford, Peterborough PE8 6JA
T: (01780) 782223
F: (01780) 783031
E: events.haycock@arcadianhotels.co.uk

WARE
Hertfordshire

Briggens House Hotel ★★★★
Briggens Park, Stanstead Road (A414), Stanstead Abbotts, Ware, Hertfordshire SG12 8LD
T: (01279) 829955
F: (01279) 793685
E: reservations@corushotels.com
I: www.corushotels.com

Marriott Hanbury Manor Hotel & Country Club ★★★★★
Ware, Hertfordshire SG12 0SD
T: (01920) 487722
F: (01920) 487692
E: angela.thurlow@marriotthotels.co.uk
I: www.marriott.com/marriott.stngs

Roebuck Hotel ★★★
Baldock Street, Ware, Hertfordshire SG12 9DR
T: (01920) 409955
F: (01920) 468016
E: roebuck@zoffanyhotels.co.uk
I: www.zoffanyhotels.co.uk

WEST RUNTON
Norfolk

Dormy House Hotel ★★
Cromer Road, West Runton, Norfolk NR27 9QA
T: (01263) 837537
F: (01263) 837537
E: j.jjarvis@freenetname.co.uk

The Links Country Park Hotel and Golf Club ★★★
Sandy Lane, West Runton, Cromer, Norfolk NR27 9QH
T: (01263) 838383
F: (01263) 838264
E: sales@links-hotel.co.uk
I: www.links-hotel.co.uk

WESTCLIFF-ON-SEA
Essex

Erlsmere Hotel ★★
24-32 Pembury Road, Westcliff-on-Sea, Essex SS0 8DS
T: (01702) 349025
F: (01702) 337724

Westcliff Hotel ★★★
Westcliff Parade, Westcliff-on-Sea, Essex SS0 7QW
T: (01702) 345247
F: (01702) 431814
E: westcliff@zoffanyhotels.co.uk
I: www.zoffanyhotels.co.uk

WISBECH
Cambridgeshire

Crown Lodge Hotel ★★
Downham Road, Outwell, Wisbech, Cambridgeshire PE14 8SE
T: (01945) 773391 & 772206
F: (01945) 772668
E: crownlodgehotel@hotmail.com
I: www.smoothhound.co.uk/hotels/crownl.html

Rose and Crown Hotel ★★
23/24 Market Place, Wisbech, Cambridgeshire PE13 1DG
T: (01945) 589800
F: (01945) 474610
E: randcwisbech@aol.com
I: www.roseandcrown.sagenet.co.uk

WITHAM
Essex

Jarvis Rivenhall Hotel ★★★
Rivenhall End, Witham, Essex CM8 3HB
T: (01376) 516969 & 0845 7303040
F: (01376) 513674
I: www.jarvis.co.uk

WOBURN
Bedfordshire

The Bedford Arms ★★★
George Street, Woburn, Milton Keynes MK17 9PX
T: (01525) 290441
F: (01525) 290432

WOODBRIDGE
Suffolk

Bull Hotel ★★
Market Hill, Woodbridge, Suffolk IP12 4LR
T: (01394) 382089 & 385688
F: (01394) 384902
E: reception@bullhotel.co.uk
I: www.bullhotel.co.uk

Seckford Hall Hotel ★★★
Woodbridge, Suffolk IP13 6NU
T: (01394) 385678
F: (01394) 380610
E: reception@seckford.co.uk
I: www.seckford.co.uk

Ufford Park Hotel Golf & Leisure ★★★
Yarmouth Road, Ufford, Woodbridge, Suffolk IP12 1QW
T: (01394) 383555
F: (01394) 383582
E: uffordparkltd@btinternet.com
I: uffordpark.co.uk

WROXHAM
Norfolk

The Broads Hotel ★★
Station Road, Wroxham, Norwich NR12 8UR
T: (01603) 782869 & 784157
F: (01603) 784066

Hotel Wroxham ★★
The Bridge, Wroxham, Norwich NR12 8AJ
T: (01603) 782061
F: (01603) 784279
I: www.hotelwroxham.co.uk

WYMONDHAM
Norfolk

Wymondham Consort Hotel ★★
28 Market Street, Wymondham, Norfolk NR18 0BB
T: (01953) 606721
F: (01953) 601361
E: wymondham@bestwestern.co.uk
I: www.hotelnet.co.uk/wymondham

YOXFORD
Suffolk

Satis House Hotel and Restaurant ★★
Yoxford, Saxmundham, Suffolk IP17 3EX
T: (01728) 668418
F: (01728) 668640
E: y.blackmore@aol.com

SOUTH WEST

ALCOMBE
Somerset

Alcombe House Hotel ★★
Bircham Road, Alcombe, Minehead, Somerset TA24 6BG
T: (01643) 705130
F: (01643) 705130
E: alcombe.house@virgin.net
I: www.alcombehouse.co.uk

ASH
Somerset

Ash House & Restaurant ★★★
41 Main Street, Ash, Martock, Somerset TA12 6PB
T: (01935) 823126 & 822036
F: (01935) 822992
E: reception@ashhousecountryhotel.co.uk
I: www.ashhousecountryhotel.co.uk

AXMINSTER
Devon

Lea Hill Hotel ★★
Membury, Axminster, Devon EX13 7AQ
T: (01404) 881881 & 881388
F: (01404) 881890
E: reception@leahillhotel.co.uk
I: www.leahillhotel.co.uk

BABBACOMBE
Devon

Exmouth View Hotel ★★
St Albans Road, Babbacombe, Torquay TQ1 3LG
T: 0800 7817817 & (01803) 327307
F: (01803) 329967
E: relax@exmouth-view.co.uk
I: www.exmouth-view.co.uk

Sefton Hotel ★★
Babbacombe Downs Road, Babbacombe, Torquay TQ1 3LH
T: (01803) 326591
F: (01803) 213860

BARNSTAPLE
Devon

Barnstaple Hotel ★★★
Braunton Road, Barnstaple,
Devon EX31 1LE
T: (01271) 376221
F: (01271) 324101

Downrew House Hotel and Restaurant ★★
Bishop's Tawton, Barnstaple,
Devon EX32 0DY
T: (01271) 342497 & 346673
F: (01271) 323947
E: downrew@globalnet.co.uk
I: www.downrew.co.uk

The Imperial ★★★★
Taw Vale Parade, Barnstaple,
Devon EX32 8NB
T: (01271) 345861
F: (01271) 324448
E: info@brend-imperial.co.uk
I: www.brendimperial.co.uk

The Park Hotel ★★★
Taw Vale, Barnstaple, Devon
EX32 8NJ
T: (01271) 372166
F: (01271) 323157
E: sales@brend-hotels.co.uk
I: www.brend-hotels.co.uk

Royal and Fortescue Hotel ★★★
Boutport Street, Barnstaple,
Devon EX31 1HG
T: (01271) 342289
F: (01271) 342289
E: info@royalfortescue.co.uk
I: www.brend-hotels.co.uk

BARWICK
Somerset

Little Barwick House ★
Barwick, Yeovil, Somerset
BA22 9TD
T: (01935) 423902
F: (01935) 420908

BATH
Bath and North East Somerset

The Abbey Hotel ★★
North Parade, Bath, BA1 1LF
T: (01225) 461603
F: (01225) 447758
E: ahres@compasshotels.co.uk

Cliffe Hotel ★★★
Crowe Hill, Limpley Stoke, Bath
BA3 6HY
T: (01225) 723226
F: (01225) 723871
E: cliffe@bestwestern.co.uk
I: www.cliffehotel.co.uk

Combe Grove Manor Hotel and Country Club ★★★★
Brassknocker Hill, Monkton
Combe, Bath BA2 7HS
T: (01225) 834644 & 835533
F: (01225) 834961
E: james.parker@
combegrovemanor.com
I: www.scoot.
co.uk/combe-grove

Haringtons Hotel ★★
8-10 Queen Street, Bath,
BA1 1HE
T: (01225) 461728
F: (01225) 444804
E: post@haringtonshotel.co.uk
I: www.haringtonshotel.co.uk

The Lansdown Grove Hotel ★★★
Lansdown Road, Bath, BA1 5EH
T: (01225) 483888
F: (01225) 483838
E: lansdown@marstonhotels.
com
I: www.marstonhotels.com

Lucknam Park ★★★★
Colerne, Chippenham, Wiltshire
SN14 8AZ
T: (01225) 742777
F: (01225) 743536
E: reservations@lucknampark.
co.uk
I: www.lucknampark.co.uk

Old Malt House Hotel ★★
Radford, Timsbury, Bath
BA2 0QF
T: (01761) 470106
F: (01761) 472726
E: hotel@oldmalthouse.co.uk
I: www.oldmalthouse.co.uk

The Old Mill Hotel ★★
Tollbridge Road, Batheaston,
Bath BA1 7DE
T: (01225) 858476
F: (01225) 852600
E: info@oldmillbath.co.uk
I: www.oldmillbath.co.uk

Queensberry Hotel ★★★
Russel Street, Bath, BA1 2QF
T: (01225) 447928
F: (01225) 446065
E: queensberry@dial.pipex.com
I: www.bathqueensberry.com

Royal Hotel ★★
Manvers Street, Bath, BA1 1JP
T: (01225) 463134
F: (01225) 442931
E: royal@rhotel.freeserve.co.uk
I: www.royalhotelbath.co.uk

Rudloe Hall Hotel ★★
Leafy Lane, Box, Corsham,
Wiltshire SN13 0PA
T: (01225) 810555
F: (01225) 811412
E: mail@rudloehall.co.uk
I: www.rudloehall.co.uk

BIDEFORD
Devon

The Orchard Hill Hotel ★★
Orchard Hill, Bideford, Devon
EX39 2QY
T: (01237) 472872
F: (01237) 423803

Riversford Hotel ★★
Limers Lane, Bideford, Devon
EX39 2RG
T: (01237) 474239
F: (01237) 421661
E: riversford@aol.com
I: www.riversford.co.uk

Royal Hotel ★★★
Barnstaple Street, Bideford,
Devon EX39 4AE
T: (01237) 472005
F: (01237) 478957
E: royalbid@btinternet.com
I: www.brend-hotels.co.uk

Tanton's Hotel ★★★
New Road, Bideford, Devon
EX39 2HR
T: (01237) 473317
F: (01237) 473387

Yeoldon House Hotel ★★
Durrant Lane, Northam,
Bideford, Devon EX39 2RL
T: (01237) 474400
F: (01237) 476618
E: yeoldonhouse@aol.com
I: www.yeoldonhousehotel.co.uk

BIGBURY-ON-SEA
Devon

The Henley Hotel ★★
Folly Hill, Bigbury-on-sea,
Kingsbridge, Devon TQ7 4AR
T: (01548) 810240
F: (01548) 810240

BILBROOK
Somerset

The Dragon House Hotel & Restaurant ★★
Dragon's Cross, Bilbrook,
Minehead, Somerset TA24 6HQ
T: (01984) 640215
F: (01984) 641340
E: info@dragonhouse.co.uk
I: www.dragonhouse.co.uk

BOSCASTLE
Cornwall

Bottreaux House Hotel and Restaurant ★★
Boscastle, Cornwall PL35 0BG
T: (01840) 250231
F: (01840) 250170
E: bothotel@dircon.co.uk
I: www.chycor.co.uk/bottreaux

BOVEY TRACEY
Devon

Coombe Cross Hotel ★★
Coombe Lane, Bovey Tracey,
Newton Abbot, Devon TQ13 9EY
T: (01626) 832476
F: (01626) 835298
E: info@coombecross.co.uk
I: www.coombecross.co.uk

Edgemoor Hotel ★★★
Haytor Road, Lowerdown Cross,
Bovey Tracey, Newton Abbot,
Devon TQ13 9LE
T: (01626) 832466
F: (01626) 834760
E: edgemoor@btinternet.com
I: www.edgemoor.co.uk

BOWER HINTON
Somerset

The Hollies ★★★
Bower Hinton, Martock,
Somerset TA12 6LG
T: (01935) 822232
F: (01935) 822249
E: thehollieshotel@ukonline.
co.uk
I: web.ukonline.
co.uk/thehollieshotel.

BRADFORD-ON-AVON
Wiltshire

Widbrook Grange
Rating Applied For
Trowbridge Road, Widbrook,
Bradford-on-Avon, Wiltshire
BA15 1UH
T: (01225) 864750 & 863173
F: (01225) 862890
E: widgra@aol.com

BRANSCOMBE
Devon

The Bulstone Hotel
Rating Applied For
Higher Bulstone, Branscombe,
Seaton, Devon EX12 3BL
T: (01297) 680446
F: (01297) 680446
E: kevinmon@aol.com
I: www.best-hotel.
co.uk/bulstone/index.html

BRIDGWATER
Somerset

Friarn Court Hotel ★★
37 St Mary Street, Bridgwater,
Somerset TA6 3LX
T: (01278) 452859
F: (01278) 452988

Walnut Tree Hotel ★★★
North Petherton, Bridgwater,
Somerset TA6 6QA
T: (01278) 662255
F: (01278) 663946
E: sales.walnuttree@btinternet.
com

BRIDPORT
Dorset

Bridge House Hotel ★
115 East Street, Bridport, Dorset
DT6 3LB
T: (01308) 423371
F: (01308) 423371

Haddon House Hotel ★★★
West Bay, Bridport, Dorset
DT6 4EL
T: (01308) 423626 & 425323
F: (01308) 427348

Roundham House Hotel ★★
Roundham Gardens, West Bay
Road, Bridport, Dorset DT6 4BD
T: (01308) 422753
F: (01308) 421500
E: cyprencom@compuserve.
com
I: www.roundhamhouse.co.uk

BRISTOL

Clifton Hotel ★★
St Paul's Road, Clifton, Bristol
BS8 1LX
T: (0117) 9736882
F: (0117) 9741082
E: clifton@cliftonhotels.com
I: www.cliftonhotels.com/clifton

Courtlands Hotel ★★
1 Redland Court Road, Redland,
Bristol BS6 7EE
T: (0117) 9424432
F: (0117) 9232432

Glenroy Hotel ★★
Victoria Square, Clifton, Bristol
BS8 4EW
T: (0117) 9739058
F: (0117) 9739058
E: admin@glenroyhotel.demon.
co.uk
I: www.glenroy@bestwest.co.uk

Henbury Lodge Hotel ★★★
Station Road, Henbury, Bristol
BS10 7QQ
T: (0117) 950 2615
F: (0117) 950 9532
E: enquiries@henburylodge.com
I: www.henburylodge.com

The Old Bowl Inn and Lilies Restaurant★★
16 Church Road, Lower Almondsbury, Almondsbury, Bristol BS32 4DT
T: (01454) 612757
F: (01454) 619910
E: reception@theoldbowlinn. co.uk
I: www.theoldbowlinn.co.uk

Redwood Lodge Hotel and Country Club★★★
Beggar Bush Lane, Failand, Bristol BS8 3TG
T: (01275) 393901
F: (01275) 392104
E: redwood.lodge@virgin.net
I: www.regalhotels. co.uk/redwoodlodge

The Town and Country Lodge ★★★
A38 Bridgwater Road, Bristol, BS13 8AG
T: (01275) 392441
F: (01275) 393362
E: reservations@tclodge.co.uk
I: www.tclodge.co.uk

BRIXHAM
Devon

The Berry Head Hotel ★★★
Berry Head Road, Brixham, Devon TQ5 9AJ
T: (01803) 853225
F: (01803) 882084
E: berryhd@aol.com
I: www.marine-hotel-leisure. com

BUDE
Cornwall

Atlantic House Hotel ★★
Summerleaze Crescent, Bude, Cornwall EX23 8HJ
T: (01288) 352451
F: (01288) 356666
E: eng@atlantichousehotel. co.uk
I: www.atlantichousehotel.co.uk

Barrel Rock Hotel ★★
41-43 Killerton Road, Bude, Cornwall EX23 8EN
T: (01288) 352252
F: (01288) 353122
E: petergoa4u@supanet.com

Edgcumbe Hotel ★★
19 Summerleaze Cres, Bude, Cornwall EX23 8HJ
T: (01288) 353846
F: (01288) 355256
E: edgcumbehotel@ netscapeonline.co.uk
I: www.smoothound. co.uk/hotels/edgecumbe.html

The Falcon Hotel ★★★
Breakwater Road, Bude, Cornwall EX23 8SD
T: (01288) 352005
F: (01288) 356359

Maer Lodge Hotel ★★
Maer Down Road, Crooklets Beach, Bude, Cornwall EX23 8NG
T: (01288) 353306
F: (01288) 354005
E: maerlodgehotel@btinternet. com
I: www.westcountry-hotels. co.uk/maerlodge

BURNHAM-ON-SEA
Somerset

Laburnum House Lodge Hotel ★★
Sloway Lane, West Huntspill, Highbridge, Somerset TA9 3RJ
T: (01278) 781830
F: (01278) 781612
E: laburnumhh@aol.com
I: www.laburnumhh.co.uk

BURRINGTON
Devon

Northcote Manor Hotel ★★★
Burrington, Umberleigh, Devon EX37 9LZ
T: (01769) 560501
F: (01769) 560770
E: rest@northcotemanor.co.uk
I: www.northcotemanor.co.uk

CAMBORNE
Cornwall

Tyacks Hotel ★★★
27 Commercial Street, Camborne, Cornwall TR14 8LD
T: (01209) 612424
F: (01209) 612435
E: tyacks@ westcountryhotelrooms.co.uk

CARLYON BAY
Cornwall

Carlyon Bay Hotel ★★★★
Sea Road, Carlyon Bay, St Austell, Cornwall PL25 3RD
T: (01726) 812304
F: (01726) 814938
E: info@carlyonbay.co.uk
I: www.carlyonbay.co.uk

CHAGFORD
Devon

Three Crowns Hotel ★★
High Street, Chagford, Newton Abbot, Devon TQ13 8AJ
T: (01647) 433444
F: (01647) 433117
E: threecrowns@msn.com
I: www.chagford-accom.co.uk

CHARD
Somerset

Lordleaze Hotel ★★★
Henderson Drive, Off Forton Road, Chard, Somerset TA20 2HW
T: (01460) 61066
F: (01460) 66468
E: lordleaze@fsbdial.co.uk
I: www.lordleazehotel.co.uk

CHARLESTOWN
Cornwall

Pier House Hotel ★★
Harbour Front, Charlestown, St Austell, Cornwall PL25 3NJ
T: (01726) 67955
F: (01726) 69246
I: www.cornishriviera. co.uk/pierhouse.asp

CHARMOUTH
Dorset

Hensleigh Hotel ★★
Lower Sea Lane, Charmouth, Bridport, Dorset DT6 6LW
T: (01297) 560207
F: (01297) 560830
E: davis2000@skynow.net

CHIDEOCK
Dorset

Chideock House Hotel ★★
Main Street, Chideock, Bridport, Dorset DT6 6JN
T: (01297) 489242
F: (01297) 489184
E: enquiries@ chideockhousehotel.com
I: www.chideockhousehotel.com

CHILLINGTON
Devon

White House Hotel ★★
Chillington, Kingsbridge, Devon TQ7 2JX
T: (01548) 580580
F: (01548) 581124
E: tinawhthse@cs.com

CHIPPENHAM
Wiltshire

Stanton Manor Hotel & Burghleys Restaurant★★★
Stanton St Quintin, Chippenham, Wiltshire SN14 6DQ
T: (01666) 837552
F: (01666) 837022
E: reception@stantonmanor. co.uk
I: www.stantonmanor.co.uk

CHITTLEHAMHOLT
Devon

Highbullen Hotel ★★★
Chittlehamholt, Umberleigh, Devon EX37 9HD
T: (01769) 540561
F: (01769) 540492
E: info@highbullen.co.uk
I: www.highbullen.co.uk

CHURCHILL
North Somerset

Lyncombe Lodge ★★
Lyncombe Drive, Churchill, North Somerset BS25 5PQ
T: (01934) 852335
F: (01934) 853314
E: info@highaction.co.uk
I: www.highaction.co.uk

Winston Manor Hotel ★★
Bristol Road, Churchill, Winscombe BS25 5NL
T: (01934) 852348
F: (01934) 852033
E: enquiries@winston-manor. co.uk
I: www.winston-manor.co.uk

CLIFTON
Bristol

Seeley's Hotel ★★
17/27 St Paul's Road, Clifton, Bristol BS8 1LX
T: (0117) 9738544
F: (0117) 9732406
E: admin@seeleys.demon.co.uk
I: www.seeleys.demon.co.uk

CLOVELLY
Devon

The New Inn ★★
High Street, Clovelly, Bideford, Devon EX39 5TQ
T: (01237) 431303
F: (01237) 431636
E: newinn@clovelly.co.uk

Red Lion Hotel ★★
The Quay, Clovelly, Bideford, Devon EX39 5TF
T: (01237) 431237
F: (01237) 431044
E: redlion@clovelly.co.uk

COMBE MARTIN
Devon

Sandy Cove Hotel ★★★
Old Coast Road, Berrynarbor, Ilfracombe, Devon EX34 9SR
T: (01271) 882243 & 882888
F: (01271) 883830
I: www.exmoor-hospitality-inns. co.uk

CONSTANTINE
Cornwall

Trengilly Wartha Inn ★★
Nancenoy, Constantine, Falmouth, Cornwall TR11 5RP
T: (01326) 340332
F: (01326) 340332
E: trengilly@compuserve.com
I: www.trengilly.co.uk

CRICKLADE
Wiltshire

White Hart Hotel ★★
High Street, Cricklade, Swindon, Wiltshire SN6 6AA
T: (01793) 750206
F: (01793) 750650

CULLOMPTON
Devon

The Manor Hotel ★★
2/4 Fore Street, Cullompton, Devon EX15 1JL
T: (01884) 32281
F: (01884) 38344

DARTMOUTH
Devon

Royal Castle Hotel ★★★
11 The Quay, Dartmouth, Devon TQ6 9PS
T: (01803) 833033
F: (01803) 835445
E: enquiry@royalcastle.co.uk
I: www.royalcastle.co.uk

Stoke Lodge Hotel ★★★
Stoke Fleming, Dartmouth, Devon TQ6 0RA
T: (01803) 770523
F: (01803) 770851
E: mail@stokelodge.co.uk
I: www.stokelodge.co.uk

Townstal Farmhouse ★★
Townstal Road, Dartmouth, Devon TQ6 9HY
T: (01803) 832300
F: (01803) 835428

DEVIZES
Wiltshire

Black Swan Hotel ★★
Market Place, Devizes, Wiltshire SN10 1JQ
T: (01380) 723259
F: (01380) 729966
E: lugg@blackswanhotel.fsnet. co.uk
I: www.blackswanhotel.fsnet. co.uk

DORCHESTER
Dorset

Wessex Royale Hotel ★★★
32 High West Street, Dorchester, Dorset DT1 1UP
T: (01305) 262660
F: (01305) 251941
E: info@wessex-royale-hotel. com
I: www.wessex-royale-hotel. com

DUNSTER
Somerset

Yarn Market Hotel (Exmoor) ★★★
25 High Street, Dunster,
Minehead, Somerset TA24 6SF
T: (01643) 821425
F: (01643) 821475
E: yarnmarket.hotel@virgin.net
I: www.s-h-systems.
co.uk/hotels/yarnmkt

EXETER
Devon

Devon Hotel ★★★
Exeter-by-Pass, Matford, Exeter,
EX2 8XU
T: (01392) 259268
F: (01392) 413142
E: info@devonhotel.co.uk
I: www.devonhotel.co.uk

Fairwinds Village House Hotel
★★
Kennford, Exeter EX6 7UD
T: (01392) 832911

Globe Hotel ★★
Fore Street, Topsham, Exeter,
Devon EX3 0HR
T: (01392) 873471
F: (01392) 873879
E: sales@globehotel.com
I: www.globehotel.com

The Great Western Hotel ★★
Station Approach, St David's,
Exeter, EX4 4NU
T: (01392) 274039
F: (01392) 425529
E: reception@
greatwesternhotel.co.uk
I: www.greatwesternhotel.co.uk

The Red House Hotel ★★
2 Whipton Village Road, Exeter,
EX4 8AR
T: (01392) 256104
F: (01392) 666145
E: redhouse.hotel@eclipse.co.uk
I: www.redhousehotelexeter.
co.uk

St Olaves Hotel and Restaurant
★★★
Mary Arches Street, Exeter,
EX4 3AZ
T: (01392) 217736
F: (01392) 413054
E: info@olaves.co.uk
I: www.olaves.co.uk

EXFORD
Somerset

Exmoor White Horse Hotel
★★★
Exford, Minehead, Somerset
TA24 7PY
T: (01643) 831229
F: (01643) 831246
E: exmoorwhitehorse.demon.
co.uk
I: www.exmoor-hospitality-inns.
co.uk

EXMOUTH
Devon

Ashton Court Hotel ★★
Louisa Terrace, Exmouth, Devon
EX8 2AQ
T: (01395) 263002
F: (01395) 263747
E: ashton.court@exmouth.co.uk
I: www.exmouth.co.uk

Devoncourt Hotel ★★★
Douglas Avenue, Exmouth,
Devon EX8 2EX
T: (01395) 272277
F: (01395) 269315

The Kerans Hotel ★
Esplanade, Exmouth, Devon
EX8 1DS
T: (01395) 275275
E: kerans@xmouth.co.uk
I: www.xmouth.co.uk

Manor Hotel ★★
The Beacon, Exmouth, Devon
EX8 2AG
T: (01395) 272549 & 274477
F: (01395) 225519

The Royal Beacon Hotel ★★★
The Beacon, Exmouth, Devon
EX8 2AF
T: (01395) 264886
F: (01395) 268890
E: reception@royalbeaconhotel.
co.uk
I: www.royalbeaconhotel.co.uk

EYPE
Dorset

Eype's Mouth Country Hotel
★★
Eype, Bridport, Dorset DT6 6AL
T: (01308) 423300
F: (01308) 420033
E: eypehotel@aol.com

FALMOUTH
Cornwall

Broadmead Hotel ★★
Kimberley Park Road, Falmouth,
Cornwall TR11 2DD
T: (01326) 315704 & 318036
F: (01326) 311048
E: broadmeadhotel@aol.com
⬆

**Budock Vean-The Hotel on the
River** ★★★★
Mawnan Smith, Falmouth,
Cornwall TR11 5LG
T: (01326) 250288 & 252100
F: (01326) 250892
E: relax@budockvean.co.uk
I: www.budockvean.co.uk

Green Lawns Hotel ★★★
Western Terrace, Falmouth,
Cornwall TR11 4QJ
T: (01326) 312734 & 312007
F: (01326) 211427
E: info@greenlawnshotel.com
I: www.greenlawnshotel.com

Gyllyngdune Manor Hotel
★★★
Melvill Road, Falmouth,
Cornwall TR11 4AR
T: (01326) 312978
F: (01326) 211881

Penmorvah Manor Hotel
★★★
Budock Water, Falmouth,
Cornwall TR11 5ED
T: (01326) 250277
F: (01326) 250509
E: reception@penmorvah.co.uk
I: www.penmorvah.co.uk

Royal Duchy Hotel ★★★★
Cliff Road, Falmouth, Cornwall
TR11 4NX
T: (01326) 313042 & 214001
F: (01326) 319420
E: infoeroyalduchy.co.uk
I: www.brend-hotels.co.uk

FOWEY
Cornwall

Cormorant on the River ★★
Golant, Fowey, Cornwall
PL23 1LL
T: (01726) 833426
F: (01726) 833426
E: relax@cormoranthotels.co.uk
I: www.cornwall-online.
co.uk/cormorant

Fowey Hotel ★★★
The Esplanade, Fowey, Cornwall
PL23 1HX
T: (01726) 832551
F: (01726) 832125
E: fowey@richardsonhotels.
co.uk
I: www.richardsonhotels.co.uk

Marina Hotel ★★
Esplanade, Fowey, Cornwall
PL23 1HY
T: (01726) 833315
F: (01726) 832779
E: marina.hotel@dial.pipex.com
I: www.cornwall-online.
co.uk/marina_hotel/

GALMPTON
Devon

The Maypool Park Hotel ★★
Maypool, Galmpton, Brixham,
Devon TQ5 0ET
T: (01803) 842442
F: (01803) 845782
E: peacock@maypoolpark.co.uk
I: www.maypoolpark.co.uk

GITTISHAM
Devon

**Combe House Hotel at
Gittisham** ★★★
Gittisham, Honiton, Devon
EX14 3AD
T: (01404) 540400
F: (01404) 46004
E: stay@thishotel.com
I: www.thishotel.com

HEASLEY MILL
Devon

Heasley House ★★
Heasley Mill, North Molton,
South Molton, Devon EX36 3LE
T: (01598) 740213
F: (01598) 740677
E: info@hensley-house.co.uk

HEDDONS MOUTH
Devon

Heddons Gate Hotel ★★
Heddons Mouth, Parracombe,
Barnstaple, Devon EX31 4PZ
T: (01598) 763313
F: (01598) 763363
E: info@hgate.co.uk
I: www.hgate.co.uk

HELSTON
Cornwall

Gwealdues Hotel ★★
Falmouth Road, Helston,
Cornwall TR13 8JX
T: (01326) 572808
F: (01326) 561388
E: gwealdueshotel@btinternet.
com
I: www.gwealdueshotel.co.uk

Nansloe Manor ★★
Meneage Road, Helston,
Cornwall TR13 0SB
T: (01326) 574691
F: (01326) 564680
E: info@nansloe-manor.co.uk
I: www.nansloe-manor.co.uk

HOLCOMBE
Somerset

Ring O' Roses ★★
Stratton Road, Holcombe, Bath,
Somerset BA3 5EB
T: (01761) 232478
F: (01761) 233737
E: ringorosesholcombe@tesco.
net
I: www.ringoroses.co.uk

HOLFORD
Somerset

Combe House Hotel ★★
Holford, Bridgwater, Somerset
TA5 1RZ
T: (01278) 741382
F: (01278) 741322
E: enquiries@combehouse.co.uk
I: www.combehouse.co.uk

HOLSWORTHY
Devon

**Court Barn Country House
Hotel** ★★
Clawton, Holsworthy, Devon
EX22 6PS
T: (01409) 271219
F: (01409) 271309
E: courtbarnhotel@talk21.com
I: www.hotels-devon.com

HONITON
Devon

The Belfry Country Hotel ★★
Yarcombe, Honiton, Devon
EX14 9BD
T: (01404) 861234
F: (01404) 861579

**Home Farm Hotel and
Restaurant** ★★
Wilmington, Honiton, Devon
EX14 9JR
T: (01404) 831278 & 831246
F: (01404) 831411
E: homefarmhotel@
breathemail.net
I: www.homefarmhotel.co.uk

Honiton Motel ★★
Turks Head Corner, Exeter Road,
Honiton, Devon EX14 1BL
T: (01404) 43440 & 45400
F: (01404) 47767

HOPE COVE
Devon

Cottage Hotel ★★
Hope Cove, Kingsbridge, Devon
TQ7 3HJ
T: (01548) 561555
F: (01548) 561455
E: info@hopecove.com
I: www.hopecove.com

Lantern Lodge Hotel ★★
Hope Cove, Kingsbridge, Devon
TQ7 3HE
T: (01548) 561280
F: (01548) 561736
I: www.lantern-lodge.co.uk

HORRABRIDGE
Devon

Overcombe Hotel ★★
Horrabridge, Yelverton, Devon
PL20 7RA
T: (01822) 853501 & 853602
F: (01822) 853501
E: overcombehotel@
horrabridge99.freeserve.co.uk
I: www.overcombehotel.co.uk
♿

ILCHESTER
Somerset

The Ilchester Arms ★★
The Square, Ilchester, Yeovil,
Somerset BA22 8LN
T: (01935) 840220
F: (01935) 841353
E: info@ilchesterarmshotel.
co.uk
I: www.ilchesterarmshotel.co.uk

ILFRACOMBE
Devon

Beechwood Hotel ★★
Torrs Park, Ilfracombe, Devon
EX34 8AZ
T: (01271) 863800
F: (01271) 863800
E: info@beechwoodhotel.co.uk
I: www.beechwoodhotel.co.uk

Cairn House Hotel ★
43 St Brannocks Road,
Ilfracombe, Devon EX34 8EH
T: (01271) 863911
F: 07070 800630

The Darnley Hotel ★★
3 Belmont Road, Ilfracombe,
Devon EX34 8DR
T: (01271) 863955
F: (01271) 864076
E: darnleyhotel@yahoo.co.uk
I: www.northdevon.com/darnley

Elmfield Hotel ★★
Torrs Park, Ilfracombe, Devon
EX34 8AZ
T: (01271) 863377
F: (01271) 866828
E: elmfieldhotel@aol.com
I: www.elmfieldhotelilfracombe.
co.uk

Granville Hotel ★
Granville Road, Ilfracombe,
Devon EX34 8AT
T: (01271) 862002 & 862015
F: (01271) 862803
E: bookings@devoniahotels.
co.uk
I: www.devoniahotels.co.uk

**The Ilfracombe Carlton Hotel
★★**
Runnacleave Road, Ilfracombe,
Devon EX34 8AR
T: (01271) 862446 & 863711
F: (01271) 865379
E: enquiries@ilfracombecarlton.
co.uk

Merlin Court Hotel ★★
Torrs Park, Ilfracombe, Devon
EX34 8AY
T: (01271) 862697 & 864295

Palm Court Hotel ★★
Wilder Road, Ilfracombe, Devon
EX34 8AR
T: (01271) 866644
F: (01271) 863581
I: www.palmcourthotel.net

St Brannocks House Hotel ★★
61 St Brannocks Road,
Ilfracombe, Devon EX34 8EQ
T: (01271) 863873
F: (01271) 863873
E: stbrannocks@aol.com
I: www.stbrannockshotel.co.uk

**Score Valley Country House
Hotel ★★**
Score Valley, Ilfracombe, Devon
EX34 8NA
T: (01271) 862195
F: (01271) 864805
E: info@scorevalley.co.uk
I: www.scorevalley.co.uk

The Torrs Hotel ★
Torrs Park, Ilfracombe, Devon
EX34 8AY
T: (01271) 862334
F: (01271) 862334
I: www.thetorrshotel.co.uk

Trimstone Manor ★★
Trimstone, Ilfracombe, Devon
EX34 8NR
T: (01271) 862841
F: (01271) 863808
E: info@trimstonemanor.
freeserve.co.uk
I: www.trimstone.co.uk

Westwell Hall Hotel ★
Torrs Park, Ilfracombe, Devon
EX34 8AZ
T: (01271) 862792
F: (01271) 862792
E: westwellh@ll.fsnet.co.uk
I: www.westwellhall.co.uk

ILLOGAN
Cornwall

Aviary Court Hotel ★★
Marys Well, Illogan, Redruth,
Cornwall TR16 4QZ
T: (01209) 842256
F: (01209) 843744
E: aviarycourt@connexions.
co.uk
I: www.connexions.
co.uk/aviarycourt/index.htm

INSTOW
Devon

The Commodore Hotel ★★★
Marine Parade, Instow, Bideford,
Devon EX39 4JN
T: (01271) 860347
F: (01271) 861233
E: admin@the-commodore.
freeserve.co.uk
I: www.commodore-instow.
co.uk

ISLES OF SCILLY

Atlantic Hotel ★★
Hugh Town, St Mary's, Isles of
Scilly TR21 0PL
T: (01720) 422417
F: (01720) 423009
E: atlantichotel@btinternet.com

Bell Rock Hotel ★★
Church Street, St Mary's, Isles of
Scilly TR21 0JS
T: (01720) 422575
F: (01720) 423093
E: bellrock.hotel@btclick.com
I: www.bellrockhotel.co.uk

Hotel Godolphin ★★
St Mary's, Isles of Scilly
TR21 0JR
T: (01720) 422316
F: (01720) 422252
E: enquiries@hotelgodolphin.
co.uk
I: www.hotelgodolphin.co.uk

Harbourside Hotel ★★
The Quay, St Mary's, Isles of
Scilly TR21 0HU
T: (01720) 422352
F: (01720) 422590
E: tony@harbourside1.
freeserve.co.uk
I: www.isles-of-scilly.co.uk

Star Castle Hotel ★★★
The Garrison, St Mary's, Isles of
Scilly TR21 0JA
T: (01720) 422317 & 423342
F: (01720) 422343

Tregarthen's Hotel ★★
St Mary's, Isles of Scilly
TR21 0PP
T: (01720) 422540
F: (01720) 422089
I: www.tregarthens/hotel.co.uk

IVYBRIDGE
Devon

Ermewood House Hotel ★★
Totnes Road, Ermington,
Ivybridge, Devon PL21 9NS
T: (01548) 830741
F: (01548) 830741
E: info@ermewood-house.co.uk
I: www.ermewood-house.co.uk

KEYNSHAM
Bath and North East Somerset

Grange Hotel ★★
42 Bath Road, Keynsham, Bristol
BS31 1SN
T: (0117) 986 9181
F: (0117) 986 6373
E: manager@grangekeynsham.
fnet.co.uk
I: www.grangekeynsham.co.uk

Long Reach House Hotel ★★
321 Bath Road, Keynsham,
Bristol BS31 1TJ
T: (01225) 400500 & 400600
F: (01225) 400700
E: lrhouse@aol.com
I: www.longreach-house-hotel.
com/

KINGSBRIDGE
Devon

Sun Bay Hotel ★★
Hope Cove, Nr Salcombe,
Kingsbridge, Devon TQ7 3HH
T: (01548) 561371
F: (01548) 561371
E: sunbayhotel@aol.co.uk

KINGSTEIGNTON
Devon

Passage House Hotel ★★★
Hackney Lane, Kingsteignton,
Newton Abbot, Devon TQ12 3QH
T: (01626) 355515
F: (01626) 363336
E: mail@passagehousehotel.
co.uk
I: www.passagehousehotel.co.uk

LANDS END
Cornwall

The Land's End Hotel ★★★
Lands End, Cornwall TR19 7AA
T: (01736) 871844
F: (01736) 871599
E: info@landsend-landmark.
co.uk
I: www.landsend-landmark.
co.uk

LIFTON
Devon

Arundell Arms Hotel ★★★
Lifton, Devon PL16 0AA
T: (01566) 784666
F: (01566) 784494
E: arundellarms@btinternet.
com

LOOE
Cornwall

Fieldhead Hotel ★★
Portuan Road, Hannafore, West
Looe, Looe, Cornwall PL13 2DR
T: (01503) 262689
F: (01503) 264114
E: field.head@virgin.net
I: www.fieldheadhotel.co.uk

Hannafore Point ★★★
Marine Drive, West Looe, Looe,
Cornwall PL13 2DG
T: (01503) 263273
F: (01503) 263272
E: hannafore@aol.com
I: www.hannaforepointhotel.
com

**Rivercroft Hotel and
Apartments ★★**
Station Road, East Looe, Looe,
Cornwall PL13 1HL
T: (01503) 262251
F: (01503) 265494
E: rivercroft.hotel@virgin.net
I: www.rivercrofthotel.co.uk

**Trelaske Hotel and Restaurant
★★★**
Polperro Road, Looe, Cornwall
PL13 2JS
T: (01503) 262159
F: (01503) 265360
E: trelaskehotel@lineone.net
I: www.trelaskehotel.net

LOSTWITHIEL
Cornwall

**Lostwithiel Hotel Golf &
Country Club★★★**
Lower Polscoe, Lostwithiel,
Cornwall PL22 0HQ
T: (01208) 873550
F: (01208) 873479
E: reception@golf-hotel.co.uk
I: www.golf-hotel.co.uk

LOXTON
North Somerset

The Webbington Hotel ★★★
Loxton, Axbridge, Somerset
BS26 2XA
T: (01934) 750100
F: (01934) 750020
E: webbington@
meridianleisure.com
I: www.meridianleisure.com

LYDFORD
Devon

Lydford House Hotel ★★
Lydford, Okehampton, Devon
EX20 4AU
T: (01822) 820347 & 820321
F: (01822) 820442
E: relax@lydfordhouse.co.uk
I: www.lydfordhouse.co.uk

LYME REGIS
Dorset

Alexandra Hotel ★★★
Pound Street, Lyme Regis,
Dorset DT7 3HZ
T: (01297) 442010
F: (01297) 443229
E: enquiries@hotelalexandra.
co.uk
I: www.hotelalexandra.co.uk

Hotel Buena Vista ★★
Pound Street, Lyme Regis,
Dorset DT7 3HZ
T: (01297) 442494

The Dower House Hotel ★★★
Rousdon, Lyme Regis, Dorset
DT7 3RB
T: (01297) 21047
F: (01297) 24748
E: mdowerhouse@aol.com
I: dower-house-hotel.co.uk

Mariners Hotel ★★
Silver Street, Lyme Regis, Dorset
DT7 3HS
T: (01297) 442753
F: (01297) 442431
E: mariners@ukgateway.net
I: www.lymeregis.com

Swallows Eaves Hotel ★★
Colyford, Colyton, Devon
EX24 6QJ
T: (01297) 553184
F: (01297) 553574
E: swallows.eaves@talk21.com

LYMPSHAM
Somerset

Batch Country Hotel ★★
Batch Lane, Lympsham, Weston-
super-Mare, Avon BS24 0EX
T: (01934) 750371
F: (01934) 750501
I: www.batchcountryhotel.co.uk

LYNMOUTH
Devon

Bath Hotel ★★
Lynmouth, Devon EX35 6EL
T: (01598) 752238
F: (01598) 752544
E: bathhotel@torslynmouth.
co.uk
I: www.torslynmouth.co.uk

**Shelley's Hotel & River
Restaurant ★★**
Watersmeet Road, Lynmouth,
Devon EX35 6EP
T: (01598) 753219
F: (01598) 753751
E: shelleyshotel@freeuk.com
I: www.shelleyshotel.co.uk

The Tors Hotel ★★★
Lynmouth, Devon EX35 6NA
T: (01598) 753236
F: (01598) 752544
E: torshotel@torslynmouth.
co.uk
I: www.torslynmouth.co.uk

LYNTON
Devon

North Cliff Hotel ★
North Walk, Lynton, Devon
EX35 6HJ
T: (01598) 752357
E: holidays@northcliffhotel.
co.uk
I: www.northcliffhotel.co.uk

Sandrock Hotel ★★
Longmead, Lynton, Devon
EX35 6DH
T: (01598) 753307
F: (01598) 752665

Seawood Hotel ★
North Walk Drive, Lynton, Devon
EX35 6HJ
T: (01598) 752272
F: (01598) 752272

MAENPORTH
Cornwall

Trelawne Hotel ★★★
Maenporth Road, Maenporth,
Falmouth, Cornwall TR11 5HS
T: (01326) 250226
F: (01326) 250909

MALMESBURY
Wiltshire

Knoll House Hotel ★★★
Swindon Road, Malmesbury,
Wiltshire SN16 9LU
T: (01666) 823114
F: (01666) 823897
E: knollhotel@malmesbury64.
freeserve.co.uk
I: www.knoll-house.com

Mayfield House Hotel ★★
Crudwell, Malmesbury, Wiltshire
SN16 9EW
T: (01666) 577409 & 577198
F: (01666) 577977
E: mayfield@callnetuk.com

The Old Rectory
Rating Applied For
Crudwell, Malmesbury, Wiltshire
SN16 9EP
T: (01666) 577194
F: (01666) 577853
E: office@oldrectorycrudwell.
co.uk
I: www.oldrectorycrudwell.co.uk

MANACCAN
Cornwall

Tregildry Hotel ★★
Gillan, Manaccan, Helston,
Cornwall TR12 6HG
T: (01326) 231378
F: (01326) 231561
E: trgildry@globalnet.co.uk
I: www.tregildryhotel.co.uk

MAWGAN PORTH
Cornwall

Tredragon Hotel ★★
Mawgan Porth, Newquay,
Cornwall TR8 4DQ
T: (01637) 860213
F: (01637) 860269
E: tredragon@btinternet.com
I: www.tredragon.co.uk

MELKSHAM
Wiltshire

Shaw Country Hotel ★★
Bath Road, Shaw, Melksham,
Wiltshire SN12 8EF
T: (01225) 702836 & 790321
F: (01225) 790275
E: info@shawcountryhotel.
fsnet.co.uk
I: www.shawcountryhotel.fsnet.
co.uk

MEVAGISSEY
Cornwall

**The Sharks Fin Hotel and
Waterside Restaurant★★**
The Quay, Mevagissey, St
Austell, Cornwall PL26 6QU
T: (01726) 843241
F: (01726) 842552
E: sharksfin@hotel.sagehost.
co.uk
I: www.sharksfinhotel.com

Tremarne Hotel ★★
Mevagissey, St Austell, Cornwall
PL26 6UY
T: (01726) 842213
F: (01726) 843420
E: tremarne@talk21.com
I: www.tremarne-hotel.co.uk

MINEHEAD
Somerset

Beaconwood Hotel ★★
Church Road, North Hill,
Minehead, Somerset TA24 5SB
T: (01643) 702032
F: (01643) 702032
E: beaconwood@madasafish.
com
I: www.beaconwoodhotel.co.uk

Channel House Hotel ★★
Church Path, Off Northfield
Road, Minehead, Somerset
TA24 5QG
T: (01643) 703229
F: (01643) 708925
E: channel.house@virgin.net
I: www.channelhouse.co.uk

The Kildare Lodge ★★
Townsend Road, Minehead,
Somerset TA24 5RQ
T: (01643) 702009
F: (01643) 706516

MONKTON
Devon

Monkton Court Inn ★★
Monkton, Honiton, Devon
EX14 9QH
T: (01404) 42309
F: (01404) 46861
E: tony@thosking.freeserve.
co.uk
I: www.travelcheck.
co.uk/hotel/1004.html

MORETONHAMPSTEAD
Devon

**Manor House Hotel and Golf
Course ★★★★**
Moretonhampstead, Newton
Abbot, Devon TQ13 8RE
T: (01647) 445000
F: (01647) 440961
I: www.principalhotels.co.uk

MORTEHOE
Devon

Rockham Bay Hotel ★★
North Morte Road, Mortehoe,
Woolacombe, Devon EX34 7EG
T: (01271) 870993
F: (01271) 870107

MULLION
Cornwall

**Polurrian Hotel, Apartments
and Leisure Club★★★**
The Lizard Peninsula, Mullion,
Helston, Cornwall TR12 7EN
T: (01326) 240421 & 240929
F: (01326) 240083
E: polurotel@aol.com
I: www.polurrianhotel.com

NEWQUAY
Cornwall

Arundell Hotel
Rating Applied For
86/90 Mount Wise, Newquay,
Cornwall TR7 2BS
T: (01637) 872481
F: (01637) 850001

Hotel Bristol ★★★
Narrowcliff, Newquay, Cornwall
TR7 2PQ
T: (01637) 875181
F: (01637) 879347
E: info@hotelbristol.co.uk
I: www.hotelbristol.co.uk

Carnmarth Hotel ★★
22 Headland Road, Fistral Beach,
Newquay, Cornwall TR7 1HN
T: (01637) 872519
F: (01637) 878770
E: carnmarth@connexions.co.uk

Cedars Hotel ★★
Mountwise, Newquay, Cornwall
TR7 2BA
T: (01637) 874225
F: (01637) 850421

Edgcumbe Hotel ★★★
Narrowcliff, Newquay, Cornwall
TR7 2RR
T: (01637) 872061
F: (01637) 852524
E: edgcumbe@silverquick.com

The Esplanade Hotel ★★★
9 Esplanade Road, Pentire,
Newquay, Cornwall TR7 1PS
T: (01637) 873333
F: (01637) 851413
E: info@newquay-hotels.co.uk
I: www.newquay-hotels.co.uk

Great Western Hotel ★★
Cliff Road, Newquay, Cornwall
TR7 2PT
T: (01637) 872010
F: (01637) 874435
I: www.chyco.
co.uk/greatwestern/

Philema Hotel ★★
1 Esplanade Road, Pentire,
Newquay, Cornwall TR7 1PY
T: (01637) 872571
F: (01637) 873188
E: info@philema.demon.co.uk
I: www.smoothhound.
co.uk/hotels/philema.html

Trebarwith Hotel ★★★
Newquay, Cornwall TR7 1BZ
T: (01637) 872288
F: (01637) 875431
E: enquiry@trebarwith-hotel.
co.uk
I: www.trebarwith-hotel.co.uk

Tregurrian Hotel ★
Watergate Bay, Newquay,
Cornwall TR8 4AB
T: (01637) 860280
F: (01637) 860540
E: tregurrian.hotel@virgin.net
I: www.holidaysincornwall.net

Tremont Hotel ★★
Pentire Avenue, Newquay,
Cornwall TR7 1PB
T: (01637) 872984
F: (01637) 851984

Hotel Victoria ★★★
East Street, Newquay, Cornwall
TR7 1DB
T: (01637) 872255
F: (01637) 859295
E: info@hotelvictoria.prestel.
co.uk
I: www.hotel-victoria.co.uk

Whipsiderry Hotel ★★
Trevelgue Road, Porth,
Newquay, Cornwall TR7 3LY
T: (01637) 874777
F: (01637) 874777
E: whipsiderry@cornwall.net
I: www.whipsiderry.com

NEWTON ABBOT
Devon

Hazelwood Hotel ★
33a Torquay Road, Newton
Abbot, Devon TQ12 2LW
T: (01626) 366130
F: (01626) 365021

OKEHAMPTON
Devon

Oxenham Arms ★★
South Zeal, Okehampton, Devon
EX20 2JT
T: (01837) 840244
F: (01837) 840791
E: jhenry1928@aol.com
I: www.hoteldevon.net

White Hart Hotel ★★
Fore Street, Okehampton, Devon
EX20 1HD
T: (01837) 52730 & 54514
F: (01837) 53979

OTTERY ST MARY
Devon

Salston Manor Hotel ★★★
Fluxton Road, Ottery St Mary,
Devon EX11 1RQ
T: (01404) 815581
F: (01404) 811245
E: enquiries@salstonhotel.co.uk
I: www.salstonhotel.co.uk

The Tumbling Weir Hotel ★★
Ottery St Mary, Devon EX11 1AQ
T: (01404) 812752
F: (01404) 812752
E: bpyoung@compuserve.com
I: www.
106120,2702@compuserve.com

PADSTOW
Cornwall

Green Waves Hotel ★★
West View, Trevone Bay,
Padstow, Cornwall PL28 8RD
T: (01841) 520114
F: (01841) 520568
E: info@greenwaveshotel.co.uk
I: www.greenwaveshotel.co.uk

The Old Ship Hotel ★★
Mill Square, Padstow, Cornwall
PL28 8AE
T: (01841) 532357
F: (01841) 533211

PAIGNTON
Devon

Goodrington Lodge Hotel ★★
23 Alta Vista Road, Paignton,
Devon TQ4 6DA
T: (01803) 558382
F: (01803) 550066

**Harwin Hotel and Apartments
★★**
Alta Vista Road, Goodrington
Sands, Paignton, Devon TQ4 6DA
T: (01803) 558771
F: 0870 8313998
E: enquiries@hotel-harwin.
co.uk
I: www.hotel-harwin.co.uk

**Marine Hotel
Rating Applied For**
Seafront, Paignton, Devon
TQ4 6AP
T: (01803) 559778
F: (01803) 559778

The Palace ★★★
Esplanade Road, Paignton,
Devon TQ4 6BJ
T: (01803) 555121
F: (01803) 527974
E: info@palacepaignton.com
I: www.palacepaignton.com

Preston Sands Hotel ★★
10/12 Marine Parade, Sea Front,
Paignton, Devon TQ3 2NU
T: (01803) 558718
F: (01803) 522875

Queens Hotel ★★
Queens Road, Paignton, Devon
TQ4 6AT
T: (01803) 551048
F: (01803) 551048

Redcliffe Hotel ★★★
Marine Drive, Paignton, Devon
TQ3 2NL
T: (01803) 526397
F: (01803) 528030
E: redclfe@aol.com
I: www.redcliffehotel.co.uk

Summerhill Hotel ★★
Braeside Road, Goodrington
Sands, Goodrington, Paignton,
Devon TQ4 6BX
T: (01803) 558101
F: (01803) 558101
E: info@summerhillhotel.co.uk
I: www.summerhillhotel.co.uk

Torbay Holiday Motel ★★
Totnes Road, Paignton, Devon
TQ4 7PP
T: (01803) 558226
F: (01803) 663375
E: enquiries@thm.co.uk
I: www.thm.co.uk

PELYNT
Cornwall

Jubilee Inn ★★
Pelynt, Looe, Cornwall PL13 2JZ
T: (01503) 220312
F: (01503) 220920
E: rickard@jubileeinn.freeserve.
co.uk

PENZANCE
Cornwall

Beachfield Hotel ★★★
The Promenade, Penzance,
Cornwall TR18 4NW
T: (01736) 362067 & 366882
F: (01736) 331100
E: office@beachfield.co.uk
I: www.beachfield.co.uk

Estoril Hotel ★
46 Morrab Road, Penzance,
Cornwall TR18 4EX
T: (01736) 362468 & 367471
F: (01736) 367471
E: estorilhotel@aol.com
I: www.estorilhotel.co.uk

**Mount Haven Hotel and
Restaurant ★★**
Turnpike Road, Marazion,
Cornwall TR17 0DQ
T: (01736) 710249
F: (01736) 711658
E: reception@mounthaven.
co.uk
I: www.mounthaven.co.uk

The Queens Hotel ★★★
The Promenade, Penzance,
Cornwall TR18 4HG
T: (01736) 362371
F: (01736) 350033
E: enquiries@queens-hotel.com
I: www.queens-hotel.com

**The Sea and Horses Hotel
Rating Applied For**
6 Alexandra Terrace, Sea Front,
Penzance, Cornwall TR18 4NX
T: (01736) 361961
F: (01736) 330499

PERRANPORTH
Cornwall

Beach Dunes Hotel ★★
Ramoth Way, Perranporth,
Cornwall TR6 0BY
T: (01872) 572263
F: (01872) 573824
E: beachdunes@argonet.co.uk
I: www.s-h-systems.
co.uk/hotels/beach_d.html

The Seiners Arms ★★
The Beach, Perranporth,
Cornwall TR6 0DP
T: (01872) 573118
F: (01872) 573024
E: kensarms@hotmail.com
I: www.seinersarms.com

PLYMOUTH
Devon

**The Copthorne Plymouth
★★★★**
Armada Way, Plymouth,
PL1 1AR
T: (01752) 224161
F: (01752) 670688
E: sales.plymouth@mill-cop.
com
I: www.millennium-hotels.com

Duke of Cornwall Hotel ★★★
Millbay Road, Plymouth,
PL1 3LG
T: (01752) 275850
F: (01752) 275854
E: duke@heritagehotels.co.uk
I: www.bhere.co.uk

The Grand Hotel ★★★
Elliot Street, The Hoe, Plymouth,
PL1 2PT
T: (01752) 661195
F: (01752) 600653
E: info@plymouthgrand.com
I: www.plymouthgrand.com

Grosvenor Park Hotel ★
114-116 North Road East,
Plymouth, PL4 6AH
T: (01752) 229312
F: (01752) 252777
I: www.smoothhound.
co.uk/hotels/grosvpk.html

Invicta Hotel ★★
11/12 Osborne Place, Lockyer
Street, The Hoe, Plymouth,
PL1 2PU
T: (01752) 664997
F: (01752) 664994
E: info@invicta-hotel.co.uk
I: www.invictahotel.co.uk

**Kitley House Hotel and
Restaurant ★★★**
Kitley Estate, Yealmpton,
Plymouth PL8 2NW
T: (01752) 881555
F: (01752) 881667
E: sales@kitleyhousehotel.com
I: www.kitleyhousehotel.com

New Continental Hotel ★★★
Millbay Road, Plymouth,
PL1 3LD
T: (01752) 220782
F: (01752) 227013
E: newconti@aol.com
I: www.newcontinental.co.uk

Novotel Plymouth ★★★
Marsh Mills, Plymouth, PL6 8NH
T: (01752) 221422
F: (01752) 223922
E: h0508@accor-hotels.com
I: www.novotel.com

Strathmore Hotel ★★★
Elliot Street, The Hoe, Plymouth,
PL1 2PR
T: (01752) 662101
F: (01752) 223690

Victoria Court Hotel ★
62/64 North Road East,
Plymouth, PL4 6AL
T: (01752) 668133
F: (01752) 668133
E: victoria.court@btinternet.
com

POLZEATH
Cornwall

Seascape Hotel ★★
Polzeath, Wadebridge, Cornwall
PL27 6SX
T: (01208) 863638 &
07968 010644
F: (01208) 862940
E: information@seascapehotel.
co.uk
I: www.seascapehotel.co.uk

PORLOCK
Somerset

Anchor and Ship Hotel ★★★
Porlock Harbour, Porlock,
Minehead, Somerset TA24 8PB
T: (01643) 862753
F: (01643) 862843
E: anchorhotel@clara.net

Porlock Vale House ★★
Porlock Weir, Minehead,
Somerset TA24 8NY
T: (01643) 862338
F: (01643) 863338
E: info@porlockvale.co.uk
I: www.porlockvale.co.uk

PORT GAVERNE
Cornwall

**Headlands Hotel
Rating Applied For**
Port Gaverne, Port Isaac,
Cornwall PL29 3SH
T: (01208) 880260
F: (01208) 880885
E: headlandpg@aol.com
I: www.westcountry-hotels.
co.uk/headlands

Port Gaverne Hotel ★★
Port Gaverne, Port Isaac,
Cornwall PL29 3SQ
T: (01208) 880244 &
0500 657867
F: (01208) 880151
E: pghotel@telinco.co.uk
I: www.chycor.
co.uk/hotels/port-gaverne

PORTH
Cornwall

**Sands Family Resort
Rating Applied For**
Porth, Newquay, Cornwall
TR7 3LX
T: (01637) 872864
F: (01637) 876365
E: trevelguehotel@btinternet.
com
I: www.trevelguehotel.co.uk

PORTLAND
Dorset

Portland Heights Hotel ★★★
Yeates Corner, Portland,
Weymouth, Dorset DT5 2EN
T: (01305) 821361
F: (01305) 860081
E: reception@phh.wdi.co.uk
I: www.portlandheights.co.uk

PORTLOE
Cornwall

**Lugger Hotel and Restaurant
★★**
Portloe, Truro, Cornwall TR2 5RD
T: (01872) 501322
F: (01872) 501691
E: office@luggerhotel.com
I: www.luggerhotel.com

REDRUTH
Cornwall

Crossroads Hotel ★★
Scorrier, Redruth, Cornwall
TR16 5BP
T: (01209) 820551
F: (01209) 820392
E: crossroads.hotel@talk21.com

ROCK
Cornwall

The Mariners Hotel ★★
The Slipway, Rock, Wadebridge,
Cornwall PL27 6LD
T: (01208) 862312
F: (01208) 863827
E: amiller767@aol.com
I: www.marinashotel.com

RUAN HIGH LANES
Cornwall

The Hundred House Hotel ★★
Ruan High Lanes, Truro,
Cornwall TR2 5JR
T: 01872 501336
F: 01872 501151
E: eccles@hundredhousehotel.
co.uk
I: www.hundredhousehotel.
co.uk

ST AGNES
Cornwall

**Rose-in-Vale Country House
Hotel★★★**
Mithian, St Agnes, Cornwall
TR5 0QD
T: (01872) 552202
F: (01872) 552700
E: reception@
rose-in-vale-hotel.co.uk
I: www.rose-in-vale-hotel.co.uk

**Sunholme Hotel
Rating Applied For**
Goonvrea Road, St Agnes,
Cornwall TR5 0NW
T: (01872) 552318
E: jefferies@sunholme.co.uk
I: www.sunholme.co.uk

ST AUSTELL
Cornwall

Cliff Head Hotel Limited ★★★
Sea Road, Carlyon Bay, St
Austell, Cornwall PL24 3RB
T: (01726) 812345
F: (01726) 815511
E: cliffheadhotel@btconnect.
com
I: www.cornishriviera.
co.uk/cliffhead

ST IVES
Cornwall

**Chy-an-Dour Hotel
Rating Applied For**
Trelyon Avenue, St Ives,
Cornwall TR26 2AD
T: (01736) 796436
F: (01736) 795772
E: chyndour@aol.com
I: www.connexions.
co.uk/chyandourhotel

**Garrack Hotel and Restaurant
★★★**
Higher Ayr, Burthallan Lane, St
Ives, Cornwall TR26 3AA
T: (01736) 796199
F: (01736) 798955
E: garrack@accuk.co.uk
I: www.garrack.com

Porthminster Hotel ★★★
The Terrace, St Ives, Cornwall
TR26 2BN
T: (01736) 795221
F: (01736) 797043
E: reception@
posthminster-hotel.co.uk
I: www.porthminster-hotel.co.uk

Tregenna Castle ★★★
Treloyan Avenue, St Ives,
Cornwall TR26 2DE
T: (01736) 795254
F: (01736) 796066
I: tregenna-castle.demon.co.uk

ST MAWES
Cornwall

The Idle Rocks Hotel ★★★
Harbourside, 1 Tredenham Road,
St Mawes, Truro, Cornwall
TR2 5AN
T: (01326) 270771 &
0800 243020
F: (01326) 270062
E: idlerocks@richardsonhotels.
co.uk
I: www.richardsonhotels.co.uk

SALCOMBE
Devon

Bolt Head Hotel ★★★
Sharpitor, Salcombe, Devon
TQ8 8LL
T: (01548) 843751
F: (01548) 843061
E: info@bolthead-salcombe.
co.uk
I: www.bolthead-salcombe.co.uk

South Sands Hotel ★★★
South Sands, Salcombe, Devon
TQ8 8LL
T: (01548) 843741
F: (01548) 842112
E: enquire@southsands.com
I: www.southsands.com

Thurlestone Hotel ★★★★
Thurlestone, Kingsbridge, Devon
TQ7 3NN
T: (01548) 560382
F: (01548) 561069
E: enquiries@thurlestone.co.uk
I: www.thurlestone.co.uk

Tides Reach Hotel ★★★★
South Sands, Salcombe, Devon
TQ8 8LJ
T: (01548) 843466
F: (01548) 843954
E: enquire@tidesreach.com
I: www.tidesreach.com

SALISBURY
Wiltshire

The Inn at High Post ★★
High Post, Salisbury, SP4 6AT
T: (01722) 782592
F: (01722) 782630
E: enquiries@theinnsalisbury.
co.uk
I: www.theinnsalisbury.co.uk

Rose and Crown Hotel ★★★
Harnham Road, Salisbury,
SP2 8JQ
T: (01722) 399955
F: (01722) 339816
E: reservations@corushotels.
com
I: www.corushotels.com

SAUNTON
Devon

Saunton Sands Hotel ★★★★
Saunton, Braunton, Devon
EX33 1LQ
T: (01271) 890212
F: (01271) 890145
E: info@sauntonsands.com
I: www.sauntonsands.com

SENNEN
Cornwall

The Old Success Inn ★★
Sennen Cove, Penzance,
Cornwall TR19 7DG
T: (01736) 871232
F: (01736) 871457
E: oldsuccess@sennencove.fs.
business.co.uk
I: www.oldsuccess.com

SHALDON
Devon

Ness House Hotel ★★
Marine Parade, Shaldon,
Teignmouth, Devon TQ14 0HP
T: (01626) 873480
F: (01626) 873486
E: nesshouse@talk21.com
I: www.nesshouse.co.uk

SHEPTON MALLET
Somerset

The Shrubbery Hotel ★★
17 Commercial Road, Shepton
Mallet, Somerset BA4 5BU
T: (01749) 346671
F: (01749) 346581

SHERBORNE
Dorset

Antelope Hotel ★★★
Greenhill, Sherborne, Dorset
DT9 4EP
T: (01935) 812077
F: (01935) 816473

The Eastbury Hotel ★★★
Long Street, Sherborne, Dorset
DT9 3BY
T: (01935) 813131
F: (01935) 817296
I: www.theeastburyhotel.co.uk

SIDBURY
Devon

**Sid Valley Country House
Hotel ★★★**
Sidbury, Sidmouth, Devon
EX10 0QJ
T: (01395) 597274 & 597587
F: (01395) 597587

SIDMOUTH
Devon

The Belmont Hotel ★★★★
The Esplanade, Sidmouth, Devon
EX10 8RX
T: (01395) 512555
F: (01395) 579101
E: info@belmont-hotel.co.uk
I: www.belmont-hotel.co.uk

Devoran Hotel ★★
The Esplanade, Sidmouth, Devon
EX10 8AU
T: (01395) 513151 &
0800 317171
F: (01395) 579929
E: devoran@cosmic.org.uk
I: www.devoran.com

Fortfield Hotel ★★★
Sidmouth, Devon EX10 8NU
T: (01395) 512403
F: (01395) 512403
E: reservations@furtfield-hotel.
demon.co.uk
I: www.fortfield-hotel.demon.
co.uk

Kingswood Hotel ★★
Esplanade, Sidmouth, Devon
EX10 8AX
T: (01395) 516367
F: (01395) 513185
E: kingswood.hotel@virgin.net
I: www.kingswood-hotel.co.uk

Hotel Riviera ★★★★
The Esplanade, Sidmouth, Devon
EX10 8AY
T: (01395) 515201
F: (01395) 577775
E: enquiries@hotelriviera.co.uk
I: www.hotelriviera.co.uk

Royal Glen Hotel ★★★
Glen Road, Sidmouth, Devon
EX10 8RW
T: (01395) 513221 & 513456
F: (01395) 514922
E: sidmouthroyalglen.hotel@
virgin.net

**Royal York and Faulkner Hotel
★★**
Esplanade, Sidmouth, Devon
EX10 8AZ
T: 0800 220714 &
(01395) 513043
F: (01395) 577472
E: yorkhotel@eclipse.co.uk
I: www.royalyorkhotel.net

**Salcombe Hill House Hotel
★★★**
Beatlands Road, Sidmouth,
Devon EX10 8JQ
T: (01395) 514697
F: (01395) 578310
E: salcombehillhousehotel@
eclipse.co.uk
I: www.salcombehillhousehotel.
co.uk

The Victoria Hotel ★★★★
The Esplanade, Sidmouth, Devon
EX10 8RY
T: (01395) 512651
F: (01395) 579154

Woodlands Hotel ★★
Cotmaton Cross, Station Road,
Sidmouth, Devon EX10 8HG
T: (01395) 513120 & 513166
F: (01395) 513348
E: info@woodlands-hotel.com
I: www.woodlands-hotel.com

SOURTON
Devon

Collaven Manor Hotel ★★
Sourton, Okehampton, Devon
EX20 4HH
T: (01837) 861522
F: (01837) 861614
I: www.collavenmanor.co.uk

STRATTON
Cornwall

Stamford Hill Hotel ★★
Stamford Hill, Stratton, Bude,
Cornwall EX23 9AY
T: (01288) 352709
F: (01288) 352709
I: www.stamfordhillhotel.co.uk

STREET
Somerset

Wessex Hotel ★★★
High Street, Street, Somerset
BA16 0EF
T: (01458) 443383 & 442227
F: (01458) 446589
E: wessex@hotel-street.
freeserve.co.uk
I: www.wessexhotel.com

SWINDON
Wiltshire

Goddard Arms Hotel ★★★
High Street, Old Town, Swindon,
SN1 3EG
T: (01793) 692313
F: (01793) 512984
E: goddardarms@zoffanyhotels.
co.uk
I: www.zoffanyhotels.co.uk

The Royston Hotel
Rating Applied For
34 Victoria Road, Oldtown,
Swindon, SN1 3AS
T: (01793) 522990
F: (01793) 522991
E: info@roystonhotel.co.uk
I: www.roystonhotel.co.uk

Villiers Inn ★★★
Moormead Road, Wroughton,
Swindon SN4 9BY
T: (01793) 814744
F: (01793) 814119
E: info@villiersinn.co.uk
I: www.villiersinn.co.uk

TAUNTON
Somerset

**Express by Holiday Inn
Taunton**
Travel Accommodation
Blackbrook Business Park,
Blackbrook Park Avenue,
Taunton, Somerset TA1 2RW
T: (01823) 624000
F: (01823) 624024
I: www.hiexpress.com/taunton

Rumwell Manor Hotel ★★★
Rumwell, Taunton, Somerset
TA4 1EL
T: (01823) 461902
F: (01823) 254861
E: reception@rumwellmanor.
co.uk
I: www.rumwellmanor.co.uk

TEFFONT EVIAS
Wiltshire

Howards House Hotel ★★
Teffont Evias, Salisbury SP3 5RJ
T: (01722) 716392 & 716821
F: (01722) 716820
E: enq@howardshousehotel.
com
I: www.howardshousehotel.
co.uk

TEIGNMOUTH
Devon

London Hotel ★★★
Bank Street, Teignmouth, Devon
TQ14 8AW
T: (01626) 776336
F: (01626) 778457

THE LIZARD
Cornwall

Housel Bay Hotel ★★★
Housel Cove, The Lizard, Helston,
Cornwall TR12 7PG
T: (01326) 290417 & 290917
F: (01326) 290359
E: info@houselbay.com
I: www.houselbay.com

TINTAGEL
Cornwall

Atlantic View Hotel ★★
Treknow, Tintagel, Cornwall
PL34 0EJ
T: (01840) 770221
F: (01840) 770995
E: atlantic-view@eclipse.co.uk
I: www.holidayscornwall.com

Bossiney House Hotel ★★
Bossiney Road, Tintagel,
Cornwall PL34 0AX
T: (01840) 770240
F: (01840) 770501
E: bossineyhh@eclipse.co.uk
I: www.cornwall-online.
co.uk/bossiney

Willapark Manor Hotel ★★
Bossiney, Tintagel, Cornwall
PL34 0BA
T: (01840) 770782

The Wootons Country Hotel
★★
Fore Street, Tintagel, Cornwall
PL34 0DQ
T: (01840) 770170
F: (01840) 770170

TIVERTON
Devon

The Tiverton Hotel ★★★
Blundells Road, Tiverton, Devon
EX16 4DB
T: (01884) 256120
F: (01884) 258101
E: sales@tivertonhotel.co.uk
I: www.tivertonhotel.co.uk

TORCROSS
Devon

Greyhomes Hotel ★
Torcross, Kingsbridge, Devon
TQ7 2TH
T: (01548) 580220
F: (01548) 580832
E: howard@greyhomeshotel.
co.uk
I: www.greyhomeshotel.co.uk

TORMARTON
Gloucestershire

Compass Inn ★★
Tormarton, Badminton, Avon
GL9 1JB
T: (01454) 218242
F: (01454) 218741
I: www.compass-inn.co.uk

TORPOINT
Cornwall

Whitsand Bay Hotel ★★
Portwrinkle, Torpoint, Cornwall
PL11 3BU
T: (01503) 230276
F: (01503) 230329

TORQUAY
Devon

Abbey Court Hotel ★★
Falkland Road, Torquay, Devon
TQ2 5JR
T: (01803) 297316
F: (01803) 297316

Abbey Lawn Hotel ★★
Scarborough Road, Torquay,
Devon TQ2 5UQ
T: (01803) 299199
F: (01803) 291460

Anstey's Lea Hotel ★★
327 Babbacombe Road, Torquay,
TQ1 3TB
T: 0800 0284953 &
(01803) 200900
F: (01803) 211150
E: info@ansteyscove.co.uk
I: www.ansteyscove.co.uk

Ashley Court Hotel ★★
107 Abbey Road, Torquay,
TQ2 5NP
T: (01803) 292417 & 296078
F: (01803) 215035
E: reception@ashleycourt.
demon.co.uk
I: www.ashleycourt.demon.co.uk

Hotel Balmoral ★★
Meadfoot Sea Road, Torquay,
Devon TQ1 2LQ
T: (01803) 299224
F: (01803) 293381

Belgrave Hotel ★★★
Belgrave Road, Torquay,
TQ2 5HE
T: (01803) 296666
F: (01803) 211308
E: info@belgrave-hotel.co.uk
I: www.belgrave-hotel.co.uk

The Berburry Hotel ★★
64 Bampfylde Road, Torquay,
Devon TQ2 5AY
T: (01803) 297494
F: (01803) 215902
E: bsellick@berburry.co.uk
I: www.berburry.co.uk

Bishops Court ★★★
Lower Warberry Road, Torquay,
Devon TQ1 1QS
T: (01803) 294649
F: (01803) 291175

Burlington Hotel ★★
462-466 Babbacombe Road,
Torquay, TQ1 1HN
T: (01803) 210950
F: (01803) 200189
E: info@burlington.hotel.co.uk
I: www.torquayholidayhotels.
co.uk

Bute Court Hotel ★★
Belgrave Road, Torquay,
TQ2 5HQ
T: (01803) 213055
F: (01803) 213429
E: bute-court-hotel@talk21.
com
I: www.bute-court-hotel.co.uk

Carlton Court Hotel ★★
18 Cleveland Road, Torquay,
TQ2 5BE
T: (01803) 297318
F: (01803) 290069
E: carltoncourt@onetel.net.uk
I: www.carlton-court.co.uk

Carlton Hotel ★★
Falkland Road, Torquay, TQ2 5JJ
T: (01803) 400300
F: (01803) 400130
E: carltonetlh.co.uk
I: www.tlh.co.uk

Hotel Cimon
Rating Applied For
82 Abbey Road, Torquay, Devon
TQ2 5NP
T: (01803) 294454
F: (01803) 201988

Corbyn Head Hotel ★★★
Torbay Road, Seafront, Torquay,
TQ2 6RH
T: (01803) 213611
F: (01803) 296152
E: info@corbynhead.com
I: www.corbynhead.com

County Hotel ★★
52/54 Belgrave Road, Torquay,
Devon TQ2 5HS
T: (01803) 294452
F: (01803) 294452

The Court Hotel ★★
Lower Warberry Road, Torquay,
TQ1 1QS
T: (01803) 212011
F: (01803) 292648
E: teresa@court-hotel
I: court-hotel.co.uk

Derwent Hotel ★★
Belgrave Road, Torquay, TQ2 5HT
T: (01803) 400100
F: (01803) 400110
E: derwent@tlh.co.uk
I: www.tlh.co.uk

Fonthill Hotel ★★
Lower Warberry Road, Torquay,
TQ1 1QP
T: (01803) 214099
F: (01803) 200609
I: www.fonthillhotel.co.uk

Frognel Hall ★★
Higher Woodfield Road,
Torquay, TQ1 2LD
T: (01803) 298339
F: (01803) 215115
E: mail@frognel.co.uk
I: www.frognel.co.uk

Hotel Gleneagles ★★★
Asheldon Road, Wellswood,
Torquay, TQ1 2QS
T: (01803) 293637 & 215621
F: (01803) 295106
E: HotelGleneagles@lineone.net
I: www.hotel-gleneagles.com

Gresham Court Hotel ★★
Babbacombe Road, Torquay,
TQ1 1HG
T: (01803) 293007 & 293658
F: (01803) 215951
E: greshamcourthotel@hotmail.
com
I: www.gresham-court-hotel.
co.uk

Hylton Court Hotel ★
109 Abbey Road, Torquay,
TQ2 5NP
T: (01803) 298643 & 264464
F: (01803) 298643

Livermead House Hotel ★★★
Sea Front, Torquay, TQ2 6QJ
T: (01803) 294361
F: (01803) 200758
E: rewhotels@aol.com
I: www.livermead.com

Manor House Hotel ★★
Seaway Lane, Torquay, TQ2 6PS
T: (01803) 605164
F: (01803) 606841
E: mark@manor-house-hotel.
co.uk
I: www.manor-house-hotel.
co.uk

Norcliffe Hotel ★★
Sea Front, Babbacombe Downs,
Torquay, TQ1 3LF
T: (01803) 328456
F: (01803) 328023

Osborne Hotel ★★★
Hesketh Crescent, Meadfoot
Beach, Torquay, TQ1 2LL
T: (01803) 213311
F: (01803) 296788
E: enq@osbourne-torquay.co.uk
I: www.osbourne-torquay.co.uk

The Overmead Hotel ★★
Daddyhole Road, Torquay,
TQ1 2EF
T: (01803) 295666
F: (01803) 211175
I: www.torbayhotels.com

Palace Hotel ★★★★
Babbacombe Road, Torquay,
TQ1 3TG
T: (01803) 200200
F: (01803) 299899
E: info@palacetorquay.co.uk
I: www.palacetorquay.co.uk

Princes Hotel ★
Park Hill Road, Torquay, Devon
TQ1 2DU
T: (01803) 291803
F: (01803) 292113
E: derek@rpinceshotel.fsnet.
co.uk

Rawlyn House Hotel ★★
Rawlyn Road, Chelston, Torquay
TQ2 6PL
T: (01803) 605208
F: (01803) 607040
E: shirleycox@genie.co.uk

Red House Hotel ★★
Rousdown Road, Chelston,
Torquay TQ2 6PB
T: (01803) 607811
F: (01803) 200592
E: stay@redhouse-hotel.co.uk
I: www.redhouse-hotel.co.uk

Richmond Hotel ★★★
27 Croft Road, Torquay,
TQ2 5UD
T: (01803) 298457
F: (01803) 215866
I: www.torquayhotels.co.uk

Roseland Hotel ★★
Warren Road, Torquay, TQ2 5TT
T: (01803) 213829
F: (01803) 291266
I: www.torquayhotels.co.uk

Seascape Hotel ★★
8-10 Tor Church Road, Torquay,
Devon TQ2 5UT
T: (01803) 292617
F: (01803) 299260
E: enquiries@torquayseascape.
co.uk
I: www.torquayseascape.co.uk

Shedden Hall Hotel ★★
Shedden Hill, Torquay, TQ2 5TX
T: (01803) 292964
F: (01803) 295306
E: sheddenhtl@aol.com
I: www.sheddenhallhotel.co.uk

Sydore Hotel ★★
Meadfoot Road, Torquay,
TQ1 2JP
T: (01803) 294758
F: (01803) 294489
E: john@sydore.co.uk
I: www.sydore.co.uk

Toorak Hotel ★★★
Chestnut Avenue, Torquay,
TQ2 5JS
T: (01803) 400400
F: (01803) 400140
E: toorak@tlh.co.uk
I: www.tlh.co.uk

Torcroft Hotel ★★
Croft Road, Torquay, TQ2 5UE
T: (01803) 298292
F: (01803) 291799
E: torcroft@torquaydevon.
fsnet.co.uk

Tormohun Hotel ★
28-30 Newton Road, Torquay,
TQ2 5BZ
T: (01803) 293681
F: (01803) 314649

Victoria Hotel
Rating Applied For
Belgrave Road, Torquay, TQ2 5HL
T: (01803) 400200
F: (01803) 400120
E: victoria@tlh.co.uk
I: www.tlh.co.uk

Westwood Hotel ★
111 Abbey Road, Torquay,
TQ2 5NP
T: (01803) 293818
F: (01803) 293818
E: reception@westwoodhotel.
co.uk
I: www.westwoodhotel.co.uk

Old Church House Inn ★★★
Torbryan, Newton Abbot, Devon
TQ12 5UR
T: (01803) 812372 & 812180
F: (01803) 812180
E: information@church-house.
co.uk
I: www.church-houseinn.co.uk

Royal Seven Stars Hotel ★★
The Plains, Totnes, Devon
TQ9 5DD
T: (01803) 862125 & 863241
F: (01803) 867925
I: www.smoothhound.
co.uk/hotels/royal7.html

Alverton Manor ★★★
Tregolls Road, Truro, Cornwall
TR1 1ZQ
T: (01872) 276633
F: (01872) 222989
E: reception@alvertonmanor.
demon.co.uk

Brookdale Hotel ★★★
Tregolls Road, Truro, Cornwall
TR1 1JZ
T: (01872) 273513
F: (01872) 272400
E: brookdale@hotelstruro.com
I: hotelstruro.com

Carlton Hotel ★★
Falmouth Road, Truro, Cornwall
TR1 2HL
T: (01872) 272450
F: (01872) 223938
E: reception@carltonhotel.co.uk
I: www.carltonhotel.co.uk

The Royal Hotel ★★★
Lemon Street, Truro, Cornwall
TR1 2QB
T: (01872) 270345
F: (01872) 242453
E: reception@
royalhotelcornwall.co.uk
I: www.royalhotelcornwall.co.uk

Prince Hall Hotel ★★
Two Bridges, PL20 6SA
T: (01822) 890403
F: (01822) 890676
E: bookings@princehall.co.uk
I: www.princehall.co.uk

**Percy's Country Hotel &
Restaurant ★★**
Virginstow, Beaworthy, Devon
EX21 5EA
T: (01409) 211236
F: (01409) 211275
E: info@percys.co.uk
I: www.percys.co.uk

**The Molesworth Arms Hotel
★★**
Molesworth Street, Wadebridge,
Cornwall PL27 7DP
T: (01208) 812055
F: (01208) 814254
E: sarah@molesworth.ision.
co.uk
I: www.molesworth.ndirect.
co.uk

Trehellas House ★★
Washaway, Bodmin, Cornwall
PL30 3AD
T: (01208) 72700 & 74499
F: (01208) 73336
I: www.trehellas.com

Downfield House Hotel ★★
16 St Decuman's Road, Watchet,
Somerset TA23 0HR
T: (01984) 631267
F: (01984) 634369
I: www.smoothhound.
co.uk/hotels/downf

Watergate Bay Hotel ★★★
Watergate Bay, Newquay,
Cornwall TR8 4AA
T: (01637) 860543
F: (01637) 860333
E: hotel@watergate.co.uk
I: www.watergate.co.uk

Ancient Gate House Hotel ★
20 Sadler Street, Wells, Somerset
BA5 2RR
T: (01749) 672029
F: (01749) 670319
E: info@ancientgatehouse.co.uk
I: www.ancientgatehouse.co.uk

Charlton House ★★★
Charlton Road, Shepton Mallet,
Somerset BA4 4PR
T: (01749) 342008
F: (01749) 346362
E: enquiry@charltonhouse.com
I: www.charltonhouse.com

The Crown at Wells ★★
Market Place, Wells, Somerset
BA5 2RP
T: (01749) 673457
F: (01749) 679792
E: reception@crownatwells.
co.uk
I: www.crownatwells.co.uk

Swan Hotel ★★★
Sadler Street, Wells, Somerset
BA5 2RX
T: (01749) 836300
F: (01749) 836301
E: swan@bhere.co.uk
I: www.bhere.co.uk

The White Hart Hotel ★★
19-21 Sadler Street, Wells,
Somerset BA5 2RR
T: (01749) 672056
F: (01749) 671074
E: info@whitehart-wells.co.uk
I: www.whitehart-wells.co.uk

The Manor Hotel ★★
West Bexington, Dorchester,
Dorset DT2 9DF
T: (01308) 897616 & 897785
F: (01308) 897035
E: themanorhotel@btconnect.
com
I: www.themanorhotel.com

Four Acres Hotel ★★★
West Coker, Yeovil, Somerset
BA22 9AJ
T: (01935) 862555
F: (01935) 863929

The Cedar Hotel ★★
Warminster Road, Westbury,
Wiltshire BA13 3PR
T: (01373) 822753
F: (01373) 858423
E: cedarwestbury@aol.com
I: www.cedarhotel.co.uk

WESTON-SUPER-MARE
North Somerset

Arosfa Hotel ★★
Lower Church Road, Weston-super-Mare, BS23 2AG
T: (01934) 419523
F: (01934) 636084
E: info@arosfahotel.co.uk
I: www.arosfahotel.co.uk

Beachlands Hotel ★★★
17 Uphill Road North, Weston-super-Mare BS23 4NG
T: (01934) 621401
F: (01934) 621966
E: info@beachlandshotel.co.uk
I: www.beachlandshotel.com

Daunceys Hotels ★★
9-14 Claremont Crescent, Weston-super-Mare, Avon BS23 2EE
T: (01934) 410180
F: (01934) 410181
E: reservations@daunceyshotel.fsnet.co.uk

The New Ocean Hotel ★★
1 Manilla Crescent, Madeira Cove, Weston-super-Mare, Avon BS23 2BS
T: (01934) 621839
F: (01934) 626474

Queenswood Hotel ★★
Victoria Park, Weston-super-Mare, Somerset BS23 2HZ
T: (01934) 416141
F: (01934) 621759
E: stay@queenswoodhotel.com
I: www.queenswoodhotel.com

WEYMOUTH
Dorset

The Glenburn Hotel ★★
42 Preston Road, Weymouth, Dorset DT3 6PZ
T: (01305) 832353
F: (01305) 835610
E: info@glenburnhotel.com
I: www.glenburnhotel.com

Hotel Rembrandt ★★★
12-18 Dorchester Road, Weymouth, Dorset DT4 7JU
T: (01305) 764000
F: (01305) 764022
E: reception@hotelrembrandt.co.uk
I: www.hotelrembrandt.co.uk

Hotel Rex ★★★
29 The Esplanade, Weymouth, Dorset DT4 8DN
T: (01305) 760400
F: (01305) 760500
E: rex@kingshotels.f9.co.uk
I: www.kingshotel.co.uk

The Sherborne Hotel
Rating Applied For
117 The Esplanade, Weymouth, Dorset DT4 7EH
T: (01305) 777888
F: (01305) 759111

WHEDDON CROSS
Somerset

Raleigh Manor Country House Hotel ★★
Wheddon Cross, Minehead, Somerset TA24 7BB
T: (01643) 841484
E: raleighmanor@hotmail.com

WICK
Gloucestershire

Tracy Park Golf & Country Club ★★★
Bath Road, Wick, Bristol BS30 5RN
T: (0117) 9372251
F: (0117) 9374288
E: hotel@tracypark.com
I: www.tracypark.com

WILLITON
Somerset

Masons Arms Hotel ★★
2 North Road, Williton, Taunton, Somerset TA4 6SN
T: (01984) 639200
F: (01984) 635933
E: themasons@richardshotels.co.uk
I: www.richardshotels.co.uk

WINCANTON
Somerset

Holbrook House Hotel ★★★
Wincanton, Somerset BA9 8BS
T: (01963) 32377
F: (01963) 32681
E: enquiries@holbrookhouse.co.uk
I: www.holbrookhouse.co.uk

WINSFORD
Somerset

Royal Oak Inn ★★★
Exmoor National Park, Winsford, Minehead, Somerset TA24 7JE
T: (01643) 851455
F: (01643) 851009
E: enquiries@royaloak-somerset.co.uk
I: www.royaloak-somerset.co.uk

WOODBURY
Devon

Woodbury Park Hotel, Golf & Country Club★★★★
Woodbury Castle, Woodbury, Exeter EX5 1JJ
T: (01395) 233382
F: (01395) 233384
E: events@woodburypark.co.uk
I: www.woodburypark.co.uk

WOOLACOMBE
Devon

Crossways Hotel ★
The Esplanade, Woolacombe, Devon EX34 7DJ
T: (01271) 870395
F: (01271) 870395
I: www.smoothhound.co.uk/hotels/crossway.html

Little Beach Hotel ★★
The Esplanade, Woolacombe, Devon EX34 7DJ
T: (01271) 870398

Narracott Grand Hotel ★★
Beach Road, Woolacombe, Devon EX34 7BS
T: (01271) 870418
F: (01271) 870600
E: enquiries@narracott.co.uk
I: www.narracott.co.uk

Pebbles Hotel and Restaurant ★
Combesgate Beach, Mortehoe, Woolacombe, Devon EX34 7EA
T: (01271) 870426
E: enquiries@pebbleshotel.com
I: www.pebbleshotel.com

Watersmeet Hotel ★★★
Mortehoe, Woolacombe, Devon EX34 7EB
T: (01271) 870333
F: (01271) 870890
E: info@watersmeethotel.co.uk
I: www.watersmeethotel.co.uk

Woolacombe Bay Hotel ★★★
South Street, Woolacombe, Devon EX34 7BN
T: (01271) 870388
F: (01271) 870613
E: woolacombe.bayhotel@btinternet.com
I: www.woolacombe-bay-hotel.co.uk

YEOVIL
Somerset

Yeovil Court Hotel ★★★
West Coker Road, Yeovil, Somerset BA22 2HE
T: (01935) 863746
F: (01935) 863990
E: verne@yeovil-courthotel.co.uk
I: www.yeovilhotel.com

SOUTH OF ENGLAND

ABINGDON
Oxfordshire

Abingdon Four Pillars Hotel ★★★
Marcham Road, Abingdon, Oxfordshire OX14 1TZ
T: (01235) 553456
F: (01235) 554117
E: abingdon@four-pillars.co.uk

ALDERSHOT
Hampshire

Potters International Hotel ★★★
1 Fleet Road, Aldershot, Hampshire GU11 2ET
T: (01252) 344000
F: (01252) 311611

ALRESFORD
Hampshire

The Swan Hotel ★★
11 West Street, Alresford, Hampshire SO24 9AD
T: (01962) 732302 & 734427
F: (01962) 735274
E: swanhotel@btinternet.com

ALTON
Hampshire

Alton Grange Hotel & Restaurant ★★★
London Road, Alton, Hampshire GU34 4EG
T: (01420) 86565
F: (01420) 541346
E: info@altongrange.co.uk
I: www.altongrange.co.uk

ANDOVER
Hampshire

The Bourne Valley Inn
Rating Applied For
St Mary Bourne, Andover, Hampshire SP11 6BT
T: (01264) 738361
F: (01264) 738126
E: bourneinn@aol.com
I: www.townpages.co.uk

The White Hart Hotel ★★★
Bridge Street, Andover, Hampshire SP10 1BH
T: (01264) 352266
F: (01264) 323767

ASCOT
Berkshire

The Highclere Hotel ★★
Kings Road, Sunninghill, Ascot, Berkshire SL5 9AD
T: (01344) 625220
F: (01344) 872528

AYLESBURY
Buckinghamshire

Posthouse Aylesbury ★★★
Aston Clinton Road, Aylesbury, Buckinghamshire HP22 5AA
T: 0870 400 9002
F: (01296) 392211

West Lodge Hotel ★★
45 London Road, Aston Clinton, Aylesbury, Buckinghamshire HP22 5HL
T: (01296) 630331 & 630362
F: (01296) 630151
E: JB@westlodge.co.uk
I: www.westlodge.co.uk

BASINGSTOKE
Hampshire

Hampshire Centrecourt ★★★
Centre Drive, Chineham, Basingstoke, Hampshire RG24 8FY
T: (01256) 816664
F: (01256) 816727
E: hampshirec@marstonhotels.com
I: www.marstonhotels.com

Hanover International Hotel & Club Basingstoke★★★★
Scures Hill, Nately Scures, Hook, Hampshire RG27 9JS
T: (01256) 764161
F: (01256) 768341
E: maxine.butler@awhotels.com
I: www.hanover-international

Establishments printed in blue have a detailed entry in this guide

Red Lion Hotel ★★★
24 London Street, Basingstoke,
Hampshire RG21 7NY
T: (01256) 328525
F: (01256) 844056
E: redlion@msihotels.co.uk
I: www.msihotels.co.uk

BEMBRIDGE
Isle of Wight

Bembridge Coast Hotel ★★★
Fishermans Walk, Bembridge,
Isle of Wight PO35 5TH
T: (01983) 873931
F: (01983) 874693
I: www.warnerholidays.co.uk

Windmill Hotels Ltd ★★
1 Steyne Road, Bembridge, Isle
of Wight PO35 5UH
T: (01983) 872875
F: (01983) 874760
E: info@thewindmillhotel.co.uk
I: www.windmill-inn.com

BLANDFORD FORUM
Dorset

Anvil Hotel & Restaurant ★★
Salisbury Road, Pimperne,
Blandford Forum, Dorset
DT11 8UQ
T: (01258) 453431 & 480182
F: (01258) 480182
E: theanvil@euphony.net

Crown Hotel ★★★
West Street, Blandford Forum,
Dorset DT11 7AJ
T: (01258) 456626
F: (01258) 451084

BOURNEMOUTH
Dorset

Babbacombe Court Hotel ★★
28 West Hill Road, West Cliff,
Bournemouth, BH2 5PG
T: (01202) 552823 & 551746
F: (01202) 789030

Bay View Court Hotel ★★★
35 East Overcliff Drive,
Bournemouth, BH1 3AH
T: (01202) 294449
F: (01202) 292883
E: enquiry@bayviewcourt.co.uk
I: www.bayviewcourt.co.uk

Belvedere Hotel ★★★
Bath Road, Bournemouth,
BH1 2EU
T: (01202) 297556 & 293336
F: (01202) 294699
E: Belvedere_Hotel@msn.com
I: www.belvedere-hotel.co.uk

**The Bournemouth Highcliff
Marriott Hotel★★★★**
St Michael's Road, West Cliff,
Bournemouth, BH2 5DU
T: (01202) 557702 & 557724
F: (01202) 292734
E: reservations.Bournemouth@
marriothotels.co.uk
I: www.marriothotels.com.
bohbm

Burley Court Hotel ★★★
Bath Road, Bournemouth,
BH1 2NP
T: (01202) 552824 & 556704
F: (01202) 298514
E: burleycourt@btclick.com
I: www.smoothhound.co.uk

Cecil Court Hotel ★★
4 Durley Road, West Cliff,
Bournemouth, BH2 5JL
T: (01202) 553160

Chesterwood Hotel ★★★
East Overcliff Drive,
Bournemouth, BH1 3AR
T: (01202) 558057
F: (01202) 556285
E: enquiry@chesterwoodhotel.
co.uk
I: www.chesterwoodhotel.co.uk

Chine Hotel ★★★
Boscombe Spa Road,
Bournemouth, BH5 1AX
T: (01202) 396234
F: (01202) 391737
E: reservations@chinehotel.
co.uk
I: www.chinehotel.co.uk

Chinehurst Hotel ★★
18-20 Studland Road, Alum
Chine, Bournemouth, Dorset
BH4 8JA
T: (01202) 764583
F: (01202) 762854

Cliffeside Hotel ★★★
East Overcliff Drive,
Bournemouth, BH1 3AQ
T: (01202) 555724
F: (01202) 314534
I: www.arthuryoung.co.uk

The Connaught Hotel ★★★
West Hill Road, West Cliff,
Bournemouth, BH2 5PH
T: (01202) 298020
F: (01202) 298028
E: sales@theconnaught.co.uk
I: www.theconnaught.co.uk

The Cottage Private Hotel ★★
12 Southern Road, Southbourne,
Bournemouth BH6 3SR
T: (01202) 422764
F: (01202) 381442
E: ron+val@rjvhalliwell.force9.
co.uk
I: www.smoothound.
co.uk/hotels/cottage3.html

Cottonwood Hotel ★★
Grove Road, East Cliff,
Bournemouth, BH1 3AP
T: (01202) 553183
F: (01202) 299225
E: cottonwood@ukonline.co.uk
I: www.cottonwood-hotel.co.uk

The County Hotel ★★
Westover Road, Bournemouth,
BH1 2BT
T: (01202) 552385
F: (01202) 297255
E: countyhotel@freeuk.com

Cumberland Hotel ★★★
East Overcliff Drive,
Bournemouth, BH1 3AF
T: (01202) 290722
F: (01202) 311394
E: cumberland@arthuryoung.
co.uk
I: www.arthuryoung.co.uk

Durley Hall Hotel ★★★
7 Durley Chine Road,
Bournemouth, BH2 5JS
T: (01202) 751000
F: (01202) 757585
E: sales@durleyhall.co.uk
I: www.durleyhall.co.uk

Durlston Court Hotel ★★★
47 Gervis Road, East Cliff,
Bournemouth, BH1 3DD
T: (01202) 316316
F: (01202) 316999
E: dch@seaviews.co.uk
I: www.seaviews.co.uk

Elstead Hotel ★★★
Knyveton Road, Bournemouth,
BH1 3QP
T: (01202) 293071
F: (01202) 293827
E: info@the-elstead.co.uk
I: www.the-elstead.co.uk

Fircroft Hotel ★★
Owls Road, Bournemouth,
BH5 1AE
T: (01202) 309771
F: (01202) 395644
E: info@fircroft.co.uk
I: www.fircrofthotel.co.uk

The Five Ways Hotel ★★
23 Argyll Road, Sea Road,
Boscombe, Bournemouth,
Dorset BH5 1EB
T: (01202) 301509 & 304971
F: (01202) 391107

The Grange Hotel ★★
Overcliff Drive, Southbourne,
Bournemouth BH6 3NL
T: (01202) 433093
F: (01202) 424228
I: www.
bournemouthgrangehotel.co.uk

Grosvenor Hotel ★★★
Bath Road, Bournemouth,
Dorset BH1 2EX
T: (01202) 558858
F: (01202) 298332
E: enquiries@
grosvenor-bournemouth.co.uk.
I: www.
grosvenor-bournemouth.co.uk

The Hermitage Hotel ★★★
Exeter Road, Bournemouth,
Dorset BH2 5AH
T: (01202) 557363
F: (01202) 559173
E: info@hermitage-hotel.co.uk
I: www.hermitage-hotel.co.uk

Hilton Bournemouth ★★★★
Westover Road, Bournemouth,
Dorset BH1 2BZ
T: (01202) 557681
F: (01202) 554918
E: general.manager@
bournemouth.stakis.co.uk
I: www.hilton.com

Hinton Firs ★★★
Manor Road, East Cliff,
Bournemouth, BH1 3HB
T: (01202) 555409
F: (01202) 299607
E: hintonfirs@bournemouth.
co.uk
I: www.pageant.co.uk

Inver House Hotel ★★
12 Priory Road, Bournemouth,
Dorset BH2 5DG
T: (01202) 553319
F: (01202) 553313

Kensington Hotel ★★
18 Durley Chine Road, West
Cliff, Bournemouth, BH2 5LE
T: (01202) 557434
F: (01202) 290562
E: kensington18@aol.com
I: www.plu44.com/o/kensington/

Kiwi Hotel ★★
West Hill Road, Bournemouth,
BH2 5EG
T: (01202) 555889
F: (01202) 789567
E: kiwihotel@aol.com
I: www.kiwihotel.co.uk

Lynden Court Hotel ★★
8 Durley Road, West Cliff,
Bournemouth, Dorset BH2 5JL
T: (01202) 553894
F: (01202) 317711

Manor House Hotel ★★
34 Manor Road, East Cliff,
Bournemouth, Dorset BH1 3EZ
T: (01202) 396669
F: (01202) 396669

Mansfield Hotel ★★
West Cliff Gardens,
Bournemouth, BH2 5HL
T: (01202) 552659
E: mail@bournemouthhotel.net
I: www.bournemouthhotel.net

Marsham Court Hotel ★★★
Russell-Cotes Road, East Cliff,
Bournemouth, BH1 3AB
T: (01202) 552111
F: (01202) 294744
E: reservations@marshamcourt.
co.uk
I: www.marshamcourt.com

Mayfair Hotel ★★★
27 Bath Road, Bournemouth,
Dorset BH1 2NW
T: (01202) 551983
F: (01202) 298459
E: info@themayfair.com
I: www.themayfair.com

New Durley Dean Hotel ★★★
West Cliff Road, Bournemouth,
BH2 5HE
T: (01202) 557711
F: (01202) 292815
I: newdurleydeanhotel.co.uk

The New Westcliff Hotel ★★
27 Chine Crescent, West Cliff,
Bournemouth, BH2 5LB
T: (01202) 551062
F: (01202) 315377

Overcliff Hotel ★★
58 Grand Avenue, Southbourne,
Bournemouth BH6 3PA
T: (01202) 428300
F: (01202) 430718

Palm Court Hotel ★★
38 Christchurch Road,
Bournemouth, BH1 3PD
T: (01202) 558088 & 268898
F: (01202) 789318
E: admin@palmcourt.freeserve.
co.uk
I: www.palmcourthotel.
freeserve.co.uk

Pavilion Hotel ★★★
22 Bath Road, Bournemouth,
BH1 2NS
T: (01202) 291266
F: (01202) 559264

The Quality Cadogan Hotel
★★★
8 Poole Road, Bournemouth,
BH2 5QU
T: (01202) 757758
F: (01202) 757756
E: ch@seaviews.co.uk
I: www.seaviews.co.uk

Queen's Hotel ★★★
Meyrick Road, East Cliff,
Bournemouth, BH1 3DL
T: (01202) 554415
F: (01202) 294810
E: hotels@arthuryoung.co.uk
I: www.arthuryoung.co.uk

Hotel Riviera ★★
West Cliff Gardens,
Bournemouth, BH2 5HL
T: (01202) 552845
F: (01202) 317717
E: info@hotel-riviera.co.uk
I: www.hotel-riviera.co.uk

Riviera Hotel ★★
12-16 Burnaby Road, Alum
Chine, Bournemouth, Dorset
BH4 8JF
T: (01202) 763653
F: (01202) 768422
I: www.smouthhound.
co.uk/calotels.html

Roysdean Manor ★★
5 Derby Road, Bournemouth,
BH1 3PT
T: (01202) 554933
F: (01202) 780916
E: sales@roysdeanmanor.co.uk
I: www.roysdeanmanor.co.uk

Russell Court Hotel ★★
Bath Road, Bournemouth,
BH1 2EP
T: (01202) 295819
F: (01202) 293457
E: russelcrt@aol.com
I: www.enterprisehotel.co.uk

Sandy Beach Hotel ★★
43 Southwood Avenue,
Southbourne, Bournemouth,
Dorset BH6 3QB
T: (01202) 424385
F: (01202) 424385
E: sandybeach@bournemouth.
co.uk

Sun Court Hotel ★★
West Hill Road, West Cliff,
Bournemouth, BH2 5PH
T: (01202) 551343
F: (01202) 316747
E: info@suncourthotel.com
I: www.suncourthotel.com

Suncliff Hotel ★★★
East Overcliff Drive,
Bournemouth, BH1 3AG
T: (01202) 291711
F: (01202) 293788
E: reservations@suncliffhotel.
co.uk
I: www.suncliffhotel.co.uk

Sydney House Hotel ★★
6 West Cliff Road, West Cliff,
Bournemouth, BH2 5EY
T: (01202) 555536
F: (01202) 555536
E: sww@fsmail.net

Tralee Hotel ★★★
West Hill Road, West Cliff,
Bournemouth, Dorset BH2 5EQ
T: (01202) 556246
F: (01202) 295229
E: hotel@tralee.co.uk

Trouville Hotel ★★★
Priory Road, West Cliff,
Bournemouth, BH2 5DH
T: (01202) 552262
F: (01202) 293324
E: reservations@trouvillehotel.
uk.com
I: www.arthuryoung.co.uk

Ullswater Hotel ★★
Westcliff Gardens,
Bournemouth, BH2 5HW
T: (01202) 555181
F: (01202) 317896
E: enq@ullswater.uk.com
I: www.ullswater.uk.com

West Cliff Sands Hotel
Rating Applied For
9 Priory Road, West Cliff,
Bournemouth, Dorset BH2 5DF
T: (01202) 557013

Westleigh Hotel ★★
26 West Hill Road, West Cliff,
Bournemouth, Dorset BH2 5PG
T: (01202) 296989
F: (01202) 296989

Winterbourne Hotel ★★★
Priory Road, Bournemouth,
BH2 5DJ
T: (01202) 296366
F: (01202) 780073
E: reservations@winterbourne.
co.uk
I: www.winterbourne.co.uk

Woodcroft Tower Hotel ★★
Gervis Road, East Cliff,
Bournemouth, BH1 3DE
T: (01202) 558202
F: (01202) 551807
E: enquiries@woodcrofthotel.
co.uk
I: www.woodcrofthotel.co.uk

BRACKNELL
Berkshire

Coppid Beech Hotel ★★★★
John Nike Way, Bracknell,
Berkshire RG12 8TF
T: (01344) 303333
F: (01344) 301200
E: reservations@
coppid-beech-hotel.co.uk
I: www.coppidbeech.com

Dial House Hotel ★★
62 Dukes Ride, Crowthorne,
Berkshire RG45 6DL
T: (01344) 778941
F: (01344) 777191
E: dhh@fardellhotels.com
I: www.fardellhotels.com

BRAMSHAW
Hampshire

Bramble Hill Hotel ★★
Bramshaw, Lyndhurst,
Hampshire SO43 7JG
T: (023) 8081 3165
F: (023) 8081 2126

BROCKENHURST
Hampshire

Cloud Hotel ★★
Meerut Road, Brockenhurst,
Hampshire SO42 7TD
T: (01590) 622165
F: (01590) 622818
E: enquiries@cloudhotel.co.uk
I: www.cloudhotel.co.uk

The Watersplash Hotel ★★
The Rise, Brockenhurst,
Hampshire SO42 7ZP
T: (01590) 622344
F: (01590) 624047
E: bookings@watersplash.co.uk
I: www.watersplash.co.uk

Whitley Ridge Country House Hotel ★★★
Beaulieu Road, Brockenhurst,
Hampshire SO42 7QL
T: (01590) 622354
F: (01590) 622856
E: whitleyridge@brockenhurst.
co.uk
I: www.whitleyridge.co.uk

BUCKINGHAM
Buckinghamshire

Buckingham Four Pillars Hotel
★★★
A421 Ring Road South,
Buckingham, Buckinghamshire
MK18 1RY
T: (01280) 822622
F: (01280) 823074
E: buckingham@four-pillars.
co.uk
I: www.four-pillars.co.uk

Villiers Hotel ★★★
3 Castle Street, Buckingham,
Buckinghamshire MK18 1BS
T: (01280) 822444
F: (01280) 822113
E: villiers@villiers-hotels.
demon.co.uk

BURFORD
Oxfordshire

The Bay Tree ★★★
Sheep Street, Burford, Oxford
OX18 4LW
T: (01993) 822791
F: (01993) 823008
E: bookings@
cotswold-inns-hotels.co.uk
I: www.cotswold-inns-hotels.
co.uk

Cotswold Gateway Hotel
★★★
Cheltenham Road, Burford,
Oxford OX18 4HX
T: (01993) 822695 & 823345
F: (01993) 823600
E: cotswold.gateway@dial.
pipex.com
I: www.cotswold-gateway.co.uk

BURLEY
Hampshire

The Burley Inn ★★
The Cross, Burley, Ringwood,
Hampshire BH24 4AB
T: (01425) 403448
F: (01425) 402058

Moorhill House Hotel ★★★
Burley, Ringwood, Hampshire
BH24 4AG
T: (01425) 403285
F: (01425) 403715
E: moorhill@carehotels.co.uk
I: www.carehotels.co.uk

CALBOURNE
Isle of Wight

Swainston Manor Hotel & Restaurant ★★★★
Calbourne, Newport, Isle of
Wight PO30 4HX
T: (01983) 521121
F: (01983) 521406
E: hotel@swainstonmanor.
freeserve.com.uk

CHALE
Isle of Wight

Clarendon Hotel & Wight Mouse Inn ★★
Nr Blackgang, Chale, Ventnor,
Isle of Wight PO38 2HA
T: (01983) 730431
F: (01983) 730431
E: info@wightmouseinns.co.uk
I: www.wightmouseinns.co.uk

CHESTERTON
Oxfordshire

Bignell Park Hotel ★★
Chesterton, Bicester, Oxfordshire
OX26 IUE
T: (01869) 241444 & 241192
F: (01869) 241444

CHIPPING NORTON
Oxfordshire

Chadlington House ★★★
Chapel Road, Chadlington,
Oxford OX7 3LZ
T: (01608) 676437
F: (01608) 676996
E: info@chadlingtonhouse.com
I: www.chadlingtonhouse.com

The Crown & Cushion Hotel, Conference & Leisure Centre
★★★
23 High Street, Chipping Norton,
Oxfordshire OX7 5AD
T: (01608) 642533
F: (01608) 642926

CHOLDERTON
Hampshire

The Red House Hotel ★★
Parkhouse Cross, Cholderton,
Salisbury, Wiltshire SP4 0EG
T: (01980) 629542
F: (01980) 629481
E: theredhouse@fsmail.net

CHRISTCHURCH
Dorset

Tyrrells Ford Hotel ★★★
Avon, Christchurch, Dorset
BH23 7BH
T: (01425) 672646
F: (01425) 672262

CORFE CASTLE
Dorset

Mortons House Hotel ★★★
East Street, Corfe Castle,
Wareham, Dorset BH20 5EE
T: (01929) 480988
F: (01929) 480820
E: stay@mortonshouse.co.uk
I: www.mortonshouse.co.uk

COWES
Isle of Wight

New Holmwood Hotel ★★★
Queens Road, Egypt Point,
Cowes, Isle of Wight PO31 8BW
T: (01983) 292508
F: (01983) 295020
E: nholnwoodh@aol.com
I: www.newholmwoodhotel.
co.uk

Rawlings Hotel ★★
30 Sun Hill, Cowes, Isle of Wight
PO31 7HY
T: (01983) 297507
F: (01983) 281701

DEDDINGTON
Oxfordshire

Holcombe Hotel & Restaurant ★★★
High Street, Deddington,
Banbury, Oxfordshire OX15 0SL
T: (01869) 338274
F: (01869) 337167
E: reception@holcombehotel.
freeserve.co.uk
I: www.bestwestern.co.uk

EASTLEIGH
Hampshire

The Concorde Club & Hotel ★★★
Ellington Lodge, Stoneham Lane,
Eastleigh, Hampshire SO50 9HQ
T: (023) 8065 1478
F: (023) 8065 1479
E: info@theconcordeclub.com
I: www.theconcordeclub.com

EMSWORTH
Hampshire

The Brookfield Hotel ★★★
Havant Road, Emsworth,
Hampshire PO10 7LF
T: (01243) 373363 & 376 383
F: (01243) 376342

FAREHAM
Hampshire

The Red Lion Hotel ★★★
East Street, Fareham, Hampshire
PO16 0BP
T: (01329) 822640
F: (01329) 823579

Upland Park Hotel ★★
Garrison Hill (A32), Droxford,
Southampton SO32 3QL
T: (01489) 878507
F: (01489) 877853
E: reservations@
uplandparkhotel.co.uk
I: www.uplandparkhotel.co.uk

FARINGDON
Oxfordshire

Faringdon Hotel ★★
Market Place, Faringdon,
Oxfordshire SN7 7HL
T: (01367) 240536
F: (01367) 243250

FARNBOROUGH
Hampshire

The Falcon Hotel ★★★
68 Farnborough Road,
Farnborough, Hampshire
GU14 6TH
T: (01252) 545378
F: (01252) 522539
E: falcon@meridian leisure.co.uk
I: www.meridianleisure.com

FENNY STRATFORD
Buckinghamshire

**Campanile Milton Keynes
Hotel**
Travel Accommodation
40 Penn Road, Fenny Stratford,
Milton Keynes MK2 2AU
T: (01908) 649819
F: (01908) 649818

FORDINGBRIDGE
Hampshire

**Ashburn Hotel & Restaurant
★★**
Fordingbridge, Hampshire
SP6 1JP
T: (01425) 652060
F: (01425) 652150
E: ashburn@mistral.co.uk
I: www.ashburn.mistral.co.uk

FRESHWATER
Isle of Wight

Albion Hotel ★★★
Freshwater Bay, Isle of Wight
PO40 9RA
T: (01983) 755755
F: (01983) 755295

Farringford Hotel ★★
Bedbury Lane, Freshwater, Isle of
Wight PO40 9PE
T: (01983) 752500 & 752700
F: (01983) 756515
E: enquiries@farringford.co.uk
I: www.farringford.co.uk

GILLINGHAM
Dorset

**Stock Hill Country House Hotel
★★★**
Stock Hill, Gillingham, Dorset
SP8 5NR
T: (01747) 823626
F: (01747) 825628
E: reception@stockhill.net
I: www.stockhill.net

GOSPORT
Hampshire

Belle Vue Hotel ★★★
39 Marine Parade East, Lee on
the Solent, Gosport, Hampshire
PO13 9BW
T: (023) 9255 0258
F: (023) 9255 2624
E: information@bellevue-hotel.
co.uk
I: www.bellevue-hotel.co.uk

The Manor Hotel ★★
Brewers Lane, Gosport,
Hampshire PO13 0JY
T: (01329) 232946
F: (01329) 220392
E: tony_lid@msn.com
I: www.smoothhounds.
co.uk/hotels/manorhtml

GREAT MILTON
Oxfordshire

**Le Manoir aux Quat' Saisons
★★★★**
Church Road, Great Milton,
Oxford, Oxfordshire OX44 7PD
T: (01844) 278881
F: (01844) 278847
E: lemanoir@blanc.com
I: www.manoir.com

HAVANT
Hampshire

Bear Hotel ★★
East Street, Havant, Hampshire
PO9 1AA
T: (023) 9248 6501
F: (023) 9247 0551

HAYLING ISLAND
Hampshire

Newtown House Hotel ★★★
Manor Road, Hayling Island,
Hampshire PO11 0QR
T: (023) 9246 6131
F: (023) 9246 1366

HECKFIELD
Hampshire

The New Inn ★★
Heckfield, Hook, Hampshire
RG27 0LE
T: (0118) 932 6374
F: (0118) 932 6550

HIGH WYCOMBE
Buckinghamshire

Abbey Lodge Hotel ★★
Priory Road, High Wycombe,
Buckinghamshire HP13 6SL
T: (01494) 471013
F: (01494) 471015

HOOK
Hampshire

Raven Hotel ★★★
Station Road, Hook, Hampshire
RG27 9HS
T: (01256) 762541
F: (01256) 768677

HUNGERFORD
Berkshire

The Bear at Hungerford ★★★
Charnham Street, Hungerford,
Berkshire RG17 0EL
T: (01488) 682512
F: (01488) 684357
I: www.jarvis.co.uk

Littlecote House Hotel ★★★
Hungerford, Berkshire RG17 0SS
T: (01488) 682509
F: (01488) 682341

KINGSTON BAGPUIZE
Oxfordshire

**Fallowfields Country House
Hotel ★★★**
Faringdon Road, Kingston
Bagpuize with Southmoor,
Oxford, OX13 5BH
T: (01865) 820416
F: (01865) 821275
E: stay@fallowfields.com
I: www.fallowfields.com

KNOWL HILL
Berkshire

Bird In Hand ★★★
Bath Road, Knowl Hill, Reading
RG10 9UP
T: (01628) 822781 & 826622
F: (01628) 826748
E: birdinhand.co.uk
I: www.birdinhand.co.uk

LIPHOOK
Hampshire

**Old Thorns Hotel, Golf &
Country Club★★★**
Griggs Green, Liphook,
Hampshire GU30 7PE
T: (01428) 724555
F: (01428) 725036
E: info@oldthorns.com
I: www.oldthorns.com

LITTLEWICK GREEN
Berkshire

**Riders Country House Hotel
Rating Applied For**
Bath Road, Littlewick Green,
Maidenhead, Berkshire SL6 3RQ
T: (01628) 822085
F: (01628) 829211
E: ridershotel@hotmail.com

LULWORTH COVE
Dorset

Cromwell House Hotel ★★
Lulworth Cove, West Lulworth,
Wareham, Dorset BH20 5RJ
T: (01929) 400253 & 400332
F: (01929) 400566
E: catriona@lulworthcove.co.uk
I: www.lulworthcove.co.uk

LYMINGTON
Hampshire

Passford House Hotel ★★★
Mount Pleasant Lane,
Lymington, Hampshire SO41 8LS
T: (01590) 682398
F: (01590) 683494
E: bookings@
passfordhousehotel.co.uk
I: www.passfordhousehotel.
co.uk

South Lawn Hotel ★★★
Lymington Road, Milford-on-
Sea, Lymington, Hampshire
SO41 0RF
T: (01590) 643911
F: (01590) 644820
E: enquiries@southlawn.co.uk
I: www.southlawn.co.uk

Stanwell House Hotel ★★★
Jane McIntyre Hotels Ltd, 15
High Street, Lymington,
Hampshire SO41 9AA
T: (01590) 677123
F: (01590) 677756
E: sales@stanwellhousehotel.
co.uk
I: www.stanwellhousehotel.
co.uk

LYNDHURST
Hampshire

Knightwood Lodge ★
Southampton Road, Lyndhurst,
Hampshire SO43 7BU
T: (023) 8028 2502
F: (023) 8028 3730

The Stag Hotel ★★
69 High Street, Lyndhurst,
Hampshire SO43 7BE
T: (023) 8028 2999
F: (023) 8028 2999

Woodlands Lodge Hotel ★★★
Bartley Road, Woodlands,
Southampton, Hampshire
SO40 7GN
T: (023) 8029 2257
F: (023) 8029 3090
E: woodlands@nortels.ltd.uk
I: www.nortels.ltd.uk

MAIDENHEAD
Berkshire

Elva Lodge Hotel ★
Castle Hill, Maidenhead,
Berkshire SL6 4AD
T: (01628) 622948
F: (01628) 778954
E: reservations@elvalodgehotel.
demon.co.uk
I: www.elvalodgehotel.demon.
co.uk

MARLOW
Buckinghamshire

**Danesfield House Hotel and
Spa ★★★★**
Henley Road, Marlow-on-
Thames, Marlow,
Buckinghamshire SL7 2EY
T: (01628) 891010
F: (01628) 890408
E: sales@danesfieldhouse.co.uk
I: www.danesfieldhouse.co.uk

MILFORD-ON-SEA
Hampshire

Westover Hall Hotel ★★★
Park Lane, Milford-on-Sea,
Lymington, Hampshire SO41 0PT
T: (01590) 643044
F: (01590) 644490
E: westoverhallhotel@barclays.
net
I: www.westoverhallhotel.com

MILTON COMMON
Oxfordshire

The Oxford Belfry ★★★★
Milton Common, Oxford
OX9 2JW
T: (01844) 279381
F: (01844) 279624
E: oxfordbelfry@marstonhotels.
com
I: www.marstonhotels.com

MILTON KEYNES
Buckinghamshire

Calverton Lodge Hotel ★★
38 Horsefair Green, Stony
Stratford, Milton Keynes
MK11 1JP
T: (01908) 261241
F: (01908) 265924
E: calvert@powernet.co.uk
I: www.calvertonlodge.co.uk.

The Different Drummer Hotel
★★
94 High Street, Stony Stratford,
Milton Keynes MK11 1AH
T: (01908) 564733
F: (01908) 260646
E: sales@thedifferentdrummer.
co.uk
I: www.thedifferentdrummer.
co.uk

Parkside Hotel ★★★
Newport Road, Woughton on
the Green, Milton Keynes
MK6 3LR
T: (01908) 661919
F: (01908) 676186
E: rooms@parkside-hotel.co.uk
I: www.parkside-hotel.co.uk

Quality Hotel Milton Keynes
★★★
Monks Way, Two Mile Ash,
Milton Keynes MK8 8LY
T: (01908) 561666
F: (01908) 568303
E: admin@gb45.u-net.com
I: www.choicehotelseurope.com

Swan Revived Hotel ★★
High Street, Newport Pagnell,
Buckinghamshire MK16 8AR
T: (01908) 610565
F: (01908) 210995
E: swanrevived@btinternet.com
I: www.swanrevived.co.uk

MINSTER LOVELL
Oxfordshire

The Mill & Old Swan ★★★
Minster Lovell, Oxford,
Oxfordshire OX8 5RN
T: (01993) 774441
F: (01993) 702002
E: themill@initialstyle.co.uk
I: www.initialstyle.co.uk

NEW MILTON
Hampshire

**Chewton Glen Hotel, Health &
Country Club** ★★★★★
Christchurch Road, New Milton,
Hamphire BH25 6QS
T: (01425) 275341
F: (01425) 272310
E: reservations@chewtonglen.
com
I: www.chewtonglen.com

NEWBURY
Berkshire

**Donnington Valley Hotel &
Golf Course** ★★★★
Old Oxford Road, Donnington,
Newbury, Berkshire RG14 3AG
T: (01635) 551199
F: (01635) 551123
E: general@donningtonvalley.
co.uk
I: www.donningtonvalley.co.uk

Regency Park Hotel ★★★★
Bowling Green Road, Thatcham,
Berkshire RG18 3RP
T: (01635) 871555
F: (01635) 871571
E: info@regencypark.co.uk
I: www.regencyparkhotel.co.uk

The Vineyard at Stockcross
★★★★★
Stockcross, Newbury, Berkshire
RG20 8JU
T: (01635) 528770
F: (01635) 528398
E: general@the-vineyard.co.uk
I: www.the-vineyard.co.uk

NITON UNDERCLIFF
Isle of Wight

The Windcliffe Manor Hotel
★★★
Sandrock Road, Niton Undercliff,
Ventnor, Isle of Wight PO38 2NG
T: (01983) 730215
F: (01983) 730215
E: enquires@windcliffe.co.uk
I: www.windcliffe.co.uk

ODIHAM
Hampshire

George Hotel ★★
High Street, Odiham, Hook,
Hampshire RG29 1LP
T: (01256) 702081
F: (01256) 704213

OXFORD
Oxfordshire

The Balkan Lodge Hotel ★★
315 Iffley Road, Oxford,
Oxfordshire OX4 4AG
T: (01865) 244524
F: (01865) 251090
I: www.oxfordcity.
co.uk/hotels/balkan

Cotswold Lodge Hotel ★★★★
66A Banbury Road, Oxford,
OX2 6JP
T: (01865) 512121
F: (01865) 512490

Mount Pleasant ★★
76 London Road, Headington,
Oxford OX3 9AJ
T: (01865) 762749
F: (01865) 762749
E: mount.pleasant@ukonline.
co.uk

Old Bank Hotel ★★★★
92-94 High Street, Oxford,
OX1 4BN
T: (01865) 799599
F: (01865) 799598
E: info@oldbank-hotel.co.uk
I: www.
oxford-hotels-restaurants.co.uk

The Old Parsonage Hotel
★★★★
Townhouse
1 Banbury Road, Oxford,
OX2 6NN
T: (01865) 811022
F: (01865) 811016
E: jwj@mogford.co.uk
I: www.
oxford-hotels-restaurants.co.uk

Otmoor Lodge Hotel ★★
Horton Hill, Horton cum Studley,
Oxford OX33 1AY
T: (01865) 351235
F: (01865) 351721
E: otmoorlodge@btinternet.
com
I: www.otmoorlodge.co.uk

Royal Oxford Hotel
Rating Applied For
Park End Street, Oxford,
OX1 1HR
T: (01865) 248432
F: (01865) 250049
E: frontdesk@royaloxfordhotel.
co.uk
I: www.royaloxfordhotel.co.uk

Studley Priory Hotel ★★★
Horton cum Studley, Oxford,
Oxfordshire OX33 1AZ
T: (01865) 351203 & 351254
F: (01865) 351613
E: res@studley-priory.co.uk
I: www.studley-priory.co.uk

Victoria Hotel ★★
180 Abingdon Road, Oxford,
Oxfordshire OX1 4RA
T: (01865) 724536
F: (01865) 794909
I: www.oxfordcity.
co.uk/hotels/victoria

Westwood Country Hotel
Rating Applied For
Hinksey Hill Top, Oxford,
Oxfordshire OX1 5BG
T: (01865) 735408
F: (01865) 736536
E: reservations@
westwoodhotel.co.uk
I: www.westwoodhotel.co.uk

PANGBOURNE
Berkshire

**The Copper Inn Hotel &
Restaurant** ★★★
Church Road, Pangbourne,
Reading RG8 7AR
T: (0118) 984 2244
F: (0118) 984 5542
E: reservations@copper-inn.
co.uk
I: www.copper-inn.co.uk

PETERSFIELD
Hampshire

Langrish House Hotel ★★
Langrish, Petersfield, Hampshire
GU32 1RN
T: (01730) 266941
F: (01730) 260543
E: frontdesk@langrishhouse.
co.uk
I: www.langrishhouse.co.uk

POOLE
Dorset

Harbour Heights Hotel ★★★
73 Haven Road, Sandbanks,
Poole, Dorset BH13 7LW
T: (01202) 707272
F: (01202) 708594

Haven Hotel ★★★★
Banks Road, Sandbanks, Poole,
Dorset BH13 7QL
T: (01202) 707333
F: (01202) 708796
E: reservations@havenhotel.
co.uk
I: www.havenhotel.co.uk

Quarterdeck Hotel ★★
2 Sandbanks Road, Poole, Dorset
BH14 8AQ
T: (01202) 740066 & 748448
F: (01202) 736780
E: reception@quarterdeckhotel.
co.uk

Sandbanks Hotel ★★★
15 Banks Road, Sandbanks,
Poole, Dorset BH13 7PS
T: (01202) 707377
F: (01202) 708885
E: reservations@
sandbankshotel.co.uk
I: www.sandbankshotel.co.uk

PORTSMOUTH & SOUTHSEA
Hampshire

Beaufort Hotel ★★
71 Festing Road, Southsea,
Portsmouth, Hampshire
PO4 0NQ
T: (023) 9282 3707
F: (023) 9287 0270
E: res/enq@beauforthotel.co.uk

Glendower Hotel
Rating Applied For
22-23 South Parade, Southsea,
Hampshire PO5 2JF
T: (023) 9282 7169
F: (023) 9283 8738
E: sylvia@yeganehs.freeserve.
co.uk

Ocean Hotel & Apartments
★★
8-10 St Helens Parade,
Southsea, Hampshire PO4 0RW
T: (023) 92734233 & 92734342
F: (023) 92297046
E: feris@oceanhotel.freeserve.
co.uk
I: www.oceanhotel.freeserve.
co.uk

The Queen's Hotel ★★★
Clarence Parade, Southsea,
Hampshire PO5 3LJ
T: (023) 9282 2466
F: (023) 9282 1901
E: bestwestqueens@aol.com
I: www.queenshotel-southsea.
co.uk

Salisbury Hotel ★
57-59 Festing Road, Southsea,
Hampshire PO4 0NQ
T: (023) 9282 3606 & 9273 4233
F: (023) 9282 0955
E: feris@oceanhotel.freeserve.
co.uk
I: www.oceanhotel.freeserve.
co.uk

The Sandringham Hotel ★★
7 Osborne Road, Southsea,
Hampshire PO5 3LR
T: (023) 9282 6969 & 9282 2914
F: (023) 9282 2330
E: reception@
sandringham-hotel.co.uk
I: www.sandringham-hotel.co.uk

Westfield Hall Hotel ★★
65 Festing Road, Southsea,
Hampshire PO4 0NQ
T: (023) 9282 6971
F: (023) 9287 0200
E: jdanie@westfield-hall-hotel.
co.uk
I: www.users.globalnet.
co.uk/~jdanie

READING
Berkshire

Comfort Inn ★★
39 Christchurch Road, Reading,
Berkshire RG2 7AN
T: (0118) 931 1311
F: (0118) 931 4136
I: www.hotelchoice.
com/travelweb

The Great House at Sonning ★★★
Thames Street, Sonning-on-
Thames, Reading, RG4 6UT
T: (0118) 969 2277
F: (0118) 944 1296
E: greathouse@btconnect.com
I: www.greathouseatsonning.
com

Rainbow Corner Hotel ★★
132-138 Caversham Road,
Reading, RG1 8AY
T: (0118) 958 8140
F: (0118) 958 6500
E: info@rainbowhotel.co.uk
I: www.rainbowhotel.co.uk

Upcross Hotel ★★★
68 Berkeley Avenue, Reading,
Berkshire RG1 6HY
T: (0118) 959 0796
F: (0118) 957 6517
E: reservations@upcrosshotel.
co.uk

RINGWOOD
Hampshire

Moortown Lodge Hotel & Restaurant ★★
244 Christchurch Road,
Ringwood, Hampshire BH24 3AS
T: (01425) 471404
F: (01425) 476052
E: enq@moortownlodge.co.uk
I: www.moortownlodge.co.uk

ROTHERWICK
Hampshire

Tylney Hall Hotel ★★★★
Rotherwick, Hook, Hampshire
RG27 9AZ
T: (01256) 764881
F: (01256) 768141
E: sales@tylneyhall.com
I: www.tylneyhall.com

RYDE
Isle of Wight

Biskra Beach Hotel & Restaurant ★★
17 St Thomas Street, Ryde, Isle
of Wight PO33 2DL
T: (01983) 567913 & 615272
F: (01983) 616976
E: info@biskra-hotel.com
I: www.biskra-hotel.com

ST LAWRENCE
Isle of Wight

Rocklands Hotel ★★
Undercliff Drive, St Lawrence,
Ventnor, Isle of Wight PO38 1XH
T: (01983) 852964
E: Holidays@rocklandshotel.
com
I: www.rocklandshotel.com

ST LEONARDS
Dorset

The St Leonards Hotel ★★
185 Ringwood Road, St
Leonards, Ringwood, Hampshire
BH24 2NP
T: (01425) 471220
F: (01425) 480274

SANDOWN
Isle of Wight

Burlington Hotel ★★
5-9 Avenue Road, Sandown, Isle
of Wight PO36 8BN
T: (01983) 403702
F: (01983) 402307
E: burlingtonhotel.sandown@
virgin.net

Chad Hill Hotel ★★
7 Hill Street, Sandown, Isle of
Wight PO36 9DD
T: (01983) 403231
F: (01983) 403231
E: chadhillhotel@supanet.com
I: www.chadhillhotel.com

Grange Hall Hotel ★★
Grange Road, Sandown, Isle of
Wight PO36 8NE
T: (01983) 403531
F: (01983) 402922
E: grangehall@c4.com

Melville Hall Hotel ★★★
Melville Street, Sandown, Isle of
Wight PO36 9DH
T: (01983) 406526
F: (01983) 407093
E: enquiries@melvillehall.co.uk
I: www.melvillehall.co.uk

Montrene Hotel ★★
Avenue Road, Sandown, Isle of
Wight PO36 8BN
T: (01983) 403722
F: (01983) 405553
E: info@montrene.co.uk
I: www.montrene.co.uk

The Ocean Hotel ★★
The Esplanade, Sandown, Isle of
Wight PO36 8AB
T: (01983) 402351 & 402352
F: (01983) 406699
E: ocean hotel@aol.com
I: www.ocean-hotel.co.uk

The Parkbury Hotel ★★★
29-31 The Broadway, Sandown,
Isle of Wight PO36 9BB
T: (01983) 402508
F: (01983) 404471
E: sean@parkbury.freeserve.
co.uk
I: www.smoothhound.
co.uk/hotels/parkbury.html

Riviera Hotel ★★
2 Royal Street, Sandown, Isle of
Wight PO36 8LP
T: (01983) 402518
F: (01983) 402518
E: riviera@hotel4326.freeserve.
co.uk

The Royal Cliff Hotel ★★
Beachfield Road, Sandown, Isle
of Wight PO36 8NA
T: (01983) 402138
F: (01983) 402138
E: bobfuller@msn.com
I: www.royalcliffhotel.co.uk

Royal Pier Hotel ★★
Esplanade, Sandown, Isle of
Wight PO36 8JP
T: (01983) 403187 & 405567
F: (01983) 408155

Sandringham Hotel ★★
Esplanade, Sandown, Isle of
Wight PO36 8AH
T: (01983) 406655
F: (01983) 404395
I: www.sandringhamhotel.co.uk

Sands Hotel ★★
Culver Parade, Sandown, Isle of
Wight PO37 8AT
T: (01983) 402305
F: (01983) 402305
E: bta@sands-hotel.co.uk
I: www.sands-hotel.co.uk

Trouville Hotel ★★
Sandown Esplanade, Sandown,
Isle of Wight PO36 8LB
T: (01983) 402141
F: (01983) 403143

SAUNDERTON
Buckinghamshire

The Rose & Crown Inn ★★
Wycombe Road, Saunderton,
Princes Risborough,
Buckinghamshire HP27 9NP
T: (01844) 345299
F: (01844) 343140
E: rose.crown@btinternet.com
I: www.rose.crown.btinternet.
co.uk

SEAVIEW
Isle of Wight

SpringVale Hotel and Restaurant ★★
Springvale, Seaview, Isle of
Wight PO34 5AN
T: (01983) 612533
F: (01983) 812905

SHAFTESBURY
Dorset

The Royal Chase Hotel ★★★
Salisbury Road, Shaftesbury,
Dorset SP7 8DB
T: (01747) 853355
F: (01747) 851969
E: royalchasehotel@btinternet.
com
I: www.theroyalchase.co.uk

Sunridge Hotel ★★
Bleke Street, Shaftesbury, Dorset
SP7 8AW
T: (01747) 853130
F: (01747) 852139
E: sunridgehotel@talk21.com

SHANKLIN
Isle of Wight

Appley Private Hotel ★★
13 Queens Road, Shanklin, Isle
of Wight PO37 6AW
T: (01983) 862666
F: (01983) 863895
E: appley.htl@lineone.net
I: www.appleyhotel.co.uk

Aqua Hotel ★★
17 The Esplanade, Shanklin, Isle
of Wight PO37 6BN
T: (01983) 863024
F: (01983) 864841
E: info@aquahotel.co.uk
I: www.aquahotel.co.uk

The Auckland Hotel ★★
10 Queens Road, Shanklin, Isle
of Wight PO37 6AN
T: (01983) 862960
F: (01983) 862175

Bay House Hotel ★★
Chine Avenue, Keats Green,
Shanklin, Isle of Wight
PO37 6AG
T: (01983) 863180
F: (01983) 866604
E: bay_house@netguides.co.uk
I: www.netguides.
co.uk/wight/super/bayhouse.
html

Bourne Hall Country Hotel ★★★
Luccombe Road, Shanklin, Isle of
Wight PO37 6RR
T: (01983) 862820
F: (01983) 865138
E: bhch@dialstart.net

Braemar Hotel ★★
1 Grange Road, Shanklin, Isle of
Wight PO37 6NN
T: (01983) 863172
F: (01983) 863172

Brunswick Hotel ★★★
Queens Road, Shanklin, Isle of
Wight PO37 6AN
T: (01983) 863245
F: (01983) 868398

Channel View Hotel ★★
Hope Road, Shanklin, Isle of
Wight PO37 6EH
T: (01983) 862309
F: (01983) 868400
E: enquiries@channelviewhotel.
co.uk
I: www.channelviewhotel.co.uk

Chine Court Hotel ★★
Popham Road, Shanklin, Isle of
Wight PO37 6RG
T: (01983) 862732
F: (01983) 866688
E: chinecourthotel@aol.com

Cliff Hall Hotel ★★
Crescent Road, Shanklin, Isle of
Wight PO37 6DH
T: (01983) 862828

Craven Court Hotel ★★
5 Highfield Road, Shanklin, Isle
of Wight PO37 6PP
T: (01983) 862009
E: craven-court@lineone.net
I: www.hotels-isle-of-wight.
com

Curraghmore Hotel ★★
22 Hope Road, Shanklin, Isle of
Wight PO37 6EA
T: (01983) 862605
F: (01983) 867431

Eastmount Hotel ★★
Eastmount Road, Shanklin, Isle
of Wight PO37 6DN
T: (01983) 862531

Fernbank Hotel ★★
Highfield Road, Shanklin, Isle of Wight PO37 6PP
T: (01983) 862790
F: (01983) 864412
E: enquiries@fernbankhotel.com
I: www.fernbankhotel.com

Hambledon Hotel ★★
11 Queens Road, Shanklin, Isle of Wight PO37 6AW
T: (01983) 862403
F: (01983) 867894
E: Enquiries@Hambledon-hotel.co.uk
I: www.Hambledon-hotel.co.uk

Harrow Lodge Hotel ★★
Eastcliff Promenade, Shanklin, Isle of Wight PO37 6BD
T: (01983) 862800
F: (01983) 868889
I: www.harrowlodge.co.uk

Hartland Hotel & Victorian Restaurant★★★
Victoria Avenue, Shanklin, Isle of Wight PO37 6LT
T: (01983) 863123
F: (01983) 865800

Heatherleigh Hotel ★★
17 Queens Road, Shanklin, Isle of Wight PO37 6AW
T: (01983) 862503 & 865 074
F: (01983) 861 373
E: aghardy@madasafish.com
I: www.heatherleigh.co.uk

Keats Green Hotel ★★★
3 Queens Road, Shanklin, Isle of Wight PO37 6AN
T: (01983) 862742
F: (01983) 868572

Luccombe Hall Hotel ★★★
Luccombe Road, Shanklin, Isle of Wight PO37 6RL
T: (01983) 862719 & 864590
F: (01983) 863082
E: reservations@luccombehall.co.uk
I: www.luccombehall.co.uk

Malton House Hotel ★★
8 Park Road, Shanklin, Isle of Wight PO37 6AY
T: (01983) 865007
F: (01983) 865576
E: christos@excite.co.uk

Marlborough Hotel ★★
16 Queens Road, Shanklin, Isle of Wight PO37 6AN
T: (01983) 862588
F: (01983) 862588

Monteagle Hotel
Rating Applied For
Priory Road, Shanklin, Isle of Wight PO37 6RJ
T: (01983) 862854
F: (01983) 865321

Orchardcroft Hotel ★★
Victoria Avenue, Shanklin, Isle of Wight PO37 6LT
T: (01983) 862133
F: (01983) 862133
E: nicklaffan@hotmail.com

Parkway Hotel
Rating Applied For
6 Park Road, Shanklin, Isle of Wight PO37 6AZ
T: (01983) 862740
F: (01983) 862740
E: parkwayhotel@msn.com

Roseberry Hotel ★★
3 Alexandra Road, Shanklin, Isle of Wight PO37 6AF
T: (01983) 862805
F: (01983) 862805

Rylstone Manor Hotel ★★★
Rylstone Gardens, Popham Road, Shanklin, Isle of Wight PO37 6RG
T: (01983) 862806
F: (01983) 862806
E: rylstone@dialstart.net
I: www.rylstone-manor.co.uk

St George's House Hotel ★★
St George's Road, Shanklin, Isle of Wight PO37 6BA
T: (01983) 863691
F: (01983) 863691
E: jawithers@aol.com

Seaways Hotel ★★
34 Prospect Road, Shanklin, Isle of Wight PO37 6AE
T: (01983) 862447

The Shanklin Hotel ★★
Clarendon Road, Shanklin, Isle of Wight PO37 6DP
T: (01983) 862286
F: (01983) 865533

Shanklin Manor House Hotel ★★★
Manor Road, Old Village, Shanklin, Isle of Wight PO37 6QX
T: (01983) 862777
F: (01983) 863464

Sherwood Court Hotel ★★
Atherley Road, Shanklin, Isle of Wight PO37 7AU
T: (01983) 862518
F: (01983) 867646

Snowdon Hotel ★★
19 Queens Road, Shanklin, Isle of Wight PO37 6AW
T: (01983) 862853 & 862026
E: mikebeston@snowdonhotel.fsnet.co.uk
I: www.snowdonhotel.co.uk

Somerton Lodge Hotel ★★
43 Victoria Avenue, Shanklin, Isle of Wight PO37 6LT
T: (01983) 862710 & 862718
F: (01983) 862710
E: somerton@talk21.com

Victoria Lodge Hotel ★★
Alexandra Road, Shanklin, Isle of Wight PO37 6AF
T: (01983) 862361
F: (01983) 862361

SHIPTON–UNDER–WYCHWOOD
Oxfordshire

Shaven Crown Hotel ★★
High Street, Shipton-under-Wychwood, Oxford OX7 6BA
T: (01993) 830330
F: (01993) 832136

SOUTHAMPTON
Hampshire

Botleigh Grange Hotel ★★★★
Grange Road, Hedge End, Southampton SO30 2GA
T: (01489) 787700
F: (01489) 788535
E: enquiries@botleighgrangehotel.co.uk
I: www.botleighgrangehotel.co.uk

Botley Park Hotel, Golf & Country Club★★★★
Winchester Road, Boorley Green, Botley, Southampton SO32 2UA
T: (01489) 780888
F: (01489) 789242
E: res.botleypark@macdonald-hotels.co.uk
I: www.macdonaldhotels.co.uk

SPARSHOLT
Hampshire

The Wessex Centre ★★
Sparsholt College, Sparsholt, Winchester, Hampshire SO21 2NF
T: (01962) 797259
F: (01962) 776636
E: info@thewessexcentre.co.uk
I: www.thewessexcentre.co.uk

STOKE POGES
Berkshire

Stoke Park Club ★★★★
Park Road, Stoke Poges, Slough SL2 4PG
T: (01753) 717171
F: (01753) 717181
E: info@stokeparkclub.com
I: www.stokeparkclub.com

STOKENCHURCH
Buckinghamshire

The King's Arms Hotel ★★★
Oxford Road, Stokenchurch, High Wycombe, Buckinghamshire HP14 3TA
T: (01494) 609090
F: (01494) 484582
E: kares@dhillonhotels.co.uk
I: www.dhillonhotels.co.uk

STONOR
Oxfordshire

The Stonor Arms Hotel ★★★
Stonor, Henley-on-Thames, Oxfordshire RG9 6HE
T: (01491) 638866
F: (01491) 638863
E: stonorarms.hotel@virgin.net
I: www.stonor-arms.co.uk

STRATFIELD TURGIS
Hampshire

The Wellington Arms ★★★
Stratfield Turgis, Hook, Hampshire RG27 0AS
T: (01256) 882214
F: (01256) 882934
E: wellington.arms@virgin.net

STREATLEY
Berkshire

The Swan Diplomat Hotel ★★★★
Streatley on Thames, Streatley, Reading, Berkshire RG8 9HR
T: (01491) 878800
F: (01491) 872554
E: sales@swan-diplomat.co.uk
I: www.swandiplomat.co.uk

STUDLAND
Dorset

The Manor House Hotel ★★
Manor Road, Studland, Swanage, Dorset BH19 3AU
T: (01929) 450288
F: (01929) 450288
E: themanorhousehotel@lineone.net
I: themanorhousehotel.com

SWANAGE
Dorset

Burlington House Hotel ★
Highcliffe Road, Swanage, Dorset BH19 1LW
T: (01929) 422422
E: burlingtonhousehotel@btinternet.com

The Grand Hotel ★★★
Burlington Road, Swanage, Dorset BH19 1LU
T: (01929) 423353
F: (01929) 427068
E: grandhotel@lineone.net
I: www.grandhotelswanage.co.uk

The Pines Hotel ★★★
Burlington Road, Swanage, Dorset BH19 1LT
T: (01929) 425211
F: (01929) 422075
E: reservations@pineshotel.co.uk
I: www.pineshotel.co.uk

Purbeck House Hotel ★★★
91 High Street, Swanage, Dorset BH19 2LZ
T: (01929) 422872
F: (01929) 421194
E: purbeckhouse@easynet.co.uk
I: www.purbeckhousehotel.co.uk

SWAY
Hampshire

String of Horses Country House Hotel★★★
Mead End Road, Sway, Lymington, Hampshire SO41 6EH
T: (01590) 682631
F: (01590) 682911
E: relax@stringofhorses.co.uk
I: www.stringofhorses.co.uk

White Rose Hotel ★★
Village Centre, Sway, Lymington, Hampshire SO41 6BA
T: (01590) 682754
F: (01590) 682955
E: whiterosesway@lineone.net

THAME
Oxfordshire

Peacock Hotel & Restaurant ★★
Henton, Oxford, Oxfordshire OX9 4AH
T: (01844) 353519
F: (01844) 353891

The Spread Eagle Hotel ★★★
Cornmarket, Thame, Oxfordshire OX9 2BW
T: (01844) 213661
F: (01844) 261380
E: enquiries@spreadeaglethame.co.uk
I: www.spreadeaglethame.co.uk

TOTLAND BAY
Isle of Wight

Country Garden Hotel ★★★
Church Hill, Totland Bay, Isle of Wight PO39 0ET
T: (01983) 754521
F: (01983) 754521
E: countrygardeniow@cs.com
I: www.thecountrygardenhotel.co.uk

VENTNOR
Isle of Wight

Bonchurch Manor ★★★
Bonchurch Shute, Bonchurch,
Ventnor, Isle of Wight PO38 1NU
T: (01983) 852868
F: (01983) 852443

Burlington Hotel ★★★
Bellevue Road, Ventnor, Isle of
Wight PO38 1DB
T: (01983) 852113
F: (01983) 853862

Eversley Hotel ★★★
Park Avenue, Ventnor, Isle of
Wight PO38 1LB
T: (01983) 852244
F: (01983) 853948
E: eversleyhotel@fsbdial.co.uk
I: www.eversleyhotel.com

Hillside Hotel ★★
Mitchell Avenue, Ventnor, Isle of
Wight PO38 1DR
T: (01983) 852271
F: (01983) 852271
E: netguides@hillside.co.uk

Leconfield Hotel ★★
85 Leeson Road, Upper
Bonchurch, Bonchurch, Ventnor,
Isle of Wight PO38 1PU
T: (01983) 852196
F: (01983) 856525
E: admin@leconfieldhotel.co.uk
I: www.leconfieldhotel.co.uk

Old Park Hotel ★★
St Lawrence, Ventnor, Isle of
Wight PO38 1XS
T: (01983) 852583
F: (01983) 854920
I: www.parkhotel.co.uk

St Maur Hotel ★★
Castle Road, Ventnor, Isle of
Wight PO38 1LG
T: (01983) 852570
F: (01983) 852306
E: sales@stmaur.co.uk
I: www.stmaur.co.uk

**The Ventnor Towers Hotel
★★★**
Madeira Road, Ventnor, Isle of
Wight PO38 1QT
T: (01983) 852277
F: (01983) 855536
E: ventnor@inc.co.uk
I: www.wightonline.
co.uk/ventnortowers

**Windsor Carlton Hotel
Rating Applied For**
Alexandra Gardens, Ventnor, Isle
of Wight PO38 1EE
T: (01983) 852543
F: (01983) 855207
E: wch@windsorcarlton.softnet.
co.uk
I: www.windsorcarlton.co.uk

WANTAGE
Oxfordshire

The Bear Hotel ★★★
Market Place, Wantage,
Oxfordshire OX12 8AB
T: (01235) 766366
F: (01235) 768826
E: thebearhotel@hotmail.com
I: www.SmoothHound.
co.uk/hotels/bear/html

WAREHAM
Dorset

**Kemps Country House Hotel
★★**
East Stoke, Wareham, Dorset
BH20 6AL
T: (01929) 462563
F: (01929) 405287
E: kemps.hotel@lineone.net
I: www.smooothhound.
co.uk/hotels/kemps.html

The Priory Hotel ★★★
Church Green, Wareham, Dorset
BH20 4ND
T: (01929) 551666
F: (01929) 554519
E: reception@theprioryhotel.
co.uk
I: www.theprioryhotel.co.uk

**Springfield Country Hotel &
Leisure Club ★★★**
Grange Road, Wareham, Dorset
BH20 5AL
T: (01929) 552177
F: (01929) 551862
E: enquiries@
springfield-country-hotel.co.uk
I: www.
springfield-country-hotel.co.uk

Worgret Manor Hotel ★★
Worgret Road, Wareham, Dorset
BH20 6AB
T: (01929) 552957
F: (01929) 554804
E: worgretmanorhotel@
freeserve.co.uk
I: www.smoothhound.
co.uk/hotels/worgret.html

WENDOVER
Buckinghamshire

The Red Lion Hotel ★★
9 High Street, Wendover,
Aylesbury, Buckinghamshire
HP22 6DU
T: (01296) 622266
F: (01296) 625077
E: redlion@regentinns.plc.uk

WEST LULWORTH
Dorset

**Shirley Hotel
Rating Applied For**
West Lulworth, Wareham,
Dorset BH20 5RL
T: (01929) 400358
F: (01929) 400167
E: durdle@aol.com
I: www.shirleyhotel.co.uk

WIMBORNE MINSTER
Dorset

**Beechleas Hotel & Restaurant
★★**
17 Poole Road, Wimborne
Minster, Dorset BH21 1QA
T: (01202) 841684
F: (01202) 849344
E: beechleas@hotmail.com
I: www.beechleas.com

WINCHESTER
Hampshire

Harestock Lodge Hotel ★★★
Harestock Road, Winchester,
Hampshire SO22 6NX
T: (01962) 881870 & 880038
F: (01962) 886959
I: www.harestocklodgehotel.com

The Wessex Hotel ★★★★
Paternoster Row, Winchester,
Hampshire SO23 9LQ
T: 0870 400 8126
F: (01962) 841503
E: heritagehotels_winchester@
forte-hotels.com
I: www.wessexhotel.co.uk

**The Winchester Royal Hotel
★★★**
Marston Hotels Ltd, St Peters
Street, Winchester, Hampshire
SO23 8BS
T: (01962) 840840
F: (01962) 841582
E: royal@marstonhotels.com
I: www.marstonhotels.com

WINDSOR
Berkshire

Aurora Garden Hotel ★★
Bolton Avenue, Windsor,
Berkshire SL4 3JF
T: (01753) 868686
F: (01753) 831394
E: aurora@auroragarden.co.uk
I: www.auroragarden.co.uk

**Fairlight Lodge Royal Windsor
Hotel ★★**
41 Frances Road, Windsor,
Berkshire SL4 3AQ
T: (01753) 861207
F: (01753) 865963
E: fairlightlodge@hotmail.com
I: www.fairlightlodge.webjump.
com

Grovefield Hotel ★★★
Taplow Common Road,
Burnham, Slough SL1 8LP
T: (01628) 603131
F: (01628) 668078
E: info@grovefield.
macdonald-hotels.co.uk
I: www.grovefieldhotel.com

Royal Adelaide Hotel ★★★
46 Kings Road, Windsor,
Berkshire SL4 2AG
T: (01753) 863916
F: (01753) 830682
E: royaladelaide@
meridianleisure.com
I: www.meridianleisure.com

**Runnymede Hotel and Spa
★★★★**
Windsor Road, Egham, Surrey
TW20 0AG
T: (01784) 436171
F: (01784) 436340
E: Info@runnymedehotel.com
I: www.runnymedehotel.com

**Sir Christopher Wren's House,
Hotel & Business Centre ★★★**
Thames Street, Windsor,
Berkshire SL4 1PX
T: (01753) 861354
F: (01753) 860172
E: hotels@wrensgroup.com
I: www.wrensgroup.com

**Stirrups Country House Hotel
★★★**
Maidens Green, Bracknell,
Berkshire RG42 6LD
T: (01344) 882284
F: (01344) 882300
E: reception@stirrupshotel.
co.uk
I: www.stirrupshotel.co.uk

WINKTON
Dorset

Fisherman's Haunt Hotel ★★
Salisbury Road, Winkton,
Christchurch, Dorset BH23 7AS
T: (01202) 477283 & 484071
F: (01202) 478883

WITNEY
Oxfordshire

The Marlborough Hotel ★★
28 Market Square, Witney,
Oxfordshire OX8 7BB
T: (01993) 776353
F: (01993) 702152

**Witney Four Pillars Hotel
★★★**
Ducklington Lane, Witney,
Oxfordshire OX8 7TJ
T: (01993) 779777
F: (01993) 703467
E: witney@four-pillars.co.uk
I: www.four_pillars.co.uk.

WOKINGHAM
Berkshire

Cantley House Hotel ★★★
Milton Road, Wokingham,
Berkshire RG40 5QG
T: (0118) 978 9912
F: (0118) 977 4294
E: reception@cantleyhotel.co.uk

WOODLANDS
Hampshire

Busketts Lawn Hotel ★★
174 Woodlands Road,
Woodlands, New Forest, Nr
Southampton, Hampshire
SO40 7GL
T: (023) 8029 2272 & 8029 3417
F: (023) 8029 2487
E: enquiries@
buskettslawnhotel.co.uk
I: www.buskettslawnhotel.co.uk

WOODSTOCK
Oxfordshire

The Bear ★★★
Park Street, Woodstock, Oxford,
Oxfordshire OX20 1SZ
T: 0870 400 8202
F: (01993) 813380
E: heritagehotels_woodstock.
bear@fortehotels.com
I: www.heritage-hotels.com

The Kings Arms Hotel ★★
19 Market Street, Woodstock,
Oxford OX20 1SU
T: (01993) 813636
F: (01993) 813737
E: enquiries@kings-woodstock.
fsnet.co.uk

YARMOUTH
Isle of Wight

The Bugle Hotel ★★
The Square, Yarmouth, Isle of
Wight PO41 0NS
T: (01983) 760272
F: (01983) 760883
I: www.buglehotel.co.uk

ALFRISTON
East Sussex

The Star Inn ★★★
Alfriston, Polegate, East Sussex
BN26 5TA
T: 0870 400 8102
F: (01323) 870922

ARUNDEL
West Sussex

The Arundel Park Hotel ★★
The Causeway, Arundel, West
Sussex BN18 9JL
T: (01903) 882588
F: (01903) 883808
E: david@arundelparkhotel.
co.uk
I: www.arundelparkhotel.co.uk

Burpham Country House Hotel
★★★
Burpham, Arundel, West Sussex
BN18 9RJ
T: (01903) 882160
F: (01903) 884627

Swan Hotel ★★★
27-29 High Street, Arundel,
West Sussex BN18 9AG
T: (01903) 882314
F: (01903) 883759
E: info@swan-hotel.co.uk
I: www.swan-hotel.co.uk

ASHFORD
Kent

Eastwell Manor Hotel ★★★★
Eastwell Park, Boughton Lees,
Ashford, Kent TN25 4HR
T: (01233) 213000
F: (01233) 635530
E: eastwell@btinternet.com
I: www.eastwellmanor.co.uk

**Holiday Inn Garden Court
Ashford/Kent** ★★★
A20 Maidstone Road, Hothfield,
Ashford, Kent TN26 1AR
T: (01233) 713333 & 713950
F: (01233) 712082

ASHINGTON
West Sussex

The Mill House Hotel ★★★
Mill Lane, Ashington,
Pulborough, West Sussex
RH20 3BX
T: (01903) 892426
F: (01903) 892855
E: mill1@netcomuk.co.uk

BEXHILL
East Sussex

The Northern Hotel ★★
72-82 Sea Road, Bexhill, East
Sussex TN40 1JL
T: (01424) 212836
F: (01424) 213036
E: reception@northernhotel.
co.uk
I: www.northernhotel.co.uk

BOGNOR REGIS
West Sussex

Aldwick Hotel ★★
Aldwick Road, Aldwick, Bognor
Regis, West Sussex PO21 2QU
T: (01243) 821945
F: (01243) 821316

Beachcroft Hotel ★★★
Clyde Road, Felpham, Bognor
Regis, West Sussex PO22 7AH
T: (01243) 827142
F: (01243) 827142
E: reservations@
beachcroft-hotel.co.uk
I: www.beachcroft-hotel.co.uk

The Royal Hotel ★★
The Esplanade, Bognor Regis,
West Sussex PO21 1SZ
T: (01243) 864665
F: (01243) 863175

The Royal Norfolk ★★
The Esplanade, Bognor Regis,
West Sussex PO21 2LH
T: (01243) 826222
F: (01243) 826325

BRIGHTON & HOVE
East Sussex

The Belgrave Hotel ★★★★
64 Kings Road, Brighton,
BN1 1NA
T: (01273) 323221
F: (01273) 321485
E: thebelgrave@cwcom.net
I: www.thebelgravehotel.
brighton.cwc.net

Brighton Hilton West Pier
★★★★
137 Kings Road, Brighton,
BN1 2JF
T: (01273) 329744
F: (01273) 775877
E: paul.nason@bedfordbright.
stakis.co.uk
I: www.hilton.com

The Granville Hotel ★★★
124 Kings Road, Brighton, East
Sussex BN1 2FA
T: (01273) 326302
F: (01273) 728294
E: granville@brighton.co.uk
I: granvillehotel.co.uk

Hilton Brighton Metropole
★★★★
Kings Road, Brighton, BN1 2FU
T: (01273) 775432
F: (01273) 207764
E: reservations@brightonmet.
stakis.co.uk

Imperial Hotel ★★★
First Avenue, Hove, Brighton
BN3 2GU
T: (01273) 777320
F: (01273) 777310
E: info@imperial-hove.com
I: www.imperial_hove.com

Jarvis Norfolk Hotel ★★★
149 Kings Road, Brighton,
BN1 2PP
T: (01273) 738201
F: (01273) 821752
I: www.jarvis.co.uk

Jarvis Preston Park Hotel
★★★
216 Preston Road, Brighton,
BN1 6UU
T: (01273) 507853
F: (01273) 540039
I: www.jarvis.co.uk

Langfords Hotel ★★★
Third Avenue, Hove, Brighton,
East Sussex BN3 2PX
T: (01273) 738222
F: (01273) 779426
E: langfords@pavilion.co.uk
I: www.langfordshotel.com

Old Ship Hotel ★★★
King's Road, Brighton, BN1 1NR
T: (01273) 329001
F: (01273) 820718
E: oldship@paramount-hotels.
co.uk
I: www.paramount-hotels.co.uk

Premier Lodge
Travel Accommodation
144 North Street, Brighton,
BN1 1DN
T: 0870 700 1334
F: 0870 700 1335
I: www.premierlodge.co.uk

Princes Marine Hotel ★★★
153 Kingsway, Hove, Brighton
BN3 4GR
T: (01273) 207660
F: (01273) 325913
E: princesmarine@bestwestern.
co.uk
I: www.brighton.
co.uk/hotels/princes

Quality Hotel Brighton ★★★
West Street, Brighton, BN1 2RQ
T: (01273) 220033
F: (01273) 778000
E: admin@gb057.u-net.com

Royal Albion Hotel ★★★
35 Old Steine, Brighton,
BN1 1NT
T: (01273) 329202
F: (01273) 748078
I: www.britanniahotels.com

St Catherines Lodge Hotel ★★
Kingsway, Hove, Brighton
BN3 2RZ
T: (01273) 778181
F: (01273) 774949

CAMBERLEY
Surrey

Burwood House Hotel ★★
15 London Road, Camberley,
Surrey GU15 3UQ
T: (01276) 685686
F: (01276) 62220
E: Burwoodhouse@supanet.
com
I: burwoodhousehotel.co.uk

CANTERBURY
Kent

**Canterbury Hotel and
Restaurant** ★★
71 New Dover Road, Canterbury,
Kent CT1 3DZ
T: (01227) 450551
F: (01227) 780145
E: canterbury.hotel@btinternet.
com
I: www.
canterbury-hotel-apartments.
co.uk

County Hotel ★★★★
High Street, Canterbury, Kent
CT1 2RX
T: (01227) 766266
F: (01227) 451512
E: info@county.
macdonald-hotels.co.uk
I: www.macdonaldhotels.
co.uk/county-hotel

Ebury Hotel ★★
65-67 New Dover Road,
Canterbury, Kent CT1 3DX
T: (01227) 768433 & 811550
F: (01227) 459187
E: info@ebury-hotel.co.uk
I: www.ebury-hotel.co.uk

The Old Coach House ★★
Dover Road (A2), Barham,
Canterbury, Kent CT4 6SA
T: (01227) 831218
F: (01227) 831932

Pointers Hotel ★★
1 London Road, Canterbury,
Kent CT2 8LR
T: (01227) 456846
F: (01227) 452786
E: pointers.hotel@dial.pipex.
com
I: www.pointers.hotel.dial.pipex.
com

Woodpeckers Country Hotel
★★
Womenswold, Canterbury, Kent
CT4 6HB
T: (01227) 831319
F: (01227) 831403
E: Woodpeckershotel@aol.com
I: www.Smoothhound.
co.uk/hotels/woodpeck.html

CHICHESTER
West Sussex

The Inglenook ★★★
255 Pagham Road, Nyetimber,
Pagham, Bognor Regis, West
Sussex PO21 3QB
T: (01243) 262495 & 265411
F: (01243) 262668
E: reception@the-inglenook.
com
I: www.the-inglenook.com

Jarvis Chichester Hotel ★★★
Westhampnett, Chichester, West
Sussex PO19 4UL
T: (01243) 786351
F: (01243) 782371
I: www.jarvis.co.uk

**Marriott Goodwood Park Hotel
& Country Club** ★★★★
Goodwood, Chichester, West
Sussex PO18 0QB
T: (01243) 775537
F: (01243) 520120
E: reservations.goodwood@
marriotthotels.co.uk
I: www.marriotthotels.
com/pmegs

Millstream Hotel & Restaurant
★★★
Bosham Lane, Bosham,
Chichester, West Sussex
PO18 8HL
T: (01243) 573234
F: (01243) 573459
E: info@millstream-hotel.co.uk
I: www.millstream-hotel.co.uk

Ship Hotel ★★★
North Street, Chichester, West
Sussex PO19 1NH
T: (01243) 778000
F: (01243) 788000
I: www.shiphotel.com

Woodstock House Hotel ★★
Charlton, Chichester, West
Sussex PO18 0HU
T: (01243) 811666
F: (01243) 811666

CLIFTONVILLE
Kent

Grand Hotel ★★
Eastern Esplanade, Cliftonville,
Margate, Kent CT9 2LE
T: (01843) 221444
F: (01843) 227073
I: www.grandhotelgroup.co.uk

Royal Hotel ★★
81 Eastern Esplanade,
Cliftonville, Margate, Kent
CT9 2JP
T: (01843) 232563
F: (01843) 229748
I: www.royalhotel.uk.com

Walpole Bay Hotel ★★
Fifth Avenue, Cliftonville,
Margate, Kent CT9 2JJ
T: (01843) 221703
F: (01843) 297399
E: info@walpolebayhotel.co.uk
I: www.walpolebayhotel.co.uk

COPTHORNE
Surrey

**Copthorne Hotel Effingham
Park ★★★★**
Copthorne Way, Copthorne,
Crawley, West Sussex RH10 3PG
T: (01342) 348800
F: (01342) 348833
E: sales.gatwick@mill-cop.com
I: www.millennium-hotels.com

CRAWLEY
West Sussex

**Jarvis International Hotel
★★★**
Tinsley Lane South, Three
Bridges, Crawley, West Sussex
RH10 8XH
T: (01293) 561186
F: (01293) 561169
I: www.jarvis.co.uk

CUCKFIELD
West Sussex

Hilton Park Hotel ★★★
Tylers Green, Cuckfield,
Haywards Heath, West Sussex
RH17 5EG
T: (01444) 454555
F: (01444) 457222
E: hiltonpark@janus-systems.
com
I: www.janus-systems.
com/hiltonpark.htm

DEAL
Kent

**Dunkerleys Restaurant and
Hotel ★★★**
19 Beach Street, Deal, Kent
CT14 7AH
T: (01304) 375016
F: (01304) 380187
E: dunkerleysofdeal@btinternet.
com
I: www.dunkerleys.co.uk

Royal Hotel ★★★
Beach Street, Deal, Kent
CT14 6JD
T: (01304) 375555
F: (01304) 375555

DORKING
Surrey

**Gatton Manor Hotel, Golf &
Country Club ★★★**
Standon Lane, Ockley, Dorking,
Surrey RH5 5PQ
T: (01306) 627555
F: (01306) 627713
E: gattonmanor@enterprise.net
I: www.smoothhound.
co.uk/hotels/gatton.html

DOVER
Kent

The Churchill ★★★
Dover Waterfront, Dover, Kent
CT17 9BP
T: (01304) 203633
F: (01304) 216320
E: enquiries@churchill-hotel.
com
I: www.churchill-hotel.com

**Walletts Court Country House
Hotel, Restaurant and Spa
★★★**
West-Cliffe, St-Margarets-at-
Cliffe, Dover, Kent CT15 6EW
T: (01304) 852424 &
0800 0351628
F: (01304) 853430
E: wc@wallettscourt.com
I: www.wallettscourt.com

EASTBOURNE
East Sussex

Carlton Court Hotel ★★
10 Wilmington Square,
Eastbourne, East Sussex
BN21 4EA
T: (01323) 430668
F: (01323) 732787
E: carlton@carltoncourthotel.
co.uk
I: www.carltoncourthotel.co.uk

Chatsworth Hotel ★★★
Grand Parade, Eastbourne, East
Sussex BN21 3YR
T: (01323) 411016
F: (01323) 643270
E: stay@chatsworth-hotel.com
I: www.chatsworth-hotel.com

Congress Hotel ★★
31-41 Carlisle Road, Eastbourne,
East Sussex BN21 4JS
T: (01323) 732118 & 644605
F: (01323) 720016

The Grand Hotel ★★★★★
King Edwards Parade,
Eastbourne, East Sussex
BN21 4EQ
T: (01323) 412345
F: (01323) 412233
E: sales@grandeastbourne.co.uk
I: www.grandeastbourne.co.uk

Hydro Hotel ★★★
Mount Road, Eastbourne, East
Sussex BN20 7HZ
T: (01323) 720643
F: (01323) 641167
E: sales@hydrohotel.com
I: www.hydrohotel.com

The Jevington Hotel ★★
7-11 Jevington Gardens,
Eastbourne, East Sussex
BN21 4HR
T: (01323) 732093
F: (01323) 431569
E: jevingtonhotel@talk21.com

Langham Hotel ★★
Royal Parade, Eastbourne, East
Sussex BN22 7AH
T: (01323) 731451
F: (01323) 646623
E: info@langhamhotel.co.uk
I: www.langhamhotel.co.uk

Lansdowne Hotel ★★★
King Edward's Parade,
Eastbourne, East Sussex
BN21 4EE
T: (01323) 725174
F: (01323) 739721
E: the.lansdowne@btinternet.
com
I: www.the.lansdowne.
btinternet.co.uk

Lathom Hotel ★★
4-6 Howard Square, Eastbourne,
East Sussex BN21 4BG
T: (01323) 641986
F: (01323) 416405

New Wilmington Hotel ★★
25 Compton Street, Eastbourne,
East Sussex BN21 4DU
T: (01323) 721219
F: (01323) 721219
E: info@new-wilmington-hotel.
co.uk
I: www.new-wilmington-hotel.
co.uk

Oban Hotel ★★
King Edward's Parade,
Eastbourne, East Sussex
BN21 4DS
T: (01323) 731581
F: (01323) 721994

York House Hotel ★★★
14-22 Royal Parade, Eastbourne,
East Sussex BN22 7AP
T: (01323) 412918
F: (01323) 646238
E: frontdesk@yorkhousehotel.
co.uk
I: www.yorkhousehotel.co.uk

EGHAM
Surrey

Great Fosters ★★★
Stroude Road, Egham, Surrey
TW20 9UR
T: (01784) 433822
F: (01784) 472455
E: enquiries@greatfosters.co.uk
I: www.greatfosters.co.uk

ENGLEFIELD GREEN
Surrey

Savill Court Hotel ★★★
Wick Lane, Englefield Green,
Egham, Surrey TW20 0XN
T: (01784) 472000
F: (01784) 472200
E: reservations@
savillcourt-macdonaldhotels.
co.uk
I: www.savillcourt.com

ESHER
Surrey

Haven Hotel ★★
Portsmouth Road, Esher, Surrey
KT10 9AR
T: (020) 8398 0023 & 8398 7793
F: (020) 8398 9463

FARNHAM
Surrey

**The Bishop's Table Hotel &
Restaurant ★★★**
27 West Street, Farnham, Surrey
GU9 7DR
T: (01252) 710222
F: (01252) 733494
E: welcome@bishopstable.com
I: www.bishopstable.com

FAWKHAM
Kent

**Brands Hatch Place Hotel
★★★**
Fawkham Valley Road,
Fawkham, Longfield, Kent
DA3 8NQ
T: (01474) 872239 & 875000
F: (01474) 879652
E: bhplace@arcadianhotels.
co.uk
I: www.macdonaldhotels.co.uk

FOLKESTONE
Kent

The Burlington Hotel ★★★
Earls Avenue, Folkestone, Kent
CT20 2HR
T: (01303) 255301
F: (01303) 251301
E: sales@theburlingtonhotel.
com
I: www.theburlingtonhotel.com

Clifton Hotel ★★★
The Leas, Clifton Gardens,
Folkestone, Kent CT20 2EB
T: (01303) 851231
F: (01303) 851231
E: reservation@cliftonhotel.com
I: www.the cliftonhotel.com

FRIMLEY GREEN
Surrey

**Lakeside International Hotel
★★★**
Wharf Road, Frimley Green,
Camberley, Surrey GU16 6JR
T: (01252) 838000
F: (01252) 837857

GRAVESEND
Kent

**The Inn on the Lake Hotel
★★★**
A2, Shorne, Gravesend, Kent
DA12 3HB
T: (01474) 823333
F: (01474) 823175
E: enquiries@innonlake.co.uk
I: www.innonlake.co.uk

Tollgate Hotel
Travel Accommodation
Watling Street, Gravesend, Kent
DA13 9RA
T: (01474) 357655
F: (01474) 567543

HADLOW
Kent

Leavers Manor Hotel ★★
Goose Green, Hadlow,
Tonbridge, Kent TN11 0JH
T: (01732) 851442
F: (01732) 851875
E: info@leaversmanor.freeserve.
co.uk
I: www.leaversmanor.co.uk

HASLEMERE
Surrey

Lythe Hill Hotel ★★★★
Petworth Road, Haslemere,
Surrey GU27 3BQ
T: (01428) 651251
F: (01428) 644131
E: lythe@lythehill.co.uk
I: www.lythehill.co.uk

HASTINGS
East Sussex

Beauport Park Hotel ★★★
Battle Road, Hastings, East
Sussex TN38 8EA
T: (01424) 851222
F: (01424) 852465
E: Reservations@
beauportprkhotel.demon.co.uk
I: www.beauportparkhotel.co.uk

The Chatsworth Hotel ★★
Carlisle Parade, Hastings, East
Sussex TN34 1JG
T: (01424) 720188
F: (01424) 445865

Cinque Ports Hotel ★★★
Summerfields, Bohemia Road,
Hastings, East Sussex TN34 1ET
T: (01424) 439222
F: (01424) 437277
E: enquiries@cinqueports.co.uk
I: www.cinqueports.co.uk

High Beech Hotel ★★★
Battle Road, St Leonards-on-
Sea, Hastings, East Sussex
TN37 7BS
T: (01424) 851383
F: (01424) 854265
E: highbeech@barbox.net
I: www.highbeechhotel.com

Lansdowne Hotel ★★
1 Robertson Terrace, Hastings,
East Sussex TN34 1JE
T: (01424) 441615
F: (01424) 447046
E: lansdowne.hotel@btinternet.
com
I: www.infotel.
co.uk/hotels/46686.htm

Yelton Hotel ★★
1-7 White Rock, Hastings, East
Sussex TN34 1JU
T: (01424) 422240
F: (01424) 432350

HAYWARDS HEATH
West Sussex

**The Birch Hotel (Heathland
Hotels) Ltd ★★★**
Lewes Road (A272), Haywards
Heath, West Sussex RH17 7SF
T: (01444) 451565
F: (01444) 440109
E: info@birch-hotel.com
I: www.birch-hotel.com

HOLLINGBOURNE
Kent

**Jarvis International Hotel
★★★**
Ashford Road, Hollingbourne,
Maidstone, Kent ME17 1RE
T: (01622) 631163

HORLEY
Surrey

Stanhill Court Hotel ★★★
Stanhill, Charlwood, Horley,
Surrey RH6 0EP
T: (01293) 862166
F: (01293) 862773
E: enquiries@stanhillcourthotel.
co.uk
I: www.stanhillcourthotel.co.uk

HORSHAM
West Sussex

Wimblehurst Hotel ★★
Wimblehurst Road, Horsham,
West Sussex RH12 2ED
T: (01403) 251122
F: (01403) 251155
E: wimble@globalnet.co.uk

HYTHE
Kent

The Hythe Imperial ★★★★
Princes Parade, Hythe, Kent
CT21 6AE
T: (01303) 267441
F: (01303) 264610
E: hytheimperial@
marstonhotels.com
I: www.marstonhotels.com

Stade Court Hotel ★★★
West Parade, Hythe, Kent
CT21 6DT
T: (01303) 268263
F: (01303) 261803
E: stadecourt@marstonhotels.
com
I: www.marstonhotels.com

LANCING
West Sussex

**Sussex Pad Hotel
Rating Applied For**
Old Shoreham Road, Lancing,
West Sussex BN15 0RH
T: (01273) 454243
F: (01273) 453010
E: sussexpad@talk21.com

LEATHERHEAD
Surrey

Bookham Grange Hotel ★★
Little Bookham Common,
Bookham, Leatherhead, Surrey
KT23 3HS
T: (01372) 452742
F: (01372) 450080
E: bookhamgrange@easynet.
co.uk
I: bookham-grange.co.uk

LENHAM
Kent

**Chilston Park Country House
Hotel ★★★★**
Sandway, Lenham, Maidstone,
Kent ME17 2BE
T: (01622) 859803
F: (01622) 858588
E: chilstonpark@arcadianhotels.
co.uk
I: www.chilstonparkhotel.co.uk

LEWES
East Sussex

Shelleys Hotel ★★★
High Street, Lewes, East Sussex
BN7 1XS
T: (01273) 472361
F: (01273) 483152
E: info@shelleys-lewes.
com
I: www.shelleys-hotel-lewes.
com

LITTLEBOURNE
Kent

**Bow Window Inn & Restaurant
★★**
50 High Street, Littlebourne,
Canterbury, Kent CT3 1ST
T: (01227) 721264
F: (01227) 721250
E: bow@windowhotel.freeserve.
co.uk

LOWER BEEDING
West Sussex

Mannings Heath Hotel ★★
Winterpit Lane, Lower Beeding,
Horsham, West Sussex RH13 6LY
T: (01403) 891191 & 891192
F: (01403) 891499
E: info@manningsheathhotel.
com
I: www.manningsheathhotel.
com

MAIDSTONE
Kent

Grangemoor Hotel ★★
St Michael's Road, Maidstone,
Kent ME16 8BS
T: (01622) 677623
F: (01622) 678246
E: reservations@grangemoor.
co.uk

MARGATE
Kent

Clintons ★★
9 Dalby Square, Cliftonville,
Margate, Kent CT9 2ER
T: (01843) 290598 & 299550

Glenwood Hotel ★★
19-25 Edgar Road, Cliftonville,
Margate, Kent CT9 2EG
T: (01843) 292137 & 228124
F: (01843) 294398

Lonsdale Court Hotel ★★
51-61 Norfolk Road, Cliftonville,
Margate, Kent CT9 2HX
T: (01843) 221053
F: (01843) 299993
E: info@courthotels.com
I: www.courthotels.com

Palm Court Hotel ★★★
Eastern Esplanade, Cliftonville,
Margate, Kent CT9
T: (01843) 229980
F: (01843) 299993
E: info@courthotels.com
I: www.courthotels.com

MINSTER-IN-SHEPPEY
Kent

**The Abbey Hotel & Conference
Centre ★★★**
The Broadway, Minster-in-
Sheppey, Sheerness, Kent
ME12 2DA
T: (01795) 872873
F: (01795) 874728
E: abbey.hotel@virgin.net
I: www.abbeyhotel.net

NEW ROMNEY
Kent

Broadacre Hotel ★★
North Street, New Romney, Kent
TN28 8DR
T: (01797) 362381
F: (01797) 362381
E: broadacrehotel@
newromney1.fsnet.co.uk
I: www.smoothound.
co.uk/hotels/broadacre.html

PEASLAKE
Surrey

The Hurtwood Inn Hotel ★★★
Peaslake, Guildford, Surrey
GU5 9RR
T: (01306) 730851
F: (01306) 731390
E: sales@hurtwoodinnhotel.
com
I: www.hurtwoodinnhotel.com

PULBOROUGH
West Sussex

Chequers Hotel ★★
Old Rectory Lane, Pulborough,
West Sussex RH20 1AD
T: (01798) 872486
F: (01798) 872715
E: chequershotel@btinternet.
com

RAMSGATE
Kent

**Ramada Jarvis Ramsgate
★★★**
Harbour Parade, Ramsgate, Kent
CT11 8LZ
T: (01843) 588276 & 572201
F: (01843) 586866
E: jmarina.rs@jarvis.co.uk
I: www.jarvis.co.uk

San Clu Hotel ★★★
Victoria Parade, East Cliff,
Ramsgate, Kent CT11 8DT
T: (01843) 592345 &
0800 5942626
F: (01843) 580157
E: sancluhotel@lineone.net
I: www.san-clu-hotel.co.uk

REDHILL
Surrey

Nutfield Priory ★★★★
Nutfield, Redhill RH1 4EL
T: (01737) 824400
F: (01737) 823321
E: nutpriory@aol.com
I: www.nutfield-priory.com

ROCHESTER
Kent

**Bridgewood Manor Hotel
★★★★**
Bridgewood Roundabout,
Walderslade Woods, Chatham,
Kent ME5 9AX
T: (01634) 201333
F: (01634) 201330
E: bridgewoodmanor@
marstonhotels.co.uk
I: www.marstonhotels.co.uk

**Gordon House Hotel
Rating Applied For**
91 High Street, Rochester, Kent
ME1 1LX
T: (01634) 831000
F: (01634) 814769
E: bookings@gordonhotel.
free-online.co.uk
I: www.gordonhotel.free-online.
co.uk

Medway Manor Hotel Ltd ★
14-16 New Road, Rochester,
Kent ME1 1BG
T: (01634) 847985
F: (01634) 832430

ROYAL TUNBRIDGE WELLS
Kent

Jarvis International Hotel
★★★
Tonbridge Road, Pembury, Royal
Tunbridge Wells, Kent TN2 4QL
T: (01892) 823567
F: (01892) 823931
I: www.jarvis.co.uk

Royal Wells Inn ★★★
Mount Ephraim, Royal
Tunbridge Wells, Kent TN4 8BE
T: (01892) 511188
F: (01892) 511908
E: info@royalwells.co.uk
I: www.royalwells.co.uk

The Spa Hotel ★★★
Mount Ephraim, Royal
Tunbridge Wells, Kent TN4 8XJ
T: (01892) 520331
F: (01892) 510575
E: info@spahotel.co.uk
I: www.spahotel.co.uk

RYE
East Sussex

**Flackley Ash Hotel &
Restaurant** ★★★
London Road, Peasmarsh, Rye,
East Sussex TN31 6YH
T: (01797) 230651
F: (01797) 230510
E: flackleyash@marstonhotels.
co.uk
I: www.marstonhotels.co.uk

The George ★★★
High Street, Rye, East Sussex
TN31 7JP
T: (01797) 222114
F: (01797) 224065

The River Haven Hotel ★★
Quayside, Winchelsea Road, Rye,
East Sussex TN31 7EL
T: (01797) 227982
F: (01797) 227983
E: bookings@riverhaven.co.uk
I: www.riverhaven.co.uk

Rye Lodge Hotel ★★★
Hilders Cliff, Rye, East Sussex
TN31 7LD
T: (01797) 223838 & 226688
F: (01797) 223585
E: info@ryelodge.co.uk
I: www.ryelodge.co.uk

ST MICHAELS
Kent

London Beach Golf Hotel
★★★★
Ashford Road, St Michaels,
Tenterden, Kent TN30 6SP
T: (01580) 766279
F: (01580) 766681
E: enquiries@londonbeach.com
I: www.londonbeach.com

SANDWICH
Kent

Bell Hotel ★★★
The Quay, Sandwich, Kent
CT13 9EF
T: (01304) 613388
F: (01304) 615308
E: hotel@princes-leisure.co.uk
I: www.princes-leisure.co.uk

**The Blazing Donkey Country
Hotel & Restaurant** ★★
Hay Hill, Ham, Deal, Kent
CT14 0ED
T: (01304) 617362
F: (01304) 615264
E: reservations@blazingdonkey.
co.uk
I: www.blazingdonkey.co.uk

SEALE
Surrey

Jarvis International Hotel
★★★
Seale, Farnham, Surrey
GU10 1EX
T: (01252) 782345
F: (01252) 783113
I: www.jarvis.co.uk

SHEPPERTON
Surrey

The Ship Hotel ★★
Russell Road, Shepperton,
Middlesex TW17 9HX
T: (01932) 227320
F: (01932) 226668

STEYNING
West Sussex

**The Old Tollgate Restaurant &
Hotel** ★★★
The Street, Bramber, Steyning,
West Sussex BN44 3WE
T: (01903) 879494
F: (01903) 813399
E: otr@fastnet.co.uk
I: www.oldtollgatehotel.com

TENTERDEN
Kent

Little Silver Country Hotel
★★★
Ashford Road, St Michaels,
Tenterden, Kent TN30 6SP
T: (01233) 850321
F: (01233) 850647
E: enquiries@little-silver.co.uk
I: www.little-silver.co.uk

TICEHURST
East Sussex

Dale Hill Hotel & Golf Club
★★★★
Ticehurst, Wadhurst, East Sussex
TN5 7DQ
T: (01580) 200112
F: (01580) 201249
E: info@dalehill.co.uk
I: www.dalehill.co.uk

WEST CHILTINGTON
West Sussex

Roundabout Hotel ★★★
Monkmead Lane, West
Chiltington, Pulborough, West
Sussex RH20 2PF
T: (01798) 813838
F: (01798) 812962
E: roundabouthotelltd@
btinternet.com
I: www.roundabouthotel.co.uk

WOKING
Surrey

Northfleet Hotel ★★
Claremont Avenue, Woking,
Surrey GU22 7SG
T: (01483) 722971
F: (01483) 756376
E: northfleet@hotmail.com
I: www.northfleet.com.uk

WORTHING
West Sussex

Cavendish Hotel ★★
115-116 Marine Parade,
Worthing, West Sussex
BN11 3QG
T: (01903) 236767
F: (01903) 823840
E: thecavendish@mistral.co.uk
I: www3.mistral.
co.uk/thecavendish/

WYCH CROSS
East Sussex

Ashdown Park Hotel ★★★★
Wych Cross, Forest Row, East
Sussex RH18 5JR
T: (01342) 824988
F: (01342) 826206
E: sales@ashdownpark.com
I: www.ashdownpark.com

Finding
accommodation
is as easy as 1 2 3

Where to Stay makes it quick and easy to find a place to stay.
There are several ways to use this guide.

1

Town Index

The town index, starting on page 366, lists all the places with
accommodation featured in the regional sections. The index gives a page
number where you can find full accommodation and contact details.

2

Colour Maps

All the place names in black on the colour maps at the front have an
entry in the regional sections. Refer to the town index for the page
number where you will find one or more establishments offering
accommodation in your chosen town or village.

3

Accommodation listing

Contact details for **all** English Tourism Council assessed accommodation
throughout England, together with their national Star rating are given in
the listing section of this guide. Establishments with a full entry in the
regional sections are shown in blue. Look in the town index for the page
number on which their full entry appears.

Information

The National
Quality Assurance
Standards

English Tourism Council

★ ★ ★
HOTEL

When you're looking for a place to stay, you need a rating system you can trust. The English Tourism Council's ratings are your clear guide to what to expect, in an easy-to-understand form. Properties are visited annually by our trained, impartial assessors, so you can have confidence that your accommodation has been thoroughly checked and rated for quality before you make a booking.

Based on the internationally recognised rating of One to Five Stars, the system puts great emphasis on quality and is based on research which shows exactly what consumers are looking for when choosing a hotel.

Ratings are awarded from One to Five Stars - the more Stars, the higher the quality and the greater the range of facilities and level of services provided.

Look out, too, for the English Tourism Council's Gold and Silver Awards, which are awarded to properties achieving the highest levels of quality within their Star rating. While the overall rating is based on a combination of facilities and quality, the Gold and Silver Awards are based solely on quality.

Star ratings are your sign of quality assurance, giving you the confidence to book the accommodation that meets your expectations.

What to expect at each rating level

In a One Star Hotel you will find an acceptable level of quality, services and a range of facilities. Moving up the One to Five Star rating scale, you will find progressively higher quality standards providing ever better guest care as well as a wider range of facilities and a higher level of services.

● At a ONE STAR hotel you will find:
Practical accommodation with a limited range of facilities and services, but a high standard of cleanliness throughout. Friendly and courteous staff to give you the help and information you need to enjoy your stay. Restaurant/eating area open to you and your guests for breakfast and dinner. Alcoholic drinks will be served in a bar or lounge. 75% of bedrooms will have en-suite or private facilities.

● At a TWO STAR hotel you will find
(in addition to what is provided at ONE STAR):
Good overnight accommodation with more comfortable bedrooms, better equipped - all with en-suite or private facilities and colour TV. A relatively straightforward range of services and a personal style of service. Food and drink is of a slightly higher standard. A restaurant/dining room for breakfast and dinner.

● At a THREE STAR hotel you will find
(in addition to what is provided at ONE and TWO STAR):
Very good accommodation offering significantly greater quality and higher standard of facilities and services, and usually more spacious public areas and bedrooms. A more formal style of service with a receptionist on duty. Room service of continental breakfast. Laundry service available. Greater attention to quality of food.

● At a FOUR STAR hotel you will find
(in addition to what is provided at ONE, TWO and THREE STAR):
Accommodation offering excellent comfort and quality; all bedrooms with en-suite bath, fitted overhead shower and WC. Strong emphasis on food and drink. Staff will have very good technical and social skills, anticipating and responding to your needs and requests. Room service of all meals and 24 hour drinks, refreshments and snacks.

● At a FIVE STAR hotel you will find
(in addition to what is provided at ONE, TWO, THREE and FOUR STAR):
Spacious, luxurious accommodation offering you the highest international quality of accommodation, facilities, services and cuisine. It will have striking accommodation throughout, with a range of extra facilities. You will feel very well cared for by professional, attentive staff providing flawless guest services. A hotel setting the highest standards for the industry, with an air of luxury, exceptional comfort and a very sophisticated ambience.

General Advice & Information

MAKING A BOOKING

When enquiring about accommodation, make sure you check prices and other important details. You will also need to state your requirements, clearly and precisely - for example:

- Arrival and departure dates, with acceptable alternatives if appropriate.
- The type of accommodation you need; for example, room with twin beds, private bathroom.
- The terms you want; for example, room only, bed and breakfast, half board, full board.
- If you have children with you; their ages, whether you want them to share your room or be next door, any other special requirements, such as a cot.
- Particular requirements you may have, such as a special diet.

Booking by letter

Misunderstandings can easily happen over the telephone, so we strongly advise you to confirm your booking in writing if there is time.

Please note that the English Tourism Council does not make reservations - you should write direct to the accommodation.

DEPOSITS

If you make your reservation weeks or months in advance, you will probably be asked for a deposit. The amount will vary according to the time of year, the number of people in your party and how long you plan to stay. The deposit will then be deducted from the final bill when you leave.

PAYMENT ON ARRIVAL

Some establishments, especially large hotels in big towns, ask you to pay for your room on arrival if you have not booked it in advance. This is especially likely to happen if you arrive late and have little or no luggage.

If you are asked to pay on arrival, it is a good idea to see your room first, to make sure it meets your requirements.

CANCELLATIONS

Legal contract

When you accept accommodation that is offered to you, by telephone or in writing, you enter a legally binding contract with the proprietor.

This means that if you cancel your booking, fail to take up the accommodation or leave early, the proprietor may be entitled to compensation if he cannot re-let for all or a good part of the booked period. You will probably forfeit any deposit you have paid, and may well be asked for an additional payment.

The proprietor cannot make a claim until after the booked period, however, and during that time every effort should be made by the proprietor to re-let the accommodation.

If there is a dispute it is sensible for both sides to seek legal advice on the matter.

If you do have to change your travel plans, it is in your own interests to let the proprietors know in writing as soon as possible, to give them a chance to re-let your accommodation.

And remember, if you book by telephone and are asked for your credit card number, you should check whether the proprietor intends charging your credit card account should you later cancel your reservation.

A proprietor should not be able to charge your credit card account with a cancellation unless he or she has made this clear at the time of your booking and you have agreed. However, to avoid later disputes, we suggest you check with the proprietor whether he or she intends to charge your credit card account if you cancel.

INSURANCE

A travel or holiday insurance policy will safeguard you if you have to cancel or change your holiday plans. You can arrange a policy quite cheaply through your insurance company or travel agent. Some hotels also offer their own insurance schemes.

ARRIVING LATE

If you know you will be arriving late in the evening, it is a good idea to say so when you book. If you are delayed on your way, a telephone call to say that you will be late will help prevent any problems when you arrive.

SERVICE CHARGES AND TIPPING

These days many places levy service charges automatically. If they do, they must clearly say so in their offer of accommodation, at the time of booking. Then the service charge becomes part of the legal contract when you accept the offer of accommodation.

If a service charge is levied automatically, there is no need to tip the staff, unless they provide some exceptional service. The usual tip for meals is ten per cent of the total bill.

TELEPHONE CHARGES

Hotels can set their own charges for telephone calls made through their switchboard or from direct-dial telephones in bedrooms. These charges are often much higher than telephone companies' standard charges (to defray the cost of providing the service).

Comparing costs

It is a condition of the quality assurance scheme, that a hotel's unit charges are on display, by the telephones or with the room information. But in practice it is not always easy to compare these charges with standard telephone rates. Before using a hotel telephone for long-distance calls, you may decide to ask how the charges compare.

SECURITY OF VALUABLES

You can deposit your valuables with the proprietor or manager during your stay, and we recommend you do this as a sensible precaution. Make sure you obtain a receipt for them.

Some places do not accept articles for safe custody, and in that case it is wisest to keep your valuables with you.

Disclaimer

Some proprietors put up a notice which disclaims liability for property brought on to their premises by a guest. In fact, they can only restrict their liability to a minimum laid down by law (The Hotel Proprietors Act 1956).

Under that Act, a proprietor is liable for the value of the loss or damage to any property (except a motor car or its contents) of a guest who has engaged overnight accommodation, but if the proprietor has the notice on display as prescribed under that Act, liability is limited to £50 for one article and a total of £100 for any one guest. The notice must be prominently displayed in the reception area or main entrance. These limits do not apply to valuables you have deposited with the proprietor for safe-keeping, or to property lost through the default, neglect of wilful act of the proprietor or his staff.

BRINGING PETS TO ENGLAND

The quarantine laws have recently changed in England and a Pet Travel Scheme (PETS) is currently in operation. Under this scheme pet dogs are able to come into Britain from over 35 countries via certain sea, air and rail routes into England.

Dogs that have been resident in these countries for more than 6 months may enter the UK under the Scheme, providing they are accompanied by the appropriate documentation.

For dogs to be able to enter the UK without quarantine under the PETS Scheme they will have to meet certain conditions and travel with the following documents: the Official PETS Certificate, a certificate of treatment against tapeworm and ticks and a declaration of residence.

For details of participating countries, routes, operators and further information about the PETS Scheme please contact the PETS Helpline, DEFRA (Department for Environment, Food and Rural Affairs), 1a Page Street, London SW1P 4PQ

Tel: +44 (0) 870 241 1710 Fax: +44 (0) 20 7904 6834 Email: pets.helpline@defra.gsi.gov.uk, or visit their web site at www.defra.gov.uk/animalh/quarantine

CODE OF CONDUCT

All the places featured in this guide have agreed to observe the following Codes of Conduct:

1 To ensure high standards of courtesy and cleanliness, catering and service appropriate to the type of establishment.

2 To describe fairly to all visitors and prospective visitors the amenities, facilities and services provided by the establishment, whether by advertisement, brochure, word of mouth or any other means. To allow visitors to see accommodation, if requested, before booking.

3 To make clear to visitors exactly what is included in all prices quoted for accommodation, meals and refreshments, including service charges, taxes and other surcharges. Details of charges, if any, for heating or additional service or facilities should also be made clear.

4 To adhere to, and not to exceed, prices current at time of occupation for accommodation or other services.

5 To advise visitors at the time of booking, and subsequently of any change, if the accommodation offered is in an unconnected annexe, or similar, or by boarding out; and to indicate the location of such accommodation and any difference in comfort or amenities from accommodation in the main establishment.

6 To give each visitor, on request, details of payments due and a receipt if required.

7 To deal promptly and courteously with all enquiries, requests, reservations, correspondence and complaints from visitors.

8 To allow an English Tourism Council representative reasonable access to the establishment, on request, to confirm that the Code of Conduct is being observed.

COMMENTS AND COMPLAINTS

Hotels and the law

Places that offer accommodation have legal and statutory responsibilities to their customers, such as providing information about prices, providing adequate fire precautions and safeguarding valuables. Like other businesses, they must also abide by the Trades Description Acts 1968 and 1972 when they describe their accommodation and facilities.

All the places featured in this guide have declared that they do fulfil all applicable statutory obligations.

Information

The proprietors themselves supply the descriptions of their establishments and other information for the entries, and they pay to be included in the regional sections of the guide. All the acommodation featured in this guide has also been assessed or has applied for assessment under the quality assurance standard.

The English Tourism Council cannot guarantee accuracy of information in this guide, and accepts no responsibility for any error or misrepresentation. All liability for loss, disappointment, negligence or other damage caused by reliance on the information contained in this guide, or in the event of bankruptcy or liquidation or cessation of trade of any company, individual or firm mentioned, is hereby excluded.

We strongly recommend that you carefully check prices and other details when you book your accommodation.

Problems

Of course, we hope you will not have cause for complaint, but problems do occur from time to time.

If you are dissatisfied with anything, make your complaint to the management immediately. Then the management can take action at once to investigate the matter and put things right. The longer you leave a complaint, the harder it is to deal with it effectively.

In certain circumstances, the English Tourism Council may look into complaints. However, the Council has no statutory control over establishments or their methods of operating. The Council cannot become involved in legal or contractual matters.

If you do have problems that have not been resolved by the proprietor and which you would like to bring to our attention, please write to: Quality Standards Department, English Tourism Council, Thames Tower, Black's Road, Hammersmith, London W6 9EL.

About the Guide Entries

LOCATIONS

Places to stay are listed under the town, city or village where they are located. If a place is out in the countryside, you may find it listed under a nearby village or town.

Town names are listed alphabetically within each regional section of the guide, along with the name of the county or unitary authority they are in (see note on page 15), and their map reference.

MAP REFERENCES

These refer to the colour location maps at the front of the guide. The first figure shown is the map number, the following letter and figure indicate the grid reference on the map.

Some entries were included just before the guide went to press, so they do not appear on the maps.

ADDRESSES

County names, which appear in the town headings, are not repeated in the entries. When you are writing, you should of course make sure you use the full address and postcode.

TELEPHONE NUMBERS

Telephone numbers are listed below the accommodation address for each entry. Area codes are shown in brackets.

PRICES

The prices shown in Where to Stay 2002 are only a general guide; they were supplied to us by proprietors in summer 2001. Remember, changes may occur after the guide goes to press, so we strongly advise you to check prices when you book your accommodation.

Prices are shown in pounds sterling and include VAT where applicable. Some places also include a service charge in their standard tariff so check this when you book.

Standardised method

There are many different ways of quoting prices for accommodation. We use a standardised method in the guide to allow you to compare prices. For example when we show:

Bed and breakfast, the prices shown are for overnight accommodation with breakfast, for single and double rooms.

The double-room price is for two people. If a double room is occupied by one person there is sometimes a reduction in price.

Half board, the prices shown are for room, breakfast and evening meal, per person per day, and are usually based on two people sharing a room.

Some places provide only a continental breakfast in the set price, and you may have to pay extra if you want a full English breakfast.

Checking prices

According to the law, hotels with at least four bedrooms or eight beds must display their overnight accommodation charges in the reception area or entrance. In your own interests, do make sure you check prices and what they include.

Children's rates

You will find that many places charge a reduced rate for children especially if they share a room with their parents.

Some places charge the full rate, however, when a child occupies a room which might otherwise have been let to an adult.

The upper age limit for reductions for children varies from one hotel to another, so check this when you book.

Seasonal packages and special promotions

Prices often vary through the year, and may be significantly lower outside peak holiday weeks. Many places offer special package rates - fully inclusive weekend breaks, for example - in the autumn, winter and spring. A number of establishments have included in their enhanced entry information about any special offers, themed breaks, etc. that are available.

You can get details of other bargain packages that may be available from the establishments themselves, the Regional Tourist Boards or your local Tourist Information Centre (TIC).

Your local travel agent may also have information, and can help you make bookings.

BATHROOMS

Each accommodation entry shows you the number of en suite and private bathrooms available, the number of private showers and the number of public bathrooms.

'En suite bathroom' means the bath or shower and WC are contained behind the main door of the bedroom. 'Private bathroom' means a bath or shower and WC solely for the occupants of one bedroom, on the same floor, reasonably close and with a key provided. 'Private shower' means a shower en suite with the bedroom but no WC.

Public bathrooms normally have a bath, sometimes with a shower attachment. If the availability of a bath is important to you, remember to check when you book.

MEALS

Evening meals are available at all establishments in this guide. It is advisable to check meal times when making your booking. Some smaller places may ask you at breakfast or midday whether you want an evening meal. The prices shown in each entry are for bed and breakfast or half board, but many places also offer lunch, as you will see indicated in the entry.

OPENING PERIOD

All places are open for the months indicated in their entry. If an opening period is not shown, please check with the establishment.

SYMBOLS

The at-a-glance symbols included at the end of each entry show many of the services and facilities available at each place. You will find the key to these symbols on the back cover flap. Open out the flap and you can check the meanings of the symbols as you go.

SMOKING

Many places provide non-smoking areas - from no-smoking bedrooms and lounges to no-smoking sections of the restaurant. Some places prefer not to accommodate smokers, and in such cases the descriptions and symbols in each entry makes this clear.

PETS

Many places accept guests with dogs, but we do advise that you check this when you book, and ask if there are any extra charges or rules about exactly where your pet is allowed. The acceptance of dogs is not always extended to cats and it is strongly advised that cat owners contact the establishment well in advance. Some establishments do not accept pets at all. Pets are welcome where you see this symbol 🐕 .

The quarantine laws have recently changed in England and pet dogs are able to come into Britain from selected European countries. For details of the Pet Travel Scheme (PETS) please turn to page 352.

CREDIT AND CHARGE CARDS

The credit and charge cards accepted by a place are listed in the entry following the letters CC.

If you do plan to pay by card, check that the establishment will take your card before you book.

Some proprietors will charge you a higher rate if you pay by credit card rather than cash or cheque. The difference is to cover the percentage paid by the proprietor to the credit card company.

If you are planning to pay by credit card, you may want to ask whether it would, in fact, be cheaper to pay by cheque or cash. When you book by telephone, you may be asked for your credit card number as 'confirmation'. But remember, the proprietor may then charge your credit card account if you cancel your booking. See under Cancellations on page 351.

CONFERENCES AND GROUPS

Places which cater for conferences and meetings are marked with the symbol ⚑. Rates are often negotiable, depending on the time of year, numbers of people involved and any special requirements you may have.

Awaiting confirmation of rating

At the time of going to press some establishments featured in this guide had not yet been assessed for their rating for the year 2002 and so their new rating could not be included. For your information, the most up-to-date information regarding these establishments' ratings is in the listings pages at the back of this guide.

Central
Reservations Offices

Some of the accommodation establishments in the regional sections of this guide are members of hotel groups or consortia which maintain a central reservations office. These are identified with the symbol ⓒⓡ, and the name of the group or consortium, which will appear in the coloured band on the right of the entry. Bookings or enquiries can be made directly with the establishment or to the central reservations office.

Best Western
Best Western Hotels
Amy Johnson Way
Clifton Moor
York YO30 4GP
Reservations: 08457 747474
Fax: (01904) 695496

Butterfly Hotels Ltd
PO Box 50
Bury St Edmonds
Suffolk IP32 7HB
Tel: (01284) 705 800
Fax: (01284) 702 545
E-mail: reception@butterflyhotels.co.uk
Internet: www.butterflyhotels.co.uk

The Circle
Independent Hospitality Marketing
20 Church Road
Horspath
Oxford OX33 1RU
Tel: (01865) 875888
Fax: (01865) 875777
E-mail: circlehotels@dial.pipex.com
Internet: www.circlehotels.co.uk

Corus and Regal Hotels
5th Floor, Elgar House
Shrub Hill Road
Worcester WR4 9EE
Tel: 0845 300 2000
Fax: (01905) 730 311
Internet: www.corushotels.co.uk
See advertisement inside front cover.

Grand Heritage Hotels
First Floor
Warwick House
181-183 Warwick Road
London W14 8PU
Tel: (020) 7244 6699
0800 0560457 (toll free)
Fax: (020) 7244 7799
E-mail: enquiries@grandheritage.com
Internet: www.grandheritage.com

The Independents
The Independents Hotel Association
Beambridge
Sampford Arundel
Wellington
Somerset TA21 0HB
Information line: (01823) 672100
Bookings: 0800 885544
Fax: (01823) 673100
E-mail: info@theindependents.co.uk
Internet: www.theindependents.co.uk

Jarvis Hotels
Jarvis Central Reservations
Castle House
Desborough Road
High Wycombe
Buckinghamshire HP11 2PR
Tel: 0845 7 30 30 40
(calls charged at local rate)
Fax: (01494) 686737

Marston Hotels
Central Reservations
The Mews
Prince's Parade
Hythe
Kent CT21 6AQ
Tel: 0845 1300 700
Fax: (01303) 266368
E-mail: res@marstonhotels.com
Internet: www.marstonhotels.com

Minotel Europe
Chemin Renou 2
CH - 1005 Lausanne
Tel: 0041 21 320 4638
Fax: 0041 21 323 5938
E-mail: europe@minotel.ch

Pride of Britain Hotels
Cowage Farm
Foxley
Wiltshire SN16 0JH
Tel: (01666) 824 666
Fax: (01666) 825 779
E-mail: info@prideofbritainhotels.com
Internet: www.prideofbritainhotels.com

Principal Hotels Group
Central Reservations Office
15A Prospect Place
Harrogate HG1 1LA
Freephone: 0800 454454
Fax: (01423) 503555

Small Luxury Hotels of the World
James House
Bridge Street
Leatherhead
Surrey KT22 7EP
Reservations Toll Free Number: 00800 525 4 8000
Internet: www.slh.com

Utell
NLA Tower
12-16 Addiscombe Road
Croydon
Surrey CR9 6DS
Tel: 08705 300200
Internet: www.utell.com or
www.hotelbook.com

Distance Chart

The distances between towns on the chart below are given to the nearest mile, and are measured along routes based on the quickest travelling time, making maximum use of motorways or dual-carriageway roads. The chart is based upon information supplied by the Automobile Association.

To calculate the distance in kilometres multiply the mileage by 1.6

For example: Brighton to Dover
82 miles x 1.6
=131.2 kilometres

	Aberdeen	Aberystwyth	Barnstaple	Birmingham	Brighton	Bristol	Cambridge	Cardiff	Carlisle	Carmarthen	Colchester	Dorchester	Dover	Edinburgh	Exeter	Fort William	Glasgow	Gloucester	Guildford	Holyhead	Hull	Inverness	Kendal	Leeds	Lincoln	Liverpool	Maidstone	Manchester	Middlesbrough	Newcastle	Norwich	Nottingham	Oxford	Penzance	Perth	Plymouth	Sheffield	Southampton	Stranraer	Taunton	York
Aberystwyth	468																																								
Barnstaple	603	214																																							
Birmingham	431	124	180																																						
Brighton	605	288	208	171																																					
Bristol	513	128	99	90	169																																				
Cambridge	462	215	267	97	120	170																																			
Cardiff	531	110	127	109	201	44	203																																		
Carlisle	231	236	372	199	375	282	257	300																																	
Carmarthen	513	48	190	171	264	106	266	67	282																																
Colchester	516	289	292	171	112	195	48	227	310	290																															
Dorchester	595	206	94	172	119	62	179	119	363	182	206																														
Dover	587	325	273	207	82	206	124	238	400	301	116	200																													
Edinburgh	125	335	470	298	473	380	333	398	98	381	385	462	458																												
Exeter	585	196	53	162	175	82	249	109	353	172	274	55	245	453																											
Fort William	156	446	581	409	584	491	466	509	209	491	518	573	590	133	563																										
Glasgow	147	333	468	296	472	379	353	397	96	379	405	461	478	49	451	102																									
Gloucester	479	111	125	56	155	35	150	61	247	124	171	117	192	347	107	456	343																								
Guildford	563	224	175	128	44	106	91	138	332	201	103	97	97	432	147	541	428	99																							
Holyhead	459	101	339	167	343	250	259	201	227	149	333	332	369	327	322	436	323	215	300																						
Hull	375	228	321	140	258	231	138	249	170	312	191	313	262	247	303	379	266	196	239	219																					
Inverness	106	494	630	457	633	540	514	558	257	540	566	622	639	158	612	66	174	505	591	485	428																				
Kendal	279	190	325	153	329	236	245	254	47	236	319	318	355	147	308	256	143	201	286	181	164	305																			
Leeds	331	174	302	121	263	212	146	230	126	220	200	294	271	202	284	335	222	177	220	165	60	383	71																		
Lincoln	387	199	276	89	216	186	95	204	182	267	147	245	220	258	258	291	278	151	173	204	46	439	176	72																	
Liverpool	357	110	274	102	277	184	193	202	126	163	268	266	304	225	256	335	222	150	235	101	128	383	79	74	140																
Maidstone	548	286	234	168	50	167	85	199	361	262	77	161	41	419	206	570	458	153	58	329	223	619	315	233	181	263															
Manchester	356	134	261	89	264	171	160	189	123	180	212	253	291	223	243	332	219	137	222	125	97	381	77	44	85	35	251														
Middlesbrough	276	245	357	177	318	268	198	286	95	291	251	350	322	147	340	280	191	233	276	236	89	308	84	63	123	145	283	115													
Newcastle	234	276	388	208	349	299	229	317	60	322	282	381	353	106	371	239	154	264	307	267	142	266	102	94	154	176	314	146	38												
Norwich	488	277	329	159	171	233	63	264	282	327	61	241	175	359	311	491	379	212	162	320	150	540	276	173	104	241	135	186	223	254											
Nottingham	393	162	234	54	195	144	86	163	188	226	139	226	218	265	216	397	284	110	153	178	92	446	164	74	38	112	179	71	129	160	119										
Oxford	503	159	170	68	109	73	81	105	271	168	124	115	146	371	152	480	367	48	67	239	189	529	225	171	130	173	106	161	226	257	144	103									
Penzance	697	308	108	274	287	194	361	221	465	284	386	167	357	565	111	674	562	219	259	433	414	723	419	396	369	367	317	355	451	482	423	328	264								
Perth	87	382	518	345	521	428	402	446	145	428	454	510	527	42	500	102	62	393	478	373	315	114	193	268	327	271	487	266	192	151	428	334	418	611							
Plymouth	628	239	67	205	218	125	292	152	396	215	316	98	288	496	45	605	492	150	190	364	345	654	350	326	300	298	248	286	382	413	354	259	195	77	542						
Sheffield	365	167	277	76	233	182	122	201	159	264	176	264	247	236	254	236	255	148	191	158	66	417	125	36	47	79	207	99	100	131	147	44	141	366	281	297					
Southampton	570	225	142	135	66	106	131	138	339	201	159	53	152	439	109	548	435	100	49	307	257	596	292	238	197	241	112	228	293	324	193	171	67	221	484	152	208				
Stranraer	232	342	478	305	481	388	363	406	106	388	415	470	487	133	460	188	86	354	439	333	276	258	153	228	288	231	448	226	201	163	388	294	378	572	146	503	265	446			
Taunton	554	165	50	132	160	51	218	79	323	142	243	45	224	423	32	532	419	77	126	291	272	581	276	253	227	225	184	212	308	339	280	186	121	144	469	75	223	94	429		
York	322	202	315	134	276	225	155	243	117	248	209	307	280	193	297	326	213	191	233	193	38	374	91	24	80	103	240	72	50	89	180	86	184	409	238	340	58	251	223	266	
London	544	238	216	120	59	120	60	152	313	215	61	128	79	413	198	522	409	102	30	281	186	571	266	198	143	215	39	202	253	284	115	131	56	310	458	241	168	80	419	167	211

National Rail network

- Principal routes
- Other selected routes
- ✈ Airport interchange
- ✈ Railair coach link with Heathrow Airport
- ⚓ Ferry interchange

LONDON TERMINALS

C	Charing Cross
E	Euston
F	Fenchurch Street
K	Kings Cross
L	Liverpool Street
M	Marylebone
P	Paddington
S	St Pancras
V	Victoria
W	Waterloo

Channel Tunnel services
LILLE, BRUSSELS, PARIS

National Rail Enquiries
08457 48 49 50
www.nationalrail.co.uk

© ATOC 2000. All rights reserved. MCD/BAJS-2S 11/00

National Rail

01/NRE/1169

A selection of events for 2002

This is a selection of the many cultural, sporting and other events that will be taking place throughout England during 2002. Please note, as changes often occur after press date, it is advisable to confirm the date and location before travelling.

* Provisional at time of going to press.

January 2002

1 January
The New Year's Day Parade - London
Parliament Square,
SW1 to Berkeley Square, London W1
Tel: (020) 8566 8586
Email: markp@londonparade.co.uk
www.londonparade.co.uk

3-13 January
London International Boat Show
Earls Court Exhibition Centre, Warwick Road,
London SW5 9TA
Tel: (01784) 472222 (Boatline)
www.bigblue.org.uk

13 January
Antique and Collectors' Fair
Alexandra Palace,
Alexandra Palace Way, London N22 7AY
Tel: (020) 8883 7061
Email: info@pigandwhistlepromotions.com
www.allypally-uk.com

27 January
Charles I Commemoration
Banqueting House,
Whitehall, London SW1A 2ER
Tel: (01430) 430695

31 January-3 February
**Wakefield Rhubarb Trail and Festival
of Rhubarb**
Various venues, Wakefield
Tel: (01924) 305841
Email: pventom@wakefield.gov.uk
www.wakefield.gov.uk

February 2002

1 February*
Cheltenham Folk Festival
Town Hall, Imperial Square, Cheltenham
Tel: (01242) 226033
Email: Antoniac@cheltenham.gov.uk
www.visitcheltenham.gov.uk

9-16 February
Jorvik Viking Festival - Jolablot 2002
Various venues - Jorvik, Coppergate, York
Tel: (01904) 643211
Email: marketing.jorvik@lineone.net
www.jorvik-viking.centre.co.uk

17 February
Chinese New Year Celebrations
Centered on Gerrard Street and Leicester Square,
London WC2
Tel: (020) 7287 1118

17 February-24 March
Lambing Sunday and Spring Bulb Days
Kentwell Hall, Long Melford, Sudbury

26 February-3 March
Fine Art and Antiques Fair
Olympia, Hammersmith Road, London W14
Tel: (020) 7370 8212
Email: olympia.antiques@eco.co.uk
www.olympia-antiques.co.uk

March 2002

6 March-1 April
Ideal Home Show
Earls Court Exhibition Centre,
Warwick Road, London SW5 9TA
Tel: (0870) 606 6080

7 March-10 March*
Crufts 2002
National Exhibition Centre, Birmingham

12 March-14 March
**Cheltenham Gold Cup National Hunt
Racing Festival**
Cheltenham Racecourse, Prestbury Park, Cheltenham
Tel: (01242) 513014
www.cheltenham.co.uk

17 March
Antique and Collectors' Fair
Alexandra Palace, Alexandra Palace Way,
London N22 7AY
Tel: (020) 8883 7061
Email: info@pigandwhistlepromotions.com
www.allypally-uk.com

23 March
Head of the River Race
River Thames, London
Tel: (01932) 220401
Email: secretary@horr.co.uk
www.horr.co.uk

23 March-24 March*
Thriplow Daffodil Weekend
Various Venues, Thriplow, Royston
Tel: (01763) 208132
Email: jmurray@thriplow.fsnet.co.uk
www.thriplow.org.uk

29 March
British and World Marbles Championship
Greyhound Public House,
Radford Road, Tinsley Green, Crawley
Tel: (01403) 730602

29 March-5 April*
Harrogate International Youth Music Festival
Various venues, Harrogate
Tel: (01306) 744360
Email: peurope@kuoni.co.uk
www.performeurope.co.uk

30 March
Oxford and Cambridge Boat Race
River Thames, London
Tel: (020) 7611 3500

April 2002

1 April
Old Custom: World Coal Carrying Championship
Start: Royal Oak Public House,
Owl Lane, Ossett
Tel: (01924) 218990
Email: bwilding@gawthorpe.ndo.co.uk
www.gawthorpe.ndo.co.uk

1 April
London Harness Horse Parade
Battersea Park, London SW11
Tel: (01733) 371156
Email: t-g@ic24.net
www.eastofengland.org.uk

4 April-6 April*
Horse-racing: Martell Grand National Festival
Aintree Racecourse,
Ormskirk Road, Aintree, Liverpool
Tel: (0151) 523 2600
Email: aintree@rht.net
www.aintree.co.uk

14 April
London Marathon
Greenwich Park, London SE10
Tel: (020) 8948 7935

18 April-20 April
Maltings Beer Festival
Tuckers Maltings, Teign Road, Newton Abbot
Tel: (01626) 334734

20 April-6 May
World Snooker Championships
Crucible Theatre, Norfolk Street, Sheffield
Tel: (0114) 249 6006
www.embassysnooker.com

24 April-27 April
Bury St Edmunds Beer Festival
Corn Exchange, Cornhill, Bury St Edmunds
Tel: (01842) 860063

May 2002

1 May-6 May*
Cheltenham International Jazz Festival
Various venues throughout Cheltenham

1 May-31 May*
Bexhill 100 Festival of Motoring
Seafront, De La Warr Parade, Bexhill
Tel: (01424) 730564
Email: brian@bexhill100.co.uk
www.bexhill100.co.uk

1 May-31 May*
Hay on Wye Literature Festival
Various Venues in Hay-on-Wye,
Hay-on-Wye, Hereford
Tel: (01497) 821299

1 May-31 May*
Jennings Keswick Jazz Festival
Keswick
Tel: (01900) 602122
Email: carnegie@allerdale.gov.uk

1 May-31 Aug
Glyndebourne Festival Opera
Glyndebourne Opera House,
Glyndebourne, Glynde, Lewes

3 May-6 May
Hastings Traditional Jack in the Green Morris Dance and Folk Festival
Various venues, Hastings
Tel: (01424) 781122
Email: greenman@britishlibrary.net
www.jack-in-the-park.co.uk

4 May-27 May*
Rhododendron and Azalea Time
Leonardslee Gardens,
Lower Beeding, Horsham
Tel: (01403) 891212
Email: leonardslee.gardens@virgin.net
www.leonardslee.com

5 May-6 May*
2002 Dover Pageant
Dover College Grounds, Dover
Tel: (01304) 242990
Email: pageant@port-of-dover.com
www.port-of-dover.com/pageant

12 May
Antique and Collectors' Fair
Alexandra Palace, Alexandra Palace Way,
London N22 7AY
Tel: (020) 8883 7061
Email: info@pigandwhistlepromotions.com
www.allypally-uk.com

15 May-19 May
Royal Windsor Horse Show
Home Park, Windsor Castle, Windsor
Tel: (01753) 860633
Email: olympia-show-jumping@eco.uk
www.olympia-show-jumping.co.uk

18 May-19 May
London Tattoo
Wembley Arena, Empire Way, Wembley
Tel: (01189) 303239
Email: normanrogerson@telinco.co.uk
www.telinco.co.uk/maestromusic

21 May-24 May
Chelsea Flower Show
Royal Hospital Chelsea,
Royal Hospital Road,
Chelsea, London SW3 4SR

25 May-26 May*
Air Fete
RAF Mildenhall,
100ARW/CV USAF, Mildenhall,
Bury St Edmunds
Tel: (01638) 543341
www.mildenhall.af.mil/airfete

26 May-27 May
Battle Medieval Fair
Abbey Green, High Street, Battle
Tel: (01424) 774447
Email: chpsmith@lineone.net

27 May-7 Jun
Isle of Man T.T. Motorcycle Festival
Various venues Isle of Man
Tel: (01624) 686801

29 May-30 May
Corpus Christi Carpet of Flowers and Floral Festival
Cathedral of Our Lady and St Philip Howard,
Cathedral House, Arundel
Tel: (01903) 882297
Email: aruncathl@aol.com

1 June-3 June*
Orange WOW
North Shields Fishquay and Town Centre, North Shields
Tel: (0191) 200 5164
Email: carol.alevroyianni@northtyneside.gov.uk
www.orangewow.co.uk

1 June-4 June*
Chatham Navy Days
The Historic Dockyard, Chatham
Tel: (01634) 823800
www.worldnavalbase.org.uk

6 June-12 June
Appleby Horse Fair
Fair Hill, Roman Road,
Appleby-in-Westmorland
Tel: (017683) 51177
Email: tic@applebytowncouncil.fsnet.co.uk
www.applebytowncouncil.fsnet.co.uk

6 June-16 June
Fine Art and Antiques Fair
Olympia, Hammersmith Road, London W14
Tel: (020) 7370 8212
Email: olympia.antiques@eco.uk
www.olympia-antiques.com

7 June-8 June*
Vodafone Derby Horse Race Meeting
Epsom Racecourse, Epsom
Tel: (01372) 470047
Email: epsom@rht.net
www.epsomderby.co.uk

12 June-18 June
Grosvenor House Art and Antiques Fair
Le Meridien Grosvenor House, Park Lane,
London W1A 3AA
Tel: (020) 7399 8100
Email: olivia@grosvenor-antiquesfair.co.uk
www.grosvenor-antiquesfair.co.uk

15 June
Trooping the Colour - The Queen's Birthday Parade
Horse Guards Parade, London SW1
Tel: (020) 7414 2479

15 June-23 June
Broadstairs Dickens Festival
Various Venues, Broadstairs
Tel: (01843) 865265
www.broadstairs.gov.uk/dickensfestival.html

18 June-21 June
Royal Ascot
Ascot Racecourse, Ascot
Tel: (01344) 876876
www.ascot.co.uk

19 June-23 June
Covent Garden Flower Festival
Covent Garden Piazza, London WC2
Tel: 09064 701 777 (60p per minute)
Email: info@cgff.co.uk
www.cgff.co.uk

21 June-30 June
Newcastle Hoppings
Town Moor, Grandstand Road, Newcastle upon Tyne
Tel: (07831) 458774

22 June
HOYA Round the Island Race
Isle of Wight Coast, c/o Island Sailing Club,
70 High Street, Cowes
Tel: (01983) 296621
Email: islandsc.org.uk
www.island.org.uk

24 June-7 July
Wimbledon Lawn Tennis Championships
All England Lawn Tennis and Croquet Club,
Church Road, London SW19 5AE
Tel: (020) 8946 2244

28 June-30 June*
The Ordnance Survey Balloon and Flower Festival
Southampton Common, The Avenue, Southampton
Tel: (023) 8083 2525
Email: southampton.gov.uk

29 June-17 July*
Chester Mystery Plays
Cathedral Green, Chester
Tel: (01244) 682617

July 2002

5 July-14 July
Lichfield International Arts Festival
Throughout City of Lichfield
Tel: (01543) 306270
Email: Lichfield.fest@Lichfield-arts.org.uk
www.lichfieldfestival.org

5 July-14 July
York Early Music Festival
Various venues, York
Tel: (01904) 645738
Email: enquiry@yorkearlymusic.org
www.yorkearlymusic.org

6 July-7 July
Sunderland International Kite Festival
Northern Area Playing Fields, District 12, Washington
Tel: (0191) 514 1235
Email: jackie.smithr@edcom.sunderland.gov.uk
www.sunderland.gov.uk/kitefestival

6 July-18 August
Cookson Country Festival
Various Venues in South Shields
Tel: (0191) 424 7985
Email: andy.buyers@s-tyneside-mbc.gov.uk
www.s-tyneside-mbc.gov.uk

10 July-14 July*
Henley Festival
Royal Regatta, Henley-on-Thames
Tel: (01491) 843400
Email: info@henley-festival.co.uk
www.henley-festival.co.uk

13 July-14 July
Tewkesbury Medieval Festival
The Gastons, Gloucester Road, Tewkesbury
Tel: (01386) 871908

19 July-14 September
BBC Henry Wood Promenade Concerts
Royal Albert Hall, Kensington Gore, London SW7 2AP
Tel: (020) 7765 5575
Email: proms@bbc.co.uk
www.bbc.co.uk/proms

25 July-4 August*
Manchester 2002
- The 17th Commonwealth Games
Various venues, Manchester
Tel: (0161) 228 2002

26 July-28 July
Gateshead Summer Flower Show
Gateshead Central Nurseries, Whickham Highway, Lobley
Hill, Gateshead
Tel: (0191) 433 3838
Email: g.scott@leisure.gatesheadmbc.gov

27 July-28 July*
Sunderland International Air Show
Promenade, Sea Front, Seaburn, Sunderland
Tel: (0191) 553 2000

31 July
Nantwich and South Cheshire Show
Dorfold Hall, Nantwich
Tel: (01270) 780306

August 2002

1 August-30 August
Last Night of the Proms Outdoor Concert
Castle Howard, York
Tel: (01653) 648444
Email: mec@castlehoward.co.uk
www.castlehoward.co.uk

1 August-31 August*
Lowther Horse Driving Trials and Country Fair
Lowther Castle , Lowther Estate, Lowther, Penrith
Tel: (01931) 712378

3 August-4 August
Woodvale International Rally
R A F Woodvale, 43 Kenilworth Road, Southport
Tel: (01704) 578816

4 August-11 August
Alnwick International Music Festival
Market-place, Alnwick
Tel: (01665) 510417
Email: jim@alnwick0.demon.co.uk

10 August-17 August
Billingham International Folklore Festival
Town Centre, Queensway, Billingham
Tel: (01642) 651060
www.billinghamfestival.co.uk

16 August-26 August*
Ross on Wye International Festival
Various venues around Ross on Wye, mainly by the
riverside, Rope Walk, Ross-on-Wye
Tel: (01594) 544446
Email: info@festival.org.uk
www.festival.org.uk

22 August-27 August
International Beatles Festival
Various venues, Liverpool
Tel: (0151) 236 9091
Email: cavern@fsb.dial.co.uk
www.cavern-liverpool.co.uk

25 August-26 August
Western Union Notting Hill Carnival
Streets around Ladbroke Grove , London W11
Tel: (020) 8964 0544

28 August-1 September
Great Dorset Steam Fair
South Down Farm, Tarrant Hinton, Blandford Forum
Tel: (01258) 860361
Email: enquiries@steam-fair.co.uk
www.steam-fair.co.uk

30 August-3 November
Blackpool Illuminations
Promenade, Blackpool
Tel: (01253) 478222
Email: tourism@blackpool.gov.uk
www.blackpooltourism.gov.uk

31 August-1 September*
Lancashire Vintage and Country Show
Hamilton House Farm, St Michael's on Wyre, Preston
Tel: (01772) 687259

September 2002

1 September*
Egremont Crab Fair and Sports
Baybarrow, Orgill, Egremont
Tel: (01946) 821554
Email: crabfair.homestead.com/mainpage.html

1 September-30 September*
Southampton International Boat Show
Western Esplanade, Southampton
Tel: (01784) 223600
Email: boatshow@boatshows.co.uk
www.bigblue.org.uk

5 September-8 September
**The Blenheim Petplan International
Three Day Event**
Blenheim Palace, Woodstock
Tel: (01993) 813335
Email: blenheimht@btconnect.com

7 September-8 September
Berwick Military Tattoo
Berwick Barracks, Berwick-upon-Tweed
Tel: (01289) 307426

7 September-8 September*
Kirkby Lonsdale Victorian Fair
Kirkby Lonsdale
Tel: (015242) 71570

13 September-15 September
Thames Festival
River Thames, London
Tel: (020) 7928 0960
Email: festival@coin-street.org
www.ThamesFestival.org

18 September-21 September*
Barnstaple Ancient Chartered Fair
Seven Brethren Bank, Barnstaple
Tel: (01271) 373311
Email: barnstaple_com_council@northdevon.gov.uk

22 September
Antique and Collectors' Fair
Alexandra Palace, Alexandra Palace Way,
London N22 7AY
Tel: (020) 8883 7061
Email: info@pigandwhistlepromotions.com
www.allypally-uk.com

October 2002

1 October-6 October
Horse of the Year Show
Wembley Arena, Empire Way, Wembley
Tel: (020) 8900 9282
Email: info@hoys.co.uk
www.hoys.co.uk

11 October-19 October
Hull Fair
Walton Street Fairground, Walton Street, Hull
Tel: (01482) 615625
Email: city.entertainments@hull.gov.uk

20 October
Trafalgar Day Parade - The Sea Cadet Corps
Trafalgar Square, London WC2
Tel: (020) 7928 8978
Email: rbusby@sea-cadets.org

November 2002

1 November-30 November*
International Guitar Festival of Great Britain
Various venues, Wirral
Tel: (0151) 666 5060
Email: rob@bestguitarfest.com
www.bestguitarfest.com

1 November-31 December*
Marwell's Winter Wonderland
Marwell Zoological Park, Colden Common, Winchester
Tel: (01962) 777407
Email: events@marwell.org.uk

3 November
London to Brighton Veteran Car Run
Hyde Park, London W2
Tel: (01753) 765035

9 November
Lord Mayor's Show
City of London, London
Tel: (020) 7606 3030

10 November
Remembrance Day Service and Parade
Cenotaph, Whitehall, London SW1
Tel: (020) 7273 3498
Email: frances.bright@homeoffice.gsi.gov.uk

16 November-23 December
Thursford Christmas Spectacular
Thursford Collection, Thursford Green,
Thursford, Fakenham
Tel: (01328) 878477

17 November
Antique and Collectors' Fair
Alexandra Palace, Alexandra Palace Way,
London N22 7AY
Tel: (020) 8883 7061
Email: info@pigandwhistlepromotions.com
www.allypally-uk.com

December 2002

18 December-22 December
**Showjumping: Olympia International
Championships**
Olympia, Hammersmith Road, London W14
Tel: (020) 7370 8206
Email: olympia-show-jumping@eco.co.uk
www.olympia-show-jumping.co.uk

Calendar 2002

JANUARY

M	T	W	T	F	S	S
	1	2	3	4	5	6
7	8	9	10	11	12	13
14	15	16	17	18	19	20
21	22	23	24	25	26	27
28	29	30	31			

FEBRUARY

M	T	W	T	F	S	S
				1	2	3
4	5	6	7	8	9	10
11	12	13	14	15	16	17
18	19	20	21	22	23	24
25	26	27	28			

MARCH

M	T	W	T	F	S	S
				1	2	3
4	5	6	7	8	9	10
11	12	13	14	15	16	17
18	19	20	21	22	23	24
25	26	27	28	**29**	30	31

APRIL

M	T	W	T	F	S	S
1	2	3	4	5	6	7
8	9	10	11	12	13	14
15	16	17	18	19	20	21
22	23	24	25	26	27	28
29	30					

MAY

M	T	W	T	F	S	S
		1	2	3	4	5
6	7	8	9	10	11	12
13	14	15	16	17	18	19
20	21	22	23	24	25	26
27	28	29	30	31		

JUNE

M	T	W	T	F	S	S
					1	2
3	**4**	5	6	7	8	9
10	11	12	13	14	15	16
17	18	19	20	21	22	23
24	25	26	27	28	29	30

JULY

M	T	W	T	F	S	S
1	2	3	4	5	6	7
8	9	10	11	12	13	14
15	16	17	18	19	20	21
22	23	24	25	26	27	28
29	30	31				

AUGUST

M	T	W	T	F	S	S
			1	2	3	4
5	6	7	8	9	10	11
12	13	14	15	16	17	18
19	20	21	22	23	24	25
26	27	28	29	30	31	

SEPTEMBER

M	T	W	T	F	S	S
30						1
2	3	4	5	6	7	8
9	10	11	12	13	14	15
16	17	18	19	20	21	22
23	24	25	26	27	28	29

OCTOBER

M	T	W	T	F	S	S
	1	2	3	4	5	6
7	8	9	10	11	12	13
14	15	16	17	18	19	20
21	22	23	24	25	26	27
28	29	30	31			

NOVEMBER

M	T	W	T	F	S	S
				1	2	3
4	5	6	7	8	9	10
11	12	13	14	15	16	17
18	19	20	21	22	23	24
25	26	27	28	29	30	

DECEMBER

M	T	W	T	F	S	S
30	31					1
2	3	4	5	6	7	8
9	10	11	12	13	14	15
16	17	18	19	20	21	22
23	24	**25**	**26**	27	28	29

TOWN INDEX

The following cities, towns and villages all have accommodation listed in this guide. If the place where you wish to stay is not shown, the location maps (starting on page 18) will help you to find somewhere suitable in the same area.

CHECK THE MAPS

The colour maps at the front of this guide show all the cities, towns and villages for which you will find accommodation entries. Refer to the town index to find the page on which it is listed.